The Last War in Albion Volume 1: The Early Work of Alan Moore and Grant Morrison

Philip Sandifer

ERUDITORUM

PRESS

To Ahania

Table of Contents

Prologue

"This is not a dream."
–Alan Moore, "Shadowplay," in *Brought to Light*, 1988.

The Last War in Albion is a history of British comics. More specifically, it is a history of the magical war between Grant Morrison and Alan Moore, a war that is on the one hand entirely of its own invention and on the other a war fought in the realm of the fictional, rendering its actual existence almost but not entirely irrelevant. Certainly the unreality of the War has not stopped it from being the most fundamental battle for the soul of Britain in the isle's long history of magical warfare.

The War, to be clear, is not the scant material residue of their verbal feud in various interviews over the years; this exists and will be picked over, but it is not the meat of the matter. Rather it is a more basic issue: how is it that two comics writers with such a clear overlap in interests, who grew up a mere three-hundred-and-forty miles (no further than from Boston to Washington) and seven years (no larger than the age difference between J.R.R. Tolkien and C.S. Lewis) apart are not friends and have not a hint of warmth in their relationship? And yet it is emphatically and undeniably the case.

Underneath this fact is a story: one of how the British comics industry unexpectedly produced a small generation of some of the most important writers of the 1980s and 90s, and in turn had a huge cultural legacy in both the US and UK. So much so that the number three grossing movie of all time, Joss Whedon's *The Avengers*, is massively and documentably indebted to a British comics industry that was, prior to the arrival of people like Alan Moore, Grant Morrison, Neil Gaiman, Warren Ellis, and Kieron Gillen, a minor backwater of the lowest order.

Within that story there are two figures that appear almost identical to even a casual observer. One, Alan Moore, is a heavily bearded self-proclaimed magician who made his name with DC Comics in 1984 writing *Swamp Thing*, an environmental-themed superhero-horror comic. The other, Grant Morrison, is a bald self-proclaimed magician who made his name with DC Comics in 1988 writing *Animal Man*, an environmental-themed superhero-horror comic. As has been mentioned, these two men are not friends. Indeed, to be blunt, they hate each other's guts. There are sensible reasons for this. Despite their intense similarities, there are fundamental aesthetic differences between Grant Morrison and Alan Moore that place them in diametric opposition for a host of issues with profound social, political, historical, and magical implications.

This latter adjective is worth remarking upon, as it is central to their differences. Both men believe in a system by which the manipulation of symbols creates material change in the real world. Both explicitly use their creative work in multiple media as an attempt to cause such change. Their comics are magic spells hurled into the culture wars, trying in their own way to reshape reality. And they are opposed. This is the story of what happens as a result of this. This is the story of the Last War in Albion.

Understanding this event as a war has several consequences. It does not entirely mean that it is a story of two generals marshalling their forces and battling on the astral plane. It is not Harry Potter versus Voldemort (more Hagrid versus Snape, really). Alan Moore and Grant Morrison are combatants, and major battles revolve around their actions, but their role is that of Austria and Serbia in World War I. The actual war is much larger and diffuse, its reach spiraling outwards through Ideaspace such that few things are left undisturbed by its fallout.

Nevertheless, *The Last War in Albion* will approach the War primarily through the lens of its outbreak and initial combatants: Alan Moore and Grant Morrison. The mildly hostile interplay of their entwined careers will be understood as the beginning of its story. There is, of course, backstory and foreshadowing to be had, but how it chronologically plays out from 1978 to the present day forms the primary plot, if you will, of the project. It is in this regard comparable to Neal Stephenson's treatment of the Newton-Leibnitz feud in *The Baroque Cycle*, his three-thousand-page magnum opus. Except this will probably be longer.

The structure of *The Last War in Albion* is self-consciously different from *TARDIS Eruditorum*, the project to which it is most obviously compared. That project is structured as an episode guide—a series of short essays on successive episodes of *Doctor Who*. *The Last War in Albion* was, at least initially, structured as a single essay, and though this collected edition has been subdivided into chapters for convenience, the overall logic of ongoing serialized narrative—a form central to the War itself—has been retained.

This means that it does not linearly cover every Grant Morrison and Alan Moore comic in publication order with distinct entries for each, although as near to every comic by both writers (as well as, in later volumes, several others) as it is feasible to discuss will be discussed. Rather, it will take longer and more oblique paths. It will inevitably return to the basic narrative of "1978 to the present day," but as the word "return" suggests, it will depart from the main thoroughfare regularly. A section talking about a seven-page comic in an anthology may be followed by one talking about 1960s new wave science fiction, followed by one about 1973 trash cinema, followed by one about a different comic published off and on from the year of the seven-pager to 1989, followed by one about William Blake, before finally moving on to the original writer's other major comics work of that year, a forgotten superhero strip for his local paper. And all of these sections may be internally digressive as well, gesturing towards other sections of the book or of future books.

The remaining nature of the War will be revealed in the telling. All that remains is the task of selecting a beginning point and commencing the narrative proper.

Chapter One: Near Myths

"To leap from one universe to another, unafraid! That's sorcerer's work!"
–Grant Morrison, *Zatanna* #1, 2005

By virtue of one of the major figures being extremely invested in the precise timing of it, that beginning point will be the publication of Grant Morrison's first paid comics work, a five-page story entitled "Time is a Four Letter Word" published in a short-lived Scottish anthology called *Near Myths* in October 1978. This is a decision with consequences. The nature of the War, as previously stated, is that its effects span much of history. "Time is a Four Letter Word" is akin to an outcrop of rock, and a seemingly tiny one at that. In truth, however, it stands upon tens of miles of buried rock— a geologic strata spanning in every direction. The visible layer is a mere fraction of the whole, apparent only due to chance events: the scouring of a glacier, the cleaving of a river valley, an editor picking up a particular story from the slush pile. These fleeting circumstances determine how the underlying tectonics of history and ideology are transmuted into surface terrain and material culture, defining the very world itself.

This is not the beginning so much as the first visible stone. Still, there is a level of arbitrariness to it. Both Morrison and Moore published non-paying work prior to October 1978. One could justify the decision to lead with either one. However, starting with Morrison has two advantages. First, it is something Morrison is passionate about. In his extended commentary on Pádraig Ó Mealóid's "Alan Moore and *Superfolks* Part 3: The Strange Case of Grant Morrison and Alan Moore," Grant Morrison insists, "In October 1978, Alan Moore had sold one illustration—a drawing of Elvis Costello to *NME*—and had not yet achieved any recognition in the comics business. In 1979, he was doing unpaid humor cartoons for the underground paper *The Back Street Bugle*. I didn't read his name in a by-line until 1982, by which time I'd been a professional writer for almost five years. Using the miracle of computer technology, you can verify any of these dates right now, if you choose to." This is a deliberately selective recounting of the facts, but it is nevertheless an accurate one, and to start with *St. Pancras Panda* or Moore's unproduced Arts Lab play *Another Suburban Romance* would be unduly partisan.

Second, any alternate ordering would remove Grant Morrison from the story for too long. While Morrison is correct to note that his first professional comic sale predated Moore's, the truth is that Morrison's early comics work consists of four short stories in an Edinburgh-based anthology that only lasted five issues before folding, a four-year run of a newspaper strip that ran exclusively in local Scottish papers and has not been collected since, and five issues of DC Thomson's *Starblazer*. Other than that, Morrison has no professional comics credits prior to 1986, by which time Moore was in the midst of *Watchmen, Marvelman/Miracleman, Swamp Thing,* and *V for Vendetta*. Morrison, in essence, spent the time from 1979 to 1986 treating comics as an occasional payday to keep the lights on while he embarked on a failed career as a rock star.

Indeed, Morrison's own vehement objections to Alan Moore describing him as an "aspiring writer" in 1983 is inadvertently revealing, as Morrison claims to have not "read his name in a byline until 1982," by which time Moore had contributed to *Doctor Who Magazine, Star Wars: The Empire*

Strikes Back Monthly, and *2000 AD*, and had been living exclusively on his writing income for three years. Morrison, however, apparently did not encounter him until the launch of Quality Communications' *Warrior*, where both *Marvelman* and *V for Vendetta* debuted. Certainly Moore was not yet a major figure in comics as of 1982 (indeed, it was those two works that really put him on the map), but to have not seen his byline anywhere indicates a surprisingly casual level of comics readership on Grant Morrison's part.

Nevertheless, the fact remains: even if Moore became a significant figure in British comics first, Morrison's professional comics career began several months earlier, and to present the War as if Morrison's career was purely a reaction to Moore's career would be fundamentally misleading. Accordingly, Grant Morrison's first paid work appeared in Galaxy Media's *Near Myths* #2. Edited by Rob King, *Near Myths* described itself as "a Science Fiction and Fantasy comic primarily for Adults, although it is suitable for older children," a threshold that almost perfectly suited the seventeen-year-old Grant Morrison, who presumably became aware of the magazine because it was a published out of Edinburgh and thus was a part of his local Scottish comics scene.

As one would expect from an adolescent writer at the start of his career, "Time is a Four Letter Word" is more interesting conceptually than in practice. Particularly compelling is its opening. It begins with a Celtic barbarian figure confronting a naked priestess at Stonehenge, where the sword-and-sorcery hero declares gravely, "I have come from Cerne Abbas and Ynis Wytrin, from Abiri and the Green Plains. I have seen the power change on the old tracks, seen the..." only to transition to a futuristic-mod office: his dialogue bubble extends off the panel, eaten by the panel below it, the words fading away, while in the next panel, a scantily clad woman listens to her grinning manager, who has his dialogue bubble begin off panel, fading in with a half-readable line "seen the ____" before he continues, "...we had at Greenwich. There's new Trixies opening up already. Christ, we've lost Oxford completely. The chronal overspill swamped a six mile radius."

The problem, it appears, is that time is collapsing such that old things are bleeding into the present and overlapping. And so the confrontation between scantily-clad post-mod heroine and her boss Quentin parallels the Celtic warrior at the start of the story and a more ambiguously time-framed protagonist who attempts to rape a corn maiden bathing in a lake. The plots blur together and switch interchangeably as Quentin and Dana arrive at Stonehenge, triggering the collapse of time. "The accumulated time store of Stonehenge breaks loose. The rush of energy spans the world, triggering the final chain reaction," as the world explodes into singularity.

It is, as mentioned, conceptually neat, but ultimately it is also hamstrung by its structure. Morrison's formal experimentalism is impressive, and his grasp of page layout sophisticated, but he's substantially weaker on the mechanics of storytelling. The introduction of the corn maiden rape plot is ultimately confusing, coming well past the halfway mark of the comic and not seeming to add any new ideas. Morrison's a decent artist, but he's not up to the task of making his three settings visually distinctive, and the transitions are thus muddy and unclear. There's some cool techniques and a good idea, but he's not yet learned how to wed them to each other.

Nevertheless, it is an impressive debut for a seventeen-year-old writer-artist, and its publication was no fluke. Morrison's talent is obvious but raw. A similar sense pervades his next story, spread out over *Near Myths* #3 and #4, featuring "Gideon Stargrave, last of the mods" in a series of excitable psychedelic action scenes entitled "The Vatican Conspiracy." Gideon Stargrave is a dandy action hero investigating, in a shock twist of titling, a conspiracy at the Vatican. He's drawn into it when the mysterious Jan Dark comes to him asking for help, followed shortly thereafter by a priest who breaks down Stargrave's door, accuses him of being a heretic, and promptly opens fire. This sets off a chain of action set pieces, including Stargrave being killed by a talking duck police officer, a helicopter chase, a snowmobile shootout chase down a mountain, Stargrave's resurrection, a gunfight with a dominatrix nun, the ritual sacrifice of Joan of Arc (the secret identity of Jan Dark), the loosing of Fenriswulf, son of Loki, and the election of a new pope. While this certainly makes for a lot of events, especially for a mere twenty-one pages, the actual plot as such is relatively thin.

There is a case to be made that a dandy action hero gunning down a dominatrix nun is something that does not require any additional justification. Certainly Morrison's later career will more than once assemble a brilliant comic out of little more than a set of slick images. He is, after all, a creator who has proclaimed, "I find my depth, paradoxically, in the surface of things." The difference is that in those future instances he will have a much clearer sense of visual storytelling, and will be working with stronger artists. More than once in "The Vatican Conspiracy" a scene transitions abruptly and across both space and time, but no clear narrative marker exists to guide this transition. Morrison's art, while retaining the stylistic innovations of "Time is a Four Letter Word," is not up to the task of clearly delineating a scene change (a trick that, to be fair, would be done more through coloring than linework these days anyway), and Morrison declines to add caption boxes establishing a jump in time, so that the comic goes casually from Stargrave killing a hooded executioner and rescuing Jan Dark to him walking into a room decorated with a Che Guevara poster and proclaiming, "It's my sister Genevieve's flat," while a dark-haired woman (Jan Dark, as it turns out, though her hair and clothing is completely different from a page ago) lies in the bed, all without so much as a "a few hours later."

This is, admittedly, a deliberate choice. In fact, Morrison uses caption boxes elsewhere, and uses them well, describing how in the streets of time-collapsed London, "The sirens still

Figure 1: Speech bubbles bleeding between characters and panels. (By Grant Morrison, from "Time is a Four Letter Word" in Near Myths #2, 1979)

Figure 2: Gideon Stargrave drawn to resemble mid-80s Grant Morrison (By Grant Morrison, from "Famine" in Food for Thought, 1985)

sound. Far off, explosions of glass and the rattle of machine gunfire move echoes in the streets. And even the slow fall of sound. Far off, explosions of glass and the rattle of machine rain cannot extinguish the napalm fires or wash away the blood in the choked gutters," before sardonically adding, "It's no joke," the first indication that it might have been. (Arguably this passage parodies Alan Moore's at times overwrought style in *Swamp Thing* some five years before that comic debuted, and the choice of blood-choked gutters has obvious parallels.) Given this, it seems as though the rapid shifts of scene are in some ways the point—that Morrison is aiming for chaotic juxtaposition. But the resulting lack of clarity is difficult to praise for anything other than its ambition.

Nevertheless, one must acknowledge the importance of the Gideon Stargrave strips. Morrison gave the character a return engagement in the first volume of *The Invisibles*, making Stargrave a fictional character created by King Mob in a three-issue arc. But even before this Morrison clearly saw the strips as the most important aspect of his *Near Myths* work, using them metonymously to talk about that work in both 1988 and 1989 interviews, years before *The Invisibles*. And it's clear that Stargrave was, in Morrison's mind, his "primary" creation, as the end of "The Vatican Conspiracy" teases his intended appearance in *Near Myths* #5, "The Entropy Concerto." This, however, was not to be—save for an appearance in a two-page strip in a 1985 benefit comic for the Ethiopian famine, Stargrave did not appear again until *The Invisibles*.

The 1985 two-pager is compelling, creating an unnerving juxtaposition between fashion photography's obsession with thinness and real famine that hinges on moments of sublime perversity, like the image of a model who "got the chance to actually fly out to Ethiopia for a photo session with some dying children," a session which gave her some "great ideas for makeup." But more interesting than the content is the shift in Stargrave as a character—here he's a photographer fairly obviously visually referenced on Grant Morrison and starkly different from his appearance in *Near Myths*— indeed, without the caption identifying the story as a Stargrave story it would be impossible to recognize it as such. This gets at why the character has such apparent significance to Morrison: he's an authorial stand-in. In the letter column to *The Invisibles* #22 Mark Millar referred to him as "Grant Morrison with a girlfriend, cool clothes and no stammer," although perhaps the more pertinent evidence is the very fact that he's an alter ego of King Mob, a character both directly modelled on Morrison and upon whom Morrison would model himself.

Regardless of Stargrave's later successes, however, "The Vatican Conspiracy" marks the end of his involvement in the War for now. Instead of "The Entropy Concerto," *Near Myths* #5, hastily edited by Bryan Talbot instead of Rob King, editor of the first four, ran a story by Morrison entitled "The Checkmate Man." "The Checkmate Man" depicts a "temporal assassin"—a cyborg constructed by the CIA—who goes back in time and murders historical figures, reshaping the present world.

It is in some ways very much like the Gideon Stargrave stories and "Time is a Four Letter Word"—full of jumps across time and space and an ever-shifting universe. But where those stories focus on the action, "The Checkmate Man" takes an entirely different approach. The only part of it that could be described as an action scene takes place on the first page, which features the assassination of Karl Marx, while the remaining nine pages consist of Conrad, the eponymous assassin, reflecting on the stress and horror of his job. It's a surprisingly intimate character piece, miles from Morrison's other *Near Myths* work. There's also a degree of thought that's been put into the setting that isn't present in Morrison's other *Near Myths* work—a throwaway bit about attempting to prevent the Lincoln assassination only to have him die in an accident the next day speaks volumes about the world of "The Checkmate Man" and the way in which the

Figure 3: Gideon Stargrave makes a surprise return decades after his almost completely forgotten debut. (Written by Grant Morrison, art by Phil Jimenez and John Stokes, from The Invisibles #17, 1996)

CIA program he's a part of only changes the world through death and destruction. The result is that the closing page, where Conrad realizes that all the George Orwell books have vanished from his bookshelf before forgetting that he even cares about it, is haunting in its scope, revealing the real effects of Conrad's CIA-backed sanitization of history.

"Mary sticks to the alleyways, where the light and noise of the city is screened out a little."
—Warren Ellis, *Transmetropolitan*, 1998

Oddly, while "The Checkmate Man" better foreshadows Morrison's future career by actually being pretty good, it is also the *Near Myths* story that Morrison has not meaningfully brought up in interviews. While he points to "Time is a Four Letter Word" as being "based around the simultaneity of time concept Alan Moore himself is so fond of these days" and returns to Stargrave in a number of ways, "The Checkmate Man" is, despite being the best of his *Near Myths* stories and the one that actually presents a credible case for the idea that Morrison was, in 1979/80, out ahead of the field, the one piece Morrison seems content to relegate to the status of juvenilia and trivia. No, it is Gideon Stargrave who, by all appearances, best captures the spirit of what Morrison was doing in *Near Myths*, and thus is most important to contextualize in the larger comics scene of 1979. The *Near Myths* stories are, after all, a small rock in a larger formation, and it is at this point more helpful to establish some of the underlying conceptual strata.

While Morrison has, in interviews, gone back and forth on what his inspirations are for Gideon Stargrave, his most common claim is Michael Moorcock. In a 1997 interview he said, of his reuse of the character in *The Invisibles*, that "King Mob's 'Gideon Stargrave' stories are direct quotes from the Michael Moorcock-inspired short stories I wrote obsessively when I was 17," which is to say, his *Near Myths* contributions. He was blunter in the letter column to *The Invisibles* #17, the first issue featuring Stargrave, describing him as "a thinly-veiled ripoff of Moorcock's 'Jerry Cornelius' character."

Moorcock, while usually generous about the use of Jerry Cornelius, took particular exception to this, memorably proclaiming that his "image of Grant Morrison is of someone wearing a mask, a flat hat and a striped jersey and carrying a bag marked SWAG." (This is not entirely hypocritical of Moorcock, who generally approved the use of Cornelius himself, as opposed to imitations thereof.) Moorcock's complaint, however, was in reference to the later use of Gideon Stargrave in *The Invisibles*, and not to the *Near Myths* material; it would be surprising if Moorcock had read it. Morrison subsequently distanced himself from Moorcock, claiming that Stargrave was "heavily but not entirely influenced by Moorcock and J.G Ballard." And this is consistent with his earlier statements, such as in a 1988 interview where he proclaimed, "Stargrave was originally based on the lead character in J. G. Ballard's 'The Day of Forever'; everyone thought he was ripped off from Jerry Cornelius, but it was Ballard."

Nevertheless, it's a thin defense. The Ballard story in question was written in 1966, four years into Ballard's writing career, and begins with the memorable sentence, "At Columbine Sept Heures it was always dusk." The story's central conceit is that the Earth has stopped rotating, thus fixing every point in the world at a particular time of day forever, such that cities are renamed with their times: London 6 p.m. and Saigon Midnight. Its main character, Halliday, "found himself obsessed by his broken dreams" of an ancient town on the Mediterranean, and a woman there, and moved from Norway to North Africa to find her. The plot is existent but oblique—Halliday lives with a couple for three months, but they move because the dusk line is slowly shifting and they wish to avoid night. He meets a woman who he decides is the one from his dreams, they have a series of cryptic conversations, and finally gets shot at a bit as he flees in a car.

The similarities to the Stargrave material are limited at best. Ballard's story is a sparse character piece, whereas Gideon Stargrave spends much of the story in fast-paced action set pieces. Halliday is written as a cipher with few overt similarities to the dandy action hero Gideon Stargrave, described in the recap page from *Near Myths* #4 as an "art time anarchist, raconteur, and wit." To say that Stargrave is based on the lead character of "The Day of Forever" is thus puzzling. More might be said for the premise, which is based on a collapse of reality that bears at least some similarity to the idea of a world where time has become a geographic feature. But even given that, it's difficult to justify Morrison's claim of having based his story on Ballard's. The most plausible explanation is that Morrison confused the short story "The Day of Forever" with some other story in the anthology by the same title, although were this the case it is difficult to see how such a hazily remembered book could be such an active influence.

Nevertheless, Morrison's larger debt to Ballard is obvious—just not his debt to that particular story (although a case could be made for "The Checkmate Man," a story that feels altogether more Ballardian). A more probable source is Ballard's 1969 book *The Atrocity Exhibition*, republished in 1990 with illustrations by San Francisco-based underground comix artist Phoebe Gloeckner. This book shares the fascination that "The Day of Forever" has with the idea of a reality that has in some sense collapsed. In "The Day of Forever" it is that time has effectively ceased, whereas in *The Atrocity Exhibition* it is that a number of ghoulish concepts have become conflated—in particular the precise machinery of cars and weapons and the extremes of human bodily experience. The book contains such memorable sections as "The Assassination of John Fitzgerald Kennedy Considered as a Downhill Motor Race," which does precisely what its title suggests. ("The course," it explains, "ran downhill from the Book Depository, below an overpass, then on to the Parkland Hospital and from there to Love Air Field. It is one of the most hazardous courses in downhill motor racing, second only to the Sarajevo track discontinued in 1914." It then pauses for a paragraph break before noting, sardonically, that "Kennedy went downhill rapidly.")

What is crucial about the collapsed world of *The Atrocity Exhibition* is that it is not collapsed in any traditionally post-apocalyptic sense, but in a more esoteric and conceptual one. The main character, whose name shifts from chapter to chapter, lives a life where his outside references have collapsed. "'Sixties iconography," the book commences in one of its characteristic lists or inventories of objects in its strange exhibition, "the nasal prepuce of LBJ, crashed helicopters, the pudenda of Ralph Nader, Eichmann in drag, the climax of a New York happening: a dead child. In the patio at the center of the maze a young woman in a flowered white dress sat behind a desk covered with catalogues," the paragraph continues, seamlessly altering its style, "her blanched skin exposed the hollow planes of her face. Like the Pilot, Talbot recognized her as a student at his seminar. Her nervous smile revealed the wound that disfigured the inside of her mouth."

This aggressively experimental prose style, very much unlike "The Day of Forever," which feels more like the lyrically magical realist tales of Jorge Luis Borges than like the harsh cuts of *The Atrocity Exhibition*, resembles nothing so much as the clever dialogue trick on page one of "Time is a Four Letter Word." This, then, is at least a plausible influence on Grant Morrison's mash-up of pop culture detritus into a violent action conspiracy story in which the structure of time has spilled chaotically out over the world. "The Day of Forever" is a vast, silent structure of a world that's come to a halt. Its outbreak of violence at the end stands as a blurry smear on an otherwise completely still textual landscape. *The Atrocity Exhibition* is brash, loud, and over-saturated in the way that Grant Morrison's world and style clearly is.

It is also closer to the work that Ballard is remembered for. At least as a sci-fi writer, Ballard is remembered for 70s work like *High Rise*, a novel in which a luxury apartment community is reduced to brutal and animalistic savagery. Its style is altogether more collected than *The Atrocity Exhibition*, but the same sense of strange hybridization persists. Consider the odd fusing of action hero and domesticity in this passage: "Wilder watched her with respect. He had tangled with these crones more than once, and was well aware that they were capable of a surprising turn of speed. Without moving, he waited as she leaned over the landing rail and emptied the slops from the champagne bucket. The cold grease spattered Wilder and the dog, but neither made any response." This is Ballard to a tee—a cracked mirror of our own material culture used to show us the cultural practices of another culture.

Ballard is part of the so-called new wave of science fiction that arose in the 1960s and 70s in both the US and UK. In the US major figures included Alfred Bester, Ursula K. LeGuin, and Harlan Ellison, but in the UK the major names were Moorcock, who edited *New Worlds*, the leading magazine of the style, and Ballard, the magazine's biggest star. For Ballard, at least, the goal of science fiction was to abandon outer space in favor of "inner space," which he defined in 1968 as "an imaginary realm in which on the one hand the outer world of reality, and on the other the inner world of the mind meet and merge. Now, in the landscapes of the surrealist painters, for example, one sees the regions of Inner Space; and increasingly I believe that we will encounter in film and literature scenes which are neither solely realistic nor fantastic. In a sense, it will be a movement in the interzone between both spheres." This sense of eccentric spaces in the margins of things again evokes the odd fused worlds of Morrison's initial stories.

Another way to approach understand Ballard and the new wave, however, is through William S. Burroughs, an American writer who provided a preface for *The Atrocity Exhibition* that declares, much in line with Morrison and Ballard, "The line between inner and outer landscapes is breaking down. Earthquakes can result from seismic upheavals within the human mind. The whole random universe of the industrial age is breaking down into cryptic fragments," though it's unclear whether he's talking about the book or the world around it. (Indeed, Morrison said, in the same 1988 interview where he cited "The Day of Forever" as an influence, that the Stargrave stories' style was "more akin to William Burroughs than Michael Moorcock.")

William S. Burroughs was the craggy end of the Beat Generation in America, the third name people pick when identifying its major writers after they've named Alan Ginsberg and Jack Kerouac. The Beats marked the first wave of postwar counterculture in America, self-identified by Kerouac in 1948. Somewhere between brilliant and screwed out of their heads with drugs, the Beats were joyfully narcissistic middle-class rebels. Perhaps their most defining moment comes in Alan Ginsberg's "Howl," which begins by describing how Ginsberg "saw the best minds of my generation destroyed by madness, starving hysterical naked / dragging themselves through the negro streets at dawn looking for an angry fix, / angelheaded hipsters burning for the ancient heavenly connection to the starry dynamo in the machinery of night, / who poverty and tatters and hollow-eyed and high sat up smoking in the supernatural darkness…" and continues in a similar vein for long enough to make it a mainstay of Intro to Poetry syllabi from English teachers looking for a work that "connects" to their late teenage students.

"This dread world and the rolling of wheels"
–William Blake, *The Book of Urizen*, 1794

Burroughs provides no such easy access route, and is beloved less by the academic consensus than by generations of committed counterculture figures who, like Ballard and Moorcock, "weren't so much influenced by him as inspired by him." At times not so much a writer than a stunningly

competent criminal, Burroughs effectively hit on the brilliant
scheme of supporting a drug habit by writing about it. Famed
for shooting his wife to death in an ill-advised drunken
William Tell impression, Burroughs's style is an obvious
antecedent for Ballard's harshly visceral lists in *The Atrocity
Exhibition*. His masterpiece is *Naked Lunch*, an unstructured
ramble of a book that was the subject of several landmark
obscenity trials, all of which were decided in its favor. It
wanders from misadventure to misadventure, steadily
dissolving reality into a paranoid dreamscape that seems to
have been Burroughs's drugfucked experience channeled
onto the page, a world where "One Friday Fats siphoned
himself into The Plaza, a translucent-grey foetal monkey,
suckers on his little soft, purple-grey hands, and a lamprey
disk mouth of cold, grey gristle lined with hollow black
erectile teeth, feeling for the scar patterns of junk," a
paragraph that exists as part of a sprawling multi-paragraph
sentence with no end in sight.

Burroughs transitioned this into a literary career such that
a reasonable circle of admirers improbably allowed him to
live a heroin-addicted lifestyle until the ripe old age of 83,
sustaining a pleasant existence in Lawrence, Kansas where he
could have his drugs without the preying cityscape waiting to
devour him. But his paranoia was not just of the perverted
rabbit hole of criminal culture that urban drug culture offered
him. Rather, he feared the very technology of language,
describing it as a "control machine" that was
indistinguishable from his own addiction in its tyranny over
his thought.

Burroughs, like many figures within and without the war,
was overtly an occultist, creating with British performance
artist Brion Gysin the cut-up technique, in which written
works are physically shredded into strips and remixed to
produce new phrases, a practice Burroughs believed to have
actual magical import, to the extent that he joined the chaos
magic organization The Illuminates of Thanateros late in life.
But while Morrison acknowledges the similarity, he resists

calling Burroughs an influence, boasting in a 1989 interview that he had "used cut-ups and non-sequiturs before I'd even read a Burroughs book," and specifically pointing to his "unreadable Gideon Stargrave" stories as an example. This suggests that any influence Burroughs had was indirect, filtered through the new wave science fiction writers Morrison was more overtly following from.

Still, it clearly establishes the tradition in which Morrison's earliest work must be positioned—a casually eschatological tradition heavy on formal experimentalism. But none of this captures the peculiar iconography of Morrison's comics: the juxtaposing of dandy secret agents and sword-and-sorcery apocalypses, or the psychedelic Bond pastiche of Gideon Stargrave. Explaining that requires turning to the influence Morrison's anxiety runs highest about, Michael Moorcock.

Moorcock is an oddity of a writer in part because he's worked in so many genres, or, perhaps more accurately, so many flavors within the basic sci-fi/fantasy genre. For the purposes of talking about Gideon Stargrave, however, it is specifically his Jerry Cornelius series that matters. Jerry Cornelius is essentially an attempt to do heroic fantasy in the style of *The Atrocity Exhibition*. Where *The Atrocity Exhibition* attempted to blur the mediated pornographies of sex and death into one psycho-cultural landscape, however, the Jerry Cornelius novels switch quickly among narrative frames and worlds, with characters dying and coming back freely and casually. Moorcock admits to the similarity: "Just as Ballard found his remedy in the form he used for *Atrocity Exhibition* and the later stories published from 1965 onwards, I felt I'd found my remedy in the form I used in *The Final Programme*," the first Cornelius novel. And so Cornelius adventures through an ever-shifting world. But what's key is that he adventures—for all the formal complexity of his world, the Jerry Cornelius books feature deceptively straightforward plots.

Moorcock has cited Mike Harrison, a friend within the *New Worlds* scene who wrote three Jerry Cornelius stories of his own, when explaining this. Harrison, as Moorcock explains it, "said that Jerry was more a technique than a character," and goes on to say that "he's a narrative device." In a 2009 interview Moorcock explained that Cornelius "is someone learning to exist, through all kinds of strategies, in our contemporary world," a character he found useful because he felt like his other writing "was able to deal with the big philosophical issues but not the specifics of modern life"—what he wanted was "a character who was able to exist in a lot of different contexts in contemporary cities, especially London." So Cornelius was a shifting cipher of a character who filled a narrative function in a story that endlessly changed what sort of world it was in.

Moorcock drew attention to this fact by basing the first Cornelius novel, *The Final Programme*, upon his earliest story with his most famous creation, Elric of Melniboné. "Since Elric was a 'myth' character," Moorcock explains, "I decided to try to write his first stories in twentieth century terms." Elric of Melniboné is already an inversion of the standard sword-and-sorcery tropes—a scrawny albino with no interest in war, partially possessed by his black blade Stormbringer, and forced to feed it souls over the course of a weary and tragic journey as a roaming warrior. Like Cornelius, he is as much a narrative structure as anything—Moorcock has always insisted that "I don't do world-building," and the stories attracted early letters complaining about the lack of detail in Melniboné's background and history. Elric is, by Moorcock's own admission, himself as a late teenager— "angsty, self-blaming, feeling I was doing harm to others around me and so on," although, in typical Moorcock style, he also cites Charles Maturin's 1820 gothic novel *Melmoth the Wanderer* and Bunyan's *Pilgrim's Progress* as inspiration.

The Elric novels are probably Moorcock's most enduring creation, serving as the centerpiece for Neil Gaiman's quasi-autobiographical short story "One Life Furnished in Early

Moorcock," which Gaiman describes as "a story about a boy a lot like I was once and his relationship with fiction... when I was twelve, Moorcock's characters were as real to me as anything else in my life." Within the story Gaiman describes the Elric tales as "honest. There was nothing going on beneath the surface there. Elric was the etiolated prince of a dead race, burning with self-pity, clutching Stormbringer, his dark-bladed broadsword—a blade which sang for lives, which ate human souls, and which gave their strength to the doomed and weakened albino."

This was itself a reasonable pastiche of Moorcock's style in the Elric novels, which were themselves an excited pastiche of the sword-and-sorcery style epitomized by Robert E. Howard's Conan the Barbarian stories. "Elric had wound a scarf around the rail and tied the other end to his wrist," Moorcock writes in the first book. "Dyvim Tvar had used a long belt for the same purpose. But still they were flung in all directions, often losing their footing as the ship bucked this way and that, and every bone in Elric's body seemed about to crack."

But this style is markedly different from that of Moorcock's other major series. In the *Dancers at the End of Time* series, for instance, Moorcock told the tales of Jherek Carnelian in the dying days of the universe itself, as it collapses inwards upon itself. Full of time travel and decadence, the *Dancers at the End of Time* line offers an almost completely different tone. "From the farmhouse came a great banging about," begins one passage in the first story, *An Alien Heat*, "shouts and barkings, and lights appeared downstairs. Mrs. Underwood grabbed Jherek by the sleeve and drew him inside the first building. In the darkness something snorted and stamped. 'It's a horse!' said Jherek. 'They always delight me and I have seen so many now.'"

It is not, crucially, that Moorcock simply maintained a wide variety of franchises and writing styles. Moorcock freely mixed his worlds together, as in the novella *Elric at the End of Time*, which, as its name suggests, thrusts Elric into the decadent world of *Dancers at the End of Time*, giddily parodying his at times monotonous angst in the process. Elric is prone to lengthy cod-epic monologues where he proclaims things like, "I am of older blood, the blood of the Bright Empire itself, the blood of R'lin K'ren A'a which Cran Liretn mocked, not understanding what it was he laughed at," and other such nonsense. And yet at the End of Time such monologues are but curiosities—when he demands to be returned to Melniboné "so that I may fulfill my own doom-laden destiny" another character looks at him "with affectionate delight. 'Aha! A fellow spirit! I too have a doom-laden destiny." His gloom giving him no particular credential here, Elric is reduced to muttering, "I doubt it is as doom-laden as mine."

The intersections of these fictional worlds is governed by an overall system Moorcock calls the Multiverse, which is based around the idea of the Eternal Champion, a figure that exists in all worlds and that all of Moorcock's protagonists are iterations of. Within the Multiverse the struggle between law and chaos (the latter represented by an eight-point star that, in 1978, was appropriated by Peter J. Carroll in *Liber Null* as the symbol of his newly created system of chaos magick) is endlessly mediated by said Champion, any given manifestation of which is just a facet of the whole. (Many, though not all of the incarnations have the initials JC, hence the similarity in names between *Dancers at the End of Time*'s Jherek Carnelian and Jerry Cornelius.)

In many ways Jerry Cornelius is the purest expression of this. As mentioned, his first book, *The Final Programme*, is written in a relatively straightforward style. But by the second volume, *A Cure for Cancer*, Moorcock found it necessary to append a reader's note that explains, "This book has an unconventional structure." Here, for example, Moorcock has a chapter entitled "Mystery of Yowling Passenger in Snob Auto" where the majority of the text consists of a man in the backseat of Jerry's car (the controls of which are "beautifully designed in diamonds, rubies, and sapphires" that respond "with delicate sensuality to his touch") who screams incoherently. "Aaaaaaaaaaaahhh! Why? Why? Aaaaaaaaaaaaaaaaaaaaaaaa aaaaaaaaaaaaaaaaaaa whyaaaaaaaaaaaaaaaaaaaaaaaaaaa aaaaaaaaaaaaaaaaaawhyaaaaaaaaaaaaaaaaaaawhyaaa," one representative passage comments, "whyaaaaaaaaaaaaaaaaaaaaaaaaaaaaaaaaaaaaaaaawhyaaaaaahhhhh! YOU WON'T GET AWAY WITH THIS YOUNG MAN! Yaaaaaaaaaaaaaaaaaaaaaaaaaaaaaaaaaaaaaaaaaaaaaa! You'll regret thisaaaaaaaaaaaaaaaaaaaaaaaaaaaaaaaa! WHY! WHY! WHY!" before continuing "AAAAAAAAAAH! Yaaaaaaaaaaaaaaaaaaaaaaaaaaaaaaaaaaaargh! Yaaaaaaaaaaaaaaaaaaaaaaaaaaaaaaaaaaaaaaaaaaaaaaaaaaaaaaaargh! THE AUTHORITIES WILL SOON CATCH UP WITH YOU, MY FRIEND!" and concluding "OOOOOOOOOOOOOOOOOOOOOOOOOOOOOOOO OOOOOOOOH. URSH! YAROOOOOOOOOOOOOOOOOOOO! I SAY, STOP IT, YOU ROTTERS! OOOOOOCH! GAARR," at which point Jerry inserts a comment, setting off another round in which the character's screams of "AAAAAAAAA" are typographically arranged so that the As themselves form larger letters A on the page.

The Cornelius books are characterized by large quantities of philosophical dialogue amidst action set pieces, which often fade towards the background. A few chapters after the yowling passenger, Cornelius recalls a conversation where "a girl had once asked him, stroking the muscles of his stomach, 'What do you achieve by the destruction of the odd library? There are so many. How much can one man do?' 'What he can,' Cornelius had told her, rolling on her. 'It's History that's caused all the trouble in the past.'" Moorcock has commented that the Cornelius books are populated by "characters who are aware of the psychological implications of their statements and actions. That is they are as aware of the unconscious as the conscious. In that sense it was a rejection of modernist techniques as found in Joyce, Woolf

5. Mystery of Yowling Passenger in Snob Auto

Jerry drove the Phantom VI convertible at a rapid lick. The controls of the car, beautifully designed in diamonds, rubies and sapphires by Gillian Packard, responded with delicate sensuality to his touch. In the back, in his chamois leather straitjacket, the transmog case continued to scream.

'EEEEEEEEEEEEEEEEEEEEEEEEEEEEEEEEEEEEEEEEEEEEEEEEHELP
MEEEEEEEEEEEEEEEEEEEEEEEEEEEEEEEEEEEEEEEEEEEEEEEEEEEE.'
'That's what we're trying to do, old lord. Hang on.'
'Aaaaaaaaaaaahh! Why? Why? Aaaaaaaaaaaaaaaaaaaaaaaaaaaaaaaaaaaaaaaaaaa
aaaaaaaaaaaaaaaawhyaaaaaaaaaaaaaaaaaaaaaaaaaaaaaaaaaaaaaaaaaaaaaaaaaaaaaaaa
aaaaaaaaaaaaaaaaaaaaaaaaaaaaawhyaaaaaaaaaaaaaaaaaawhyaaaaaaaaaaaaaaaaaaaaaaaa
whyaaaaaaaaaaaaaaaaaaaaaaaaaaaaaaaaaaaaaaaaawhyaaaaaaaaaaaaaaaaaaaaa ahhhh!
YOU WON'T GET AWAY WITH THIS, YOUNG MAN!
Yaaaaaaaaaaaaaaaaaaaaaaaaaaaaaaaaaaaaaaaaaaaaaaaaaaaaaaaaaaa! You'll regret
thisaaaaaaaaaaaaaaaaaaaaaaaaaaaaaaaaaaaaaaaaaaaaaaaaa! WHY! WHY! WHY!
AAAAAAAAAAAAAAAAH! Yaaaaaaaaaaaaaaaaaaaaaaaaaaaaaaaaaaaaaaaaargh!
Yaaaaaaaaaaaaaaaaaaaaaaaaaaaaaaaaaaaaaaaaaaaaaaaaaaaaaaaaaaaaaaaaargh!
THE AUTHORITIES WILL SOON CATCH UP WITH
YOU, MY FRIEND! OOOOOOOOOOOOOOOOOOOOOOOOO
OOOOOOOOOOOOOH. URSH! YAROOOOOOOOOOOOO!
I SAY, STOP IT, YOU ROTTERS! OOOOOOOOOOOOCH!
GAARR! EEEEEEEEEEEEEEEEEEEEEEEEEEEEEEEEEEEEEEEEEEEEE
EEEEEEEEEEEEEEEEEEEEEEEEEEEEK! DO YOU KNOW WHO I
AM??????'
'Do you? That's what we're trying to fix. Be quiet, there's a
good chap.'
'AAAAAAAAAAAAAAAAAAAAAAAAAAAAAAAAAAAAAAAAAAAAA
AAAAAAAAAAAAAAAAAAAAAAAAAAAAAAAAAAAAAAAAAAAAA
AAAAAAAAAAAAAAAAAAAAAAAAAAAAAAAAAAAAAAAAAAAAA
```
        A          A          A          A
      A  A       A  A        A  A        A  A
     A    A     A    A      A    A      A    A
     AAAAAAA   AAAAAAA    AAAAAAA    AAAAAAA
    A    A A      A  A       A  A      A  A      A
   A      A      A          A          A          A
```
AAAAAAAAAAAAAAAAAAAAAAAAAAAAAAAAAAAAAAAAAAAAA
AAAAAAAAAAAAAAAAAAAAAAAAAAAAAAAAAAAAAAAAAAAAA
AAAAAAAAAAAAAAAAAAAAAAAAAAAAAAAAAAAAAAAAAAAAA
HHHHHHHHH!' said the ex-chairman defiantly.

: 164 :

Figure 4: Text as visual object (A Cure for Cancer, *1969*)

and so on. My view was that we had moved on from needing to make that sort of observation." Instead Moorcock's characters, as he describes it, "tend to anticipate one another's statements and short-cut their own," engaging in an endlessly anticipated and reiterated philosophical dialogue that plays out over the superficial frame of the heroic fantasy stories.

"This Zen-crazed aerial madman just won't take no for an answer!"
–Grant Morrison, *The Invisibles* #18, 1996

To suggest that it is possible that a fictional multiverse in which one primary character is a dandy action hero who lives in an eternally shifting world and another—the most prominent, in fact—is a sword-and-sorcery barbarian figure whose world blends in with the present day at times might have been an influence on the writer of the Gideon Stargrave stories or "Time is a Four Letter Word" seems almost too obvious to mention. Of course Moorcock was a major influence on Grant Morrison's earliest comics work, and, more to the point, on much of his subsequent work.

The question of why Moorcock, who was after all usually perfectly happy to let others play with his fictional terms, lashed out so angrily at Morrison for his Cornelius pastiche is interesting, but not entirely germane at this point in the War's development. Suffice it to say that Morrison is quite justified in his exasperation when he points to his later works and asks, "Can anyone tell me from which Michael Moorcock novels *Zenith* and *Animal Man* were plagiarized?" and that Morrison was influenced by the entire new wave literary tradition Moorcock came out of, not just Moorcock in particular. All the same it is in many ways very easy to draw direct and specific links between Moorcock's work and his, especially in his earliest stuff.

But it is also important to realize that for Morrison it is more the interplay of iconography that fascinates than the actual content. So while Morrison may include a flashback to

Stargrave and his sister Genevieve arguing, whereby Genevieve proclaims that "Love is a lie! A justification for sex! Sex is all there is! Sex! Sex! Sex! You're out of synch with the world, love. Obsolete..."—a scene with marked similarities to the sorts of twists the Cornelius books take—this is, for Morrison, just a visual and narrative trope to riff off of, as opposed to a considered meditation on contemporary sexuality.

In this regard it is perhaps more significant to look at the degree to which Cornelius had filtered out into the larger culture, throughout which the concept echoes. Most obvious is the 1973 film *The Final Programme*, a Moorcock-disclaimed adaptation of the first Cornelius book starring Jon Finch. The film was a disposable piece of 70s trash cinema, and its execution rarely matched the giddy ambition of the books, but it still grounded Cornelius's adventures in what seems like their natural environment: the world of cultural images out of which his adventures are built. (Morrison, for his part, cites the film as equally important to his aesthetic and self-conception as the books when he mentions them in *Supergods*, although given how many times the Moorcock issue had come up by that time that may well just be him trolling Moorcock.)

If the film of *The Final Programme* was a cheap-looking version of the Cornelius stories then it compares sensibly with the other obvious Cornelius analogue in 1973's popular culture, Jon Pertwee's portrayal of classic sci-fi hero Doctor Who as a ruffled shirt-wearing dandy whose magical blue box moved him rapidly from setting to setting, and who never quite fit in, always seeming more like an alien doing a drag performance of the manly action hero—the sort whose cool car was in fact an antique roadster, and whose action sequences consisted of shouting "Hai!" a lot as people fell over. This idea of an alien drag performance also describes the glam rock period of David Bowie's career, which seems in many regards a decade-long real life performance of a Jerry Cornelius story, complete with an end-of-decade

*Figure 5: Jon Finch's rendition of Jerry Cornelius talks assassination in a pinball arcade. (*The Final Programme, *1973)*

transformation into Pierot the Clown. In other words, if Cornelius is less a character than a technique then the technique was a standard approach of 1970s media, and Morrison, who is clearly deeply invested in the visual style of things, would have picked it up from far more places than just some novels.

This marks a profound difference between Morrison and Moorcock. Moorcock is aggressively literary in his influences—from his perspective "the *Commedia dell'arte*," an Italian style of theater based around stock and trope characters, "has been one of my chief influences, especially in relation to the Cornelius books. I have a large collection of commedia material as well as French and English versions. I have some of those old commedia plot books which can be very stimulating when mulling over the structure of a story." Elsewhere he lists his influences as Ronald Firbank, a post-decadent British author of the early 20th century heavily inspired by Oscar Wilde, and Burroughs, who he remarks are "two not dissimilar figures in my estimation." The difference between this profoundly bookish approach and Morrison's, who in 2005 declared that "I haven't had any interest in science fiction since a brief but inspirational teenage obsession with the 'New Wave' generation of Moorcock, Ballard, and Ellison" and that "these days I just read comics and watch DVDs for my fiction dose," is self-evident. However similar the material the two writers treat, in other words, there are fundamental divergences in their interests and approaches.

Rather than focusing on the specific question of direct influence, it is more useful to consider the general question of interplay between the new wave that Moorcock and Ballard belonged to—a movement that had demonstrably broad impact on the culture—and British comics in 1979, particularly in the context of *Near Myths*. If this means going beyond Moorcock's work to understand the context then it also means going beyond Morrison's, as Gideon Stargrave is only the second most significant character in *Near Myths* primarily inspired by Jerry Cornelius. The other, greater Moorcock riff is Luther Arkwright, eponymous hero of Bryan Talbot's universe-hopping epic *The Adventures of Luther Arkwright*. Talbot is, largely unfairly, a forgotten man of British comics; unlike both Moore and Morrison, who abandoned drawing their own comics due to their lack of speed and talent, Talbot remained known primarily as an illustrator, from his work on *Nemesis the Warlock* for *2000 A.D.* to his credits in things like Vertigo Comics' *Sandman*, *Hellblazer*, and *Fables*. But his solo work is of equal note, particularly *Alice in Sunderland*, *The Tale of One Bad Rat*, and *The Adventures of Luther Arkwright*.

Luther Arkwright did not begin in *Near Myths*, but in *Brainstorm Comix*, a mid-70s underground book put out under the Alchemy Press label and dominated by Talbot's early work. A seven-pager whose debt to Cornelius is not even thinly veiled, "The Papist Affair" did not bristle with promise, and Talbot has largely cast it out of the Arkwright canon. Still, its mix of motorbikes and period detail in an alternate history in which the villain is the church is a close mirror of Grant Morrison's "The Vatican Conspiracy." (This fact is not lost on Bryan Talbot, who in 2009 referred to "a kung fu fight with a fascist archbishop—a scene later plagiarized by Grant Morrison in one of his *Near Myths* strips." Talbot overstates the case, but more has been made out of narrower similarities in the course of the War.)

Still, all of this would be an odd footnote were it not for the fact that Talbot resurrected the character for a strip in *Near Myths*, which debuted in the first issue and continued into issue number five, which Talbot himself edited in a last, desperate, and failed attempt to get the magazine into usable shape. Talbot tried it again in *psssst!*, when it was interrupted by the magazine folding out from under it again, before the existing material was collected along with several issues of new material by Valkyrie Press from 1987-89, and eventually Dark Horse Comics in a manner not dissimilar to DC's eventual handling of Alan Moore's *V For Vendetta*.

Figure 6: *Gunplay with nuns in the first appearance of Bryan Talbot's*
Adventures of Luther Arkwright, *"The Papist Affair," from his mid-70s*
work in Brainstorm Comix…

Figure 7: *…and in Grant Morrison's second Gideon Stargrave strip (From*
Near Myths #4, 1979)

Although few would suggest, particularly in the light of the latter's appropriation by Anonymous and the Occupy movement, that *The Adventures of Luther Arkwright* has had the same degree of influence as *V for Vendetta*, the comparison is not entirely inapt. Certainly *The Adventures of Luther Arkwright* has what might be described as friends where it counts— Michael Moorcock, Alan Moore, Neil Gaiman, Rick Veitch, and Garth Ennis provided fan mail for the letter column of the first issue of the Arkwright sequel *Heart of Empire*. Moore and Moorcock further provided introductions to the Valkyrie press editions of *The Adventures of Luther Arkwright*, where Moore tipped his hat to Talbot for being "a crucial stepping stone" and positioning Talbot as the genesis of the entire wave of British comics writers and artists that was cresting in 1987 when his introduction was written. Moorcock declares him "one of my own personal favorites," while Warren Ellis goes so far as to proclaim *Arkwright* to be "the single most influential graphic novel to come out of Britain to date." Even Grant Morrison, whose relationship with potential influences can be strained, defends Talbot in a 2002 interview, crediting him over Alan Moore for comics' abandonment of thought bubbles, and defending him when the interviewer proclaims, "I don't rate Luther Arkwright," saying that "I just thought it was fantastic" and "I like Bryan Talbot's work. It kinda resonated with stuff I was into."

Clearly *The Adventures of Luther Arkwright* is a landmark text, and, by most reasonable standards, serves as a better claim to cultural significance for *Near Myths* than the appearance of Morrison's juvenilia. But these proper Luther Arkwright stories follow from what is almost an incidental detail of "The Papist Affair," which is mostly, as Talbot described it in 2009, "a daft romp." In the course of its heavily armed motorcycle nun antics the story almost incidentally introduces its premise of parallel worlds. This is sensible enough—"The Papist Affair" is an admitted Cornelius riff, and thus it's essentially impossible that parallel worlds weren't in Talbot's head as he was writing it.

But Talbot became intrigued by this concept and decided to develop Arkwright into a character who could anchor a sustained narrative. In the course of this he moved the character away from his Moorcockian roots. So the Luther Arkwright of *Near Myths* is a more austere character, still modern, but rendered in a less period-dated style. Talbot also swapped the cartoony, exaggerated style of the *Brainstorm Comix* iteration of the character in favor of a shadowy style dominated by intricate inkwork and photorealist faces, and abandoned the simple grid he used for his straightforward action romp in favor of an experimental style heavily reliant on layering objects on top of objects and including snatches of documents that exist only within the world of the story.

Like Morrison's work there's a high degree of formal complexity to Luther Arkwright. And like Morrison's work this complexity is turned towards a specifically psychedelic approach in which the hopping between parallel universes turns into an intensive spiritual enlightenment. This culminates in issue #6 of the nine-issue Valkyrie Press series, in which Arkwright has a near-death experience and spiritual rebirth. Splash pages dominated by blocks of text abound, walls of stream of consciousness and ecstatic visions juxtaposed with Blakean horrors rendered in what Morrison describes as Talbot's "meticulous drawing style," comparing it to Albrecht Dürer.

The text becomes a cut-up invocation that puts Burroughs to shame, describing how "in the garden of Gethsemene Kali becomes Miranda take this my ankh the Egyptian sign of life renounce the ways of violence Luther the tabla beat faster the star changes to a distant Balalaika Siberian winds howl" against a backdrop of copulating demons drawn in sinewy shadow. This was not, to be clear, an influence on Morrison—*The Adventures of Luther Arkwright* #6 is entirely a product of the late 80s. Rather, it shows the extent to which Morrison's early strips fit firmly and coherently into a defined literary tradition that defies simple attempts to pin down specific and discrete influences.

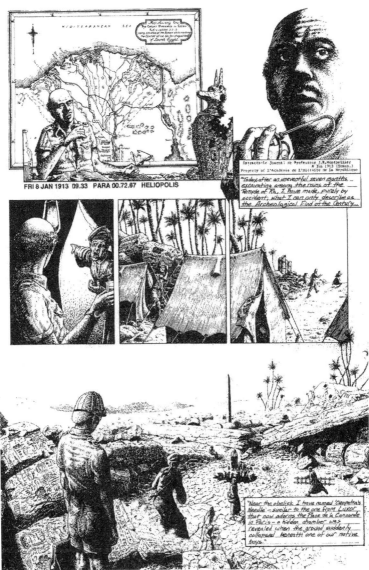

Figure 8: Talbot's second go at Luther Arkwright featured stylistic flourishes such as textual artifacts from within the fictional world and tight, detailed linework.(From The Adventures of Luther Arkwright #1, *by Bryan Talbot, 1987, original from* Near Myths, *1979)*

"Not born so much as ground like pigment from his times"
–Alan Moore, *Angel Passage,* 2001

Even still, for all that Morrison insists, admittedly with self-deprecating panache, that he dismissed Talbot because "I was a punk, and I didn't need things to be slick as long as they had conviction and personality," the direct influence is compelling. Morrison's artwork evolves over his time on *Near Myths,* adopting a heavier shadow and thicker line that owes a clear debt to Talbot (as well as to the squarer-jawed action style of then-DC Comics based superhero artist Neal Adams, discussions of whose work bookend the chapter of *Supergods* in which Talbot and *Near Myths* are discussed). Indeed, Morrison's final *Near Myths* story, "The Checkmate Man," feels more than a little like Luther Arkwright, both in its structure and style. (Indeed, Morrison's copyright notice explicitly distinguishes between the 1979 art and 1977 script, as though mindful of the similarities and wanting to make sure everybody knew he'd come up with it independently.)

But the anxiety of influence is not particularly interesting in this case, as we've seen. Morrison's work fits clearly into an overall tradition in which dandy secret agents leaping among worlds and having psychedelic revelations were relatively common. What's interesting is not the question of precisely when Morrison became aware of Talbot's work any more than whether Ballard or Moorcock is the larger influence on Gideon Stargrave. There's no reason not to believe Morrison when he says that *Near Myths* "introduced me to Bryan Talbot," a statement that seems to consciously hedge against the possibility that "The Vatican Conspiracy" is, as Talbot alleges, indebted to "The Papist Affair." Given that Stargrave appears in issue #3 of *Near Myths* several months after Arkwright's debut, it's entirely possible that Morrison was self-consciously tweaking the comic's head feature with a glitzed-up experimental parody of its abandoned first version; it would, after all, be a perfect reflection of Jerry Cornelius's first story's status as a rewrite of some early Elric yarns.

Equally, however, it's just possible that Morrison and Talbot individually hit what was obviously hanging in the air like cannabis smoke over social meetings in Edinburgh's Science Fiction Bookshop. In the end there's not really a difference.

What is more significant is the fact that Talbot and Morrison had visibly different interests within this basic nexus of themes. *The Adventures of Luther Arkwright* seems overtly concerned with the content of its psychedelic event, bathing it in a textual and semiotic excess that renders it particular and precise. The paratexts of the comic reinforce this—*The Adventures of Luther Arkwright* #6 ends with an essay by Mike Kidson about the psychedelia of the death/rebirth sequence. In it he provides a dense inventory of occult details therein, blazing in one paragraph through Timothy Leary, DNA, the symbol of the caduceus, Pythagoras, the chakra system, the musical scale, Kabbalah, the tarot, and the number of the Beast. Like Talbot's tight-knit linework, the hyper-density of the references marks this as a work concerned with details.

It is not that Morrison's work is not detail oriented; "The Checkmate Man" shows that Morrison was a savvy observer of other people's work. But Morrison's focus is, as always, less on substance than on visual style. The high point of "The Checkmate Man" comes in its first page, a perfectly staged visual set piece of the eponymous assassin taking down Karl Marx with a high-powered sniper rifle. Although both textual narrative ("his briefcase bursts open, the papers within caught by the wind are blown like the leaves. The sky is reflected, in the swelling puddle around Marx's head") and visual components are competent, the central brilliance of the scene is simply the mad and giddy perversity of its basic existence.

Morrison, in other words, is the David Bowie to Talbot's Brian Eno, an energetic populist opposite a meticulous craftsman. But this constitutes, in a sense, the logical final form of the new wave aesthetic. The collapse into images is simply the furthest possible reach of treating the genre markers of a story as mere decoration to be cut-up and

Figure 9: The unexpected assassination of Karl Marx. (By Grant Morrison, from "The Checkmate Man" in Near Myths *#5, 1980)*

reworked. Morrison plays entirely within the frenetic interchanging of images. It's the exact inversion of Moorcock's approach: where Moorcock sets out to demonstrate that the story exists regardless of its frame, Morrison sets out to demonstrate that the story is just a dummy to be adorned with clothing.

In this regard the most telling statement in his discussion of Bryan Talbot in *Supergods* is his suggestion that Talbot was "a better writer than he was an artist," a statement that applies equally well (and indeed far better) to Morrison himself. Morrison's implied suggestion is that Talbot's mistake was to not pursue writing as he did, and that the Luther Arkwright stories were in their own way just as superficial as his Gideon Stargrave strips. Certainly Morrison took a swipe at it in the review he put out in *Ark* #28, which he describes as "five pages of autobiography, and then a bit where I have to say something about Luther Arkwright" before trailing off and suggesting he fell asleep at that point of writing the review.

This tension between writing and art underlies a lot of British comics—both Morrison and Moore, after all, started as writer-artists before reinventing themselves as pure writers. And understanding the War through them necessarily puts the focus on that aspect of what comics are. But the art is a massive dimension of it, and one that is easily overlooked. Comics are, in point of fact, a visual medium, and talking about them is, as they say, like talking about sex. Indeed, much of what makes Moore and Morrison so good is the fact that they are sufficiently trained as artists to think substantively and innovatively about the visual dimensions of their work.

As an example of how this art/writing divide dramatically affects how a given figure within the War is understood, consider William Blake, one of the key figures in the British magical tradition that defines the contours of the War. Blake was an artist-writer in a protocomic form of illuminated manuscripts, within which he crafted prophetic visions of a mythology shaped in his own head, spinning tales of demonic Urizen and rebellious Orc and how the shifting of power among them would shape the future of Albion. Indeed, his influence is felt clearly in the page-sized images with prose accompaniment of *The Adventures of Luther Arkwright* #6, where the writhing masses of demonic figures he drew in his illustrations for Dante's *Divine Comedy* are transmuted by Talbot into crisp detail without losing any of their libidinous terror.

This connection was explicitly commented upon by Dave Thorpe, a primary developer of Captain Britain for Marvel UK, in the *Arkeology* volume that reprinted various essays on the comics that Valkyrie Press published. His two-page essay entitled "A Vision of Albion" quoted Blake passages alongside an interpretation of Luther Arkwright and some poor black and white reproductions of Blake's art (as well as, of all things, a 1989 sketch of Luther Arkwright by Grant Morrison that Morrison, when asked about it, boasted was a "five minute scribble") and discussed the relatively thin fact that both of them are British and based on visionary, psychedelic experiences. Still, if the understanding of Blake's system is thin the similarities are still relatively straightforward. In an interview with Roger Whitson for *ImageTexT,* Talbot admitted to a "resonance" between his work and Blake's on the fundamentally technical level of "the strong image, dramatic composition and dynamic line—plus the use of text in his illustrated poems."

But there's an even more basic point of intersection between Blake and the new wave tradition that Morrison and Talbot follow from: central to Blake's visionary mythology is the notion of Albion, a primeval humanity that has not been divided and split into its fallen form. This sense of unity as the elements of a thing are gathered back together and allowed to coexist, contradictions and all, that it becomes, in Blakean terms, a part of Eternity—is an obvious precursor to the composite landscapes of Burroughs's cut-ups, Ballard's pataphoric lists, or Moorcock's shifting facets of the Eternal

Figure 10: Demons in Blake. (From his illustrations to the Divine Comedy, *c. 1824-27)*

Figure 11: Demons in Talbot. (From The Adventures of Luther Arkwright #6, *c. 1982)*

Champion. In Blake's mythology characters repeatedly fragment, are turned into their emanations or others, or otherwise transform so that their role in the narrative is completely new, such that a name like "Enitharmon" can refer to both the child of the Zoa Tharmas and his emanation, Enion, and to the emanation of Los, the fallen form of the Zoa Urthona. Enitharmon, with Los, gives birth to Orc, the fallen form of the Zoa Luvah, who, along with Urizen, the fourth Zoa, are the four divisions of Albion, the primeval man. The similarities to Moorcock's fragmented Eternal Champion, or to the uncertain and shifting reality of the Jerry Cornelius stories could not be any more blatant.

Blake succeeded as a working artist for his entire life, though his income was meager and he lived in borderline poverty. The practical result of this was that his work was split between his prophetic illuminated manuscripts and freelance illustration jobs, some interesting and provocative like his illustrations for Edward Young's largely forgotten *Night-Thoughts*, others rather less so. Blake's relationship to this work was at times tense, as was his relationship to the poverty he felt harmed his work. But more significant is the way in which this split in his career between writing, illustrating his own writing, and illustrating other people's writings has affected his reputation, fragmented him into various disciplines andcareers. For most people he's the writer of "The Tyger" and perhaps also "The Lamb," and rarely credited with anything outside *Songs of Innocence* and *Songs of Experience*, which are transmuted from an entwined pair of illuminated books into the base lead of poetry anthologies.

The visionary nature of William Blake defies the usual genre divisions and, perhaps more problematically, subject divisions. It is simply not accurate to treat him as a poet or as an artist, nor even as a comics creator, although comics scholars have produced some of the most compelling work on Blake of recent years. In truth Blake belonged to a category poorly appreciated by history—the working creator.

Blake was, as Peter Ackroyd put it, "a lower-middle-class tradesman, a mystic intimately involved in the world of commerce and craft," and his career as an engraver, working with varnishes, oils, and acids was "hard and continuous physical labour. Words were for him objects carved out of metal, and it could be said that the technical requirements of his trade—the need for strong outline, for example, and the importance of minute particulars—helped him to formulate an entire metaphysical system." So when Blake writes

> I rest not from my great task!
> To open the Eternal Worlds, to open the immortal Eyes
> Of Man inwards into the Worlds of Thought: into Eternity
> Ever expanding in the Bosom of God, the Human Imagination
> O Saviour pour upon me thy Spirit of meekness & love:
> Annihilate the Selfhood in me, be thou all my life!

the annihilation of selfhood should be taken not merely as a mystical experience but as work—the great task alluded to some lines earlier. Nor is this work merely the creative business of sitting around waiting for a vision to strike him. To open the immortal Eyes Of Man inwards into the Worlds of Thought and into Eternity Ever expanding in the Bosom of God requires the brutal, burning, acrid physical labor of page, creating prints and engravings, of framing and laying out the and of perfecting the linework of each individual page, of which there were a hundred in *Jerusalem*, always to be hand colored, unique from any other copy. It involves laboring for sixteen years on the poem, plus another eight on the unfinished *Vala, or the Four Zoas*, elements of which were repurposed into *Jerusalem*, in at times crushing near-poverty, dependent completely on patrons and commissions thrown his way as much out of sympathy as out of regard for his talent. It is not merely vision but the brutality of what Alan Moore calls the world's blunt engine that produces Blake's art, and to understand it as anything other than material creation is to violently misunderstand it.

This reality makes the work of a visionary comics producer harder. The need to take on commissions and side work means that Talbot, instead of creating works of pioneering vision, has spent much of his career on Judge Dredd and Batman stories or illustrating cards for Wizards of the Coast's *Magic: The Gathering* money factory. Even in his later personal work the sense of vision at times chokes and drowns underneath the realities of modern comics production. *Heart of Empire*, his 1999 sequel to *The Adventures of Luther Arkwright*, retains none of the original's experimental or psychedelic heft; Talbot's obsessive linework vanishes beneath Angue McKie's digital coloring, making the pages look like nothing more special than his illustration work for Neil Gaiman's *Sandman*, and even when the comic embarks on psychedelic vision there's a muted cleanliness to it.

This is a pity, as Talbot is, in practice, every bit the skilled genius of Moore, Ellis, Morrison, and Gaiman. The trouble is that Talbot's great work is a narrow band—the two Arkwright stories, *The Tale of One Bad Rat*, and *Alice in Sunderland* providing the bulk of it. Talbot has, save for four issues of *Sandman* spin-off *The Dreaming*, never written comics for others to draw. His vision is, like Blake's, suited only to his own hand, unlike that of Morrison and Moore, who quickly came to conclude that their vision was best realized through the eyes and lines of other men.

Chapter Two: Captain Clyde and Starblazer

"A society where nothing can change because it takes superhuman effort to keep things the way they are"
–Warren Ellis, 1999

Morrison's self-illustrated work consists of the four *Near Myths* strips, a single issue of *Starblazer*, and his four-year run doing *Captain Clyde* for various local Scottish papers. His reasons for abandoning art are simple—as he put it, "When you're writing, you can do so much more." Unlike Moore, who proclaimed that he abandoned drawing his own material because he was neither fast nor good enough, Morrison maintains that he could have made it as an artist, declaring in 1990 that he "could've been better than most people who're drawing today" and that "sometimes I do thumbnails before I write a story, and the thumbnails look better than the finished art."

Regardless of his reasons for abandoning art, the *Captain Clyde* strips and *Starblazer* issue are interesting both for providing the remaining body of Morrison's work that carries no influence whatsoever from Alan Moore and for providing the last major glimpses of Morrison's vision of himself as a writer-artist in the Bryan Talbot mould. They also mark the introduction of one of the most important concepts in the War, the tradition of pulp heroics, and specifically of superheroes. This is in some ways strange: the superhero was not in and of itself big in the UK—certainly not in the same way that, for instance, *2000 AD* or *Eagle* were. American superhero comics, on the other hand, were for a crucial period quite popular, albeit for idiosyncratic reasons. The usual story, which is perhaps more folklore than sound economic analysis, is that copies of American superhero comics in excess of what sold in America were repurposed as ballast for trans-Atlantic shipping. Once they were in the UK they were typically sold off as an afterthought, entering the markets through idiosyncratic distribution at cut-rate prices. (Interestingly, Morrison has suggested that the nearby American submarine bases in Faslane and Holy Loch meant that American comics were particularly likely to be available in Glasgow, claiming that the Yankee Book Store in Paisley was the first store in the UK to stock them.)

That's in print, at least. On television, the Adam West-fronted *Batman* television series was a perennial bit of televisual ballast. So while the idea of the superhero was well known, it was firmly an imported concept. The only British superhero of any significant note was Mick Angelo's Marvelman, who, by 1979, had not been published in sixteen years, and even he was just a cheat to work around the consequences of the *National Comics Publications v. Fawcett Publications* debacle. Superheroes were an American thing that some British children enjoyed alongside the existing selection of British comics.

Among these British children, however, were both Grant Morrison and Alan Moore, a detail upon which the entire War hinges. This cannot be stated unequivocally enough—without both of their loves for American superhero comics, none of this would ever have happened. In this regard, being asked to write *Captain Clyde* was a huge deal for Morrison, who had been designing superheroes since his teens. But it is also worth stressing the degree to which its genre further places *Captain Clyde* outside any mainstream conception of the British comics industry at the time.

Still, it is worth discussing the superhero, both for its later influence upon the War and to provide a broader context for

Morrison's early work. The superhero is generally considered to have been invented by Jerry Siegel and Joe Shuster in 1938 for *Action Comics* #1, which was headlined with the first appearance of Superman. On one level this is unequivocally true and the only sensible understanding of the origin of superheroes. Certainly this is the origin story Grant Morrison used in *Supergods*, his at times compelling and at times maddening history of the superhero, which he opens with the text of the Superman Code. And it makes sense—Superman was the first of DC Comics's wave of superheroes, followed quickly by Batman, Wonder Woman, and the first versions of the Flash, Green Lantern, and other heroes. The basic paradigm was copied tentatively by one of their rivals, Timely Comics, which quickly churned out the Sub-Mariner (by Bill Everett, who is often claimed to have descended from William Blake, a misleading claim given that Blake had no children, although he is a distant relative), the Human Torch, and Captain America.

Superhero comics were popular in World War II, then declined: Timely (by then Atlas Comics) canceled all of its superheroes, and DC whittled its roster down to Superman, Batman, and Wonder Woman—which is still treated as the nominal Holy Trinity of DC's superhero line. But in the 1950s a team of DC editors and writers including Julius Schwartz, Gardner Fox, Carmine Infantino, Robert Kanigher, and John Broome created Barry Allen, a new version of World War II-era superhero the Flash, kicking off the Silver Age of American superhero comics. Atlas once again followed suit, but this time hit on massive success with what is now the Marvel Universe, featuring the Fantastic Four, the X-Men, Iron Man, Thor, Spider-Man, and a revamped Captain America. The history of superheroes from there to the present day is relatively easy to infer the broad strokes of, and its relevant details can be left for later.

Upon closer inspection, however, the release of *Action Comics* #1 is not quite the *sui generis* debut of the superhero that it might appear. Superman clearly fits into a tradition of masked crime-fighters like Zorro, the Green Hornet, and the Shadow, who are themselves subsets of a larger category of pulp heroes including Doc Savage, John Carter, and Conan the Barbarian. Superman is original inasmuch as he's both costumed and superpowered. But it's impossible to create a definition out of these two facts. Costumes alone fail to distinguish the post-Superman characters from the pre-Superman ones. But equally, Powers are not a requirement of the post-Superman ones, nor absent from the pre-Superman ones. The second step in the standard history of superheroes, Batman, has no powers and is essentially indistinguishable from the Green Hornet or the Shadow, save for the fact that he happened to debut after Superman. And while nothing on quite the scale of Superman's powers existed, there's not a sizable difference between Superman's powers and Doc Savage's training since birth to be the absolute theoretical peak of human ability. Yes, Superman is an alien, but the situation is visibly just the reverse of Edgar Rice Burroughs's John Carter, who has vast physical abilities when transported to Mars because his body is better adapted to the planet. Jerry Siegel even admits to the inspiration, and Superman's powers were far less impressive in the early days than they are now. Even absolutely demanding the fantastic origin of the powers doesn't work—the Shadow, when transported to radio, had what were blatantly supernatural powers.

So neither costumes nor powers are original to Siegel and Shuster. Nor does the idea of combining them adequately explain the invention of superheroes. Costumes are not sufficient to define superheroes, and powers are not necessary. Whatever the idea of the superhero is, it resists a straightforward definition that links it inextricably to Superman. It is, however, telling that superheroes are inexorably associated with one particular medium: comic books. This separates them from almost any other popular genre, and suggests a more useful way of isolating them from adjacent genres. Superheroes have a visual dimension. This is also not an absolute rule—Batman and Superman both had radio shows, and novels like Robert Mayer's *Superfolks* clearly featured superheroes despite not being illustrated.

For the purposes of understanding the War, however, an absolute rule that can be used to separate superheroes from non-superheroes is less useful than an explanation of why the terrain is how it is. Clearly the publication of *Action Comics* #1 was a landmark event in the development of superheroes. It defines the terrain upon which much of the War is fought. What matters is not what the terrain looks like, nor even what precise creative decisions caused it to look that way, but rather a larger question: why is this terrain worth fighting over? The answer to *that* question, at least, can be understood straightforwardly through visual aesthetics.

What *Action Comics* #1 indisputably was is the first massively successful attempt at the pulp hero to be defined by colorful visual representation. Technologically speaking, this was not popular until cheap four-color printing was possible. Accordingly, it was in 1930s comic books that it happened. The cleverness of Superman was that he used color well. He was bright—even lurid—and Siegel and Shuster had what was, for the time, a shockingly kinetic style of visual storytelling. What was crucial was not the idea of a costumed hero with special powers, but the fact that this particular costumed hero was interesting because he looked good. Grant Morrison tacitly confirms as much in *Supergods*, where he spends pages analyzing the visual composition of the cover of *Action Comics* #1, writing in ecstatic tones of "the vivid yellow background with a jagged corona of red" in its background and linking its visual design to "the gateway of the *loa* (or spirit) Legba, another manifestation of the 'god' known variously as Mercury, Thoth, Ganesh, Odin, or Ogma," the latter being, predictably, a figure from the *Cath Maighe Tuireadh*, a 9th century Celtic text.

The superhero is thus best used to describe a type of pulp hero story that emerged out of 1930s American comic books. Not all superheroes have their origins in comic books, but enough do that it is a reasonably challenging game to identify

Figure 12: The cover of Action Comics #1, *generally considered the first superhero comic.* (By Joe Shuster)

ones who first appeared in another medium, especially ones that have any degree of popularity today. They are defined primarily by a visual intensity and a sense of heritage tracing back to *Action Comics* #1. And they are worth fighting over because pulp heroes of that sort are a large part of contemporary culture, and have come to almost completely dominate the American comic book industry, in which large swaths of the War are fought.

But the War starts in Britain and remains, in the end, fought in Albion. And in British comics culture superheroes never gained the absolute dominance over the comics industry that they did in America. In British comics the first massively popular instance of highly visual pulp storytelling was *Eagle*, an anthology comic featuring stories in several genres headlined by the colorful adventures of *Dan Dare: Pilot of the Future*, and, crucially, dating to 1950, not 1938. And 1950 was squarely in the dead period of superhero comics between their World War II popularity and their Silver Age revivals. This meant that the British comics industry had several years in which to develop its own styles of highly visual pulp storytelling without any influence from American superheroes.

"Believe in the Stars."
–Alan Moore, *Dodgem Logic* #4, 2010

Which meant, in turn, that in 1979 Grant Morrison could submit a story to *Starblazer*, a comic that simply would not have ever existed in the late 70s American comic book industry. *Starblazer* debuted in April of 1979, and became a twice-monthly title in July of the same year. Its concept is simple—single-issue sci-fi stories (later broadened to include fantasy as well) sold in what's known as "digest" format. Measuring at 13.5 x 17.5 centimeters (or roughly 5 x 7 inches), digests were about the height of a mass market paperback, but slightly wider at the base—similar to the formats used for science fiction magazines like *Galaxy* and

New Worlds as well as American "digest" comics, the most famous of which were Gold Key's efforts. Within British comics, digests were an interesting format: unlike the usual comics magazines, they actually told single stories in a single issue instead of serializing several stories per issue. Also unlike the usual anthologies, digests generally told bespoke stories in each issue. Some characters might appear for multiple engagements, but there was no expectation that consecutively numbered issues would feature any of the same characters or plots.

Starblazer was published from 1979 to 1991 by DC Thomson, a Dundee-based publisher most known for popular children's comics *The Beano* and *The Dandy*, the former of which is still published and is currently the longest-running comic in the UK (the honor having been held by *The Dandy* until its 2012 cancellation). *Starblazer* was the sci-fi focused sister publication of the definitive digest-sized British comic *Commando*, first published in 1961 and still running today. *Commando*, as its title suggests, was primarily focused on war comics, and its basic format of a sixty-four page war story in a single digest-sized issue became something of a standard for the form. Fleetway published scads of them under the generic "Picture Library" header, including *War Picture Library*, *Valiant Picture Library*, *Top Secret Picture Library*, *Thriller Picture Library*, *Space Picture Library*, and *Lion Picture Library*, some of which were devoted to particular genres, while others switched among multiple genres.

Grant Morrison's first contribution to *Starblazer* was in issue #15, entitled "Algol the Terrible," and is the only one that he drew himself. Over the next decade he contributed seven more stories, culminating in 1987's "The Ring of Gofannon," his one fantasy story. These comics mark his only major comics work during the gap between the cancellation of *Captain Clyde* in 1982 and his return to the industry in 1985, and thus the only real bridge between his juvenilia and his later career. Despite this, they are in some ways the most ephemeral of Morrison's early work. Where

Figure 13: Grant Morrison's cover to his debut Starblazer *story.*

the *Near Myths* material tied into his career-defining work on *The Invisibles* and *Captain Clyde* foreshadowed his later superhero work (and gave him a convenient cudgel in his priority dispute with Alan Moore), his *Starblazer* work amounts to 512 pages of formulaic space action. (Or, rather, 448 pages of that and sixty-four of sword-and-sorcery adventure.) Nevertheless, Morrison, in several interviews, has suggested that *Starblazer* was a formative experience. In 2003 he discussed "learning the basics of comic storytelling from the expert editors at Thomson," though a 2013 comment that all of his scripts for *Starblazer* got the same editorial note— "more space combat"—suggests that the description of "expert editors" may have been slightly tongue-in-cheek.

Still, on the whole, Morrison's account of DC Thomson is on balance positive. In a 1988 interview he admits to having "a lot of fights" with his editors over things like his attempt to do a *Starblazer* story with a pacifist hero, and, more troublingly, his attempt to do a black hero, and complains that the pay for a *Starblazer* script was "ludicrously small." But he also says, "I must admit to having a fondness for *Starblazer* and I try to contribute whenever I get the chance," which is demonstrably true given that it was the only comics work he did from 1982-85. And it's telling that, in an interview for Mark Salisbury's 1999 anthology *Writers on Comics Scriptwriting*, he described how he "had two outlets from the start. One for the avant-garde stuff, where I could just blow out any shit from my head onto paper, and one for really mainstream commercial work." What's striking about this quote is the relative disdain with which he treats the *Near Myths* work. It is surely in part self-deprecating humor (the interview comes from a period where he had a similar split between his profoundly avant-garde work on *The Invisibles* and his exuberantly traditionalist *JLA*), but it reveals a clear investment in the mainstream and the value of the mainstream. And it's true that the *Starblazer* comics show a narrative discipline that Morrison's other early work does not. They are sixty-four page action stories done in the same model as all of the other digest comics of the time, only with space combat.

It is worth summarizing the contents of Morrison's 512 pages of *Starblazer* work. His first story, as mentioned, is "Algol the Terrible," which features a peaceful space alliance attacked by evil warlords led by, of all people, Algol the Terrible. "The Last Man on Earth," in *Starblazer* #28, is about a young man named Gaunt who goes on a mission to retrieve "the Stardust Equation" (which has the secret of immortality), but who eventually has to double back and destroy the mad computer that sent him on the mission. "Operation Overkill," from issue #45, features Kayn, a sunglasses-clad hero hunting an escaped criminal with a horde of terrifying creatures. Issue #86 featured "The Cosmic Outlaw," which brings back the protagonist of "Algol the Terrible," Herne, for a routine engagement fighting one of the last surviving Starbarons (also from "Algol the Terrible"). 1984's "The Death Reaper," in issue #127, features the return of Kayn from "Operation Overkill," now given an origin and established as a blind ex-cop known "for methods to be found in no book." This time he's trying to solve the murder of his ex-partner, and ends up meeting Cinnibar, a sword-and-sorcery warrior in the Red Sonja mould. The pair returns in #167 for "Mind Bender," where Kayn is called in by the very police that fired him to unravel a conspiracy. And the two appear again in "The Midas Mystery" ten issues later, this time investigating who blew up an office building. And finally there's "The Ring of Gofannon," Morrison's one sword-and-sorcery story, in issue #209, which features Goll, a Conan-esque warrior, searching for the titular ring.

Many of these stories, though by no means all of them, have interesting twists within their premises. "The Ring of Gofannon," for instance, hinges on the revelation that the ring is not, in fact, a piece of jewelry, but rather the route Goll and his servant take, which when travelled releases powerful magical energies. "The Last Man on Earth" features a not entirely dissimilar twist of a quest given in bad faith, such that the hero journeys out and back, finally confronting the evil questgiver over the true nature of the quest and using the power the villain sought against them. But in most of these stories the cleverness of the premise does not really seem to be the point. What is more important is the way the plot progresses through a series of action set pieces. The plot of Morrison's first story is representative.

It opens with Algol's robotic servants attacking a group of ships and being interrupted by Herne, a lone fighter, who defeats them. There he's given a medal by a dying astronaut and told to take it to Gondwane. Herne obliges, fighting more Starbarons on his way to Gondwane. In Gondwane he starts looking for Kelvin, the man he's been sent to find, when he's attacked by assassins sent by Algol. After dispatching them he gets information that Kelvin is at the north pole, so heads there, where his bar fight to get information about Kelvin is interrupted by another Starbaron attack, which is held off by the people of Hammerfest while Herne escapes. Algol nukes Hammerfest in revenge, then follows Herne to Thule, the planet mentioned by an old prospector in the bar as Kelvin's next destination. There, after Kelvin explains how the power of the medallion can destroy the Starbarons, Herne is attacked by Algol's forces, prompting a race to the hidden weapon on Thule's surface. Herne and his friends withstand a siege by Algol's forces as they ready the weapon to fire, and manage to destroy Algol's fleet before Algol can destroy the planet. Having accomplished this, Herne flies off to further adventure.

The plot, as this description surely makes clear, is mostly just a series of contrivances to get the heroes from battle to battle. That is not to say that the story is lacking in wit. Herne is drawn from a ghost named in Shakespeare, and popularly linked to the larger Celtic concept of the horned god Cernunnos—this referencing of European folklore and mysticism is common in Morrison's *Starblazer* scripts, which

Figure 14: Space combat. (From Starblazer #15, *by Grant Morrison, 1979)*

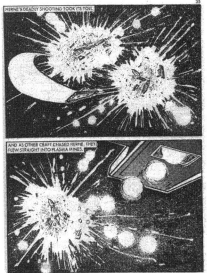

Figure 15: More space combat. (From Starblazer #15, *by Grant Morrison, 1979)*

also namecheck Norse mythology, Hindu cosmology, and the genre collisions. The Hammerfest sequence of "Algol the Terrible," for instance, is a satisfying bit of a Western mixed into the sci-fi, while the Kayn stories regularly have sword-and-sorcery elements abutting their ostensible film-noir-in-space premises. Indeed, the basic concept of Kayn as a sci-fi noir hero is quite clever, and it's worth pointing out that DC Thomson used both Kayn and Cinnibar for a series of adventures after Morrison left the title, lending credence to Morrison's claim to Salisbury that *Starblazer* taught him that "if you don't have a strong character your story is in trouble." (This cannot even be attributed to wanting to bank on Morrison's later reputation, as *Starblazer* stories all went out anonymously, and even when *Starblazer* listed credits years after the fact, Morrison was credited as G.T. Morrison.) This genre blending is more similar to the "avant-garde" material Morrison was doing for *Near Myths* than he lets on.

There is a larger question lurking amongst this issue of formulaic action plots and genre-bending that informs much of what has transpired in these early maneuverings of the War. It is telling that the War begins over the subject of repetitive stories that blend genre tropes willy-nilly and are comprised of action set-pieces. For one thing, this is 1979, and the craze of *Star Wars* is at its height. That comics would nick its basic structure of "take a bunch of genre tropes and smash them together with lots of fight scenes" seems obvious. Fittingly, when Alan Moore finally arrives on the scene during this segment of the British comics industry, one of his first gigs is for Marvel UK's *Star Wars* title. But both *Star Wars* and *Starblazer* are just late 70s instances of a much longer tradition: the pulps.

Attempts to precisely divide up the subject matter under discussion into, for instance, a strict definition of pulp magazines and how they relate to penny dreadfuls and other forms of cheap fiction are doomed to failure. Suffice it to say that comics belong in a tradition of printed materials that offered fictional stories to the masses. If one wants to pretend at precision, the penny dreadfuls were a British invention—mid-19th century downmarket serialized fiction for the working class that couldn't afford Dickens. Out of these came Sweeney Todd, made into a musical by Stephen Sondheim, and Sexton Blake, an enduring Sherlock Holmes knockoff.

In the United States, meanwhile, the analogous trend was pulp magazines, named for the low-quality paper they were printed on. The first to market was Frank Munsey with a revamp of his magazine *Argosy* in the dying days of the 19th century. In 1903, Street & Smith (absorbed into Condé Nast in 1959) came to market with the cheekily titled *The Popular Magazine*, which secured the US publication rights to H. Rider Haggard's sequel to his landmark *She* for publication in 1903. Haggard created one of the first proper pulp genres, the "Lost World" stories, which filled the pressing need to find new things for the British to colonize, having visibly run out of places left on Earth. In these a distinguished Victorian adventurer would discover some remote pocket of a civilization that was previously undiscovered or thought extinct. The iconic one came in 1885 with *King Solomon's Mines*, which introduced Haggard's most enduring creation, Allan Quatermain, who, along with no shortage of other pulp characters, will re-emerge much later in the War with *The League of Extraordinary Gentlemen*.

The pulps were home to a raft of developments essential to the War. Robert E. Howard invented the "sword and sorcery" subgenre with Conan the Barbarian in *Weird Tales*, also the home of H.P Lovecraft; Dashiell Hammett and Raymond Chandler created Sam Spade and Philip Marlowe in *Black Mask*; Robert Heinlein, Isaac Asimov, and Alfred Bester published in magazines like *Galaxy* and *Astounding Science Fiction*, creating the so-called golden age of that genre; and Edgar Rice Burroughs created both Tarzan and John Carter for *The All-Story*, a sister magazine of Munsey's *Argosy*. All of which is to say that the diversity of what was published under the banner of "the pulps" was tremendous. But one of the basic bread-and-butter structures of the pulps remained adventure stories of the sort that Haggard's "Lost World" stories provided. Both of Burroughs's creations fit squarely into this genre, but so, in their own way, did stories of Conan the Barbarian's exploits in the ancient Hyborian Age.

What these stories had in common was largely a feature of their serialization. The pulps were weekly magazines, meant to be scooped up excitedly by their readers. What we now read as novels like *A Princess of Mars* or *King Solomon's Mines* were released over time, a chapter every week. The enduring classics of pulp literature sat alongside forgettable tripe of the highest order. For every classic Lovecraft story published in *Weird Tales* there are dozens of stories with cover descriptions like "THE ALBINO DEATHS—weird tortures in a ghastly abode of horrors—by Ronal Kayser," which are, it seems likely, in deserved obscurity. But the breathlessness of that description is instructive. Consider the beginning of Howard's first Conan story, with its epic thunder: "Know, oh prince, that between the years when the oceans drank Atlantis and the gleaming cities, and the years of the rise of the Sons of Aryas, there was an age undreamed of, when shining kingdoms lay spread across the world like blue mantles beneath the stars," before unleashing a torrent of names: "Nemedia, Ophir, Brythunia, Hyperborea, Zamora with its dark-haired women and towers of spiderhaunted mystery, Zingara with its chivalry"—and note how the line has such poetic cadence, creating a near-rhyme between "mystery" and "chivalry," then leading into "Koth that bordered on the pastoral lands of Shem, Stygia with its shadow-guarded tombs, Hyrkania whose riders wore steel and silk and gold," continuing its trend of precise and strangely-worded details: tombs that are guarded by shadows and riders in steel and luxury—and finally concluding, "but the proudest kingdom of the world was Aquilonia, reigning supreme in the dreaming west. Hither came Conan, the Cimmerian, black-haired, sullen-eyed, sword in hand, a thief, a reaver, a slayer, with gigantic melancholies and gigantic mirth, to tread the jeweled thrones of the Earth under his sandaled feet," a setup after which the audience knows Conan with a sort of breathless intimacy that demands further exploration.

Equally effective is the hard-boiled patter of Sam Spade or Philip Marlowe, pulling the reader forward with a wry self-confidence, or Edgar Rice Burroughs's mystery-laden introduction to John Carter: "I am a very old man; how old I do not know. Possibly I am a hundred, possibly more; but I cannot tell because I have never aged as other men, nor do I remember any childhood." One simply must know more. Indeed, the absence of this hypnotic prose in favor of banal action set pieces provides at least part of the explanation for why the *John Carter* film was so singularly unable to replicate the narrative magic of its source text. These texts were a sort of verbal spectacle, doing the same thing to language that Siegel and Shuster did for the comics page.

But the chief engine of the narrative was the cliffhanger.

"Wiping Moscow from the face of the Earth would be fine."
–Warren Ellis, recounting editorial guidance from Hasbro,
2008

A story's job was to be exciting for a certain number of words, then to end on a big cliffhanger so the reader would want to see what happens next week. Their cryptic introductions serve as replacements for the lead-ins from previous installments, and the stories quickly get into their own distinctive rhythms. Chapter Four of *A Princess of Mars* ends with the revelation of a creature described as "about the size of a Shetland pony, but its head bore a slight resemblance to that of a frog, except that the jaws were equipped with three rows of long, sharp tusks." The chapter then leaves off, more questions than answers.

This structure survived the pulps' gradual evolution into comics. In the UK the successors were things like *The Beano* and *The Dandy*, but also titles like *Eagle*, Marcus Morris's 1950 comics magazine headlined by two brightly colored pages of

Frank Hampson and his studio's *Dan Dare, Pilot of the Future*. Dan Dare is one of the most iconic figures in British comics, and will appear several times in the course of the War. A square-jawed pilot meant to evoke the heroism of the RAF in the still-vividly remembered Battle of Britain, Dan Dare fought the villainous Treens, coded blatantly as space Nazis and led by the fiendish Mekon. Dare was in the tradition of action heroes like Flash Gordon—Alex Raymond's 1930s newspaper comic. In the US, anthologies like *Action Comics* featured adventures of various different heroic figures, some ending in cliffhangers, while other stories resolved with emphatic promises of the further exploits of popular characters like Superman.

Even these shorter stories had their breathless quality, however, and it's telling that the digest format, which didn't serialize its stories, got a similarly punctuated effect by its small page sizes. Because it's difficult to get more than three panels onto a single page and complex page layouts are simply impossible (to say nothing of improbable on the cheap wages and fast schedule of *Starblazer*), stories acquire a momentum. Grant Morrison uses this format to reasonable effect, executing fast shifts among settings to cram more action into his comic, and the short bursts of plot exposition punctuated by action sequences serve all the same narrative functions as cliffhangers.

What Morrison does that's particularly clever, though, is to use the genre-blending techniques he was already experimenting with in *Near Myths* on the space combat action of *Starblazer*. This is why Herne can wander through a landscape that is obviously taken from a western, only set in a frozen northland in the course of a story about robotic space conquerors. The episodic structure of the plot lets Morrison switch among genre codes, so that, for instance, a hard-boiled detective in the Hammett/Marlowe style can meet a barbarian princess straight out of Robert E. Howard as they race around space stations like a Flash Gordon serial.

But these elisions of genre had always been part of the pulps. Robert E. Howard's sword-and-sorcery epics were close cousins of H.P. Lovecraft's cosmic horror, and Burroughs's planetary romances were in many ways Conan stories reworked into outer space, only with a Civil War veteran as the main character. Michael Moorcock's genre experiments are, in this regard, the natural extension of his boyhood days editing the *Sexton Blake Library* and *Tarzan Adventures*, to which he contributed his own Sojan the Swordsman "sword and sorcery" character, the decision to launch Jerry Cornelius with a rewritten Elric of Melniboné story coming off as a wry joke about just how interchangeable the plots of all of these are. The mass success of *Star Wars* is nothing more than George Lucas realizing that cinema was capable of executing the genre fusion of monks wielding laser swords in a space-set Errol Flynn movie about a young farmboy, and that what worked in the pulps would probably work on the screen. Sure enough, it did.

But there's a question in all of this that may be non-obvious, which is why is it so easy to switch around among the seemingly disparate genres of noir detectives, sword-and-sorcery fantasy, and space adventure. These genres are clearly natural fits for each other in practice, but what is it that enables them to work so well together? More broadly, why does genre-crossing work in the first place?

First it is necessary to understand genre, a word with two distinct but related meanings. In a classical sense, at least, genre describes structure as much as content. This is true even to the extent that Aristotle, in *The Poetics*, discusses how epics are distinct from tragedies not just in their plot structure, but in the fact that epics are written in hexameter. That is to say, it's not merely the fact that tragedies have a particular plot structure about "a man who is not eminently good and just, yet whose misfortune is brought about not by vice or depravity, but by some error or frailty," but that tragedies are distinct from epics on the basic level of the rhythm of language used within them. Even today this

Figure 16: A Western-style shootout in the frozen northland. (From Starblazer #15, by Grant Morrison, 1979)

$$\gamma^1\beta^1\delta^1 A^1 C \uparrow \left\{ \begin{array}{c} [DE^1 neg.Fneg.] \\ d^7 E^7 F^9 \end{array} \right\} G^4 K^1 \downarrow [Pr^1 D^1 E^1 F^9 = Rs^4]^8$$

Figure 17: Narrative as understood by Vladimir Propp.

distinction applies to a significant extent—consider, for instance, the way in which personal and autobiographical comics will use a sparser visual style that suggests a single artist compared to the slickly stylized approach of American superhero comics, where even though the distinctive styles of individual artists are discernible the imagery is processed so as to (quite accurately) look like it comes from a corporate gestalt and not a single visionary. Different types of stories are told in fundamentally different ways.

In the early 20th century this sort of approach to genre was in vogue thanks to a set of critics known as structuralists. Structuralists were interested in describing things in terms of larger, often deterministic structures. A representative example is Russian folklorist Vladimir Propp, whose 1928 landmark *Morphology of the Folktale* attempted to create a generalized schema that all Russian folktales followed, thus allowing the folktales to be represented as quasi-mathematical formulas. Individual plot elements were assigned letters, so that "I" represents victory over the villain, with I^1 referring to "victory in open battle," I^2 to "victory or superiority in a contest," I^3 to "winning at cards," and I^4 to "superiority in weighing." Notably, however, within this any amount of variation in particulars can exist—any plot incident in which the hero defeats the villain in a contest is an I^2 regardless of whether the contest is a test of strength, an archery competition, or any other competition. A given Proppian formula, in other words, can be filled in with an infinite number of possible details.

Indeed, one can even expand the Proppian formula to include details that would be anachronistic to a Russian folktale. There is no inherent reason one could not construct a story that strictly followed Proppian structure, but where the open battle of I^1 is a spaceship battle, or a shootout in the wild west. Such a story would fail to be a Russian folktale only for the incidental reason that spaceships and the wild west were not popular concerns of 19th century Russian storytellers. What matters, in this sense of genre, is only the broadest and most abstracted shape of the plot.

There is, however, a second sense of genre in which the word refers not to the structure of stories but to certain elements within them. These are genres like fantasy, science-fiction, and westerns that are defined by the presence of magic or spaceships or a particular geographic/historical setting as opposed to by what happens in them. These genres are characterized by an almost infinite level of granularity, so that fantasy can be broken down into "high fantasy," "dark fantasy, "sword and sorcery," et cetera, allowing for no end of debate as to whether or not *A Princess of Mars* is most accurately described as "planetary romance" or "sword and planet." But these genres do not define the plots of their stories so much as the tone generated by the plot devices. It is worth comparing two of Morrison's *Starblazer* stories in this regard: "The Ring of Gofannon" and "The Last Man on Earth." Both involve a lengthy journey to recover a powerful object—the eponymous Ring of Gofannon and the Stardust Equation. In each case, the journey has multiple distinct steps in which the protagonist encounters and overcomes new threats. The difference is that in one the threats are spaceships and mercenaries with laser guns, and in the other they're air elementals and dragons.

It would, however, be trivial to switch them. A fantasy story in which some mad king sends a hero on a quest for a powerful weapon that the hero eventually uses to overthrow the king is as easy to imagine as a sci-fi one in which the central twist of the "ring" being sought is not a piece of jewelry but a circuitous route on a map. The basic content of the two stories, in other words, is not genre-specific, and either one could trivially be reworked into another genre. Arguably, in fact, one is simply Morrison reworking the other.

All of this conspires to make an important point about the terrain the War is fought on. The comics industries that Grant Morrison and Alan Moore affected were ahead of the trend in a general shift of the nature of popular culture. What might broadly be called tales of the fantastic—science fiction, fantasy, and horror, but really a wide swath of genres that developed in cheap serialized print media in the 20th century, including superheroes—became increasingly popular in film over the late 20th and early 21st centuries. Consider the ten top-grossing movies of each of the years following the end of World War II—a significant period of cultural shift in both America and the United Kingdom. This requires some marginal calls—does *Song of the South* count as fantasy, for instance? But a general narrative can be traced. From 1946-1979, the average number of top-ten grossing films featuring some sort of sci-fi/fantasy elements was 0.88, while from 1979—the year Moore and Morrison got their professional starts—to 1987—the year of *Watchmen* (and the year before *Animal Man*)—the number was 2.3... and 1987 is the last year to date that there were no sci-fi/fantasy films in the top ten. From 1988-2000, the turn of the millennium, and the end-date of *The Invisibles* (and in the middle of *Promethea*) it was 3.8; 2000 also marked the release of *X-Men*, the film that launched the contemporary superhero boom. From 2001 to the present day, using the current 2013 numbers, it has been 6.5, 2001 having been the first year to have a majority of its top-ten films be sci-fi/fantasy.

These numbers do not, to be clear, represent a rise in pulp-derived action/adventure films. Rather, they represent an increase in the presence of specifically fantastic elements in films, most of which but not all of which are also action/adventure films. Nor do they suggest some direct causality whereby Grant Morrison's sigilistic working in *The Invisibles* causally increased the number of sci-fi films being made, although it is certainly the case that they did increase sharply the year after that comic finished. The rise of sci-fi/fantasy happened gradually over decades. However, it is most certainly the case that the people who produced this increasing torrent of sci-fi/fantasy were influenced by the pulps and cheap serialized material that existed during their childhoods.

So in the late 1970s, as this tide began in film with things like *Star Wars*, *Close Encounters of the Third Kind*, and *Alien*, major filmmakers in the genre like George Lucas, Steven Spielberg, and Ridley Scott were inspired by the pulp fiction of their childhoods—1950s America for George Lucas and Steven Spielberg, and late 40s/early 50s Britain for Ridley Scott. All of this took place in the context of other historical shifts, of course, but it was the trend that Moore and Morrison were swept up in, and, eventually, came to find themselves appearing to steer. Film and serialized print, after all, had always been bedfellows. Film adapted popular serialized print stories and genres—the films that were popular in the 1940s, 50s, and 60s were still action-adventure stories derived from the pulps, but they were war stories and westerns that lacked sci-fi/fantasy elements.

But the lines between these pulp genres often blur, much as the line between superheroes and the pulps blurs. *Starblazer* was the sci-fi/fantasy sister title to the straight war digest *Commando*, also published by DC Thomson. The American comics industry of the 40s-60s had superheroes, but also had westerns, crime comics, horror, and other genres. Edgar Rice Burroughs wrote sci-fi when he did the Barsoom stories, but more straight adventure when he did Tarzan. Grant Morrison can feature a noirish private eye in a Flash Gordon story. *Eagle* ran *Dan Dare* alongside stories of the French Foreign Legion. Adventure stories taken from the pulps have always been a subset of film, and sci-fi/fantasy has always been a subset of adventure stories. It is both crucial and obvious to point out that the pulps and film are, however, very different media. Further, it is important to point out that they have very different narrative forms.

> *"She realized the real problem with stories—if you keep them going long enough, they always end in death."*
> —Neil Gaiman, *Sandman* #6, 1989

This is best explained in terms of ancient Greece. Virtually all thought about narrative structure is a reaction to Aristotle's *Poetics*, and, to a lesser extent, his *Rhetoric*. Some works restate or expand upon the *Poetics*, others fly in the face of it, but there is little that has been said about narrative structure over the past two-and-a-third millennia that has not been substantially engaged with Aristotle. Even today, any guide to screenwriting or novel writing that one purchases will be, essentially, a collection of self-help tips wrapped around an explanation of Aristotelean plot structure. Much of this stems from the fact that Aristotle was the first person to codify some very important things. For instance, Aristotle proclaims that "a whole is that which has a beginning, a middle, and an end. A beginning is that which does not itself follow anything by causal necessity, but after which something naturally is or comes to be. An end, on the contrary, is that which itself naturally follows some other thing, either by necessity, or as a rule, but has nothing following it. A middle is that which follows something as some other thing follows it." This may sound terribly obvious, but that is in most regards the point; Aristotle in essence codified the basic idea of plot structure that is taken for granted today.

Aristotelean plotting, summarized briefly, and incorporating several developments postdating Aristotle himself, works thusly: a plot should follow a single action, albeit a complex action in which a character goes through several moments of "recognition and reversal" in which they learn something and, accordingly, have their fate reversed. Events at the beginning of the story should make events at the end likely, while events at the end should justify the inclusion of events at the beginning, a rule succinctly restated by Anton Chekov, who orders writers to "remove everything that has no relevance to the story. If you say in the first chapter that there is a rifle hanging on the wall, in the second or third chapter it absolutely must go off. If it's not going to be fired, it shouldn't be hanging there." Equally important are the dramatic unities, which require that the action take place over one continuous period of time and in one place. These rules have loosened since Aristotle's time—proper Aristotelean narrative should take place in one room, with no breaks in time at all, whereas more contemporary treatments treat unity of time and place as injunctions not to include events that aren't part of the single action that the plot is about.

The point, within Aristotle, is to engender a catharsis of pity and fear that occurs when the audience sees a well-depicted imitation of a noble human life brought down by his own flaws and imperfections. Crucial to this structure is the act of imitation, or mimesis, which is where Aristotle begins the *Poetics*. For Aristotle what defines narrative is the fact that it is an imitation of human action, stemming from the fact that man "is the most imitative of living creatures, and through imitations learns his earliest lessons; and no less universal is the pleasure felt in things imitated." By watching an imitation of a tragic downfall, in Aristotle, we are able to engage with the emotions of pity and fear in a cathartic, cleansing way that produces a spiritually validating feeling that is poorly captured by Aristotle's prose—which is, in practice, merely the adapted lecture notes taken by his students at the Lyceum.

All of this sounds very sensible, but it's important to note that Aristotelean plot structure applies to the specific genre of tragedy. Aristotle spends much of the start of the *Poetics* meticulously differentiating tragedy from other genres such as comedy and the epic. Aristotle clearly has detailed views on how both comedy and the epic function, but these views are not expressed within the *Poetics*, and, more importantly, are not expressed in any surviving work of Aristotle's, although his views on comedy are widely believed to survive in a manuscript called the *Tractatus Coislinianus*. Epics, however, are trickier. Aristotle is largely dismissive of the epic, saying that "epic poets were succeeded by Tragedians, since the drama was a larger and higher form of art." The difference, as

Aristotle explains it, is that while "Tragedy endeavors, as far as possible, to confine itself to a single revolution of the sun... the Epic action has no limits of time." Another way of framing this is that the epic has multiple plots as opposed to tragedy's single-minded focus. This, in turn, comes close to his remarks elsewhere in the *Poetics*, where he proclaims that "of all plots and actions the episodic are the worst. I call a plot episodic in which the episodes or acts succeed one another without probable or necessary sequence."

Aristotle's value judgment regarding tragedy and epics has, perhaps improbably, survived the 2335 years since Aristotle's death. Proper and literary fiction works according to broadly Aristotelean lines, with a tight unity of plot that builds to a definitive ending. The sort of fiction that just goes on and on, meanwhile, is largely frowned upon, or, at least, would be if self-proclaimed paragons of taste paid enough attention to it to frown. But it hasn't gone away in the least—the narrative structure of the pulps is visually based on the epic. In many ways the core difference between the epic and tragedy—a genre that should really be broadened to "literary" fiction in general—is the issue of endings. Literary fiction is written towards a moment of eventual resolution that will satisfy what Aristotle describes as "the instinct for harmony and rhythm," whereas epics (now more usually referred to as pulps) are written for serialization, building not towards an ending but towards the periodic punctuation of the cliffhanger.

This is true even when they are not serialized—*Starblazer*, after all, clearly uses the structure of the epic within a given issue, offering a largely episodic plot in which various adventures take place, building to a conclusion that is determined more by the page number than by any sense of narrative progression. There's no inherent reason why "The Last Man on Earth" has to reach Earth proper when it does, as opposed to adding another two or three planets to Gaunt's arrival on Earth, nor, for that matter, is there a reason one or more events of the story couldn't be excised. The plot is fundamentally just a series of encounters strung together, and the point of the encounters is less to build towards the eventual resolution and more to fulfill what Grant Morrison has described as the only note he ever got from DC Thomson: "More space combat."

This gets at the limitations of the epic/pulp format: they are by and large suitable for storytelling based around what Aristotle calls spectacle, but rather lacking in most other regards. They're fantastic if what you want is space combat (or some other form of exciting action and spectacle), but visibly lacking in character depth or complex plotting. Ultimately the virtue of any major pulp hero is that they are usable to tell a lot of stories with exciting events, not that any one of these stories is particularly emotionally moving. This is not a problem as such—clearly epic/pulp genres have been getting along for more than two thousand years without having to assimilate completely to tragedy's structure. But it remains a fundamental divide between two types of storytelling. And this divide carries with it a wealth of value judgments, with the epic/pulp structure being a lower, coarser genre for mass appeal, and the literary/tragic structure being more refined.

For the most part, comics are a medium that is, in practice, naturally inclined towards pulp genres. In many ways the War is fought over that inclination, and, more to the point, over a desire to reverse and resist that inclination, writing stories that are on the one hand using genre iconography associated with the pulps, but that are structured like literary fiction, and, ideally, that are widely recognized as literary fiction. The techniques developed in the course of the War were not the first such techniques—George Lucas's wedding of space opera iconography to the "hero's journey" structure developed by Joseph Campbell in *Star Wars* accomplished the same goal. But a by-product of the War was a massive profusion in techniques to accomplish literary-structured fiction with pulp iconography within visual media, many of which led to enormously successful films mostly (though not entirely) featuring American superheroes. Inasmuch as the War can be explained simply as the product of developments in what might be broadly described as "aesthetic technology," the development of these techniques serves to explain it.

In this regard, it is worth turning to *Captain Clyde*, especially given that Morrison, in discussing the strip, makes much of the way in which it culminates in a "rain-soaked, lightning-wracked epic of Fall and Redemption" in which Captain Clyde heroically sacrifices his life, bringing the story to exactly the sort of end that eternally serialized pulp narratives do not generally reach. But by Morrison's own admission, this ending was "a far cry" from how the strip began, which was basically as a gimmick of a strip for *The Govan Press*, a local newspaper for an ex-burgh of Glasgow that had been around since 1851 (the paper, that is—Govan itself dates back to the 5th or 6th century). Grant Morrison, recommended by his local political agitator of a father, was asked to provide a comic strip, specifically a superhero local to Glasgow. The editors, Colin Tough, apparently wanted something in the style of the 1960s Adam West *Batman* series that had been popular in the UK a decade earlier and was still being rerun on ITV as schedule filler, but did not care enough to actually edit or enforce this desire on Grant Morrison. Morrison instead took a lightly satirical angle on the source material, writing the exploits of Chris Melville, an unemployed lout of a young Scottish man who comes "into direct contact with the ancient magic of Britain's pagan countryside," as Morrison put it in *Supergods*, and becomes the eponymous Captain Clyde.

This reflects a crucial oddity of *Captain Clyde* and of Grant Morrison's early work—a quirk that makes him distinctive within his generation of British comics writers: Morrison is Scottish. This is a part of his identity in the same way that Alan Moore's Northampton roots shape his interests and career. *Captain Clyde*, in particular, reflects that fact. The discussion of "Britain's pagan countryside" evokes the classic horror film *The Wicker Man*, made in 1973 and, in fact, rereleased in 1979 in America to considerable acclaim, and also run occasionally on ITV in the late 1970s. *The Wicker Man* was set on a fictional Scottish island called Summerisle, difficult to access from the mainland. A police officer comes to Summerisle to investigate a disappearance, and finds himself caught up in a mystery set within the initially charming-seeming rural village. The police officer is a devout Christian, creating initial tension with the island's adherence to old pagan practices, and as the film unfolds the pagan celebrations take a sinister turn that amounts to a nipple-heavy version of 1960s classic *The Prisoner*'s take on vacation destinations. Ultimately, the police officer is burnt alive in the eponymous wicker man by the villainous Lord Summerisle, played with relish by Christopher Lee, while the villagers cheerily sing an old folk song, "Summer is Icumun In." As Morrison put it in 2013, "In Scotland, we're pretty weird."

The Wicker Man fit into an entire history of 1970s countryside horror that included the early Tom Baker era of *Doctor Who*, the disturbing children's serial *Children of the Stones*, and a wealth of other period horror. These stories typically meshed the pagan history of Britain with the modern day, suggesting a lurking horror or power in the lost pagan lore. This, however, raises the question of what this lost pagan lore is. Which, in turn, requires a general history of Great Britain. Great Britain generally refers to the largest island of the United Kingdom, which contains the individual countries (but not sovereign states) of England, Scotland, and Wales. England is the most populous of these, and in essence consists of the territory seized and held by the Norman invasion of William the Conqueror in 1066, and previously populated largely by the Anglo-Saxon population that dominated mainland Europe. Wales and Scotland consist of territories that at least initially held out against English rule.

English rule consisted not only of the racial distinction between the Norman English and the Celtic Scots, but between the largely Christian (and previously Norse) population of England and the Celtic pagan tradition of both Scotland and Wales. These populations were not less Christian by any measure, but they had a different flavor of Christianity that, by British self-mythology, ought be considered an entirely distinct church from the Roman Catholic church, although this claim is historically dubious. The suppressed Celtic religions, however, took on a mythic standing for the eventual material suppression of the Scottish and Welsh populations as the Norman English flexed their political and military muscle over the island. By the end of the 16th century all of Wales was annexed to England, and in the early 18th century Scotland was fully unified with England under Queen Anne, having previously been hastily cobbled together in a sort of political shotgun marriage in 1603 when King James VI of Scotland further acquired the title of James I of England following the death of Queen Elizabeth, last of the Tudor monarchs, becoming the first of the Scottish Stewarts. Anne herself was the last of the Stewart monarchs, and was succeeded by the German George I. This sequence of events did not go down entirely well with all portions of the legendarily, nay, stereotypically feisty Scottish population—as Morrison joked in a convention Q&A, "My fucking country… my country has been ruled by the fucking English for five hundred years, so don't tokenise me, okay?!" a self-conscious overreaction that served as a loving parody of certain flavors of Scottish identity.

The long and short of it is that both Scotland and Wales maintained a sense of cultural independence after their forced mergers, but culturally, politically, and economically they were both treated as second class citizens of the newborn Great Britain (later the United Kingdom following the 19th century appendage of Ireland, which broke up partially in the early 20th century when Ireland split off, followed by the counter-secession of Northern Ireland in 1922). Scotland largely fared better than Wales; in the mid-18th century Edinburgh, the capital, was the heart of the Scottish Enlightenment, contributing major thinkers like David Hume and Adam

Smith to the world. Capitalism was literally invented by the Scottish, as, in many ways, was the industrial revolution, which led to a 19th century economic boom in Glasgow, Scotland's largest city.

Glasgow is the more industrial city to Edinburgh's upper class sheen. Situated on the River Clyde with easy shipping access to the Atlantic Ocean through the Firth of Clyde, it was a center not just of industrial money but of labour-focused politics. It is in Glasgow that Scotland's two major football teams, Celtic F.C. and Rangers F.C., play; their rivalry is known as the Old Firm. Both had a heyday in European soccer, with Celtic winning the European Cup along with both Scottish cups and a league cup in 1967, but carries with it a deeply unpleasant racial and religious dimension—Rangers F.C. have had to take active measures to crack down on the singing of sectarian chants like "Billy Boys," a song that boasts that "we are the Billy Boys, hullo, hullo. You'll know us by our noise. We're up to our knees in fenian blood, surrender or you'll die." Fenian, in this case, refers to Irish nationalists, and explains why, in 2006, Rangers were forced by footballing authorities to explicitly forbid singing of the song.

The cultural successes of Glasgow and Edinburgh did not disguise the degree to which Scotland was widely treated as a bit of a cultural punchline by the politically more powerful England. *Doctor Who* sent it up in the 1976 story *Terror of the Zygons*, in which the Loch Ness Monster is, predictably, revealed as an alien cyborg. Three years earlier, *The Wicker Man* made unsettling horror out of the otherwise seemingly innocuous practices of maypole rituals and folk music. And then there's 1979, the year a seventeen-year-old Grant Morrison started *Captain Clyde* for a local paper in the outskirts of Glasgow, and two further small papers in syndication—one in Renfrew, six miles west of Glasgow, and another in Clydebank, which, as its name suggests, abuts Glasgow on the River Clyde.

"Wales and Scotland shrink themselves to the west and to the north!
Mourning for fear of the warriors in the Vale of Entuthon-Benython."
–William Blake, *Jerusalem*, 1820

The strip took the superficial glitz of superhero comics filtered through the requested Adam West *Batman* series, but situated it in the working class realities of late-20th century Scottish life. Begun in 1979, the first year of the Thatcher government, *Captain Clyde* started as a lightly satirical roman à clef, with Chris Melville unapologetically modeled on Morrison, and fitting his self-description of himself at the time as "a dole casualty, another of Thatcher's victims, a statistic," only simultaneously living the should-be glitzy life of the superhero. He was paid £4 a week for the strip, less than Alan Moore was getting for his far simpler-to-draw weekly *Maxwell the Magic Cat* strips at basically the same time, and while he eventually got a raise to £6, he grew frustrated with the strip fairly quickly, and by the end was dashing out the strip "in the eight hours before handing it in." It lingered in near complete obscurity—nobody ever wrote in about it, leading the paper to run a competition to solicit comments, for which only three people wrote in, two of them members of Morrison's family, and the third failing to actually mention the strip. The result, as Morrison tells the story, is that he attempted increasingly outlandish plots in a bid to get a reaction out of anybody until the strip came to contain "baby-eating demons and murderous skull-faced horrors"; he was eventually sacked three years into the strip by a new editor at *The Govan Press* after the strip was dropped in both of the other papers, which he describes as surely being a welcome development for "traumatized readers who could once more consult the TV listings without being assaulted by satanic imagery and blasted skeletons."

Perhaps unsurprisingly, Morrison is mythologizing things a bit here, although as much to make himself look a bit ridiculous as to bolster his reputation. It's not that he's wrong to describe the final villain of Captain Clyde as Satanic—his face is a horned skull, he's got a burning trident symbol on his chest, and he's introduced as "Moloch, Prince of Chaos." But Morrison's account of innocent Glaswegian pensioners being scarred for life by what sounds less like a superhero comic than a death metal album is overstating the case— Moloch is still fundamentally a character nobody would blink at if he appeared in a children's cartoon. And he's not just talking up how transgressive *Captain Clyde* was—the idea that this marked any sort of significant turn in the later period of the strip is hard to support. While his crack about baby-eating horrors can be written off as straightforward exaggeration, it's worth noting that Morrison starts off two storylines with strips in which the various residents of Glasgow are gruesomely murdered in classic "first reel of a horror movie" style, including one in which a kid is torn apart. It's just that these are actually the first two stories of the run, as opposed to the end.

The result of this self-mythologizing is interesting. On the one hand, as mentioned, it mostly serves to make Morrison look slightly ridiculous, long on bad judgment and unprofessional conduct. But this narrative of self-sabotage has an obvious advantage when one considers the more obvious explanation for why a strip like *Captain Clyde* might not have taken off, which is simply that it was a not very good strip in an obscure local paper. To be fair, Morrison never really denies this, and it's clear from his self-deprecation that he remembers the idea of the strip rather more fondly than the execution. But he's still fundamentally spinning the story as one about him being too edgy and punk for the paper's audience of "the elderly, the chronically unemployed, and other vulnerable members of society," a move highlighted by the way in which his description of the strip's end (in which Captain Clyde "succumbed to full-scale diabolic possession before assuming a new identity as the self-proclaimed 'Black Messiah.' Poised to destroy the world, until redeemed by Alison's unswerving devotion, he killed the Devil himself before tumbling from the sky to expire in the

Figure 18: James Marshall is brutally murdered by monsters. (From Captain Clyde, by Grant Morrison, 1980)

Figure 19: The inoffensively Satanic Moloch. (From Captain Clyde, by Grant Morrison, 1982, blurriness due to source)

arms of his beloved") slyly neglects to mention that all of this takes place in the last two strips, with the length of Clyde's demonic possession being precisely six panels.

But while nobody, Morrison included, would seriously try to rank *Captain Clyde* among his greatest works, there's clear potential within it. Morrison is right, for instance, to highlight his decision to make Chris Melville, as he puts it in *Supergods*, a "young man on the dole who thought small and fought small," especially in contrast to the kitschy Adam West *Batman* knock-off proposed by his editor, a jokey gimmick that would surely have run dry quickly. Given his description of the paper's audience, this can even be argued as a potentially savvy decision to make the story closer to many of their lived experiences. Admittedly, Morrison never really finds anything to do with this thread beyond a couple of superficial gags (he takes outsized pleasure in a strip in which Melville visits the dentist, who is baffled by the fact that the drill can't get into his teeth), and by the later strips it's dropped out of the mix almost entirely, but the fact that he had such a strong idea so early in his career, and moreover the guts to stand up for it over editorial skepticism, speaks well of him.

And there's no shortage of other strong concepts in *Captain Clyde*. For instance, the villain Trinity, who Morrison described in a 1985 interview as "a schizophrenic with a triple personality who was able to divide his body into three—each with a different power and facet of the personality," was a concept he'd return to in 1989 when he created Crazy Jane for *Doom Patrol*. And there's a pleasantly inventive moment when Captain Clyde defeats one of Trinity's three facets—the one that can expand in size—by tricking him into expanding to where his bones break from the load, a borderline-stereotypical bit of superhero deconstruction, but one that still clearly shows Morrison was thinking about this sort of thing. The strip also shows off the wide range of Morrison's influences. The second storyline, for instance, involves what are for the most part fairly generic subterranean monsters that are killing people from beneath the Govan Cross Underground Station, but Morrison enlivens the plot by having them be the Deros, a race of monstrous savages described by Richard Shaver in the pages of *Amazing Stories*, whose editor Ray Palmer presented Shaver's tales (which he insisted were true descriptions based on years spent as a prisoner of the Deros) as the Shaver Mystery over the course of several years, to considerable (and more importantly, profitable) controversy.

Morrison's interest in the Shaver Mystery points to a larger influence on him during this period, namely his first magical experience, which occurred after his uncle gave him the Aleister Crowley/Frieda Harris *Thoth Tarot* for his nineteenth birthday, which led him to subscribe to *The Lamp of Thoth* and attempt what he describes as "a traditional ritual" resulting in "a blazing, angelic lion head... growling out the words 'I am neither North nor South.'" And this influence shows through in other places in *Captain Clyde*, perhaps most obviously in the character's origin story, which involves him taking a walking tour of some stone circles and receiving a visitation from "Elen, Goddess of the old straight tracks and sacred stones," who offers him the "powers of earth and fire" if he can defeat her champion, Magna.

There's an altogether more obvious source for Captain Clyde's origin story than this, however: Chris Claremont's 1976 creation of Captain Britain, whose origin shares numerous major elements with Captain Clyde's: the stone circle, the visitation from a pagan figure, the battle with an opposing champion, and an explicit choice between violence and peace. There's a weird caginess to the way Morrison engages with this influence, however. In *Supergods*, for instance, the section immediately prior to his discussion of *Captain Clyde* is a lengthy one on Claremont that culminates in a brief and derisive mention of Captain Britain, suggesting that Claremont "had intuited perhaps where the lightning would strike next. Something that felt like a movement was stirring in the fields of Albion and Caledon." But in a 1985

Figure 20: *Captain Clyde defeats one of Trinity's personas with an old standard of realism. (From* Captain Clyde, *by Grant Morrison, 1981, shading problems due to source)*

Figure 21: *Captain Clyde recalls the details of Richard Shaver's Deros. (From* Captain Clyde, *by Grant Morrison, 1980)*

interview about *Captain Clyde* he notes that Claremont had done a concept similar to Trinity, joking that "it was my idea first, so up yours Claremont," while conspicuously declining to mention any influence on Captain Clyde's origins save for his own interest in "ley lines and earth magic and all that pseudo-mystical hippy shit."

If one is to talk about Morrison's anxiety of influence with regards to *Captain Clyde*, however, there's a much larger one to grapple with. So large, in fact, that it constitutes a vast and multidimensional occult war for the soul of Albion itself: Alan Moore. The overwhelming point of Morrison's preferred version of the *Captain Clyde* story, after all, is to establish it as a forgotten precursor to Moore's breakout work on *Marvelman* in *Warrior*. As he puts it in *Supergods*, "For me, *Marvelman* was the next stage beyond the kitchen sink naturalism of *Captain Clyde*." And fair play to Morrison—its supposed realism is absolutely one of the most frequently praised elements of *Marvelman*, and Morrison's concept of an on-the-dole superhero really does predate it by about a year and a half. As with the basic question of who got their professional career started first, in the raw and brutal terms of a priority dispute, Morrison got there first. But what Morrison does not mention in any interviews and what is easy to miss given that *Captain Clyde* remains not only out of print but virtually impossible to read without trekking to the Mitchell Library in Glasgow and looking at their archive of *The Govan Press*, is the extent to which Moore's influence is visible in Morrison's final arc on *Captain Clyde*, which ran in mid-to-late 1982 after Moore had begun his famous *Marvelman* run.

These final strips are marked by what Morrison describes as "portentous valedictory captions." For instance, one cliffhanger reads, "The wind begins to rise and it tastes bad, as though blown from a slaughterhouse. Captain Clyde's scalp bristles, his flesh creeps and he turns slowly to confront the leering, snarling face of a thousand childhood nightmares. The face of the Lord of Darkness, the Fallen Angel, the Face of Satan!!!" Overly exuberant use of exclamation points aside, this is blatantly inspired by Moore's similarly portentous but far more remembered captions in *Warrior #3*, which came out a few months before that installment of *Captain Clyde*, and which features a cliffhanger with narration like, "It's here, black and terrible inside his skull. Its tendrils roil behind his eyes, dragging him down into the dark," and, in its final caption, "The cold lightning of fear skewers them and they feel the terrible hunger in the heart of the storm... they see the smile on the face of the tiger."

And this, in the end, reveals the sad truth of Morrison's early career: it was never going to work. Following the 1981 cancellation of *Captain Clyde* and the 1980 collapse of *Near Myths*, Morrison essentially departed comics until 1985, turning in the occasional *Starblazer* script for spare cash. Nominally this was to pursue a career in music, but it must be said that Morrison cannot have looked at his output since 1978 and seen anything with a serious chance of providing a steady income, nor, for that matter, a sense of creative satisfaction. Particularly stinging must have been his dismissal from *Captain Clyde*, given that *The Govan Press* had, in 1976, run a feature on Morrison's interest in comics with the endearingly bad pun of a title, "He's Quick on the Draw— That's Grant," that eagerly showed off some of his work and proclaimed that "you'd be excused for thinking that the characters featured here had been dreamed up by a top comic strip writer. And had been drawn by a professional cartoonist. **But they are, in fact, the brainchild and the work of a local, 16-year-old artist.**" (In fact only two are; the third's a drawing of Marvel's Iron Fist.) The brief feature goes on to eagerly declare that "a lad with a great future is Grant Morrison." And just five years later they were firing him, his superhero strip for them having been deemed an overly expensive failure at six quid a week.

For all his later bluster about this early stage of his comics career, it has to be said that Morrison's early attempts in the industry were not successful, and that failure must have

Figure 22: A 1976 Govan Press *article on Grant Morrison.*

stung. Certainly it's easy to see why his firing from *Captain Clyde* would disturb his previous rock solid confidence, expressed to that very paper as, "I'm hoping to take up art as a career. If that doesn't come off I've nothing else in mind." A break from comics to follow another passion makes perfect sense in the context. It's clear that Morrison did not pay much attention to the larger comics industry during his four-year sabbatical, seemingly buying only Dez Skinn's *Warrior* anthology, where he encountered a revival of *Marvelman* that did much of what he had attempted for *The Govan Press*. This failure was not, clearly, for lack of ideas—Morrison's work, in fact, amounts to a near-miss version of Bryan Talbot's successful *The Adventures of Luther Arkwright*, a near-miss of *Marvelman*, and some perfectly competent single issues tailored to a specific market, albeit one that didn't pay enough to make a living. Failures these early works may be, but their problem is not lack of ambition; Morrison was never short on that. It is not even lack of talent—they are no worse than the juvenilia of any other writer, and a good deal better than the juvenilia of most. Their problem is altogether more existential. Simply put, Morrison's career could not take off until Moore's already had.

The problem, to be clear, is not that Morrison needed Moore as an influence. He was profoundly influenced by Moore, yes, but to reduce Moore's importance to Morrison to mere influence is, in the end, to do a disservice to both men. But what Morrison needed from Moore was something more fundamental—something hinted at in his unwavering fascination with the avant-garde, and displayed clearly in his constant, at times petulant rebellion against the expectations of *The Govan Press* and its readership. Morrison's nature is at its core rebellious. He is nothing without a rival; a dramatic foil he can define himself by defying. And so Morrison would have to wait for his great adversary's career to bloom before his own could.

Chapter Three: The Underground Comix of Alan Moore

"A detective, a man we could trust, even with our children."
–Grant Morrison, *Supergods*, 2011

That began happening on March 31ˢᵗ, 1979, five months after Grant Morrison's career took off, when Spotlight Publication's national music weekly *Sounds* published the first installment of *Roscoe Moscow: Who Killed Rock n' Roll*. Less than five months later, on the 25ᵗʰ of August, 1979, the local Northampton paper *The Northants Post* began a weekly comic strip titled *Maxwell the Magic Cat*. *Sounds* was paying £35 a week, while the *Northants Post* paid £10, making a combined £45 a week—£2.50 greater than the unemployment benefits Alan Moore had previously been drawing, and officially marking the beginning of his career as a full-time comics writer.

The revolution that this event heralded was, at first, wholly invisible. *Roscoe Moscow* was published under the name of Curt Vile, an obvious parody of German composer Kurt Weill, best known for his work with Bertolt Brecht on *The Threepenny Opera*, while *Maxwell the Magic Cat* featured the more obscurely humorous pen name Jill de Ray. The reasons for the pseudonyms are simple and rooted in Moore's early biography. In 1978 he was an office clerk at a local gas company with vague long-term plans to get out of what he viewed as dispiriting and degrading jobs and make a career as an artist. Between the soberingly awful economic situation of late-70s Britain, which would eventually lead to the 1979 election of Margaret Thatcher, and the impending arrival of his first daughter, Leah, Moore took the risky decision to quit his job and live on the £42.50 a week of benefit payments while he tried to establish himself as a comics creator, reasoning that "I know the limits of my courage. I wouldn't have been up for doing it after I've got these big, imploring eyes staring up at me." His benefits—approximately £200 in contemporary terms—were described as "the bare minimum what we needed to live on—paying the rent, the baby, all the rest of it." His threshold for success as a comics creator was both simple and pragmatic: if he could make more money than that, he'd succeeded.

The problem was that any money he made while trying to get to £42.50 a week would be illegal under the rules of his benefits, and so to keep that income under the table he adopted pseudonyms. ("I presume that there's a statute of limitations upon these things and—hell, let them find me and fine me; I can probably pay it now," he quipped in 2003, while explaining the ruse.) The result, however, is that these strips are treated as an oddly disposable artifact of Moore's career that aren't "proper" Moore—not even published under his real name. Instead, the start of his career is largely recognized as beginning with his work for Marvel UK and IPC's *2000 AD*, his first work as a writer instead of as a writer-artist, and in the sci-fi/fantasy genre style in which he made his name. His *Sounds* and *Maxwell the Magic Cat* work is generally treated as the equivalent of Grant Morrison's *Near Myths* and *Captain Clyde*—a juvenile prelude to the main event.

This, however, is nonsense. For one thing, Moore was not a juvenile in 1979. Although their careers and thus the War started at the same time, Moore is seven years Morrison's senior, and he was already twenty-five when he started *Roscoe Moscow*, not the seventeen that Morrison was when he sold "Time is a Four Letter Word." More to the point, Moore didn't take the early-80s sabbatical from comics that Morrison did. *Roscoe Moscow* and the *Maxwell the Magic Cat* strips are Moore's earliest regular paid comics work, but they do not mark some discrete early stage of his career. The last *Roscoe Moscow* strip ran in the June 28th, 1980 issue of *Sounds*, by which time Moore had already begun his work on *Doctor Who Magazine*. The first installment of *Skizz* saw print in Prog 308 of *2000 AD* on the same day that his second *Sounds* strip, *The Stars My Degradation* wrapped: March 19th, 1983; at that point, Moore was in the midst of his run on Captain Britain in *The Daredevils* for Marvel UK and had seen nine chapters of *Marvelman* and *V for Vendetta* come out in *Warrior*. (Indeed, the final strip of *The Stars My Degradation* contains a joke about Unstuck Simpson destroying the universe during sexual congress with Ginda Bojeffries of the still forthcoming *Bojeffries Saga*.) And by the time of the final *Maxwell the Magic Cat* strip, on October 9th, 1986, Moore was deep into *Watchmen*.

Roscoe Moscow and *Maxwell the Magic Cat*, in other words, are not merely Alan Moore's first professional comics work—they are the beginning of an uninterrupted career as a professional comics creator. Which means that they also mark the point where the War stops being anything like a strict linear sequence of events; from this point on, nothing happens in its own bubble, independent from other concerns. Nevertheless, his work for *Sounds* and on *Maxwell the Magic Cat* is distinct from the bulk of his career in that it forms the only substantial body of work that he's illustrated himself. Moore never completely abandoned drawing—he did a one-pager for Harvey Pekar's *American Splendour* in 1990, and both a cover and a small comic called *Astounding Weird Penises* for *Dodgem Logic* in 2010. But like Grant Morrison, after an initial flirtation with being a writer-artist, Moore settled on simply writing. The reasons for this are similar to Morrison's—as Moore puts it, he noticed that his friend Steve Moore (it is at this point traditional to say "no relation") was doing just fine as a writer and that, unlike Moore, he "never worked beyond four in the afternoon." But unlike Morrison, Moore

Figure 23: Although writing under a pen name, Alan Moore alluded to his true identity in a cryptic crossword clue, referencing one of Steve Moore's pen names on the front of the paper. (From Roscoe Moscow: Who Killed Rock n' Roll, *by Alan Moore as Curt Vile, 1979)*

Figure 24: Titles hidden in buildings by Alan Moore in Roscoe Moscow *(left) and by Will Eisner in* The Spirit *(right).*

acknowledges a second major flaw in being a writer-artist, which is that he, as he put it, "can't draw very well." He relied heavily on the technique of stippling—the use of tiny dots for shading—which, as he wryly noted, "editors loved." But this only further slowed his production down, and was a fairly transparent ruse to cover the underlying frailties of his technique.

Still, for all that Moore self-deprecates his art skills, *Roscoe Moscow* demonstrates an admirable determination to push himself. Early on in the strip he abandoned all notion of a consistent layout for the strip's title. The ninth installment pastiches *Weird Tales*, the pulp magazine in which H.P. Lovecraft did the bulk of his work; the thirteenth is an homage to Will Eisner's *The Spirit*, and particularly to Eisner's tendency to work the strip's logo into an existing panel; others involved detailed collages and intricate panel layouts. While there is admittedly something of an upper bound to Moore's artistic skill, on the whole *Roscoe Moscow* is visibly the work of an artist stretching himself, improving, and trying increasingly ambitious things. Moore's description of this as "doing an apprenticeship in public, learning the ropes" is apt—it very much feels like the work of someone who is actively honing their craft. Moore visibly sets stylistic challenges for himself and then attempts to meet them, already demonstrating the methodical focus on structure and technique that would come to characterize his entire career.

Repeatedly, when reading *Roscoe Moscow*, one is struck by moments in which Alan Moore's future work seems prefigured. It is not just the technical complexity of some of the later strips, which rivals his work on *Swamp Thing* and *Promethea* in concept, if not in execution—the *Weird Tales* strip and depiction of David Bowie as a Lovecraftian horror prefigures an entire career of Lovecraft pastiches, for instance. Indeed, one could, if one was truly determined, argue that the revelation of "David Boko, the giant bisexual tentacled nightmare" lurking in the sewers late in the run was directly recycled by Moore to create the subterranean penis

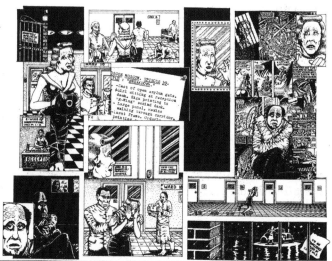

Figure 25: Moore's Roscoe Moscow *work demonstrates his early interest in intricate panel layouts. (From* Roscoe Moscow: Who Killed Rock 'n Roll, *by Alan Moore as Curt Vile, 1980)*

Figure 26: Prophetic birds in Roscoe Moscow, *prefiguring Moore's work on* Swamp Thing. *(From* Roscoe Moscow: Who Killed Rock 'n Roll, *by Alan Moore as Curt Vile, 1979)*

monster in *Neonomicon*, although it's possible that doing so would reveal more about one's self than about Alan Moore. Perhaps a more immediate comparison comes in the thirty-sixth installment of *Roscoe Moscow*, where Roscoe has a dream vision of Wiggy Pulp full of grotesque imagery of the sort he'd lean heavily on in *Swamp Thing*.

On the surface this makes Moore's claim that his *Sounds* work "will probably remain unpublished" as "to put it out as a piece of work by Alan Moore, it would be crap, because it wouldn't be the Alan Moore that people are expecting" sound odd. But this claim requires context—Moore has never done anything like renounce his early work. Rather, it reflects a characteristically complex ethical calculation on Moore's part. The actual claim that Moore makes when asked about republishing his *Sounds* material is, "I don't want to make any money out of it because I don't think it's good enough." (This claim was, admittedly, made in 2008, at which point Moore's *Watchmen* income made self-sacrificing ethical stances much more viable.)

So Moore's position is based in part on the luxury of not having to try to make a profit from his old *Sounds* work. Indeed, when Pádraig Ó Méalóid checked with Moore to see if it was okay to preserve the arcana of Moore's career online, Moore explicitly said that "it's nice that it's out there on the 'net... I'm really glad that it's out there, so people can see." Moore's position, in other words, is not that there is anything *wrong* with his *Sounds* work as such, but rather that he simply doesn't see it as appropriate to profit off of it given that he was still learning how to do comics. (Moore made a similar stand much earlier in his career, in fact, when he donated his proceeds for Acme Press's *Maxwell the Magic Cat* reprints to Greenpeace, joking that "the guilt at having been paid twice for this stuff would honestly be more than I could bear, and I would almost certainly burn in hell forever.")

In many ways the process of "learning to do comics" amounted to learning a degree of stylistic flexibility. The central joke of *Roscoe Moscow*, so to speak, is not just its many *Mad Magazine* style musical parodies like Rafiawerk and Brain One (Brian Eno), which Moore explains by saying, "I was suffering under the naïve impression that a strip in a music paper might be required to actually be about music. Consequently I included lots of terribly unfunny parodies of musicians that would have been better excluded." Instead, the basic humor of *Roscoe Moscow* came from the wide variety of subject matter that it might parody in a given week— American high school sex comedies of the *Grease* and *Happy Days* style one week, Jack Kirby's cover to *Sgt. Fury and His Howling Commandos* #1 the next, and so on. It was, in other words, a strip in which Moore quickly established his range as a creator, and demonstrated that he could make a credible case for his ability to tailor his work to any brief. There is a profound sense of tactical nous in *Roscoe Moscow*—it's difficult to imagine a savvier choice to launch one's career. On the one hand, the estimated distribution of *Sounds* means that this work is actually some of the highest selling of Moore's career; on the other, *Sounds* was a place where he could safely experiment as opposed to having to fit into a clear structure himself. Moore has commented that "*Sounds* didn't care what I did as long as it was funny and looked okay," a satisfyingly low bar to clear.

"*Hawdy haw! You glassy-assed jokers are a pushover!*"
–Alan Moore, *Astounding Weird Penises*, 2010

Much of this is due to the nature of *Sounds* as a magazine. It is, of course, primarily a music magazine, which means that its comics section was largely an afterthought. It was also, in many ways, the third-rate music magazine of the late 1970s. The big two magazines were *NME*—the *New Musical Express*, to which Moore made his first professional sale: a drawing of Elvis Costello—and *Melody Maker*. These magazines were not meaningfully competitors; both were published by IPC (which published *2000 AD*) and presented a reasonable dichotomy. Those with traditional and more conservative taste could go to *Melody Maker*, edited by Ray Coleman, which was still embracing prog rock and getting very excited about Bruce Springsteen. Those favoring a more progressive, avant garde approach had *NME*, which was openly political and had a bevy of music writers who went on to become the sorts of elder statesmen that *The Guardian* likes to hire.

So when Jack Hutton and Peter Wilkinson left *Melody Maker* in 1970 to start their own company, this was the closed system they confronted. The approach they eventually settled on was straightforward: they were the magazine that would embrace brash, new music. *Sounds* was the first of the three music magazines to embrace punk, and eventually spun off a heavy metal magazine called *Kerrang!* that, unlike *Sounds*, continues to be published today. *Sounds* was originally conceived of as a left-wing magazine, but by the late 1970s had become something of a mishmash—it heavily covered the Oi! subgenre of punk extensively, to the point of, in 1981, releasing a compilation called *Strength Through Oi!*, a reference to the Nazi slogan, "Strength through joy." This might plausibly have been called subversion had they not featured gay neo-Nazi Nicky Crane on the cover. Crane was, at the time, serving a prison sentence for having violently attacked more black people than was socially acceptable. (*Sounds* and the album's compiler, writer Garry Bushell, insisted that this was just a misunderstanding, and that they were unaware of the identity of the skinhead chosen for the cover. The incident was not, in any case, sufficient to drive the usually reliably leftist Moore away from the magazine—for two years after *Strength Through Oi!* he kept working for *Sounds*.)

On the other hand, *Sounds* still had enough of a leftist following that in the May 3rd, 1980 issue it ran a letter from reader Derek Hitchcock savaging *Roscoe Moscow* for being "insulting to anyone with a minimum of intelligence because of their cheapness and because of their blatant mocking prejudice," specifically calling the strip out for a series of jokes in the fiftieth installment in which Moscow bemoans being trapped "down a sewer with a hommerseckshul space-monster," complete with crude puns about being "willing to bend over backwards in order to help you." Moore responded two issues later with characteristic vehemence, pointing out that Moscow is "not meant to be a very nice character. He's terrified of women, he's terrified of homosexuals, he has a deep and xenophobic loathing of foreigners, he's a card carrying Republican who campaigned for Nixon, he's an alcoholic, sexually inadequate neurotic who can't hold down a job and dresses up like a private eye as part of a pathetic attempt at self-respect," and blasts Hitchcock for his "arse-backwards conclusions delivered in a more-liberal-than-thou tone of righteous indignation," while, equally characteristic of Moore, self-deprecatingly disclaiming that he was "not claiming that Roscoe Moscow is a good comic strip, or even a mildly funny one."

For all Moore's adamance that he had enough respect for the readership of *Sounds* not to run a disclaimer to this effect, it is perhaps telling that he wound down the strip soon after, replacing it with the sci-fi themed *The Stars My Degradation*. Perhaps more telling than the mere fact that he ended it, however, is the emphatic anger with which he did. Not long after his exchange with Hitchcock, Moore has Roscoe Moscow suffer a complete nervous breakdown and carted away to an asylum, where he's shown as a broken figure, restrained in a straitjacket and drooling helplessly on himself. The final strip features a flash forward of Roscoe Moscow's rehabilitation into the stifling banality of an ordinary life working at the chicken fat canning company juxtaposed with photos of Alan Moore telling a lame joke to enliven a strip he admits is "not that funny… I mean, none of them have been that funny, but this one's really grim." It's difficult to escape the sense that Moore is on the one hand trying to conclusively demonstrate how wrong Hitchcock is, and on the other suddenly finding the strip just as unpleasant as its detractors did.

That Moore's strip should get caught in accusations of right-wing bigotry is not only fitting given the later travails of *Sounds*, it is fitting given the obvious influences on Moore's work for them. For all that *Roscoe Moscow* delighted in its stylistic imitations of other material, its basic style was drawn from the underground comix scene—a scene with its own complex history of being accused of bigotry.

The figure most associated with the underground comix scene is Robert Crumb, often credited simply as R. Crumb, and the movement is generally said to have started with his publication of *Zap Comix* #1 in 1968. As with most things, the truth is more complicated, but *Zap* was undeniably a revelatory comic, blending a shocking level of confessionalism and obscenity with the meticulous draftsmanship of R. Crumb. So central is Crumb's artistic abilities and style to *Zap*'s success that it is not difficult to see why he's treated as the visionary founder of the style. Crumb is an immaculately talented artist who combines expressive naturalism with a fluid, cartoonish elasticity that lets him move seamlessly from the intensely human to the perversely grotesque. Combined with the iconoclastic obscenity that was perfectly in step with the times in 1968, this put Crumb at the crest of the same wave that had J.G. Ballard writing "Why I Want to Fuck Ronald Reagan" in the same year. In many ways it was a matter of being in the right place in the right time: *Zap* was published in San Francisco in the autumn of 1968, while it was still at the forefront of hippie culture.

In practice its publication owed much to the countercultural infrastructure already in place from San Francisco's embrace of the Beat scene a decade earlier. *Zap* was printed by Apex Novelties, whose owner Don Donahue got Beat poet Charles Plymell to print the comic by giving him his hi-fi tape player. It was similarly enmeshed in the hippie scene—*Zap* was preceded by Crumb's work in a paper called *Yarrowstalks*, which Crumb describes as "corny hippy spiritual stuff." Crumb credits the transformation between his earlier work and his late 60s stuff to his taking LSD in 1966.

But *Zap* isn't even the point where these countercultural movements and comics intersected for the first time. Crumb got his start in comics on Harvey Kurtzman's *Help* in 1964. Kurtzman, for his part, pioneered a satirical style of comedy in the 1950s with a particular focus on ornate sight gags (ideally executed by artist Wally Wood) via *Mad*, which he oversaw for the first several years of its publication. *Mad* lacked the over-the-top obscenity of Crumb's work (which is for the best—its publisher, William Gaines's EC, had enough problems being made the scapegoat for a moral panic in the American comics industry following the 1954 publication of Fredric Wertham's *Seduction of the Innocent*), but it shared the madcap sensibility and aesthetic of the grotesque. Certainly *Mad*'s basic format of satirical parodies of pop culture subjects is a visible inspiration for *Roscoe Moscow*.

Although the first issue of *Zap* consisted entirely of Crumb's work, in *Zap* #2 Crumb was accompanied by other cartoonists working in the same spirit. Of particular note in *Zap* #2 was the debut of the scene's second leading light, S. Clay Wilson. Crumb describes his initial impression of Wilson's work as "something I'd never seen before, anywhere, the level of mayhem, violence, dismemberment, naked women, loose body parts, huge, obscene sex organs, a nightmare vision of hell-on-earth never so graphically illustrated before in the history of art," and goes on to admit that "suddenly my own work seemed insipid." Crumb was not to be outdone, and his own work became accordingly more viscerally depraved. Wilson's style favored intricate tableaus of demons engaged in staggeringly depraved acts of sex and violence, and was the subject of a direct homage within *Roscoe Moscow*.

But the underground artist most straightforwardly linked to *Roscoe Moscow* was Art Spiegelman, whose collection of the first few installments of *Maus* is typically grouped with Frank Miller's *The Dark Knight Returns* and Moore and Dave Gibbons's *Watchmen* in arguing for the idea that 1986 was the annus mirabilis of comics. Spiegelman's story, "Ace Hole:

Figure 27: One of S. Clay Wilson's characteristic tableaus of demonic sexual horrors.

Figure 28: Moore's homage to S. Clay Wilson (From Roscoe Moscow: Who Killed Rock 'n Roll, *by Alan Moore as Curt Vile, 1979)*

Midget Detective," is a straightforward and admitted inspiration for *Roscoe Moscow*. Like Roscoe, Ace was a Mickey Spillane-style noir investigator who wound his way through a formulaic narrative decorated not by the deformed detritus of the music industry, but by the world of modern art, particularly the work of Pablo Picasso.

That a single movement should incorporate both the aggressive obscenity of S. Clay Wilson and the literate erudition of Art Spiegelman demonstrates that the scene had considerable breadth. Indeed, for all that it's associated with San Francisco, the underground movement at large had a far broader reach. In the UK, at least, the vanguards of this were the counterculture publications *Oz* and the *International Times*. *Oz*, in particular, pushed the scene, launching *Cozmic Comics* in 1972 to reprint classic American underground work alongside original British comics. *Cozmic Comics* provided early bylines for artists like Brian Bolland and Bryan Talbot. (Moore, in fact, enthused about working with Talbot on an aborted serial for *Warrior* because Talbot's "background is as solidly rooted in the underground" as Moore's.) Indeed, it was the cover of *Oz* #16 that provided Moore his first glimpse of Crumb's work in the form of an illustration of Crumb's recurring (and grotesquely racist) Angelfood McSpade character.

But Moore's most sustained engagement with Crumb came in the form of *Arcade*, a relatively late entry in the underground comix scene. By the time of its 1975 debut the countercultural claims of the underground were firmly on the retreat; between the 1973 *Miller v. California* Supreme Court ruling that allowed local communities to set their own standards for obscenity and a crackdown on the head shops in which underground comix were distributed, the distribution networks that had allowed the comics to thrive were withering. Meanwhile, the mainstream was already starting to recuperate the subversive energy of the underground. Marvel, in 1974, launched *Comix Book*, which featured artists like Art Spiegelman and S. Clay Wilson doing anodyne iterations of their usual work. *Comix Book* floundered, but in 1976 Marvel tried again with *Howard the Duck*, which featured Steve Gerber and (after a few issues) Gene Colan doing funny animal satire in a decidedly post-underground vein.

Arcade, spearheaded by Art Spiegelman and Bill Griffiths, was, as Crumb put it, "an attempt to pull together the rapidly disintegrating 'underground movement.'" This sense of decline in the movement was explicitly shared by Spiegelman, who said that in the 70s, "What had seemed like a revolution simply deflated into a lifestyle. Underground comics were stereotyped as dealing only with Sex, Dope and Cheap Thrills. They got stuffed back into the closet, along with bong pipes and love beads, as Things Started To Get Uglier." *Arcade*, then, was his effort to move past that. It's important to note that both Spiegelman and Griffiths had careers that went beyond the underground. Spiegelman, on the back of *Maus*, eventually transformed himself into an icon of literary respectability, while Griffiths transitioned from the underground to a widely syndicated newspaper strip, taking his Zippy the Pinhead character from the pages of underground publications like *Real Pulp Comix* to King Features Syndicates, who send daily installments to mainstream newspapers alongside pinnacles of suburban banality like *Blondie*, *Rex Morgan M.D.*, and *Family Circus*.

"There's no going back. We've unpicked the thread of the world."
–Grant Morrison, *The Invisibles* #2, 1994

Although it predates their breakout success by a decade, *Arcade* shares this sort of ambition. As Moore put it in his appreciation of the magazine, "Too Avant Garde for the Mafia" (the title comes from Griffiths's reply to a letter Moore had sent the magazine), "*Arcade* served as a rallying point for those cartoonists who were more concerned with their art than their bank balances," although in the case of both Griffiths and Spiegelman (and for that matter Moore),

Figure 29: R. Crumb's cover to Oz *#18 was Alan Moore's first exposure to his work.*

Figure 30: Racist caricatures persist even in Crumb's less overtly parodic material. (From "That's Life!", by R. Crumb, 1975)

it's perhaps more accurate to say that they were concerned with the idea that the two might be interrelated.

Nevertheless, Moore is wholly correct: *Arcade* was the venue for a wealth of impressive comics. Moore singles out several, not just by Crumb, but also by second string underground artists like Spain Rodriguez, Justin Green, and Kim Deitch. But it is Moore's praise of Crumb's contributions to *Arcade* that is perhaps the most fascinating. Moore singles out a story in the third issue of *Arcade* entitled "That's Life," which tells the story of Tommy Grady, an obscure blues singer who recorded one record before being shot and killed in a barroom confrontation, then segues into a depiction of Crumb finding Grady's lone record and playing it. As Moore describes it, "The last panel shows a crowd of rich white-American blues scholars smiling blissfully as Tommy Grady's voice drifts around the elegant apartment: 'Po-o boy, lo-ong way fum home... Po-o boy lo-ong way fum home...' A lone caption reminds us of the title: '...And that's life!' Crumb at his manic-depressive zenith."

None of this is wrong as such. "That's Life" is a well-worked story that builds skillfully to its bitter slap of a conclusion. But there's an unsettling issue underneath this. Crumb's depiction of Grady is clearly based on the tradition of racist blackface cartoons, much as his Angelfood McSpade drawings are. And while Moore makes excuses for Angelfood McSpade, saying that her design was "so exaggerated that it called attention to the racialism inherent in all descriptions," this argument falls flat when applied to the non-satirical depictions in "That's Life," if indeed it carries much weight when applied to McSpade. The fact of the matter is, Crumb likes drawing black people in a caricatured style that is generally recognized as grotesquely racist, and Moore's willingness to provide an apologia for it does him no favors. And although Moore singles out several female cartoonists in the underground scene for praise (including Melinda Gebbie, who he'd not yet met) in his 1983 essay "Invisible Girls and Phantom Ladies," in both his 1988 "Comments on Crumb" essay and his 1984 "Too Avant Garde for the Mafia" piece he is utterly silent on the rampant misogyny that's present in Crumb's work.

More damningly, these problems are not unique to Crumb. S. Clay Wilson's work is similarly drenched in disturbing misogyny. Trina Robbins, an accomplished underground cartoonist in her own right and the force behind *Wimmen's Comix*, an openly feminist underground comic, has complained vocally of "how willing people are to overlook the hideous darkness in Crumb's work," and blamed him directly for how "the underground comix of the Seventies [were] so full of hatred towards women; rape; degradation; murder and torture." This suggestion of deeply entrenched misogyny is echoed by Melinda Gebbie, who describes the tremendous hostility directed at female comics artists, recounting a conversation in which S. Clay Wilson told her bluntly, "Women aren't supposed to be artists. They have babies, that's what women are for."

Moore is hardly alone in praising Crumb and Wilson and yet overlooking their more disturbing aspects—the world of comics is awash with Crumb apologists. Still, Moore's relative silence on this issue is uncharacteristic. While there is a rich tradition of feminist criticism of Moore's work, even his harshest feminist critics would largely agree that Moore is a committed feminist who makes some significant errors—far from Crumb, who, as Trina Robbins is quick to point out, openly admits that he's "hostile to women." Indeed, "Invisible Girls and Phantom Ladies" is an extended critique of the long and unfortunate history of sexism in comics. But despite pages of criticism about how female characters in superhero comics were "pale and limp carbon copies of their male counterparts" and of the countless "comic cuties who have been featured in ongoing gags-and-straps situations," the extent of criticism he's willing to subject the underground to is the staggering understatement that "whatever their other merits, I doubt anyone would hold up any of S. Clay Wilson's panoramas of abused and dismembered women as a blow for feminism."

One reason Moore might have been inclined to give Crumb and Wilson a pass is that he had obvious regard for the visionary quality of their work. In Crumb's case, the bizarre sexuality of his comics work reflects his own issues, neuroses, and fetishes in a way that John Carlin describes as "not just directly autobiographical, but psychologically (and literally) naked... no one before Crumb made comics that were so directly about themselves and their own mental state." The appeal is simple: Crumb could see things that others could not, and, specifically, could see them precisely because of the odd contours of his own internal psychological state. Crumb's golden age began following his experimentations with LSD in the 1960s, which he credits with driving him into a "fuzzy state of mind" where "the barrier betwixt the conscious and the subconscious was broken open somehow. A grotesque kaleidoscope, a tawdry carnival of disassociated images kept sputtering to the surface... especially if I was sitting and staring, which I often did." Crumb admits that "it was difficult to function in this condition" and says, "I was certifiably crazy. I sat staring on the couch at Marty's apartment, or on long aimless bus rides around Chicago." Lest one think the experience was pleasant, he clarifies, "These jerky animated cartoons in my mind were not beautiful, poetic or spiritual, they were like an out-of-tune player piano that you couldn't shut off... pretty disturbing..." Yet out of this madness he created "all the main characters I would be using in my comics for the next ten years," and he describes the overall period as "a once-in-a-lifetime experience, like a religious vision that changes someone's life, but in my case it was the psychotic manifestation of some grimy part of America's collective unconscious."

The War is littered with experiences analogous to this. Moore has described several over the years, many shared with Steve Moore, perhaps most obviously his first encounter with Glycon, which took place on January 7th, 1994: "The ceiling's gone, the room now opening upon a space above that isn't night, and something stoops, leans in from outside, gathering identity with its approach. It pushes its unfathomable face down into our aquarium, displacing world, spilling reality on heaven's front-room floor." And Morrison had a comparable experience a few months later in Kathmandu in which he "began to lose contact with the physical reality of the room, seeing in its place cranky ancient streets, and leaning ceramic houses haunted by gnomish presences, the current dragging me deeper through hallucinatory ancestral wynds and crabby cobbled alleyways that felt like the archaic half-remembered dreams of childhood."

And there is ample history of such experiences in Albion, most notably in the life of William Blake, who, for instance, describes a visitation from the archangel Gabriel: "I looked whence the voice came, and was then aware of a shining shape, with bright wings, who diffused much light. As I looked, the shape dilated more and more: he waved his hands; the roof of my study opened; he ascended into heaven; he stood in the sun, and beckoning to me, moved the universe." Blake had such visions throughout his life, and depicted them in his work, as in *Milton* where he describes how

Walking in my Cottage Garden, sudden I beheld
The Virgin Ololon & address'd her as a Daughter of Beulah
Virgin of Providence fear not to enter into my Cottage
What is thy message to thy friend? what am I now to do
Is it again to plunge into deeper affliction? behold me
Ready to obey, but pity thou my Shadow of Delight
Enter my Cottage. comfort her, for she is sick with fatigue

There is a power to these lines. The Shadow of Delight refers to Blake's wife, Catherine, a marriage Peter Ackroyd describes as "one of the most poignant relationships in literary history." The image of Blake begging his angelic visitor to think of Catherine's suffering while simultaneously admitting his willingness "to plunge into deeper affliction" if that is what should be asked of him is a haunting portrait of the delicate balance of sanity that such visionary creativity entails. Blake further suffered from what he described as "Nervous Fear," which frequently manifested as a searing anger that did an often faltering career few favors.

For Crumb, the visionary potential of psychotropic substances blended unnervingly with mental illness. Crumb's two siblings also had artistic careers, but theirs were more visibly pocked by madness. His brother Maxon is a reasonably successful artist in his own right, but his working habits speak to deep-lying troubles beyond Crumb's. He sits upon a bed of nails to stimulate focus and engages in twelve-hour meditations; he describes his working habits as a fugue state in which he'll forget to eat for long periods. In Terry Zwigoff's 1995 documentary *Crumb*, Maxon recounts following and physically assaulting a woman, and he continues to practice a cleansing ritual in which he swallows a long strip of cloth to alleviate stomach pains that he believes to be karmic debt incurred from his father's shooting of a beggar in 1938. Robert Crumb's older brother Charles, meanwhile, was a non-offending pedophile who lived with his mother for his entire life. He continued to draw, but his artwork displayed an obsessive distaste for negative space common to those with mental illnesses. In 1993, Charles Crumb committed suicide, having failed in several earlier attempts described in the Zwigoff film.

So for all the problems posed by its racial and sexual politics, it is easy to see why Crumb's work appealed to Moore, who had been kicked out of school in 1971 for dealing LSD "purely for ideological reasons." This period clearly involved some profound psychological experiences for Moore. Although he rarely talks about it in detail, he's noted that "the problem with being an LSD dealer, if you're sampling your own product, is your view of reality will probably become horribly distorted and you may believe you have supernatural powers and you are completely immune to any form of retaliation and prosecution, which is not the case." In other interviews he's described himself as "sociopathic" during this period. Although this period did not give Moore the clarifying mystic visions that his later magical work did, the experience was still profound for him. As he put it, "LSD was an incredible experience... it hammered home to me that reality was not a fixed thing. That the reality that we saw about us every day was one reality, and a valid one—but that there were other, different perspectives where different things have meanings that were just as valid."

For all his obvious affection for psychotropic substances, Moore's discussions of his drug use demonstrate an investment in balancing visionary madness with practicality. He speaks witheringly of recreational drug use, and distinguishes "between drawings inspired by LSD and drawings attempted while under the effects of LSD." Moore's comments in *Promethea* on the decline of 1960s psychedelia are apropos in more ways than one: "Alas the zeitgeist's solar flash / scorched most such visionaries to ash / their lives, confused, addicted, lame, / drugged melodramas now became." Moore's 1971 expulsion seems to have been a literally sobering lesson to him—he eventually stopped using LSD, and restricts his use of psilocybin to ritual contexts, noting that he does proper, formal ritual increasingly rarely.

> *"But they are fictions. They are uncontaminated by effect and consequence. Why, they are almost innocent."*
> –Alan Moore, *Lost Girls*, 2006

While the underground clearly appealed to Moore on an ideological level despite the ethical failings of its leading lights, it is also worth discussing the aesthetic appeal. The gratuitous excess of the underground in and of itself is an odd fit for someone as focused on intricate structure as Moore. The tone of his praise in "Too Avant Garde for the Mafia" is telling—when he praises artists, it's for things like being "creatively self-conscious in his use of the medium," and the moments he chooses to single out are things like the final images of a biography of Stalin: "The narrative caption boxes relate how, during his final years, Stalin would travel by car along highways built for his solitary personal use across Russia. Wherever he stopped along the way there would be a room waiting for him specially constructed so as to be an exact duplicate of his room in the Kremlin, right down to the book lying open on the bedside table. While this is sinking in, we see three pictures, showing a simple side elevation of a sparsely furnished, neat-looking bedroom. Each picture is identical to the others except that they get progressively smaller." He goes on to describe the impact, "In effect, we get the impression of an endless series of identical rooms stretching away into the empty distance, proving an unnerving glimpse into the mind of someone who once controlled half of the world." When he does praise an artist of excess like R. Crumb, even that's on stylistic grounds—such as singling out "a selection of unpublished drawings from his sketchbook that proved every bit a meticulous and fascinating as his comic work."

The final key appeal of the underground to Moore was surely the means of production: the fact that artists got creative control, that work was produced for local scenes, and, of course, that it was uncensored. Censorship was, throughout the 70s and 80s, a problem for the UK comics industry. The heyday of this was the early 1970s, when the Metropolitan Police's Obscene Publications Squad brought the idea of police corruption to levels far more obscene than anything you could buy in the porn shops they took protection money from. This resulted in the police spending much more time busting magazines like Oz than in prosecuting the actual pornography industry that had largely overtaken Soho. A raid by the Obscene Publications Squad over work by Crumb and Wilson, for instance, led to the 1973 shutdown of Bookends, described by Moore as "a science fiction/comic/head shop out at Chepstow Place" in

Figure 31: Spain's grim depiction of the end of Stalin's life. (From Arcade *#4, 1975)*

Figure 32: R. Crumb's "Grand Opening of the Great Intercontinental Fuck-In and Orgy Riot," which led to an obscenity prosecution of The International Times

Notting Hill, an event which left Moore's close friend Steve Moore with five thousand pounds of debt. But to treat the 1970s as the extent of censorship in the UK is inaccurate. Even in the 1980s, Knockabout Comics (which would eventually end up handling the UK publication of the bulk of his late career comics work) ran into trouble importing his future wife's *Fresca Zizis*, all copies of which were confiscated and burned.

These prosecutions often ran into more complex times in the courts, however. *Oz* was successfully prosecuted in 1971 over a particularly provocative issue that had been edited by school children. The three editors of *Oz*, Jim Anderson, Richard Neville, and Felix Dennis were given substantial fifteen-month sentences (Dennis's was slightly less because the judge declared that he was "very much less intelligent" than the other two), and, in a particularly vicious move, had their heads shaven, a gesture that amounted to little more than an overt warning to any other dirty hippies who might get ideas. The case went to appeal, where the conviction was quashed, in part based on the observation that the Obscene Publications Squad was spending an awful lot of time busting satirical magazines and art galleries while leaving the pornography industry conspicuously unmolested.

Another prosecution based on a 1971 raid of the *International Times* offices led to the staff being hauled to the Old Bailey for the contents of *Nasty Tales*, a magazine primarily concerned with reprinting American underground material. Of particular objection was a single-panel strip by Crumb entitled "Grand Opening of the Great Intercontinental Fuck-In and Orgy-Riot" that was essentially Crumb's take on S. Clay Wilson's tableaus of perversity. To say that the courtroom was hostile to the material is an understatement—the judge, Alan King-Hamilton, is famed for his later overseeing of Mary Whitehouse's prosecution over *Gay News*'s 1976 publication of James Kirkup's "The Love That Dares to Speak its Name," a poem written from the perspective of a Roman centurion that opens with a description of Jesus being taken down from the cross "beardless, breathless, / but well hung," and goes on to describe a necrophilic dalliance with Christ, whose "shaft, still throbbed, anointed / with death's final ejaculation." King-Hamilton was quite literally a censor, having worked in that capacity for the Ministry of Information during the Second World War, and in the trial expressed astonishment that anybody would defend the literary or artistic merit of the magazine, dryly remarking that "the world is full of surprises." In giving instructions to the jury he told them that the experts summoned to discuss the merit of the magazine were not actually independent, suggested that Joy Farren, an employee of the *International Times* would "have been better employed in helping young hippies get back to their parents," and bluntly declared that "the pendulum of permissiveness has gone too far and it is time it began to swing back again."

Despite the judge's aggressive attempts to swing the verdict, the editors of the *International Times* were acquitted by a 10-2 vote of the jury, in one of the more celebrated victories against censorship of the period. All of this would surely have appealed to Moore. But his interest in the underground scene dates back a good few years earlier, and while the anti-censorship position surely helped, it cannot be the source of his infatuation. Simply put, the underground was valuable because it was an avant-garde artistic scene. Certainly Moore was seeking similar scenes out for himself in the 1970s. Moore got involved in comics fandom in the late 60s, and got involved in the fanzine scene, where he met Steve Moore, around the same time.

This was also the period where he was editing a poetry magazine for his school called *Embryo*, a few issues of which survive and circulate online. *Embryo* is not great—Moore describes his work as "angsty, breast-beating things about the tragedy of nuclear war, but [that] were actually about the tragedy of me not being able to find a girlfriend." Still, based on the surviving evidence, it was better than his peers. It's churlish to criticize at length the poetry of an amateur poet whose only real literary sin was to appear in an obscure Northampton zine alongside someone who happens to have been very good at something else ten years later, and who attracted a set of fans obsessive enough to hunt down and scan his obscure early 70s zines for the Internet's consumption. Nonetheless, it is worth recognizing the intensely inclusive attitude that the magazine embraced such that Moore's "PARANOPOLIS," which describes

> BabelGod stiltowing in distortion a billion maniac miles
>   above the road.
> Electricrackling whip, cruel and phosphorstreaking in
>   silhouette,
> through the screaming neonlight.
> THE [unreadable]MOBILES HELLHOWL WITH
> ROADBLOODLUST, SCREECHING INTO
> MANIAC WHITELINEATING
> MOTORMATTERWAY

shares a page with "A Shady Problem," a greeting-card sociology of race of that reflects, "My skin is black, your skin is white, / I don't want to have to fight / for everything that is my right." Moore's contributions are mostly unimpressive, though like the work Grant Morrison was producing at a similar age, there are moments where, knowing the writer's future, one can see the seeds. Unlike the other contributors to *Embryo* #2, Moore's work displays a range of styles and approaches that reflect the obsessive focus on craft that would come to define him, turning in a reasonably competent imitation of the beat poets in "PARANOPOLIS" alongside a bit of cod-epic fantasy in "The Spires of Ishon." Already there are visible thematic concerns: his interest in genre fiction comes through both in "The Spires of Ishon" and in "Moonshadow," which is drenched in science fiction references, while "Deathshead" contains an off-handed mention of Asmodeus.

This aggressively open approach made him a solid fit for the Arts Lab scene that was cropping up throughout the UK at the time. (David Bowie, notably, ran one out of a Beckenham pub, and his "Cygnet Committee," a deep cut on the *Space Oddity* album, was an embittered farewell to the scene.) As Moore describes the Northampton one, "It was like a spontaneous kind of multimedia group where we decided that we were going to put on some performance, or we were going to put out a magazine, some event, or whatever, and then we all just worked toward it doing whatever we felt like doing." Moore tried out different things, drifting into bands, doing poetry readings, drawing covers to zines, taking stabs at theater, et cetera. His account of the scene is tinged with a clear utopian nostalgia, admitting that the product of the Arts Lab was often rubbish, but praising its experimentalism and willingness to take risks, and clearly treating it as an influence. He specifically mentions the acting skills he picked up from the Arts Lab in a 2002 interview, where he describes his early technique of acting character parts out in front of a mirror to get a feel for them. It was also during his Arts Lab phase that he attempted to start a zine of his own to be called *Dodgem Logic*, for which he sent musician and multimedia experimenter Brian Eno a lengthy bevy of interview questions, and subsequently leading him to sheepishly apologize for never actually getting the magazine out a quarter-century later when he interviewed Eno for BBC Radio 4's *Chain Reaction* program.

As with most expressions of 60s utopian idealism, the Arts Lab scene fizzled by the mid-70s. But Moore continued to be demonstrably invested in the collaborative and experimental aesthetic of it. He worked with several collaborators, including Arts Lab pal and future *Hellblazer* scribe Jamie Delano, to write a play entitled *Another Suburban Romance*. Among the songs Moore contributed to *Another Suburban Romance* was a recycled version of a song he'd written in 1973, "Old Gangsters Never Die." This, then, is the earliest piece of Moore's work to become at all famous or well-known—a rendition of it served as the B-side to the 1983 release of "March of the Sinister Ducks," which was also accompanied by an eight-page comic adaptation by Lloyd Thatcher. The rendition was used in turn for the 1987 episode of Central's *England Their England*. The song had a second comics adaptation overseen by Antony Johnston and drawn by Juan Jose Ryp by Avatar Press in 2003, along with two other songs from *Another Suburban Romance*—the title number, and a piece called "Judy Switched Off the TV," and got another performance on Scoobius Pip's *Distraction Pieces* podcast in 2014.

That "Old Gangsters Never Die" should enjoy such an extended afterlife is not entirely surprising—it is, in point of fact, quite good. Moore quickly develops a style and voice for his narrator, and displays the deftness of language and image that his later writing is known for, imagining "some old speakeasy in the 1920s where they never pulled aside the blind and looked outside to find that fifty years had washed away all the legends and the blood stains and the zoot suits like some fistful of dead roses someone left there with the hat check girl." It by no means marks some magical turning point in which the "proper" Alan Moore arrives on the scene, but nevertheless, it shows more than just a flicker of Moore's larger ability.

> *"I don't have to have a cat die in order to produce a good work."*
> –Grant Morrison, 2013

But in many ways the most obvious precedent for *Roscoe Moscow* from his pre-professional period is the series of eleven comics entitled *St. Pancras Panda* that he did for the *Back Street Bugle*, an alternative newspaper out of Oxford. Conceptually, *St. Pancras Panda* is a straightforward parody of Michael Bond and Peggy Fortnum's Paddington Bear, although, like *Roscoe Moscow*, the parody does not bother staying narrowly focused, and the strip is instead an opportunity for Moore to cram in a wealth of gags, allusions, and parodies of institutional power.

More broadly, if *Roscoe Moscow* is Moore visibly working out the stylistic and storytelling skills that define his later work, *St. Pancras Panda* is Moore working out the skills he'd need to start *Roscoe Moscow*. It is, in every regard, a slightly more primitive version of the strip—the art is scratchier, the storytelling is less clear, the jokes are less sharp. But it demonstrates that the underground comix style affected for *Roscoe Moscow* was not just a one-time thing selected for a specific job. To some extent it may be a matter of basic convenience—Moore is endlessly self-deprecating about his artistic skills, claiming that "I was barely capable of drawing even simple objects in a way by which they might be recognized... I wasn't really sure how many ribs people had or where the muscles were in the arms and legs." This is, as is characteristic for Moore, an overstatement, but it is the case that Moore is not a first-rate artist, nor even really a second-rate one. Given this, the underground style's affinity for the grotesque meant that it was a style in which Moore's artistic shortcomings were, if not erased, at least minimized. Certainly the amount of work he's done in the underground style that he's not drawn himself is minimal. The biggest problem, in many ways, was simply that the opportunities for a middling underground-style cartoonist in the late 70s/early 80s were limited. Yes, he sold work to *Sounds* and a few one-panel humor strips to a 1979 Marvel UK winter special, but at this point he'd basically saturated the UK market for work in that style.

This work within the Arts Lab scene (broadly considered) also provides vital context for his other early professional gig, *Maxwell the Magic Cat*. As with *St. Pancras Panda* and *Roscoe Moscow*, there was precedent for *Maxwell the Magic Cat* in Moore's earlier work, specifically in his five strips of *Anon E. Mouse* for *ANoN*, the Alternative Newspaper of Northampton in 1975. *Anon E. Mouse* is not particularly good—Moore hadn't yet figured out how to work around the limitations of his drawing ability. He was also, apparently, running into aggressive editorial interference, such that his

Figure 33: The beginning of St. Pancras Panda, *Moore's short-running strip for the* Back Street Bugle. *(1978)*

Figure 34: The sole existing strip of Nutters Ruin, a macabre parody of soap operas which The Northants Post *rejected, suggesting Moore try a children's strip instead.*

time on the strip was largely unhappy. But in 1979 he tried again, under relatively bizarre circumstances. In short, a representative from the local paper, the *Northants Post*, informed Moore that the paper wanted a regular strip. It turned out that this was in no way even remotely true, and that the representative had already been sacked for being a serial liar, but the paper graciously looked at Moore's work anyway. His submission (a parody soap opera called *Nutter's Ruin*) was rejected, as the paper was apparently not particularly enthused by a parody of *The Archers* that featured a serial killer vicar and "Adolph Hilton, a kindly old Austrian gent who moved to Nutter's Ruin just after the war" and who helped out with the public speaking society. Instead, they asked for "something geared more towards children, perhaps a strip about a little cat."

The result was *Maxwell the Magic Cat*, which ran from August 1979 to October 1986. Moore bristled demonstrably atthe editorial mandate, and decided against using his "Curt Vile" pseudonym (which he'd signed *Nutter's Ruin* with) in favor of Jill de Ray. This choice goes a long way towards explaining his thinking and goals with the strip: Gilles de Rais was a 15th century French nobleman and ally of Joan of Arc who over the last eight years of his life killed upwards of eighty children by hanging them from ropes, masturbating on them, and slitting their throats. Towards the end of his murder spree he experimented in demonic summoning, offering a demon named Barron assorted body parts of children in a glass vessel, but was apparently unsatisfied with the result. After an ill-advised kidnapping of a cleric in 1440, Rais was investigated by the Bishop of Nantes, who concluded that he was, in fact, a horrific child murderer, and he was simultaneously hanged and burnt at the stake in October of that year. Clearly, Moore was not planning on being child-friendly in the conventional sense of the word.

The obvious points of comparison for *Maxwell the Magic Cat* are not as helpful as they might appear. Gary Spencer Millidge's *Alan Moore: Storyteller* claims that the strip was conceived in opposition to Jim Davis's *Garfield*. This is, however, dubious. *Garfield* launched in June of 1978 in just forty-five US papers. Its ascent was rapid, but not so rapid that a jobbing comics artist in Northampton would likely be defining his work in overt opposition to it just fourteen months later. In many ways the early strips, which focus on the young boy Norman Nesbitt interacting with his talking cat, and which quickly introduce Mangler Mullins, a thuggish school bully, more resemble what Bill Watterson's *Calvin and Hobbes* might have looked like if Watterson wasn't one of the best cartoonists of his generation, but, of course, given that Watterson's strip debuted in 1985, that line of influence seems even more chronologically unlikely. Charles Schultz's *Peanuts*, suggested by Millidge alongside *Garfield* as an influence, is certainly more likely, though the similarity is more in the wry fatalism that the strips affect and less, as Millidge would have it, in the visuals. By and large, however, Moore's strip seems to have been mainly of his own invention—it is not, after all, as though "humor strip with a funny animal" is the most blisteringly original concept in history—for *Maxwell the Magic Cat* is, in fact, Moore's third attempt at it, after *Anon E. Mouse* and *St. Pancras Panda*. Talking cats of various forms have a history in comics and animation, going back to Otto Messmer's 1919 creation of Felix the Cat, and Moore, in particular, would surely have had Robert Crumb's Fritz the Cat firmly in mind when grumpily writing a talking cat.

But the real obvious influences for *Maxwell the Magic Cat* come from the larger context of children's comics that Moore was shoved into. The definitive set of British children's comics were DC Thomson's suite of comics: *The Beano, The Beezer, The Dandy*, and *The Topper*, of which *The Beano* and *The Dandy* were the oldest and best known. *The Dandy* dates to 1937, and *The Beano* to 1938, with the latter still in print today. When the *Northants Post* asked Moore for a children's strip about a cat, what both they and Moore surely had in mind was *Korky the Cat*, the cover strip for *The Dandy*. Korky is a relatively odd character. He's mischievous, certainly, but is a relatively anodyne trickster. He might cause a bit of trouble, but only of a mild sort, and he's just as likely to be the victim of a prank as the perpetrator. *Korky the Cat*, in other words, is less a defined style of humor and more a framework in which various jokes can be made. In this regard, the difference between it and *Maxwell the Magic Cat* is largely the sorts of jokes that are made. *Korky the Cat* delights in lowbrow humor and punchlines of people (or cats) smashing into things or getting comically mangled, or, occasionally, in open racism, as in a strip where a caricatured Chinese character appears to ask for a "mandolin" but in fact wants a mandarin orange. *Maxwell the Magic Cat*, on the other hand, is based around political humor and complex jokes about the structure of comics. More than anything this constitutes Moore's rebellion against the structure of children's comics, and it's part and parcel of a larger rebellion against *The Beano* and *The Dandy*.

On the one hand, *The Beano* and *The Dandy* were influences on Moore—he described them in an interview as the first comics he ever read. But there's a big difference between that and liking them, and he elsewhere described them as "almost a staple part of working class existence. They were something like rickets. They were just something you had." This obviously low opinion of them appears to be based on what Moore, even from an early age, recognized as a dangerous and unsettling dynamic of power and control. In Moore's account, these comics "mainly featured working class children in working class environments, and generally being spanked by their parents and teacher, which was a peculiar fixation," and that "they presented a world that was almost indistinguishable from the one that I lived in." Unlike *Garfield*, this presents a credible account of Moore's reservations about doing a children's comic.

But the nature of this dynamic is more complex than Moore lets on in his interview quips. While strips in *The Beano* often featured resolutions that involved mischievous children getting spanked, this has to be taken in the context of the behavior exhibited on the way to being spanked. The two most relevant strips here—and surely the two Moore was specifically referring to when talking about the comics' spanking fixation—are *The Bash Street Kids*, which features the exploits of a rebellious group of schoolchildren who are frequently spanked by their schoolteacher, and *Dennis the Menace*, who is usually spanked by his father.

(It is worth clarifying for the sake of some readers that the *Dennis the Menace* strip in *The Beano* is a completely separate phenomenon from Hank Ketcham's American comic strip of the same name. Both feature the same basic premise—a young boy named Dennis and his troublemaking exploits—although the American Dennis is a well-meaning child who inadvertently causes trouble, whereas the British one, created by artist Davey Law and *Beano* editor Ian Chisholm, is more of an unreconstructed sociopath. The two characters are wholly unrelated, with Law/Chisholm and Ketcham hitting on the name independently. Chisholm was apparently inspired by a music hall song entitled "Dennis the Menace in Venice," while Ketcham named the character after his own son. The strips debuted in the same week, with the American one starting on March 12th, 1951, and the British one five days later in the March 17th issue of *The Beano*.)

These are not unique strips by any means—their focus on naughty schoolchildren was shared by other *Beano* strips like *Roger the Dodger* and *Minnie the Minx*. *The Dandy* skewed towards a slightly different aesthetic; though it had strips like *Winker Watson* and *The Smasher* that were in the same style, they aren't the strips *The Dandy* is famous for, whereas *Dennis the Menace* and *The Bash Street Kids* are the iconic strips of *The Beano*. Reading them, then, what jumps out is not so much the corporal punishment that many strips end with as the giddily destructive antics preceding. *The Bash Street Kids*, for instance, feature in misadventures like crashing a miniature train at an amusement park into a beehive, or letting an elephant loose in the classroom. *Dennis the Menace*, meanwhile, appears in adventures with a similar tone (he has his own

Figure 35: *Mayhem and corporal punishment in a 1962 installment of* Dennis the Menace. *(From* The Beano*)*

Figure 36: *Maxwell and Norman find themselves cleaning up after the exploits of Peregrine the Pleasant Panther. (From* Maxwell the Magic Cat, *by Alan Moore as Jill de Ray, 1983)*

"releasing bees" story less than a month after *The Bash Street Kids* get one), but also in ones in which he's more overtly malevolent, such as, for instance, when he systematically tortures his neighbor Walter on a birdwatching exhibition for no particular reason, finally unleashing a herd of wild turkeys and laughing as he's attacked by them.

It's not hard to draw a link between this sort of destructive revelry and bits of *Maxwell the Magic Cat*— especially in the early days where it was more straightforwardly a kids comic. The difference is that where *The Beano* and *The Dandy* revel in displaying the destructive antics, showing the scenes of chaos, Moore's approach is to leave the destruction off panel. Even in the strip's latter days, Moore would go back to the "rampant destruction for comedy purposes" trope. For instance, Maxwell's intensely violent cousin, Peregrine the Pleasant Panther, tends to do things like eat zookeepers.

The fifth panel reveal of Peregrine's murderous rampage follows four oblique panels showing the dirt that Maxwell and Norman are throwing into the air as they dig the murdered zookeeper's grave, allowing Moore to obliquely build to his humorous/murderous punchline. This has two advantages. First, it makes the joke into something more nuanced and subtle. Instead of just being a joke about how hilarious it is to see innocent bystanders violently ripped apart by wild animals, it becomes a joke about piecing together what's actually happening in a story that at least initially seems to be about how Peregrine has gone home. Second, it prevents Alan Moore from having to spend time drawing something difficult like a panther mauling. This approach is typical of *Maxwell the Magic Cat*—even during the sections where Moore reworks it into being a political satire, the basic joke is typically the level of remove between what's depicted in the strip and the cultural subject matter being joked about. For instance, a strip mocking the upcoming wedding of Prince Andrew is done in the form of Maxwell talking on the phone to (presumably) the Queen about his idea for "Andy and Fergy Airsickness Bags."

But this merely accounts for the starting point that Moore rebelled against. Before long, any resemblance between *Maxwell the Magic Cat* and a children's comic was gone, and eventually the *Northants Post* conceded the point and moved the strip off the children's page entirely. It's not that the strip was ever child-unfriendly as such, though after a few months it becomes hard to imagine any child particularly enjoying the jokes about pairing red wine with fish or Robert Mitchum. By the time Moore got to tins of cat food sitting on death row and the tragic end of Liver Chunks in Oyster Sauce, any pretense that the strip was aimed at children was firmly out the window. Instead, Moore turned it into a general gag-a-week strip that wandered through any number of interests: politics, complex formal play with the structure of the comics medium, and bleak existential jokes (a captured mouse asks Maxwell what happens after death, and Maxwell describes cat heaven. The mouse admits that this doesn't sound that bad, and asks where mice go when they die. "Oh, they go to cat heaven as well.") And, of course, wonderfully dreadful puns.

By and large, this worked. Moore's intensely structural approach lends itself well to comedy. This is something that even a cursory examination of interviews with him reveals: he is a terribly funny man. Even when Moore is working with a bit of a shaggy dog punchline he frames it in a precisely worked set of comic beats. *Maxwell the Magic Cat* isn't spectacularly drawn, but it's reliably funny. Even when it gets political, it does so with the sort of mass market subversiveness that characterizes classic American newspaper strips of the same era like *Doonesbury* and *Bloom County*—it's cheeky, but never over the line of what can be published in a community newspaper. Moments like Moore's suggestion that laws regarding inbreeding don't apply to "cats and the Royal Family" might generate an angry letter or two, but it's not like he was including satanic imagery and blasted skeletons. The edgiest the strip ever got was a ten-week series

Figure 37: Liver Chunks in Oyster Sauce walks his last mile. (From
Maxwell the Magic Cat, *by Alan Moore as Jill de Ray, c. 1981)*

Figure 38: A late Maxwell the Magic Cat *strip that plays with the formal*
constraints of the comics medium. (By Alan Moore as Jill de Ray, 1986)

Figure 39: Alan Moore's acerbic commentary on the Falklands War. (From
Maxwell the Magic Cat, *by Alan Moore as Jill de Ray, 1982)*

satirizing the then-current Falklands War, in which a storyline about redundancies resulting in supporting characters being given their notice is derailed by a sudden and arbitrary cat/mouse war that causes everyone to forget about the unemployment crisis. Clever stuff, certainly, but given that Moore was busy launching *V for Vendetta* at the same time, it's hard to suggest that it's particularly incendiary.

> *"I fed her with an unused can of Monster's cat food,*
> *which I spooned into Monster's dusty cat bowl."*
> –Neil Gaiman, *The Ocean at the End of the Lane*, 2013

As mentioned, *Maxwell the Magic Cat* ran until late 1986. The official word in Acme Press's second volume of collected *Maxwell* strips is that "Moore dropped the strip due to the pressure of other work, and the *Post*'s stance on homosexuals' place in the community. It didn't feel there should be one." Both of these reasons are largely believable. Certainly Moore's workload by 1986 was such that he probably was looking for an excuse. Equally, Moore's passion on the issue of gay rights is documented (*AARGH!* came out just two years after he quit *Maxwell*, and he had already penned the "Valerie" episode of *V for Vendetta*), as is his propensity for taking decisive action over at times esoteric moral principles. It is also perhaps telling that the well of interesting ideas for *Maxwell* was visibly drying up towards its end. As the comic wore on, Moore frequently put out strips based on fairly pedestrian puns and rather flat gags. One strip consists of Maxwell sniffing a female cat for three panels and then asking if she's a Sagittarius. As this is only four panels, an opening panel consisting of Maxwell standing and whistling is added to bring it to five. Also, "Sagittarius" is misspelled. But even towards the end there were gems—three weeks later Moore has a particularly clever iteration of his frequent swipes at his own drawing ability.

In many ways, then, what's more remarkable than the question of why he quit is why it took him until 1986 to do so. He had, after all, left the higher-paying *Sounds* job over three years earlier. Admittedly the *Sounds* strips were considerably more elaborate, and the art was surely a bigger time sink for Moore, but by the time that the second issue of *Watchmen* was out the £12.50 a week that *Maxwell the Magic Cat* was pulling in (roughly £31 in contemporary money) cannot have been a significant portion of the Moores' monthly income. Moore, for his part, joked towards the end of the run that "I sprinkle shredded dollar bills over my cornflakes these days." One is left to wonder, then, why he persisted with the strip.

The answer proposed by Eddie Campbell in the first Acme collection is likely a lot of it: *Maxwell* provided Moore the opportunity for "immediate representation of [his] thoughts and idle notions; many samples are throwaway ideas, playful jokes about the technicalities of comics—balloons, frames, title-headings—but they reach us without being modified by a collaborator or the complicated requirements of the big publishing houses, nor are they spoiled by the accompanying tiresome acrimony of the soured involvements of the smaller publishing houses." Or, as Moore put it more simply in a 1991 interview, "*Maxwell The Cat* was fun, though. I carried on doing it long after it was profitable for me to do so."

But in many ways there is an even simpler explanation for Moore's strange perseverance with the strip: it was for his local paper. Moore has, throughout his career, maintained active connections with the local community of Northampton, from his Arts Lab work in the mid-70s through to *Dodgem Logic*'s endearing commercially naïve localism. It is not, to be clear, that the strip gave him some sort of practical power in the community—apparently the only reader comment he ever got came four years into the run, which mistook the Jill de Ray pseudonym as a real person and declared her a "frustrated old bitch," to which Moore sardonically commented that it was "scarcely fair considering I'd only just turned thirty at the time." Rather, it seems to be the basic virtue and value of writing something for and about his local community. That someone who would go on to pen a 75,000-word novel about a small portion of Northampton would persist in penning a comic strip for the local paper as long as his ethics allowed hardly seems surprising. It was, to quote Moore, "quick, disposable, and enables me to respond quickly on a local level to anything I feel like mouthing off again," and "not so much a comic strip, I suppose, but more a primal scream session."

It is difficult, if not impossible, to imagine any of the other combatants in the War doing something like this. Certainly one struggles to imagine Morrison, even if he'd not been sacked, continuing to do *Captain Clyde* well into his *Animal Man* run. And unlike *Captain Clyde*, *Maxwell the Magic Cat* is not some passion project for Moore. Its value was not the extent to which he was creating something he'd always wished had existed, but rather the extent to which it provided a material engagement with the local world around him. In this regard his eventual departure from the strip was wholly consistent with the strip: a howl of rage embedded firmly in the local community.

The other substantial work of Moore's that falls into this early period is *The Stars My Degradation*, the second and far longer-running of his two *Sounds* strips. (Although he did a handful of one-offs for the Christmas issues of *Sounds*, all but one of these were in the same setting as *The Stars My Degradation*.) On one level *The Stars My Degradation* is a clear transitional work between Moore's earliest work on *Roscoe Moscow* and *Maxwell the Magic Cat* and the later sci-fi/fantasy/horror stuff for which he's best known. But it's still firmly in the underground style of *Roscoe Moscow*, the strip it directly replaces. Where *Roscoe Moscow* was based on Moore's assessment of what *Sounds* wanted (presumably based largely on the strip he was accompanying on the *Sounds* comic page, Savage Pencil's *Rock 'n Roll Zoo*), and *Maxwell the Magic Cat* was devised in response to a specific commission, *The Stars My Degradation* is the first time in Moore's professional work that he's gotten to shape a comic to his own interests, namely science fiction.

The problem, of course, is that the chronology of Moore's career doesn't support the idea that *The Stars My Degradation* marks any sort of turning point for Moore. As noted, by the time *The Stars My Degradation* started Moore had already begun work for *Doctor Who Magazine*, with his first story, "Black Legacy," wrapping around the same time as *Roscoe Moscow*. Within a few months of its beginning Moore would begin work for *2000 AD*, and while working on *The Stars My Degradation* he'd do his work with *Star Wars*, and begin his work for both *Marvel UK* and *Warrior*. *The Stars My Degradation* is, in other words, not a transitional strip, but something Moore undertook while already in the process of switching from his initial career as a writer-artist to a career primarily as a writer. Further complicating this transition is that the end of *The Stars My Degradation* wasn't even written by Moore—as of 1982 he was only doing art chores on the strip with the writing done by the pseudonymous Pedro Henry, essentially the only time in his career where he was employed as an artist instead of a writer.

Where *Roscoe Moscow* demonstrates Moore pushing himself, like challenging himself with increasingly elaborate title splashes, *The Stars My Degradation* consistently feels like a safer, more conservative strip. This becomes clear almost immediately, as every installment of *The Stars My Degradation* began with a brief comedic rhyme: "Dempster Dingbunger is my name / Sputwang is my nation. / The depths of space gob in my face...", with the strip's title completing the verse. Similarly, Moore largely abandons the complex and ambitious layouts and structures he employed in *Roscoe Moscow* for a simpler and more direct sort of storytelling, occasionally punctuated by jokes about how he's blowing his deadlines. Some strips are self-evidently constructed so as to allow him to hit them with minimal effort, such as one that consists of five tight close-ups of characters' faces with lengthy captions providing their thoughts.

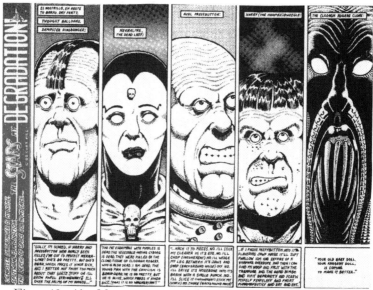

Figure 40: Alan Moor saves time in The Stars my Degradation. *(By Alan Moore as Curt Vile, 1981)*

Figure 41: Another S. Clay Wilson homage, this time featuring cameos of all of Alan Moore's characters to date. (From The Stars My Degradation, *by Alan Moore as Curt Vile, 1981)*

In this regard *The Stars My Degradation* feels less like an artistic transition and more like a comics writer taking an extra gig because his kids need new shoes. When he started it, his *Sounds* work was still the bulk of his income—the ten quid *Maxwell the Magic Cat* was making him was a necessary supplement, and whatever he made off of his eight pages of *Doctor Who* work would have been little more than a nice bonus. The sci-fi conceit put the comic closer to Moore's own interests than *Roscoe Moscow*, but the overall impression is of Moore making time while he waits to get established doing what he had by this point realized he should be doing, namely writing strips for other artists to draw.

This is not to say that *The Stars My Degradation* lacks interesting moments. Moore occasionally embraced structural complexity in *The Stars My Degradation*, and there are several strips he clearly spent time on, most notably a single panel fight scene in the mould of his S. Clay Wilson tribute in *Roscoe Moscow*, this one including his parody of Marvel Comics's X-Men alongside cameo appearances from Roscoe Moscow, St. Pancras Panda, Maxwell, and his recurring *2000 AD* character Abelaard Snazz. He frequently had clever plots as well, particularly early on—for instance, a murderously psychotic cyborg Axel Pressbutton infiltrates an anarchist cell consisting entirely of police informants trying to infiltrate an anarchist cell. (The plot culminates with one informant, depicted as a stereotypically masked anarchist with a wide-brimmed hat who in his first appearance is actually clutching a lit bomb, having his supposedly impossible plan to blow up the Central Justice Building actually work and leading to the revolution inadvertently taking place.)

But in the end, where *Roscoe Moscow* felt like early work of someone with vast capabilities in their craft, *The Stars My Degradation* feels like a man getting paid. It is, of course, impossible to take this as a significant criticism. Artistic production is first and foremost a form of work and labor, and Moore had a family to feed. At the time he started on *The Stars My Degradation* he had one kid, and his second was on the way. To criticize him for "merely" doing a comic for the fact that it kept his family from starving is to miss the fact that the War is not merely an abstracted phenomenon of textual play, but a real sequence of events that happened to actual people. In this regard *The Stars My Degradation* marks the point where Moore manages to accomplish what Morrison failed to in all of his inventive juvenilia: to turn out "good enough" material on a regular enough schedule to make a living doing it, and to demonstrate the discipline needed to do so past the point where the work is fun or intellectually satisfying. To continue to come up with inventive page layouts and subversive cat gags week in and week out is one thing. To labour excessively on a reasonably humorous sci-fi parody strip, eventually taking it as a pure artistic gig when you've already come to terms with the fact that art isn't your strong suit, is another.

There's something strangely apropos in Moore's choice of parody subjects in *The Stars My Degradation*, then. The title—indeed the entire opening rhyme—is a parody of Alfred Bester's 1956 novel *The Stars My Destination* (originally serialized under the title *Tiger! Tiger!*). Bester is very much ascience fiction fan's science fiction writer—one who enjoys rather more renown within science fiction fandom than without. To name *The Stars My Destination* as one's favorite science fiction novel is not in the least bit controversial—Samuel Delany, William Gibson, and Michael Moorcock number among those who have. But unlike writers such as Isaac Asimov, Robert Heinlein, and Arthur C. Clarke, Bester is not widely known outside of science fiction circles, and *The Stars My Destination* is in many ways the definition of a cult classic.

On one level, *The Stars My Destination* is a fairly straightforward pulp-style novel, serialized over four issues of *Galaxy* and featuring the sort of episodic content familiar to such material. What elevates it is the character arc of its protagonist, Gully Foyle. Foyle is not a well-rounded character in the conventional, literary sense. In fact, he is largely a cipher. At any given time his motives are utterly transparent and simple, and he is typically single-mindedly consumed by them. At first Foyle is seen floating in space, described as "one hundred and seventy days dying and not yet dead" and as struggling to survive "with the passion of a beast in a trap." When a passing spaceship ignores his distress call his motivation changes to revenge. Over the course of the novel his motivations shift and evolve further—he learns to act as a socialite, renaming himself Geoffrey Fourmyle, and eventually learns to control his emotions so that the remnants of an extensive facial tattoo of a tiger he is forcibly given early in the novel stops appearing on his skin. Eventually he has a quasi-mystical experience as he's trapped in a burning building, causing him to teleport throughout space and time (limited teleportation, called jaunting, being one of the basic conceits of the novel) while burning, before finally becoming a sort of cosmic holy man, living peacefully in the stars to see if mankind ascends to his level.

In other words, while the novel lacks any sort of intricate character work, it still has a clear character arc that grants a greater sense of unity and development than many contemporary novels. Its central conceit is that the various bits of sci-fi technology Bester posits allow a single man to go from an animalistic creature driven only by his survival instinct to a figure of profound spiritual enlightenment. This is compelling in its reach, and presages the then yet-to-emerge new wave of science fiction that Moorcock and Ballard would eventually exemplify, where science fiction concepts were not merely logic games about hypothetical technology, but metaphors for psychological and sociological phenomena, more interesting for the ways it can comment on human consciousness than for the comparatively banal questions of how imaginary science works.

"It contains such cheerfully protocyber elements as multinational corporate intrigue; a dangerous, mysterious, hyperscientific McGuffin (PyrE); an amoral hero; a supercool thief woman."

–Neil Gaiman, on *The Stars My Destination*

In this regard what is most interesting in *The Stars My Destination* is the section in which Foyle is jaunted through space and time, intersecting his past timeline. Through this period he experiences synesthesia, such that "the cold was the taste of lemons and the vacuum was a rake of talons on his skin. The sun and the stars were a shaking ague that racked his bones." His journey here is described as "hurtling along the geodesical space lines of the curving universe at the speed of thought, far exceeding that of light. His spatial velocity was so frightful that his time axis was twisted from the vertical line drawn from the Past through Now to the Future. He went flickering along the new near horizontal axis, this new space-time geodesic, driven by the miracle of a human mind no longer inhibited by concepts of the impossible." This vision of traumatic enlightenment prefigures the visions of eternity that Morrison and Talbot played with in *Near Myths*, to say nothing of Moore's future work like *The Moon and Serpent Grand Egyptian Theatre of Marvels* and *Promethea*.

Throughout it, however, is the peculiar image of Gully Foyle himself. The tiger tattoo and his incandescent jaunt through space and history are clearly drawn from the same poem that Bester took his original title from: William Blake's "The Tyger," the first stanza of which provides the novel's epigraph. The poem is Blake's best known, and comes from *Songs of Experience*, the counterpart to his *Songs of Innocence*. As the titles suggest, these two books are intimately connected, with several poems in each sharing titles or otherwise mirroring each other, the earlier *Songs of Innocence* presenting a lilting, pastoral view of childhood, the later and more bitter *Songs of Experience* revealing scenes of crushing poverty and cruelty.

"The Tyger" is *Songs of Experience*'s retort to "The Lamb," a pleasant bit of verse reflecting on the eponymous ewe's "clothing of delight, / Softest clothing wooly bright," and how it's a reflection of Christ's kindness. In contrast, "The

Tyger" provides an image of monstrous divinity: a beast of fire and rage. Blake's verse at once recoils from the beast and stares at it in awe, but more importantly at whatever divinity created such a terror, asking "In what distant deeps or skies, / Burnt the fires of thine eyes? / On what wings dare he aspire? / What the hand, dare sieze the fire?" The Tyger itself is a terror, yes, but merely a mundane one of sinew and flame, in the end no different than the tragic poverty Blake depicts elsewhere in *Songs of Experience*. The true terror is the monstrous god that created this beast, and the terrifying order of things in which it exists, a sentiment expressed in the poem's penultimate verse, which asks if "When the stars threw down their spears / and water'd heaven with their tears; / Did he smile his work to see? / Did he who made the Lamb make thee?"

And yet through all of this Blake's sense of awe and wonder at this divinity comes through. "The Tyger" evokes the horror of God, but it never even contemplates rejecting or rebuking God for these horrors. Instead the terrified awe becomes a new form of worship. This is, in the end, the point of *The Stars My Destination*: not merely that Foyle has this visionary experience, but the monstrous world of corrupt corporations and human depravity that steadily moves him from his innocuous beginnings to his eventual enlightenment. Its vision of enlightenment is as terrible as it is desirable, and emerges from Foyle's engagement with the material world, a social progression from base animal to enlightened being.

On the surface *The Stars My Degradation* is a grim and cynical inversion of this. The social order that Dempster Dingbunger encounters does not provide him any sort of enlightenment: merely humiliation and, as the title puts it, degradation. It is the work of someone who is barely clawing a living together, and who has suffered mightily at the hands of authority figures such as the headmaster who didn't just expel him in 1971, but who hounded him for years afterwards, writing "the anti-matter equivalent of references" that went so far as to accuse him of sociopathy, which resulted in him having to take degrading jobs, like one at a tannery described thusly: "We had to turn up at 7.30 AM and drag these blood-stained sheepskins out of these vats of freezing cold water, blood, and various animal by-products. Many were the happy hour that we had throwing sheep's testicles at each other," or, as put elsewhere, "the job down at the skinning yards where men with hands bright blue from caustic dye trade nigger jokes." Even eight years removed from that, as Moore navigated the beginnings of a freelance artistic career, trying to avoid the threatening gaze of Thatcher's newly elected government and its savage cuts to the social safety net he was still dependent on, the sense of a world whose machinations led not to any sort of spiritual enlightenment but towards suffering, disappointment, and being cheated by the people you trusted would have been clear. Hence Dingbunger's world of kangaroo courts and forced labor, where no matter what apparent victories he wins in surviving he will never encounter anything but celestial degradation.

And yet in practice Moore was, unbeknownst to him, on the other path—the one mapped out in Bester's original. It is not that he was wrong about the brutal cruelty of the world, any more than Blake was wrong when he described the crushing poverty of young chimney sweepers: "A little black thing among the snow: / Crying weep, weep. In notes of woe!", and savaging those who "praise God & his Priest & King / who make up a heaven of our misery." As Moore makes his way through the landscape of the War he will encounter far more instances of abuse and exploitation. And yet in hindsight *The Stars My Degradation* is a rung on a ladder that would lead Moore from the impoverished desperation of a freelancer to the heights of artistic genius and, for that matter, financial success. In time he would find himself staring into the same monstrous light gazed upon by Blake and Foyle. Like both Blake and Foyle, his path into that light wound through the material cruelty of the world. But it also wound past it. Moore kept working, producing comics at a furious rate. His work for Marvel UK, IPC, and Dez Skinn's *Warrior* would provide enough income that he could drop the time-intensive *The Stars My Degradation*, but even then he replaced it with yet more work. Even while doing *The Stars My Degradation* he took on other jobs, writing a variety of reviews and interviews for *Sounds*.

But it would be a mistake to treat Moore's eventual success as some supreme act of individual will, just as it would be to treat Blake's artistic career as the product of a wholly independent man, or, for that matter, to treat Foyle's enlightenment that way. At a key moment in Foyle's space-time jaunting he encounters Robin Wednesbury, a one-way telepath he'd encountered several times previously in the novel, and, crucially, treated with shocking cruelty on more than one occasion. And yet Robin, when she meets the jaunting and burning Gully Foyle, explains to him what's happening and tells him what he needs to know in order to save himself and escape the burning building he's trapped in. This establishes an essential point in Bester's narrative, which is that for all that the cruelty of the world set Foyle on his path, Foyle is in no way a completely isolated individual. Indeed, he depends on a variety of friends and allies, all of whom work together to get him out of the burning building.

Moore's ascent from a grubby £45-a-week freelance existence to becoming one of the most successful and acclaimed artists of his era was similarly dependent on a variety of friends and helpers, of which perhaps the earliest and most significant was Steve Moore, who he first met in the late 1960s, and who provided the model for his eventual transition into being a writer instead of a writer-artist. Steve Moore, in fact, is the writer behind the Pedro Henry pseudonym, and stepped in to help Moore manage his workload by plotting the final year of *The Stars My Degradation*. But Steve Moore's influence on the strip extends beyond his credited assistance. One of the major characters of *The Stars My Degradation* is Axel Pressbutton, an extravagantly violent cyborg who made his first appearance in a strip called "Three

Eyes McGurk and his Death Planet Commandos," another early non-paying gig Moore did for the minor British music magazine *Dark Star*. Moore had been working on a strip called *The Avenging Hunchback*, a superhero parody, but the second installment of that strip was lost when the editor's car was stolen, and Moore was too disheartened to repeat all of his delicate stippling. Accordingly, Steve Moore stepped in to help his friend, writing "Three Eyes McGurk" as a replacement strip, and co-creating the Pressbutton character. (Moore in fact based Pressbutton's visual design on Lex Loopy, a Lex Luthor parody designed for *The Avenging Hunchback*.) "Three Eyes McGurk" ended up being Moore's first American publication, getting a reprint in a 1981 anthology edited by Gilbert Shelton, and Moore went on to incorporate the character (earlier in his life, as he dies at the end of his original appearance) into *The Stars My Degradation*.

As mentioned, it was Steve Moore who taught Alan Moore to write comics scripts, and whose career was the early model for Moore's transition away from being a writer-artist. But perhaps the most crucial intervention Steve Moore made in Alan Moore's early career was utterly pragmatic, as he tipped Moore off to an imminent job vacancy at Marvel UK's *Doctor Who Magazine*.

Chapter Four: Doctor Who and Star Wars

"There's nobody there, was never anybody there except a fluctuation in the visual purple, a perceptual misunderstanding, trick of moonlight."
–Alan Moore, *Unearthing*, 2006

It is not quite accurate to describe Steve Moore as a major combatant in the War. Much of the War's practical impact concerns the movement of British comics creators into the American market. Steve Moore, however, never really did that much in American comics, and what he did was largely stuff directly in Alan Moore's orbit. He is relatively reclusive—only a handful of interviews with him are readily available. Perhaps most significantly, it is difficult to identify any clear "major work" of his on which to anchor his performance. All of the other protagonists of the War have clear landmarks—major contributions to the psychic culture that constitute the primary battles of the War around which the lesser skirmishes orbit. But Steve Moore has at best minimal involvement in the major battles of the War. His career looks like that of the eternal journeyman: he contributed to a wealth of British comics, but never in a headlining role. His work is at times arcane—much was written under pseudonyms, including some of his best-known work like the *Laser Eraser and Pressbutton* strips for *Warrior*. Inasmuch as it is famous, it is largely because of his connection with Alan Moore.

On the one hand, this is unfair to a creator who was successful and interesting in his own right. On the other, there is an awful lot to that connection: Steve Moore is by far the most constant and consistent of Alan Moore's friends and collaborators. He was present at the earliest stages of Alan Moore's career, scripting things like "Three Eyes McGurk," and remained so until his death in 2014, serving as the initial editor for *Jerusalem* and co-authoring *The Moon and Serpent Bumper Book of Magic*. Alan Moore, for his part, has been consistently effusive in crediting Steve Moore, saying in one interview, "When I was starting out he was an invaluable help. When I decided to move from being a cartoonist to being a writer, it was Steve who read through my early scripts and told me to lose half the words and gave me a lot of pointers on how to do it. And then later it was him who inspired me to become a practising magician. In many ways, he's completely ruined my life!" But all of this exists primarily in the realm of influence.

In this regard Steve Moore's impact upon the War is more akin to that of Glycon or the Vajra Hotel aliens than to that of someone like Warren Ellis or Kieron Gillen, or even, for that matter, someone like Garth Ennis or Peter Milligan. He is a guide and mentor to one of the War's primary protagonists, in both a spiritual and practical sense. It is merely that, unlike Glycon, Steve Moore's physical instantiation consists of more than just a Roman glove puppet. And yet this career is merely the visible evidence of a larger and stranger entity. As Alan Moore puts it in his introduction to Steve Moore's 2011 novel *Somnium*, "I began to realize that the waking part of Steve Moore's life, the part I knew, was just the iceberg's tip. There was another life going on below the waterline." This other life is further expanded in Alan Moore's essay-turned-spoken-word-piece-turned-fumetti *Unearthing*, which unveils the full extent of Steve Moore's mythic life. But for now what is relevant is his material, waking life.

Steve Moore was born on the 11th of June in 1949 in a house situated on a close just off the main road of Shooter's Hill, across from the old Memorial Hospital. Shooter's Hill, the tenth highest point in London, is located in the southeastern portion of the city, about four miles into the eastern hemisphere, perfectly situated to get a complimentary Olympic Games missile battery installed in 2012. The nearest Underground stop is North Greenwich, on the Jubilee line, though the saner course of action would be the two-mile walk from Woolwich Arsenal on the Docklands Light Railroad, or, if you prefer a cab, to get off at Lewisham, where there's a cab rack. (The latter is Alan Moore's preference in *Unearthing*.) He lived in this house for his entire life, save for a three-month stretch in Westcliff-on-Sea in 1984.

Much of Steve Moore's later life seems to extend inexorably from his two childhood interests: the ancient world and outer space. In both cases, he engaged those interests as a voracious reader, steadily packing his house with books. (Alan Moore describes how, in the late 1960s, his friend's growing library resulted in his older brother being ousted from his bedroom and "banished to the boxroom, a comfort-fit coffin just across the tiny landing.) He left school at sixteen, his only qualifications in science, and promptly found himself working for Rank Hovis McDougall in a laboratory job in Deptford, a mile and a half across the border into the western hemisphere.

Around the same time, in the earliest days of the new wave, he became active in science fiction fandom, attending meetings of the British Science Fiction Association before heading home on the tube along with John Carnell, Michael Moorcock's predecessor as the editor of *New Worlds*. He got into fanzines, discovering Marvel Comics through an article in Charles Platt's *Beyond*, then finding copies and eventually starting his own fanzine, the comics-focused *Ka-Pow*. This led to him helping organize the first two British comics conventions. Alan Moore missed the first of these, although he was recognized in the program as a non-attending member, but at the age of fifteen made the second one at the Waverly Hotel in London, by the Great Ormond Street Hospital, where he first met Steve Moore, with whom he'd previously exchanged letters.

By this time Steve Moore had left his job as a flour grader for Rank Hovis McDougall and taken work at Odhams Press. Odhams was the first licensed republisher of Marvel Comics in the UK, repackaging Spider-Man and Hulk comics alongside sub-*Beano* and *Dandy* kids comics under the Power Comics label by rearranging the panels to fit the size of a British comics page and occasionally relettering them or redrawing portions to remove caption boxes and credits. Moore worked on *Pow!*, *Fantastic*, and *Smash!*, contributing his first story to *Pow!* #45 at the end of 1967. The Power Comics label was a fairly slavish imitation of the Marvel Comics aesthetic; "Bullpen Bulletins" became "From the Floor of 64," in lieu of the editorial presence of Smilin' Stan Lee they had Alf, Bart, and Cos, and Steve Moore was duly embarrassed with his own alliterative nickname of Sunny Steve Moore, "with the planetary attribution so exactly wrong," as Alan Moore wryly notes.

In 1969 Odhams faltered and was sold off to IPC, with Moore going to work under their Fleetway banner. From there he bounced around various titles—a stretch on *Valiant*, another on *Tiger*, a brief run on *War Picture Weekly*, and then on to *Whizzer and Chips* and other humor magazines, one of which, *Cor!*, led to him working with Dez Skinn for the first time. In 1972 he decided to quit the editorial side of comics and take his chances on what Alan Moore drolly describes as "the listing death-trap scaffolding of a freelance existence," where he proceeded to churn out stories and articles across a vast number of genres and publications: *The Legend of the Seven Golden Vampires* in Thorpe and Porter's *House of Hammer* (under Skinn again), *Orek the Outlander* for *Target Magazine*, an underground piece called "The Void" for *Cozmic Comics*, an article on "Kung fu Girls" in *Game*, and an entirely fabricated account of sex tourism in Bangkok for *Titbits* that marked the

Figure 42: Power Comics would frequently alter and rearrange panels from Marvel's originals. (Top from Daredevil #5, *written by Stan Lee and Wally Wood, art by Wally Wood, 1964. Bottom from* Smash #85, *1967)*

first use of his Pedro Henry pseudonym; he supported himself in lean times by working at Bram Stokes's Dark They Were & Golden Eyed bookshop. And come 1979 Steve Moore had moved full circle, once again working on UK reprints of Marvel Comics material, this time at Marvel UK and, for the second time in his career, under Dez Skinn, who put him on the Hulk and Nick Fury strips of *Hulk Comic*, Marvel UK's firstattempt at producing original material, and, in October, on the backup strip for the newly launched *Doctor Who Weekly*.

Doctor Who is a longstanding and peculiarly British feature of the sci-fi landscape. It emerged in late 1963 as part of a broader initiative on the part of the BBC to attempt literate, intelligent sci-fi that collided headlong with the need for an adventure serial to show on Saturdays around teatime. The result was an idiosyncratic but flexible format—an elderly alien time traveler (the eponymous Doctor Who), his granddaughter, and two middle-aged British schoolteachers travel through space and time in a ship that appears to be a London police box on the outside, but that houses vast interior dimensions. What would have been a 60s curiosity running a few years inadvertently got an extended lease on life in 1966 when BBC executives had the idea to remove the ailing and difficult to work with William Hartnell from the lead role and replace him with Patrick Troughton, explaining this sudden change as a previously unknown aspect of Doctor Who's alien nature. The combination of its extremely flexible premise, its ability to recast its leading man at will, and Troughton's bold willingness to play the part in a starkly different manner from William Hartnell's patrician take resulted in a show that could run indefinitely. It became a British staple and icon.

By 1980, however, *Doctor Who* was a show in decline. Its leading man, Tom Baker, had been in the part for six years. Previously its sustaining genius had been its ability to reinvent itself for the times, but with Baker in place for so long it had begun to ossify into a familiar format. In his 1975 debut,

Baker was a breath of fresh air, mixing a magnetic charisma and sense of humor with a raft of well-produced stories that unabashedly nicked their aesthetic from Hammer Film's horror movies. But by 1980 the show was finishing its seventeenth season, and Baker was visibly spending most of his time on autopilot. On top of that, the economic malaise that hammered the UK in the late 1970s took its toll on the BBC budgets, and the show's visual aesthetic, never its strong suit to begin with, plummeted. When the eighteenth season kicked off in the fall of 1980, it found itself getting hammered in the ratings by the American import of *Buck Rogers in the 25th Century* on ITV.

It was in this context that Marvel UK, in 1979, acquired the then-dormant license to do Doctor Who comics, and came out with *Doctor Who Weekly*. Its first issue, in October of 1979, ran twenty-eight pages, fourteen of which were comics. The lead feature was "Doctor Who and the Iron Legion," featuring the magazine's main coup: Pat Mills and John Wagner, co-creators of Judge Dredd for IPC's *2000 AD*, wrote the strip, with Dave Gibbons, a rising star at *2000 AD*, on art duties. The strip was striking both in the over-the-top mania of its concepts (the first story arc involves robotic soldiers attacking England from an alternate dimension where Rome never fell; a later story called "The Star Beast," featured the villainous Beep the Meep, a galactic conqueror who happens to look like an adorable, innocent fluffball of an alien) and in its willingness to engage in a level of violence that would never fly on the television series, for reasons of both budget and taste.

Supporting the main feature was a five-page chapter of a Chris Claremont-penned comics adaptation of *War of the Worlds* framed as a "Tale from the TARDIS," and the first installment of "Return of the Daleks," a four-pager by Steve Moore in which a futuristic movie mogul's Dalek movie is overrun by actual Daleks, but not featuring Doctor Who himself except as a first-panel narrator to introduce the story. This basic setup of a Wagner/Mills lead and a Steve Moore-penned backup without Doctor Who himself remained in place for the first thirty-four issues, although the "Tales from the TARDIS" feature was eventually replaced by lightly illustrated prose stories featuring Doctor Who, and reprints of old 1960s Dalek comics.

Moore's backing material was, in general, solid, often with a humorous touch. In "Return of the Daleks" he milks some solid comedy out of the Daleks mistaking the actor playing Nor-Din, the great general who defeated them, for the real thing. Similarly entertaining is a daft one-parter offering a solo adventure of K-9, the Doctor's robotic dog. That is not to say that comedy was Moore's only tone—his second story, "Throwback: The Soul of a Cyberman," is a surprisingly touching story about a Cyberman (a race of human-like creatures who steadily replaced themselves with mechanical parts and became emotionless robots) who malfunctions and acquires emotions. And elsewhere he indulges in spectacle aimed at *Doctor Who* fans, as with his two-part story pitting the Cybermen against one of the silliest *Doctor Who* monsters, the Ice Warriors, who are quite literally green lizard men from Mars.

"Oh, and by the way, Pedro Henry is really Steve – HEY!! Leave it out, you! This is my typewriter! My typ1/2.*/"£5/8£,- &'(?)WEX*≈≈"
—Warren Ellis, fan letter to *Warrior*, 1983

The most significant of Steve Moore's backup strips, however, were a pair of stories introducing the character Abslom Daak. Daak's first appearance was in *Doctor Who Weekly* #17 in a strip illustrated by Steve Dillon and titled simply "Abslom Daak... Dalek-Killer." It opens with Daak being convicted of "murder, pillage, piracy, massacre, and other crimes too horrible to bring to the public attention" and being sentenced to his choice of "death by vaporisation or exile D-K." Daak's response is that "vaporisation doesn't hurt," and so he is teleported to a planet occupied by Daleks and ordered to kill as many as he can before they inevitably kill him.

And so Daak and his chain-sword (like a chainsaw, only a sword) plunge to the Dalek-occupied world of Mazam, where Daak meets Taiyin and rescues her from Daleks. The story consists of Daak repeatedly trying to engage in suicidal assaults against the Daleks, openly wanting to die, and Taiyin steadily falling in love with him and trying to save him from his self-destructive impulses. Daak remains an over-the-top character throughout: wise-cracking, violent, lightly misogynistic, and virtually unkillable. The story ends with one of the handful of Daleks that Daak has not murdered killing Taiyin just as she admits her love for Daak. With her dying breath she tells him to live his life, leading him to scream his promise to "kill every damned, stinking Dalek in the galaxy!"

Daak's story picks up about two months later in Moore's *Star Tigers*, the first installment of which speaks volumes about how pleased Marvel UK was with Daak's first appearance. Daak is carefully omitted from both the cover and the table of contents' description of the strip, deeming his appearance a big enough treat to be worth keeping as a surprise. The first installment features a bunch of Draconians (obscure lizard people from a 1973 *Doctor Who* episode) watching as a group of Dalek ships enter Draconian space, claiming to be in pursuit of a criminal. The Draconians watch as the fleeing criminal evades all of the Dalek ships and shoots them out of the sky. The Draconians invite the criminal to land, and in the last two panels of the strip it becomes clear that the ship is piloted by a drunken Abslom Daak. Eventually Daak gets caught up in Draconian political intrigue and flees the planet with Prince Salander, a Draconian who has fallen out of political favor. This forms the plot of the first four of *Star Tigers'* seven installments, at which point it took a roughly three-month hiatus. By the time it returned, Steve Moore had replaced Mills and Wagner in writing the lead feature for Dave Gibbons, Alan Moore had written two backup series, and the magazine had gone from

Figure 43: Abslom Daak chooses his fate. (From Doctor Who Weekly *#17, written by Steve Moore, art by Steve Dillon, 1980)*

Figure 44: Daak's solemn vow. (From Doctor Who Weekly *#20, written by Steve Moore, art by Steve Dillon, 1980)*

the artwork, when Dez Skinn realized belatedly that the rights to them were actually owned by Terry Nation, who wrote their first story, and not the BBC. The Dalek version was reinstated in the trade paperback, and indeed return in the very next issue). The final installment features this rag-tag team destroying a Dalek fleet, ending with a "The end... for now..." caption box teasing future adventures, which, as it happened, never materialized under Steve Moore's pen.

This was not, however, due to any problem with Daak himself; quite the opposite, as Daak was a markedly popular supporting character. Indeed, Daak was sufficiently popular that *Doctor Who* fans, a typically myopic lot, cling tenaciously to the idea that Axel Pressbutton, who Steve Moore reteamed with Steve Dillon to write for *Warrior*, was a clone of Daak created after Moore's attempt to take the character away from Marvel UK failed. Moore, for his part, rubbishes the claim, pointing out that "before *Warrior*, no one in mainstream British comics owned the characters they created, and Daak and the Star Tigers were always going to belong to Marvel/*Doctor Who*." In fact, Pressbutton predates Daak, who first appeared in 1980, a year after "Three-Eyes McGurk and his Death-Planet Commandos." That's not to say that the similarities don't exist, however: Alan Moore directly parodies the scene at the start of the first strip in which Daak is convicted and sentenced to his choice of vaporization or becoming a Dalek Killer in *The Stars My Degradation*, for instance (Steve Moore sardonically notes that "you can imagine how outraged I was by the fact that, later, when he asked me to write *Stars* for him, I said yes straight away. He was paying me £10 a week, after all!"), while Moore and Dillon had Daak cameo for a brief gag in *Laser-Eraser and Pressbutton*.

But it is easy to make too much of the similarities between Daak and Pressbutton. For all that Steve Moore talks about the personal nature of the Daak stories, saying that "at the time I was deeply depressed over a broken romance, and a lot of that angst went into the first Daak

Figure 45: *Alan Moore parodies Abslom Daak's sentencing in* The Stars My Degradation *(Alan Moore, as Curt Vile, 1980)*

Figure 46: *Honoring the connection between the two characters, Steve Moore and Steve Dillon wrote an Abslom Daak cameo into* Laser Eraser and Pressbutton. *(From* Warrior #6, 1982)

story," as originally conceived, Abslom Daak was at least partially a joke about both *Doctor Who* and *Doctor Who Weekly*. Pressbutton, after all, was hardly the only extremely violent character in British comics. It is worth recalling that when Daak debuted in the backup feature, the lead feature of *Doctor Who Weekly* was written by a superstar team from IPC's *2000 AD*, which, by 1979, was the hottest thing in British comics. Given the overall influence on *Doctor Who Weekly*, the decision to insert a heavily violent character in the vein of Bill Savage's *Invasion!* strip from *2000 AD*, or, for that matter, in the vein of Judge Dredd, albeit without that strip's particular social commentary, into what Dez Skinn described as "the somewhat light-weight Doctor Who" must be taken as a rather inspired bit of snark and pastiche, made all the sharper by how much the character inverted the comparative non-violence of the Daleks' usual opponent.

For all that he's a satirical character, however, Moore clearly took Daak seriously. At one point he plotted out a sprawling ten-issue miniseries to be called *After Daak*, which would have involved Daak reviving Taiyin and spending three days with her before she died again. This was to be paralleled by a story set in the future as two scholars investigated the legends of Abslom Daak, which would have ended with an aged and retired Daak dying what Moore's outline describes as "a quiet, pathetic death... no heroics." *After Daak* was abandoned after a dispute about length—Marvel was phasing out ten-issue series, and wanted Moore to contract it to four issues that focused on, as editor John Freeman suggested, "what Daak does best," which, as Moore put it, meant "he wanted a thug with a chainsaw"—a far cry from Moore's far more somber story of death and redemption.

Moore has spoken at length about the symbolism intended in the character names: Taiyin, Daak's lover, who dies in his arms after being gunned down by a Dalek at the end of Daak's first storyline, "was a title of the moon in Chinese... the moon, being beautiful but out of reach, symbolised the woman I'd lost," and that "I was still carrying a lot of grief about the lady in question by the time I began writing *Star Tigers*, so Daak carried the dead Taiyin round with him too, in hope of reviving their love." The lunar imagery at play in Taiyin's name speaks further volumes given the fact that by 1980 Moore had already had his first major magical experience, in which he was named as Endymion, the mortal shepherd who'd fallen in love with the moon goddess Selene, with whom Moore himself would eventually have a romance with. (He worked this into the Daak narrative in *Doctor Who Weekly* #18, where Daak reveals that Taiyin reminds him of an old lost love named Selene).

Daak's popularity helps explain why, when Mills and Wagner departed the lead strip after *Doctor Who Weekly* #34, during the pause in the midst of "Star Tigers," Steve Moore was promptly promoted to take over the main feature. Steve Moore's take on the main Doctor Who comic was on the whole lighter than Mills and Wagner's. Under Mills and Wagner the *Doctor Who Weekly* comic felt like a strange hybrid of *Doctor Who* and *2000 AD*—which was, after all, the point of the exercise. Steve Moore's stories, on the other hand, have an altogether more poetic lilt to them. His first strip, "Doctor Who and the Time Witch," features Doctor Who locked in a mental battle with a quasi-sorceress, and culminates in a scene in which the sorceress's brutish henchman is split into two by Doctor Who and the sorceress giving him conflicting commands (she wants him to kill Doctor Who, who in turn wants him to make a cup of tea), which results in two identical henchmen pounding on each other. Another story features Doctor Who meeting what appears to be the literal Greek gods (including, inevitably, Selene), and ends with him rescuing Prometheus from a prison on Olympus so he can seed the galaxy with life.

It would be a mistake, however, to suggest that Steve Moore wrote only "funny" stories for *Doctor Who Weekly* (and, subsequently, *Doctor Who Monthly*). His second story, "Dragon's Claw," was a properly sprawling epic that mashed up the Sontarans, a particularly duff *Doctor Who* monster, with the kung fu movies that fascinated Moore, who was a noted *I Ching* scholar on top of everything else in his career. This is particularly welcome, as on television *Doctor Who* never really managed to engage kung fu movies in its fifty years of genre pastiches, and when it has looked to China it's been in an infamously Sinophobic way. Similarly serious is Moore's final story for *Doctor Who Monthly*, "Spider-God," a stinging eight-pager in which Doctor Who watches in horror as human surveyors butcher a colony of aliens purely because they fail to understand the nature of the alien society and lifecycle.

The promotion of Steve Moore, meanwhile, left a vacancy on the backup feature. Steve Moore informed Alan Moore, who he knew was looking to break into script-writing, of the opportunity, and passed his trial script (entitled "Black Legacy") on to editor Paul Neary. And thus the first two-page installment appeared in *Doctor Who Weekly* #35, marking Alan Moore's first job as a writer instead of as a writer/artist. "Black Legacy" is a fairly straightforward horror story: a team of Cybermen arrive on a barren planet seeking the terrifying weapons created by the long-dead Deathsmiths of Goth. Over the course of four two-page installments they are steadily picked off by an unseen force, the Deathsmiths' "Apocalypse Device," which turns out to be a sentient weapon that desires to be used. The Deathsmiths had in fact destroyed their own spaceships to trap the Apocalypse Device on their planet, and since then the Apocalypse Device has been waiting for someone to come to Goth so it could steal their spaceship and finally unleash itself on the universe. In desperation the last surviving Cyberman destroys its ship, trapping the Apocalypse Device, only to have, in the epilogue, the Sontarans arrive seeking the weapons. The story ends with the Device musing, "This time it will escape to spread its blight across the heavens, free to do the job it was created for. It will not wait forever. That is the problem with ultimate weapons…"

On art duties for the story was David Lloyd, who had served as an occasional artist on Steve Moore's backup strips, and who Alan Moore was familiar with due to their mutual contributions to the fanzine *Shadow*. This would soon prove to be a fruitful artistic collaboration, and even in 1980 Moore regarded Lloyd as an underrated artist with "a really powerful sense of storytelling and a starkness in his contrasts of black and white" and who "had an experimental bent that was complementary to mine." This is a fair assessment. Lloyd brings a moody line to the strip, casting Goth in deep shadows that befit the name. He draws the Cybermen with a lithe precision, taking them away from the clanking robots they had steadily become on the television series and helping to sell the script's concept of emotionless machine men who nevertheless are overtaken by fear and paranoia.

For Moore, at least, the appeal of the gig was in part the constraints. Having squandered the first year of his attempt at becoming a professional comics creator on a story to be called *Sun Dodgers*, that was to be a massive epic "that made *Lord of the Rings* look like a five-minute read," only to in that time complete roughly half a page of it, Moore found the discipline required in two-pagers refreshing: "You've got to kind of establish everything and have each little two-page section come to its own dramatic conclusion. It was trickier than it looked but it was a great way of learning how to write comics." This view that short-form comics provide a useful sense of self-discipline is an oft-repeated mantra of Moore's—in another interview, he speaks about how "if there's some way that you could do an apprenticeship that involves short stories that is probably the best way in. It teaches you so much as a writer. In a short story you have to develop all of the characters, you have to develop the situation and bring it to an interesting conclusion, all in three or four pages. So you have to do all of the things that you will have to do in a bigger work but in a much more constrained space, which teaches you an awful lot that you can then expand should you get the opportunity to turn it into a bigger and more ambitious work."

Moore followed "Black Legacy" with "Business as Usual," another four-parter comprised of two-page chapters. This one featured the Autons, villains made of living plastic created by Robert Holmes for a pair of stories featuring Jon Pertwee's Doctor Who in the early 1970s when the use of plastics was rapidly expanding. In Holmes's original stories, plastic was a metaphor for the fake and artificial—the first of them, *Spearhead from Space*, literalized this by having the Autons replace people with plastic duplicates. Its iconic scene of mannequins smashing their way out of high street shops to slaughter people on the road proved to be one of *Doctor Who*'s most enduring images, recycled by Russell T Davies in his 2005 revival of the show. The second, *Terror of the Autons*, broadened the reach, having not just plastic people, but various consumer products that turned lethal: plastic chairs, plastic daffodils, children's dolls, et cetera, and contrasted these with a joyfully gaudy celebration of the newfound possibilities of color television in what is arguably one of the first iconic documents of the glam rock era (itself an era concerned with questions of artifice and superficiality). But even *Spearhead from Space* played with this broad conceptual space, setting major scenes at a plastics factory, thus tying the themes of artificiality to industrialization.

Coming to the same themes in 1980, Moore took an appropriately updated approach. Instead of concerning himself with the by-then dated issue of the rise of plastic as a consumer product, Moore focused on the Autons' role as monsters made out of industrial practices. "Business as Usual" is ultimately about corporate intrigue, telling the story of Max Fischer, an industrial spy sent by a company called Interchem to investigate the rapidly growing Galaxy Chemicals. Its central conceit is that the ostensible alien invasion is portrayed as indistinguishable from the normal operations of a large company—business as usual, as it were. The story is a wry joke, with the Autons staging a hostile takeover in both the real-world and sci-fi senses of the phrase. (Or, as Moore put it, recalling the strip in an interview

Figure 47: Under David Lloyd's pen, the Cybermen became lithe and sleek creatures, in contrast to the decaying horror of the Apocalypse Device. (From "Black Legacy" in Doctor Who Weekly *#35, written by Alan Moore, art by David Lloyd, 1980)*

Figure 48: David Lloyd subtly communicates the sense that something is wrong with Winston Blunt even as Moore's captions speak of how normal this all is. (From "Business as Usual" in Doctor Who Weekly *#40, 1980)*

with Gareth Kavanagh, "I suppose it was me making a clumsy attempt at making some sort of satirical or political comment about commercialism and big business and plasticity.")

Conceptually, at least, it's possibly the best *Doctor Who* story of 1980. It's in the execution that it falters. Moore is at times a bit too proud of his own cleverness (a problem that will arguably dog him for his entire career), pushing his observations a touch too far in places. Little justifies the opening line of the third installment, which proclaims that Fischer "had always thought a killing was something one made on the stock market... until he discovered Autons!" And the cleverness largely fades in later installments, as the inventive premise gives way to a fairly drab and extended action sequence as Fischer tries and nearly succeeds in escaping from the Autons' wrath.

But whatever might be said about the later chapters, the first chapter is sheer genius. Moore employs one of his usual tricks of having narration that contrasts significantly with what's being depicted in the panel, and using that contrast to reveal new sorts of information. So while the narration calmly explains how perfectly ordinary the events of the story are (in the first page Moore proclaims that "there was no-one to notice," "there was no-one to be surprised," "no-one raised an eyebrow," "and it was quite normal"), while the events themselves, to a reasonably sci-fi attuned reader, are clearly the early stages of an alien invasion. This sort of contrast is further highlighted by the art of David Lloyd, who is adept at using small details to make seemingly ordinary images incongruous. So, for instance, as the Auton-controlled Winston Blunt approaches the receptionist of Interchem, his eyes are drawn as wide-open, his head tilted at an angle (which matches the angle at which the entire panel below it is drawn), and his mouth is closed, giving a clear sense that something is wrong. Likewise, when Blunt appoints his successor at Galaxy Plastics, the new manager's face is portrayed with no shadows on it whatsoever, and he stands in a rigid position such that he looks slightly wrong. Later drawings of the same character give him a face that is not dissimilar to the way that Lloyd would later draw the anarchist terrorist V in *V for Vendetta*.

Moore's prose also displays techniques that will recur throughout his career. His tendency towards a poetic, rhythmic narration is often commented on, and is perfectly visible as early as "Black Legacy." Consider this passage (with stressed syllables underlined): "but concealed within the shadows of the withered vegetation, It watches them. It watches them, these glittering machine men, as they erect their flimsy shelters." It is not perfectly metered by any measure, but there's a clear cadence to it. It's driven mainly by iambs, save for an occasional trailing unstressed syllable at the ends of phrases (a common feature in poetry as well). Similarly, Moore's use of repetition creates a sense of rhythm, as in passages like "Cyberleader Maxel is many things… a brutal tyrant, an enslaver of worlds, a callous mass murderer," which uses a well-groomed three item list for rhetorical effect. This is the technique that Douglas Wolk has identified in Moore's work in general, noting that "whenever he or one of his characters has something meaningful to say, the language Moore uses shifts into an iambic gallop."

What's immediately interesting about Moore's early *Doctor Who* work is that his second story is no less metered in its narrative, but that it has an entirely different tone. Where "Black Legacy" is mostly iambic, "Business as Usual" goes for dactyls and trochees, as with the line, "No one raised an eyebrow when Blunt invested his capital in founding his own plastics company. It was just sound business."

Again, the meter is not strict, but it repeatedly puts the emphasis at the beginnings of phrases, favoring three-syllable feet with words like "capital" and "company." These longer feet give the work a very different feel, as does the triple stressed syllable in "just sound business," which draws considerable attention to that specific and seemingly mundane phrase, quietly exposing the underlying deception, namely that, far from being ordinary sound business, Blunt's decision is in fact part and parcel of an alien invasion. The narration of "Black Legacy" feels clipped, and like it's working in a more classical, epic sense, where "Business as Usual" sounds mundane and conversational. It's slightly too wordy, resembling the obfuscatory language of stereotypical corporate jargon. "Business as Usual" also features, in places, highly alliterative phrasing such as "the sinister, smiling figure steps noiselessly forward. Behind, in the shadows, something stirs." In twenty-three syllables Moore manages to get nine that feature an s sound. The effect fits perfectly into the milieu of sales and corporate branding that the larger story utilizes, highlighting its satirical bite.

> *"Increasingly observers describe the War as a shape rather than a sequence of events, a map of causality."*
> –Lawrence Miles, *The Book of the War*

But for all the cleverness of these two stories and all that Moore learned from the two-page chapter structure, it is, in the end, a limitation. "Business as Usual" suffers badly from having to recap its basic premise every other page. Where the first chapter can luxuriate in its droll humor and contrasts, once it has to start recapping its tone while simultaneously moving forward it begins to falter. On top of that, the fact that Moore is stuck writing *Doctor Who* stories without Doctor Who in them is a problem. Using the Autons as a comment on 1980s corporate culture is a phenomenal idea. Indeed, when Russell T Davies brought the Autons back for the first episode of the 2005 *Doctor Who* revival he almost directly apes Moore's central joke, having Doctor Who explain to his companion, who speculates that the aliens are "trying to take over Britain's shops," that "it's not a price war. They want to overthrow the human race." But with eight pages and no Doctor Who there's not much that Moore can do beyond have it descend into a fairly basic story about a man and an evil alien fighting and blowing things up. It's not that Moore handles it badly so much as that there's something of an upper bound to the inventiveness available to a story told in four two-page chapters.

This two-page structure, however, was a peculiar artifact of where *Doctor Who Weekly* was at the time. The final installment of "Business as Usual" appeared in *Doctor Who Weekly* #43, the last issue before it abandoned weekly publication and rebranded itself as *Doctor Who Monthly*. As *Doctor Who Weekly* the magazine was primarily a comics magazine, cramming in reprints of old Marvel stories as "Dr. Who's Time Tales" and reprints of 1960s Dalek strips alongside pages like "Fantastic Facts," which dutifully informed the reader of such important if contextless facts like "the egg of the ostrich is six to seven inches long and (if you were thinking of having one for breakfast) they take 40 minutes to boil." As part of the profusion of comic strips the backup feature for the final few months was shortened to two-page chapters from its previously longer length.

Come issue #44, with the magazine renamed *Doctor Who Monthly*, the magazine expanded to thirty-six pages, jumped to 30p, and began featuring more detailed behind-the-scenes features and synopses of old stories. Sillier features like Fantastic Facts persisted, but the comics were pared back to two features, a main one starring Doctor Who and a backup feature, initially the tail end of Steve Moore's *Star Tigers*. By the time of Moore's final contribution in *Doctor Who Monthly* #57 silly features like "Fantastic Facts" were banished entirely, and instead the magazine was comprised almost entirely of behind-the-scenes features and retrospectives on the program. Over this transformative year Moore published three further backup features: "Star Death," "The 4-D War," and "Black Sun Rising." These three stories are typically described as the 4-D War Cycle, and tell related but bespoke stories about a war fought by the Time Lords against the mysterious Order of the Black Sun.

The first of these stories, "Star Death," goes back to the earliest days of the Time Lords (Doctor Who's species)—

indeed, to the very point at which they became "lords of time": when they harnessed the energy of Qqaba, a star in the process of collapsing into a black hole. Their preparations are interrupted by a mercenary named Fenris, who has traveled back in time to undo the Time Lords by sabotaging their experiments by disrupting the "protective haloes" keeping the Gallifreyans' ships from plunging into the black hole. But Fenris's sabotage is stopped when Rassilon (the founder of the Time Lords, in *Doctor Who* lore) proves unexpectedly able to reactivate the haloes with his mind. Rassilon calmly dispatches Fenris with lightning from his finger ('He would call it electro-direction. We would call it magic.") that knocks off his belt so that he cannot control his time travel anymore, resulting in him having his atoms "spread from one end of eternity to the other." But though the basic power of time travel is now the Gallifreyans', they still have not created a means of controlling their travel. Rassilon, meanwhile, ponders the belt he shot off of Fenris, and calmly takes the directional control off of it in order to create the desired means, thus creating a neat little temporal paradox.

The second, "4-D War," takes place twenty years after "Star Death," and features Rema-Du, the daughter of two of the characters in that story, teaming up with Wardog, a member of the Special Executive, to plunge into the void and retrieve Fenris so he can be interrogated, revealing to the Time Lords who attacked them. They do so, but just as the Time Lords discover the names of their opponents, the Order of the Black Sun, the Order itself shows up en masse, killing eleven (including Fenris) and severing Wardog's arm. (When this is pointed out to him, he laconically responds, "Great God, my Lady! So they have!") When Rema-Du anguishedly demands to know why this has happened, proclaiming that the Time Lords have done nothing to deserve this attack, her father sadly notes that they have not *yet* done anything to deserve it.

Finally there's "Black Sun Rising," which features a trade conference between the Time Lords and the still-peaceful

Order of the Black Sun, which the Sontarans attempt to sabotage by mind-controlling a member of the Special Executive to assassinate the leader of the Order. But instead of sabotaging relations and driving the two groups to war, Wardog figures out the ruse and kills the Sontaran, suggesting that the Order of the Black Sun and the Time Lords are, for now at least, allies.

There is something altogether more interesting going on in the 4-D War Cycle, however. Although each story is a self-contained number that builds to a mild twist ending, they are chapters of a larger story that is demonstrably being told out of order. The story gestures constantly towards a grander epic with the scale of his abandoned *Sun Dodgers*, but one that has been broken into manageable parts and is masquerading as a series of short stories. Given that these are still some of the earliest things Moore has written ("Star Death" appeared at the end of 1980, at which point Moore's only other writing-only credits were a quartet of short stories for *2000 AD*), this confidence is impressive, and subtly belies his suggestion that a sizable apprenticeship on short stories is a vital step in learning to write comics.

And yet the 4-D War Cycle is, in the end, still a collection of short stories. In many ways this makes the swaggering scope of it all the more impressive. It would be one thing to, after a handful of short works, go right back to attempting a three-hundred-page epic. It's quite another to decide to merge the vast, epic structure with another mode of storytelling. It's also worth noting the inventiveness of what Moore does in these comics. At the time he wrote them, *Doctor Who*, despite having been on the air for over seventeen years, had never really done a story focusing on time travel as anything other than the MacGuffin needed to start a story. As Moore noted, in the Kavanagh interview, "I was trying to take the time travel seriously, which was something that I always thought was a bit of a flaw in Doctor Who. No, not a flaw. But I would have enjoyed it more if they had made more use of mind-bending or mind-boggling time paradoxes." Instead, however, Doctor Who simply uses his time machine to arrive at the location of a given adventure, and with only a handful of exceptions as of 1980 the time machine is never involved in the plot after that.

As Moore notes, this is not a problem as such for *Doctor Who*—there are ultimately more stories to be done in the mould of "Doctor Who shows up somewhere and has an adventure" than there are using the well-worn tropes of time travel. But it's still telling that Moore dramatically expanded the scope of what *Doctor Who* could do in the course of some backup features in a comic magazine, doubly so given how flexible a format *Doctor Who* was to begin with. It's also telling that Moore's expansion of *Doctor Who*'s premise stuck and had considerable influence. The idea of a "time war" became a major feature of *Doctor Who* in the 1990s when it reincarnated as a series of novels after the television series was cancelled, and has been a fundamental element of the mythology in its post-2005 incarnation, which, particularly under writer Steven Moffat, uses causality paradoxes and non-linear storytelling with the same sort of frequency that Alan Moore uses iambs. And the similarity is not accidental— Russell T Davies, who established the Time War for the post-2005 series, is a die-hard comics fan who explicitly referenced the Deathsmiths of Goth from "Black Legacy" in a *Doctor Who* prose piece he wrote. Nor is Davies the first person involved in *Doctor Who* to draw from Alan Moore. Lawrence Miles, who wrote much of the "time war" stuff in the 90s, which he spun off into the independent Faction Paradox franchise, has cited Moore as a major influence on his work, while Andrew Cartmel, who script-edited the series for its final years at the end of the 80s, drew from Moore's work repeatedly, and even invited Moore to write for the show, an offer Moore declined. (Cartmel would go on to script one portion of Alan Moore's *The Worm*.)

Admittedly, some of this influence is simply the fact that Alan Moore is, along with Douglas Adams and Neil Gaiman, one of a tiny handful of respectable literary writers to have gone anywhere near *Doctor Who*, and his involvement with it, even if it's only twenty-eight pages of out-of-print comics from the earliest days of his career, has a certain weight, especially during the sixteen years *Doctor Who* was off the air and had a small legion of fans desperate for the show to be taken more seriously. Given this it is perhaps telling that Christopher Priest, another "proper" literary writer, made extensive use of causality paradoxes in *Sealed Orders*, his abandoned script for the television series written around the same time as Moore's comics. The ideas Moore offered, in other words, were in many ways simply the sort of ideas smart people had about *Doctor Who* at the time, and it's overstating the case to treat his ideas here as entirely novel and visionary. By his own admission, the Order of the Black Sun is an unsubtle rip-off of DC's Green Lantern Corps, which Moore, as a British writer, assumed he was never going to get to write. What's innovative here is not so much the ideas themselves as applying them to *Doctor Who*.

Furthermore, on the evidence available, it's impossible to judge Moore's larger ambition. The three existent stories leave much about the 4-D War unexplained. The nature of Rassilon's seemingly magical and godlike powers in the opening chapter hints at some larger and more mysterious role intended for him. The actual provocation of the war between the Time Lords and the Order of the Black Sun remains unclear. As does the actual outcome of the war. Moore did not write a sprawling epic of a non-linear war; he wrote a couple of early chapters of something that could plausibly have expanded into one.

Moore was, apparently, intending to write further tales in the cycle, but circumstances intervened. Instead he left the title along with Steve Moore, who had worked extensively on a plot outline for a third Abslom Daak story only to discover that the editor, Alan McKenzie, had already begun writing a story of his own with the characters. Angered by this, Steve Moore abruptly quit the main strip (to be replaced by future *Bojeffries Saga* artist Steve Parkhouse) and Alan Moore

Figure 49: The Order of the Black Sun's logo and powers owed a heavy debt to the Green Lantern Corps. (From "4-D War" in Doctor Who Monthly #51, written by Alan Moore, art by David Lloyd, 1981)

followed suit in what Steve Moore has referred to as "a wonderful gesture of support that was remarkable for someone at that early a stage in their career."

"So this Zealot comes to my door, all glazed eyes and clean reproductive organs, asking me if I ever think about God. So I tell him I killed God. I tracked God down like a rabid dog, hacked off his legs with a hedge trimmer, raped him with a corncob, and boiled off his corpse in an acid bath. So he pulls an alternating- current taser on me and tells me that only the Official Serbian Church of Tesla can save my polyphase intrinsic electric field, known to non-engineers as 'the soul.' So I hit him. What would you do?"
–Warren Ellis, *Transmetropolitan*, 1998

While it's true that Moore, who had not come close to establishing himself as a writer, took a genuine professional risk in quitting, the fact that he did so early in his career is the only remarkable thing here. It is, in fact, the first of many such gestures. Indeed, within comics, Moore's tendency to get into professional feuds is almost as large a part of his legacy as his actual comics work, and as it has for his comics work, his capacity for umbrage ultimately serves as one of the primary casus belli of the War.

It is worth looking, then, at this first dispute in order to better understand the nature of Moore's umbrage. First of all, there is no way to frame this dispute as being over a slight to Moore himself. If anything, Steve Moore's departure would probably have been an opportunity for Moore, who would have been an obvious frontrunner for the vacancy. His decision to walk away from *Doctor Who Monthly*, in other words, really was an act of pure and genuine solidarity with his friend made, if not at great cost to himself, at least significant risk to his still-nascent career. This, at least, is characteristic of all of Moore's feuds and disputes; it is difficult to think of any in which he has materially benefitted from his stance. The archetypal Alan Moore feud is one in which Moore furiously leaves money, often quite large amounts of it, on the table in pursuit of subtler ideological goals.

This highlights the second interesting part of the dispute, which is the nature of the Moores' grievance. It is manifestly not that McKenzie was using Steve Moore's characters without his permission. Steve Moore was well aware that he didn't own Daak or his fellow Star Tigers. He had no objection to the characters being dusted off eight years later, although he notes that he appreciated that Richard Starkings, the then-editor of *Doctor Who Magazine*, asked him if he'd mind Daak coming back before proceeding with the story. And as previously mentioned, Moore was well aware that he was working on other people's property and that they could continue his work without him.

Rather, the objection was to allowing Moore to waste time developing a Daak story only to find out that the editor who had given him the task had quietly taken the job for himself without telling him. There's a subtle distinction here, which is characteristic of many of Alan Moore's disputes. It does not hinge on a question of what McKenzie was legally allowed to do, but rather on the fact that McKenzie behaved in a manner that struck both Moores as dishonest and deceitful. This is a distinction that Moore makes often, and that is equally often lost on his critics. He rarely objects to specific practices so much as he objects to people who change the rules on him when he feels he's upheld his side of a bargain. It is, with Moore, almost always intensely and intimately personal. This fact often gives his disputes an oddly disproportionate character, and explains what can otherwise seem like Moore's erratic behavior during them, with Moore objecting vigorously to what often seems like minor slights. What appears in many cases to be professional disputes are, in practice, deeply personal grievances based in Moore's belief that someone he trusted had betrayed him. The implications and causes of this odd tendency will become clearer over the course of the War.

Still, in the case of *Doctor Who Monthly* the dispute was ultimately minor. Moore left one publication and almost immediately took up work at the same company on another title in a smooth lateral transition to writing five-page backup features about a different major science fiction franchise. Like much of its audience, Alan Moore had moved from *Doctor Who* to *Star Wars*, specifically *The Empire Strikes Back Monthly*.

There are few external events as significant to the War as the 1977 release of George Lucas's science fiction epic *Star Wars*. The movie almost single-handedly changed both the default aesthetics of science fiction and the economic climate in which science fiction was made, not only in film, but in other media. From a business perspective, *Star Wars* is a dividing line in the history of film. The boom in sci-fi/fantasy film that started in the late 1970s is almost entirely due to the impact of *Star Wars*, which grossed what was then a staggering $300 million, nearly double what the next highest grossing film (*Close Encounters of the Third Kind*) had made. From that point on, science fiction was box office gold. But the film's real impact came from George Lucas's decision to take a half-million dollar cut to his fee for directing the film in favor of retaining the merchandising rights, which he subsequently exploited ruthlessly and to the tune of far more than half a million dollars. And his first move in this regard was to get the novelization and the first issues of the Marvel Comics version of the film out ahead of the film's release.

This alone was a big deal. The American comics industry was in rocky shape in the late 1970s, and the success of Marvel's *Star Wars* adaptation was credited by Jim Shooter, who took over as Editor-in-Chief in the 1980s, for keeping the company afloat, though Shooter claims it was Roy Thomas who single-handedly saved the company by securing the rights. Even more significant, however, was the toy line, the license for which went to Kenner. The toys were so popular that Kenner was hopelessly swamped by demand, and spent Christmas 1977 selling certificates that could be redeemed for toys in the new year. That year the toys were so successful that, if they were a film, their gross sales would have made them the fifth biggest of the year.

Star Wars, in other words, was not merely a successful film—it was a successful business model. It created the idea of science fiction films as a large-scale franchise. This was not an entirely original idea—Gerry Anderson spent the 1960s and early 70s running a small television empire based on promoting his shows in multiple media, making sure to have official comics magazines and the like that tied in and advertised the shows. But *Star Wars* brought things to a new level. The larger franchise of toys, comics, books, and, with later films, every other sort of merchandise imaginable became bigger sources of income than the films themselves, such that a new film was in many ways simply an advertisement for the much larger set of marketing it inspired. This was the logic under which *Doctor Who* acquired its own comics magazine, and was similarly the logic under which *The Empire Strikes Back Weekly* (later *The Empire Strikes Back Monthly*) existed as well. In short, science fiction properties weren't just texts in their own right—they were big businesses in their own right.

But *Star Wars* had another sort of influence, one that was largely aesthetic. This is usually described in terms of a shift towards big-budget, special effects-laden blockbusters. This is true, but in many ways just a subset of a larger transformation. The real aesthetic shift that *Star Wars* offers is that it marked a decisive move away from science fiction as a genre in the sense of plot structure and back towards the original pulp sense of it as an iconography. There was a brief moment, generally referred to as the Golden Age of Science Fiction, in which science fiction existed to tell a particular type of story in which thinking about science was foregrounded. These stories tended to fall into two basic categories. The first is basically the logic puzzle, in which some technological snafu is solved through clever thinking about well-defined rules. The canonical example is Isaac Asimov's novel/short story collection *I, Robot*, in which basically all of the stories take this tack, playing with Asimov's invention of the "Three Laws of Robotics," which state, in order, that a robot can never allow a human to be hurt, must always obey humans, and must protect its own existence, with each law being trumped by the preceding one(s).Take the story "Runaround," for instance. A particularly expensive robot is put in a peculiar situation when a rather casually given command conflicts with its third law of self-protection, one that has been bolstered in the robot so that "his allergy to danger is unusually high." This results in a sort of feedback loop that the robot cannot escape from. The solution, of course, is for one of the human characters to throw themselves in danger in the presence of the robot, thus triggering the sacrosanct First Law of Robotics which breaks the robot from its cycle.

The other sort of story can be described as a "thought experiment." On the short story level it includes things like Arthur C. Clarke's "The Star," which describes an expedition exploring the remnants of a supernova and discovering a scorched planet with the ruins of a civilization in its orbit. The story is a straightforward twist-ending piece, continuing for roughly 2500 words as the narrator, a futuristic Jesuit monk, tells of the expedition and its discovery of some awful truth that will shake the Catholic faith to its core. In the final paragraph it's revealed that the narrator has successfully dated the explosion of the supernova. Clarke writes, "There can be no reasonable doubt: the ancient mystery is solved at last. Yet, oh God, there were so many stars you could have used. What was the need to give these people to the fire, that the symbol of their passing might shine above Bethlehem?" But this structure is suitable for more than just twist-ending short stories. Walter M. Miller's acclaimed *A Canticle for Leibowitz* holds to the same basic structure, imagining a monastic community after a nuclear war has devastated the world poring over memorabilia and artifacts and interpreting detritus like shopping lists as holy relics. The story has numerous moments of moving humanity, but its sheer scope—the novel takes place over 1200 years—means that it cannot be treated as a character piece. It is instead an imagined history—an attempt not to tell a story about people but about what might happen following a particular set of events.

Both types of stories were, if not unique to science fiction as a genre, at least distinct narrative forms that existed on their own terms. They were also, however, a vanishingly brief moment in literary history, belonging squarely to the dreams of technocratic utopia that flourished in the aftermath of World War II. The 1960s New Wave of science fiction writers like Michael Moorcock and J.G. Ballard challenged it thoroughly, bringing in a literary sensibility, and by 1976 the "golden" style had been on the wane. But *Star Wars* went in a markedly different direction, namely backwards to the classic pulp model. Much of *Star Wars* could just as easily be done as a sword-and-sorcery epic (indeed, the interchangeability of the two genres was the underlying premise of DC Thompson's *Starblazer*) or as a swashbuckling pirate story.

In this regard what is significant is not so much that *Star Wars* was full of visual spectacle, but that the visual spectacle was often a direct homage to the vibrant cover art of old pulp sci-fi magazines. The irony here is considerable—the film that finally killed off the Golden Age aesthetic for good did so by mimicking the cover art of the very magazines that had housed much of the Golden Age. There are moments in *Star Wars* where one can practically identify the exact cover of *Astounding Science Fiction* that inspired the shot. But the genius of *Star Wars* was not simply in its use of visual spectacle. What *Star Wars* did was to take the plot elements of the pulp epic and fit them together into a film with a compelling storyline that hung together like literary fiction. The way it did this was by using a plot structure called "the hero's journey," established by Joseph Campbell in his book *The Hero With a Thousand Faces*.

On one level Campbell was a critic not unlike Vladimir Propp, in that he argued for the existence of a single plot structure that described a large number of stories. But while Propp was content to describe Russian folk tales and Russian folk tales alone, Campbell's ambition was nothing short of describing the overall structure of all mythology, an ambition that is realized in an ecstatically mystical tone that contrasts sharply with Propp's clinical pseudo-equations. His underlying structure is a simple one. A hero receives a "call to adventure," leaves the Ordinary World to retrieve a boon from some Special Other Place, and encounters a series of obstacles that culminates with, in Campbell's telling, the Meeting with the Goddess, the Atonement with the Father, and Apotheosis. Having secured the Boon, the hero must escape from the Special Other Place and reintegrate himself (and his Boon) into the Ordinary World before earning the Freedom to Live.

Campbell describes all of these in his characteristically flowery language. The Meeting with the Goddess, for instance, is "a mystical marriage of the triumphant hero-soul with the Queen Goddess of the World" that is "the crisis at the nadir, the zenith, or at the uttermost edge of the earth, at the central point of the cosmos, in the tabernacle of the temple, or within the darkness of the deepest chamber of the heart." The figure is a sort of sacred feminine akin to what is represented Kabbalistically in the Sephirah of Binah, or Understanding. Campbell's description of one manifestation, the Lady of the House of Sleep, is telling: "She is the paragon of all paragons of beauty, the reply to all desire, the bliss-bestowing goal of every hero's earthly and unearthly quest. She is mother, sister, mistress, bride. Whatever in the world has lured, whatever has seemed to promise joy, has been premonitory of her existence... Time sealed her away, yet she is dwelling still, like one who sleeps in timelessness, at the bottom of the timeless sea." This invocation of the sea closely mirrors Dion Fortune's description of Binah as "the Great Mother, sometimes also called Marah, the Great Sea... She is the archetypal womb through which life comes into manifestation."

"God is one and all. God is all. One is all. One perfect moment."
—Alan Moore, *Promethea,* 2002

Within Campbell, however, this event is paralleled by another immediately after, which he calls Woman as the Temptress. After encountering the Goddess there comes a point where women "become the symbols no longer of victory but of defeat," for "no longer can the hero rest in innocence with the goddess of the flesh; for she is become the queen of sin." This evokes the virgin/whore complex at the heart of many depictions of the sacred feminine, captured chillingly in the revelation given to Edward Kelley while scrying in the seventh aethyr that drove him to abandon magic:

"I am the daughter of Fortitude, and ravished every hour from my youth. For behold I am Understanding and science dwelleth in me; and the heavens oppress me. They cover and desire me with infinite appetite; for none that are earthly have embraced me, for I am shadowed with the Circle of the Stars and covered with the morning clouds. My feet are swifter than the winds, and my hands are sweeter than the morning dew. My garments are from the beginning, and my dwelling place is in myself. The Lion knoweth not where I walk, neither do the beast of the fields understand me. I am deflowered, yet a virgin; I sanctify and am not sanctified. Happy is he that embraceth me: for in the night season I am sweet, and in the day full of pleasure. My company is a harmony of many symbols and my lips sweeter than health itself. I am a harlot for such as ravish me, and a virgin with such as know me not. For lo, I am loved of many, and I am a lover to many; and as many as come unto me as they should do, have entertainment."

Predictably, after this encounter with the sacred feminine comes the (in Campbell's eyes at least) more important encounter with the divine masculine, Atonement with the Father. This is in essence a parallel with the Sephirah of Chokmah. Campbell introduces the concept by quoting Jonathan Edwards's "Sinners in the Hands of an Angry God," talking about how God's "wrath towards you burns like Fire; he looks upon you as Worthy of nothing else but to be cast into the fire; he is of purer Eyes than to bear to have you in his Sight." But as Fortune says in *The Mystic Qabalah*, "although the sight of the Divine Father blasts mortals with fire, the Divine Son comes familiarly among them and can be invoked by the appropriate rites." Or, as Campbell puts it, "The magic of the sacraments (made effective through the passion of Jesus Christ, or by the virtue of the meditations of the Buddha), the protective power of primitive amulets and charms, and the supernatural helpers of the myths and fairy tales of the world, are mankind's assurances that the arrow, the flames, and the flood are not as brutal as they seem." Thus, in this stage, the hero is able to reconcile with the father and to be initiated into the world such that "he has become himself the father."

This accomplished, the hero may achieve Apotheosis, ascending to a state of divine grace himself such that "having surpassed the delusions of his formerly self-assertive, self-defensive, self-concerned ego, he knows without and within the same repose. What he beholds without is the visual aspect of the magnitudinous, thought-transcending emptiness on which his own experiences of ego, form, perceptions, speech, conceptions, and knowledge ride." Or, as Dion Fortune puts it in her description of Kether, the highest Sephirah, it is "the intensest form of existence, pure being unlimited by form or reaction; but it is existence of another type than that to which we are accustomed, and therefore it appears to us as non-existence."

The climactic scenes of *Star Wars* follow this pattern with deliberate precision. As the film approaches its denouement, Luke Skywalker encounters the white-clad Princess Leia, who turns out to be more capable and competent than the entire group of adventurers who rescued her. (In earlier drafts, Leia was explicitly a member of a mystic order, increasing her goddess-like nature.) Subsequently, Luke comes to a reconciliation with the film's father figure, as Obi-Wan Kenobi sacrifices himself in a battle with Darth Vader to allow Luke and the others to escape. After this Luke himself attains the ability to "use the Force" and, with this newfound spiritual power, is able to destroy the Death Star (a name dripping with mystical implications).

The problem with all of this is not that it doesn't work—indeed, the Hero's Journey as described by Campbell is a fairly basic and usable narrative of mystical ascension. Rather, the problem comes from the sprawling nature of Campbell's ambition. Campbell baldly declares that the purpose of his work is "to bring together a host of myths and folk tales from every corner of the world" and "develop a vast and amazingly constant statement of the basic truths by which man has lived throughout the millenniums of his residence on the planet." Thus he describes the journey as the Monomyth, "the one, shape-shifting yet marvelously constant story that we find." Campbell grounds his theory in Freudian and Jungian psychoanalysis, using the psycho-sexual relations spelled out in their work as the foundational document for a singular, all-encompassing vision of human desire. The reality, however, is that Campbell's account of mythology is ludicrously selective and Eurocentric, essentially dismissing all eastern mythology as bastardized Egyptian mythology. And that's on top of the obviously patriarchal view of mythology that he espouses. The truth is that Campbell found a story about death and resurrection that he liked, identified numerous variations of it, and then took to world mythology with the characteristic glee of a man with a hammer unleashed into a world of nails. It is exactly what William Blake (whose complex and visionary mythology goes wholly unmentioned in Campbell's work) speaks of when he begs that "God us keep from single vision and Newtons sleep."

No wonder, then, that Alan Moore considered *Star Wars* to be "an utterly dreary film" that he had "no interest" in. But this did not mean that his approach to writing the comics was cynical—as he put it, "Don't turn anything down. If it isn't something that's interesting to you, then try to do something clever with it that will make it interesting to you." This is consistent with everything else Moore was doing in this period: writing comics was a job, valuable because it paid the bills. The point of writing *Star Wars* comics wasn't the deep and abiding passion he had for the material, but that it was a more pleasant way to put food on the table than a dreary office job. At the time Moore did his five *Star Wars* comics they were still sporadic windfalls to be taken alongside his earliest IPC work—irregular paydays that supplemented the week-in/week-out income of his self-drawn work, which he didn't really start to back away from until he got regular assignments. In other words, he unashamedly needed the money. Accordingly, he approached the job as a professional. Indeed, it's arguable that his relative detachment from the material improved his work. The process of finding a way to make *Star Wars* interesting to himself and the process of finding an innovative take on the material are, after all, relatively similar.

This does not, however, mean that Moore succeeded straightforwardly. Indeed, his first *Star Wars* comic, in *The Empire Strikes Back Monthly*, is a deeply insipid affair. At fifteen pages it was by some measure the longest single narrative Moore had written by that point in his career, and there's a sense that the structural complexities opened by having that much space to play with simply overwhelmed him. The story has Moore's usual poetic lilt—he describes how the planet of Attahox "stank of poverty of and disease, of blood and bad wine. It stank of rotten fruit and loveless passion. And this was not the worst of it… For Attahox was a world whose soul had festered in its own futility. And the soul of Attahox stank above all other things." But this description, compelling as it is, is part of a five-page lead-in to

Moore's main plot in which essentially nothing happens. It's the sort of thing Moore more capably dispatches in a panel or two when he's actually under space constraints, but here he allows it to bloat.

The strip's actual idea is a ship occupied by a group that describes themselves by simply saying "we are five"—a group that worships "the Left-Handed God. The Soulworm. The Lady with the Locust Heart." The story traces Han Solo, Chewbacca, and Leia as they try to escape from this horrific ship, which they ultimately accomplish by freeing Wutzek, a demon imprisoned onboard. Wutzek destroys the five and frees our heroes, who fly off, glad that whatever they've done by unleashing Wutzek's might, "they've done it in an Empire-held section of space." The ideas here are interesting enough, but the plot structure is flaccid. There is no sense of build or development, no gathering sense of tension as the characters are pulled deeper into the depraved world of the five.

But once Moore settled back down to the short story length, his structural strengths returned. "Dark Lord's Conscience," for instance, is a tight little six-pager (although it was originally published with its final page missing due to an editorial mistake) focusing on Darth Vader. The story features Vader facing off against a talking octopus named Lady Dhol in a game called Firepath, where pieces are routinely consumed in flames. Paralleled to this is the story of a plot against Vader's life. In the story's final two pages Vader turns the tables as it turns out he has been playing the game so as to allow him to incinerate both his would-be assassin and Lady Dhol herself, who was in on the conspiracy. It is, on the whole, a nice little piece, and the one most grounded in *Star Wars* itself, focusing as it does primarily on the character of Darth Vader as opposed to introducing strange new concepts to the *Star Wars* universe.

A similarly tight structure is obvious in "Rust Never Sleeps," Moore's penultimate *Star Wars* strip and the first time in his career that he worked with Alan Davis, who would be a short-running but major collaborator for him. The

Figure 50: The accidentally omitted final page of Alan Moore and John Stokes's "Dark Lord's Conscience." (From Classic Star Wars: Devilworlds, *1996,* meant to have been printed in The Empire Strikes Back Monthly *#154, 1982)*

strip is a model of tight plotting: C-3PO travels to a planet dominated by a junkyard for defective droids in order to warn them of the Empire's desire to strip the planet of metals. He meets the ostensible leader of the droid civilization, Brother Fivelines, who informs him that the droids are a pacifist society who consider the junkyard to be "the living body of God," as the myriad of abandoned droids "corroded and fused together" to become "the sum total of all droidkind's hopes and aspirations, the resting place of our souls." Inevitably, the Stormtroopers arrive and promptly vaporize Fivelines, at which point his belief that the planet is a living god is borne out as the planet begins pelting the Storm Troopers with bolts from abandoned droids before the ground itself opens to swallow them.

There's a calm efficiency to this structure. First the story's premise is introduced—a planet of abandoned droids with its own strange religion. C-3PO expresses disbelief in the religion. Antagonists show up, and C-3PO's doubts are shown to be wrong. The end. Its plot differs from "Black Legacy" only inasmuch as in "Black Legacy" the central characters are the villains, and so their failure to appreciate the supernatural forces around them means they die horribly, whereas in "Rust Never Sleeps" the central character is the sympathetic C-3PO, and so instead he watches as other people who are cruel in their disbelief die horribly. Structurally both are straight lifts of countless horror stories. "Rust Never Sleeps" fits in with things like "The Fall of the House of Usher" and *At the Mountains of Madness* in which the story is narrated by a lone survivor, whereas "Black Legacy" fits more with "The Shadow Over Innsmouth" or *Frankenstein* in which the bulk of the story is told from the perspective of a character who does not make it out, the story serving as a sort of last document of the doomed protagonists.

But the cleverness of "Rust Never Sleeps" is not primarily in the fact that it is a by-the-books horror story. Rather, it is in the fact that it is not a horror story at all, even though its basic plot structure is straightforwardly lifted from one. The structure is really just a platform for the real point, which is an exploration of the basic idea of a robot god. Tellingly, C-3PO drops out of the narrative at the end. Once the Stormtroopers arrive at the end of the third page, his role is superfluous. He begs Brother Fivelines not to confront them and bemoans how Fivelines didn't listen to him while he's vaporized, but that's his final line. The remaining page and a half of the story consist only of the droid god's rising up to defeat the Stormtroopers. C-3PO doesn't even get a full appearance after it—he appears cut-off on the side of one panel on the last page, but the story has nothing to do with him. Instead it focuses on an extended narration ruminating on the nature of the god of the droids.

This narration is interesting in a large part because it gives the sense of recreating Moore's own process in hatching the story, starting from the premise of the droids having a god, and then speculating that "surely it would be as meek and subservient as the droids themselves. It would not be a god of wrath. It would not be a god of vengeance. Would it?" And from there it imagines what sort of vengeance such a god might take if the premises the story started with (that "droids have no hearts. No bones to bend beneath the load that is too heavy. No souls to rail against the indignity that is unbearable") are finally discarded. This is the real conceptual framework of the story—the game of what-if.

It is tempting to describe this approach as formulaic. Moore's short stories ultimately all tend to work the same way: they have some high concept central twist such that a character misreads their circumstances, leading to a denouement in which the real nature of things is revealed to them, often in such a way as to impressively kill the villains. And yet even across Moore's four *Star Wars* five-pagers there's an impressive variety. "Tilotny Throws a Shape" is ultimately humorous. "Rust Never Sleeps" and "Dark Lord's Conscience" are less thoroughly funny, but are nevertheless both primarily set up for a wry twist ending. His final *Star*

Wars story, "Blind Fury," on the other hand, is a grim-faced horror story. Moore is not recycling the same story, but using a fairly tight-knit plot structure to explore a variety of ideas. When the idea is a horror story, as in "Blind Fury," the structure ends up with the feel of a Robert E. Howard Conan tale. When the idea is more abstract and philosophical, as in "Rust Never Sleeps," the structure produces a different mood. In the end, it is not so much that Moore is writing formulaic stories as that Moore is, at this stage in his career, writing five-pagers, and a five-page comic story simply doesn't leave much room for variety. Twist endings are the only approach that's realistically available.

Moore, however, was clearly never entirely happy with *Star Wars*. The limits of Moore's patience with the franchise become clear by the time of "Blind Fury." It traces Luke Skywalker's encounter with the last survivor of the Order of the Terrible Glare, which apparently fought a war against the Jedi several thousand years ago. Where Moore's other stories move around their twist endings with relative grace, "Blind Fury" blunders about, depending on Luke repeatedly trying to remember why he's heard of the planet he's investigating, and only doing so when it comes time for someone to explain the plot. The central twist—that the last surviving member of the Order has been saved in a computer and doesn't realize that the war is thousands of years old and the Jedi have died out— is a science fiction staple, resulting in a fairly dull resolution. The closing narration as Luke stares into the burning rubble of the tower in which he found the computer seems to sum up the degree to which Moore is at a loss, reading, "There is a lesson here, somewhere. Perhaps if he stares into the flames for long enough it will be revealed to him. Perhaps…" Or, as it happens, perhaps not.

Other times, however, Moore's obvious frustration with the *Star Wars* title led him to push into a strange sort of creativity. This is most notable in his second and by far best *Star Wars* strip, "Tilotny Throws a Shape." After a one-page opening in which Princess Leia finds herself chased by

Figure 51: The wrath of a meek and subservient god. (From "Rust Never Sleeps" in Star Wars: The Empire Strikes Back Monthly #155, *written by Alan Moore, art by Alan Davis, 1982)*

Figure 52: Splendid Ap finds time difficult. (From "Tilotny Throws a Shape," in Star Wars: The Empire Strikes Back Monthly #154, *written by Alan Moore, art by John Stokes, 1982)*

Stormtroopers on a seemingly abandoned dusty planet, Moore's caption rather archly notes, "In a universe as old as this one, the death of a princess is scarcely new. It has happened before. What follows hasn't." This is something of an understatement. What follows is set of four entities whose nature is never really explained, but who apparently exist outside of space and time. Or, at least, usually do, as at the start of the story one of them, Tilotny, declares that she has "thrown a shape" and boasts, "I've invented form! I've invented mass! Oh, cleverest Tilotny! Everything has edges! And... and things happen one after another! Tilotny has invented time!" Tilotny's shape—a humanoid figure—is quickly mimicked by her compatriots as Horliss-Horliss (who can, as Tilotny observes, metastyle, but who has never thrown a shape) manifests as an abstract shape, followed by Cold Danda (inventor of anti-concepts) manifesting as an orb with a face in the style of the Green Man, and finally Splendid Ap (who is, Tilotny later notes, stupid, and who misunderstands time and thus accidentally exists in many places at once) who takes the shape of a pyramid (colored a memorable bright pink by Pamela Rambo for Dark Horse's 1996 reprint).

The four proceed to cavort until their revels are intruded upon by Leia and her pursuing Stormtroopers, the latter of which cause a bit of an uproar as Cold Danda accuses Tilotny of repeating a shape. She quickly begins altering the Stormtroopers, at which point Horliss-Horliss joins in, killing Princess Leia by turning her heart into a diamond. Tilotny then merges the storm troopers into a single being, at which point they get bored of shapes and abandon the planet, leaving Splendid Ap to clean up the mess and bring everyone back to life. It is, in other words, a story in which *Star Wars* is almost, if not entirely, irrelevant. Much of it amounts to cosmic beings of seemingly limitless power bickering childishly over a creative priority dispute; indeed, the whole story could be read as the War in a microcosm, with Horliss-Horliss, who comes second to throwing shapes and whose more abstract shape Tilotny poo-poohs "isn't even a good shape! It does not have as much shapeness" (to which Horliss-Horliss sniffs that Tilotny doesn't "perceive the subtlety of my form"), standing in for Grant Morrison. Superficially, of course, this is refuted by chronology, but one ought recall that Horliss-Horliss and Tilotny are both beings who normally exist outside the flow of chronologic time, experimenting with it only for the brief duration of "Tilotny Throws a Shape," and thus this problem is in no way a meaningful obstacle.

Moore's rejection of the style of *Star Wars* must also be understood as an embrace of starkly different forms of science fiction narrative. Where *Star Wars* embraced the ability of science fiction to do rollicking adventure yarns, "Tilotny Throws a Shape" harkens to an older model of science fiction in which the point of the genre was to play with interesting intellectual concepts. The approach of "Tilotny Throws a Shape" amounts to crashing *Star Wars* into the sort of science fiction written by Italo Calvino, whose short story collections *Cosmicomics* and *t zero* are mostly narrated by Qfwfq, an entity as old as the universe who casually reincarnates in a variety of forms throughout time and who reminisces about various events in cosmic history, talking about how, as a child, "I was acquainted with all the hydrogen atoms, one by one, and when a new atom cropped up, I noticed it right away," and how he played games with the atoms. "Since space was curved," Qfwfq explains, "we sent the atoms rolling along its curve, like so many marbles, and the kid whose atom went furthest won the game." The story goes on to describe the formation of galaxies as a consequence of Qfwfq's games: he took a bunch of hydrogen atoms "and flung them into space. At first they seemed to scatter, then they thickened together into a kind of light cloud, and the cloud swelled and swelled, and inside it some incandescent condensations were formed, and they whirled and whirled and at a certain point became a spiral of constellations never seen before, a spiral that poised, opening in a gust, then sped away as I held on to its tail and ran after it."

It is not merely this sort of vast cosmic sweep that Moore borrows from Calvino, however. Like Moore, Calvino's stories frame the cosmic in human terms, deriving humor from the contrast. In one story, for instance, Qfwfq compares his current life ("At Penn Station I get off the train, I take the subway, I stand and grasp the strap with one hand to keep my balance while I hold my newspaper up in the other, folded so I can glance over the figures of the stock market quotations") with his memories of the primordial state of the Earth when "the substance of things changed around us every minute; the atoms, that is, passed from one state of disorder to another state of disorder and then another still: or rather, practically speaking, everything remained always the same. The only real change would have been the atoms arranging themselves in some sort of order." In another, "The Aquatic Uncle," he tells the story of how his family had made the transition from living in the sea to living on dry land, all save for one stubborn uncle, N'ba N'ga, who is portrayed as a cantankerous and slightly embarrassing old man. The story describes how Qfwfq found himself with the difficulty of introducing his fiancée because "I hadn't yet dared tell Lll that my great-uncle was a fish," before his fiancée eventually leaves him for his great uncle, having been seduced by the romance of the old sea.

In other words, as with his 4-D War Cycle for *Doctor Who Monthly* it is not so much the ideas that are innovative here as it is where Moore opts to deploy them. Extra-dimensional beings playing games with the fundamental forces of the universe aren't in and of themselves innovative, but throwing them into the universe of *Star Wars* is not only innovative but also a witty commentary on the limitations of that universe. And yet "Tilotny Throws a Shape" is not some angry howl of protest against Moore's assignment. Its structure is still a tight little five-pager with a clear setup and punchline; on page one Leia encounters a Stormtrooper helmet and a pile of bones that, impossibly, look like they've been around for millennia. At the end the Stormtroopers pursuing her are accidentally sent millennia into the past by Splendid Ap, who is, as the narration notes, confused by time and space. The closing two panels feature Leia recovering and making her way back towards her ship, the Stormtrooper bones lying in the dust, neatly tying off the story's premise and setup. Structurally it's as straightforward an execution of the short-form comic story as exists. It's just that its content is, by the standards of *Star Wars*, completely and utterly barmy.

But while the idea may not be startlingly original, Moore handles it well. The humor and casually vast metaphysical implications of the story prove a compelling playground for Moore, and he handles the tension between the grotesque fates suffered by Leia and the Stormtroopers and the fundamental humor of the strip well. Given four characters whose nature is fundamentally inconceivable, Moore manages to make them all distinct, and with very little space to do it in. It has clear influences, but it is not a slavish imitation of those influences by any measure. Beyond that, it is a mistake to treat the existence of influence as a problem in any sense; all creative works have influences. What is clear from Moore's work is that his influences are particularly broad. Even at this early stage of his career they include underground comix, golden age science fiction, American superhero comics, HP Lovecraft, Brechtian theater, film noir, Victorian horror, time travel fiction, and Italian postmodernism. Beyond that, he has combined these influences in unexpected and startling ways. This constitutes a laudable achievement for someone whose professional work consists of some comic strips for a second tier music magazine and some filler about *Doctor Who* and *Star Wars*.

And yet it also suggests that Moore is not best served by writing in such narrow genres as "*Star Wars* tie-ins" or "*Doctor Who* stories that don't feature Doctor Who." It is both telling and compelling, then, that a far larger body of Alan Moore's early work comes in the form of bespoke short stories for

2000 AD published under the header of *Tharg's Future Shocks.* It is not that this format allowed unfettered creativity by any measure. But it was a structure that allowed Moore to stretch his creative wings, as well as to work with a compelling variety of artists.

Chapter Five: Future Shocks

*"Sound clarions of war. Call Vala from her close recess in all her dark deceit." –*William Blake, *The Four Zoas*, 1807

The dawn of Moore's work for *2000 AD* marks a subtle but significant change to the nature of the War's narrative. Prior to this point in the narrative the material under discussion has been only sporadically collected. None of Grant Morrison's early works have been reprinted at all, nor, for all practical purposes, has Moore's *Doctor Who* work. *Roscoe Moscow* and *The Stars My Degradation*, meanwhile, have been put up for free on the Internet with Moore's blessing, *Maxwell the Magic Cat* has a long-out-of-print reprint series, and Moore's *Star Wars* material briefly found a home in an omnibus published by Dark Horse Comics, but has, ironically, gone back out of print since Marvel regained the *Star Wars* license. But from this point on the overwhelming majority of the texts that constitute the War are readily available in some form or another, and thus form a coherent and reasonably well-known body of texts, all of which were published in the same general period.

This shift coincides almost perfectly with the portion of Alan Moore's career in which he wrote for IPC's *2000 AD*, a period which lasted from July of 1980 through April of 1986, when Moore abandoned *The Ballad of Halo Jones*. This marks a significant dividing line in both Moore's career and the War, serving as the last thing he wrote for the mainstream British comics industry in which he got his start, and furthermore happening a month after the first major battle of the War broke out with the publication of *Watchmen* #1 by DC Comics. If one were to impose a structure of "phases" on a career that in practice consisted of multiple overlapping gigs, April of 1986 would mark one of the few genuinely obvious candidates.

But Moore's career from 1980 to 1986—what might be called the IPC Years, although none of the three biggest works of the period were published by IPC—also contains two distinct phases. The first of these goes from July of 1980, with the publication of his first story, "Killer in the Cab" in Prog 170, through September of 1983, when his final one-off story, the two-page "Look Before You Leap!" appeared in Prog 332. For the bulk of this period Moore's career consisted of essentially four jobs. He was always at one time or another writing something for Marvel UK—initially the *Doctor Who Weekly* work, then his *Star Wars* strips, and finally his run on *Captain Britain* in various magazines. He was also still doing the two jobs he started in 1979—the *Sounds* comics (*The Stars My Degradation* by this point) and *Maxwell the Magic Cat*. Finally, he did a smattering of one-off (and occasionally two-off) strips for *2000 AD*, mostly, though not entirely, under the *Tharg's Future Shocks* banner. This provided a stable career plan for Moore for just under two years.

The first significant change to this setup came in March of 1982, when he added another gig to the rotation, writing a pair of strips for *Warrior* every month (strips which eventually migrated to the US following *Warrior*'s implosion, and which will thus be dealt with later). This was counterbalanced by him handing off writing duties on *The Stars My Degradation* to Steve Moore, giving £10 of his £35-a-week pay to him—Moore's only extended stint as an artist of someone else's scripts. On March 19th, 1983, things changed again as he began work on *Skizz*, his first ongoing strip for *2000 AD*; the same day, *Sounds* published the last installment of *The Stars My Degradation.*

In the short term, Moore threw himself into *2000 AD* work to fill the gap. Prog 308, in which *Skizz* debuted, also featured "The Reversible Man," the first of Moore's short stories to go out under the *Time Twisters* banner instead of as one of *Tharg's Future Shocks,* and a story that marks a visible shift in his style. (Of his remaining sixteen short stories for *2000 AD*, nine went out under the *Time Twisters* banner.) For the next six months Moore was frequently contributing two stories per issue—an installment of *Skizz* and a short story. The end of *Skizz* in August of 1983, however was quickly followed by the publication of Moore's first work for the American market, *Saga of the Swamp Thing* #20. This, in turn, marked the point where Moore ceased doing short stories for IPC, and moved into the second phase of his work for them, consisting of only long-form stories—first a series of stories featuring his characters of D.R. & Quinch in the first half of 1984, and then, starting in July of 1984, *The Ballad of Halo Jones.* In one sense this is simply a divide between a "pure" UK phase and a hybrid UK-US phase, and one certainly can look at Moore's career through that lens. But in many ways it is more helpful to view Moore's *Swamp Thing* work as a largely unexpected twist of fate that changed the direction of a career otherwise understandable on its own terms, a career defined first and foremost by the magazine *2000 AD.*

The first issue, or prog (short for "programme," as the covers refer to themselves) of *2000 AD* was cover-dated February 26th, 1977, but the history of the magazine begins slightly earlier, in 1974. That was the year that DC Thompson, publishers of *Starblazer* and *The Beano,* debuted *Warlord.* *Warlord* was a shot in the arm for an essentially moribund British boys comics industry in which there had been few major innovations since *Eagle* in 1950. The fact that *Eagle* had itself entered a steady decline and been cancelled by new owner IPC in 1969, some five years earlier, did not stop it from being essentially the sole functional model for boys comics, especially at IPC, where the boys group was dominated by Jack Le Grand, a staunch traditionalist who was thoroughly uninterested in innovation or modernization. In the face of such a stodgy market, *Warlord*, while still a war comic in the traditional mould, went for an increased degree of grit and violence, which proved a substantial success.

Caught flat-footed, IPC decided to break outside its usual methods and hired a pair of freelancers, John Wagner and Pat Mills, to create a *Warlord* competitor. That magazine was *Battle Picture Weekly*. In order to avoid the stodginess in the boys group, the comic was actually created in secret, in the office space belonging to the girls group where Mills and Wagner both also worked. Even there, they gave a sense of the iconoclastic cheek that they would bring to their more famous endeavors. Alan Moore suggests that their time on girls comics had led them to grow "cynical and possibly actually evil," and fondly remembers a comic called *The Blind Ballerina* in the IPC magazine *Jinty*. The comic was on the whole accurately titled—it focused on a girl who wanted to become a ballerina despite being blind. As Moore puts it, with some embellishment, "John [Wagner] would just try to put her into increasingly worse situations. At the end of each episode you'd have her evil Uncle saying, 'Yes, come with me. You're going out onto the stage of the Albert Hall where you're going to give your premiere performance,' and it's the fast lane of the M1. And she's sort of pirouetting and there's trucks bearing down on her."

This gleeful love of the inappropriate served Wagner and Mills well in creating a suitably violent war comic, and *Battle Picture Weekly* #1 comes off as a piece of precision engineering. *D-Day Dawson* features a strapping, square-jawed soldier who is critically injured so that there's a bullet lodged in his chest that will, eventually, work its way to his heart and kill him. The medic who diagnoses him, however, is quickly killed in a shell attack while Dawson escapes. Dawson proceeds to rejoin the front line, declaring to himself, "The Germans had better watch out... they're up against a man with nothing to lose!" This, then, became the occasion for a comic in which Dawson took increasingly absurd and heroic risks to protect his men. *Lofty's One-Man Luftwaffe* features a British soldier who, in an impressive series of contrivances, manages to infiltrate the Luftwaffe so that he can "give the Hun a real pasting—from the inside!" *The Flight of the Golden Hinde* provided the comic's most inventively weird premise— a reconstruction of Sir Francis Drake's ship, which was out to sea when the war broke out, joins the war efforts and single-handedly takes down a Nazi ship. *Battle Honours* provided a patina of respectability by retelling stories of great (that is, violent) British military victories, while *Day of the Eagle* (the title unapologetically nicked from Frederick Forsyth's *The Day of the Jackal*) provided a change of pace with an espionage story, and got the middle two-page spread (printed in color). *Rat Pack*, singled out by Garth Ennis as one of his favorite strips, is an unalloyed *Dirty Dozen* knock-off by Gerry Finley-Day (who would go on to do a ton of work for *2000 AD*) and Judge Dredd co-creator Carlos Ezquerra, featuring four hardened criminals recruited to become a team of crack commandos. And then there's *The Terror Behind The Bamboo Curtain*, in which Sado, a grotesquely stereotyped Japanese soldier sends British POWs into a complex maze of death traps known as the Bamboo Curtain, which leads "big Jim Blake, a crack jungle fighter" to get himself sent behind the curtain so he can stop Sado's sadistic games.

It is *The Bootneck Boy*, however, which most exemplifies the sort of approach that Mills and Wagner could pull off. In it, a scrawny lad named Danny Budd tries to join the marines, but is rejected. Budd is an archetypal Mills/Wagner hero—a scrappy iconoclast who breaks the rules and gets rewarded for it. The strip takes care to establish Budd's inherent goodness—on the first page he rescues an old man trapped under the rubble of a bombed-out building. But despite his good deeds he's abused by his uncle at work, and gets into a fight with his cousin Ron (nicknamed Piggy) when Ron insults his deceased father's medals. After stoically enduring a

Figure 53: Danny Budd, the Bootneck Boy, impresses a recruiting sergeant with his working class grit. (From Battle Picture Weekly *#1, 1975)*

beating from his uncle, Danny goes to deliver some coal, at which point he's accosted by a group of boys who blame him for something or other Piggy did. Danny takes on all three boys, shouting at a marine who rushes in to help him to "keep off, Mister! They started this fight—an' Im gonna finish it meself!" The marine, who turns out to be the recruiting sergeant who rejected him at the start of the strip, is so impressed with Danny's fighting that he changes his mind and accepts him into the armed forces, where his adventures continue.

What is significant about *The Bootneck Boy* is not merely the adeptness with which Mills and Wagner find spurious justifications for violence, but the nature of its hero—from "the tough northern town of Tynecastle." Danny is an explicitly working class lad whose heroism comes not only from his good nature, but from his disregard for illegitimate authority and his common sense. It's notable that he's beaten by his uncle for fighting with Piggy—the same sort of corporal punishment that working class kids suffered routinely in *The Beano* and *The Dandy*. But instead of being a violent end to a carnivalesque inversion of social roles, the beating is just a badge of honor Danny wears as he stubbornly holds to his own moral code. It's not plucky inventiveness or a tendency to "keep calm and carry on" that saves the day, but hard-edged working class grit and bottle. In other words, the working class audience of the comic is reassured that they, not the people in charge, are the real heroes of the story.

"The client's head, contained inside the sack, came free with a loud smack where the spine parted company with the skull."
—Warren Ellis, *Dead Pig Collector*, 2013

Battle Picture Weekly was an unambiguous success, much to the chagrin of Le Grand and the old guard (although this may have had as much to do with Pat Mills's impressive pay package, which exceeded that of John Sanders, the man who hired him, as it did with any actual creative differences). But money always speaks louder than tradition, and Mills and Wagner quickly found more work within IPC. Wagner was tapped to lead an only semi-successful revamp of *Valiant*, an old adventure magazine that was, despite Wagner's efforts, merged into *Battle* in 1976. Mills, on the other hand, was tasked with creating another book that would go even further in the direction pioneered by *Warlord* and *Battle Picture Weekly*, to be called *Action*, which debuted in February of 1976.

British comics were by and large a working class medium, as Alan Moore has observed—that was part and parcel of why *The Bootneck Boy* worked. But *Action* took this to a new level, targeting the working class population directly and elevating the anti-authority attitudes of *The Bootneck Boy* to a fundamental tenet. The book's famed centerpiece was *Hook Jaw*, which was ostensibly a *Jaws* knockoff. Featuring a giant shark named, fittingly enough, Hook Jaw, the strip inverted the *Jaws* formula—where Spielberg reveled in keeping the shark off-screen for as long as possible and building up suspense, *Hook Jaw* puts the giant shark in the first panel, and proceeds to revel gratuitously in the fact that, as the color center spread, it could use large swaths of red ink whenever the shark snatched a new victim. But for all the strip's glorious violence, Mills was insistent that it be an "ecological" story in which Hook Jaw is the protagonist, who would take bloody vengeance against evil and corrupt humans on behalf of the untamed nature he represents. This was central to *Action*'s appeal and logic—it was not merely a comic about reveling in gratuitous violence, but one about reveling in gratuitous violence against authority figures.

In this regard the most iconoclastic story in its first issue was perhaps *Hellman of Hammer Force*, which took as its protagonist a German tank commander in World War II. Hellman, however, was an honorable soldier who insisted he was "a soldier, not a butcher," and as such clashed repeatedly with the Nazi hierarchy and had little love for Hitler. The story thus presents a bizarre inversion of standard war comics in which the reader is asked to root for a German soldier fighting the British, but where the German behaves like a stereotypical British war comics hero, thus leaving the underlying moral principles of the genre intact.

The anti-authority tendencies exemplified by this sort of story were on full display throughout the rest of the magazine. A regular feature was *Twit of the Week*, in which readers could propose various celebrities to be deemed twits for their annoying excesses. And so beloved icons like Bruce Forsyth (a reader "can't bear his catch-phrases"), Kojak ("he's always sucking a lolly"), and Lee Majors ("Bionic Berk") are roundly mocked. On the same page the comic would feature banal facts akin to the later *Fantastic Facts* series in *Doctor Who Weekly*, only with someone asking "So What?" in response to empty trivia like "Irishmen in the 9th century used to pay a 'Nose Tax' to the Danes," such that the feature became about mocking the stupid filler of other magazines.

Later issues of *Action* introduced features like *Look Out for Lefty*, a football strip penned by Tom Tully that focused on a working class hothead, Kenny "Lefty" Lampton, and his travails on and off the pitch. It was, to say the least, a very different sort of football strip to the relentlessly earnest *Roy of the Rovers*—at one point Lefty's girlfriend takes revenge on a player who's deliberately sabotaging his game so as to keep him in the reserves by throwing a Coke bottle at his head. The effect of this was a piece in *The Daily Mail*, where a Football League secretary proclaimed, "It is really appalling that there are people so brainless as to sell comics to children with stuff like this inside them. The man responsible ought to be hit over the head with a bottle himself," while other supposed experts compared the comic to pornography and called for it to be banned. This was, of course, more or less exactly the response *Action* was going for, and almost everyone involved with the comic would have worn their condemnation in *The Daily Mail*—a staggeringly reactionary paper that memorably ran a front-page headline in July of 1934 proclaiming "Hurrah for the Blackshirts" and speaking

Figure 54: Lefty's girlfriend throws a Coke bottle at a player's head, which Football League secretary Alan Hardaker called an "appalling and brainless" image. (From Look Out for Lefty *in* Action #32, *written by Tom Tully, artist uncredited, 1976)*

Figure 55: Key elements of the Kids Rule OK! *formula were the choice of adults to kill at the outset (a judge, a cop, and a teacher) and the satisfyingly gruesome corpses they leave behind. (From* Action #31, 1976)

enthusiastically about how Oswald Mosley, founder of the British Union of Fascists, had a "sound, commonsense, Conservative doctrine" (an editorial stance that had, a few months earlier, earned editor Harold Harmsworth, Lord Rothermere, a fan letter from Adolf Hitler thanking him for his "wise and beneficial public support" of "a policy that we all hope will contribute to the enduring pacification of Europe"), and which, more recently, lambasted Neil Gaiman's wife Amanda Palmer for a moment during her Glastonbury performance where her left nipple was visible, to which Palmer wrote and performed a scathing musical response in which she called them a "misogynistic pile of twats" shortly after ripping off her kimono and exposing the bulk of her naked body to a rapturous round of applause from her audience—as a badge of honor.

Such criticism, however, eventually had its effect. *The Daily Mail*'s criticism was echoed by the *Evening Standard* and by *The Sun*, which proclaimed *Action* to be "The Sevenpenny Nightmare," and trotted out Ted Willis, creator of *Dixon of Dock Green*, and famed bullying public moralizer Mary Whitehouse to condemn it. Of particular concern was *Kids Rule OK!*, a strip debuting in issue #31 of *Action*. The premise of *Kids Rule OK!* is that increased pollution has caused adults to suddenly drop dead and immediately turn to dust, leaving only people below the age of twenty alive. "As we die," a medical expert explains, "the children grow contemptuous of us. Law and order is breaking down. Soon, civilisation, as we know it, will be in ruins," before he promptly drops dead himself. The resulting story was basically a festival of teenage gangs imaginatively killing each other, and its attitude was well captured by the cover to *Action* #32, which featured a rioting group of kids led by a boy whipping a fallen adult with a chain, a policeman's helmet on the ground beside him, clearly suggesting the occupation of the victim. The caption, "Aggro! is a way of life in *Kids Rule OK!*" went well with the captions along the top of the cover such as "Wow! Blood

Flows as Green Fights on!" and "Wow! Disembowelled by Hook Jaw!"

The pressure against it quickly grew to be too much, and before long a direct action group called Delegates Opposing Violent Education was going around and defacing newsstand copies of *Action* with stickers that proclaimed, "CAUTION. This is a BLACKED publication. Certain writings in this work are not cleared by DOVE as being pro-child, in that they are either by direct meaning, context or by implication, an incitement for adults to breach the primary FUNDAMENTAL written principles of the Children & Young Persons Act 1933 Section 1 (1) which clearly prohibits: 'Assault. ill-treatment, abandonment. neglect and/or mental derangement' of the child to age 16. In the interests of Free Speech this publication remains undamaged. DIRECT ACTION by DOVE. Totnes, Devon. 'On the side of the child only—Britain's Future'." A few weeks after the debut of *Kids Rule OK!* the BBC had IPC editor John Sanders on *Nationwide*, its evening news magazine program, where he was brutally grilled by presenter Frank Bough, who went off the pre-discussed format to condemn *Action*. Shortly thereafter the magazine was the subject of debate in the House of Commons. When WH Smith reportedly threatened to drop all IPC titles from its stores if *Action* was not taken off the shelves, Jack Le Grand, with Sanders on vacation in Italy, took the opportunity to order the October 23rd, 1976 issue pulped, and the magazine vanished for six weeks before returning in a neutered form, with *Kids Rule OK!* simply vanishing from its pages, along with most of the graphic violence and, for that matter, the point of the comic. The magazine limped on for another year before it was finally put out of its misery.

For all that *Action* ended ignobly, however, it was still a sales success, and Mills quickly found himself tasked with a new job—developing a science fiction comic to take advantage of the growing popularity of sci-fi films spearheaded by *Star Wars*, a job that had been kicking around

IPC offices for a while due to a memo by a staffer named Kelvin Gosnell that was initially ignored (by Jack Le Grand, of course) but finally picked up on by Sanders. Mills quickly hit on the idea of using a revival of Dan Dare, late of *Eagle* and still owned by IPC, as a flagship strip, and set about coming up with a variety of other strips to accompany it. In August of 1976, two months before *Action* imploded, Mills presented IPC management with a dummy issue of the magazine that featured unlettered art from various strips, only four of which survived (in altered forms) to the first issue six months later. Two others—*The Visible Man* (a rather grotesque strip about a man whose skin becomes transparent) and *Shako* (a fairly straightforward clone of *Hook Jaw* featuring a polar bear instead of a shark, with the memorable tagline of "The only bear on the CIA Death List!") would be held to fill gaps later in the magazine's run, and so when the magazine actually debuted it had a total of five strips.

The four surviving strips included the revamped *Dan Dare* (which never really worked or fit in *2000 AD*, and was finally abandoned after two years), the fairly forgettable *M.A.C.H. 1* (a *Six Million Dollar Man* knock-off), and *Harlem Heroes* (a futuristic sports strip notable only for its early art by Dave Gibbons, who credits his getting the gig over numerous other artists for his familiarity with US comics and the fact that he "gave the Harlem Heroes a sort of American superhero costume"). None were particularly landmark. The fourth, however, was rather more promising. Called *Invasion*, it kicked off the first issue of *2000 AD* with a stunning splash page, drawn by Jesus Blasco, of Volgan paratroopers invading Great Britain. The Volgans were, in practice, thinly veiled Russians, and the invasion itself lasts all of four pages before the swarming troops overrun the country and establish martial law. The strip is firmly in the tradition of *Action*, complete with giddily excessive violence—the fifth page has a thinly veiled Margaret Thatcher being executed on the steps of St. Paul's Cathedral—and a working class rebel of a hero, Bill Savage, who discovers that a Volgan tank blew up his house and killed his family. "There's nothing left," his friend exclaims, to which Savage laconically points out that he's got "one thing left... me shotgun!" and promptly uses it to gun down a Volgan patrol. "You're crazy, Savage!" his friend implores. "You can't fight the Volgs alone. Britain's surrendered! The war is over!" To which Savage replies, "I'm opening it again—*my war's just begun!!*" And indeed, the strip features exactly that—Savage, armed only with a shotgun and working class grit, proceeds to organize the resistance and lead the takeback of his country.

The fifth strip in the first issue, on the other hand, was added after the dummy issue. Titled *Flesh*, it tells the story of time-travelling hunters who go back in time to kill dinosaurs, and of Old One Eye, a massive T-Rex who marauds them. Combining the over the top gore of *Hook Jaw* with a high concept premise and a visual aesthetic drawn from Western films, *Flesh* was unapologetically lurid, using its sci-fi premise to mash up a ridiculous mismatch of concepts and imagery into an attractively weird package. But it was not until the second issue of *2000 AD* that its true starring strip, the one that would encapsulate its aesthetic and approach, debuted. That strip was *Judge Dredd*, created by Mills and Wagner alongside artist Carlos Ezquerra (although the first published strip was drawn by Mike McMahon, to Ezquerra's considerable irritation), and it would prove to be one of the most enduring creations of British comics.

Judge Dredd's success is in many ways down to its peculiar inversion of the established formula Mills and Wagner pioneered back in *The Bootneck Boy*. Aware of the growing criticism of *Action*, Mills and Wagner designed *Judge Dredd* to be able to deflect the usual line of argument against the magazine. And so instead of massive amounts of anti-authority violence of the style of *Kids Rule OK!*, *Judge Dredd* featured massive amounts of violence committed by a futuristic police officer against criminals. In addition to removing the obvious political objection to the violence, *Judge Dredd* also couched it in jokey excess via the outlandish world of Mega-City One, a futuristic city sprawling across the entire American eastern seaboard in which vast city blocks, typically named after 20th century celebrities and television characters, would often feud and go to war with one another. (So, for instance, in the famed 1981 *Block Mania* storyline, the Enid Blyton and Dan Tanna blocks went to war.)

"The Tek-Judges of Anubis have eaten a poison-weed and they shall die soon."
–Grant Morrison and Mark Millar, *Judge Dredd: Book of the Dead,* 1993

But the heart of the strip's appeal came in its combination of the anti-authority leanings of *Kid Rule OK* or *Look Out For Lefty* with the noble bad guy protagonist of *Hellman of Hammer Force*. The standard set-up of a *Judge Dredd* story involves Dredd going to great lengths to bust some "creep" whose crime seems relatively minor. Even if there is a proper villain, it's not uncommon for a *Judge Dredd* strip to end with some minor accomplice getting arrested by Dredd, with any pleas for mercy being inevitably rejected. An early story, for instance, ends with Dredd arresting a man for receiving an illegal but presumably life-saving organ transplant, proclaiming him to be one of "the real villains" in the illegal transplant ring he's busting.

The strip, in other words, is an aggressive satire of what would become known as the broken windows theory of policing, in which focusing on small crimes against the social order—vandalism being the textbook example—was believed to reduce crime in general. In practice, of course, broken window policing became an excuse for police forces to focus on petty crime committed by poorer people, and was little more than an excuse for neoliberal crypto-fascists like Ronald Reagan and Margaret Thatcher to arrest more racial minorities. Dredd predates both Thatcher's Britain, which came into power in 1979, and the broken windows theory, first codified in 1982, but this only added to its power. It meant that when Thatcherism rose to power the artistic resistance to it was already worked out and ready.

It's unsurprising, then, that when Alan Moore encountered Prog 11 on a newsstand, he fell in love. Initially, at least, he was drawn in by the cover—a Brian Bolland number featuring the villain from that week's *Dan Dare*. Bolland—who would go on to find acclaim as an interior artist, primarily on *Judge Dredd*—combines meticulous, clean linework with incredible depth in its shading, and with a flair for the grotesque that can render even the most outlandish of visual concepts in intricate and captivating detail. His cover to Prog 11 is further boosted by a heavy use of reds, oranges, and yellows, and a satisfyingly pulpy speech balloon as the ashen, red-eyed man on the cover proclaims, "Follow me into the sun… you will share *the death of a Martian warrior!*"

But this was May of 1977, and Moore, sci-fi fan that he might be, was twenty-four and rather old to be drawn in just by lurid sci-fi pulpiness. This was the year after he'd been writing the avant-garde play *Another Suburban Romance*, and after he'd sent his fan letter in to Bill Griffiths at *Arcade*. The sorts of things that appealed to him weren't just violence and cool imagery. Indeed, Moore describes the appeal of the magazine to his twenty-four-year-old self in terms of the "really funny, cynical writers working on *2000 AD* at the time," and how he "thought these people were intelligent" due to the "satirical stuff" in the magazine. In Prog 11, at least, it's fairly clear what strip he would have been talking about, and, unsurprisingly, it's *Judge Dredd*, which was in the midst of its first multi-part story, *The Robot Wars*.

The Robot Wars concerns a robot uprising in Mega-City One and Judge Dredd's actions in stopping it. It is a self-consciously over-the-top affair, with lots of gratuitous violence, but all of it stylized—the strip doesn't even try to pretend that the robots are there for anything other than letting them get away with the sort of violence that got *Action* cancelled. But this time it's couched in a cartoonish, openly silly aesthetic of big, humorously named robots. The story

Figure 56: Brian Bolland's cover to 2000 AD *#11, which caught Alan Moore's eye and got him reading the magazine.*

Figure 57: Prior to the start of The Robot Wars, *Judge Dredd made the moral legitimacy of the robot rebellion unequivocal. (From 2000 AD #9, written by John Wagner, art by Ron Turner, 1977)*

culminates with an installment drawn by Ian Gibson, whose sketchy, slightly cartoonish style morphs into a dead-on Jack Kirby parody for the dramatic finale, as Dredd and the robot messiah Call-Me-Kenneth have a showdown on an aerial oil tanker. It's a big, frothy cops-and-robbers spectacular with robot criminals and sci-fi cops.

Except that the script makes no effort to hide the underlying ethics. The issue before the war kicks off is a story that opens with a robot named George begging for his life, pleading his master not to order him to set himself on fire and melt. His master does not relent, ordering him to kill himself, and so the robot weeps and burns to death as a crowd of onlookers watch the marketing demo of this new vintage of "K Series Robots," which "are almost human. They think, they feel... but they obey!" Having shown this grotesque horror, the entire story line that follows is about Judge Dredd trying to stop these robots from rebelling against these conditions. Call-Me-Kenneth is, in this regard, a troubling figure. Like any good villain, his demands are totally sensible—he does not want to be a slave. He inspires other robots to overthrow their enslavers. Yes, they do so violently, but given the horrors imposed on them, even this seems wholly reasonable. Tellingly, Call-Me-Kenneth is said to have been a carpenter robot—which is to say, he is explicitly positioned as the robotic equivalent of what William Blake describes as "Jesus our Lord, who is the God of Fire and Lord of Love to whom the Ancients look'd and saw his day afar off, with trembling and amazement."

Blake, for his part, loved a good riot, or at least did in his youth. A lifelong political radical (though his politics were, in the end, ensnared in the same labyrinth of visions as the rest of his genius), at the age of twenty-two he found himself swept up in the 1780 Gordon riots, in which a bit of anti-Catholicism stirred up by Lord George Gordon marched en masse upon Parliament to protest a bill relieving Catholics of several long-standing penalties dating back to the Popery Act of 1698, which, among other things, placed a bounty on

Catholic priests. A riot broke out, and, as riots do, quickly spread to encompass other causes. Blake found himself swept up in a crowd and witness to the burning of Newgate Prison, in which Lord Gordon would die, jailed not for the Gordon Riots (where he was acquitted of high treason due to the effective legal defense from his cousin Thomas, Lord Erskine, based on the argument that the form of treason Lord Gordon was accused of was not technically treason under the Treason Act 1351, a defense that saw Lord Erskine quickly become the star lawyer of London) but for defaming Marie Antoinette. In later life, Blake himself would stand trial for treason after getting into a fight with a drunken soldier, John Schofield, who Blake would go on to fantasize about being "bound in iron armour before Reuben's Gate" in his epic *Milton*. And Call-Me-Kenneth largely exists in the same tradition, at least on first appearance.

Or, as Judge Dredd explains it, "We give robots the ability to think, give them human shape, and emotions. How long before they develop that other human trait—evil!" And Dredd's position never wavers—he unhesitatingly fights the robots like they are the greatest evil ever to come to the world. Sure enough, Call-Me-Kenneth eventually positions himself as a robotic despot, torturing and killing robots in scenes actively reminiscent of George a few issues earlier, and actively comparing himself to Hitler. Once he does that, of course, all moral nuance is gone, and the audience is free to root for Judge Dredd as he reprograms Call-Me-Kenneth's robots so that they all begin chanting, "I am the slave of humans!" With slavery restored, the loyal robots of the world are given pleasure circuits rewarding them for their servitude, and Judge Dredd is left with a funny robotic sidekick named Walter in the style of Doctor Who's annoying robotic dog K-9.

The strip makes zero effort to have a coherent morality—by any reasonable standard the audience should be on the side of the robots, but the strip never once allows for the possibility that the robots might have anything resembling a point. The revelation that Call-Me-Kenneth is a Hitler-esque despot is totally extraneous to the plot, shoved in to create a vague moral justification, but the entire point of the strip is to call the reader's attention to that fact, bringing them in on the joke. "OK, you got *Action* canned because it was full of violent working class fantasies," the strip says, "so we'll write violent fantasies you like instead." Or, as Blake put it in *The Marriage of Heaven and Hell*, "Improvement makes strait roads, but the crooked roads without Improvement, are roads of Genius."

So it is hardly a surprise that such a bleakly multi-layered satire would appeal to Moore. Or to anyone else—*2000 AD* was a runaway success, with *Judge Dredd* quickly establishing itself as its star strip. And so when Moore devoted himself to a comics career, his initial plan—the never-started *Sun Dodgers*—was imagined as a pitch to *2000 AD*. Once he turned to scripting he took steps to land this dream assignment again, but was advised by Steve Moore to start with a smaller script, and so he produced a short *Judge Dredd* script, which his friend helped him look over, and which he then sent to IPC. Alan Grant, then a sub-editor, thought it showed promise, but politely explained that *Judge Dredd* was John Wagner's baby ("Which I should have realized," Moore notes in hindsight) and that Moore might try his hand at a different type of script.

But this narrative, oft-reported as it is, does not quite hold together. For one thing, this submission would have been in late 1979/early 1980, at which point John Wagner had several gaps in his streak of writing the character, including the massive *Cursed Earth* epic written by Pat Mills, and Jack Adrian was doing semi-regular fill-ins on the character. Moore would have known this, because in 1977, in Prog 36, *2000 AD* took the largely unprecedented step of giving its writers and artists credits, albeit with the humorous conceit that they were not people but "script robots" and "art robots" working under the lash of fictitious extraterrestrial editor Tharg the Mighty. And so Moore had every reason to think *Judge Dredd* might be a strip he could write. Certainly if it was as out of the question as Grant's account suggests, one wonders why Steve Moore, who mentored Moore on the script and who had already offered guidance about what *2000 AD* would and wouldn't buy, didn't think to mention this.

To some extent one suspects the reason is simply that the script, "Something Nasty in Mega-City One" (Moore specifies that "if possible, the word "NASTY" should look as if it has been sculpted from decomposing flesh… vile, worm-infested, and just about to crawl off the page and into the readers [sic] lap."), isn't all that good. It's a competent piece of setup for a presumably multi-part story about Judge Dredd fighting an alien monster, but it has none of the satirical bite that Moore so admired in *Judge Dredd*. But it's not as though this were the case with every *Judge Dredd* story, so this isn't disqualifying as such. The truth, one suspects, is not so much that Grant wouldn't consider another freelancer on *Judge Dredd* as that Grant wasn't going to put this particular promising face onto the magazine's flagship strip for his first go at things. And Moore's script, while good, is not so good as to make that a difficult decision to understand at all.

After all, there were loads else in *2000 AD—Judge Dredd* may have been the magazine's flagship product, but over the years it was joined by other classic strips. *2000 AD* was a weekly comic, and thus existed on the slippery tightrope of perpetual deadlines. Strips that didn't seem popular were ruthlessly culled, and new ones sprung up regularly to replace them. The nature of the industry, particularly under IPC, was that entire magazines went under regularly, and when one was popular there were always a rush of clones. When these clones faltered they were summarily chopped, typically by merging them into a more popular title, which would print a few installments of the cancelled title's most popular strips under a joint masthead before quietly axing them and the cancelled magazine's space in the title. *2000 AD* was involved in this twice over the years, becoming, fleetingly, *2000*

AD/Starlord and *2000 AD/Tornado* as those two publications were cancelled and folded in.

Starlord actually ended up being the source of some of the other major and famous strips in *2000 AD*, such as *Strontium Dog*, another strip featuring a nomadic loner, and the *Ro-Busters*, a robotic rescue squad bearing more than a slight resemblance to Gerry Anderson's *Thunderbirds* franchise. *Ro-Busters* later spun off the *ABC Warriors*, which had design work from Kevin O'Neill, who would in turn go on to create *Nemesis the Warlock* with Pat Mills, which in turn provided a major stepping stone for Bryan Talbot's career when he succeeded the punishingly slow O'Neill on art duties. (*Nemesis*, idiosyncratically, is a spin-off of The Jam's song "Going Underground," which *2000 AD* used as the pilot of an aborted series called *Comic Rock* that loosely adapted pop songs as comic stories.) Other stand-out *2000 AD* strips included *Rogue Trooper*, originally by Gerry Finley-Day and Dave Gibbons, which told the story of a genetically modified soldier who carried with him the minds of his three fallen comrades (Gunnar, Bagman, and Helm) embedded in computer chips mounted, fittingly, on his gun, backpack, and helmet, and *Sláine*, a sword-and-sorcery gorefest created by Pat Mills and his then wife Angela Kincaid, which provided a breakthrough opportunity for *Preacher* cover artist Glenn Fabry. These were supplemented by a wealth of short-run stories both classic and deservedly obscure.

Moore contributed numerous one-offs for several of these features in various *2000 AD* Annuals, writing *Ro-Busters* tales in the 1982, '83, and '84 *2000 AD* annuals (all published in December of the year before, the annual being designed as a Christmas present), *Rogue Trooper* in the 1983 and 84 ones, and *ABC Warriors* in the 1985 annual. He acquitted himself well in all cases. His first such story, the *Ro-Busters* story "Bax the Burner," is a decent tale about an abusive mutant boyfriend, which Moore, in a very early interview, took special pride in, noting that it "was the only one in which I've hung the plot around a strong emotional content and not had the whole thing come off as being incredibly trite and sentimental," which is a fair self-assessment. His subsequent two *Ro-Busters* strips were more humorous—one in which the robot Hammerstein accidentally reverts to his *ABC Warriors*-era persona and starts smashing things, and another in which the Ro-Busters go up against the Stormeagles, an even less thinly veiled ripoff of *Thunderbirds*.

> *"Jeez, y'know, that felt good. There don't seem to be so many laughs around these days."*
> *"Well what do you expect? The Comedian is dead."*
> —Alan Moore, *Watchmen*, 1986

Moore's *Rogue Trooper* work is an altogether more somber affair. The first, "Pray for War," tells of Gunnar having to kill another soldier who calls himself "Pray for War" because, as he says, "War is the best thing that ever happened to me" and "Combat is what makes me happy," ending with Rogue reassuring Gunnar, "You only killed part of him—the ugly part. The war killed any humanity left in him long ago." The second, "First of the Few," involves Rogue finding one of the abandoned prototypes of the Genetic Infantrymen, for whom he allows the mercy of death, actively declining to load his consciousness into his gun or helmet. Both are straightforward anti-war stories; "First of the Few" describes the hellish world of Nu Earth as "the ultimate monument to war. The land is scorched bare and the air is a poisonous soup," Moore writes with obvious relish, crafting a dour and pleasureless war story that subverts the genre.

Moore is even more somber in his *ABC Warriors* story, "Red Planet Blues," which has Hammerstein investigating a problem on Mars. The problem turns out to be that the planet still has life on it, and the solution of the humans that hire Hammerstein is to simply burn the weeds in which the lifeforms live. Hammerstein reflects at the end, "We burned the whole undergrowth and we only found one dead Martian animal. I figure even that was a fluke." Nevertheless,

Hammerstein opts to bury the animal, admitting that he's "getting old" and "getting soft." The story ends as a haunting dirge about the nature of colonial genocide, as Hammerstein warns the dead alien, "The humans are coming, and soon all your tribe will lie as still as you. There's nothing you can do about it. It's their planet now."

But while Moore dabbled with these characters, the bulk of his *2000 AD* work was either on the three strips he created—*Skizz*, *D.R. & Quinch*, and *The Ballad of Halo Jones*—or short stories, mainly under the banner of *Tharg's Future Shocks*. These short stories were a pragmatic necessity owing to the hectic pace of *2000 AD*'s weekly schedule. In between longer strips, or when an artist on a longer strip was running late and replacing him was unfeasible, the magazine would run bespoke short stories. The first of these was in Prog 25, where it filed the hole left by *Dan Dare* going on hiatus, and was penned by an uncredited Steve Moore. It tells the story of a war between red-haired and black-haired people, both cave tribes with swords. This goes on for two pages before a final page reveals that the humans are in a glass box kept by giant ants, who watch their antics with amusement and muse over how "they work together... and fight... I'd swear they were almost as intelligent as us ants" before concluding that, no, "it's just instinct."

The underlying structure of this short-form story is one pioneered in American comics of the 1950s, particularly those published by EC, which maintained a line of horror comics like *Tales from the Crypt* featuring short stories, generally with twist endings in which the protagonist suffers some ghastly fate at the hands of forces he has failed to adequately understand. Moore's story of giant ants playing with humans has several antecedents in EC—for instance, a story in *Vault of Horror* #22 in which a fisherman goes to pick up a candy bar lying on the shore, only to find out that it's a lure, and that he's being dragged out into the ocean by some aquatic land-fisher. The structure is mirrored right down to the conceit that the stories are narrated and presented by the fictitious editor. It's these stories that Alan Grant recommended Moore to work on after rejecting his *Judge Dredd* script, and it was with one of them that Moore first got published in his beloved *2000 AD*.

Moore's first published work with *2000 AD* was actually the second one he had accepted—a short called "A Holiday in Hell," which appeared in the *2000 AD Sci-Fi Special* in 1980. It is in many ways a textbook example of the *Future Shocks* formula. The story depicts a futuristic world where Earth has become "a world without war, without crime, without bloodshed," meaning that people vacation on Murderworld (formerly known as Mars) to blow off steam killing robots. The story tracks a husband and wife who go on vacation there, but at the end of the vacation the wife, Gabrielle, begins acting strangely. After returning home she proceeds to kill her husband, and, at the end of the story, it's revealed that from time to time the robots take a vacation by going to Earth and killing humans. The story is unremarkable, but competent and interesting: there's a clever commentary under the hood, and it's at once smart and over the top. Though not an extraordinary story by any measure, it's a good one, and it's easy enough to see why Alan Grant accepted it for publication.

Moore's first accepted story, on the other hand, was "Killer in the Cab," which came out in Prog 170, published in July of 1980, a month after he'd begun work on *Doctor Who Weekly*. The summer of 1980 was not, by any standard, a golden age for the magazine. Shackled with the title of *2000 AD/Tornado* following the merger with a floundering IPC stablemate, the magazine consisted of an adaptation of Harry Harrison's *Stainless Steel Rat* books, a wretched Tom Tully number called *The Mind of Wolfie Smith*, the rather better *Sam Slade, Robot Hunter*, and, most promisingly, a middle installment of the sprawling *Judge Dredd* epic "The Judge Child." With the Gerry Finley-Day series *The V.C.s* on a one-issue hiatus, however, there was room for a one-off strip, which Alan Moore provided under the banner of *Ro-Jaws'*

Robo-Tales, which was in effect being used in place of *Tharg's Future Shocks* at this point in the magazine's history. The basic plot is a space trucker (named Sundodger, in a nod to Moore's aborted epic) whose truck's automated defense systems have wrongly determined that he's trying to hijack the truck, and are thus trying to kill him. Working via the futuristic equivalent of the CB with another trucker, the female Andromeda Angel, the trucker is able to disable the security system and regain control of his truck. In the final panel it's revealed that the Andromeda Angel is herself a robot, a fact that will presumably frustrate Sundodger's clearly desired romantic relations with her when they meet in a week's time at Max Drax's Palace O'Potions.

The strip is a straightforward adventure story with a small twist pinned onto the end, but its craftsmanship runs deeper than its unremarkable surface features. Structurally, the strip is a procedural—the action focuses on Sundodger and the Andromeda Angel figuring out how to retake Sundodger's rig, and on the technical steps taken to accomplish this. But given that this is a procedural based around an entirely fictive world—there are not, in fact, space trucks on remote, dead planets—this is no mean feat. Moore has to simultaneously introduce the rules of the space trucking world and show Sundodger and the Andromeda Angel figuring out how to work within those rules. The mechanism of having Sundodger explain everything he sees and does to the absent Andromeda Angel goes a long way towards making that easy, though it's by no measure a subtle or nuanced accomplishment—yet there's an impressive grasp of storytelling here, and the entire exercise is entertainingly enlivened by Moore's thick use of trucker dialect, a body of knowledge he'd put to use a few years later when he contributed two pieces to the 1983 *BJ and the Bear Annual.*

Six progs later, Moore was back again with "The Dating Game," another *Robo-Tale.* Prog 176 is an unusual one for the magazine—fully three of the stories were shorts, as *The V.C.s* had ended the issue prior, the current *Sam Slade, Robot Hunter* story the week before that, and *The Mind of Wolfie Smith* was on a week's break, leaving only *The Stainless Steel Rat Saves the World* and "The Judge Child" to anchor the magazine. "The Dating Game" was the final strip in the issue, and the second *Ro-Jaws' Robo-Tales* in it. Comparing it to the earlier story, "The Robo-Shrink" by C.P. Rice, it's easy to see why Moore rose through the ranks at *2000 A.D.* "The Robo-Shrink" is a three-pager about a robotic therapist who has clearly gone round the bend itself, advising patients to "murder the creep" and to "take an axe, go to your neighbor's apartment—AND SMASH HIS HI-FI TO PIECES!" Ultimately, after failing to find a mechanical fault in the therapist, the mechanics send it to be analyzed itself. And that's the end. There's nothing that can quite be called a resolution, nor any real development over the course of the story. Indeed, it barely deserves to be called a story—it is in essence three pages of incident that do not evolve or develop at all. The ending seems to be going for humor, but it's not clear what the joke is—that the obviously malfunctioning robotic therapist should get psychiatric treatment? That it should be charged for it?

While "The Dating Game," on the other hand, can't be called a great story, it at least makes a point of coming to a humorous ending where the joke makes sense, and gets decent mileage out of its premise until then. It tells the story of Myron Fooble, who seeks romance via a dating agency only to have the agency match him up with the central city computer, which controls every aspect of the city. Fooble eventually spurns the computer, which promptly becomes a jilted and homicidal ex, trying to run Fooble down with automated taxi cabs and scald him in the shower. "Every machine in the city is after my blood," he laments. "Even my electric toothbrush," which proceeds to bounce towards him, growling. Eventually he flees the city to become a scavenger, only to be eaten by a computerized litter bin. "True love may never run smooth," Ro-Jaws reflects, "but atomic-powered stainless steel garbage grinders certainly do." It's a simple strip, and indeed a faintly misogynistic one, trading as it does on the stereotype of women as irrationally and violently jealous, but notably, unlike "The Robo-Shrink," it demonstrates a basic coherence to its storytelling. That this should be something that immediately puts Moore ahead of the pack says, as Moore readily suggests in countless interviews, more about the unfortunate state of British comics in 1980 than it does about Moore's skills. Nevertheless, it's clear even at this early stage that Moore is a rising talent.

The most notable thing about "The Dating Game," however, is that it marks the first collaboration between Alan Moore and Dave Gibbons. Gibbons was a long-time veteran on *2000 AD*, having made his debut in the first issue as the artist on Tom Tully's *Harlem Heroes*. Since then he bounced around the magazine, drawing a slew of *Dan Dare* strips, a couple of *Judge Dredd*s, and various *Future Shocks*. Like Brian Bolland, Gibbons's style is characterized by an intense level of detail and an exceedingly clean line. Where Bolland specializes in the grotesque, however, Gibbons's strength is, as Moore cheekily puts it, that he was "prepared to draw whatever absurd amount of detail you should ask for, however ludicrous and impractical." It is not merely his willingness, however, but his skill at it—the cleanliness of Gibbons's line-work makes the absurd depths of detail crystal clear. On *2000 AD*, at least, Moore mostly used this talent for humorous effect. Of their half-dozen collaborations, four came in a period from May to July of 1982, shortly after Gibbons left Gerry Finley-Day's *Rogue Trooper*. All four were two-page jokes, often with straightforward punch lines. "Skirmish," for instance, depicts a group of alien invaders being cut to ribbons by human defenders with "terrible weapons that make such a ridiculous noise," which turn out to be the machinations of a kid playing *Space Invaders*. (*Space Invaders* is actually a recurring theme in Moore's work around this time—the game features in a joke in the fourth Abelard Snazz strip, and in a *Maxwell the Magic Cat* strip, all during the 1982-83 period when the game was at its most popular. [This

Figure 58: Myron Fooble is plagued by the angry yet amorous advances of his newly feral toothbrush. (From "The Dating Game," in 2000 AD #176, written by Alan Moore, art by Dave Gibbons, 1980)

Figure 59: The Clone Ranger dispatches Billy the Squid. (From "The Wild Frontier," in 2000 AD #269, written by Alan Moore, art by Dave Gibbons, 1982)

strip is one of several *Maxwell the Magic Cats* to use recycled punchlines from Moore's *Future Shocks*. A month or two earlier he did a strip in which an *ET*-like alien is squashed by Maxwell, revealing that it's only four centimeters tall. This is the same basic punchline as the June 1982 *Future Shock* "The Big Day," in which aliens prophesize the return of their gods only to be crushed by said gods, which turn out to be Apollo 11 astronauts who dwarf the microscopic aliens.] This makes it the only video game to get any sort of attention from Moore save for an appearance by Pac-Man in the penultimate *Maxwell the Magic Cat*. This information surely allows a dedicated researcher to track the precise progression of what arcade machines were owned by some pub in Northampton during the mid-1980s.)

These strips culminate in "The Wild Frontier," a story that demonstrates straightforwardly how Gibbons's art style lends itself to Moore's style of comedy. Moore describes the strip as "one of those stupid things you do when you hear that Dave Gibbons will be drawing a job." "The Wild Frontier" is a two- page bit of larking about on the premise of a space-western, complete with jokes about "the octobandits led by that cephalopod sidewinder... Billy the Squid!" and the Clone Ranger, a vast stampede of identical masked men with their catchphrase of "Hiyoo, Chromium! Hawaay!" All of this is depicted by Gibbons in comically ludicrous detail that not only emphasizes the ridiculousness of the concept but wallows in its glorious excess, encouraging readers to dwell on panels to catch all of the sight gags Gibbons has managed to cram in. But even as early as "The Dating Game" Gibbons was showing his propensity for detail, making sure to put the bouquet of Saturnian Singing Orchids that the computer gives Myron in as many panels as possible (and thus allowing Moore to create more deliciously awful plant rhymes such as "Who cares if the greenfly bite? / I've got you to hold me tight. / You're my man, I don't mean maybe... / You're my fertilizer baby") and, of course, depicting the sublime lunacy of Myron's homicidal toothbrush.

"You're saying the Sentinels lied about all them space wars? Well what have they been doin' all these years?"
–Alan Moore, *Top Ten*, 2001

Unfortunately, for all that Moore was clearly better at them than other writers, there simply weren't a ton of slots for short stories at this period in the magazine's history. *Tharg's Future Shocks* hadn't appeared since Prog 135 in late 1979, and wouldn't make a return until March of 1981, at which point Moore began getting published in *2000 AD* with considerably more regularity. If his earliest 1980 shorts were merely competent, his 1981 work must be recognized as a genuinely extraordinary run of stories, and a key turning point in the emergence of Moore as a writer. Properly, his hot streak began in December of 1980 with the publication of "Final Solution," the first of his six stories to feature Abelard Snazz, a genius known for his "two-storey brain" whose schemes inevitably end in humorous catastrophe. This was followed by a run of six consecutive *Future Shocks* interspersed with two more Snazz stories that constitute the most sustained run of quality and creativity that the *Future Shocks* line ever had.

The claim that *Future Shocks* trade on twist endings is often repeated, and it's certainly true that they appear a lot. But in Moore's best work the twist ending is not the point of the exercise, instead providing a narrative resolution to a story that is otherwise about exploring other ideas. For a short story of only four or five pages, a twist ending is a natural fit—the length is almost exactly long enough to reasonably develop an idea, but not really long enough to develop a second one. And so the natural structure is to develop the idea, take it in a surprising direction, and then stop without having to worry about the consequences of that change. Often this is the point of the exercise—there's few ways to explain "A Holiday in Hell," for instance, except in terms of its final revelation. But other times the twist ending is just a frame to hold a different sort of story.

"Grawks Bearing Gifts," the first of Moore's stories to actually bear the *Tharg's Future Shocks* label, is a prime example. The story has a twist ending, to be sure, but the twist comes halfway down the penultimate page. The ending panel is still there for a comedic punchline, but it's not a plot twist in the least. The basic form of a twist ending is still there—several pages of fleshing out an idea only to reveal a key detail about the idea that casts everything in a new light. But the story isn't built to emphasize that. Instead the point of the story is the nature of the twist. The story concerns a race of aliens called the Grawks (which Moore impishly notes are depicted via "a lot of terrible racist slurs directed at Australians" and offers "no defense for this, and, in the tradition of Conservative cabinet-ministers when asked why they were card-carrying members of the National Front until three weeks previously," declares that he will "put it down to the indiscretions of a reckless youth") who arrive on Earth and act like stereotypical dumb tourists, in particular freely handing out large amounts of gold for the privilege of buying various major landmarks. Until, on the fourth page, the Grawks produce a page of trans-galactic law that explains that "purchase of properties on all planets shall be considered binding if the seller and signatory is a bona-fide member of the planet in question" and that "ignorance of this clause may not be deemed an excuse." Having acquired the entirety of the planet and collapsed the economy by flooding it with gold, they proceed to rename the planet, rework various landmarks in their own image, and shove the human population into reservations, leading to a final panel where Margaret Thatcher consoles a broken-hearted general who failed to plan for this eventuality while a Grawk stands outside a sign saying "Earthling Resettlement Area No. 2085," snaps a picture, and happily exclaims, "Coo-eeee!"

With the twist coming comparatively early in the story and without any real suddenness (page three is already mostly about the degree to which Grawks are taking over things), the story stops being about the cleverness and starts being about the nature of what the Grawks are doing. The twist is a means to an end, that end being a story that takes a variety of things Europeans, and particularly the British, have done to any number of cultures over the years. The point of the story is to show Britain (and the world at large, though notably Moore only depicts European and American areas being taken over by Grawks) on the receiving end of treatment it has historically dished out. The twist isn't a surprise, but rather a tool for Moore to engage in scathing cultural commentary.

Moore's next *Future Shock*, "The English/Phlondrutian Phrasebook," challenges the usual plot structure of a *Future Shock* even further—enough so, in fact, that it went out without any sort of banner. The story is presented as a found object—each page contains an image of a "Vocosonics Futura Transliterator" that is presenting the eponymous phrasebook (one of the characters can be seen to be holding the device in several of Brendan McCarthy's delightfully barmy images in Moore's sole collaboration with the legendary artist). The story consists of a series of helpful Phlondrutian phrases for a potential traveler, divided into sections like "At the Spaceport," "At the Hotel," "On the Beach," and, later, "While Being Arrested" and "On the Slave Satellite." The plot, then, exists as an implication—the images depict one hapless pair of tourists as they go through the nightmarish vacation suggested by that progression of sections, but the story is not so much about one specific Kafka-esque vacation so much as it is about the underlying joke of a planet where "Waiter, my soup is giggling," and "Sign a confession? But we are innocent!" are both essential phrases for the prospective traveler. The strip is an experiment in style and technique—an attempt to see how changing the underlying structure of a narrative changes the

Figure 60: The Grawks, designed as parodies of Australian tourists, step out of their spaceship. (From "Grawks Bearing Gifts," in 2000 AD #83, written by Alan Moore, art by Ian Gibson as Q. Twerk, 1981)

Figure 61: Rocket Redglare is not the lithe action hero he used to be. (From "The Regrettable Ruse of Rocket Redglare," in 2000 AD #234, written by Alan Moore, art by Mike White, 1981)

stories that can be told. This sort of careful focus on structure and particularly on structural experimentation will go on to become one of the most fundamental techniques in Moore's repertoire.

This is not to suggest, however, that Moore avoided the straightforward twist ending entirely. "The Regrettable Ruse of Rocket Redglare," for instance, plays its ending very straight. Rocket Redglare is a Flash Gordon-style hero who's well over the hill, and is first shown struggling to lace his middle-aged flab into a corset so he can don the old costume to open a Mega-Market. Desperate to prove his relevance, he contacts his old arch-foe Lumis Logar, and proposes that Logar fake an invasion of Earth for Redglare to repel, thus restoring his faded glory. Logar accepts the proposal cheerily, asking rhetorically, "Who could bear a grudge for thirty years?" The answer, as revealed in the final panel, is that Logar could: he ends up launching a real invasion and casually killing off Redglare.

The story recognizably employs one of Moore's standard techniques—the reconsideration of an existing pulp narrative from a quasi-realist perspective, usually one that assumes the passage of time. He'll go on, of course, to use the same basic premise to vast critical acclaim on both *Marvelman* and *Watchmen*. The "quasi" here is, in fact, important. There is little that is actually realistic about "Rocket Redglare." The idea that Redglare's nemesis needed Rocket's regrettable ruse in orderto launch his revenge barely holds up to any scrutiny, and the world of the story strikes a compelling but fundamentally preposterous balance between treating Redglare and Logar as actual people in the world and treating them as fictional characters. It's telling that Redglare's scheme is not one to make money, but rather one to regain his popularity. His problem, in other words, is one faced as a fictional character—he's declined in popularity and has in effect been cancelled. His financial success comes the same way any franchise does—toys, t-shirts, bubblegum cards, and films. His marriage, tellingly, was fixed up by his and his wife's mutual agent. He is, in effect, an actor whose movie franchise has stalled, but where his movie franchise also has potentially deadly real-world implications. The point is not a gritty, realist, "Let's pretend these fictional characters existed in the real world," but rather a riff on what would happen if a single real-world concept—the sense of being over the hill— were imported into a fictional setting. Within that, it uses another classic and well-worn plot structure: the con man whose unethical scheme blows up in his face.

"The Last Rumble of the Platinum Horde" is a similarly basic twist-ending story in which the Karbongian Empire, lacking anyone left to conquer, sends out its last great army, the Platinum Horde, to sweep across the universe until they reach the edge of space itself. Space turns out to be curved, however, and after generations of slaughter the Platinum Horde circles back on the decaying remains of the Karbongian Empire itself, the all-conquering serpent biting down hard upon its own tail. Moore, in his typically self-deprecating manner, notes that he'd "like to claim that it was a bitter and satirical attack upon the mindless brutalities of war," but that "it was really just plain bloody violent," and laid most of the praise at the feet of future *Watchmen* colorist John Higgins, who he claims "did a sterling job in depicting the lighter side of genocide." (Moore also notes that since writing the story he's discovered that the title "was partially stolen from a Norman Spinrad story which, if you can find it, is much better than this one." The story in question is "The Last Hurrah of the Golden Horde," reprinted in the now easy to find short story collection by the same name, and makes an interesting counterpoint to Moore's.

Spinrad's story features the character of Jerry Cornelius, created by Michael Moorcock [whose *New Worlds* published Spinrad's controversial novel *Bug Jack Barron* when other publishers wouldn't touch it, resulting in *New Worlds* taking heat in the House of Commons due to its partial funding from the British Arts Council], being dragged into a convoluted web of double crosses and intrigue in Maoist

China, which he resolves by using a specially made violin to induce a massive outbreak of violence, resulting in a scene whereby "Major Sung shrieked: 'Capitalistic running dogs of the demographic People's revisionist lackeys of Elvis Presley have over-run the ideological manifestations of decadent elements within the amplifier of the pagoda!' and committed hari-kiri," while "The Rock began smashing slot machines with a baseball bat" and "Starlets tore off their bikinis and chased terrified hatchet men around the poolside" as "The Human Wave reached the pool, dove in, and proceeded to beat moribund crocodiles to death with their gunbutts" alongside "a suicide squad" that "hurled itself through the plate glass window of a trailer and devoured the rug" while simultaneously "Cadillacs circled the boxcar of heroin like hostile Indians, filling the air with hot lead" contemporaneously with the moment "The sopping remnants of the human wave reached the trailer camp and began beating thugs to death with dead crocodiles" synchronized with the point when "Red Guards showered the C-5A with ink bottles" concomitantly with "Tongues of flame were everywhere" and "Explosions, contusions, fire, gore, curses, looting, rape," all of which, in the original manuscript, are treated as distinct paragraphs.

"Robots couldn't really give a fuck if you live or die. Seriously. I mean, what are you thinking? 'Ooh, I must protect the bag of meat at all costs because I couldn't possibly plug in the charger all on my own.' Shut the fuck up."
–Warren Ellis, 2007

This cacophony of violence is finally stumbled upon by the "two hundred decrepit remnants of what had once been the glorious Golden Horde, most of them incoherent with exhaustion." The horde, who, in addition to being in the title, have lurked in the background of the story, with occasional paragraphs describing their slow and pathetic march, charge gamely into the combat only to discover that "to their chagrin that there was precious little unburnt, unpillaged, unraped, unkilled" and they all die pathetically. The story ends with Cornelius attempting to ride off on the horse of the last Khan of the Golden Horde, which is said to have "waddled forward a few steps, puked, and died." And that's basically that.

That this apparently inadvertent coincidence of titles should take place around a Jerry Cornelius story written by someone other than Michael Moorcock is ironic, given that one of the most superficially obvious conflagrations in the War centers on Grant Morrison's Gideon Stargrave character and the degree to which it and his larger work are or are not rip-offs of Moorcock's work. Essentially no plot elements coincide between Spinrad and Moore's stories. And yet there is a thematic kinship between them. Both are ruminations on the nature of violence that hinge on an over-the-top display of it which is revealed to be fundamentally hollow. The end effect is to highlight the impressive diversity of potential in storytelling. Two writers with relatively similar ideas—a rumination on the banality of violence featuring the iconography of the Mongol hordes—ended up in profoundly different places. Even the similarity of title is wholly understandable—there really was a 13th century Mongol Khanate known as the Golden Horde, so it's hardly surprising that two separate writers working with Mongol iconography riffed on the same famous and poetic name from history.

This was, however, not always the case for Moore's *Future Shocks*. Two months before "The Last Rumble of the Platinum Horde" Moore penned "The Return of the Two-Storey Brain," his second story featuring Abelard Snazz. Unlike "The Last Rumble of the Platinum Horde," which Moore was content to have reprinted in the *Shocking Futures* collection with a self-deprecating note in the introduction, Moore asked for "The Return of the Two-Storey Brain" not to be reprinted alongside the other five Abelard Snazz tales in the *Twisted Times* collection because, as he puts it, "Some while after the sequel was published, I reread a story by the incandescent R.A. Lafferty and was horrified to learn that, unknowingly, two of the story's three main ideas had been stolen wholesale. This phenomenon," he explains, of "being unable to remember which stories are yours and which belong to someone else happens frequently among high-output writers and is probably unavoidable to some degree." However, he declares, "that's certainly no reason to compound the unintentional plagiarism by reprinting the story here." As with "The Last Rumble of the Platinum Horde" and Spinrad, Moore ends by suggesting readers track down some Lafferty, calling him the better writer.

Moore revisited the issue in a later interview, explaining how "just occasionally you'll come up with an idea and you'll think, 'That's brilliant! That's a great idea! It must be mine!' And you don't recognize it as, 'Now, wait a moment, that's a story that I've read by somebody else.'" He notes that he publicly admitted the incident and asked for the story not to be reprinted, and explained that "when you're having to write to deadlines and turn out a lot of stories, you have to think fast. And maybe if I'd had a couple more days, I'd have remembered the R.A. Lafferty story," but that instead it was "only some weeks later" that he realized the problem. Interestingly, in this interview he goes on to criticize a Man Booker Prize-winner whose book, it was pointed out, "was actually William Faulkner's *As I Lay Dying*, right down to the structure of the individual chapters," taking a dim view of the author's defense that it was an homage, and noting that "these things happen, but once it happens once or twice or whatever, you have to become a lot stricter on yourself." [Moore, in the interview, misidentifies the book as James Kellman's 1994 prize-winning *How Late it Was, How Late*—in fact the book in question is the 1996 winner, Graham Swift's *Last Orders.*]

All of this raises an interesting issue within the War, however. Much of the conflict within the War, after all, comes from various creative priority disputes between Moore and Morrison. As the War develops, a major concern will be

Moore's late-career disdain both for working on properties he does not himself own and his outrage at projects like *Before Watchmen* that make use of his ideas. Given this, the existence of a plagiarism issue early in Moore's career is interesting, not least because of the opportunities it offers Moore's adversaries in the War to cry hypocrisy and let slip the dogs of internet commentary.

It is first worth actually looking at the similarities. Contrary to Moore's recollection, the story in question is not in fact from an anthology of Lafferty's work, but from his 1968 novel *Space Chantey*, which presents a sci-fi adventure modeled after *The Odyssey*. The fourth chapter of this book features Captain Roadstrum, the lead character of the work, using a device that lets him rewind time slightly to cheat at gambling. Eventually he becomes a multi-billionaire, as well as an emperor who owns a thousand different worlds, only to lose it all to a restroom attendant as he attempts to get the attendant to give him a piece of toilet paper with the Emperor's Crest on it, for which the attendant wants a single coin. Roadstrum, determined not to pay [despite his massive wealth] proceeds to get involved in a series of double or nothing bets despite not having his time-rewinding device on him, and this eventually bankrupts him, and indeed leaves him twenty-four worlds in debt to the attendant, who is said to "still own those worlds today. He is High Emperor and he administers his worlds competently. He is a man of talent."

Moore's story, on the other hand, features Abelard Snazz being rescued from certain death by Hoolio Moolabar, who has recently lost his life savings at a casino. Snazz contrives to help him by creating a small time machine in the chest cavity of his robotic servant Edwin and uses it in the same manner that Lafferty's character does—to rewind time at the casino and thus win games with foreknowledge of what will happen. When it comes time to go, however, the doorman declines to get their spaceship, citing house rules against it. Snazz proceeds to make a bet with him, but, unable to rewind time because Edwin is off getting drunk with a robotic dancer, proceeds to lose everything in an ever-escalating game of double or nothing. Moolabar, having lost all of his money again, rewinds time to before he rescues Snazz and Edwin and leaves them once again to die.

There are, to be fair, differences between the stories. Lafferty's story makes no indication of how the restroom attendant is so lucky, whereas Moore's is shown to have an "Acme Probability Scrambler" that explains why the coin flip always comes out heads. Moore's story, on the other hand, lacks the rather charming detail of high-roller gamblers playing for planets instead of just for money, and indeed also lacks the bizarre cast of gamblers that Roadstrum faces down such as "Johnny Greeneyes, who could see every invisible marking on cards with his odd optics," and "Pyotr Igrokovitch," who, "following heavy losses in his youth… shot himself through the head." Whenever Pyotr loses he shoots himself again, though always through the same passage. "It was rather a weird thing when seen by one for the first time," Lafferty writes, "and Pyotr very often killed spectators standing behind him."

But these are small details. Moore is on the whole correct—"The Return of the Two-Storey Brain" is a fairly straightforward lift of an incident out of *Space Chantey*. That details are changed does not ultimately distract from the fact that Moore wrote a story with the same basic effect as Lafferty's—someone has a clever but dishonest idea and gets their comeuppance by being overly arrogant to the wrong person. This in and of itself is not a problem—every Abelard Snazz story has a plot along these lines. The problem is that Moore runs the plot in the same setting—a sci-fi casino—and with the same dishonest idea. Unlike his inadvertent overlap with Spinrad, where the two writers ended up with stories that are as different as two stories using the iconography of the Mongol hordes to make a comment on the hollowness of violence could plausibly be, here Moore is working with the same basic images as another writer and trying to produce the same basic effect.

Figure 62: Abelaard Snazz, who Moore designed specifically to be unnerving to look at. (Art by Steve Dillon)

Figure 63: A parking lot attendant thwarts Abelard Snazz's get-rich scheme in a plot twist inadvertently nicked from R.A. Lafferty. (From "The Return of the Two-Storey Brain," in 2000 AD #209, written by Alan Moore, art by Mike White, 1981)

Figure 64: "Bad Timing" is a spoof of Superman's origin story that ends in the Earth's destruction. (From 2000 AD #291, written by Alan Moore, art by Mike White, 1982)

This marks a useful line in trying to understand how influence works. None of Moore's stories, nor indeed anyone's stories, exist in a vacuum devoid of influence. "The Regrettable Ruse of Rocket Redglare," for instance, is transparently modeled off of Flash Gordon, just as the later "Bad Timing" is expressly based around Superman. But the entire point of the story is that it's taking the Flash Gordon style of story and twisting it into a cynically entertaining parody of itself. The problem with "The Return of the Two-Storey Brain" isn't that it shares so many concepts with Lafferty, but that it does nothing with those concepts that Lafferty hadn't already done, and indeed, recreates his central premise. In this regard it is markedly different from even the work of Moore's that most obviously takes concepts from other writers, which can almost never be described as an imitation of those writers. Moore's sense of an obligation to be stricter on himself in future work is one that he appears to have taken quite seriously.

It is also worth reiterating that the shared point between *Space Chantey* and "The Return of the Two-Storey Brain" is one that is central to Abelard Snazz in general. This does not, however, imply that Snazz is in any way a rip-off character. Indeed, Snazz is a satisfyingly original concept, and the fact that what constituted a satisfying incident in *Space Chantey* and what constituted a satisfying Abelard Snazz story were similar is largely coincidental.

Snazz, for his part, made his first appearance ten progs prior to "The Return of the Two-Storey Brain" in the first part of a two-part *Ro-Jaws Robo-Tale* called "Final Solution" that marked Moore's fourth contribution to *2000 AD*. The story concerns a planet on which crime has gotten completely out of control. In desperation, the Prime Minister turns to Abelard Snazz, whose distinctive double decker brain means that he has two stacked sets of eyes. Snazz promptly designs giant police robots, who proceed to eliminate crime, only to then go on arresting people for comically minor infractions like breaking the laws of etiquette by using the wrong spoon.

Desperate to stop this latest calamity, the planet turns to Snazz again, and he creates criminal robots for the police robots to arrest. Which is all well and good until people get caught in the crossfire between the robots, leading Snazz to propose robotic civilians to get caught in the crossfire instead. At this point the planet becomes too crowded for human habitation and everyone flees, pausing only to jettison Snazz and his fawning robotic companion Edwin out the airlock before they can get too far on their idea for a robotic planet.

The central joke of "Final Solution" is one about technocracy and the tendency of people in charge to favor overly elaborate and engineered solutions. More broadly, it's an indictment of the same logic behind what Moore's later-career collaborator Iain Sinclair describes as grand projects. Sinclair's beloved bugbear is of course the 2012 London Olympics, but they are for him only the biggest image of "the grand project of New Labour and lottery money," which he describes as "top-heavy schemes <that> are imposed down from the top" in the name of "a legacy that offers little more than what was there already." Describing the Olympics, Sinclair notes that "the games are just empty buildings," but that this is functional because people are used to living among ruins. Of the grand project, Sinclair says, "They were just ruins. They were never anything else." This sense of hollowness describes Snazz's scheme as well—the replacement of progressively more aspects of society with robot duplicates until society itself is crowded out.

"I actually had plans. We had just sort of opened up very, very preliminary negotiations to find out if Gorey would be interested in illustrating it. And the day I finished it, he died. I mean literally. I finished it and the news was that Edward Gorey died."
–Neil Gaiman, on *Coraline*

But it's a mistake to treat Snazz as the sole culprit of the piece. Yes, Snazz exists to satirize over-elaborate top-down thinking, but it's important to note that Snazz is merely a consultant working for the government—a government that never once pipes up to say, "Wouldn't just decommissioning the robot cops make more sense?" or "Why don't we reprogram the buggers so they don't arrest people for wearing ugly ties?" just as in "The Return of the Two-Storey Brain" Hoolio Moolabar never steps in to say, "Erm, why don't we just go get the car instead of betting every penny we have with the doorman?" Snazz, in other words, is not so much a villain as a parodic version of a particular societal tendency that allows people like him to function in the first place.

Moore, reflecting on Snazz, rejects the idea that Snazz works because he's "a symbol of irresponsible science run amok, a sort of boffo Frankenstein," noting that "anybody who can bring about the downfall of entire civilizations armed only with good intentions can't be *all* bad," and that "he is nowhere near as irredeemably stupid as the people who listen to him."

This tendency is reinforced by the later Snazz stories, which focus less on the preposterous schemes Snazz comes up with and more on the sorts of places Snazz ends up. For instance, the fourth Abelaard Snazz story, "Halfway to Paradise," has Snazz acting as an image consultant to a variety of gods [including a lisping Thoth whose name, it is thus implied, might actually be pronounced the same as "sauce"], and the next story, two months later, features him building giant robot tennis players for a bunch of parodic Californians under the title "The Multi-Storey Mind Mellows Out." [Moore notes that there is "nothing that really compares with the sublime pinnacle of creative ecstasy that I experienced upon coining the phrase 'Jog for your life'."] In both stories Snazz's scheme is hardly the focus—it's not even flawed, as such, in "Halfway to Paradise." Instead the point is to show new sorts of people stupid enough to listen to Snazz.

That is not, of course, to say that Snazz is above reproach. A recurring theme in the Abelard Snazz stories is Snazz's arrogance. As early as "The Return of the Two-Storey Brain," Snazz is compounding his troubles with hubris. It's

Figure 65: The sublime pinnacle of creative ecstasy. (From "The Multi-Storey mind Mellows Out," in 2000 AD #254, written by Alan Moore, art by Paul Neary, 1982)

Figure 66: An elaborate crossover among Moore's 2000 AD work. (From "The Double-Decker Dome Strikes Back, in 2000 AD #237, written by Alan Moore, art by Mike White, 1981)

not any flaw in his scheme that leads to his bankruptcy, but rather his insistence that a man as rich as he is shouldn't have to get his own car. Likewise, in the next Snazz misadventure, "The Double-Decker Dome Strikes Back," Snazz's scheme only falls apart when his scheme to use the good will of the Farbian Crottle Worms, described as "the most saintly and good-natured beings in known space," to power the machinery of the Farbians [a people whose culture consists entirely of their own self pity—they are first depicted rowing a space ship as they sing, "Our crops won't grow / our cattle are starving / and we owe money to our in-laws. / Our shoes do not fit / But we have lost the receipt / Maybe tomorrow will be better, but frankly we doubt it." The explanation for their misery is revealed in a narrated section that describes how their previous homeworlds were flattened by the Platinum Horde, invaded by Grawks, and wiped out by a Rigelian cleaner as depicted in "They Sweep the Spaceways," another early instance of Moore indulging in crossovers amongst his creations] falls apart when he reacts angrily to the Farbians praising the worms, declaring that "if it hadn't been for me those greasy little glory-grabbers would still be baiting fish-hooks!" This, it turns out, is finally enough to piss the crottle worms off, and their good will evaporates, dooming Snazz.

A similar plot unfolds in "Genius is Pain," the final Snazz story, which spends three pages and change acting as though Snazz has been put on trial for his various crimes, which are listed off in great detail, only to have it turn out that he's been summoned to celebrate his six millionth birthday. His present for reaching this ripe old age [mainly through long periods of time spent in extra-dimensional pocket universes or suspended animation] is "the one gift that will make you happier than anything in the world," which, in the eyes of the Manager of the Universe, turns out to be just a reconstructed Edwin, who proceeds to repeat his one meaningful line, praising Snazz's genius, as Snazz angrily beats the poor robot. The story serves not only to emphasize the myriad of properly awful things Snazz has been responsible for, but to show the degree to which Snazz is a selfish boor. And yet even here, the reader is forced to admit that Edwin was somewhat annoyingly fawning, and Moore admits that he'd killed him off at the start of "The Double-Decker Dome Strikes Back" "before he had the chance to become tiresome." Snazz remains, at least, comical in his malignancy, a satisfyingly entertaining mirror of society's worst impulses.) This is perhaps unfair, however—"The Last Rumble of the Platinum Horde" may hinge on a fairly predictable twist, but equally, the story does have a reasonably sharp edge, encapsulating all the supposed glories of war and empire in an embittered joke. The ending, in which the Platinum Horde, lacking any better ideas, sets off once again is particularly cutting.

In other stories, however, Moore evaded the twist ending structure outright. "They Sweep the Spaceways," for instance, does not even have a plot as such, little yet a twist at the end. It's an example of what Moore describes as "a list story, in which you just think of an absurd topic or situation and then list as many funny or engaging ideas as you can relate to it." A list story does not necessarily have to be plotless—the one Moore coined the term to describe, the later "Sunburn" from Prog 282 in September of 1982, is ostensibly the story of Rorschach Skubbs, who has killed his wife and is attempting to dispose of the body, only to end up perishing. But this is in practice just an excuse for a chase across Moore's setting for the story, a holiday camp on the sun, where Moore can unveil various jokes: pallor-parlours "where the fashionable go to lose their suntans," asbestos-based clothing, lava surfers who shout "magma's up," and so forth.

"They Sweep the Spaceways," however, lacks even this meager narrative frame. It consists merely of a description of the job of inter-galactic janitor, a role best performed by the Rigelians, who are larger than suns. "Like all Rigellians, Quargol"—the example janitor of the piece—"has an almost indefinite lifespan. This is just as well, as Quargol's working

Figure 67: "They Sweep the Spaceways" ended with a humorous job application for the cosmic janitorial position it describes. (From 2000 AD #219, written by Alan Moore, art by Garry Leach, 1981)

Figure 68: The giddily macabre antics of Timothy Tate, Moore's contribution to a long and glorious literary tradition of gruesome rhymes about children. (From "A Cautionary Fable" in 2000 AD #240, written by Alan Moore, art by Paul Neary, 1981)

'day' is over eight million years long." Quargol is a mildly grumpy working class janitor who spackles over black holes, replaces burnt out suns, and tries to kill off outbreaks of "that most virulent of galactic pests—civilization." The piece ends, after a fairly transparent bit of product placement for "Big Bang," described by Quargol as "the new miracle cleaning fluid" that "destroys 99.999% of all known civilizations," with a card that the reader can fill out to apply for the job, which, Moore notes, many readers did, even checking the box claiming that they were over 870,000 miles tall. Moore jokingly describes the story as "a calculated attempt to incite the working class population of this country to full scale revolution by rubbing their noses in their joblessness," which, hyperbole aside, gets at the point of the story, which is to juxtapose vast cosmic phenomena and sci-fi iconography with menial working class drudgery. Its effectiveness is, on the whole, only increased by the structural innovation of avoiding a plot altogether.

The last story in Moore's early run of hits, "A Cautionary Fable," is similarly playful with structure. It tells "the tale of Timothy Tate, a child too vile to contemplate." Tate is a glutton, who goes from standard-issue excessive appetite to the point where "he'd munch, with unashamed glee, through carpets and upholstery, and household pets too slow to flee would often vanish utterly." Eventually he encounters a UFO landing, eats the aliens, and grows to monstrous size, at which point he begins eating people and buildings in the course of an urban rampage. Eventually he topples from the spire of a skyscraper, plummeting to his death, at which point "Mr. Horace Bloggs of Forebone's Food for Healthy Dogs" shows up to clear his carcass. "We dare not show what hideous fate befell the shell of Timmy Tate," the story ends, macabrely, "but happy pets, in sated bliss, still lick their chops and reminisce."

As the quotes show, the defining feature of the story is that it's told in rhyme, featuring distinct phrases consisting of four iambic or anapestal feet in an AABB rhyme scheme, positioned beneath Paul Neary's illustrations, which manage to evoke a combination of classic Victorian children's literature and a giddy sense of the grotesque. The approach is simple—it is essentially, as Moore describes it, "Hilaire Belloc for the eighties," and uses the same meter, rhyme scheme, and, more to the point, perversity as Belloc's *Cautionary Tales for Children* (for instance, "Jim, Who Ran Away from his Nurse and was Eaten by a Lion," has his final fate described thusly: "The lion having reached his Head, / The Miserable Boy was dead!"), only with a lightly sci-fi twist appropriate for *2000 AD*. As with most of Moore's successful *Future Shocks*, the appeal is largely in the choice of subjects to contrast, mixing together two types of narratives in order to produce surprising effects.

None of these stories are great and major works by Alan Moore. But there is only so much that a bespoke four-to-six page humor piece can accomplish, and Moore's 1981 *Future Shocks* by and large sit comfortably at the upper limits of that. Certainly they were far above the standard set by Moore's contemporaries. One of the other major contributors of *Future Shocks* in 1981 was Kelvin Gosnell, whose short stories were barely coherent. "The Sound of Silence," in Prog 207, is indicative. It features a man being driven to distraction by the overly loud music of his neighbors, prompting him to invent a machine that cancels out all sound. He, for no reason set up anywhere in the preceding two-and-a-half pages, proceeds to use his machine to embark on a life of crime. Predictably, he gets caught and ends up sharing a cell with the son of the overly loud family who kicked off the story—a family that had been utterly unmentioned in the story at any point after the main character turned to a life of crime. The story ostensibly has the same sort of elliptical shape that Moore's twist endings do, but without any of the actual work put into setting it up. The twist is, in effect, that the part of the story that was casually thrown away at the halfway point to be replaced with a completely different story comes back. And this is par for the course for Gosnell—three issues later he offers "The Collector," which proceeds through three pages of generic war story featuring American pilots in the Vietnam War before revealing that the pilot of a mysterious unmarked plane is in fact the devil and that the pilots are all dead. It is not that this is a bad twist so much as that nothing whatsoever in the first three pages even remotely sets it up.

Gosnell is perhaps an easy target (and it should be noted that Gosnell's writing elsewhere is much more capable), but even other writers of repute floundered on the *Future Shocks*. Steve Moore and Peter Milligan both penned *Future Shocks* in 1981, and while they lacked the aggressive incompetence of Gosnell's writing, they also lacked the creative panache of Moore's stories. In a magazine like *2000 AD*, where the appeal is often more in the quality of the concepts than in the execution as such, this is a significant flaw. Moore is essentially the only writer of *Future Shocks* who used them to try to come up with arresting ideas while also focusing on tight, disciplined storytelling. Moore, indeed, used these stories to push and challenge himself. This did not always work out—also from this period is "Southern Comfort" in the 1981 *Sci-Fi Special*, a strip that Moore had his name taken off of (it went out instead under the rather bitter name of R.E. Wright) due to his dissatisfaction with the finished art by Walter Howarth. Identifying exactly what went wrong is tricky—Moore, in interviews, refers discretely to "a guy who obviously has enough problems already." But the strip Moore describes trying to write—one spurred by editor Steve McManus who, "in an ingenious attempt to curb the flow of shimmering and lucid metaphor that I used to give the humblest caption box a certain poetry and élan, asked me to do a two-part story without captions." What went wrong between Moore's script, which he describes as "a superb Swiss-precision piece of Graphic Narrative," and the finished product, which uses repeated caption boxes, is not entirely clear, although given Howarth's art one suspects it is simply that the script as drawn was not capable of telling its story without Moore (or someone) adding numerous captions to explain what the plot was supposed to be. Still, for all that the strip failed, it's telling that Moore was so willing to experiment in the first place.

That he stood out for doing so only emphasizes the truth, which is that *2000 AD* was largely setting a low bar for Moore to clear. Yes, "The English/Phlondrutian Phrasebook" is terribly clever, but its stablemates include forgettable pap like *Meltdown Man* (A SAS officer, who's been transported to the future in a nuclear explosion, fights to liberate the humanoid animals of the future from their evil human captors) and *Return to Armageddon* (a prequel to the Book of Genesis featuring space pirates; it's nowhere near as good as that sounds). Mere competence was enough to be the third-best strip in Prog 214. Admittedly the other two strips in that issue—an installment of a lengthy *Judge Dredd* series called "The Mega-Rackets," and the twelfth part of the sprawling *Strontium Dog* origin story "Portrait of a Mutant"—can credibly be called classics of the magazine. "Portrait of a Mutant" has a reasonably entertaining sci-fi concept—guns that send their target back a few minutes into the past, at which point the Earth has hurtled forward in space, leaving the target dead in the vacuum, and *Judge Dredd* features the ever-popular conceit of Umpty Candy. But neither are particular high points. "Portrait of a Mutant" is terribly long, and the twelfth part is an exercise in getting the plot from point A to point B. And *Judge Dredd*, though good, is doing nothing the strip hadn't done in its two-hundred-and-twelve previous iterations. Shining brightly among such competition is not something any comics writer could do, but equally, it doesn't take the best of the best to flourish.

It is important, however, to understand why one would want to flourish on these stories. The purpose of *Future Shocks* is, after all, straightforward. As Grant Morrison put it in a 1989 interview, "There's a sort of apprenticeship—you're forced to do *Future Shocks* (notoriously tedious one-off filler sci-fi stories)." In Morrison's account, "They usually get you to do two years of work on those before you're let loose on a proper strip." But for Morrison, at least, the process was accelerated—he would only toil on *Future Shocks* for a year or so, penning sixteen before being given *Zenith*. Moore, meanwhile, waited from July of 1980 until March of 1983, over two-and-a-half years, in which he penned thirty-six short stories, at which point he was finally honored with the thrilling brief of creating a clone of *E.T.*—before the movie actually came out. Had Moore been given the year-long apprenticeship Morrison would eventually get, he'd have moved on to a regular series around the time of "They Sweep the Spaceways."

Instead he was left on *Future Shocks* long after his best ideas had visibly been used. Indeed, the transition point where Moore's ideas run out is unnervingly clear. After a run of six brilliant strips punctuated by a couple of Abelard Snazz stories and the unfortunate business of "Southern Comfort," Moore ended 1981 with "Mister Could You Use a Squonge," in which satisfyingly hideous-looking alien life-forms nicknamed Squonges turn out to grant profound intelligence to anyone who wears them. The twist ending—that the Squonges were all completely insane and drove their wearers uselessly mad—is largely flat, and the story has a curious lack of point. This is not in and of itself significant—any writer, given a massive number of short stories to write—will turn out a few duds. But "Mister Could You Use a Squonge" still marks the end of the period in which Moore would reliably score a hit every time.

In many ways this comes down to a simple matter of numbers. In 1981 Moore penned nine strips for *2000 AD*. In 1982 he penned twenty-one, a rate that meant he appeared in nearly half of the fifty-two issues of *2000 AD* published that year. Yes, many of his 1982 strips were comparatively shorter two-pagers, but the sheer volume of output in 1982 almost necessarily came at the expense of quality. It is not, however, that this middle period was devoid of good stories. Prog 247's "Salad Days," for instance, spends two pages getting more mileage than would seem possible out of a pun whereby a bunch of alien vegetables eat humans because they are "humanitarians." Prog 278's "Hot Item" is an effective list story about the heat death of the universe in which numerous jokes are made about the lack of any sort of energy available such that small distances take enormous amounts of time to cross. ("It's no good! They've put centimetres between us while we've been nattering!") The story's ending, in which the energy crisis is forestalled by the discovery of old issues of *2000 AD* whose thrill-power "never wanes nor grows dim" and "will give our people all the energy they need for years to come" is perhaps more than a little self-serving, but the story still sparkles. And Prog 252's "American Werewolf in Space," in which what looks like it will be a blood-soaked yarn about a werewolf massacring people on a spaceship turns into a bizarre farce when it's revealed that the entire two-thousand person crew of the *Hermes* are all werewolves, and the entire mission was just an excuse to jettison the werewolves from the planet, is improbably inventive.

"We have camera eyes that speed up, slow down, and even reverse the flow of time, allowing us to see what no one prior to the twentieth century had ever seen — the thermodynamic miracle of broken shards and a puddle gathering themselves up from the floor to assemble a half-full wineglass."
–Grant Morrison, *Supergods*, 2012

But many other stories in the period are flat at best. "A Second Chance," a two-pager in which the last man on Earth finds a woman, is utterly devoid of any point. "All of Them Were Empty," in which a siege on a American truck stop is revealed to be conducted by sentient cars wanting a fill-up, is similarly uninspiring, as is "No Picnic," in which a man is buried alive on Easter Island to become one of the famed heads. And when Moore did hit gold, it was often by rehashing his own previous work. One of his best stories of 1982, "The Wages of Sin," is a redo of "They Sweep the Spaceways," this time focusing on the training that would-be galactic conquerors go through. It's not that it's a pale imitation of "They Sweep the Spaceways." In fact, its jokes are a step sharper, and the art by Bryan Talbot is superlative. But it's still just a refinement of an earlier strip.

For the most part this stretch of Moore's work is characterized by a heavy reliance on straightforward twist endings. Some of these are reasonably clever—"The Beastly Beliefs of Benjamin Blint" for instance, uses the basic twist of the classic *Twilight Zone* episode "The Eye of the Beholder," whereby the eponymous Benjamin Blint tells his therapist about the horrible creature that periodically appears to him. The strip shows several such encounters, between a typically square-jawed man and a suitably horrible looking creature. The final panel reveals that Blint is in fact the monstrous creature, haunted by the "hideous" ordinary human, who Blint finally admits can't possibly be real, because "there just isn't room in the real world for creatures as stomach-turning and loathsome as that." "The Bounty Hunters," four issues later, is a similarly straightforward twist ending—soldiers hunting a homicidal shape-changing alien grow increasingly jumpy, suspecting the planet's foliage, each other, and even the planet itself of being the alien. Eventually they admit defeat and return to their ship, which promptly devours them, having been the alien all along.

Both of these stories are broadly competent, but they are straight-laced twist ending stories with little to trade on other than the hope that their twist is clever. In practice, it usually was, or at least clever enough to work. If anything, Moore was likely to end up being a bit too clever, as in the straightforwardly named "Twist Ending," in which a writer is interviewed by a journalist who is convinced the writer is secretly an alien. The eponymous twist ending is that while the writer is not an alien, his typewriter is in fact a sentient alien life form who is the real author of works like "Invasion of the Death Gerbils." It makes about as much sense as one would expect, and, given the title, seems almost a deliberate mockery of the twist ending formula for *Future Shocks*.

But mock the format as he might have, the truth is that Moore was largely unable to escape it in this period. Indeed, it's telling that Moore's tendency to self-plagiarize extended to duplicating the same idea within 1982. "Return of the Thing," in Prog 265, uses almost the exact same twist as "The Beastly Beliefs of Benjamin Blint," this time having a strip that appears to be about a woman cowering in horror as a massive alien monster lumbers into her house, only to have it turn out that her concern was simply that she hadn't finished making dinner yet, and that the alien is in fact her husband returning home. It's clever, but it's also the second time in sixteen weeks that Moore has relied on the trick of having what appears to be a monster in fact be something else. And it's a not entirely clear or coherent strip either—it's never quite clear why the husband enters his house by kicking the door down, for instance.

But Moore's stagnation is wholly understandable. The same month as "The Wages of Sin" came out, he picked up two regular strips in *Warrior* #1. *Warrior* was a young upstart of a magazine (hence it turning to largely untested talent for two of its launch titles), but it quickly established itself as a critical darling, and Moore's career accelerated. As he puts it, "Once *2000 AD* and Marvel knew I was being given series work by somebody else, they became more inclined to give me series work as well." But this isn't quite true. Yes, Marvel UK gave him *Captain Britain* three months after *Warrior* #1. But IPC spent an entire year letting Moore write two-pagers about things like an exploration of a brick wall discovered at the edge of the universe that turns out to have some message written on it, which, after considerable effort, is revealed to be graffiti reading "Big George rules, OK?" By the time they got around to offering him *Skizz*, he was on the cusp of winning his first Eagle award. (That year's awards would prove quite a rebuke to IPC, who were essentially shut out. Brian Bolland's victory as best artist was cold comfort, given that he had by that time made the jump to US comics, which meant that the only award they won was "Character Most

Worthy of Own Title" for Judge Anderson. Another way to put it, of course, is that IPC's only win was for what people wished they were doing instead of what they were doing. The rest of the awards went to *Warrior*, most notably to Alan Moore for his work on *Marvelman*.)

Nor was IPC particularly interested in utilizing Moore elsewhere in its stable of magazines. The only other place it found to house Moore's work was in their revived version of *Eagle*, where he contributed a pair of fumetti—"Trash!" and "Profits of Doom"—under the banner of *The Collector*, which provided *Future Shocks*-style short stories about various horrible and supernatural fates befalling collectors of things. The former story concerns a man who throws out all of his grandmother's papers and memories in a pique, only to be killed when the papers reincarnate in her house and drown him. The latter features a collector who cheats a man out of a valuable comic, which turns out to have never been actually published. The collector reads of himself in the comic, and is promptly eaten by tentacles from within it. The two stories are among the most ephemeral and marginal work of Moore's career, and show the degree to which IPC mostly used him for disposable filler.

This is one of the points where the overlapping chronology of Moore's early work obscures the actual narrative, however. It is true that *2000 AD* was among the first professional work Moore did as a pure writer—"Killer in the Cab" came out two weeks into *Business As Usual* for *Doctor Who Weekly*. But other than publishing there early on, essentially none of Moore's big breaks took place in the magazine. Far from being Moore's big break at long-form storytelling, *Skizz* was in fact the fourth ongoing strip he'd written, post-dating *V for Vendetta* and *Marvelman* by an entire year. In this light, Moore's middle-period work for *2000 AD* takes on a new tone. Moore—always confident of his abilities (as early as 1984 he was willing to casually proclaim that there were "maybe a dozen people in the Western world who know as much or more than I do about writing comics," although he clarified that "this says more about the paucity of the medium than it does about my personal talents")—must have chafed looking at Prog 240 and realizing that "A Cautionary Fable" wasn't going to lead to him getting a regular strip because the magazine would rather give that honor to Tom Tully, who was busily penning the barely readable *The Mean Arena*. (To be fair to IPC, it is not clear they had a choice. Artist Robin Smith recalls that "Tully was one of those blokes who had this deal whereby they were entitled to have a story in so many titles," meaning that, in effect, cancelling one of Tully's numerous banal series was a pointless endeavor, as it would have to be replaced by another Tom Tully story.)

To be crowded out by lesser writers even as Moore visibly proved himself with other companies can only have been a frustrating experience, especially given that *2000 AD* was a magazine Moore had such regard for and so wanted to succeed at. And when IPC finally offered Moore a strip, it was as a sop after he pitched a *Judge Dredd* spin-off to be called *Badlander*. In other words, instead of being promoted on the basis of his talent, Moore was given a derisory promotion only when it was clear that he was agitating for one and unsatisfied with toiling on *Future Shocks*.

Regardless, acquiring his first regular strip for *2000 AD* had demonstrable benefits for Moore's writing, not least because it coincided with a new sort of short story format for the magazine focused primarily on time travel, called *Time Twisters*. In some ways this turn was prefigured earlier—one of Moore's better 1982 stories was "The Disturbed Digestions of Doctor Dibworthy," a three-pager with art by Dave Gibbons in which Doctor Dibworthy, staring at a piece of paper, feels himself on the verge of a great insight, at which point a horde of future versions of himself show up to implore him not to invent the time machine he's about to come up with the idea for. Eventually, in horror, Dibworthy throws out the piece of paper, only to find himself on the verge of a similar insight in the flow patterns of his glass of port. As is typical of Moore/Gibbons collaborations in *2000*

AD, the story is a comedy, and Gibbons's propensity for detail enables several panels of a small crowd of Dibworthys, all with suitably unique facial expressions and postures. But unlike many of Moore's other short stories in 1982, there's an undercurrent of deeper poignancy and horror to the story, and the twist ending, rather than being funny, is ever so slightly unnerving. In any case, Moore liked the character enough to bring him back in a proper *Time Twisters* ten months later, in which he continually attempts to change the past, only to be disappointed by his apparent failure when, in reality, his memories change with the past and he fails to notice the profound differences in the room around him as he makes increasingly drastic alterations, starting with murdering an "obscure Turkish diplomat in 1057 A.D." and escalating to killing King John prior to signing the Magna Carta and preventing the invention of the Steam Engine. The story ends with Dibworthy preventing the Big Bang, and being disappointed when "nothing happened. Nothing at all."

But while the first Dibworthy story shows the broad potential of what Moore could do when writing about time, it's not until Prog 308 in March of 1983 that the renaissance of Moore's later *2000 AD* work truly kicks off. That issue contained both the first installment of *Skizz*, and his first proper *Time Twister*, a four-pager called "The Reversible Man." This is, by most reckonings, also one of his best stories. The premise is simple enough—it's just the events of a perfectly ordinary man's life, only told in reverse so that his first memory is of getting up off the pavement, feeling a sharp pain, and then walking backwards with an ice cream cone that reforms and jumps up into his hand. As he walks he explains how "ice cream seemed to be dribbling off my tongue and re-filling the cone in my hand." The story progresses as he gets bored of retirement and gets an office job ("the manager smiled and stole my gold watch," he notes), disinters an old woman (his mother, in fact) from the cemetery and takes her to the hospital where she slowly recovers and moves in with him, watches as his children grow young and finally go off to the hospital with their mother, never to return, marries his wife (and thus has to move out), goes back to school ("it was very pleasant forgetting things that had never been any use to me, like Latin and chemistry," he notes, with Moore's relish at the line positively dripping off the page), and finally becomes an infant, at which point he's slapped on the back and stops breathing.

Moore has commented of the story that it was "pathetically easy to write," and that he was resultantly surprised by its reception, speculating that its popularity was because "the events of our lives become dulled by repetition and it takes an unusual view of them for us to see life and its emotional implications anew," disclaiming that the story's success "had very little to do with me as a writer." This is, perhaps, false modesty, however—elsewhere he proclaims it "one of the best stories I've ever done," and boasts of how "during their lunch hour, the day that came out, it had all the secretaries weeping." But even in that interview, where he breathlessly describes the emotional effect of how "an ordinary little scene of two people meeting, their first meeting... becomes their final departure," he suggests that the story came mainly out of his inclination to "do something to see what will happen" and to experiment within the confines of the format.

"The flood of animal emotions surging in the street. Present desires precipitated. Curdled to sea foam."
–Alan Moore, *The Highbury Working*, 1997

The story may have been straightforward to write, but the suggestion that there is no writerly skill involved in its success is clearly untrue. Much of the story's power comes not just from the way in which it frames the events of a man's life, but in the specific choices of what events to frame and how to frame them. For instance, when the narrator's father is dug up and brought to the hospital and eventually goes home, the narrator's mother, understandably, moves out to live with her newly un-dead husband. The narration describes how "they took several of our things with them to furnish their home. Mostly antique furniture. We didn't mind." The choice of the furniture as a detail for this reversed event—the death of the narrator's father—is a carefully chosen one. There are many things that accompany the death of a parent, but the choice of a mundane, material thing like dealing with their old furniture is a well-chosen one, such that the word "antiques" speaks volumes. Similarly, the description of how "work got progressively easier and I had to give less and less money to the firm every Friday night" is not the only way that one could describe reversing one's career path, but it's a particularly sharp one, preserving the sense of frustrating drudgery even in reverse.

More to the point, Moore's claim that "The Reversible Man" was "a classic example of one of those stories that just lie around waiting for someone to trip over them and commit them to paper" overlooks the fact that he is neither the first nor the last writer to tackle this basic idea. In 1922, F. Scott Fitzgerald wrote a similar story with "The Curious Case of Benjamin Button," and mentioned in the introduction that after writing the story he saw a similar idea in Samuel Butler's notebooks. This is a reference to some notes Butler wrote for his 1872 novel *Erewhon* (which is widely considered the first work to think seriously about the possibility of artificial intelligence), where he suggested that the people of Erewhon might "live their lives backwards, beginning, as old men and women, with little more knowledge of the past than we have of the future, and foreseeing the future about as clearly as we see the past, winding up by entering into the womb as though being buried. But delicacy forbids me to pursue this subject further: the upshot is that it comes to much the same thing, provided one is used to it." The idea also appears in T.H. White's *The Once and Future King*, a revisioning of Arthurian legend first published in 1938, in which Merlin lives backwards in time. And after Moore the idea had life as well—Martin Amis won a Man Booker Prize in 1991 with

*Figure 69: The narrator of "The Reversible Man" meets his wife in reverse.
(From* 2000 AD *#308, written by Alan Moore, art by Mike White, 1983)*

*Figure 70: One of the most astonishingly bleak panels in Moore's early career.
(From "One Christmas During Eternity," in* 2000 AD *#271, written by
Alan Moore, art by Redondo, 1982)*

Time's Arrow, a novel that uses the same basic premise. And, of course, there are the films *Memento* and *Irréversible*, which tell their narratives backwards, even though the characters do not experience them that way.

All of this points to the fact that Moore's story works not just because he executed a reasonably common idea, but because he did it well. Likewise, Martin Amis didn't win a Man Booker Prize for nicking an obscure old idea out of a boys comics magazine, but because he chose as the subject for his backwards life a doctor who worked at Auschwitz, describing how he helped create a race, the Jews: first he created their bodies in ovens and animated them in fake showers, then he personally removed Zyklon B pellets from their flesh, and finally, for many, perfected their dental work, given freely from his own personal supplies of gold to craft fillings for them. "I *knew* my gold had a sacred efficacy," the narrator enthuses. "All those years I amassed it, and polished it with my mind: for the Jews' teeth." This shocking inversion of the Holocaust, where all of the degradations and atrocities become acts of life-giving kindness, gives it new power to horrify by creating a new and startlingly perverse perspective to look at them, much as Moore inverts the major events of life to fill them with new poignancy. The suggestion that this potency comes merely from the idea and not the particulars of the execution is demonstrably false.

But the power of "The Reversible Man" is also worth looking at in context with another fact: it is only the second short story Moore wrote for *2000 AD* that cannot plausibly be described as a comedy. In the previous two-and-a-half years of writing strips for the magazine, the only other time he did something decisively non-comedic came in July of 1982, when in Prog 271 he penned "One Christmas During Eternity"—a bleak number about a family of immortals celebrating Christmas with their son, in which it turns out that the son is a robot they rented for the day and had to return, and that they do not even get the same robot year-to-year. Both stories are elevated by the fact that they have ambitions beyond merely demonstrating a clever idea. "The Reversible Man" does not merely stand out in contrast to the rest of Moore's short stories, though—its quiet poignancy marks it out from the rest of *2000 AD*. In Prog 308 the other stories were: a story in which an alien barely survives a crash landing, with a final panel revealing the strip's punchline of the alien having landed in Birmingham; a Judge Dredd story featuring the Prankster, who commits elaborate and destructive practical jokes; the first installment of *Invasion of the Thrill-Snatchers*, in which the Greater Spotted Thrill-Sucker is lured to Earth to do battle with Tharg the Mighty; and the seventeenth part of a *Rogue Trooper* storyline called "Fort Neuro", in which Rogue has to help defend a base of insane soldiers. All of these stories foreground action and comedy in a way that makes Moore's story of ordinary human life stand out sharply.

Two issues after "The Reversible Man" Moore penned what he later considered to be his favorite *Time Twister*, "Chrono-Cops." The sixth and final of his IPC collaborations with Dave Gibbons, "Chrono-Cops" is in many ways the most Alan Mooreish of his *2000 AD* strips. Moore has always been a writer with a keen focus on questions of structure, and what Grant Morrison describes as his "love of obvious structure" is a thread that extends all the way to his hyper-elaborate games with the idea of the comics page in works like *Promethea*. "Chrono-Cops" can only be read in this context—in just five pages Moore constructs an elaborate farce of intersecting timelines in which characters repeatedly bump into their future and past selves resulting in a convoluted comedy of errors.

The plot is, by design, a mouthful. Joe Saturday and his partner, Ed Thursday, are police officers dealing with crimes against the timeline. On their way back from busting a perp for "the attempted murder of your own great grandfather" they encounter themselves about to leave on that very assignment. On their way to their next assignment, accordingly, they meet themselves going back, and are warned that on that assignment Ed will receive a black eye, and it's suggested that they go pick up some raw steak before setting out. Doing so, they encounter a temporal car crash on the 1997 flyover (presumably related to *The Highbury Working*) where Ed is assaulted by Zanzibar Z. Ziggurat, who punches him in the face while proclaiming that he's "never forgotten what you did to me" and that he should "wait till you find out what happens to your career!"

A deeply shaken Ed holds the steak to his black eye in the canteen as his earlier self buys it in the background before he and his partner head off on another mission (after inadvertently intersecting their future selves warning their past selves about the black eye, which they handle by hiding in the bushes). On this mission they are attempting to apprehend Yolanda Y. Yorty, a "long-term interest bandit" who would "deposit a pound note in her bank account, jump three hundred years into the future, and collect the accumulated interest." The easiest way to apprehend Yorty turns out to be to arrest her as an infant, but a shaken Ed grabs the wrong baby, inadvertently accosting an infant Zanzibar Ziggurat, thus causing Ziggurat's trauma that resulted in his earlier assault of Ed. At this point the stress proves to be too much for Ed, and he attempts to travel back in time and marry his own grandmother. Joe Saturday is tasked with bringing the rogue Chrono-Cop in, and ends up marrying Ed's grandmother himself and thus becoming Ed's grandfather. "Funny how things worked out," Saturday reflects, while acknowledging that "Ed didn't think it was funny. He gets out in four more years… he says he's gonna kill me."

By the larger standards of baroque time travel plots this is not a massive headscratcher, but for a five-page story Moore works in an impressive amount of depth. He's aided, of course, by Gibbons, whose attention to detail and clean artwork communicates with a clarity that enables Moore's intricately worked plot to come across straightforwardly despite its complexity. Gibbons also imbues the story with a strong sense of cartooning-based comedy. Joe Saturday and Ed Tuesday are given clear and distinct visual designs so that they're always immediately recognizable, and Gibbons puts considerable thought into the design of the minor characters so that even a largely insubstantial character like the guy they arrest on the first page is a detailed, lush creation.

But in the end the story's success is largely down to Moore. He is hardly the only person ever to write a time travel farce, but the decision to wed that farce to a parody of a *Dragnet*-style cop story is fresh and innovative. The story isn't just well-done, it's inventive and alluring, combining elements that, on the surface, don't go together into a coherent package. The strip is densely packed with both comedy and complexity, in a way that makes it stand out from the rest of what *2000 AD* was doing.

But it would be a mistake to suggest that the arrival of the *Time Twisters* banner marked some absolute turning point for Moore's *2000 AD* work. Yes, "The Reversible Man" and "Chrono-Cops" are each strong contenders for being considered the best of Moore's short pieces for the magazine, but it is not as though his post-*Skizz* work is universally brilliant. Sandwiched in between "The Reversible Man" and "Chrono-Cops" in Prog 309, for instance, is an untitled *Time Twister* in which aliens set up a Historical Zoo on a desolate and abandoned Earth, featuring reconstructions of historical Earth figures. Out of curiosity the aliens construct two copies of Albert Einstein "to see if they were smart enough to work out what had happened to them. You know... being dead and then being alive again." They are, as it happens, and so go off to liberate the humans in the Military Enclosure, at which point the humans drive the aliens away and retake their planet. It is, to say the least, not one of Moore's most impressive outings.

On the other hand, the final six months of Moore's short story writing do contain a cluster of quality stories not really seen since the impressive 1981 run from "Grawks Bearing Gifts" through "A Cautionary Fable." In addition to "The

Figure 71: This panel appears twice in "Chrono-Cops" as different sets of the main characters reach the point in the story where this scene takes place. On the first pass, it's not clear what the nuns in the background are up to, while by the second the reader has realized that the nuns are in fact a third version of Ed and Joe that the two in the foreground are unaware of. (From "Chrono-Cops," in 2000 AD #310, written by Alan Moore, art by Dave Gibbons, 1983)

Figure 72: It becomes obvious that Harry Bentley's "time machine" is in fact his death. (From "Time Machine," in 2000 AD #324, written by Alan Moore, art by Redondo, 1983)

Reversible Man" and "Chrono-Cops" there's "The Big Clock," the first D.R. & Quinch story (a *Time Twister*, much as the first Abelard Snazz was in fact a *Ro-Jaws Robo-Tale*), "Ring Road," "Eureka," and the sublimely bleak "The Time Machine." All of these are solid—even the weakest of them, "Ring Road," is strangely moody piece, with art by Jesus Redondo, a Spanish artist and *2000 AD* standard. Redondo's characters have what Moore describes as "dark emotional realism" and "a sort of sleazy credibility," an effect generated by his propensity for heavily shaded panels with large patches of black and a wealth of scratchy hatching. This serves as a good fit for the most literally elliptical of Moore's stories, which features an escaped criminal violently hijacking a car and driving off, not realizing that she is driving through time. She starts in 1935, and winds her way past a 1950s diner, picks up a hippie hitchhiker, and passes some angry punks before seeing the flash of atomic armageddon and driving through a post-apocalyptic wasteland. From there she circles back to pre-historic times before finally pulling up to help a young girl standing by the roadside who is, of course, her younger self from the start of the story. It's a straightforward twist ending story, but Redondo's grim linework elevates it.

Redondo is also on hand four issues later for "The Time Machine," which is easily the most depressing story Moore wrote for *2000 AD*. It begins with a man, Harry Bentley, who is falling through a "freezing black," that is "cold and crushing like interstellar space, without light, without stars," but is unphased by it due to his sheer joy that his time machine worked. Over the next few pages he revisits moments in his life, going through all the regrets and sorrows of his past—losing Duffo, his stuffed clown, and failing to kiss Jackie Rutherford when he had the chance. Then the reader learns about his failed marriage, which came apart under financial strain and his obsession with building a time machine to get back to what he remembered as a happier childhood. And then, at the end, it's revealed that the time machine never worked, and that he has thrown himself off a bridge in despair, and the functioning time machine is in fact his life flashing before his eyes as he drowns in Redondo's river of sweeping black ink.

"Don't move. For almost sixty years, don't move. Stand still and turn to urban furniture, to your own monument, to landscape."
—Alan Moore, *Unearthing*, 2006

But the uptick in the quality of Moore's stories cannot be attributed entirely to a propensity for seriousness. D.R. & Quinch, after all, are thoroughly comedic, as is "Chrono-Cops." "The Big Clock" takes a positively whimsical tone. It's a guide to how time functions, which turns out to be because of the work of people living in a giant clock "suspended at the center of eternity" that's run by a gentleman named Arthur Seck. Seck takes the reader on a tour of the facility, showing them the process by which time is dug up, the fate sisters who weave time once it's been processed into fine wires, the people who sort it into good times and bad times, and so on. It is unabashedly a list story—a plotless exploration of various entertaining concepts of how time might work. The best is Cyril, whose job it is "to remember everything in the whole of existence. If he forgets something, it vanishes from living memory," which is exactly what happens when Seck interrupts him by asking how it's going, leading to everybody in the cosmos losing their ballpoint pens. ("Portuguese dramatist Gil Vicente was born in 1470... Mrs Booth of Islington has to cancel her milk tomorrow... Stalactites grow down, not up...," he mutters to himself, trying to keep track of the rest of it). The story ends with Seck realizing that he's behind on winding up the mainspring of the clock, leading to it running down and, presumably, time stopping entirely. It is unabashedly a slender thing, but it's terribly charming and memorable.

Also memorable is "Eureka," one of Moore's later *Future Shocks*, which tells of a ship fruitlessly searching for alien life. Eventually one of the crewmen suggests that "an alien could be anything," wondering "if an alien is just a concept? Something that doesn't even exist in any physical sense." A few months later the same crewman, Marty Kessler, proclaims that he's "had an idea. It just popped into my head. And it wasn't human! No human mind could have conceived of it unaided. That idea was an alien… and the alien's in my mind right now!" Steadily the crew comes to realize that Kessler is right as he explains his idea to them, and they too proceed to become possessed by the alien. Eventually the narrator is the only one left, until he's cornered by the crew who, in unison, explain the idea to him, converting him as well.

Several aspects of the story jump out. First, Moore conjures up an impressively tangible sense of possession out of just a few small details. The narrator mentions that Kessler always says "I mean," and, when he's talking about the possibility that an alien is just an idea he does just that, repeating "I mean" twelve times on a single page. But when Kessler proclaims that he's "made contact with the aliens" he doesn't say "I mean" once. Further giving a clear sense of possession is the fact that everybody who hears the idea starts smiling, in marked contrast to the grumpy misery on the ship at first. (They hadn't found any aliens, the narrator notes, "but we had each found fifteen other human beings that we didn't much like.") But secondly, and more broadly interesting, is the nature of the alien idea. The idea is never stated in full—the story's punchline is Tharg deciding that "this Future Shock is too dangerous to continue" just as the narrator is going to explain the idea. But the beginning of the idea is stated: "if all time is simultaneous and all events happen in a single instant, then time is but a figment of the mind, and…"

And what, though? The answer may be unstated in "Eureka," but a look at his larger work explores this in greater detail. He describes his mammoth novel *Jerusalem* in almost identical terms, explaining that "the universe is a four-dimensional solid in which nothing is moving and nothing is changing. The only thing that is moving through that solid along the time axis is our consciousness. The past is still there, the future has always been here, and, in this gigantic solid, every moment that has ever existed or will ever exist is all existing conterminously at the same moment." This is almost exactly what the "Eureka" alien seems to be pointing towards. Moore's conclusion in his later work is that this "completely solves the minor problem of death" as "when our consciousness gets to the end of our life, there's nowhere for it to go other than back to the beginning... we have our lives over and over again an infinite number of times and, each time, we are having exactly the same thoughts, saying exactly the same things," which, in Moore's view, makes us immortal. "You're welcome," he notes.

Much as this idea comes out of Moore's later, explicitly mystical thought, the underlying concepts are vividly present in Moore's earliest work. "The Reversible Man" is, in many ways, an illustration of the idea of consciousness having to go back to the beginning of life at the end, only with the added detail of consciousness having to travel backwards instead of simply leaping back seamlessly. "Ring Road," the plot of which is a literal illustration of this idea, and indeed Moore's propensity for elliptical narrative structure in general, is similar evidence that these concerns have been present throughout his career. Nor is the idea original to him—in interviews he references an Einstein quote he was told, which he paraphrases as Einstein saying that "death isn't really a big thing because I understand the persistent illusion of transience." In fiction the idea can be traced back easily to the British new wave of science fiction and stories like Ballard's "The Day of Forever," set in a world where time has stopped, and which Grant Morrison claimed as the inspiration for his Gideon Stargrave character. Morrison, for his part, has snarked that his professionally published comic, "Time is a Four-Letter Word," was "based around the simultaneity of time concept Alan Moore himself is so fond of these days and which informs his in-progress novel *Jerusalem*," which, while an accurate description of "Time is a Four-Letter Word," largely ignores the fact that Moore had visibly been playing with these concepts since the early 1980s, when Morrison was largely out of comics and playing in a succession of failed rock bands.

More to the point, it is clear that the introduction of time as an available theme for Moore enlivened his *2000 AD* work considerably. Moore admits as much, saying that he "received the news that *2000 AD*'s staple *Future Shocks* would henceforth be augmented with the chronological convolutions of the *Time Twisters* series with undiluted glee." Moore further explains his glee, expressing a lifelong interest in time and telling of childhood memories of "doggedly staring at an hour hand for what seemed like entire afternoons in the hope of seeing it move, even slightly" and "the awe and delight accompanying any cinematic display of a flower speeded up, a gull slowed down, or almost anything running backwards." But for all of Moore's interest in time, it's striking how often his work seems a refutation of it. By most definitions, after all, time is fundamentally related to the notion of change. And yet in Moore's conception time becomes a fixed and absolute thing.

This tendency is clear by the time of *Jerusalem*, but is still visible in his *2000 AD* work as well. In "Ring Road," for instance, the entire point is that the story lacks a meaningful beginning or end, instead looping around on itself such that every event is its own cause and effect. "Chrono-Cops" is the same way, albeit with a deliberately tangled construction. The fifth panel of the story depicts a meeting in the lobby in which, in the background, two nuns are walking by. This same event appears as the first panel of the final page, where it finally becomes clear that the nuns are in fact a disguised Saturday and Thursday, and that Thursday has just come back from the assignment that drives/drove him over the edge into madness. What's important to notice here is not just the comically recursive structure, but the fact that when the story starts the events of its ending have, in fact, already happened.

The story may be full of incident, but almost every incident within it is one that has already taken place at the outset. It is not so much that anything happens as it is that Moore's narrative slowly pans across a segment of time in which everything has already happened. A similar thing takes place in "Going Native," a *Time Twister* from May of 1983 in which a man is sent back in time to discover the missing link between Neanderthals and Cro-magnons and who, in the course of looking for it, falls in love with a Neanderthal and becomes the missing link. In this case, it is not merely the events of the story that become looped and immutable, but the entire sweep of human history from its beginnings to its far future in the 63rd century.

"The Big Clock" takes this tendency towards fixity even further. Its conceit—that time is run out of a physical clock—represents time not as a process of change but as a singular, physical location. Time becomes matter, physically mined out of a several millennia large "time-seam." Time, in other words, becomes a material object, much like the four dimensional solid Moore talks about in his later career. It's interesting that Moore describes this story as the "closest to the way that I saw time as a child" and "nearest to the source from which the other stories flow," suggesting that even Moore's notion of time was not something that evolved and changed over the course of his life, but rather some pre-existing idea that Moore merely came to better understand the shape of over his career. Understood this way, Moore's career ceases to be a progression of events at all, instead becoming a single concept that has been threaded into the psychic geography of Albion, winding serpent-like through its history. From this perspective, it becomes possible that Moore is not even a combatant in the War at all, but rather a pre-existing portion of it, and that the entire War exists as a confusion over the distinction between the battle and the battlefield. His sole set of tactics in the War amount to a steadfast refusal to move or change in any way.

But Moore's temporal renaissance was ultimately short-lived, as, indeed, was his interest in continuing to do short stories for IPC. By June of 1983 he was turning in one-note fare like "The Hyperhistoric Headbang!" which is to *This Is Spinal Tap* what D.R. & Quinch are to O.C. & Stiggs, which is to say, a sci-fi upgrade adding thermonuclear weapons. As with D.R. & Quinch, Alan Davis provides some entertaining visuals, but it is hard to escape the sense that its inclusion in the *Shocking Futures* collection is due mainly to a desire to be able to put Davis's name on the book, as the listless story itself is a list story without a particularly interesting list. Its only two ideas of note are a planet in which every inhabitant has been genetically engineered to scream at a certain pitch, which is subsequently destroyed by a stylus playing it like a record, causing the animals to scream, and a drum line consisting of time-travelling past major explosions in galactic history. Similarly uninspired is the next issue's "The Lethal Laziness of Lobelia Loam," which amounts to an attempt to redo "A Cautionary Fable" with a light time travel twist. His final *Time Twister*, "The Startling Success of Sideways Scuttleton," is likewise flaccid—a five-pager about a con man who can "wiggle me back in a certain way" to step between alternate realities, but whose life of crime comes to an end when he throws his back out and can no longer control his dimension hopping. Although a potentially novel concept—Moore writes excellent con men—the story lacks much of a plot and ends with a half-hearted twist.

Moore's remaining three *Future Shocks* are all two-pagers. The first, "Dad," is about a man standing outside a space station where he's been locked out by a "father" that's demanding he apologize. As the comic shows the scene from different angles it eventually becomes clear that the father is just a computer, and that the spaceman has been dead for years, having had a meteorite shatter his helmet. It's bleak little number, to be sure. But its context only really becomes clear in light of Moore's next two stories, "Buzz Off!" and "Look Before You Leap!" Both are almost entirely wordless—"Look Before You Leap!" only has non-verbal sounds like a bird going "Gluwook-Gluwook!" or a man laughing, and "Buzz Off!" consists only of buzzing-noises, sound effects, and a final, very small caption offering the story a pithy punchline. In this context "Dad," which features only a single computer voice and no captions, becomes clearer. Moore, in his final stories, is pushing his stylistic envelope again, working to tell stories in ways that trust the visuals more. Ironically, this is what he was trying to do back with "Southern Comfort." In these stories the visuals support him better than Howarth's did, but the point is the same.

In that regard, then, Moore finished his time doing shorts for IPC the way he began it—by trying to learn new storytelling techniques. In this regard his comments about "doing an apprenticeship in public" and using short stories to learn "to do all the things that you will have to do in a bigger work but in a much more constrained space" are very much on target through and through. He used his time at IPC to learn his trade and craft. That not all of his experiments came off is, in many ways, proof of this fact. But notably, many of the experiments that did come off demonstrate techniques he would later make considerable use of, up to and including his confidence in purely visual storytelling that he was clearly trying to build in his last few strips. The effect is not entirely unlike the old story about Michelangelo creating the David by taking a block of marble and removing everything that wasn't the David. The figure that is Alan Moore visibly emerges into the narrative, and comes ever more into focus over the course of these dozens of short stories.

Chapter Six: Skizz and D.R. & Quinch

"Best bet is to set your fantasies in the here and now and then, if challenged, claim to be writing Magical Realism." –Neil Gaiman

Indeed, it's clear that by the time he was done with his *Future Shocks* he had, in practice, emerged, having stopped them in order to focus on his new and much higher-paying gig doing *Swamp Thing* at DC Comics. There is no serious way to describe Alan Moore in the autumn of 1983 as a tentative journeyman. And, as noted, even within the period working on *Future Shocks* for *2000 AD* there is a clear dividing line in March of 1983, when Moore began writing *Skizz*, his first ongoing series for *2000 AD*. Within the standard mythology of these things, *Skizz* is part of Alan Moore's apprenticeship—where he cut his teeth learning to tell stories. Much of this is simply the fact that *2000 AD* and their current owners tell this story in a particular way. The trade paperback collection of *Skizz* boasts that "*2000 AD* was the proving ground for a host of A-list British writers and artists, now recognised both sides of the Atlantic. Luminaries to emerge from under the wing of Tharg the Mighty (*2000 AD*'s alien editor for the uninitiated) include Brian Bolland, Garth Ennis, Alan Grant, Alan Moore, Grant Morrison, Frank Quitely, and many, many more." Which is, of course, a good marketing line—*2000 AD* is where Moore's career began, in this telling.

This is, of course, nonsense. Moore's career began in *Sounds*, and then in *Doctor Who Weekly*. The bits of his *2000 AD* that can be described as early, prototypic work consist of a handful of *Future Shocks* in 1981 and 1982. But at any point after March of 1982, when *Warrior* #1 hit, containing the first installments of both *Marvelman* and *V for Vendetta*, it is ludicrous to suggest that Alan Moore is a developing talent who was still learning the ropes. As of that month he was producing two iconic, career-defining works, each of which can make credible cases to be the most important, influential, and transformative comics in the world at the time of their publication. So when, a year later, he began writing *Skizz* for *2000 AD* he was not emerging from the wing of Tharg the Mighty—he was a major talent at the top of his game writing an *E.T.* knockoff for a magazine he was sentimentally attached to (a reason not entirely dissimilar to why he was still working on *Maxwell the Magic Cat*).

As noted, in fact, *2000 AD* was oddly reticent to give Moore an ongoing strip. *Skizz* was the fourth ongoing that Moore worked on, after *V for Vendetta*, *Marvelman*, and *Captain Britain*, and by all appearances it was only given to him to mollify him when he started to (correctly) reason that he was perhaps being wasted on an endless progression of *Future Shocks*. It is, in other words, firmly the work of a mature talent. On the other hand, Moore has generally been disdainful of the strip, referring to it just eight months after it started as "horrible." It is not a strip he talks about at any significant length, and indeed can be described with reasonable accuracy as his first real flop of an ongoing. From this perspective, *2000 AD*'s quiet rebranding of it as part of Moore's self-described apprenticeship in comics is wholly sensible, because there's just not another good way to reimagine this as a major piece of work worth buying. It is a historical curiosity, and thus its historical bona fides must be bolstered somehow.

There are two points of inspiration that everybody agrees upon for *Skizz*, and these usually serve as both the starting and ending point for discussion of the strip. The first fits in with the longstanding practice within British comics of imitating popular media. Just as *Action*'s star feature, *Hookjaw*, was an unsubtle rip-off of *Jaws*, *Skizz* is a rip-off of Steven Spielberg's *E.T.*, by pretty much everyone's agreement. Indeed, in his interview on the subject in the 1984 annual, Moore, tongue visibly in cheek even through the mass of beard, describes how "the Mighty One noticed all of the recent books and films about aliens on Earth," which, in the context of the mega-hit that *E.T.* was, is thoroughly unsubtle. Moore elsewhere was more explicit, describing it as a "horrible *E.T.* rip-off," and the comic's readers were scarcely kinder, commenting on the similarities for the letters page and suggesting that *2000 AD* was "losing its touch" and "could have come up with something much better." And yet for all this criticism, Moore is well-insulated from plagiarism charges through the clever strategy on his part of simply not actually watching the film. This was, however, as much by necessity as creative integrity: *Skizz* was offered to Moore in the period between *E.T.*'s June 1982 debut in the United States and its UK run six months later, and was well into production when the film finally did see UK release, which meant that Moore was stuck writing an *E.T.* imitation without actually having any ability to watch the film he was supposed to be ripping off.

Lacking the ability to actually rip off his intended source material (a setup that speaks volumes about the degree to which *Skizz* was a minimal sop to Moore's desire to expand his work), Moore improvised, instead lifting from the then-popular BBC Two drama *Boys from the Blackstuff*, which is the second major and agreed upon influence on *Skizz*. Moore, as is typical when dealing with instances of overt inspiration, is open about this, saying that "there's an awful lot in there that owes far too much to Alan Bleasdale," the writer of *Boys from the Blackstuff*, and that while "*Skizz* wasn't an Alan Bleasdale-ripoff, one character in there and some of the atmosphere owed a lot" to the writer. "It was derivative," Moore concludes, and "a case of admiring something and not having the taste or tact to know when I was going too far," although not, he stressed, "evil or wrong" (and thus unlike, say, the Lafferty lift in the second Abelard Snazz story).

In hindsight Moore's vocal debt to Bleasdale seems like a necessary corrective for the fan audience that has spared *Skizz* the obscurity of other short-run *2000 AD* strips. The truth is that almost anyone who picks up *Skizz* because Alan Moore's name is on it—which is to say, anyone who picked up *Skizz* after 1983—would immediately recognize the influence of *E.T.* in a way they might not a BBC Two drama about working class Liverpudlians. Despite having not seen the film, Moore ended up writing something with a broadly similar plot. Both stories feature an alien stranded on Earth who befriends a young human. Both feature major scenes in which the alien begins learning English, scenes in which the alien is overwhelmed by sensory input, and sequences where the alien falls ill. They use the same basic antagonist—government agents investigating the alien—and culminate in a chase sequence followed by the alien successfully escaping the planet after a sentimental farewell. Superficially, at least, it is only the fact that Moore wrote *Skizz* without seeing *E.T.* that stops this from being a lift on the scale of "Return of the Two-Storey Brain." But a closer inspection reveals that *Skizz* does precisely what "Return of the Two-Storey Brain" does not: use the basic components of a story to tell a substantively different story.

The most significant difference between *Skizz* and *E.T.* comes from their basic perspective. The first installment of *Skizz* is told entirely from the perspective of the titular character as he crashes his ship and escapes from the wreckage. No human characters, or, indeed, characters at all besides Skizz and his ship's computer appear, and it is not until the final panel that any sort of hint is made as to actual setting of the story, namely Birmingham. It's not until the third installment that Roxy, the human protagonist of the strip, is actually introduced, and not until the fourth strip that

Figure 73: Roxy and Skizz overcome their communication barrier. (From Skizz, in 2000 AD #311, written by Alan Moore, art by Jim Baikie, 1983)

the reader actually sees Skizz from Roxy's perspective instead of the world from Skizz's perspective. And even that comes in a divided episode—the first two pages of the strip show Roxy from Skizz's perspective, followed by two pages of Skizz from Roxy's. This makes sense given the context in which *Skizz* appeared, which is to say, in a comics magazine dedicated to science fiction. What's really telling is the first installment. From the first page, the focus is on Skizz, with a narration that displays a casual confidence in an audience familiar with sci-fi jargon. Within one page Moore mentions plasmotors, polarized gravity buffers, the sacred equations, shield-fungus, prysms, hydrocircuitry, luxate, formalhaut ore, and lymph-batteries. None of this is explained in any detail— the reader is expected to just accept that this (wholly invented) sci-fi jargon makes sense in the same way that gamma grenades and chem-swap, to take two similar bits of jargon from elsewhere in Prog 308, make sense. Instead the twist in the first installment of *Skizz* is that the alien has landed in a place as mundane as Birmingham.

This is the exact opposite of how *E.T.* approaches it. The opening sequence of *E.T.* does focus on the aliens, but from a removed distance, treating them as objects of wonder. The opening shot is of a starry night, the camera panning down past the tree line and to a glowing spaceship nestled among the trees. The aliens are first seen occluded and in the distance—the camera peers at them through trees, and it is not entirely clear what they look like. Once this establishing sequence is done, the film approaches the aliens from the perspective of the story's main character, Eliot. A key scene comes when Eliot tosses his baseball into the shed and it is thrown back out at him—instead of seeing any glimpse of E.T., there's one of Spielberg's trademark shots: a closeup on a human face reacting to something. The same basic shot is used when Eliot first properly encounters E.T. in the cornfield—there are shots of E.T., but they're interspersed with Eliot's reactions, so that the focus of the scene becomes the human gazing upon the alien. The final shot of the film, similarly, is a close-up on Eliot's face as he watches the alien ship depart.

Spielberg, in other words, is very careful to make sure that nobody misses the point that this is a story about Eliot's childlike wonder at the marvels of the universe and not about aliens as such. *E.T.* is consciously and deliberately a movie in which the science fiction concepts are firmly and carefully embedded in the real world. Its blockbuster success can hardly be called a surprise—1982 is the third year in a row that a genre film was number one in the box office, following on *Star Wars: The Empire Strikes Back* and *Raiders of the Lost Ark*, and the trend would continue for several years to come (*Return of the Jedi*, *Ghostbusters*, and *Back to the Future* were the top films of the next three years). It came at a time when sci-fi was huge, in other words. But for all that its success rode the wave pioneered by *Star Wars* in 1977, as a film *E.T.* continually resists the sci-fi approach. *E.T.* is instead, in effect, a piece of magical realism.

As a literary genre, magical realism is most associated with Latin American writers of the mid-20th century, with its iconically major practitioners being Jorge Luis Borges and Gabriel García Márquez. The first major attempt to formulate a definition of the genre came with the 1955 publication of Angel Flores's essay, "Magical Realism in Spanish American Fiction," where he identifies the genre as beginning with the publication of Borges's 1935 short story collection *Historia universal de la infamia*, generally translated in English as *A Universal History of Infamy*. The genre as Flores describes it is defined by "the amalgamation of realism and fantasy" so as to produce the "transformation of the common and the everyday into the awesome and the unreal." The same year that Flores defined the genre Márquez published his short story, "Un señor muy viejo con unas alas enormes," typically translated as "A Very Old Man With Enormous Wings," which has been widely anthologized and serves as the standard representative text in teaching the genre in high school and university level literature classes.

"England was a scary place. No wonder it produced a scary culture."
–Warren Ellis, *Planetary*, 1999

"A Very Old Man With Enormous Wings" tells the story of a winged man who crashes to ground in the courtyard of Pelayo and Elisenda. But the story focuses resolutely on Pelayo and Elisenda's experience and not on the nature of the winged man in their courtyard. Its memorable first paragraph carefully holds the titular detail back until the end so that it becomes just one of a host of details about their lives. "On the third day of rain," Márquez writes, "they had killed so many crabs inside the house that Pelayo had to cross his drenched courtyard and throw them into the sea, because the newborn child had a temperature all night and they thought it was due to the stench."

Only at the end of the paragraph about this rainstorm does the narration turn to the fact that there was " a very old man, lying face down in the mud, who, in spite of his tremendous efforts, couldn't get up, impeded by his enormous wings." The story never moves beyond this approach: the nature of the old man is not explored. Instead the story tells of how Elisenda thinks to charge for admission to see the old man, who is proclaimed over the objections of the local priest to be an angel. But over time the old man becomes commonplace—his status as the town's star attraction is usurped by a "woman who had been changed into a spider for having disobeyed her parents," and who had none of the old man's reticence about being a carnival attraction. The old man, meanwhile, only musters up a few odd miracles "like the blind man who didn't recover his sight but grew three new teeth, or the paralytic who didn't get to walk but almost won the lottery, and the leper whose sores sprouted sunflowers." In time he convalesces and flies away without explanation, and the story ends, never having stopped to consider much of anything beyond the question of what it is like for a poor family to have an old man with wings literally crash into their lives.

The influence of this approach on *E.T.* is clear enough. *E.T.* is a movie interested not in the alien, but the way in which Eliot and his family's lives change upon meeting the alien. This is not, it must be reiterated, due to Spielberg not being a sci-fi person. Spielberg's later career and indeed his earlier one both make clear that he has the same instinctual understanding of science fiction that Moore's jargon-laced intro to *Skizz* assumes. But for *E.T.* he sets this aside and tells a story in a magical realist mode, albeit one that eschews the cynicism of Márquez's quasi-angel in favor of an unabashed embrace of childlike wonder.

Moore, however, changes things significantly. The biggest change stems from the nature of the human character encountered by the alien. Eliot is a ten-year-old boy, whereas Roxy is a fifteen-year-old girl. The difference is massive—the reader is first introduced to Roxy rejecting the advances of a boy outside her window—a boy she later decks when he spreads the story that he'd spent the weekend at her place while her parents were out of town. The decision to position Roxy as a character who has come of age changes the narrative considerably. Where *E.T.* is about a figure of innocence encountering wondrous things, *Skizz* is about a character who is defined not by her innocence but by her ethics and compassion. Eliot investigates E.T. further because he's curious. Roxy, meanwhile, takes in Skizz and cares for him for no seeming reason other than kindness and the desire to help.

It is notable that one can scour Alan Moore's career at considerable length and find few examples of Moore writing something from the perspective of a child. When he deals with childhood as a theme, as in *Lost Girls* or *The Birth Caul*, it is always in retrospect—childhood is looked back on from a position of adulthood. The only real exception prior to *Jerusalem* is the first installment of *Monster*, a serial for the IPC magazine *Scream* about a twelve-year-old boy's attempts to

Figure 74: The introduction of Roxy at the start of the third installment of Skizz, a sequence that depends on the decision to go with a female protagonist for their human lead. (From 2000 AD *#310, written by Alan Moore, art by Jim Baikie, 1983)*

hide his deformed and puissant Uncle Terry in the attic, and it is notable that after penning the first installment Moore departed the strip and was replaced by John Wagner. And so it was never particularly likely that Moore would go with the same "boy and his alien" plot of *E.T.*

In the absence of a plot centered on the experience of gazing upon the alien, then, Moore provides a story about an alien's perspective on the ordinary world. Skizz reacts with horror and fear at his surroundings, recoiling as he watches some punks stumble out of a pub and fight, begging to himself, "Oh no, please. Don't let it be! Don't let them be that primitive!" Even after he meets Roxy he's afraid—he accidentally burns himself on a cup of coffee she gives him, and as he screams the captions note that "it hurt him. He knew it. He knew the creature would try to hurt him." As Roxy yells in frustration at the coffee stain on her carpet, Skizz cowers in the corner, looking at Roxy and thinking, "Here it comes. The animal's teeth are bared... the sharp teeth of a meat-eater. Its paws clench into clubs. Its posture radiates hostility. It's going to kill him. Perhaps it's going to eat him..." And even after Skizz learns English and firmly befriends Roxy, the story repeatedly reverts to his perspective in order to shed light on the world he has come to inhabit.

But ultimately, the influence of *E.T.* on *Skizz* is one of iconography, and any similarities really do amount to there being certain things that are reasonably obvious aspects of the "alien lost on Earth and befriended by a young innocent" plot. In terms of things Moore consciously drew on in writing *Skizz* the obvious point of influence is, as mentioned, Alan Bleasdale's *Boys from the Blackstuff*. It is not that Bleasdale is a major influence on the plot—that would, in truth, be difficult. Rather, Bleasdale has visible influence on the tone Moore adopted in writing *Skizz*. To fully understand the tone of *Boys from the Blackstuff*, however, it is necessary to understand the tone of 1982 in Great Britain, which is to say, Thatcherism.

Margaret Hilda Thatcher, born Margaret Hilda Roberts, was the daughter of a grocery shop owner in Lincolnshire who started her political career running doomed campaigns against a safe Labour seat in Kent, and who finally got handed the safe conservative seat of Finchley in 1958. After twelve years of rising through the ranks of the Conservative Party she became Education Secretary in 1970 when Edward Heath unseated the Wilson government. In that capacity she decided to cut education spending by ending the free milk program for children between the ages of seven and eleven, resulting in the tabloid nickname of "Thatcher the Milk Snatcher." Despite, or perhaps because of this reputation, she was elected Leader of the Conservative party in 1975 after Heath's Government fell the year before, due largely to its unsuccessful navigation of the energy crisis caused by the 1973 strike of the National Union of Miners.

In May 1979, two days before the publication of the sixth installment of *Roscoe Moscow: Who Killed Rock n' Roll?* and following the collapse of the Labour-led Callaghan government in the face of the so-called Winter of Discontent, in which a series of industrial disputes led to widespread uncertainty, culminating in an unofficial strike of the gravediggers in Liverpool that resulted in 150 bodies being stored in a warehouse in Speke and the perhaps ill-advised decision for a mid-level bureaucrat in the Liverpool health system to publicly speculate that if the strike continued they might have to take up burial at sea, as well as a London waste collector's strike that resulted in Leicester Square in the heart of the West End of London being used as a temporary garbage dump by the city's Conservative-led council, Margaret Thatcher became the Prime Minister of the United Kingdom of Great Britain and Northern Ireland, a position she would hold until her ouster in a 1990 party coup.

Thatcher holds the interesting distinction of being the political figure with the most pop songs celebrating her death written while she was still alive, a fact that speaks volumes about her cultural impact. Morrissey closed his first solo album, *Viva Hate*, with "Margaret at the Guillotine," asking insistently, "When will you die?" while Elvis Costello vowed to stand on her grave and "Tramp the Dirt Down" on his 1989 *Spike*. Pete Wylie and Hefner had the similarly titled "The Day That Margaret Thatcher Dies" and "The Day that Thatcher Dies," the latter of which was an interpolation of "Ding Dong, the Witch is Dead" from *The Wizard of Oz* that inspired the movement to get that song to chart the week of her death in 2013—it rose to number two and forced the BBC to awkwardly explain why a song from a 1939 film was playing in the chart countdown between Duke Dumont and Pink. The experience of living under Thatcherism has been memorably described by Warren Ellis on more than one occasion, including his claim that "we would look out the window every morning to make sure the bitch hadn't put Daleks in the streets yet," and all of Alan Moore, Jamie Delano, and Grant Morrison at various times heaped indignities on her in their work.

It's easy enough to see why. The earliest years of the Thatcher era began with massive unemployment due to Thatcher's decision to prioritize monetary policy over employment in her economic strategy. By the summer of 1981, as riots began breaking out in particularly hard-hit areas such as Brixton, unemployment had surged to more than eleven percent, over triple what it had been a decade ago, and double what it had been just two years earlier as Moore was starting his professional comics career. Some of Thatcher's political advisers suggested partially evacuating Liverpool, where the July Toxteth riots hit and, and allowing it to fall into "managed decline," a proposal that was ultimately rejected in favor of a hard-edged police response due in part to Thatcher's belief that the rioters showed excessive hostility to the police, whose repeated racial profiling of Toxteth youth was widely credited for the toxic environment out of which the riots sprung, and whose tactics to manage the riot involved driving vehicles into the crowds at high speeds.

In April of 1982, the same month as the second issue of *Warrior* hit, Thatcher's government entered a war with Argentina over the ownership of some South Atlantic islands settled in the 18th century called, alternately, the Falkland Islands or, to the Argentinians, the Malvinas. The conflict, memorably described by Borges as "a fight between two bald men over a comb," was nevertheless one of the defining events of 1982. Argentina's post-Peron military junta, also suffering from an economic recession, contrived to invade the islands in an attempt to bolster patriotic sentiment and on the assumption that the UK would not respond militarily. Thatcher proved these assumptions wrong, kicking off a two-month war in which just a bit over nine hundred people died, most of them Argentinian, and nearly half of those in the controversial sinking of the ARA *General Belgrano*. The Falklands War, named, inevitably, by the victor, was viewed by many on the political left as a craven but ultimately successful ploy to win back popularity lost to Thatcher due to the unemployment rate, by then up to 12.6% and on its way to a high of 14%; Moore wrote a several-week satire of the events in *Maxwell the Magic Cat*. Thatcher, in any case, won re-election handily the same week that Prog 320 of *2000 AD* came out, featuring Moore's "Ring Road" *Time Twister* and the thirteenth installment of *Skizz*, in which Roxy begs Cornelius and Loz to help her rescue Skizz from the government.

Neither *Boys from the Blackstuff* nor *Skizz* depict Thatcher directly, but both are deeply informed by the cultural mood that her Premiership instilled. *Boys from the Blackstuff* is a prime example of the grand BBC tradition of creating social realist dramas to highlight the conditions faced by marginalized members of society, a style of television whose pinnacle was the 1966 television play *Cathy Come Home*, an early work by filmmaker Ken Loach that documented the eponymous Cathy's slow descent into poverty and homelessness, culminating in a shockingly upsetting scene in which Cathy's children are seized by social services in the middle of a railway station. *Boys from the Blackstuff* actually predates the Thatcher era slightly—it originated as simply *The Black Stuff*, a 1978-produced and 1980-aired episode for the *Play for Today* anthology, a series of television plays. The series was the successor to *The Wednesday Play*, the banner under which *Cathy Come Home* came out, and differed mainly in that it did not always air on Wednesdays; it featured work by numerous high-profile British writers, often, though by no means always, with a focus on social realism. This was certainly the tradition that Alan Bleasdale's *The Black Stuff* came out of. *The Black Stuff* featured six tarmac layers from Liverpool working in Middlesbrough who get drawn into a scam working a second, non-union job, that results in them getting sacked. After a 1981 stand-alone piece called *The Muscle Market*, the characters were brought back in 1982 for the five-episode *Boys from the Blackstuff*. The first of these reintroduced the main characters from *The Black Stuff*, and each of the subsequent four focused closely on a single character's story.

> *"I could still walk away from this. I could say I was kidnapped.*
> *I could say I was forced to do things. I'm at an impressionable age.*
> *And I haven't killed anyone. Not yet."*
> –Grant Morrison, *Kill Your Boyfriend*, 1995

As with *The Black Stuff*, the point of *Boys from the Blackstuff* was the depiction of the difficulty of working class existence at that particular moment of British history. It is not a show about diagnosing the underlying causes of unemployment—there are no thorough and informative debates over monetarism, or close-readings of Friedrich Hayek. It simply attempts to show the experience of living at the bottom of society when times are getting harder. Its iconic episode was its fourth, "Yosser's Story," which focused on Yosser Hughes, the character responsible for getting them drawn into the scam back in *The Black Stuff*. In "Yosser's Story" he is reduced to a broken shell of a man, and, over the course of the hour-long episode, broken down further as his children are taken away and he continues to fail at finding employment. The character becomes steadily unhinged and erratic, unwilling or unable to grasp that his increasing desperation is making his situation worse at every turn. The episode culminates with Yosser attempting suicide by jumping into a lake, only to be hauled out by the police, the final shot being his face as he screams in horror at the realization that he's survived.

"Yosser's Story" works by combining this brutally bleak story with the superlative acting of Bernard Hill, who sells the anguish of a simple man who never had much trying to make sense of having it all taken away from him. Hill's performance makes Yosser at once pathetic and eminently quotable, especially with Bleasdale's deft use of the catchphrases "Gizza job," (that is, "give us a job") and "I can do that," often spoken in rapid succession as he fruitlessly hounds someone for employment. The episode is also rife with deliciously dark humor, such as a scene in which Yosser goes to a priest, pleading, "I'm desperate, father!" The priest says to call him Dan, and so Yosser, obligingly, declares, "I'm desperate, Dan!"—Desperate Dan being the mascot of *The Dandy*. The result was in effect *Cathy Come Home* for the 80s— a story of tragic circumstance, only now with a frenzied, grim sense of humor and the feeling of the entire world becoming unglued.

For all that Moore emphasizes the influence of *Boys from the Blackstuff* on *Skizz*, it must be said that the influence is not one that pervades the whole of the comic In reality there is only one close point of comparison, and that is the character of Cornelius, who is clearly based on Yosser Hughes. Instead of saying "gizza job" and "I can do that," Cornelius's catchphrase is "I've got my pride," and he lacks Bernard Hill's distinctive moustache, but the underlying concept is the same—Cornelius has lost his job as a pipe-fitter, and seems constantly on the brink of a complete breakdown, a line he nearly crosses on more than one occasion in the comic. Indeed, this seems the major underlying concept of *Skizz*—to take *E.T.* and have him meet Yosser Hughes from *Boys From the Blackstuff*.

This collision of genres, however, has more of a consequence on the tone of the story than might be

Figure 75: The final image of "Yosser's Story" is a freeze frame on Yosser's grotesquely contorted anguish at his own survival.

Figure 76: Cornelius's improbable return, pride and all. (From Skizz *in* 2000 AD *#330, written by Alan Moore, art by Jim Baikie, 1983)*

immediately apparent. For all that *Skizz* does, in fact, share the same basic plot structure as *E.T.*, the fact that one is a movie about childish wonder in suburban America while the other is about the bleak pointlessness of coming of age in Thatcher's Britain has considerable impact on the way that the two stories function. The sense of childlike wonder that *E.T.* is based around simply cannot plausibly exist in a world like Bleasdale's, and *Skizz* exists to demonstrate this, demanding, in effect, a different and more cynical take on the alien/human encounter.

The best moments of this come when *Skizz* takes moments from *Boys from the Blackstuff* and refactors it into being about aliens. So instead of a moving sequence where Yosser finally speaks out loud his growing understanding that the world is broken and failing him—he declares that "the trouble is, most of us either talk to ourselves or through our ass. I found that out. I'm thirty-six years old and I found that out. Unless you're somebody," a personal revelation delivered in the back of a squad car—we get a speech from Cornelius when asked by Roxy to help rescue Skizz from a government facility: "I didn't understand before," he says, "but I do now. It's great when you can understand things. I can't understand things at all. When I can, it's great. That's why I feel sorry for your mate. I bet there's lots of things that he can't understand. There's lots of things I can't understand, and I live here." Similarly, Yosser's ending—an attempted suicide that he comes back from—is mirrored in Cornelius's. In the penultimate installment, he's shot, apparently fatally, but then, improbably comes back to defeat the story's main villain. In both cases, there's a strange and uncanny comedy to it. The tropes of the working class social realist drama playing out on a sci-fi scale are not entirely out of keeping with Bleasdale's own sense of humor.

But the moments taken directly from *E.T.* are changed too. *E.T.* is a coming of age story—the alien serves as a vehicle for Eliot to transform himself into, if not an adult, at least an altogether more mature character. *Skizz*, on the other hand, rejects the idea that encountering the alien might present some sort of transformative experience. Nothing in the end of the story gives any real indication that Roxy's life, or indeed anyone else's, is going to be changed by having met Skizz. Cornelius still doesn't have a job, Roxy is still fifteen and growing up in Thatcher's Britain, and though one nasty and sadistic government employee is summarily thrown off a bridge by Cornelius, one does not get the sense that this has effected any lasting change. Where there has been a change (such as with Cornelius's epiphany that "there's nothing as important" as outer space, "not even pipe-fitting!") the change is pointedly useless. Cornelius is still on Earth at the end of the story, and while he may understand the vital importance of outer space, such importance is as inaccessible to him as before. Where Eliot has had a moving coming-of-age story, everyone involved in *Skizz* seems to have been left completely unchanged by the experience. This is, of course, in keeping with the tone of socially realist dramas like *Boys from the Blackstuff*.

The problem is that it's not a terribly satisfying ending. Moore is trying to merge two very different plot structures with actively conflicting needs. *Boys from the Blackstuff*-style social realism is fundamentally a story of inertia. The entire point of sternly depicting the awful conditions of working class folk in the north is to present the problem as intractable so that the viewing audience is moved to care about and engage with the real world. An ending based on the transformative properties of an alien who descends from the sky is the exact opposite of what a story like Yosser Hughes's demands. *E.T.*, on the other hand, is at its heart still a sci-fi film in the Joseph Campbell/Hero's Journey tradition, hitting all the requisite plot beats with banal methodicism. In that story the entire point is that Eliot is forever changed by his encounter with the alien and that he will now return to his life having grown up. That's what a coming-of-age story (which is really the plot structure the Hero's Journey is meant to emulate) does, just as surely as a socially realist story depicts inescapable conditions. And Moore is stuck trying to make both outcomes work.

Moore's ending, in which Skizz is rescued at the climactic moment by the confluence of Cornelius's unexpected lack of being dead and the arrival of a spaceship of Tau-Cetians to rescue him, ultimately fails to hit the balance. Moore has complained in interviews of the editorial interference that led to the insertion of dialogue over his planned wordless parting between Roxy and Skizz. As Moore describes it, "I just wanted them to look at each other, then he reaches forward, and they just kiss each other, and then he's gone. There's no words at all." Instead, however, Skizz begins to say something to Roxy, and Roxy replies, "No words, Skizz. Just... farewell." As Moore puts it, "Can you imagine that a big, strapping, working-class lad like myself would write dialogue like that!? What really rankled me was that my name was on the script. People were going to believe that I wrote, 'No words, Skizz. Just farewell.' They're gonna beat me up in the street."

Moore is not wrong that the altered dialogue is banal, trite, and moronic—not least because "farewell" is, in point of fact, a word. But Moore's concern over the possibility of being jumped by a mob of working class comics fans from the Boroughs are surely not helped by the ending he did write one page later, in which Skizz explains humanity to his rescuers, saying that "they were cruel and ugly. There was so much hate and despair... and so much love. What are they like, Shipmaster? I will tell you. Some of them have style. And some of them have their pride. And some of them... some of them are stars." While it is true that this monologue, unlike the editorially inserted dialogue between Roxy and Skizz, moves along with Moore's trademark well-metered lilt (note in particular the repetition of "some of them" in the closing sentences), the fact is that it is not actually any less mawkish.

The real problem is that Moore, in this ending, completely fails to live up to the satirical promise that drew him to 2000 AD in the first place. It is worth comparing the ending of *Skizz* to the iconic *Robot Wars* storyline that was running in the magazine when Moore discovered it in 1977. *The Robot Wars* memorably ended with the messianic robot liberator Call-Me-Kenneth being thoroughly defeated by Judge Dredd, who emphatically reestablishes slavery for robots. The satirical bite was ferocious: the story pretends to be a story about the merits of law and order and tough policing, but that reading falls apart upon inspection, revealing the degree to which the protagonist is the clear villain of the piece. Moore certainly could have come up with a similarly embittered ending in which the naively innocent coming of age drama runs painfully aground against the reality of Thatcher's Britain and comes undone. But instead Moore embraced the sentimentality of *E.T.* over the spiky anger of *Boys from the Blackstuff* and ended up with a mediocrity.

It must be remembered, however, that while *Skizz* was Moore's fourth ongoing strip to start, it is notable for being the first one to end. Moore would not have to deal with the prospect of wrapping up *Marvelman* or *V for Vendetta* until 1989, and his run on Captain Britain extended to 1984. *Skizz*, on the other hand, wrapped in August of 1983, five months after it started. At ninety-four pages, it was by some margin the longest thing he'd ever written, aside from his humor strips for *Sounds*, which are a fundamentally different sort of narrative. Much as his early *Star Wars* strip "The Pandora Effect" suffered from his obvious floundering at the length, *Skizz* shows a writer encountering an ending outside the context of short twist-of-fate stories for the first time and not quite making it. (Though truth be told, the accusation that endings are something of a weak point for Moore is not especially hard to back up with evidence—even among Moore's agreed upon classics it is notable that the iconic moments tend to come somewhat early in the narratives, and Eddie Campbell notes that Alan Moore "tends to trail off towards the end of the project" in terms of his speed in writing.)

Given this, the degree to which he flounders is impressive in its triviality. Moore's only real failing with *Skizz* is that the two aggressively different narratives he mashes up don't quite cohere in the ending. The strip is by no means a classic of the medium, but it's good enough that *2000 AD*'s various owners over the years have been able to turn a reasonable profit selling it as a historical curiosity, and that Jim Baikie produced two (entirely forgettable) sequels as a writer-artist in the early 1990s. Certainly the strip has moments of real and impressive quality, even if the whole is somewhat less than the sum of its parts.

If *Skizz* is ultimately hampered by its satirical toothlessness, Moore's *D.R. & Quinch*, his other early ongoing for *2000 AD*, goes a long way towards rebuking such criticism. That said, it is not entirely straightforward to call *D.R. & Quinch* an ongoing series. In most regards it is closer to the Abelard Snazz stories—a series of short stories featuring a recurring set of characters and a common underlying gag. There are in fact six distinct *D.R. & Quinch* stories, ranging in length from a single installment to a pair of five-parters, "D.R. & Quinch Get Drafted" and "D.R. & Quinch Go to Hollywood." The strip's longest sustained run was a stretch of three stories that ran over ten consecutive issues in 1984, starting with "D.R. & Quinch Go Straight," which began in Prog 350, and ending with the last part of "D.R. & Quinch Get Drafted" in Prog 359.

The strip's origins, however, come in Prog 317 in 1983, where, alongside one of the middle installments of *Skizz*, Moore penned what at the time appeared to be a perfectly ordinary *Time Twister* entitled "D.R. & Quinch Have Fun on Earth." Over six pages, it tells the story of Ernie Quinch and his friend Waldo "D.R" Dobbs (the D.R. is for "diminished responsibility") as they take an elaborate sort of revenge on Dean Fusk, who suspended the pair from college when he "found all the fur-coats and lasers" that Quinch had been hiding in his locker. Their scheme involves traveling back in time for several pages of sociopathic fun that incidentally results in orchestrating the entire history of Earth: shaping the continents with "a thermo-nuclear bazooka," teaching Neanderthals to beat each other up, and trying to grab aircraft with a tractor beam off the coast of Bermuda, which mostly just results in the aircraft being destroyed. At the end it turns out that as a result of their interference, humanity is having their first encounter with aliens, which results in a big reception that Dean Fusk attends. It further turns out that the shape of the continents on Earth spells out several nasty messages about Dean Fusk, resulting in the atomization of Earth and D.R. and Quinch being readmitted to college due to the suspicion that Fusk planted the evidence in Quinch's locker.

Several influences collide in "D.R. & Quinch Have Fun on Earth." The first is, as Moore himself puts it, "the great British comic tradition of making heroes out of juvenile delinquents; if you imagine *Dennis the Menace* with a thermonuclear capacity, you're probably pretty close to the idea of *D.R. & Quinch*." But there is more to the conceit than just that. *Dennis the Menace* itself belongs to the tradition of British children's comics such as *The Beano* and *The Dandy* that Moore described as being about "working class children in working class environments, and generally being spanked by their parents and teacher, which was a peculiar fixation." Which is to say that the comics Moore is extending the logic of were largely about the restoration of order. *Dennis the Menace* or *The Bash Street Kids* work in a sort of carnivalesque tradition where the entertaining and chaotic antics of the title characters are a short-lived inversion of the social order that is fun while it lasts, but always corrected in the end so that everyone knows their place. But *D.R. & Quinch* makes no effort to restore the social order. It is not just that D.R. and Quinch use thermo-nuclear bazookas instead of just leaving people to trip on soap, but that the sheer extent of mayhem that they get up to removes all possibility of restoring order. The worst thing that *Dennis the Menace* is ever going to do to anybody is make them fall into a lake or get slightly mauled by wild animals, which, at least in the context of a comic strip, is hardly a ghastly fate. "D.R. & Quinch Have Fun on Earth," on the other hand, culminates in the casual destruction of the planet. Giving them a spanking isn't really a suitable restoration of order at that point.

The second major influence is the *National Lampoon*'s recurring feature *O.C. and Stiggs*, an influence that *D.R. & Quinch* largely wears on its sleeve, or, at least, in its title. Like *D.R. & Quinch*, *O.C. and Stiggs* tells the story of two socially maladapted college students and their mayhem-causing adventures. For instance, at the start of their most iconic adventure, *The Utterly Monstrous, Mind-Roasting Summer of O.C. and Stiggs*, which took up the entire October 1982 issue of the *National Lampoon*, the narrator O.C. describes "the small inconvenience of having to attend the wedding reception of Schwab's sister, Lenora, a totally white-skinned harpist and ballet deviate with nostrils that look like old-fashioned key holes, who never appears anywhere without a ribbon on her somewhere, usually on her head, and usually four or five of them." He goes on to explain that "because Lenora was so artistic and withdrawn and delicate, and totally unable to function anyplace where there were any people or any windows or anything else that might suck her into a connection with the world, me and Stiggs got her an Uzi submachine gun for a wedding present, with a twenty-round clip and a detachable stock." This turns out to be a prime example of starting as one means to go on.

"He dropped acid bombs from little hatches in the base of his testicles, pissed dissembler all over them, blinded them with organ-specific toxins sprayed from his nipples, and claimed he did it all for the Virgin Mary—who, he said, lived down his street and wore indian army boots."
–Warren Ellis, *Transmetropolitan*, 1999

Once again, the obvious difference is in the sort of technology, although if one is being honest the presence of submachine guns already puts *O.C. and Stiggs* in a class closer to *D.R. & Quinch* than *Dennis the Menace*. But on the whole, *O.C. and Stiggs* takes a markedly different approach than *D.R. & Quinch*. Whereas D.R. and Quinch revel fairly purely in the destruction they cause, largely seeing it as an end in itself, O.C. and Stiggs are visibly motivated by an outright hatred for the people they harass. When D.R. and Quinch take revenge on someone it is inevitably because that person has done something terrible to them like kick them out of school or say mean things about them at a legal hearing. More often, however, they simply cause destruction for its own sake. O.C. and Stiggs, on the other hand, are arbitrarily malicious towards people. For instance, they describe the main target of their antics, Randall Schwab Jr., as "the most uncoordinated, whining, unacceptable goon in existence. Me and Stiggs have been torturing him and his family for over half of our lives. This is for two simple reasons: 1) he lives close to us, 2) he has an enormous head." It is not, of course, that expelling them from school for their hidden cache of weapons is a particularly good reason for D.R. and Quinch to take revenge on Dean Fusk, but there is at least a certain internal logic to it. O.C. and Stiggs, on the other hand, seem wholly capricious in their targets and antics. They just pick people they don't like very much and torment them.

On top of that, *O.C. and Stiggs* has a rather nastier edge to its humor. They indulge in sexist, racist, and homophobic behavior at considerable length, describing characters as "the Sluts de Box Car" and "two totally maladjusted nymphos," and describing things like a tuxedo store that's "a 100 percent Negro operation, limited exclusively to colors, substances, and textures alluring to Negroes only," neighboring "a filthy ethnic barbershop." At one point, deciding to reenact bits of *The Adventures of Huckleberry Finn*, they declare that "Barney had to be Nigger Jim on our voyage, so we made him wear lots of black goo," while "Stiggs refused to be Tom Sawyer, who, he said, was a homo pantywaist." This results in an encounter with "some Indian cops sleeping in the bushes" who "wanted our beer, so we told them that the Negro

Figure 77: Randall Schwab Jr. discovers the Uzi that O.C. and Stiggs left for his sister as a wedding present. (From The Utterly Monstrous, Mind-Roasting Summer of O.C. and Stiggs, *1982)*

Figure 78: The sort of ugly racial humor that is typical of O.C. and Stiggs. (From The Utterly Monstrous, Mind-Roasting Summer of O.C. and Stiggs, *1982)*

owned the beer and he was making us drink it because he was afraid he would become an alcoholic if he drank alone. By the time they processed this in their highly mystical and alcoholic Indian minds, however, we had drifted out of range, so they resumed sleeping." Certainly some of the humor is in precisely how awful all of these things are to say and in the degree to which O.C. and Stiggs are terrible people, but the sheer quantity of punching down is tough to swallow.

Moore, unsurprisingly, does not go in for deliberate offensiveness of this sort. More to the point, where the central joke of *O.C. and Stiggs* is just how utterly horrible the main characters are as people, *D.R. & Quinch* is on the whole more sympathetic to its protagonists. As Moore puts it, "a lot of people identify with these two ugly acne-ridden alien individuals who find no greater fun in life than going around and bombing expensive foreign restaurants," and with good reason: D.R. and Quinch are terribly fun. They are, at their core, sci-fi iterations of the anarchic youth *Action* foregrounded during its heyday in strips like *Look out for Lefty* and *Kids Rule OK!* It's a strip about joyfully dealing outsized retribution to the established social order, and as such fits perfectly into *2000 AD* in a way that *Skizz*, with its odd tension between its two goals, never quite could.

Fueling this bite is Moore's use of an unreliable narrator. A key part of the humor in *D.R. & Quinch* is the fact that what D.R. and Quinch say in their narration is not to be completely trusted. This is made clear in the first panel of the first story, when Quinch says, "I like guns and starting fights. My psychiatrist says I'm a psychotic deviant. But that doesn't mean I'm a bad person, right?" The entire joke, of course, is that this is precisely what being a psychotic deviant who likes guns and starting fights means. And this sort of humor continues throughout the comic. When, for instance, Quinch describes how they "pulled over in the late pre-Cambrian and checked out all the stuff that was starting to wriggle about in the radioactive mud. It was incredibly disgusting. But then, like D.R. said, 'That's life'," the line is funny because D.R. is being more accurate than the narration recognizes: D.R. and Quinch are, at that point in the strip, literally examining and occasionally shooting the earliest forms of life on Earth.

Of particular creative note is the fact that Moore is able to generate a subtly different sort of humor from the narration of each of his characters. "D.R. & Quinch Have Fun on Earth" is narrated by Quinch, and in it, as noted, the humor stems largely from Quinch's earnest obliviousness to his own malevolence. The humor is largely down to the fact that Quinch honestly does not appear to have any understanding of the fact that he is an absolutely horrible person. But as a result, the reader is only ahead of Quinch on a moment-to-moment basis. That is to say, whenever Quinch comments on a given incident, such as, "We tried to grab a couple of their planes with the tractor beam, to look at while we were cruising just off of Bermuda. But they were, like, really inferior merchandise, and they, like, fell to bits," the reader understands that Moore is giving a fictitious explanation of the Bermuda Triangle even though Quinch does not. But when, at the end of the story, it turns out that the shape that D.R. and Quinch bombed the continents into provides an insult against Dean Fusk, this is not set up. The reader knows more than Quinch describes about any given thing, but Quinch's tendency towards a simple, episodic narrative obscures the overall arc of things.

The pair's second story, "D.R. & Quinch Go Straight," has the same basic plot of "D.R. & Quinch Have Fun on Earth." D.R. and Quinch are punished by an authority figure (a judge this time), and take elaborate revenge. In this case the plot is lifted more directly from *The Utterly Monstrous, Mind-Roasting Summer of O.C. and Stiggs*, specifically the incident towards the end of the story in which O.C. and Stiggs take elaborate revenge on one of their nemeses by opening a drug rehab clinic next door to his house—not to mention the side character of Pulger, a "distressed war veteran" with an "alarmingly volatile condition" as "a result of his experiences during the recently-ended Ghoyogi Slime Jungle Wars,"

Figure 79: D.R. and Quinch blow up several emergent life forms on Earth. (From "D.R. & Quinch Have Fun on Earth," in 2000 AD *#317, written by Alan Moore, art by Alan Davis, 1983)*

which, in practice, means that he is the sort of person who, for "a quad-engine Strato-Chopper and thirty air-to-ground warpedos for his personal use," a characterization fairly clearly based on Howard Sponson, who O.C. describes as "Vietnam vet with roasted brains. He guards pot plantations and helps us out when we need stuff like Israeli machine guns and air-to-ground missiles." But more important than the plot is the way in which the style of narration changes.

"D.R. & Quinch Go Straight" is narrated by D.R. instead of by Quinch, and has a substantially different style. Where Quinch's narration comes in from the start and presents the entire story as, in effect, an essay that some comic artist has drawn pictures to accompany (there is in fact no dialogue to speak of in "D.R. & Quinch Have Fun on Earth"), D.R. merely provides commentary on the story, not even directly addressing the reader until page three. More to the point, where the humor in "D.R. & Quinch Have Fun on Earth" largely derives from the fact that Quinch does not fully understand what is happening or the implications of it, "D.R. & Quinch Go Straight" largely depends on the fact that D.R. has a clear scheme in mind from the outset, and that he is repeatedly lying. So when he declares that he "forgot that I had arranged a visit by the Ghoyogian Diplomatic Party" and that "I suppose I should have told Pulger about the Ghoyogian visit in advance," the humor is that the reader can see clearly (and has in fact been able to see since the end of the previous installment of the story) that this is going to end with Pulger and his fellow violent ex-servicemen proceeding to unleash a massive and comical spree of destruction against the visiting Ghoyogians in such a way as to cause a pleasant amount of horrifying property damage to the actually perfectly reasonable Judge Thorkwung. Where Quinch appears largely naïve about his horrible nature, D.R. positively revels in it, admitting things like, "Had I suspected then the truly horrifying suffering and amazing loss of life that would be caused by our well-meaning enterprise… I'd have done it anyway. Only more so." It's a similar sort of

Figure 80: A major plot point in the second D.R. & Quinch *story is the construction of Massacre House right next door to the pair's nemesis… (From "D.R. & Quinch Go Straight," in* 2000 AD *#350, written by Alan Moore, art by Alan Davis, 1984)*

Figure 81: …a plot point that is nearly identical to one from The Utterly Monstrous, Mind-Roasting Summer of O.C. and Stiggs. *(1982)*

humor to that of Quinch's narration, but with the emphasis subtly shifted so as to freshen the material. Instead of being unaware of the implications of what he's saying, D.R. is hyper-aware of them and communicating primarily through the subtext.

Also important, of course, is the material itself. The anarchic glee that *D.R. and Quinch* builds its humor out of is an ideology that must surely have appealed to Alan Moore. The detail that the two lead characters have been kicked out of school makes this one of the earliest of relatively few instances in Moore's career where one is compelled to read a story at least partially autobiographically. Moore, after all, was himself kicked out of school, and, if not under similar circumstances to those of D.R. and Quinch (he was only caught dealing acid, as opposed to harboring an extensive stash of high energy weapons), at least under a similar rhetoric. "The headmaster who had dealt with my expulsion had, I think, taken me rather personally," Moore explains. "He had written to all of the colleges and schools that I might have thought of applying to and told them that they should under no circumstances accept me as a pupil because it would be a corrupting influence upon the morals of the other students. I believe that he did at one point in the letter refer to me as sociopathic, which I think was rather harsh."

"Kid-With-Knife is behind you with an AK-47."
–Kieron Gillen, *Phonogram: The Singles Club*, 2009

It is difficult not to find certain parallels between Moore's wry interview humor in 2005 and the opening gag of "D.R. & Quinch Have Fun on Earth," where Quinch explains that "my psychiatrist says I'm a psychotic deviant. But that doesn't mean I'm a bad person, right?" Similarly, in another interview, Moore describes how "I was just convinced I must get my revenge upon society, no matter what" for being kicked out, making it clear that his animosity was for "the government, it was the structure of everything." Although this is delivered with similar humor (Moore encourages the interviewer to "try to picture, if you will, a little 17-year-old Alan sitting there, kind of staring, hallucinating"), the similarity between it and D.R. and Quinch's worldview is striking. And more to the point, understandable—the result of Moore's headmaster's aggression against him was his consignment to a seeming lifetime of jobs "that didn't give a damn who they employed," essentially ripping away all his seeming prospects and future over, in effect, one transgression.

In other words, for all that D.R. and Quinch are self-evidently irredeemable sociopaths, it's in no way surprising that Moore would find the pair broadly sympathetic simply because they are irredeemable sociopaths who hate the right people. More to the point, the nature of the humor within *D.R. & Quinch* becomes more subtle and nuanced when taken in this light. The game of what is said, and what is deliberately unsaid, whether by author or character, becomes altogether more complex. The structure of any given joke within *D.R. & Quinch* is based, in effect, on the audience's ability to recognize the layers of irony in place and to in turn recognize themselves as the sort of people clever enough to see the real joke beneath the surface language. This goes hand in hand with the sense of being angry at the right people that the strip (and *2000 AD* at large) fosters: if you're clever enough to get the joke, you're also clever enough to know who the world's assholes are and to appreciate the fantasy of shooting them with a ZZ-50 Mono-Nucleic Pulveriser.

The problem, however, is that, as Moore put it, "They were originally supposed to be a one-off," and were never designed for ongoing adventures. There is really only one joke to the characters, and Moore knew it. Even by the third *D.R. & Quinch* strip, the premise of the strip was drifting. Where the first two stories had been about reveling in comedy violence against the Man, the third strip, "D.R. & Quinch Go Girl Crazy," takes an entirely different approach. In this case, the story is focused on Quinch's discovery that

D.R. has fallen for a girl named Chrysoprasia. Chrysoprasia is a clean cut, perfectly nice girl, or, as Quinch puts it, "a worthless, simpering zombie," and, accordingly, D.R. has opted to clean up his act and stop hanging out with Quinch. Offended by this, Quinch sets out to get his friend back by showing Chrysoprasia how horrible a person her boyfriend actually is. The central gag at the rough halfway point of the strip is that the result is not, in fact, that she leaves D.R., but that she redubs herself Crazy Chryssie and becomes as sociopathically violent as D.R. and Quinch, bursting into the theatre she and D.R. were meant to perform in while shouting "grab your ankles and prepare to eat photon oblivion, you incredibly boring old people!"

Certainly the strip is funny, but its denouement, in which D.R. shamelessly and without hesitation sells out Chryssie and lets her go to prison to protect Quinch, rather takes the air out of the joke. Indeed, it marks a real turning point in *D.R. & Quinch*, in that it's the first point where D.R. and Quinch get revenge on someone who is portrayed as basically sympathetic. That this is also the first substantive female character in the story makes the ugliness of this even more pronounced. It's a fundamentally different sort of humor. In many ways the twist, in which Chrysoprasia turns delinquent, highlights the nature of the shift involved. In the first two strips the sort of gag that opens "D.R. & Quinch Go Girl Crazy," where Quinch explains that his mother "says I'm emotionally deprived with accordant behavioural aberrations. This means that I like stealing things and destroying vehicles and terrorising people who have never done me any harm whatsoever. This is why everybody hates me, and that's why I'm emotionally deprived," is the norm. In that sort of gag there's a careful balance of knowledge. Quinch may be oblivious to the irony involved in his words, but he's not *wrong* as such. D.R. and Quinch are, in this sort of joke, possibly oblivious or liars, but they're still basically allied with the strip's implied author.

Figure 82: Chrysoprasia is (at first) not entirely well-adapted to Quinch's violent tendencies... (From "D.R. & Quinch Go Girl Crazy," in 2000 AD #353, written by Alan Moore, art by Alan Davis, 1984)

Figure 83: but after her transformation into Crazy Chryssie (made a brilliant sight gag by Alan Davis) she gets the hang of rampant sociopathy. (From "D.R. & Quinch Go Girl Crazy," in 2000 AD #353, written by Alan Moore, 1984)

But once Quinch gets caught flatfooted by Chryssie's heel turn this dissolves. The strip is no longer going along with D.R. and Quinch's antics with an eyebrow raised at the ironic excess. Instead, D.R. and Quinch have become fallible characters in a narrative that expects them to overcome adversity, and, more disturbingly, characters with interiority who the audience is meant to empathize with in subtle and complex ways. This is, in most circumstances, a sign of a more mature story, but in this case it's a step towards the disintegration of the basic premise of the strip. The joke that binds the whole thing together has been removed. This is understandable—there really aren't that many more variations on it to be had after the first two strips—but it also reveals the fact that there's not actually a lot more potential in the characters.

In many ways this problem is highlighted perfectly by the fourth *D.R. & Quinch* story, "D.R. & Quinch Get Drafted." The idea of this story is straightforward and compelling enough, and largely does what it says on the tin—the pair get drafted into the Ghoyogian war that they started two strips earlier. There is, within this, a substantial and quality idea. Pitting the anarchic and ironic violence of *D.R. & Quinch* against the banal violence of an actual war is clever and, more to the point, very much worth doing. But stretched over five separate installments the subversive cleverness largely found itself lost in the mix. Tellingly, parts two and three end with essentially identical cliffhangers: D.R. & Quinch run into a supporting character from a past story on Ghoyogia. First they find themselves thrown in jail with Pulger, the violent ex-grunt who D.R and Quinch manipulated into setting off the war back in "D.R. & Quinch Go Straight," and then they find themselves sharing an escape tunnel with Chryssie.

What's really revealing about these two gags is that they are devoid of any substance besides the iconography of *D.R. & Quinch* itself. Instead of humor based on the strip and reader indulging in a shared recognition of the irony involved, the strip and reader are now indulging in a shared memory of past *D.R. & Quinch* strips. The humor comes not from substance but from reference—from a nostalgia for the great *D.R. & Quinch* strips of, if not old, at least of a month or so ago. It's not even that the jokes don't work, but merely that they are visibly the jokes of a strip that has run its course. It is tempting to recall Moore's later criticism of DC Comics' predilection for creating stories that repurpose concepts originally developed by Moore as resembling them "going through my trashcan like raccoons in the dead of the night," except to note that Moore is not grabbing quarter-century old ideas but stuff from just a few weeks earlier in the very same magazine. Given Moore's sense of the creative bankruptcy involved in the former, the latter must have been a depressing experience.

None of this is to say that "D.R. & Quinch Get Drafted" is a failure, even in terms of its subversive and satirical messages. For all the messiness, there are moments of real charm. The moment where D.R. scoffs at the low quality of weaponry on display and, in doing so, impresses the draft office with his seeming dedication to war is truly charming, if self-evidently repurposed from Arlo Guthrie's 1967 pacifist hit "Alice's Restaurant." And the strip's denouement, in which a standoff between Ghyogians and the space marines from which D.R. and Quinch have gone AWOL, in which D.R., Quinch, Pulger, and Chryssie are, predictably, caught in the middle is resolved when Quinch's very wealthy mother descends from a spaceship, casually crushing the two opposing armies, and rescues her "dummy-dumpling," inviting him and his friends "inside my cosy inter-cosmic mega-palace" to "have a nice cup of tea and a scone." The ridiculous *deus ex machina* (or, at least, giant alien ex machina) is a self-consciously lousy and arbitrary resolution that breaks the inherent deadlock in a contrast between *D.R. & Quinch*'s fun, satirical violence and the awful and cruel violence of war. Instead of trying to balance them out, Moore simply introduces a ludicrous device that highlights exactly how stupid and pointless war is—a point he reiterates with D.R.'s

Figure 84: Quinch's mother arrives to "save" the day. (From "D.R. &
Quinch Get Drafted," in 2000 AD #359, written by Alan Moore, art by
Alan Davis, 1984)

final monologue, where he talks about how "as the mega-palace drifted among the stars, I thought about war and rich people and all the utterly fantastic things that had, like, happened to me. All at once I understood why it is that men fight each other. I suddenly saw the answer to all this senseless violence that afflicts us! But, like, I didn't write it down or anything... and, like, y'know how it is—next morning I had totally forgotten what it was, man." It's withering and funny, and while it doesn't balance out the staleness of the four strips worth of buildup, it is, at the very least, quite good on its own merits.

The final ongoing *D.R. & Quinch* strip, "D.R. & Quinch Go to Hollywood," presents an even larger problem. More than one critic has identified it as the pinnacle of *D.R. & Quinch*, and not without reason. It's a gleefully over-the-top parody of the world of Hollywood in which D.R. and Quinch come into possession of the last script of Torquetto Jubbli, a formerly brilliant and acclaimed screenwriter who is back from ten years of writers block, or at least would have been if he hadn't dropped dead in front of D.R. & Quinch. Despite the screenplay being completely illegible (D.R. is fairly certain that the third word of the title is "oranges," and the line "Close the curtains, Geoffrey, I'm amphibious" definitely appears at the end, but the remaining 51,100 pages of the screenplay are utterly unreadable), D.R. & Quinch are able to browbeat and con their way into production, helped by the fact that their star, a not-actually-remotely veiled Marlon Brando, is, as his manager explains, "totally unable to read or write," a secret that has been successfully kept because "no one can understand a word he says anyway."

Despite this, his apparently moving performance of the script, which he renders as "Uhguh dmnuh yuh, buh rudduh mnugh. Whuvuh suh thuh zuh furruh shunduhluh! Muzwuh ruh, huh? Yuh... Yuh... Abuh Luh Vuhruhduh? Vuhruhduh, huh? Sgucuh Nuh Juhnuh! Uhmuh Puh Rhunu... buh nuh thuh pyuhnuh... Uhnuh ruh cuhduh, duh fuhmuh whuh. Nuh muh... nuh muh...," causes the film to be immediately greenlit, leading D.R., when asked to "be bried and honest" in describing what the film is like, to say simply, "It's a disaster movie, man." This proves largely prophetic, as during filming Marlon fails to read the twelve meter high fluorescent signs placed around the pyramid of sixteen thousand oranges that pronounce "Danger! Do not touch these monstrously hazardous citrus fruits, man," and, despite his manager's plaintive cry to "mind the oranges, Marlon," takes one to eat, leading him to be crushed to death under several hundred tons of oranges. In his honor, D.R. names the film "Mind the Oranges, Marlon," and it proceeds to become a massive cult hit that nets D.R. & Quinch a spectacular sum of money.

The strip marks a significant change in the nature of *D.R. & Quinch* in several regards. The sociopathic tendencies of the pair are significantly ratcheted down. They're not even in the midst of some elaborately violent scheme when they get distracted by Hollywood—they meet Torquetto Jubbli in a bus depot, and in this instance are portrayed more as laconic conmen than hyper-violent juvenile delinquents. Their approach to getting the movie made is on one level not that different from their elaborate con in "D.R. & Quinch Go Straight," but there's still a sizable distinction to be made. In "D.R. & Quinch Go Straight" the pair pretend to be reformed versions of themselves. In "D.R. & Quinch Go to Hollywood," on the other hand, they dress in somewhat elaborate costumes (the sight gag of D.R. with a monocle and beret is, admittedly, brilliant) and fake their way to a social role. The trick to doing so, D.R. explains in narration, is "to impress people with your good taste and forceful personality," and so he orders "fifteen emperor lobsters," which are all to be "wearing little knitted waistcoats... in Prussian blue," and then explodes with rage when the coats are cerulean blue.

It's an entertaining satire, but this sort of blending in through ludicrous exaggeration is not a tactic that is a natural fit with D.R. & Quinch's approach to things at any point prior to this in the narrative. The reason for this is simple enough, which is that "D.R. & Quinch Go to Hollywood" is not really in the same vein as the other *D.R. & Quinch* stories at all, and instead appropriates its structure and sense of humor from another source entirely. While the other *D.R. & Quinch* stories are subversions of the longstanding British comic tradition of juvenile delinquents, "D.R. & Quinch Go to Hollywood" is at heart an execution of a style of comedy drawn from *MAD Magazine*.

> *"We confuse rebellion with a hairstyle. Nightmare of the teenage jobscape, suddenly made stupid, weak, and clumsy there among the calloused adults."*
> —Alan Moore, *The Birth Caul*, 1995

The specific style in question dates to *MAD* #4, from 1953, and from the acclaimed story "Superduperman," although following the success of that story it became the house style for *MAD*. Still, "Superduperman" is a known influence for Moore, who has credited it as such for both *Marvelman* and *Watchmen*, and is as good a vehicle to describe the style as any. In many ways "Superduperman" reflects the style of short story that Moore characterized as a "list story" when writing Future Shocks for *2000 AD*. Its structure is in effect a frame for going through a bunch of parodied aspects of Superman and, later, Captain Marvel.

In rapid succession the strip introduces Clark Bent, Lois Pain, and Billy Spafon, who with the magic word SHAZOOOM!—Strength, Health, Aptitude, Zeal, Ox (power of), Ox (power of another), and Money—becomes Captain Marbles and proceeds to have an extended fight with Superduperman. The story drips with irony: Superduperman's chest insignia constantly changes from panel to panel, often serving as various corporate logos or notes that the space is for sale, while Captain Marbles has openly given up being a superhero in favor of making money. All of this is a barely veiled parody of the then-current legal case between National Comics (the then-owners of Superman) and Fawcett

Figure 85: Wally Wood's extremely detailed art packs in a number of entertaining sight gags. (From "Superduperman," in Mad #4, written by Harvey Kurtzman, art by Wally Wood, 1953)

Publications, who owned the (at the time) more popular Captain Marvel.

Although there is a plot—Superduperman meets and fights Captain Marbles and finally defeats him by tricking him into punching himself in the head, only to find out that Lois Pain still considers him (quite correctly, given his habit of using his X-Ray vision to spy on the women's room) a creep—the plot is, like that of "Sunburn" or "They Sweep the Spaceways," mainly an excuse to pack in jokes, including elaborate sight gags within Wally Woods' hyper-detailed art and various suitably awful puns in the vein of Clark Bent. The story is just a frame for this parodic work. And this describes the basic approach—*MAD* #10's "G.I. Shmoe," #7's "Shermlock Shomes," or #13's "Prince Violent" are all basically the same structure: stories that exist to pack in a large number of humorous distortions of recognizable characters and figures.

This also perfectly describes "D.R. & Quinch Go to Hollywood," which manages to shoehorn in parodies not just of Marlon Brando but of Alfred Hitchcock and of some well-known British film critics. This is the main point of the strip—D.R. & Quinch are in effect just an occasion for Moore to write an extended list story about Hollywood. But for all that the strip is quite funny, it's also clear that any meaningful satirical bite the story might have has been well and truly drained out of it by this point. Hollywood is, in practice, just about the safest target imaginable, and Moore is ultimately adding a not particularly notable entry to a massively large genre of Hollywood parodies. In May of 1984, when the story wrapped, Moore had never even been to the US, and was still years out from the wealth of frustrating experiences with Hollywood that he would go on to have. "D.R. & Quinch Go to Hollywood" is, in other words, not the work of someone who has had even the slightest firsthand experience with Hollywood; it's just a bunch of clichés and media images of Hollywood reflected back through the eyes of an admittedly highly competent humorist.

However entertaining the results, it's miles from the furious satire of "D.R. & Quinch Have Fun on Earth" and "D.R. & Quinch Go Straight," which visibly extended from his own experience with being branded as a sociopathic juvenile delinquent, and his continual anger at "the man."

But in truth, Moore's own investment in that humor was rapidly waning. Over time Moore came to conclude that, as he put in a later interview, *D.R. & Quinch* was "something that I don't think has any redeeming social value. It makes violence funny, which I don't think is right. I have to question the point where I'm actually talking about thermonuclear weapons as a source of humor." This decision fits with Moore's larger career arc at this time; by the time *D.R. & Quinch* became an ongoing series for *2000 AD*, Moore was deep into work on *Swamp Thing*, a comic he filled with ecological sentiment. The final *D.R. & Quinch* story, "D.R. & Quinch Get Back to Nature," came out in the *2000 AD Sci-Fi Special '85*, the same year as his famed "Nukeface Papers" story in *Swamp Thing*, in which artist Steve Bissette wove chilling present-day newspaper headlines about the horrific effects of nuclear power into the art. The idea that Moore would decide that *D.R. & Quinch* "is humorous in a kind of an *Animal House* way, socially irresponsible kind of way, but I'm not really that comfortable about making jokes about nuclear weapons" is wholly believable.

But there's a broader turn in place here. By the time that Moore put *D.R. & Quinch* in place he was also deep into *V for Vendetta*, a comic that existed, as Moore put it, to interrogate the British "tradition of making heroes out of criminals," and ultimately to conclude that "killing people is always wrong" and to envision a different sort of anarchic hero who rejected violence. His rejection of *D.R. & Quinch* is clearly a parallel to that process, itself a parallel to William Blake's eventual rejection of Orc, the embodiment of revolution itself, as a viable opposition to Urizen's cold and tyrannical reason. Blake described Orc's efforts at revolution thusly: "Fury! rage! madness! in a wind swept through America / And the red flames of Orc that folded roaring fierce around / The angry shores, and the fierce rushing of th'inhabitants together," leading to the point where "Then had America been lost, o'erwhelm'd by the Atlantic, / And Earth had lost another portion of the infinite."

Beyond that, though, as Moore notes, "I probably got as many laughs out of it as I could." By the final *D.R. & Quinch* strip Moore was reduced to recreating the sense of ridiculous violence of the first few strips by putting D.R. and Quinch in charge of a summer camp and having a strip narrated by one of the traumatized campers who writes home assuring his parents that "I sure am having a swell time at this summer camp you sent me to, and I am not being maltreated in any way." As with the first few *D.R. & Quinch* stories, the humor lies in the fact that the reader is clever enough to grasp the irony in lines like this and the camper's assertion that "our supervisors are responsible adults who certainly never get drunk and shoot out all the windows in the dormitory block." But while this approach succeeds in restoring the central joke of *D.R. & Quinch* that had been largely absent since the conclusion of "D.R. & Quinch Go Straight," the satirical bite remains gone. No longer are D.R. & Quinch railing ridiculously at the horrors of conventional authority: they're just torturing kids by throwing them into patches of "mind-wrenchingly painful poison-stingwort." Whatever philosophical objections Moore might have had to the nature of *D.R. & Quinch*'s brand of satire seem beside the point when that satire has been so completely bled out of the series through excessive repetition. *2000 AD*'s 1987 attempt to revive the pair as a series of one-page gags under the banner *D.R. & Quinch's Agony Page*, written by Jamie Delano, proved similarly unpromising despite what is, on the surface at least, a nearly solid gold premise.

While Moore's writing may have flagged over the course of *D.R. & Quinch*, however, the work of his collaborator, Alan Davis, never did. Davis had been active and acclaimed for several years by the point of *D.R. & Quinch*, having done work with Alan Moore for both Marvel UK and *Warrior*, as well as a run on the Gerry Finley-Day *2000 AD* series *Harry Twenty on the High Rock*. But these jobs had largely established Davis as, in his own words, "the gritty realistic artist." Certainly *Harry Twenty on the High Rock* supports this—it's a quite grim prison escape story with the sci-fi twist that the prison is "a hundred miles above the earth" and "crammed with 10,000 of the hardest, most vicious criminals from the world below." The protagonist, Harry Twenty, formerly Harry Thompson, was sent to prison for smuggling food to starving islanders, and spends the bulk of the strip trying to escape. It is, as one would expect, violent and full of unsavory figures. The strip culminates with the prison being blown out of Earth's orbit in the course of a prison riot, and ends with Harry effectively in charge of the prison where he declares, in a straight-up ripoff of *The Prisoner*, "I ain't a number any longer. I'm a free man!" The ending leaves plenty of room for a continuation, but the strip was an acknowledged mess— Finley-Day's scripts were described charitably as "in need of battening down and knocking into shape," and less charitably as borderline incoherent: "The sentences don't make sense," said Alan Grant, who had the unenviable job of rewriting Finley-Day's already paid-for scripts. It wrapped in Prog 307, and was at that point replaced with *Skizz*.

Davis describes the experience as stressful. "When Richard [Burton] got me along to the *2000 AD* offices, Steve [MacManus] wasn't really too impressed with what I was doing. He didn't really like the idea of having an American-style artist for *2000 AD*. I was almost on probation, in a way." The spectacle of an increasingly acclaimed and popular artist who was doing fantastic work for two of IPC's competitors being given a script that had been festering in the IPC inventory since 1982 because of its obvious problems closely mirrors the strange failure of IPC to give Moore ongoing work until he was on the brink of getting poached by American companies as well.

Eventually IPC deigned to give the pair, who were well into their Eagle Award winning run on *Marvelman* over at *Warrior*, a *Time Twisters* to do, which resulted in "D.R. & Quinch Have Fun on Earth." Davis, for his part, was eager to shake off the reputation for grit he had acquired and, as he put it, "prove I could draw other styles of art," and based his approach on Leo Baxendale's *Grimly Feendish* strip from Odhams' *Smash!* and *Wham!* titles. Feendish, "The Rottenest Crook in the World," originated as a villain in *Wham!*'s *Eagle-Eye Junior Spy* before getting his own strip in *Smash!*, and was a would-be supervillain whose overly elaborate schemes inevitably ended tragically for him. Depicted as a short, fat, grotesque with fangs, his influence on *D.R. & Quinch* is evident in Davis's design for Quinch.

Davis's non-comedic work had always benefited in part from his knack for drawing facial expressions, and he parlayed this skill into *D.R. & Quinch*, crafting the characters so that their faces were at once alien and tremendously expressive. Quinch generally remained impassive, as befitted his taciturn nature (virtually all of his lines across the series are simply "S'right."), but D.R.'s supremely expressive face sells countless sight gags. Similarly, the transition of Chrysoprasia to Crazy Chryssie in "D.R. & Quinch Go Girl Crazy" is accomplished largely through one single facial expression, emphasized by one of the few times Quinch's stoic grin breaks down.

The transition is also helped, however, by Davis's excellent sense of silhouette. All of Davis's primary characters in *D.R. & Quinch* have instantly recognizable outlines, and the Chrsoprasia/Chryssie transition is handled by substantially altering Chryssie's so that her previously downturned ears stick straight up (mirroring D.R.'s) and her neatly tied bun at the front of her head explodes into a front-hanging ponytail. D.R. and Quinch themselves, meanwhile, are constructed as a classic double act, with Quinch being the large and round character while D.R. is small and skinny. D.R.'s expressive face is framed by an instantly recognizable pair of sharply

Figure 86: Leo Baxendale's Grimly Feendish, the visual inspiration for Quinch.

Figure 87: D.R.'s ridiculous pompadour and massive ears give him an immediately recognizable (and funny) silhouette, a key aspect of cartooning. (From 2000 AD #355, 1984)

pointed ears and a comically large pompadour in the Elvis Presley/James Dean mould, tying him implicitly to a long history of rebellious youth. The art is crisp, clean, and entertainingly grotesque, giving the absurd excesses of Moore's script a note-perfect execution.

But this is hardly surprising for what was, by the time of *D.R. & Quinch*, a well-honed creative partnership. Moore and Davis had been working together since June of 1982 when Moore, having made his bones on the *Star Wars* and *Doctor Who* titles published by Marvel UK, was given the reins of Marvel UK's *Captain Britain*, at the time an ongoing series in the monthly anthology *Marvel Superheroes*. Davis had been drawing *Captain Britain* for the comic since September of 1981, where he made his mainstream debut illustrating a script by Dave Thorpe that served as the character's first appearance in that title. But the history of that character stretches back considerably further.

Chapter Seven: Captain Britain

"The Promethean age had been announced; the time of men as gods who bore fire in the palms of their hands had come."
–Grant Morrison, *Supergods*, 2011

To understand the nature of Captain Britain as a character, it is necessary to understand Marvel UK, which in turn requires an understanding of Marvel Comics. The company originated out of the broader publishing portfolio of Martin Goodman, born Moses Goodman in 1908 to Lithuanian immigrants to the United States. Goodman's family was large and poor, and Goodman had to drop out of school in the fifth grade to enter the workforce. He started traveling the country as a teenager, riding the rails and staying in hobo camps throughout the Great Depression. Eventually he returned to enter the publishing industry, rising through the ranks at Eastern Distributing Corporation before jumping ship to form his own company, Newsstand Publications, with Archie Comics cofounder Louis Silberkleit. In 1934 Newsstand Publications went bankrupt when their distributor went under, which led to Silberkleit departing the company, but Goodman managed to convince creditors that he could turn the company around, which he proceeded to do.

Goodman's business model was based on trend-surfing. He changed the insignias on his titles regularly, creating different lines to house different sorts of books, and was ruthless about pushing out clones of successful titles. The bulk of his magazines were pulps in the classic model: *All Star Adventure Fiction, Ka-Zar, Two-Gun Western, Uncanny Tales*, and, in a title that Goodman would use later to more success, *Marvel Tales*. In 1939, he added a comics line to capitalize on the success that National Publications was having with *Action Comics*, and so Timely Comics launched with *Marvel Comics* #1, which featured the debuts of a variety of superheroes: the android Human Torch, Bill Everett's Namor the Sub-Mariner, and a costumed detective named The Angel.

The comics sold adequately, but were not quite the hits that Goodman had hoped for. That came at the end of 1940, when writer Joe Simon and artist Jack Kirby created Captain America, a superhero designed with the simple and direct goal of providing thrilling superhero adventure stories about fighting the Nazi menace, turning the Siegel and Shuster formula of colorful action adventures towards a jingoistic patriotism that proved lucrative. But Goodman turned out to be pinching more than just a visual and literary style from National Comics, which famously bought Superman off of Siegel and Shuster for $130 (roughly £1300 today) before making billions of dollars off of the property—he leveraged all of the losses that Timely was accruing across all of its titles against profits on *Captain America*, and thus avoided having to pay Simon and Kirby as much in royalties.

Understandably displeased with this, Simon and Kirby began renting a cheap hotel room near the Timely offices and used their after work and lunch hours to develop characters to try to sell to DC Comics, a sister company to National that offered them a $500-a-week deal. Goodman had given Simon and Kirby a seventeen-year-old assistant by the name of Stanley Lieber, an aspiring writer who emptied Simon and Kirby's ash trays in between writing the text pieces that were needed to get magazine postal rates on *Captain America* under the Americanized pen name under which he would become famous: Stan Lee. Lieber had gotten the job through classic nepotism—he was Goodman's wife's cousin, and his mother had used her family connections to get him a job at Timely after he was fired from a job manufacturing trousers. Lieber eventually figured out that Simon and Kirby were working on a side project during lunch, and insisted on tagging along.

Displaying the cronyist tendencies that would eventually bring him to great heights in the comics industry, Lieber promptly ratted out Simon and Kirby, which resulted in not only their being summarily fired, but also Lieber's promotion to editor, still using his Stan Lee byline. When he returned to Timely in 1945 after a break in the army where he wrote training material and posters, the company had largely moved away from superheroes towards a more diverse pool of comics, reflecting the post-War decline in popularity of superheroes that eventually decimated National/DC's line to where, of their large pool of superhero characters, only Superman, Batman, and Wonder Woman still had titles. Lee oversaw a massively productive department that worked on funny animals as well as girls' comics like *Tessie the Typist* and *Millie the Model.* By the end of the decade, Marvel wasn't even publishing any superhero books, although Captain America's name remained on *Captain America's Weird Tales* despite his lack of any appearances in the comic.

Lee rang in the 1950s by doing Goodman's dirty work yet again, this time firing the entire comics department after Goodman discovered that Lee had stockpiled finished comics without publishing them, which Goodman reasoned meant there was no need to be paying writers and artists for new comics. Goodman took the occasion to rebrand the line from Timely Comics to Atlas Comics, with the ever loyal Lee still in charge of the line. But just a few years later the line was decimated again after Frederic Wertham, a pop psychologist, raised a moral panic about the corrupting influence of comics that resulted in a popular backlash and the shuttering of most of the industry. This, combined with the collapse of Goodman's distributor in 1957, forced Goodman to seek distribution with Independent News, a company owned by DC Comics, which thus stipulated that Goodman could only publish eight titles a month. Goodman promptly took a vacation in Florida and left Lee to fire the entire staff for the second time in a decade, which, of course, he did.

Lee kept the comics line running with a variety of generic anthologies that featured titles like *Tales to Astonish* and *Journey into Mystery*, all of them based on a standardized formula where issues would open with a monster story drawn by Jack Kirby (who came back to Lee when other work dried up), a couple of *Twilight Zone* knockoff twist ending stories, and a more surreal closing story penned by Steve Ditko. But the line was a minor part of Goodman's business, and Lee was rapidly finding himself on the fringes of the company. All of this changed, however, in 1961.

As legend tells it, Martin Goodman played a golf game with Jack Liebowitz, his counterpart at DC Comics. DC had, following the moral panic of the mid-50s, made a steady return to superhero comics, viewing them as natural and wholesome replacements for the crime comics that had been particularly targeted by Fredric Wertham and his followers. In 1960, DC launched *Justice League of America*, a comic that put their most popular superheroes together on a single team, and found considerable success with it, a fact he supposedly imparted to Goodman during this alleged golf game. In any case, whether he was tipped off by Liebowitz or just noticed the sales figures himself, Goodman proceeded to assign Lee the task of creating a knockoff title. This, however, posed a significant challenge—DC's title worked by putting existing characters together in one book, much like it had done with the Justice Society of America in the Golden Age *All-Star Comics*. But Marvel, in 1961, didn't have any currently running superhero comics, so Lee's imitation required him to create some bespoke heroes of his own.

The result was *The Fantastic Four*, featuring art by Jack Kirby. Indeed, it is easy to understate the importance of Jack Kirby to the comic. Lee was responsible for writing almost the entirety of the Atlas line, and his approach to this, later refined into the so-called Marvel Method, was to delegate a

Figure 88: Although Lee and Kirby departed significantly from the formula of Justice League of America *(left) with* The Fantastic Four *(right), it is notable that Kirby's cover to the first issue borrows its composition from DC's book.*

lot of the writing to artists. Lee would write a plot synopsis, sometimes an exceedingly vague one (by legend, Lee's plot for the famed Galactus arc of *The Fantastic Four* read simply "have them fight God"), and the artist would proceed to work the details out, with Lee adding dialogue or, at times, simply revising the artist's words. This is especially important for *The Fantastic Four*, a comic where the grotesquery of the characters is part of the premise. Featuring a new version of the Human Torch, the monstrous orange rock man called the Thing, the fairly self-explanatory Invisible Woman, and Mister Fantastic, whose body could stretch and deform at will, the team was based as much on circus sideshow acts as anything, making them tacit mirrors of the first issue's villains, a legion of monsters controlled by the evil Moleman. Kirby provided a typically classic design for all of it, giving the book a strange and uncanny kineticism.

This sense of energy was matched by Lee, whose writing featured a level of distinct and vibrant characterization that had not previously been seen in superhero comics. This was in many ways a very low bar to clear—Alan Moore has sarcastically described Lee's writing by saying that he looked at a field of one-dimensional comics characters and "had this huge breakthrough of two-dimensional characters"—but the fact remained that unlike the *Justice League of America*, which featured a team of iconic but, at least in terms of characterization, largely interchangeable square-jawed heroes (Wonder Woman included), Lee's team of freaks had a creative spark that was liberating. Mister Fantastic was a noble-hearted and at times ponderous scientist, while his girlfriend, Susan Storm, was a hapless housewife. Her brother, Johnny Storm, was a loudmouth and (literally) hotheaded youth, while Ben Grimm, the Thing, was a furious beast perpetually on the seeming edge of losing his shit and smashing everything in sight.

The approach was a hit, and Goodman's comics imprint, now renamed once again to Marvel Comics, quickly spun out clones, killing lower-selling titles like *Teen-Age Romance* to make room for *The Incredible Hulk*. Other existing titles like *Journey into Mystery* and *Tales to Astonish* acquired superhero-based lead features. Lee saw to it that the titles maintained a clear sense of identity based largely on his own skill at self-promotion. With the third issue of *The Fantastic Four*, for instance, the title boldly proclaimed itself "The greatest comic magazine in the world!!" and boasted of the issue's status as a "great, collectors'-item issue." Thor's debut in *Journey into Mystery* #83 was tagged as "The most exciting super hero of all time," while Iron Man's debut in *Tales of Suspense* #39 was "The newest, most breath-taking, most sensational super-hero of all," with a cover that made sure the reader knew it was "From the talented bull-pen where the Fantastic Four, Spider-Man, Thor and your other favorite super-heroes were born!" This image of the Marvel Bullpen was central to Lee's jovial public persona, and in the tenth issue of *The Fantastic Four* Lee and Kirby tore down the fourth wall entirely by having Doctor Doom show up in Lee and Kirby's studio demanding to see Mister Fantastic.

Inside, the comics were just as chatty, with Lee using captions to directly address the reader—the first page of Spider-Man's debut story, for instance, asks the reader, "Like costumed heroes? Confidentially, we in the comic mag business refer to them as 'long underwear characters'! And, as you know, they're a dime a dozen! But we think you may find our Spider-Man just a bit… different!" This false camaraderie with the reader, with the ludicrous claim that information plastered on the first page of a national publication was in some way confidential, helped give Marvel both a distinctive brand identity and, just as important, gave the sense of Marvel as a subversive and cooler alternative to DC's line. This was reflected in a growing engagement with adult fans, particularly college students, with Lee setting up the Merry Marvel Marching Society, a Marvel fan club, which saw forty thousand people shell out a dollar for a membership kit that included a pin "designed to look great when worn next to your Phi Beta Kappa key!"

With the exception of Spider-Man, which was drawn by Steve Ditko, all of the Marvel titles were originated by Jack Kirby, with other artists being brought in later. Kirby was both a staggeringly productive workhorse and astonishingly versatile in character design. Famously, Kirby rarely recycled characters out of the belief that it was faster to just design a new character than to reference what he'd done before, and his design work was integral to the success of the line. But, as is the norm in the history of the American comics industry, credit was hard to come by. Lee, enmeshed as he was in the corporate structure of Marvel, had all sorts of perks, but Kirby's work was freely exploited and built on by others while he never got more than a standard freelancer's check. Towards the end of the decade, Kirby agreed to testify against Joe Simon in a lawsuit over the copyright to Captain America in exchange for Marvel giving him a payment of equivalent size to any settlement Marvel reached with Simon. By this time Goodman had sold the company, and the new boss, Sheldon Feinberg, proved less than magnanimous, offering Jack Kirby a derisive contract that led to Kirby finally leaving the company in March of 1970.

"Flying was the best bit. The rest of it was fraught with more misery and self pity than the entire recorded output of Les Smiths."
–Grant Morrison, "Captain Granbretan," 1986

By this time Marvel had largely moved to a second generation of talent (with Stan Lee taking on fewer and fewer writing responsibilities, though his name was still plastered all over the branding) and was looking for new things to try. They dabbled with underground comics, attempted a return to horror, and finally managing to unseat DC as the largest comics company in the US via a brutally duplicitous move that involved colluding with DC on a price increase from twenty to twenty-five cents only to pull out of it while giving the newsstands a better cut of profits, which resulted in DC's more expensive comics being shoved to the margins of the racks. As part of this corporate expansion, Marvel decided to look into foreign markets, specifically the United Kingdom.

Short of Odhams' *Power Comics* line that gave Steve Moore his comics industry breakthrough, Marvel comics had no official UK distribution, famously arriving as ballast on ships that was then sold off in an entirely unlicensed and functionally unregulated market that made following individual series difficult. In 1972, three years after Odhams was absorbed by IPC and dropped the Marvel license, Marvel decided to take matters into their own hands by creating a UK-based publisher that would distribute Marvel work for the UK comics market. Recognizing that the British and American comics markets were fundamentally different media, with the UK dominated by weekly black and white anthologies as opposed to monthly color comics featuring a single story, Marvel UK kicked off its line at the end of September with *The Mighty World of Marvel*, an anthology that initially featured Spider-Man, the Fantastic Four, and the Hulk. Five months later they added *Spider-Man Comics Weekly* to the line-up, bringing Thor and Iron Man to the UK market as well.

The initial model of Marvel UK was straightforward—comics were printed in Europe, but were edited in New York alongside Marvel's other fare. They consisted of black and white reprints of Marvel material, with stories that filled a single US monthly issue getting cut up over multiple UK weekly installments. And they built straightforwardly on the Stan Lee-style hype machine, with *The Mighty World of Marvel* #1 containing a Stan Lee-penned editorial assuring readers in his usual manner that "As a mad Marvelite, you're more than just a reader—you're a friend," and breathlessly proclaiming that "You've entered the Mighty Marvel Age of Comics."

By 1974, Marvel UK was up to three weeklies, with *The Avengers* joining the other two. With the US branch of Marvel having a minor hit with their *Tomb of Dracula* series, launched in the wake of a revision of the stringent Comics Code that slightly loosened the restrictions on horror comics, it was decided that Marvel UK would expand to include both *Dracula Lives* and *Planet of the Apes*, following the recent US launch of that title as well. These were joined a few months later, in March of 1975, by *Savage Sword of Conan*, which provided Marvel UK with its first flop. Still, one flop was a better rate than Marvel's US division, which was hemorrhaging money and facing a dubious financial future. As one Marvel writer, Chris Claremont, put it, "We all figured by 1980 we'd all be out looking for a real job."

Claremont was responsible for the one bright spot in Marvel's 1975—a relaunch of the low-selling *The Uncanny X-Men* that featured an almost entirely new cast of characters cooked up by outgoing editor-in-chief Len Wein and Dave Cockrum. Claremont quickly settled into a distinctive style that retained the soap opera elements that Stan Lee had perfected in *The Amazing Spider-Man*, but used the considerably larger cast of *The Uncanny X-Men* to build a much vaster drama, carefully managing plot lines so that stories began with minor details touched on in a couple of panels, slowly dominating more and more of a given issue until they finally moved into the spotlight as the primary feature of a run of issues, by which time more stories would be seeded in the background featuring characters not focused on as intently by the main plot. *The Uncanny X-Men* would quickly move from a low-selling disaster to Marvel's flagship book, and Claremont would remain on the title for sixteen years.

In addition to being a breath of creative fresh air, Claremont had been born in London, although he moved to the US at the age of three and held US citizenship. And so it was not a surprise that Marvel turned to him in 1976 as the writer for their first attempt at original content for the UK market, *Captain Britain*. In 1976, however, the comics landscape for Marvel UK had changed substantially. Having expanded to too many titles, and with the UK economy in sufficient freefall that the UK had to take a loan from the IMF, Marvel UK spent much of the year cancelling and merging titles in the grand British tradition. *Super-Heroes*, a new title featuring more obscure characters, was merged into *Spectacular Spider-Man Weekly* (formerly *Spider-Man Comics Weekly*), which then became *Spectacular Spider-Man Weekly and the Super-Heroes*. *Dracula Lives* was cancelled and merged into the bizarre amalgamation of *Planet of the Apes and Dracula Lives*, and the failed Conan title was shoved into *The Avengers*, which was then dropped and merged into *Mighty World of Marvel*. The revolving door of titles meant that individual features were shuffled around madly—comics featuring the Avengers went from being published in *The Avengers* itself to *Mighty World of Marvel* before, three months later, getting shuffled off to *Super Spider-Man and the Titans*, which is what the Spider-Man comic had become after absorbing yet another failed title. It was at this time that Marvel brought in Stan Lee's younger brother, Larry Lieber, who had served as Lee's right-hand man in the early days of the Marvel line, as editor of the Marvel UK line, albeit still working from the US.

In the midst of this chaos Marvel UK's UK-based editor, Neil Tennant (later of the Pet Shop Boys), suggested that Marvel might want to create an original war comic for the British market. This was an eminently sensible suggestion—unsurprising given that Tennant would have a long career based on his ability to sense popular trends. IPC had just reinvigorated the genre with *Battle Picture Weekly*, and it had always been an extremely popular genre within the UK. Marvel was only partially taken with the suggestion, however, and decided that it would create original content for the UK market, but that this content would remain in the superhero genre that Marvel was most identified with. And so on October 13th, 1976, Marvel debuted *Captain Britain*.

The first appearance of Captain Britain is a strange thing. Capped at seven pages (that being the length of the color section), it's forced to rush through its introduction. It begins *in media res*, with Captain Britain squaring up against a golden-armored knight apparently named Reaver. But Captain Britain's thoughts betray that he's profoundly new to this—

he reacts in shock at the strength of his staff and at how he's "reacting with the speed of thought... I'm battling these thugs as if I've been fighting all my life. But I haven't! I'm a physicist, not some... super-hero!" Displaying a questionable sense of priorities for someone being attacked by an armored man with a giant sword, he decides, "I must think if I'm to survive. I must... remember...," which prompts a five-page flashback in which it's revealed that he was, just a few minutes ago, Brian Braddock, a student at Thames University helping out at a nuclear complex on Dartmoor. The complex is attacked by supervillains who proceed to stun everyone save for Braddock, who flees on a motorcycle, which he unfortunately crashes off a cliff, landing in a fiery wreck. When he improbably comes to, he hears a voice proclaiming, "I who am the beauty of the green Earth and the white moon amongst the stars and the mystery of the waters, and the desire of the heart of man, I call unto thy soul to arise and come unto me. For I am the soul of nature who giveth life to the universe; from me all things proceed... and unto me all things must return." But instead of the Wiccan coven that one might expect given that this monologue is lifted straight from Doreen Valiente's "Charge of the Goddess" from her 1956 revision of the Gardnerian *Book of Shadows*, Braddock is then confronted by two spectral figures who explain that he is in a circle of power and here to be judged, and that he must "choose either the amulet or the sword... life or death—for thee and mayhap for thy world as well!" At which point the strip leaves off as a cliffhanger, Captain Britain's origin not even completed.

With reprints of *The Fantastic Four* and of Jim Steranko's iconic run on *Nick Fury, Agent of S.H.I.E.L.D.* included as backup features, *Captain Britain* enthusiastically proclaimed its own self-importance as "the greatest comics weekly of all time" in the course of its "personal message from Stan Lee." But this personal message betrays the larger problem with the comic as well. "All of Britain has been waiting for him," it declares, "and now he's here at last... specially written and drawn just for you!" The nature of the "you" is ambiguous, but in context the comic appears to be claiming that Marvel's American staff has nicely created a superhero for Britain, as a sort of gift. The implication—that Britain could never do this itself—is perhaps not entirely inaccurate. It had, at least, not really done it since Mick Anglo's studio stopped creating original material in 1959, and Anglo's main creation, Marvelman, was just a barely veiled ripoff of Fawcett's Captain Marvel. Whether this was because Britain could not create their own superhero or the more likely reason—that the British public was largely more interested in other genres of comic such that nobody thought to—is largely irrelevant, however. What jumps out is the condescending hubris of it— the idea that Captain Britain has been created by Marvel as a generous sop to a poor, misguided country that couldn't even manage its own superhero. It is a tone that on the one hand resonates all too well with the UK's weakened status in 1976 and on the other feels altogether too much like a comic book reenactment of the humiliation of crawling to the International Monetary Fund for a bailout.

Certainly the sense that *Captain Britain* might have been receiving somewhat less than the full attention of Marvel Comics is present as early as the second issue, where the strip exceeds its seven-page limit, resulting in the climactic moment of Captain Britain's fight with Reaver being printed in black and white with the rather farcical header proclaiming, "Special bonus this week: a Captain Britain do-it-yourself colour page!" Still, at least Captain Britain's origin is completed as he chooses the amulet over the sword, declaring "I'm no killer—no slayer of men!" And so he is transformed into Captain Britain, and made a brother of the Round Table. Which means in practice that he has a big red jumpsuit with Union Jack bracelets, a lion on his chest, a full face mask with a Union Jack headband, and a magical staff. It's not that any of this is particularly bad. Claremont writes standard-issue superhero stuff that, while it lacks much spark, is at least competent. But any spark in it is, like the copious Kirby

Figure 89: Merlin appears to Brian Braddock in a flash of Kirby Krackle. (From Captain Britain *#1, written by Chris Claremont, art by Herb Trimpe, 1976)*

Figure 90: This cover, in which Captain Britain hits the Red Skull with his butt, is one of many unfortunate covers in the run. (Art by Herb Trimpe)

Krackle of Herb Trimpe's artwork, merely the borrowed fire from other, altogether more successful sources. Certainly nobody's heart seemed in it—Claremont departed over creative differences after only ten issues, and Trimpe has admitted that he thought the character "was a really stupid idea, but there was a paycheck in it." As Alan Moore put it in his 1982 recap of the character's history, Captain Britain was nothing more than "an American superhero wrapped up in a union jack."

This sense would only increase when Gary Friedrich took over the strip for the eleventh installment, following Claremont's departure. Friedrich, who would go on to be yet another grisly casualty of the comic industry's labor practices when he was sued out of even being allowed to claim that he co-created one of his most popular creations, Ghost Rider, was a longstanding Marvel writer who was nevertheless used mostly on either non-superhero work (he did extensive work on Marvel's war comics and westerns) or titles that were faltering, and his arrival on *Captain Britain* suggests that things were already coming apart for it. After a few issues that quickly wrapped up Claremont's trailing plotlines, Friedrich began an extended storyline in which Captain Britain teams up with Nick Fury and Captain America to fight the Red Skull. This arc, which makes up nearly a third of the issues of *Captain Britain*, is mostly notable for an impressive run of truly awful covers and for an equally impressive screw-up in which issue #17 was misprinted so that it contained the pages from issue #18, which was correctly printed again the next week, leaving the proper issue #17 entirely unpublished.

"I am Elen, Goddess of the old straight tracks and the standing stones! Once only in seven times seven score years can mortal man gain the powers of Earth and ire from the stones of this place."
—Grant Morrison, *Captain Clyde*, 1979

The fact that only sixteen issues into his own series Captain Britain not only needed to be propped up with a high profile guest star, but had to be propped up by the exact character he was demonstrably designed as an imitation of speaks volumes about the problems the series was facing. And these problems can hardly be called a surprise—of course a series with a hook of "Britain's very own superhero" is going to be lackluster when it's produced by a bunch of Americans with a minimal-at-best connection to Britain.

At least Claremont was born in the UK, even if he moved away too young to have any meaningful memories of it—but Herb Trimpe's UK bona fides consisted of having vacationed there once, an experience that seems to have mostly left him with the view that he "didn't believe that a superhero could be popular in England." But as tenuous as the initial creative team's connection to the UK was, Friedrich's arrival marked the point where the series became a revolving door of creators with no connection whatsoever—Trimpe left after issue #23, with John Buscema, a longstanding artist most associated with *The Avengers*, drawing seven issues before being replaced by Ron Wilson, around which point writing duties became a complete mess. Issue #36 was plotted by Friedrich but had dialogue entirely written by Larry Lieber; issue #37 was scripted by Len Wein, with Larry Lieber joining Bob Budiansky for plotting duties; and issues #38 and 39 were plotted by Bob Budiansky, with dialogue by Jim Lawrence. By this point the comic had long since deteriorated to where it was no longer profitable to print it in color, and with issue #39 it was cancelled entirely and, in the usual Marvel UK way, merged with another title, in this case the newly reminted *Super Spider-Man and Captain Britain.*

The only surprise here is that Captain Britain wasn't abandoned entirely. The series had by this point become thoroughly dire, with Captain Britain facing such ludicrous foes as Lord Hawk (who mostly just attacks people with a robotic hawk) and the Highwayman (a motorcycle-based character described as being "like a stallion-borne brigand of old") and the plot had become effectively incoherent. As Moore puts it, "At this point in the Captain's history he had two writers and three artists. This possibly explains why Merlin, previously thought to be an ancient Celtic warlock suddenly reveals himself to be an extra dimensional space traveler." So the character limped through seventeen issues of *Super Spider-Man and Captain Britain*, most of them written by Larry Lieber again, and featuring some of the most appallingly generic superhero material ever written. Moore sardonically describes it as a "spectacle of The Captain losing his last shreds of credibility at the hands of The Highwayman, The Manipulator, Dr. Claw and his Evil Mutants, The Loch Ness Monster, a bunch of Aliens, Werewolves, Vampires, Slaymaster, and of course that much-loved old stand-by the Devil Himself," a description that is unfair largely because it wrongly makes it sound vaguely interesting.

Meanwhile, in the United States, Chris Claremont used his gig writing *Marvel Team-Up Featuring Spider-Man* (a series in which Spider-Man teams up with various Marvel heroes) to take another stab at writing Captain Britain, and had him show up for a two-issue run. The story was a straightforward execution of the standard tropes of superhero team-ups—the first issue features Captain Britain and Spider-Man slugging each other over a misunderstanding, while the second involves them actually teaming up against a villain—in this case the overly elaborate assassin Arcade, who Claremont would go on to use fairly regularly in his 1980s X-Men comics. These two issues were serialized over six installments of *Super Spider-Man and Captain Britain* at nearly the exact same time they were coming out in the US, and this refreshing return to mediocrity served as the character's last appearance for over a year.

With Marvel UK in a tailspin, Marvel hired Dez Skinn, a British industry veteran, to investigate and explain what was going wrong. In Skinn's account, his report was successful and straightforward enough that Stan Lee offered him the job of editing the line, which for the first time moved editorial control of Marvel UK to the UK itself. Skinn launched a bevy of initiatives, including the acquisition of the *Doctor Who*

Figure 91: *Perhaps unsurprisingly, given the mess that makes up the credits on his first appearance, Lord Hawk did not become a classic Marvel villain. (From* Captain Britain *#28, 1977)*

Figure 92: *The traditional beginning of any superhero team-up, in which the two heroes pound the crap out of each other. (Written by Chris Claremont, art by John Byrne and Dave Hunt, in* Marvel Team-Up *#65, 1977)*

license and the launch of *Doctor Who Weekly* in October of 1979. But his first and in many ways most significant move was the March 1979 launch of *Hulk Comic*, Marvel UK's second attempt at producing original content. Where *Captain Britain* was an American comic published for British audiences, however, *Hulk Comic* featured a lineup of British creators doing their own takes on Marvel's characters. The comic led with a Hulk story by Steve Moore and Dave Gibbons, backed up by a Steve Moore-penned Nick Fury strip with the art of a sixteen-year-old Steve Dillon, a Steve Parkhouse/David Lloyd strip featuring their original creation of a noir superhero named Night Raven, and some reprints of 1960s Ant-Man comics from the US. Most of the original material faltered after about twenty issues, but the fifth strip, featuring the Black Knight as written by Steve Parkhouse and drawn by John Stokes, continued throughout the sixty-three issue run of the comic.

The Black Knight, a perennial also-ran within Marvel who first appeared in 1955 as a character in a five-issue Stan Lee-written medieval adventure serial featuring Sir Percy of Scandia, was a knight in King Arthur's court who wielded the Ebony Blade, forged by Merlin from a meteorite. In 1964, Lee created a second version of the character, descended from the original, who served as the villain for a story featuring Giant Man in *Tales to Astonish* #52. This villain kicked around for about two years before being killed in an Iron Man story, and about two years after that Roy Thomas created a third iteration, the nephew of the second, who was heroic again, and served as a recurring character in *The Avengers*.

It was this version that Dez Skinn dusted off for use in *Hulk Comic*. Reasoning, as he put it, that the Black Knight "would suit an Arthurian mystery story far better than a Manhattan skyline," Skinn turned the strip over to Steve Parkhouse, who had a noted affection for Celtic and Arthurian legend. Realizing that the Black Knight and Captain Britain, although developed independently, both had origin stories based in Arthurian mythology, Skinn suggested that Captain Britain be a co-star of the strip. But the details of this were held back—instead the Black Knight encountered a mysterious Stranger, who lurked in a cave in Cornwall. It is not until the third installment of the strip that it's finally revealed that the Stranger is in fact an amnesiac Captain Britain, and not until issue #42 that his amnesia is finally explained as the product of a psychic attack he suffered on the plane ride home from his adventure with Spider-Man, which led him to leap out of the plane and wash up on the coast of Cornwall.

Over the course of fifty installments the Black Knight and Captain Britain go on an extended adventure into Otherworld to rescue Camelot from a siege on the part of the demon Necromon, whose attack was responsible for Captain Britain's amnesia. By the end Captain Britain has died and been resurrected, the Black Knight has come to wield Excalibur itself, and the pair have found themselves accompanied by a cheeky elf named Jackdaw. As with much of Parkhouse's work, it doesn't hold up when artificially strung together into a single extended narrative, but as a weekly serial it served up satisfying slices of epic bombast elevated by Stokes's meticulous artwork, which realized the fantastic monsters in a rich style that evoked the woodcut engravings used to illustrate 19th and 20th century volumes of fairy tale and legend, thus placing the comic in the same tradition as Gustav Doré's illustrations for *Idylls of the King* or Henry Justice Ford's illustrations for Andrew Lang's *Fairy Books*. "It was magnificent," Moore declared straightforwardly in his overview of Captain Britain's comics, and it is in truth hard to argue. Certainly, for the first time, the UK had a story featuring Captain Britain that felt British, drenched in an understanding of lore and Celtic mythology that, while amplified to a bombastic tone suitable for Marvel comics, was still clearly the work of someone who grew up reading the Arthurian legends as opposed to by someone who had seen

Figure 93: The Black Knight *strip in* Hulk Comic *was elevated tremendously by John Stokes's moody artwork. (From* The Incredible Hulk Weekly *#51, written by Steve Parkhouse, 1980)*

Lerner and Loewe's *Camelot* and Disney's *The Sword and the Stone* at the cinema once. Captain Britain departed the Black Knight strip in issue #60 of what was now named *The Incredible Hulk Weekly*, sent back to Earth alongside Jackdaw by the newly resurrected King Arthur three installments before the Black Knight and King Arthur finally defeat Necromon, creating another sizable gap in his publication history. By this time Dez Skinn had leftMarvel UK (his last credited issue of *The Incredible Hulk Weekly* was #52, which came out the last week of February 1980) having effectively revamped the line. On the one hand, his approach was a committed imitation of the US Marvel approach—indeed, even in 2014 his website declares him to be "the British Stan Lee." Following from Lee, he introduced a regular column in parallel to "Stan's Soapbox": "Sez Dez," written with the same sense of unceasingly enthusiastic hype, laying out an elaborate (and ever expanding) plan for the "Marvel Revolution." By the time of *Hulk Comic* #46 at the start of 1980 he had seven "phases" to his revolution under his belt, and was hyping the eighth and (as it turned out) final one. *The Incredible Hulk Weekly* wound down in May of 1980, three months after Skinn's departure. One month later, in June of 1980, Alan Moore got his start as a comics scriptwriter in *Doctor Who Weekly*. Skinn, in the meantime, went on to run his own company, Studio System, which provided consulting services for art design. About a year after leaving Marvel he decided to get back into comics under the company name Quality Communications. And in April of 1981, Skinn began work on a new anthology series to be called *Warrior*.

There are several accounts of the exact concept behind the strips in *Warrior*, but it is generally agreed upon that the magazine was modeled directly off of Skinn's earlier work. In Skinn's account, "Instead of Captain Britain, we had *Marvelman*. Instead of Night Raven, we had *V for Vendetta*. Instead of Abslom Daak, a character we created for the *Doctor Who* comic, we had Axel Pressbutton. And instead of Conan we had Shandor." In what will prove a recurring theme when dealing with Dez Skinn, this is difficult to reconcile with factual reality. Abslom Daak's first appearance, for instance, came in the February 6th, 1980 issue of *Doctor Who Weekly*, which means that Skinn only ever edited the first story of the character. It is far more likely, as Alan Moore claims, that the comic was modeled almost entirely on *Hulk Comic*. As Moore points out, "The only inclusion of Captain Britain [in Skinn's work] had been in Steve Parkhouse's Black Knight strip in *Hulk Weekly*," suggesting that Parkhouse's *The Spiral Path* was the intended descendent of that, and that *Laser Eraser and Pressbutton* was modeled on the Moore/Dillon Nick Fury comics from *Hulk Comic*, with "Marvelman as a stand-in for the Hulk" and a couple of other ideas like *Father Shandor, Demon Stalker* coming from earlier comics Skinn had edited.

Just a month after Skinn started work on *Warrior*, Alan Moore gave an interview to David Lloyd for the newsletter of The Society of Strip Illustration, a professional organization for British comics creators. Although Moore had been in the comics industry proper for less than a year, Lloyd identified him as being among "five of the most respected and reputable strip writers in British comics" alongside Steve Parkhouse, Steve Moore, Pat Mills, and Angus Allan. This was, to be sure, high praise—Moore had, by that time, only published eight stories in *2000 AD* along with four in *Doctor Who Weekly*, but for all his greenness, Moore answered the questions in the sort of detailed length that would characterize his later interviews. In his answer to the final question, "What ambitions do you have for 'strips' as a whole?" Moore concluded by noting that his "greatest personal hope is that someone will revive *Marvelman*, and I'll get to write it."

This was, obviously, a shockingly well-timed interview comment—Skinn had, in fact, just recently decided to put a Marvelman revival into *Warrior* (even if he had not been particularly diligent in securing the rights). The strip was originally intended to go to a high-profile and well-known creative team—Steve Moore, Steve Parkhouse, Dave

Gibbons, and Brian Bolland were all sounded out, but turned the offer down. Exactly how Alan Moore came to be offered the gig is somewhat muddy. Moore suggests that Skinn might have read the SSI interview, whereas Skinn suggests that Steve Moore, when declining the series, told him that "he had a friend who would kill to write Marvelman," stressing that he'd not even heard of Alan Moore prior to that. Lance Parkin points out that this is at least somewhat strained as a claim—it requires both that Skinn forget having hired Moore for the *Frantic Winter Special* while at Marvel UK (admittedly plausible) and that Skinn did not realize that the Axel Pressbutton character he was arranging to have Steve Moore write for *Warrior* had made most of his appearances under Alan Moore's pen (also plausible given that Moore was working under a pseudonym in *Sounds*). Regardless, Skinn allowed Moore to pitch for *Marvelman* and then to write a script on spec before hiring him to write it, and, subsequently, the *Night Raven*-style strip, now called *V for Vendetta*, with David Lloyd on art. Moore's work on these two comics would turn out to span the entire decade and eventually form two of the most important texts of Moore's career, but at this point they were exceedingly well-received comics in a highly respected publication, albeit one with chronic distribution problems. They were, in other words, earning Moore acclaim among serious comics fans.

"We're not supposed to be a country that instinctively hates the foreign and spies on itself."
–Warren Ellis, *Jack Cross*, 2005

Meanwhile, during the nine months in which *Warrior* was under development, Marvel had decided to try again with Captain Britain, picking up where Steve Parkhouse had left the character in his *Black Knight* serial, namely being sent back to Earth accompanied by the elf Jackdaw. Helming the strip were a pair of fresh faces—Dave Thorpe, who had mulled around Marvel UK's editorial staff for a year and change waiting for a writing gig to open, and Alan Davis, making his artistic debut. Like many British comics creators of the time, Davis was a part-timer who came to comics as a second job, in Davis's case alongside driving forklifts for a warehouse. Famously, Davis was unaware that comics pages were typically drawn on oversized sheets and shrunk down for reproduction and so drew the art for his first issue at print size, resulting in there not being enough room for the dialogue and in the strip having to be printed in six pages instead of the intended five.

Nevertheless, Davis's style is recognizable and distinctive from the start, with the cartooning influence that would characterize his later *D.R. & Quinch* work already in evidence. He's immediately adept at character design, managing to introduce the strip's villains, Mad Jim Jaspers and his Crazy Gang, in crisp detail despite the small size of his page. He shows an immediate aptitude for drawing expressive faces and particularly fluid action—in his first page he manages a visual gag in which Captain Britain and Jackdaw land on what appears to be Earth, with Jackdaw, who lays back as though reclining, crashing onto the ground while Captain Britain lands in a dynamic pose, already prepared to fight.

This is a common element of Davis's work—he draws less ostentatiously muscular heroes than many artists, and instead focuses on drawing the whole figure, thinking clearly about the overall shape of the body. Moore, in one interview, describes watching Davis doing a character design and thinking out loud about her on an anatomical level: "She'll have a build like some of those older Russian athletes, and that means that her torso is pushed up and the rib-cage is really thick, and there'll be a little extra muscle there, and that means she'll probably stand like this," which Moore characterizes as Davis getting to the point where "he was inside the character from the bone outwards" such that he drew "the character inside out."

This skill at character design was put to immediate work by Marvel, who made a redesign of Captain Britain's costume

Figure 94: Despite his significant error in drawing the page at print size, Davis's first published comics page showed his skill and inventiveness with a memorable Z-shaped panel layout. (From Marvel Super-Heroes #377, *1981)*

one of Davis's first priorities. As Davis drolly puts it, the costume redesign was "generally accepted as a priority by everyone at Marvel UK, if not all of British fandom," as the lion rampant that formed Captain Britain's original insignia was primarily associated with an ad campaign for the Egg Marketing Board designed by author Fay Weldon, which led to Captain Britain being the subject of a number of terrible puns involving eggs. More broadly, Davis complained that the costume was "a pastiche of costume clichés, with a lion rampant and flag thrown in for cultural relevance." Davis, for his part, began the design from the perspective of military regalia, basing it on the Horse Guards of Buckingham Palace, only with a coat and helmet modeled off of the Union Jack.

Dave Thorpe, meanwhile, was a longtime comics fan who had written into *Captain Britain* back in 1977, a letter which appeared in issue #17. In it, Thorpe at least partially tipped his hand about where he intended to go with the character, complaining that Captain Britain was overly formulaic, but also noting the banality inherent in the idea and suggesting that the character be shown to be "thinking about what it means to be a 'Captain Britain,'" paralleling this with the way in which Captain America was handled in US comics. (Captain America had recently gone through a storyline where his faith in America had been shaken by the Marvel equivalent of Watergate, so he abandoned the name Captain America and instead became Nomad for several issues before resuming the name Captain America, having decided that his duty was to face "any and all threats to the American dream," and that this dream, not the government, was where his loyalties lay.)

Coming to actually write the character four years later, Thorpe was adamant that "nationalism had to be avoided," and viewed Captain Britain as "a muscle-bound upper class twit with a brain the size of a pea draped in a Union Jack," both views that are clearly anticipated in his earlier claim that the idea of a Captain Britain was fundamentally flawed. In a particularly damning claim, he noted that Captain Britain had to be starkly different from Captain America: "Americans are generally prepared to be much more nationalistic than us and use their flag patriotically. Over here only fascists do that with the Union Jack," a viewpoint that seemingly puts him at odds with his artist's ideas in redesigning Captain Britain's costume. And, in a view that would come back to haunt him in a big way, he expressed in his letter that "the intriguing questions I keep asking myself are 'where would Captain Britain stand on the Northern Ireland question?'"

But it would be a mistake to characterize Thorpe's take on Captain Britain as exclusively defined by the political. Thorpe's background included a degree studying Dada and Surrealism, and his attempt to make the character something other than an off-brand Captain America were, in his words, based on the "British surreality" of "Jonathan Swift, Lewis Carroll, Charles Dickens, HG Wells, John Wyndham, and *Doctor Who*." This connected well with editor Paul Neary's idea to put Captain Britain in an alternate universe Britain. Thorpe developed a supporting cast, starting with the editorially imposed Jackdaw, who was slated as a comedic sidekick. He introduced a set of villains in his first installment, Mad Jim Jaspers and his Crazy Gang, and subsequently unveiled Saturnyne, a mysterious figure from another dimension. But alongside this cosmic weirdness and surreal kick was an ever-present political theme. The first real clue that Captain Britain has landed on an alternate world was the revelation that the British National Party now ran Britain, and the monarch was now Queen Margaret I. (This is particularly cheeky, managing to ambiguously split the difference between the idea that Thatcher has become the Queen or that Queen Elizabeth's sister, Princess Margaret, has assumed the throne.) His third story, "The Junkheap That Walked Like a Man," was, in his description, an exploration of "an environmental theme," and he also prided himself on a story with "a multicultural flavour" that involved "Captain Britain taking a young afro-Caribbean girl for a fly-around, to convey a sense of wonder." (In practice, this story includes the rather unnerving scene of Captain Britain cradling a grinning black girl who tells her white savior, "I always knew that someone 'ad... that someone like you'd come and take me and me dad away from this mess." The comic gives no indication that Captain Britain actually does so.)

More intriguing (and disturbing) was the plot thread explaining Saturnyne and her goals. Saturnyne's job is to enact "the Push," a plan to forcibly improve the fascist world Captain Britain has landed in, which is "the most primitive of all the series of alternate earths" so that the entire set of earths can enter "an era of reason, peace, and enlightenment." The conservative dystopia that Captain Britain is stuck on is "retarding the whole series," and so she has developed a potion that will give the entire planet an evolutionary push so that it is redeemed into a more progressive and pleasant place. For better or for worse, however, this never panned out due to Thorpe being removed from the series after only nine installments.

The exact sequence of events at this point is murky. Bernie Jaye, the editor on the book, says, "The managing editor was concerned about the political content of *Captain Britain* and read the riot act," and that Thorpe, unwilling to make changes, walked off the book. Davis, however, suggests that he instigated the split over a story in which Captain Britain was to go to Northern Ireland, which Davis objected to. Thorpe describes the story as having been based on "a sad, true story, which seemed to epitomise the tragedy of the province, of two children who had met and become friends while away on holiday. But when they returned home to Belfast they realised that they came from opposite sides of the divide," leading to one child being attacked while visiting the other's neighborhood. In Thorpe's story, Captain Britain would see this fight break out and intervene. Thorpe stressed that the story was "even-handed" and did not take sides, but neither Jaye nor Davis were OK with the strip. As Davis tells it, Thorpe rewrote the script such that "Belfast became Fablest, Protestants became Rottenpasts and the Catholics

Figure 95: Captain Britain plays white savior to a poor black girl, who he does not, by all appearances, actually take away from this mess. (From Marvel Super-Heroes #383, written by Dave Thorpe, art by Alan Davis, 1982)

Figure 96: This sequence, in which Jackdaw uses magic to make everybody drink tea that civilizes them, was apparently Dave Thorpe's intended resolution to a story about the Irish Troubles. (From Marvel Super-Heroes #386, writing credited to Dave Thorpe, art by Alan Davis, 1982)

became Coalitch. The Rottenpasts were orange growers and Coalitch were potato growers. This is when I got angry because I was insulted that anyone might think I couldn't see through something so transparent," and so he threatened to walk from the strip (which was at the time a side job for him, with his main income coming from working in the aforementioned warehouse driving forklifts) only to have Marvel UK side with him and sack Thorpe instead. (Thorpe, for his part, not-so-subtly implies that this was because Davis was heavily invested in the conflict, noting in two separate interviews that Davis lived in an area with a significant number of Northern Ireland supporters.) This overstates it—both Thorpe and Jaye note that she had objections as well, and in Thorpe's account he was not fired so much as politely driven out by an editorial staff that repeatedly declined to approve any of Thorpe's story ideas.

The result was that *Marvel Super-Heroes* #385 was turned over to a Paul Neary-penned story set while Captain Britain was traveling from Otherworld to the alternate universe Thorpe set his stories in, and issue #386 contained a neutered version of Thorpe's Northern Ireland story in which Captain Britain breaks up a random gang fight, with the issue finally resolved by Jackdaw "using his mental powers harder than ever before" to get everybody to drink tea laced with Saturnyne's enhancing fluid, which caused everybody to magically start getting along. Captain Britain and Jackdaw return to Saturnyne's complex to celebrate the successful Push, only to have Alan Moore take over the strip and bring back the thoroughly minor character of Mad Jim Jaspers from Thorpe's first strip, who in a "mistake of terrible consequence" attacks the Push so that "the insanity within" Jaspers's mind comes "sluicing outwards... it ripples outwards across the city, across the nation, a tidal wave of writhing lunacy."

Some ambiguity exists over how exactly Alan Moore was hired. Jaye suggests that Paul Neary and Alan Davis each independently vouched for Moore, but in Davis's telling he only "had met Alan a week or so earlier, when Des [sic] Skinn asked me to help Garry Leach on the *Marvelman* art." Dez Skinn remembers things in the exact opposite order, claiming that Moore suggested Davis as Leach's replacement on *Marvelman*, much to Skinn's consternation, as he thought that "there are only two super-heroes strips in one country of 55 million people. You can't have the same pair of guys doing both." Moore, for his part, openly admits to not remembering the order of events. Any of these orders are possible, ultimately—Davis's first *Marvelman* art appeared in the *Warrior* Summer Special for 1982, Moore's first *Captain Britain* in July of that year, and Davis took over the art on *Marvelman* full time in October. Regardless of how he got the job, however, it's important to note that Moore's work on *Marvelman* predates his *Captain Britain* work. His basic approach in both comics is, after all, the same—a swift reconceptualization of the character created by examining and cherry picking aspects from a chaotic and only hazily remembered past.

> *"Uncharted pantheons, past legislation's Newgate reach,*
> *in cryptic masks to sing his teeming mind behind."*
> –Alan Moore, *Angel Passage*, 2001

With *Marvelman*, however, Moore had the marked advantage of starting his story with a more or less blank slate. Indeed, Skinn openly recycled the trick from *Hulk Comic*'s *Black Knight* strip of holding the reveal of the character back, instead teasing a silhouetted figure as "a hero reborn" on the cover and avoiding mentioning the character in the table of contents, even though the revelation of the character's identity is spilled on the sixth page. The result was that Marvelman started, in effect, with a tabula rasa. At the outset of the first installment of that strip, "A Dream of Flying," Michael Moran has grown up and forgotten how to turn into Marvelman and indeed that he ever was Marvelman, which allowed Moore to rebuild the character with considerable leeway.

With *Captain Britain*, however, Moore found himself taking over just ten strips after Captain Britain had already been rebooted and reimagined by Dave Thorpe and Alan Davis. Indeed, the circumstances of Thorpe's departure meant that Moore was taking over the strip midway through a storyline—one that, in his own words, "he'd neither inaugurated nor completely understood." In practice, however, he does not particularly follow that storyline, appropriating its iconography for his own purposes. The idea of the Push is quickly abandoned in favor of Jaspers's reality-warping attack, and at the start of his first proper strip in *Marvel Super-Heroes* #387, Moore introduces a new element, the Fury, described as "an unstoppable amalgam of flesh and metal" designed to kill superheroes—and responsible for the extermination of them on the alternate Earth where Thorpe's stories took place. Moore has the Fury attack Saturnyne and Captain Britain, leading Saturnyne to abandon Captain Britain and Jackdaw. Moore goes on to slaughter the rest of Thorpe's supporting cast, most notably Jackdaw in a sequence where the Fury atomizes his legs; he dies in Captain Britain's arms insisting, "Any minute now Merlin will fix everything up," which would be heartrendingly bleak if it weren't an annoying elf sidekick with a bright yellow J on his chest that was dying.

Moore's second *Captain Britain* strip was also the last one to appear in *Marvel Super-Heroes*, and provided a particularly impressive denouement to the strip's run in that magazine. After a few pages of Jaspers explaining the plot (he's a reality-warping mutant who had the Fury built to kill all the other superheroes so nobody could stop him) Moore has Jaspers drop Captain Britain in a cemetery full of the graves of the world's dead superheroes, where the Fury walks up behind him and obliterates him as he cries out to Merlin demanding to know why he's been abandoned to die.

Having efficiently engineered the complete destruction of Captain Britain in just ten pages and two strips, Moore was

Figure 97: The grimly funny death of Jackdaw. (From "The Twisted World,"
in Marvel Super-Heroes #387, *written by Alan Moore, art by Alan*
Davis, 1982)

Figure 98: As he is wont to do, Moore opened his run on Captain Britain *by*
killing him. (From "Graveyard Shift," in Marvel Super-Heroes #388,
written by Alan Moore, art by Alan Davis, 1982)

now faced with the business of definitively reinventing him for his first appearance in the newly launched title *The Daredevils*, where the strip was moving. On the one hand, Moore's career is full of tasks along these lines, whether literal reimaginings of existing characters as with *Captain Britain*, *Marvelman*, and *Swamp Thing*, or with more indirect reworkings such as *V for Vendetta*, *Watchmen*, and *Promethea*. Indeed, Moore's specific approach to Captain Britain is one that he would hew to closely in his next major attempt at a character reinvention—as he put it, "I tend to kill off characters I take over," explaining that "I feel I can't do anything with a character until I've destroyed and rebuilt him from the ground up." On the other hand, however, revamping Captain Britain meant that Moore would have to engage with what it meant to be Captain Britain—a question that entails not only having a clear vision of what Britain is, but also of what it means to be the Captain of this envisioned Britain. In this regard, Moore found himself pondering a question previously explored not just by people like Davie Thorpe and Chris Claremont, but, albeit under a different phrasing, by William Blake.

But Blake's engagement with the question of how to define and depict Britain came from the position of an artist and printmaker trying desperately (and not entirely successfully) to make a living. The material Britain that Blake depicted in his work was the same Britain that had to at least partially support and desire his work. Instead he was largely dismissed—one of the few contemporary reviews of his work callously described him as "an unfortunate lunatic," while another said his work what that of "the ebullitions of a distempered brain," and he spent his life at best barely avoiding poverty and at worst failing utterly to do so.

This is a marked contrast to Moore, who seems to have found his career at this juncture nothing short of exuberant. In the 1981 interview in which he longed to get the chance to write *Marvelman* he claimed that he was "grossly overpaid," noting that he "can turn out a four-or-five page script in a single day and get a return of somewhere between sixty and ninety quid for my efforts." It was to be sure a modest life, but it was one Moore earned entirely on his own terms, and by the time he took over *Captain Britain* a year later he was doing even better, contributing regularly to three separate titles. He had a head full of ambition, certainly, but also a clear sense of satisfaction. In this regard at least he could have stopped. Had his career peaked at this point, so long as he could keep selling material he could have been basically successful. This is essentially the point at which Steve Moore's career plateaued, and indeed at which most writing careers level off. There would have been no War.

Blake never had that choice. Raging against his poverty, determined to show the world that he could be a functional artist, he made his one fleeting attempt at a commercial work: *Songs of Innocence*, a sort of children's primer. Much of it consisted of liltingly pastoral material, most famously "The Lamb," a poem addressed to a sheep: "Little Lamb, who made thee / Dost thou know who made thee," and then concluding that it is Christ, who "calls Himself a lamb: / He is meek, and he is mild, / He became a little child." But *Songs of Innocence* was not entirely innocent itself, hiding more than a few barbs and stings from a man who was a year out from marrying Heaven and Hell. "The Chimney Sweeper," for instance, is positively cutting, telling the tale of chimney sweepers literally working themselves to death. The pastoral imagery characteristic of most of *Songs of Innocence* only appears after the arrival of an angel:

And by came an Angel who had a bright key
And he opened the coffins and set them all free.
Then down a green plain leaping laughing they run
And wash in a river and shine in the Sun.
Then naked and white, all their bags left behind,
They rise upon clouds and sport in the wind.

The poem ends with the chimney sweepers rising before dawn and heading off to work in the cold morning, warmed by the knowledge that when they die early deaths they will get to play in a pretty field with God.

"Of course I was angry," Blake says in a 2014 séance. "I didn't understand how anybody could look at the world and not be angry. I still don't." Blake explains that he "envied the children in the poems." And it was only a few years later that Blake had transformed *Songs of Innocence*, binding it in combination with the monstrous and furious *Songs of Experience*. Blake created the plates for *Songs of Experience* on the reverse sides of the plates for *Songs of Innocence*, at once a necessary money-saving move ("Copper's not cheap," he is quick to point out) and a symbolic gesture that is paralleled in the way in which *Songs of Experience* serves as a reply and corruption of *Songs of Innocence*. Multiple poems in each volume have matching titles—"Nurse's Song," "The Little Boy Lost," and "Holy Thursday" appear in both, while others, such as *Songs of Experience*'s "Infant Sorrow" are clear sequels to poems in *Songs of Innocence*. Most famous is "The Tyger," a revisiting of "The Lamb" that asks not who made the lamb with its "clothing of delight / Softest clothing wooly bright," but rather who made the "Tyger, burning bright / In the forests of the night." *Songs of Experience* is a savage, bitter pill, taking every drop of joy from *Songs of Innocence* and turning it to ash, reflected back at the reader, daring them to look away. It was, in practice, a dare far too many of Blake's contemporaries were willing to take.

Both books contain a poem entitled "The Chimney Sweeper," but in *Songs of Experience* the poem is a full-throated attack on the material world in which the exploitation depicted in the *Songs of Innocence* version takes place. "And because I am happy and dance and sing," the poem snarls, "They think they have done me no injury; / And are gone to praise God and his priest and king / Who make up a heaven of our misery." But within this response is a more complicated engagement. It is not, after all, that *Songs of*

Innocence is unaware of the issues of material exploitation that animate *Songs of Experience*. The *Songs of Innocence* iteration of "The Chimney Sweeper" is acutely aware of the abject material conditions of its child laborers—it heartbreakingly describes "little Tom Dacre, who cried when his head / That curled like a lamb's back, was shaved, so I said: / 'Hush, Tom! never mind it, for when your head's bare / You know that the soot cannot spoil your white hair," and the irony implicit in its bucolic afterlife is cutting. Indeed, by any reasonable definition it is the *Songs of Innocence* version of "The Chimney Sweeper" that seems the more nuanced and developed poem, framing its anger in ironies and ambiguities that the *Songs of Experience* version eschews in favor of a direct and furious attack. In this regard, the relationship between the two books grows more complicated, with each book seemingly a response to the other so that Innocence is not a lost state replaced by Experience, but rather something that has always existed in an uneasy relationship with it.

In another of the *Songs of Experience*, "A Little Boy Lost," Blake makes the target of his condemnation clear, describing the horrific fate of a child cruelly accused of blasphemy and burnt "in a holy place / Where many had been burned before" before concluding, icily, "Are such things done on Albion's shore?" Albion, here, is a stand-in for Britain as a whole, the name dating back to the 4th or 6th century BC. Its use in the context of a politically aggressive poem is thus nuanced. On the one hand, it puts things at a slight remove. "A Little Boy Lost" becomes at least partially allegorical, taking place not in the contemporary England in which Blake lived but in a displaced past. As is appropriate—it is not as though British children were being burnt alive for blasphemy on a regular basis in 1794, after all. And yet in the context of *Songs of Experience*'s furious anger, it cannot be taken as some defanged hypothetical either. Rather it is another instance of embittered irony. Albion on the one hand invokes an idealized and mythic version of Britain and on the other hints at a fundamental sickness that is not merely an instance of venal corruption but something that is inherently and deeply wrong with the world—a sense that is only heightened by the outsized moral obscenity of setting fire to small children.

> *"The terror answered: I am Orc, wreath'd round the accursed tree:*
> *The times are ended."*
> — William Blake, *America a Prophecy*, 1793

The year before he finished adding *Songs of Experience* to *Songs of Innocence* Blake published two further works using the word "Albion." First was *America a Prophecy*, which was followed up in 1794 by *Europe a Prophecy*. These "continental prophecies" adapted and repurposed American and European history to talk about revolution in a more absolute sense, exploring Blake's character of Orc, the furious spirit of revolution who is both the eldest son of Los and Enitharmon and the fallen form of Luvah. In these poems Albion is simply used to describe Britain. While Albion has princes, angels, and guardians, and while it is described at one point as growing sick, it is nevertheless clearly a land possessing a shore and cliffs.

But in *Visions of the Daughters of Albion*, also published in 1793, Blake sets up a different relationship. Albion itself does not appear in the poem, which would gesture towards reading Albion as simply a metonym of Britain, with the daughters not being biological offspring so much as British women in general. But the fact that the main character of the poem, Oothoon, is explicitly described as "the soft soul of America" suggests at least some measure of personification, a viewpoint that Blake confirms: while making clear that *Visions of the Daughters of Albion* is, in his view, an "early, minor work" characterized by his being "too timid to say what he means" and simultaneously "not meaning much of anything anyway," he admits that Albion is "not entirely passive" within the prophecy. This would suggest that his daughters—whose only real role in the poem is to serve as witnesses to the story of Oothoon—fail to do ever more than "hear her woes, and echo back her sighs" not because of a rejection of Oothoon (who transforms over the course of the poem from traumatized rape victim to a triumphant advocate of freedom who calls for people to "Arise you little glancing wings, and sing your infant joy! / Arise and drink your bliss, for everything that lives is holy!" a transformation that parallels the *Songs of Innocence/Songs of Experience* dualism, again placing Innocence, not Experience, as the end state) but because of the fundamental difference between her liberated American soul and their British nature. And just three years later he pushed this view further in *A Large Book of Designs*, which opened with "Albion rose," an image that clearly depicts Albion as a person and not merely as a land.

This more personified vision of Albion found fuller expression in Blake's later, longer prophecies *Milton a Poem*, *The Four Zoas*, and, most obviously *Jerusalem the Emanation of the Giant Albion*. In these works Albion is one of the major characters, treated as a primordial giant in a tradition dating back to Geoffrey of Monmouth, who described the island "then called Albion" as "inhabited by none but a few giants." In *The Four Zoas* he is described at the opening of the second night, and later in that section it is said that "From Albions Loins fled all Peoples and Nations of the Earth." It is when Albion turns "his Eyes outward to Self, losing the Divine Vision" that Urizen, Blake's "shadow of horror" representing Newtonian reason, assumes power. Albion is largely absent from the rest of *The Four Zoas*, returning only in the ninth and final night where he oversees the resurrection of Urizen's emanation Ahania, whose restoration finally tempers the demiurge's madness. *Milton a Poem* tells a different account of Albion's redemption from eternal sleep, describing how "Milton fell thro Albions heart, travelling outside of Humanity / Beyond the Stars in Chaos in Caverns of the Mundane Shell."

But *Milton* also makes it clear that Albion's bodily existence does not keep him from being a metonym for

Figure 99: Albion Rose *(From* A Large Book of Designs, *by William Blake, 1796)*

Britain. When he awakens late in *Milton*, his body is described in terms of Great Britain:

> London & Bath & Legions & Edinburgh
> Are the four pillars of his Throne; his left foot near London
> Covers the shades of Tyburn; his instep from Windsor
> To Primrose Hill stretching to Highgate & Holloway
> London is between his knees: its basements fourfold
> His right foot stretches to the sea on Dover cliffs, his heel
> On Canterburys ruins; his right hand covers lofty Wales
> His left Scotland; his bosom girt with gold involves
> York, Edinburgh, Durham & Carlisle & on the front
> Bath, Oxford, Cambridge Norwich; his right elbow
> Leans on the Rocks of Erins Land, Ireland ancient nation
> His head bends over London.

There is, in all of this, a clear differentiation between land and giant—Albion is said to have "movd his right foot to Cornwall, his left to the Rocks of Bognor," but the metonymous nature of the figure is clear.

Jerusalem, as its title suggests, focuses even more extensively on the figure of Albion, and specifically the relationship between him and his emanation Jerusalem. The twenty-sixth plate of *Jerusalem* proclaims baldly that "Jerusalem is Liberty," a point reiterated later in the poem when Blake writes that "Jerusalem is called Liberty among the Children of Albion," and that she is the light of Divine Vision incarnated in the individual. *Jerusalem* opens with Christ calling upon Albion to awaken and return, and, more to the point, to return Jerusalem, who he has hidden away from Jesus, whom she is to wed. Again, the metonymy between Albion the character and the land is made clear:

> The banks of the Thames are clouded! the ancient porches
>   of Albion are
> Darken'd! they are drawn thro' unbounded space, scatter'd
>   upon
> The Void in incohererent despair! Cambridge & Oxford &

London,
Are driven among the starry Wheels, rent away and
    dissipated,
In Chasms & Abysses of sorrow, enlarg'd without
    dimension, terrible
Albions mountains run with blood, the cries of war & of
    tumult
Resound into the unbounded night, every Human
    perfection
Of mountain & river & city, are small & wither'd &
    darken'd
Cam is a little stream! Ely is almost swallowd up!
Lincoln & Norwich stand trembling on the brink of Udan-
    Adan!
Wales and Scotland shrink themselves to the west and to
    the north!
Mourning for fear of the warriors in the Vale of Entuthon-
    Benython.

As one might expect, the metonymy continues to Albion's
emanation, Jerusalem, who "is scatterd abroad like a cloud of
smoke thro' non-entity: / Moab & Ammon & Amalek &
Canaan & Egypt & Aram / Recieve her little-ones for
sacrifices and the delights of cruelty."

But while Jerusalem is associated with the geographical
regions one would expect, there is a troubling detail in this
description, namely that these lands constitute her being
"scatterd abroad," away from her "proper" home in Britain.
This is a repeated claim in Blake's mythology—*The Four Zoas*
describes the confinement of "Jerusalems Children in the
dungeons of Babylon," and *Milton* clarifies that "Jerusalems
foundations began" in Lambeth's Vale, but that she is now "a
wandering Harlot in the streets" who is "bound in chains, in
the Dens of Babylon." When Jerusalem is reunited with Vala,
the emanation of Luvah, she becomes Britannia and rejoins
Albion, restoring Eternity and the undivided, whole nature of
all things.

All of this becomes even more problematic in the poem "Jerusalem," which serves as part of the preface to some versions of *Milton a Poem*. This poem, made famous by a 20th century musical setting by Richard Parry, calls for the construction of "Jerusalem In Englands green & pleasant Land" as an alternative to the "dark Satanic Mills" that currently blight it. Framed in terms of the mythic image of Christ visiting an ancient England, the poem calls for a "Mental Fight" to build Jerusalem, a call that is contextualized by the rest of the preface as an attack on "Hirelings in the Camp, the Court, & the University: who would if they could, for ever depress Mental & prolong Corporeal War," and whose "whole delight is in Destroying." This is visibly the same attack on Urizenic reason that animates most of Blake's work, but its framing in a fetishized "pastoral" Britain that is the true home of Jerusalem carries an unsettling vein of the same nationalism that animates the imperialist Britain that Blake so often railed against. The idea that departing Britain and entering a fallen state were coextensive, or that one serves as a metaphor for the other is a deeply poisonous one that reveals the fundamental inequalities implicit in any Liberty that Jerusalem might offer.

But in succumbing to this temptation Blake was merely falling afoul of a line that has confounded everyone who has gone to Mental War to defend their vision of Albion. This is the same conundrum that Thorpe faced when revamping *Captain Britain* in 1981 and trying to figure out how to do a Captain Britain comic that avoided any nationalism and the problematic use of the Union Jack by fascist groups. And these are surely tendencies that Moore would have been well aware of and actively eager to avoid falling afoul of.

Moore's first *Captain Britain* strip for *The Daredevils*, the memorably titled "A Rag, A Bone, A Hank of Hair," ultimately avoids the questions of defining Britain and Braddock's relationship to it, instead taking the sensible decision that defining Brian Braddock was the first priority. Having just penned "A History of Britain," in which he highlighted the excessively tumultuous creative history of the character, the lack of a satisfying origin for Braddock was clearly at the forefront of his mind, and is what he opted to tackle first. Moore thus has Merlin and Roma set about reconstructing Captain Britain's body and mind from the eponymous relics. Merlin wryly admits that Brian Braddock is "a very complex man as humans go," but sets about retelling his story, framing his earliest adventures in terms of the conflict between his scientific training and the mystic role he embraced as Captain Britain. "It must have been strange for him," Merlin notes, "a rational and coldly scientific creature, suddenly transmuted by an amulet that was the product of magic." This tension is then used to explain his leaping out of a plane off the coast of Cornwall, with his Steve Parkhouse-penned adventures alongside the Black Knight becoming the occasion for healing his mental injuries when "the two opposing halves of his warring sword were at last reconciled into one whole being." Finally, Dave Thorpe's brief run is reframed as a "final test" on the part of Merlin "before he could face the task for which he had been created." His death is thus explained as part of Merlin's plans, existing to give him hints about the nature of "the greatest battle of Captain Britain's life," which is implied to have more than a little to do with the Fury.

But having completed this necessary mysticism, Moore makes the interesting decision to spend his next three stories revisiting aspects of Captain Britain's past, further emphasizing the sense of continuity from his earliest Claremont/Trimpe appearances to the present day. First Braddock returns to the seeming ruins of Braddock Manor, where he confronts some hallucinatory visions of his parents before finally determining that the manor's apparent destruction way back in 1977's *Captain Britain* #18 has long since been repaired by the intermittently malevolent supercomputer his dead parents built in the manor's basement. In the next story, from *The Daredevils* #3, Moore brings back Captain Britain's psychic sister, Betsy Braddock, similarly unseen since 1977, with a plot involving the infiltration of S.T.R.I.K.E. (the British equivalent of S.H.I.E.L.D., and Betsy's employer) and the hiring of an assassin to hunt down S.T.R.I.K.E.'s psi division, who were the only people aware of the steady takeover of the organization. That installment ends with the revelation that the assassin is Slaymaster, who in his first appearance in *Super Spider-Man and Captain Britain* #243 described himself as "the master assassin of our time." *The Daredevils* #4's strip, "Killing Ground," consists mostly of a fight scene between the two, and in turn ends with a tease suggesting that Arcade, the villain debuted in Claremont's two-issue arc of *Marvel Team-Up*, will be accepting a contract on Captain Britain's life.

This plot never plays out, and the series takes a visible turn in *The Daredevils* #5, but it is worth highlighting the effect and importance of this three-issue stretch, if only because of how out of step it is with the rest of Moore's *Captain Britain* run, which Davis fondly describes as "jettisoning any hint of the political reality and ramping up the cosmic weirdness." Certainly the death and resurrection of Captain Britain qualifies as cosmic weirdness, but other than the first page of "An Englishman's Home" in *The Daredevils* #2, which consists of a trio of three-panel prologues setting up Moore's later arc, *The Daredevils* #2-4 are thoroughly devoid of any cosmic weirdness. It is also worth stressing that these three installments are based largely around resolving and revisiting plots that had gone utterly unmentioned (and frankly unmourned) for the last six years.

This, however, is just an extreme case of a tendency that Moore displays throughout his *Captain Britain* run. It is not that he doesn't introduce new characters. But all of them are clear extensions of characters that predated his run. The Fury is a solid enough villain, but he's also created to explain where the superheroes of the alternate earth went. Captain UK, one of those superheroes, was mentioned in passing by Dave Thorpe back in *Marvel Super-Heroes* #379, and her husband, Miracleman, is a barely veiled Marvelman. Vixen herself may

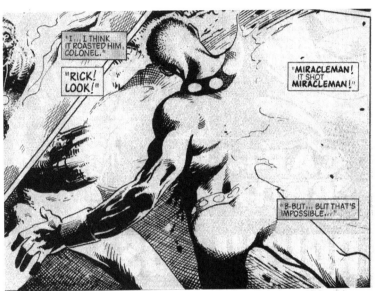

Figure 100: The Fury kills Miracleman, a thinly-veiled clone of Marvelman. (From "Rough Justice," in The Daredevils #7, *written by Alan Moore, art by Alan Davis, 1983)*

be an original character, but Vixen's gang appeared all the way back in *Captain Britain* #3. Even the Special Executive are borrowed from Moore's earlier *Doctor Who* work. Moore's *Captain Britain* is populated entirely out of the existing comic book world of *Captain Britain*. In this regard, Moore manages to largely sidestep the question of what Britain is. Britain isn't even depicted in this comic—certainly it takes several steps backwards from the overt political content of the Thorpe era. The Britain of which Braddock is Captain is, in other words, firmly a comic book realm and not a real one. As Moore puts it, "he's pure Marvel! He's there in the Marvel Universe with a billion other super characters all around him. You can't get that same realism."

> "These strands… you're made of them too… everything's made of them… silky, luminous cobwebs."
> —Alan Moore, *Swamp Thing*, 1984

In many ways, then, Alan Davis's account of things is correct in the broad strokes, but incomplete. Moore ramps down the politics and ramps up the cosmic weirdness, yes, but only as part of ramping up the general superheroishness of the strip. In this regard he is closer to Thorpe's approach than he lets on: where Thorpe attempted to ramp up both politicsand his "peculiarly British surrealty," Moore opts only for the latter. It is tempting to accuse this approach of being apolitical—a dangerous accusation when dealing with an intrinsically nationalist symbol like Captain Britain. But the British surrealism suggested would almost necessarily carry a more politicized edge to someone kicked out of school and effectively forced to work in a tannery for selling acid, and who has said, "It's difficult to overstate the impact of psychedelic drugs upon my life and work." Whimsy is not inherently apolitical, and certainly not in this context.

Indeed, it is when the "cosmic weirdness" starts to kick up in *The Daredevils* #5 that the influence of psychedelia becomes clear. That issue's *Captain Britain* strip, "Executive

Action," introduces the Special Executive, minor characters from Moore's aborted "4-D War" arc for *Doctor Who Monthly*, who proceed to kidnap Captain Britain so that he can testify at the trial of Saturnyne. The Special Executive includes Wardog and Zeitgeist, both from the *Doctor Who* strips, but also adds Cobweb and Fascination, who have overtly psychedelic powers. Cobweb "is in constant psychic contact with a number of past and future selves," which gives her the ability to see the future and past, and also means that within her mind "time has no meaning" and "past, present and future melt into a terrifying kaleidoscope." This is a return to the familiar image of time as a structure in which all events happen simultaneously, an idea that fits well within the psychedelic aesthetic. Similarly, Fascination's ability is described as making it so that "time distorts around her. Motion breaks down into juddering stroboscopic images... seconds stretch into centuries. Aeons condense into instants." Or, in other words, she gets people really high. In both cases, there are clear echoes of Moore's explanation of the value of LSD in his work: "It hammered home to me that reality was not a fixed thing."

But Moore is hardly the first to introduce a psychedelic aesthetic to Marvel comics. Indeed, it's more accurate to say that the psychedelic weirdness that the Special Executive's arrival augurs is Moore paying tribute to a rich history of psychedelia within Marvel comics. From the start, Jack Kirby's artistic style had a visionary quality to it that would only increase over the course of his career. His work drawing *Thor* for *Journey into Mystery* is indicative, with the Norse Gods ensconced in a gleaming sci-fi city at the end of a rainbow that perfectly fused the mythological underpinnings of the character to a hyper-modern sci-fi aesthetic. But equally important are the stories by Stan Lee and Larry Lieber, with plots like the January 1963 issue of *Journey Into Mystery*, in which Loki escapes from Asgard to bring mischief to Earth and does things like turn people "into blank beings" such that an entire city street becomes occupied by white outlines of

Figure 101: Betsy Braddock falls under the psychedelic spell of Cobweb. (From "Executive Action" in The Daredevils #5, *written by Alan Moore, art by Alan Davis, 1983)*

people screaming about how "we—we're turning into nothings!! It's madness! Impossible!" or turns all the objects on a street into candy and ice cream, so the whole street is a kaleidoscope of colors slowly melting and sluicing away to nothing. If psychedelia is to be framed in terms of Moore's claim that it reveals reality as something other than a fixed thing, then this story, with its threat of an otherworldly being coming to earth and deforming reality, is a clear enough example.

But it is not just when dealing with the overtly mythological and fantastic that Kirby's style tends towards the psychedelic. Many of the iconic and defining aspects of Kirby's art are ones that resonate with the aesthetics of psychedelia, whether it be his twisting, fractal-like designs for giant machines—his tendency to use clusters of solid black dots to convey massive amounts of energy, a technique that's come to be known as Kirby Krackle—or his experiments with collage and montage, Kirby's art takes the four-color action aesthetic that originally defined superhero comics and expands it to a lurid world comprised of sheer kineticism. The pinnacle of this, at least in Marvel's early days, is the three-issue run of *Fantastic Four* #48 through #50, in which Lee and Kirby introduce the planet-eating Galactus and his servant, the Silver Surfer. The story culminates with the Human Torch being sent to explore outside of time itself and past "the celestial barriers known as Un-Life" and "the final dimension curtain" in order to retrieve a weapon powerful enough to stop Galactus. When he returns he is shaken by the experience, explaining that he "traveled through worlds... so big... so big... there... there aren't words..! We're like ants... just ants.. *ants!!*"

Nor was Kirby the only Marvel artist with a psychedelic bent. Steve Ditko's run of stories featuring Doctor Strange in *Strange Tales* was just as soaked in psychedelia. Where Kirby presented a world brimming endlessly with ever stranger and more outlandish concepts, Ditko's work is based much more on a moody, shadowy space that bristles with tension and anxiety. The surreal mystic spaces that Doctor Strange explores are just as weird as the products of Kirby's imagination, but under Ditko's pen the focus is not on the mystic vastness as such, but on Doctor Strange's experience of it. Ditko doesn't just draw weird spaces, he draws Doctor Strange looking at weird spaces, framing the psychedelic weirdness in the act of individual vision, and in doing so comes closer to the ideology of psychedelia than Kirby (even if the focus on individual vision is, for Ditko, more a product of his fascination with Ayn Rand's philosophy of Objectivism than a product of psychedelia), and it is no surprise that Ditko's *Doctor Strange* was a favorite of Ken Kesey.

Marvel, always adept at chasing trends, was by 1968 actively catering towards the psychedelic aesthetic, launching a solo *Silver Surfer* series along with the similarly cosmic (and more importantly trademark protecting) *Captain Marvel*, and as the 1970s dawned, the psychedelic tendencies only increased. By this point Marvel had moved to its second generation of writers and artists, with both Ditko and Kirby having left the company, and their successors were concerned largely with somewhat cleaner and less edgy imitations of their styles. It is one of these heirs to Kirby and Ditko, Jim Starlin, who ended up perfecting the psychedelic style within Marvel with a pair of iconic runs as a writer-artist on *Captain Marvel* and, subsequently, *Warlock*. Both of the series were based in outer space, and featured an inventiveness comparable to that of Kirby or Ditko's work, spinning vast cosmic epics of mad tyrants wanting to become gods, and weird, twisted pocket universes.

Starlin's style, by his own admission, owes a lot to both artists, but with a more disciplined, intricate line than either. This was common among the second generation of Marvel artists, who copied Kirby's style, dutifully adding large patches of Krackle to their panels, but with a cleaner line that smooths away the rough edges that made Kirby's art so groundbreaking. Starlin combined this cleaner line work with writing that was as mad and inventive as anything Lee or

Figure 102: Jim Starlin's combination of clean linework and psychedelic imagery established him as one of the most influential creators at Marvel in the 1970s. (From Captain Marvel #28, by Jim Starlin, 1973)

Kirby ever cooked up, and used his role as a writer/artist to work out intricate page layouts beyond anything Kirby would ever attempt. Moore, by this time, had already done several imitations of Starlin's style, particularly his panel layouts in *The Stars My Degradation*.

So Moore's expansion into vast cosmic weirdness, like everything else in his *Captain Britain* run, extends out of the larger history of Marvel comics. But in this case it ties further into the question of who Captain Britain is and what he signifies. The psychedelic phase of Moore's *Captain Britain* focuses on the idea of multiple earths that inherited from Dave Thorpe, and specifically on the idea, implicit in Thorpe's work, that there's an equivalent of Captain Britain in every one of these universes. This has the effect of changing Captain Britain from a seemingly patriotic hero to one based in the idea of multiplicity and the idea that there are a potentially infinite number of visions of what Britain could be. This, of course, extends straightforwardly from Moore's fascination with psychedelia: reality is not a fixed thing, and thus neither is Britain.

This is a major theme for Moore, who begins setting it up early on in his run when he reveals that Merlin, the mystical figure upon which this entire mythologized Britain rests, is not one person but a succession of identities and figures such that Captain Britain would not even truly know Merlin if he met him. This changes the nature of the mystical source of Captain Britain's power, making it not a single authority but a nexus of signifiers and concepts with no central or definable authority. For all that Captain Britain, with his militaristic uniform and upper class dignity, seems to extend out of a sense of noble authority, this stands in marked contrast to the world he finds himself in, and it is this contrast that Moore focuses on. Or, as he puts it, "The English stiffness and jut-jawed pompousness which Alan Davis quite intentionally instilled in Captain Britain and Brian Braddock makes him a near-perfect straight man for the chaos and absurdity exploding all around him."

This is a heady message, and a far cry from the banal political points that Thorpe was attempting to score. But by this time Moore was writing the strip for *The Daredevils*, and *The Daredevils* was, from the start, designed as a different sort of comics magazine. For one thing, it's a lot less of a comics magazine. Its first issue uses only thirty-two of its fifty-six pages for comics, or a bit shy of 60% of the magazine. In contrast, *Marvel Super-Heroes* #377, where Davis's run on *Captain Britain* began, uses forty-one of its fifty-two pages for comics, or nearly 80%. And the final issue of *The Incredible Hulk Weekly* used twenty-nine of thirty-two pages, or just over 90% of its page count, for comics. By the end of *The Daredevils* there were only two actual comic strips running in it—*Captain Britain* and the eponymous *Daredevil* strip, although both were relatively long (the comic was reprinting full issues of *Daredevil* alongside twelve-page original *Captain Britain* strips). But what is significant about *The Daredevils* is not merely the unusually large amount of non-comic material but the sort of it.

To pick an issue more or less at random, *The Daredevils* #7 featured eleven pages of *Captain Britain*, a three-page overview of Japanese comics by Steve Moore, a two-page letter column, two pages of fanzine reviews, a four-page illustrated story featuring Night Raven, a page of broader news about the comics industry (looking at both Marvel and DC), a page of Steve Dillon's childhood artwork, seventeen pages of *Daredevil*, a four-page reprint of a strip from *Doctor Who Monthly*, and a few pages of house ads, back issue sales, classifieds, and the like. What jumps out about this list is the audience for whom a lot of it is aimed. The piece on Japanese comics, the fanzine reviews, and even the look at the early work of a major British artist (a recurring feature that in other issues covered Dave Gibbons, Alan Davis, and Garry Leach, among others) are all clearly targeted not just at comics readers, but at dedicated fans of the medium.

In this regard it is perhaps easiest to think of *The Daredevils* as Marvel UK's conscious response to Dez Skinn's

Figure 103: A page highlighting Steve Dillon's early artwork from The Daredevils #7, *typical of the sort of oddball fan-targeted content in that magazine.*

success with *Warrior*. While *Warrior* was always a mess in terms of its finances, the buzz and attention it drew turned plenty of heads. The problem was that *Warrior* made its name off of original content, whereas Marvel UK was still first and foremost a company that existed to publish reprints of American comic books.

"Noo Yawk is grim, and gritty, and realistic. There are big black buildings with little white squares on, and water towers, and manholes and lots of other gritty stuff."
–Alan Moore, "Grit," 1983

And so for all that *The Daredevils* was Marvel's attempt to create a magazine for adult comic fans who liked *Warrior*, it had to do so without actually having the budget to publish original British material like *Warrior*. All it could afford for original comics content was Moore and Davis's *Captain Britain* strip. And so it focused on its non-comics text pieces, taking a cue from the fanzine culture that existed within the UK. Fanzines—a portmanteau of "fan" and "magazine"—are fan-produced publications discussing popular media, often though not always within the broad auspices of "geek culture," with comics being a particularly common focus, although fanzines focusing on all sorts of popular culture exist. Ostensibly sold at cost with no profit being involved, fanzines were typically distributed either by mail order or at conventions, and proved a training ground for numerous creators: Dez Skinn, Alan Moore, Steve Moore, and Grant Morrison all did work for or on fanzines early in their careers. Featuring a mix of original cartoons, fan fiction, interviews, historical features, reviews, criticism, and outright whimsy, fanzine culture was at once vibrant and strange.

And this, perhaps more to the point, was something *The Daredevils* actively kept track of with its *Fanzine Reviews* column. Indeed, that column gives a sense of the broad inventiveness of fanzines as it describes their contents: interviews with war comic artists Joe Colquhoun and Kevin

O'Neill, fan fiction, reviews of Carl Sagan's *Cosmos*, comics by Eddie Campbell, a retrospective on Steve Ditko's *Hawk and Dove* comic for DC, trivia quizzes, satirical comics about *Doctor Who*, an episode guide to the 1960s *Batman* series, a compendium of ludicrous dialogue from the same series, an article on DC's 1968 *The Geek* ("one of the most brain-blisteringly awful comic books ever produced by human beings," Moore explains), reprints of iconically dumb comic book panels, a review of *Zippy the Pinhead*, a cover by Bryan Talbot, and a one-page strip by Savage Pencil are all specific features mentioned among the reviews of dozens of fanzines. Many of the text features throughout *The Daredevils* would have been perfectly at home among any number of these features, although largely those on the more serious-minded end of what was a diverse fanzine culture.

Implicit in this is the fact that *The Daredevils* was consciously targeting an older audience, and, at 65p, had a price point to match. This, in turn, explains the magazine's title feature, reprints of *Daredevil* comics from Frank Miller's iconic run on the title from 1979-83, first as an artist and then, later, as a writer-artist. Within American comics, Miller's *Daredevil* run was transformative. For all that Marvel Comics honored the long legacy of exploiting creative labor in American comics, one of the most significant differences between Marvel and DC when Marvel began launching their books was the focus on the creators of those books. DC spent the early 1960s still crediting its Batman comics to Bob Kane (who was only ever a co-creator of the character) and using a series of uncredited ghost artists on the strip, while titles like *Justice League of America* went out with no creator credits at all. Marvel, on the other hand, not only gave credits to its creators, it reveled in them. A *Doctor Strange* strip would not just be credited to Stan Lee and Steve Ditko, but would proclaim the comic to be written by "Stan Lee, Master of Macabre Menace" and drawn by "Steve Ditko, Weaver of Wondrous Witchcraft," whereas an issue of *Fantastic Four* might be by "Smilin' Stan Lee and Jolly Jack Kirby."

But the rise of Frank Miller on *Daredevil* took this auteur-based model of comics further than anyone had previously done in the American industry. By the time Miller came onto the book as a penciller in 1979, *Daredevil* was a middling title of little interest to much of anybody. His initial creative partnership with writer Roger McKenzie was rocky at best, and Miller nearly quit the book only to have editor Dennis O'Neil correctly discern which of McKenzie and Miller was the biggest talent; he sacked McKenzie instead and gave full creative control to Miller. Almost immediately, Miller turned sales around and went on to write the book for twenty-three issues, a comic run that still stands as one of the most acclaimed of all time.

Miller's work is typically described in terms of its "noir" look, a description that, while not strictly speaking inaccurate, is not quite the whole story. The most noir touches of Miller's *Daredevil* work are largely the province of inker Klaus Janson and colorist Glynis Wein, who took Miller's pencils and built a chiaroscuro world of moody shadows out of them. But it is true that Miller's art is aware of light and shadow in a way that few other artists of the time were, giving his pages a grim edge that stood out. And certainly once Miller took over writing the book his tales of femme fatales and assassins playing out in the rooftops and back alleys of Manhattan showcased his longstanding interest in noir.

But initially what jumped out about Miller's style was an altogether subtler thing: he favored smaller panels featuring close-ups whereas his predecessor on *Daredevil*, the legendary Gene Colan, favored bigger and more action-packed panels, focusing on full body shots of characters in dynamic poses. Miller frequently used long series of small panels, each showing a close-up detail of action, so that instead of a big panel of Daredevil in costume there's a series of small panels of Matt Murdock breaking his cane down into a billy club, pulling on the mask and a red glove, taking the costume off a hanger, et cetera. Instead of the normative comics approach of action panels featuring big, dynamic movements, Miller

Figure 104: Miller showed Daredevil's dynamic motion by adding numerous shadow versions of the character to a single panel. (From Daredevil #163, *written by Roger McKenzie, art by Frank Miller, 1980)*

Figure 105: Alan Moore singled this selection of panels out as a high point of Frank Miller's art in his essay "The Importance of Being Frank." (From Daredevil #164, *written by Roger McKenzie, 1980)*

would draw Daredevil writhing and twisting in midair, often including intermediate poses in a lighter outline, thus giving a much broader sense of motion and dynamism.

The result produced some truly impressive scenes. Alan Moore, talking about Miller's work in the first issue of *The Daredevils*, highlights a sequence from *Daredevil* #164 in which a reporter figures out Daredevil's secret identity, and confronts Daredevil with it by challenging him to describe a photograph he holds up to him, thus proving that Daredevil is blind. As Moore describes it, "In six tiny, narrow frames we see Daredevil turn first one way and then the other as if in an attempt to escape having to admit that he cannot see the picture, which remains unmoving and unwavering in the foreground throughout the entire six frame sequence. Eventually Daredevil is forced to turn and face it, admitting his blindness. Through the way in which Miller arranges the shots we are made to feel the anguish of Daredevil's decision in a manner which makes the speech balloons almost redundant." Elsewhere he praises a pair of wide-shot panels in which some low-life gangsters are shooting pool, and a single red-gloved hand reaches out of the darkness to stop their shot as Daredevil begins asking questions. This use of small moments as the transitions between panels is trademark Miller, and moves the focus away from big colorful action scenes and towards an intimate and more anxious sort of storytelling.

Once Miller took over as writer as well his propensity for small, tightly composed panels only increased. Pages with twelve, fifteen, or more panels became increasingly common, many of them tiny and narrow panels capable of showing only one or two objects. In this regard Miller brought the cinematic technique of montage to the comic book page, so that the action takes place not in gaudy splash panels, but in the gaps between panels, as an action of implication. It was, for the time, a startlingly mature and developed take on the medium, and one that garnered a lot of attention, much of it focused on Miller as a comics auteur. The appeal was not, in other words, *Daredevil* itself, nor the consistency of the Marvel line (as was the case in the days of Lee and Kirby), but rather on Miller as a singular talent—one whose readers would follow him to other companies and to creator-owned work like *Ronin* that featured no established characters at all. Miller had become a figure adopted by serious comics fans, with a reputation that rapidly spread beyond just comics fans and into the general public—a transformation of the American comics landscape that Moore would soon find himself taking full advantage of.

Over time, Moore's *Captain Britain* work changed to where it was more in tune with its darker co-feature (although Moore never fully embraced the neo-noir of Miller's approach either in *Captain Britain* or in his later work, and indeed wrote an uproarious piss-take of Miller's style for *The Daredevils* #8 entitled "Grit"). While the beginning of the Special Executive plot was energetically psychedelic, after the first two installments the strip began advancing the subplot of Linda McQuillan, the disappeared Captain UK from the Earth on which Captain Britain died. While Captain Britain is off having whimsical adventures with the solidly entertaining Special Executive, both the Fury and the rise of "Sir James Jaspers," this Earth's equivalent to Mad Jim Jaspers from the *Marvel Super-Heroes* days of the strip, make their return. As Jaspers rises to political prominence, he gives a speech about how superheroes "are frighteningly powerful and they are not our friends," which Linda explains is the exact speech that the Jaspers on her Earth gave before the world went horribly wrong and descended into a fascist horror. As Merlin and Roma make their reappearance as well, the Fury finally attacks. In the resulting two-issue battle, two of the Special Executive are killed, Wardog has his arm ripped off, and in the end the Special Executive storm off, abandoning Captain Britain to solve all of this himself.

This also served as the end of *The Daredevils*. *Captain Britain* migrated to *The Mighty World of Marvel*, which, for four issues, branded itself as *The Mighty World of Marvel Featuring the*

Daredevils, and the *Fanzine Reviews* and *Night Raven* features followed *Captain Britain* over, along with the serialization of the 1982 Chris Claremont/Frank Miller *Wolverine* series, which, although *The Mighty World of Marvel* was up to the third issue when *The Daredevils* merged in, was still, due to Miller's art, firmly within the aesthetic of *The Daredevils* as well. As when moving from *Marvel Super-Heroes* to *The Daredevils,* Moore used the occasion to move his storyline forward significantly. "But They Never Really Die" leaves off with Jaspers as a looming threat who has seemingly just begun to understand his powers, while "The Candlelight Dialogues," the first story in *The Mighty World of Marvel,* begins with Jaspers already in charge and having instituted detention camps for superhumans, a sizable jump in the narrative. The final panel of "But They Never Really Die" shows the Special Executive trudging off into the snow, whereas "The Candlelight Dialogues" consists entirely of two superhuman prisoners swapping stories about Captain Britain in the hopes that someday he'll come and rescue them, with Captain Britain only appearing as a feature of their tales; the Special Executive goes without mention.

Behind this jump is another issue. The end of *The Daredevils* coincided with the departure of editor Bernie Jaye, who had been integral to Moore's deep involvement with the title. Moore went so far as to write a letter for the letter column praising her on the occasion of her departure. Certainly the two had a warm working relationship—so much so that Moore recounted "her insane offer to pay for some original work out of her own pocket when it didn't look as if the budget was going to stretch far enough," an offer he ultimately responded to by crafting large swaths of the extra material for *The Daredevils* "for next to nothing" and agreeing to "give her more artwork or more scripts for the same money." Jaye, in an interview, described Moore as "a consummate professional" for whom "nothing was too much trouble." Her departure, over the fact that *The Daredevils* was merged into *The Mighty World of Marvel* without anyone talking to her about it, was a blow for Moore, and the jump to a climactic showdown between Captain Britain and Jaspers as soon as she departed feels very much like an attempt to speed up the tail end of his plot so he could be done faster.

Moore was by this point writing *Swamp Thing*, which made him substantially more money than anything in the British market. This financial security allowed him, for the first time in his career, the luxury of being selective in his work, and like his *Future Shocks* for *2000 AD*, his Marvel UK work simply became something he was uninterested in pursuing further. Indeed, "A Funeral on Otherworld" was his last work for Marvel, with whom he would eventually have an irrevocable falling out over the trademark to the name Marvelman that ended with Moore cheekily changing the name to Miracleman, the name of the Marvelman clone he wrote into the backstory of Captain UK.

None of this is to say that the resolution was rushed—Moore still turned out an additional sixty-three pages of story over seven issues, including a fifteen-page penultimate installment in which the Fury figures out a way to kill Jaspers before being killed by Captain Britain and, ultimately, Captain UK, who finally puts her fears aside and wades into battle against the machine that killed her husband. Perhaps more to the point, Moore's work in these final seven installments is as complex and nuanced as anywhere else in his run. The climactic "Endgame" features one of the most outlandishly creative fights in the history of superheroes as the hyper-adaptable Fury and the reality-warping Jaspers battle, with Moore visibly delighting in giving Davis ridiculous things to draw such as the moment when "the asylum-god transmogrifies into a metal cloud, the cloud becomes a harp of molten glass, the glass grows feathers, sprouts teeth, extends luminous claws, and tries to kill the thing that cannot die." One double-page spread includes scenes set on the moon, the bottom of the ocean, the sun, "a river of tar in a landscape of chromium," and "a plain of fused and cryptic flesh." Moore had been building towards this conflict for

Figure 106: The bizarre and surreal final fight between Mad Jim Jaspers and the Fury. (From The Mighty World of Marvel *#12, 1984)*

some time, and he pays it off in full with a suitably epic finale that culminates in a crazed and tearful Captain UK tearing at the Fury, smashing it into smaller and smaller pieces until Captain Britain finally pulls her off, saying, "It's dead, Linda. It's been dead for ten minutes. You killed it."

It is necessary in discussing the concluding period of Moore's run on *Captain Britain* to pause for a moment on the 21st of October, 1983. *The Daredevils* hovers between issues #9 and #10 (both #10 and #11 are dated November, while #9 is dated September). Moore has completed *Skizz* and published his last *Future Shock*, and is still two months away from bringing back *D.R. & Quinch*. *Warrior* is up to issue #14, with "The Veil" and "One of Those Quiet Moments" by Moore, while the first *Bojeffries Saga* had wrapped in the preceding issue. Moore has been working on *Swamp Thing* for two months, although he's still a month out from his first issue being published. Margaret Thatcher is four months into her second term. Culture Club's "Karma Chameleon" is at number one, with Siouxsie and the Banshees ("Dear Prudence") and David Bowie ("Modern Love") also charting.

"Until very recently it had been my opinion that the best way to see Glasgow was from an aeroplane, or, at the very least, by driving through at eighty miles an hour with the windows wound up."
–Alan Moore, "I Belong to Glasgow," 1984

On October 21st, Moore attended a Comics Mart in Glasgow. An account of this trip is printed in *Mighty World of Marvel* #9 under the title "I Belong to Glasgow," alongside the *Captain Britain* strip "Among These Dark Satanic Mills," a title that quotes Blake's poem "Jerusalem" about attempting to build Jerusalem (by then imagined as Liberty, the emanation of the giant progenitor of all humanity Albion) within England via a mental war of creative effort. There he met a twenty-three-year-old comics fan and sometime writer named Grant Morrison.

After a promising beginning writing and drawing avant garde stories in the new wave science fiction style and a superhero strip for his local paper, as well as a couple of stories in the space action digest *Starblazer*, Morrison had not published a comic in a year, and was at the time more interested in a music career, but he was also active in the fanzine scene, and gave Moore a copy of his fanzine *Bombs Away Batman*, which contained both some positive reviews of Moore's comics work and an interview with Morrison's band, The Mixers, in which Morrison claims Aleister Crowley as one of his influences while one of his bandmates cites Jerry Cornelius.

Moore's account of the event in "I Belong To Glasgow" is primarily a glowingly comedic take in which he goes on for several paragraphs suggesting that he was only at the event because he was bribed, and makes fairly generic if well-executed jokes about the Scottish ("While incest, murder and cannibalism have been outlawed for centuries in our own land, in Scotland they are still very much a part of everyday family life,") before settling into the meat of the piece in which he praises "the level of friendliness that we encountered," a paragraph about Bob Napier's *AKA* fanzine, and the declaration that "we had an incredible time" in Glasgow. Neither Grant Morrison nor his fanzine are mentioned at all.

Morrison's aim in bending Moore's ear was presumably related to the fact that Moore was then writing the *Fanzine Reviews* column for *The Daredevils*, and thus had the potential of giving Morrison's work a publicity boost at a period when he was beginning to transition from a music career back to comics. Said publicity never happened, although it is worth noting that Moore was transitioning away from *Fanzine Reviews* even as Morrison slipped him a copy of *Bombs Away Batman*. Beyond that, the two, from fleeting third-party accounts, had a relatively substantial conversation, with Moore giving Morrison various bits of advice and guidance. This is neither unexpected nor particularly notable—much as

Moore grew to dislike the convention scene, his generosity with fans is well documented. His apparent lack of memory of the encounter (Moore only remembers meeting Morrison once, at a dinner event after a signing—Morrison dates that encounter to 1987) is unsurprising, as for Moore someone giving him a fanzine and bending his ear for advice about the comics industry was by this time a routine experience. For Morrison, on the other hand, it was clearly not routine—Morrison would rapidly begin establishing a comics career almost precisely according to the path Moore had taken up to the point of their meeting, and this conversation in which Moore gave him advice was almost certainly tremendously influential.

But even though that October neither party noticed the War into which they were being inexorably drawn, the battle lines were rapidly forming around them. Morrison had already completed his own superhero work, *Captain Clyde*, for the *Govan Press*, and while this was not an entirely happy experience, it is still worth pointing out that there is a basic similarity between the idea of Captain Clyde, effectively the superhero of Glasgow, and the idea of Captain Britain. Even if Captain Clyde is only the superhero of a metropolitan area and not a nation, both are characters consumed by questions of place and cultural identity. And the grim and violent finale of Moore's *Captain Britain* run (in which Captain Britain must face all the enemies who had previously defeated him as they'd annihilated an entire universe) parallels Morrison's account of his *Captain Clyde* finale as "a rain-soaked, lightning-wracked epic of Fall and Redemption."

Any suggestion that *Captain Clyde* was an inspiration for *Captain Britain* requires what is at best an implausible sequence of events. Even if one assumes that Moore is downplaying his memories of Morrison and, as Morrison suggests, outright lying about not paying attention to his work, a narrative in which Moore comes into possession of a substantial run of *fin de décennie* copies of the *Govan Press* and is so taken by the hyper-apocalyptic ending that he cribs it for

Captain Britain is not even remotely likely. Indeed, it's just as reasonable—more so, really—to point out that Captain Clyde's Morrison did a "death and resurrection" story in *Captain Clyde* at almost the exact same time that Steve Parkhouse did one with Captain Britain for *Hulk Comic*, especially given that Morrison fairly blatantly nicked Captain Clyde's origin from the original Claremont strips.

Still, this does not mean that similarities between Moore's and Morrison's early takes on superheroes were coincidental either. The easiest suggestion is simply that there was something in the conceptual geography of Albion in the early 1980s that meant that attempts to engage with a superhero who served metonymously for all or part of Albion were fated to end in apocalyptic showdowns. *The Black Knight* was similarly fraught, after all. Certainly the zeitgeist was prime for it. Thatcher's Britain was a dark and scary place for the counterculture, and while in practice this meant that it thrived for having something to properly rail against, it also meant that the counterculture, which both Moore and Morrison were profoundly indebted to, became an unsettling and dark place in its own right.

The superhero facing a dark and apocalyptic moment, in other words, was very much in keeping with the spirit of the times, and crediting either Moore or Morrison with it is misleading at best, not least because it wrongly gives the impression that *Captain Clyde* and *Captain Britain* are essentially the same texts. In *Captain Clyde*, the dark ending was in essence an angry and petulant swipe at an indifferent audience, intended mainly to shock and get a reaction after the more orthodox and sincere attempts at superhero storytelling that Morrison had previously employed had failed. In *Captain Britain*, on the other hand, the grim climax serves to resolve what was initially set up. It's wholly appropriate and built to. Morrison's finale to *Captain Clyde* was designed to leave a bitter taste in the mouths of its non-existent readers; Moore's finale to *Captain Britain* was designed to be thrilling and fun.

And yet there is an impishness to Moore's finale that is not entirely unlike that of Grant Morrison's. It is worth reflecting on how Moore actually resolves the plot once the Fury manages to kill Jasper, which is to have Captain UK be the one to finally kill the Fury. This means that both of the major villains in Moore's run are defeated by someone other than Captain Britain. This furthers the sense of refusing to make Captain Britain into the obvious trap Moore described shortly after starting on the title: "a superhero wrapped up in a union jack." With the encounter also killing Merlin, there's a real sense in the finale of turning away from any absolute vision of what Britain is. The final Moore-penned story, "A Funeral in Otherworld," returns to the idea of multiple earths each with their own iterations of Captain Britain. A large splash page suggests a genuine variety to these figures, with many not immediately recognizable as Captain Britain. The lineup includes some solidly unnerving concepts—Captain Airstrip One (who featured solo in a story Moore did for a 1986 fanzine) hails from what is visibly a *1984*-inspired world, speaking Orwell's Newspeak, while Kommandant Englander is blatantly a Nazi. It is not a far cry from the angry Scottish boy who'd been fired from the daft little newspaper comic he'd been pouring his heart into and that nobody read, and who lashed out at his audience of zero with a story boiling over with blood and satanism.

The result of this is to heavily decouple Captain Britain from any sort of nationalist ideology, or even from a straightforward linkage of Albion and the idea of heroism. It may be a version of Captain Britain that saves the day, but equally, the day gets saved moments earlier by a homicidal robot. By this point the defining feature of Captain Britain compared to other superheroes is that he exists as one of a seemingly infinite number of alternatives to himself, all of which are rather more fleshed out than he is. The mythic tradition he hails from is by now downplayed, and, more to the point, revealed to be a not really straightforward mythic tradition at all, what with Merlin turning out to have a host of other names and faces and, more to the point, now being dead. He can't even be easily defined via opposition to his enemies, who, under Moore, consist of a robot defined only by its desire to kill Captain Britain and Mad Jim Jaspers, who, while ostensibly a political figure, is defined entirely in terms of the non-existent issue of superhero rights, and who is ultimately changed from being a metaphor for fascism to just being completely and utterly insane. One can still read a vague anti-fascism parable into the latter bits of Moore's *Captain Britain*, but it's a faint theme at best. First and foremost, Moore's run is defined by a refusal to straightforwardly be what is expected from the idea of Captain Britain while nevertheless telling an engaging superhero story.

And indeed, by the end, this non-ideological bent takes on an ideological quality of its own just by how carefully worked out it is. The fact that Captain Britain's world is built entirely out of other comics, that there's next to no attempt at real world political engagement, and that the nationalistic title character is largely irrelevant to proceedings goes so far in the direction of being apolitical that its silence speaks volumes. In this light, the decision to end with a vast and epic battle in which Captain Britain himself ultimately accomplishes nothing seems pointed and deliberate, a final emphatic refusal on Moore's part to allow anything other than fun and exciting superheroics into his story, thus saving the character from the American-style jingoism that originally defined him and that, in the era of the Falklands War and Thatcher's unabashed embrace of patriotism, could easily have threatened to overwhelm the character entirely.

But for all that Moore's final strip ends with a long shot of Captain Britain and Captain UK going their separate ways out of a stone circle on a hill in Darkmoor while a caption proclaims "Never The End," the truth is that Moore's deliberate evasion of expectations doesn't leave the character much room to grow after his departure. Moore's run is held together by little more than his own inventiveness and his

Figure 107: The overtly Nazi Kommandant Englander shows Moore's tendency to avoid making Captain Britain a straightforwardly benevolent concept. (From The Mighty World of Marvel #13, *written by Alan Moore, art by Alan Davis, 1984)*

Figure 108: Joan is comically unphased by the devastation of her flat. (From The Mighty World of Marvel #15, *by Alan Davis, 1984)*

ability to continually build looming threats in the same way that Claremont did on *The Uncanny X-Men*. His zeal to avoid coming to any sort of nationalist sentiment about what Captain Britain might mean results in, at the end, a character who is largely without meaningful definition. The result is that Moore's run is a tough act to follow.

Captain Britain only made three more appearances in *The Mighty World of Marvel* anyway, all of them written and drawn by Alan Davis, who had always retained a significant amount of creative power with Captain Britain. These mostly consisted of setting up plot threads, with Davis bringing back Meggan, the shapeshifting mutant from Moore's "The Candlelight Dialogues." The most interesting of these three strips is the second, "Tea and Sympathy," which consists of Captain Britain calling upon a family in a grim council flat to apologize for the fact that in the previous issue his fight with Meggan resulted in their son's death. Joan, the mother of the family, proves impossibly hospitable, immediately forgiving Captain Britain and offering him a cup of tea. There he sits and listens to Joan's husband explain about how the "trouble with folk today is no patriotism" and that back in his day "we didn't go cap in hand to any common market begging for handouts"; Captain Britain apologizes that "for the last three years I've rubbed shoulders with cosmic beings, fighting to save the universe. I'd forgotten my responsibility to ordinary people." Lest this be mistaken as an investment in some political cause, Joan reassures him that "you can't shoulder the world's problems. You're still only one man. This is real life, not some childish comic-strip." The childish comic strip then ends with armored warriors crashing into Joan's flat and destroying it, which Joan shrugs off, saying that "the council will have to rehouse us. We'll be out of this slum at last," and offering everybody more tea.

Davis saw out *Captain Britain*'s run in *The Mighty World of Marvel* with a strip that reintroduces Braddock's family, which ends with a series of teases of future plots, specifically the return of Slaymaster, the Crazy Gang, and Chief Inspector

Dai Thomas—an anti-superhero cop from the comic's original 1977 run. Three months later, Marvel UK relaunched *Captain Britain* as a comic in its own right, with the idea being that the comic would also get US distribution and feature exclusively UK-created material. In practice this meant that Captain Britain was accompanied by a reprint of Steve Moore's Abslom Daak strips from *Doctor Who Weekly*, a reprint of the first *Night Raven* strip from *Hulk Comic*, and a strip featuring the Free-Fall Warriors—obscure backing characters from a *Doctor Who Monthly* strip written by Steve Parkhouse.

"I always knew I was a special, lovelier-than-average person. It only makes sense that Jesus would turn out to be someone fabulous like me."
—Alan Moore

This time around, Captain Britain was written on Moore's recommendation by Jamie Delano, who had impressed with some *Night Raven* text pieces after Moore gave them up. Delano's run faces the exact problem one would expect following Moore's, which is that there's not a lot to work with besides bringing back Moore's own concepts. Sure enough the Crazy Gang appears, as set up by Davis, allowing Davis to recycle his best panel from *Marvel Super-Heroes* #377, followed by a version of the Special Executive from a hundred years earlier than the original called Gatecrasher's Technet. By Davis's account, it was not an especially happy collaboration—Davis described Delano's scripts as "dark, strange, cerebral," tales that "didn't fit in the super hero genre," and claims that he "was the senior partner, initially supplying plots and long story, then mutilating and reworking Jamie's scripts," which led to Delano departing the title after only thirteen issues. Davis, by this time, had found work in the US and was largely uninterested in continuing to work for Marvel UK wages anyway, which led to the demise of the series after its fourteenth issue, a conclusion written and drawn by Davis. After that the character reverted to the

American superhero he always in reality was, making a couple of appearances in Claremont-penned X-Men annuals and a suitably dreadful two-issue appearance in *Captain America* before Claremont and Davis used him along with some X-Men castoffs to create *Excalibur*, a supposedly British superhero team that was written and published in the United States and consisted 80% of characters created by Americans, a move that essentially brought the character full circle a decade after his creation.

This, however, is not quite the entire story. It is worth returning to "I Belong to Glasgow," not so much for its content as its context. It is one of several text pieces that Moore contributed to Marvel UK as part of his willingness to help Bernie Jaye get *The Daredevils* together. (Although it appears in *The Mighty World of Marvel*, the convention in question took place during the *Daredevils* run, and presumably Moore was commissioned for the piece under Jaye only to have it held back—it is, in any case, the only text piece he wrote for *The Mighty World of Marvel*.) As mentioned, "I Belong to Glasgow" is in many regards an extension of his time writing the *Fanzine Reviews* column for *The Daredevils*. Moore had some experience in the fanzine community: he'd attempted to launch a fanzine called *Dodgem Logic* in 1975 and got as far as completing an interview with Brian Eno for it, and he had subscribed to and bought numerous others over the years. But his fanzine reviews were only a part of a larger campaign that had the effective result of turning *The Daredevils* into Moore's personal fanzine, culminating in *The Daredevils* #5, in which twenty-three pages of the fifty-four page magazine were written by Alan Moore. That magazine included a reprint of his *Doctor Who Monthly* story "Star Death," two pages of fanzine reviews, a one-page overview of the Special Executive, a three-page article entitled "O Superman: Music & Comics," three pages of a serialized essay entitled "Invisible Girls and Phantom Ladies" about sexism in comics, and ten pages of *Captain Britain*.

All told, over the eleven issues of *The Daredevils*, Moore provided sixty-two pages worth of original material in addition to his *Captain Britain* strips. This surprisingly large body of work consists of several pages of fanzine reviews, the aforementioned essays "O Superman" and "Invisible Girls and Phantom Ladies," a two-part essay on Stan Lee, a six-page essay on Frank Miller, several text pieces featuring Night Raven, and a short comic story parodying Frank Miller's *Daredevil*. This is a significant amount of work to produce in a year, doubly so when that year involved a near sweep of the Eagle Awards that October. It is often said that getting an ongoing strip in *2000 AD* is the crown jewel in a British comics career, but in terms of Alan Moore's 1983 *Skizz* isn't even one of the most prominent features. It was an astonishingly good year for Moore, and, perhaps more to the point, it's clear that Moore appreciated how well he was doing—in a 1984 interview he declared, with not uncharacteristic hubris, "I reckon there are maybe a dozen people in the Western world who know as much or more than I do about writing comics," while admitting that "this says more about the paucity of the medium than it does about my personal talents." Whatever the arrogance involved in such a boast, however, it is difficult to argue that Moore's stock was rapidly rising over the course of 1983.

Given this, the fact that he spend 1983 producing so much work (and in particular so much prose work) for *The Daredevils* is significant. In the year that Alan Moore broke out as a superstar in the field of British comics and crossed over to the much larger American industry, *The Daredevils* was where Alan Moore most gave a sense of himself as a person. Indeed, it is arguable that *The Daredevils* provided an essential component to Moore's meteoric rise to global comics superstar, in that it allowed Moore to craft a persona that unified his disparate bylines into, for lack of a better word, a brand. Certainly that is the effect of the first *Fanzine Reviews* column in *The Daredevils* #1, which culminates in a picture of a young Alan Moore with distinctive beard and hair. "You have been listening to Alan Moore," the caption proclaims, cementing the effect.

In many ways, however, it is not the content of Moore's text pieces that's significant. Nobody will be surprised, after all, to learn that Moore believes that women in comics have consistently gotten the short end of the stick, although the degree to which Moore's criticisms apply thirty years after he wrote them, essentially needing no updating to, is unnerving in its own right. Similarly, given his longstanding influence on the particulars of comics as a medium, it is not a revelation that Moore is capable of an insightful and meticulous dissection of the merits of Frank Miller's art for visual storytelling. Moore's positions mark himself out as, at times, "a wimpy, indecisive, burned-out wooley-minded liberal old hippy who eats quiche, saves whales, is friendly to the Earth and subscribes to Spare Rib, The Black One-Parent Gay Catholic Gazette, and Animal Welfare Against Nuking the Nazis Quarterly," as he self-identifies at the start of "Invisible Girls and Phantom Ladies," but little of what he says is particularly controversial, and even less is shocking or outside the norm. Given the things Moore would eventually come to say in interviews, his Marvel UK pieces are positively models of discretion.

Instead what jumps out about Moore's text pieces is the tone, which is full of a carefully worked sense of irony and self-deprecation. His first piece, "The Importance of Being Frank," opens with the declaration, "Listen, don't you kids try to talk to *me* about comics! I've been reading the damn things for the past twenty two years and I'm bitter, jaded and cynical in terminal proportions." Later he describes himself as "old, cranky and unreasonable," furthering the joke. This basic approach appears in most of his text pieces. In his first *Fanzine Reviews* column he opens by saying, "Fanzines, from my elevated and near-godlike perspective, are curious creatures," goes on to talk about his "two holiday homes in the Azores" and his mass of servants, and closes with the advice that "fanzines with headlines along the lines of 'Alan

Moore: Genius or Demi-God?' or 'Alan Moore: Is He Too Good For Us, Or What?' will obviously get a fairer shake down than the rest." Moore plays this character consistently in his text pieces, and indeed continues to do so throughout his career.

But this self-deprecation is consistently paired with an erudite tone, a meticulous insight, and a casual confidence about a broad variety of topics. "Invisible Girls and Phantom Ladies" is in many regards his masterpiece in this regard, wandering from mainstream superhero comics to lengthy historical commentary on the genre to discussions of the Underground Comix scene while remaining clear and informative. "The Importance of Being Frank" is particularly sharp in this regard, offering detailed and precise accounts of why Frank Miller's *Daredevil* work is so groundbreaking. This clarity is combined with sharply insightful jabs like the observation that he is skeptical whether "Supergirl could change Streaky the Supercat's litter tray without looking like something from the Ziegfeld Follies."

This combination of ironic self-deprecation and eloquent clarity is a compelling persona for Moore to take. For one thing, it immediately protects Moore from any accusations of arrogance or pretension that might accompany his increasing prominence. Certainly at least some backlash existed along these lines: a letter in *The Daredevils* #8, for instance, gripes, "OK, so Mr. Moore is a great writer by British standards but do we have to endure so much of him?" while another complains that his writing is "on the same intellectual level as *The Texas Chainsaw Massacre*." More broadly, Moore's writing, with its often florid caption boxes and literary tone, does leave itself open to the accusation of pomposity. By ironically emphasizing his high regard for himself, Moore blunts the criticism, making it a shared joke with the reader as opposed to a case of Moore simply showing off.

But Moore's self-branding in *The Daredevils* cannot be taken as a purely defensive measure. More than his tone insulates him from certain types of criticism, the public image he cultivated over the course of 1983 is simply affable and appealing. He is in turns funny, insightful, and, when writing fiction instead of nonfiction, terribly clever. Beyond that, the inclusiveness of features like *Fanzine Reviews*, which engaged actively with the larger body of comics fandom, made it all the easier to be taken in by Moore's charms. And sure enough, it worked: while there were occasional critical letters published, overall the letters in *The Daredevils* are effusive in their praise for Moore, reiterating the consensus that he was the best comics writer in Britain at the time. Perhaps more impressive than the acclaim, however, was the degree to which the letters showed investment not merely in Moore's work, but in Moore as a person—one writer talks about how meeting Moore at a convention changed his mind on Moore's work, while another jokes about signing off a letter "until Alan Moore turns bald, Make Mine Marvel," a line that demonstrates that the readers were not only aware of Moore as a byline on work, but were aware of him as a person and celebrity.

There is, of course, an obvious source of inspiration for Moore in crafting this public persona: Stan Lee himself. Moore writes on this exact topic in an essay entitled "Stan Lee: Blinded By the Hype," subtitled "an affectionate character assassination." This subtitle is not entirely accurate—the only way in which Moore's treatment of Lee might be called "affectionate" is in contrast to his decades-later discussions of Lee, where he has suggested outright that he detests Lee. Moore proclaims him a "flawed genius" in his second paragraph, and suggests, after praising Lee's influence, that "on the other hand, without Stan Lee you wouldn't have to sit through such marrow-chilling dreck as the Spider-Man television show. I suppose it's a case of having to take the rough with the smooth." Little barbs like this dot the essay—Moore leavens all of his praise of Lee's writing with his usual self-deprecation, for instance, joking that he so enjoyed his first *Fantastic Four* comic (which his mother had bought him by mistake—he'd requested DC's *Blackhawk*) "that that evening I threw mother an extra lump of raw meat and agreed to consider putting a couple of extra links in her chair." It's typical humor for Moore's public persona in *The Daredevils*, but it's worth noting that in this instance the self-deprecation comes alongside Moore's discussions of how much he liked the comic, thus tacitly calling that very enjoyment into doubt.

But Moore does highlight a specific skill of Lee's, admitting that, in childhood, "like most readers of that period" he "had become totally brainwashed by the sheer bellowing overkill of the Marvel publicity machine," and later talking about "Lee's genius for publicity." Key to this genius, of course, was Lee's careful maintenance of the illusion of a personal connection with the reader. As Moore puts it, "each successive cover" of a Marvel comic "boasted that *this issue* was destined to be 'The Greatest Super Heroic Slugfest in the Mighty Marvel Age of Comics,'" and that "like the ninnies we were, we believed it" long after the comics had declined to the point where every issue "featured the same old mindless fight scenes that we'd been through a hundred times before." And the reason for this is explicitly Stan Lee. "After all," Moore muses, "when had Stan ever lied to us?"

Moore's persona is, of course, far from the sort of bombastic hype that Lee favored in suggesting every single installment of every single comic to be the greatest comic ever, if not the greatest story in any medium ever. Where Lee favored a breathless optimism about everything, Moore was in turns sarcastic, heavily ironic, and prone to leavening any moment of self-praise with two more in which he pokes fun at himself. This is in marked contrast to, say, Dez Skinn, whose approach was to copy Lee's continual effusiveness directly. Moore's public persona cuts an altogether more nuanced figure, and perhaps more importantly, one rather more well-suited to British culture.

But Moore's take on Lee is in the end focused on considerably more than Lee's capacity for promoting the line. For all that Moore's praise of Lee is deeply backhanded, he does unequivocally praise the way in which Lee "managed to hold on to his audience long after they had grown beyond the age range usually associated with comic book readers" via "a constant application of change, modification, and development" that meant "no comic book was allowed to remain static for long," and he talks about the ways in which Lee's characterization was far ahead of anything that had come before. (Admittedly, Moore was rather less kind elsewhere, suggesting that to Marvel, characterization consisted of saying, "Let's be realistic and give them human characters. We'll let them have one characteristic," such that "if they haven't got anything mentally wrong with them like that, something physically wrong with them will do—perhaps a bad leg or dodgy kidneys, or something like that. To Marvel, that's characterization." In the same interview, Moore takes particular relish skewering Chris Claremont [who he identifies as one of Lee's imitators in "Blinded By the Hype"]: "He makes all his X-Men foreign. One's a Russian... They're incredibly Russian. They sort of sit there and let you know how Russian they are by thinking" things like "'How I miss the happy camaraderie of the bread queues and the surprise purges.'")

This is also the note Moore opts to end his piece on, concluding that Lee "has had an influence upon the medium which is as benign as it is poisonous" due to the fact that much of American comics were by 1983 simply slavish imitations of the Stan Lee format. "In effect," he complains, "we have two big companies who are both Marvel comics to all intents and purposes but merely have different names," describing comics as a "field populated solely by the pale ghosts of Lee's former glories." In all of this, he notes, Lee's actual qualities as a writer are overlooked. "Stan Lee, in his heyday," Moore explains, "did something wildly and radically *different*." Moore concludes by asking who might step up and offer a similar revolution for the 1980s: "Any takers?"

Lance Parkin suggests that Moore had a very specific one in mind: himself. This isn't unreasonable. As Parkin points out, an increasing number of UK creators, including Brian Bolland and Dave Gibbons, had been making the move to American comics. And in many ways, Moore did seem to be angling for it. Moore's textual presence in *The Daredevils* was, after all, a sly updating of the Stan Lee formula, and his increasingly high profile across the British comics scene was giving him a visible degree of power within it. He was popular and he knew it. The idea that he could follow the course of other popular UK comics creators and break into America must have occurred to him.

Perhaps more significantly, of course, he had prior form. Not two years ago, in his very first interview, he'd seemingly summoned the *Marvelman* job out of thin air, expressing interest in the character at the exact moment that an opportunity to write it came up. So if he did intend to hook a fish out of the aether with his impish suggestion that what American comic books could really use was a creative genius to completely upend everything, he did a good job with it— the very next month he received a phone call offering him the opportunity to do just that.

Chapter Eight: Swamp Thing

"It's a secret story. It's a story of two brothers."
–Neil Gaiman, *Sandman*, 1992

Several accounts exist of how Len Wein came to decide that, of the many English language comics writers of the world, Alan Moore was the one who should take over a failing book about a plant monster living in the Louisiana bayou. Three suggestions are regularly made. The first of these is Moore's *2000 AD* work. Certainly this was a respected publication, and Wein was familiar with it, as he'd already poached Brian Bolland to illustrate Mike Barr's *Camelot 3000* and worked with Dave Gibbons, who had already been in the early stages of some pitches with Moore to work on some then-disused properties, none of which had been formally submitted by the time Len Wein made his call in May of 1983. But Moore's contributions to *2000 AD* at this point were a bunch of *Future Shocks* and part of *Skizz*, the latter of which was listed among Moore's past credits when he was announced as the comic's next writer. Although certainly good, this is not what Moore built his reputation on in the UK, and it is in some ways difficult to imagine it impressing a US editor quite enough to make the leap that Len Wein did.

This reputation amounts to the second reason given for Moore's hiring—his winning of multiple Eagle Awards, a claim that mostly exists in the form of an oft-told joke on

Moore's part in which he suggests that "the Americans tend to think that every award is an Oscar and didn't realize that the comic industry awards are all voted for by thirty people in anoraks with dreadful social lives." While it is true that several covers of *Swamp Thing* trumpeted his Eagle Awards, the ceremony in which he nearly swept them was in October of 1983, five months after Wein's call. (Several sources suggest that he won Favorite Writer in 1982. This persistent claim appears to be a confusion owing to the fact that the 1983 awards were awarded for work written in 1982. [A similar problem exists in many bibliographies regarding Moore's work for the 1982 *BJ and the Bear Annual*, which is often listed as being for the nonexistent 1983 annual.] Certainly a win in 1982 seems unlikely, as the awards would have been for material published in 1981, a year in which Moore's oeuvre consisted of some of his early *Future Shocks*, including two Abelard Snazz stories, and some of his *Doctor Who* work.)

Those Eagle Awards were mainly for his work in *Warrior*, which forms the third oft-cited reason for Wein's decision. This, in many ways, seems the most plausible explanation. For all its many logistical problems, *Warrior* had relatively good distribution in the United States; Moore's work on it was at least passingly familiar to Steve Bissette, the penciller for *Swamp Thing*. And Moore's work on *Marvelman* in that comic showed exactly the skills that someone looking to revamp a flagging property with a seemingly unpromising premise would need. And, of course, *Warrior* was where he was making his biggest impact with comics fandom, which would include Bolland and Gibbons, the latter of whom actually provided Moore's phone number to Wein. As Moore tells the story, he initially assumed the call was a prank call from his other *Warrior* collaborator David Lloyd, but eventually Wein convinced him of his authenticity and invited him to pitch for *Saga of the Swamp Thing*. (Perhaps ironically, Moore's work on *Captain Britain*, the job he'd done with the most obvious similarities to American superhero work and a character Wein in fact worked on during its first gradual downward spiral in the late 1970s, is the one thing that nobody has ever suggested played a part in his getting the *Swamp Thing* gig.)

It is also important to note that a very different sort of character enters the narrative at this point, namely DC Comics. It is quite unlike Grant Morrison and Alan Moore, who are broadly coextensive with the notion of being recognizable individuals. Nevertheless, DC is clearly a combatant. Crucially, it is both an agent in the narrative and a defined section of Ideaspace containing certain fictional characters, locations, and stories both written and unwritten. Inasmuch as it is an agent, its first major act within the War was to create the superhero in 1938, although its first major act within the chronology of Grant Morrison's professional comics career was Len Wein's phone call to Alan Moore. Inasmuch as it is a territory, however, its first major act within the War will be to be thoroughly, massively, and overwhelmingly conquered by Alan Moore.

The Time Warner subsidiary known as DC Comics has its origins in the merger between National Comics, itself a merger of two companies initially formed in the mid-1930s by Malcolm Wheeler-Nicholson, a World War I veteran turned pulp writer, and All-American Publications, which, at the time of their merger was co-owned by Jack Liebowitz, who had also come to own National Comics after forcing Wheeler-Nicholson out. National Comics' two major publications were *Action Comics* and *Detective Comics*, the latter of which was the title that had given Liebowitz a stake in the company, as he underwrote its publication. All-American Publications, meanwhile, was a 1938 partnership between Liebowitz and Max Gaines, and published a number of other significant characters: the Flash, Green Lantern, and Wonder Woman, most notably. The companies, due to the shared presence of Liebowitz, were always stablemates, but after Liebowitz bought Gaines out, leaving him free to create the competing EC Comics, they officially merged into one company in 1944 under the official name of National Periodical Publications, although they were by this time generally referred to as DC Comics, a name they'd officially adopt in 1977.

During its early days, unlike what would eventually become its sole major competitor, DC invested hard in superheroes, churning out characters to follow its initial smash success with the adventures of Superman in *Action Comics*. This began with Batman, who appeared in *Detective Comics*, created by Bill Finger with Bob Kane on art, and eventually expanded to a large and familiar stable of characters. The breadth and success of this line meant that when superheroes went out of fashion at the end of World War II, DC, unlike Marvel/Timely, did not entirely abandon the genre; they published titles featuring Superman, Batman, and Wonder Woman continually through the 1940s and 50s. And when the superhero comic proved a useful way of getting around the censorship imposed on the industry in the wake of psychologist and public intellectual Frederic Wertham's 1954 attack on comic books, it was DC that first jumped back upon that bandwagon, developing new versions of many of its old superhero properties and eventually, in 1960, teaming several of them up in the Justice League of America, a move that prompted Stan Lee and Jack Kirby to create the Fantastic Four for Marvel.

In 1968, reacting to some loosening on the restrictions imposed on comics, DC decided to get back into one of the genres that had largely been abandoned in favor of superhero comics, namely horror comics. These had been the specialty of Gaines's EC Comics, and had been one of the categories of comics most savaged by Wertham and his supporters, but in 1968 DC poached former EC editor Joe Orlando to edit *House of Mystery*, a once-horror book that had by that point become a superhero anthology. Orlando returned the book to its horror roots, introducing a new narrator in the grand tradition of EC's Crypt Keeper and Old Witch—the biblical Cain, who served as caretaker for the eponymous House of Mystery. Shortly thereafter, Orlando oversaw the revival of a sister book, *House of Secrets*, which was, fittingly, narrated by Abel.

In April of 1971, in issue 92 of *House of Secrets*, there appeared a short story entitled "Swamp Thing," written by Len Wein and drawn by Bernie Wrightson, both creators who had broken into comics under Joe Orlando in his early DC days. "Swamp Thing" tells the tale of Alex Olsen, an early 20th century scientist betrayed by his seeming friend, who, out of lust for Olsen's wife, engineered a lab accident that gravely wounded Alec, then buried his body out in the swamps. As the former friend concludes that Linda, Olsen's wife, has begun to suspect him and that he must thus murder her, it is revealed that Alex is not, in fact, dead, but has become a swamp monster, who rescues Linda but then retreats back into the swamps when he realizes that he terrifies her and that his humanity is truly gone.

Although this premise is hardly the height of creative genius, Wein and Wrightson made a good show of it with the story, which features three nested narratives. The bulk of the story is narrated in the second person, beginning, "You smile because he expects you to—but in the shadowed corridors of your heart there is no real joy—there never can be… Your name is Linda Olsen Ridge," forcibly allying the reader with a character with whom (given the demographics of DC's readership) they had numerous major differences, to say the least. This section of the story breaks off midway for a lengthy narration from Damian, Alex's treacherous friend, who explains his nefarious plot in a sequence that begins and ends as a sequence of thought bubbles, but turns to narrative captions in the middle. Linda's sequence, meanwhile is focused on how she longs for her dead husband, and on her growing paranoia. But Linda's sequence is framed by a third narrative, written in the first person from the perspective of Alex, the swamp monster. This narrative carries an altogether more mournful and haunting tone, beginning, "I cannot remember the morning any more—but I know the evening well! I belong to it now…" and continuing in a similar tone that Moore would eventually characterize as that of "Hamlet covered in snot." But the slightly baroque storytelling and Wrightson's versatile art, which has a paranoid line characterized by expanses of hatched shadow for the middle sections—though that turns faintly ridiculous for the drawings of the swamp monster himself, who looks out at the world through two meloncholy eyes set in an expanse of moss that results in a visage not unlike a sad cartoon dog— gave the story a memorable punch that stood out from the generic twist-of-fate shorts that mostly populated *House of Secrets*.

Indeed, the story was strong and popular enough that in August of 1972 DC launched an ongoing *Swamp Thing* series by Wein and Wrightson. This was not actually a continuation of the story in *House of Secrets* #92, but rather a reworking of it, set in the present day as opposed to a romanticized past. The broad structure is the same—it starts with narration from the Swamp Thing, and concludes with him trudging off into the swamp, accepting that his humanity is gone. But many of the details are changed, sometimes significantly. Instead of Alex Olsen it is Alec Holland who serves as the lead character, and it's specified how he became a swamp man, namely that he was drenched in the "bio-restorative formula" that he was working on when he was killed by a bomb planted by gangsters trying to steal his formula. Stumbling out into the swamp, burning from the bomb blast, Holland collapses into the swamp, only to emerge as a plant monster and, upon discovering his wife's body, to vow revenge on those who did this to him. And Swamp Thing himself is designed differently, with a distinct mouth and a capacity for more varied facial expressions, making him a more human-like figure. But the broad strokes are the same as that of the first Swamp Thing story.

(Notably, they also had several similarities to the origin story of a Marvel character called Man-Thing, a character whose second appearance was written by Wein in between Swamp Thing's debut in *House of Secrets* and the first issue of

Figure 109: Swamp Thing's original design featured a somewhat cartoonish, hangdog expression. (From House of Secrets #92, *written by Len Wein, art by Bernie Wrightson, 1971)*

Figure 110: Swamp Thing, and for that matter the reader, are ambushed by the bizarre Un-Men. (From Swamp Thing #2, *written by Len Wein, art by Bernie Wrightson, 1972)*

Philip Sandifer

his own series, a similarity that has been pointed out by Man-Thing's co-creator Gerry Conway, who was also Wein's roommate at the time. It is, however, worth noting that the history of swamp monsters is a lengthy one, going back, in comics at least, to a 1942 monster published by Hillman Periodicals called The Heap. Moore, coincidentally, had done a thought experiment about how he might relaunch obscure American properties in the same way that he'd done *Marvelman* just a few weeks before Wein's phone call, and had used The Heap as his subject, although he only remembered this coincidence after he'd completed his *Swamp Thing* pitch. Drawing the line of influence into an amusing circle, in 1998 Todd McFarlane debuted a new version of The Heap in *Spawn #72*, having obtained the rights to the character in his ill-fated attempt to acquire Marvelman by purchasing the smoldering remnants of Eclipse Comics. This new version had the power to transport people to a place called Greenworld, a concept that owes no small debt to Moore's transformation of *Swamp Thing*.)

There are, however, some additional plot points in *Swamp Thing #1* with no correspondence to anything in *House of Mystery #92*. The first is one of Holland's assistants, Matt Cable, who mistakenly believes that it is Swamp Thing that has killed his friends Alec and Linda, and who vows to hunt Swamp Thing down. The second is the final panel reveal, a cliffhanger leading into the second issue where, "countless miles away, in a tower at the top of the world," a clawed hand, presumably that of some sorcerer, gestures at a scrying glass showing Swamp Thing's solitary journey out into the muck and orders the creatures amassed around the glass, "Fetch him, my pets! Bring him here... to me!" This claw, in the second issue, is revealed to belong to Anton Arcane, and the creatures he commands are the Un-Men, a host of bizarre critters who, on Arcane's command, jump Swamp Thing, subdue him, and have him brought across the ocean to Arcane's lair in a standard-issue gothic castle.

It is difficult to overstate the visual impact of the Un-Men's appearance. Among Wrightson's many gifts as an artist is a flair for the grotesque, and he outdoes himself with the Un-Men, producing a dozen or so distinct designs for them, many impressively misshapen wrecks that do things like walk on their hands or have a second face where their stomach should be. One, a brain with a face that has the five fingers of a hand in lieu of legs, shouts, "swiftly, my Un-men—capture him swiftly! The Master will not tolerate your failure!" It is an almost literally stunning panel, coming as it does with minimal setup or grounding in anything the book had done up to this point. Within a couple of pages it has completely traded in the Louisiana bayou setting of its first issue for gothic horror with a heavy debt to *Frankenstein*, and two issues later it casually changed again, albeit after having introduced Abigail Arcane, the niece of the villainous mad scientist, who joins Matt Cable on his quest to hunt down Swamp Thing.

This flexibility would prove to be the animating spirit of the Wein/Wrightson run on the character, with each issue moving to a new setting or concept, so that Swamp Thing jumped from confronting aliens to witch hunters to Batman, all of them drawn in Wrightson's endearingly grotesque style. These stories were held together by Wein's characterization of Swamp Thing, which made the character long on thought balloons despite largely remaining silent within the issues, giving him a sort of detached and philosophical view on proceedings that is nevertheless animated by his continuing desires for revenge, survival, and the restoration of his humanity. It was an iconic and influential run of comics that concluded in Wrightson's final issue with the character, *Swamp Thing* #10, which featured a revived Anton Arcane, now in the twisted and Frankenstein-esque form of his own Patchwork Men. With that story, however, Wrightson departed, and after three issues with his replacement, the perfectly adequate Nestor Redondo, so did Wein. What followed were a stretch of largely serviceable single-issue horror stories, but none of them managed to capture the mad energy of the Wein/Wrightson tales, nor their giddy creativity, and the book was cancelled in 1976 with its twenty-fourth issue.

"In the end, the darkness swallows everything. Space vanishes. Time is no longer even a memory. All is lost in the numb and silent depths of forever. Captain Britain is dead."
—Alan Moore, *Captain Britain*, 1982

The character would likely have lain in obscurity for a while at that point, except that in 1982 Embassy Pictures released a film adaptation of Swamp Thing, headed by acclaimed horror director Wes Craven. The film is not what one would call a major work of Craven's, and seems to have been viewed by Craven mostly as a calling card piece to show that he could do action sequences and handle a budget. Swamp Thing, played by Dick Durock in a rubber suit in the grand cinematic tradition of Gill-man, pines for and protects Alice Cable, a composite of Abby Arcane and Matt Cable who is the sole survivor of the attack on the lab that creates Swamp Thing. He ultimately defeats Anton Arcane, who's reworked to be the force behind the attack and, in the film's final act, a giant wolf monster transformed by the same bio-restorative formula that made Swamp Thing. The story draws from several of the early Wein/Wrightson stories, but smooths out the splendid variety that animated them into a fairly generic action film with a gratuitous nude scene for Adrienne Barbeau. Its sole significant contribution to the overall Swamp Thing mythos is the decision to have Alice fall in love with Swamp Thing, a romance Swamp Thing rejects in favor of his comfortably tragic solitude, but it's nevertheless an idea that Moore would eventually expand on mightily.

It would not do, however, for DC to not have a *Swamp Thing* comic in publication to go along with the movie (despite onerous conditions related to the sale of the movie rights that meant DC could not actually produce any merchandise related to Swamp Thing whatsoever beyond a comic book), and so in 1982 a new title, *Saga of the Swamp Thing*, was started with scripts by Martin Pasko, an industry veteran with decades of experience, and art by relative newcomer Tom Yeates. Under Pasko the book was a horror anthology in the same general vein as the Wein/Wrightson issues (albeit with a seventeen-page cap on the stories due to backup stories featuring another cult DC horror character, the Phantom Stranger) and a rather convoluted metaplot involving a spooky child with supernatural powers, a villainous group called the Sunderland Corporation that was hunting Swamp Thing, a reporter named Elizabeth Tremayne and her partner, a doctor named Dennis, both of whom were also trying to find Swamp Thing, and a mysterious illness that was slowly killing Swamp Thing.

Many, though not all of these plot points were resolved in the thirteenth issue of the title, the last with Tom Yeates on art. After two issues by a guest creative team, Pasko picked up his remaining plot lines, mostly focusing on the Sunderland Corporation, in *Saga of the Swamp Thing* #16, now joined by a new artistic team of Stephen Bissette and John Totleben. Almost immediately, however, tensions began to arise. Bissette had a lifelong love of drawing monsters, and so it was in many ways a natural fit for him, but he and Totleben also came onto the project with ideas for what they wanted to draw, which they sent to Pasko. Pasko was, by both his own account and Bissette's, less than impressed. The exact nature of these ideas is, however, less than clear. As Bissette tells it, "We were reading Ramsey Campbell and Stephen King, and we were loving that new wave of horror films that was hitting around then—*The Howling* and David Cronenberg. I was like, 'Man, this should be transformational! This should be about embracing change, instead of constantly longing for what was lost.'" Pasko, on the other hand, pointedly describes an incident in which he was "constantly fighting an uphill battle because the artist wants to draw dinosaurs" and getting into "terribly demoralizing" conversations with the artists over their apparent dinosaur obsession.

In any case, with sales on the book dwindling and Pasko facing increasing commitments from his other career as a television writer, he stepped off the book after a story bringing back Anton Arcane, this time as a giant spider monster. By this point the book was DC's lowest-selling title and was inches from cancellation, but Wein, perhaps out of some fondness for a title he had, after all, originally created a decade earlier, decided to give the book one last chance by using it to try out a new writer, prompting his May 1983 phone call to Northampton.

It is important to understand just how low the expectations were for this endeavor. The deadline for Moore's first issue, in fact, was so absolute that the entire book would have been cancelled without a single issue of Moore's being published had he and the art team (who were facing a variety of personal events such as impending fatherhood for Bissette and impending marriage for Totleben) missed it. Adding to the tension was the fact that Pasko was falling increasingly behind on his scripts, to the point where Bissette was stuck drawing Pasko's final issue, *Saga of the Swamp Thing* #19, in three-page stretches from plots dictated over the phone, as opposed to from full scripts. That all of this chaos was happening on such a low-selling book meant that Moore, realistically, was probably going to get a handful of issues before the comic was cancelled and, if he was deemed to have fallen on his sword with sufficient grace, might get a slightly less tragically doomed job on a followup.

Moore, however, approached the situation with his characteristic gusto. After his conversation with Wein, Moore received a package containing the Pasko run, and he immediately set out writing a fifteen-page assessment of everything that was wrong with it and how he intended to fix it. The first and biggest problem Moore identified was that the root idea of *Swamp Thing*, though good for a few stories, was profoundly limited in the long-run. This analysis included

Moore's description of the character as "Hamlet covered in
snot. He just walks around feeling sorry for himself. That's
understandable, I mean I would too, but everybody knows
that his quest to regain his lost humanity, that's never going
to happen. Because as soon as he does that, the book
finishes." But beyond that, Moore noted that there were
larger problems, such as the fact that, "Other than being a bit
lumpy and kind of greenish, the only thing that you can say
about him is that he's very strong. Which in the DC
Universe—which back then had lots of people who could
play ball with planets—being strong was quite vanilla, really,"
and that "we had to come up with a better way for the
Swamp Thing to travel around, rather than constantly moving
around the country upon freight trains or in the boot of a car
or in some truck." He also touched base with Bissette and
Totleben, and found that he, unlike Pasko, was very much on
the same page as his artists. They were eager to draw more
horror content, and his desire to take greater advantage of
Swamp Thing's status as a vegetable monster found an
immediate resonance in John Totleben's desire to explore the
fact that Swamp Thing was "this guy made out of moss and
mud and these weeds and junk growing on him."

But for all the ambition, he still had to avoid crashing and
burning on his way out of the gate. This was no small task.
His first script, for *Saga of the Swamp Thing* #20, was drawn
over a roughly two-week period in July during which Wein
was on vacation, having left with the instruction that the issue
would be cancelled if it wasn't on his desk when he got back.
The script was presumably submitted at some point in June—
like most of Moore's scripts, it's written as a direct and
conversational address to the artist, and its concluding
sentence, "Love to everybody over there, hope you have
better luck with your next Presidential elections than we've
just had with ours, and I'll speak to you soon," dates it to
sometime in the immediate aftermath of the June 9th general
election in which Margaret Thatcher's government won a
substantially enlarged majority.

Another consequence of the jumbled production schedule by this point was that the production of issues #19, 20, and 21 overlapped. Bissette was penciling #19, and since #21 was always envisioned by Moore as the proper start to his run, issue #20 served largely to wrap up the stray plot lines of Pasko's run in much the same way that his first two *Captain Britain* strips had cleaned up the debris of the aborted Thorpe run. This meant that issue #20 had to be penciled by a guest artist, although John Totleben provided inks, thus maintaining a consistency of style. (It is worth noting that the Bissette/Totleben team was a more collaborative pencil/ink team than many, and that Totleben had an unusually large degree of freedom to rework pages.) Moore was thus left in the uncomfortable position of writing his first issue for an unknown artist, meaning, as he admitted in the script, that "I'm afraid I haven't been able to tailor it to your specific style as I would have done normally." Moore also included his usual caveat regarding his infamously dense scripts, "Since you're the guy actually sitting at the drawing board, you're the one with the final say on what's going to work and what isn't. All my descriptions are really meant to do is give you a place to start out from if you happen to be drawing this on the monday [sic] after your entire family has been wiped out by Hurricane Tracey and you don't have one good idea in your head. So don't worry too much about the specifics... just try and pick up on the mood and the dramatic pace of the story and I'll be happy."

On top of the question marks over who the creative team on *Saga of the Swamp Thing* #20 would actually be and the fact that if the production schedule didn't come off perfectly Moore would be out of a job without a single issue being published, Moore was faced with a third and more abstract problem, which was that *Swamp Thing* gave Moore a much larger canvas to work with than the short stories that he was accustomed to writing for UK audiences. Prior to *Swamp Thing*, his only piece of comics narrative of comparable length was his *Star Wars* story "The Pandora Effect," which is,

Figure 111: Dan Day's original pencils for the first page of Alan Moore's Swamp Thing *debut (left) and the published page reworked by John Totleben from Day's layout (right, from* Saga of the Swamp Thing #20, 1983)

Figure 112: One of the many double-page spreads in Alan Moore's first issue, in this case with the second page's structure broken by a massive explosion. (From Saga of the Swamp Thing #20, *art by Dan Day and John Totleben, 1983)*

charitably, not one of the highlights of his early career, in no small part because of how the extended page count sapped Moore's usual gift for structure and momentum. And for many of the earliest issues of his *Swamp Thing* run one can see him consciously working through the possibilities of the extended form. Indeed, when sending the script for his first issue to Len Wein he noted, "It'll take me another couple of issues to feel out the potential of having twenty three whole pages to work with each month, as opposed to the seven or eight that I'm used to."

Given all of this, it would hardly have been a surprise if Moore had a rough start. And to be fair, there are very few people who would argue with a straight face that "Loose Ends," his first Swamp Thing story, is a better issue than *Saga of the Swamp Thing* #21, the legendary "The Anatomy Lesson," or indeed that "Loose Ends" is a highlight of Moore's run at all. Much of this is that the comic is oddly obscure, having been omitted from the collected editions of Moore's *Swamp Thing* run until 2009. It is, after all, what its title suggests: an issue concerned with wrapping up the loose ends of the Pasko era so that Moore can begin properly with the next issue, a meticulous piece of self-contained horror designed to be a fresh start.

The most striking thing about "Loose Ends" is its composition. Of its twenty-two panels, fully eighteen are based around double-page spreads, giving the issue a tight and intricate sense of structure. Not all of this was down to Moore—his original script called for a splash page on page two as part of a three-page opening sequence, which penciller Dan Day reworked to open with a non-story splash page of Swamp Thing, putting all of the three-page sequence in a single double page spread that would have been two discrete pages in Moore's original plan. And in other places the execution of the spreads is jumbled—one is bisected in print by an advertisement, and in several others the paralleled panel structures are disrupted by a failure to have the panels quite line up from page to page. But elsewhere Moore uses the two-page format to clever effect, such as a sequence that begins as two paralleled pages, but just over halfway through the second page is disrupted as a massive explosion takes place in the story, breaking the symmetry.

The effect is that the seemingly vast canvas afforded by a twenty-three page story instead becomes a series of concrete encounters and exchanges that have their own discrete structures. In effect, Moore broke the bulk of his first issue into a series of two-page strips, as though he were writing an eleven-part series in the style of his early strips for *Doctor Who Weekly*. The issue is not quite as simplistic as that—he doesn't do anything gratuitous like pack in cliffhangers every two pages—but one can nevertheless see Moore finding a way to ease himself into the structure. For the most part, however, the issue is somewhat pedestrian—it attempts to establish a new status quo for the major characters. Some of these bits of end-tying would take years to pay off—the character of Dwight Wicker, for example, vanishes for more than thirty issues after this. Liz and Dennis vanish for even longer, their last appearance being an ominous sequence narrated as, "'All we have in common is the horror in our lives, Dennis.' That's what she said. But maybe horror was all it took. Maybe they didn't need anything else to make it work. Maybe things would be okay between them just so long as they never ran out of horrors. She leans against him, scared, vulnerable, the way a woman should be. And Dennis Barclay runs. And Dennis Barclay smiles." But the main one comes in the final pages, when Sunderland's soldiers track down Swamp Thing and shoot him dead. This rather abrupt and unexpected resolution was the plot point that would set up Moore's second, and altogether more famous issue.

"The plaques that explained who they were also told me that the majority of them had murdered their families and sold their bodies to anatomy. It was then that the word anatomy garnered its own edge of horror for me. I did not know what anatomy was. I knew only that anatomy made people kill their children."

—Neil Gaiman, *The Ocean at the End of the Lane*, 2013

Saga of the Swamp Thing #21, also known as "The Anatomy Lesson," is a regular on critics' lists of the best single issues in the history of comics. This is entirely understandable. Upon release it was a revelation to the handful of readers who were actually buying *Saga of the Swamp Thing*, and its impact upon them (and upon DC editorial, who began aggressively promoting the title in the wake of Moore's early issues) is largely responsible for how Moore took a book that was near cancellation and turned it into one of the gems of DC's line. Beyond that, however, "The Anatomy Lesson" is simply a brilliant comic. Even over thirty years later, when almost every trick and device Moore employs has become every bit as much of a comic book cliché as the twenty-year-old Stan Lee style that Moore championed moving on from, the comic buzzes with power, its sense of freshness and originality undimmed by its countless imitators. It is visibly and unequivocally a work of genius—a shot across the bow at the precise moment in Moore's career where he most needed to demonstrate just how good he was.

Under the hood, of course, "The Anatomy Lesson" is simply "A Rag, a Bone, a Hank of Hair" wrapped in a *Future Shock*. Moore is in many ways straightforwardly repeating the start of his run on *Captain Britain* here, killing the main character in an initial story that focused on wrapping up inherited plot lines and then resurrecting him in his second story. Like "A Rag, a Bone, a Hank of Hair," "The Anatomy Lesson" spends much of its time paralleling a forensic and clinical analysis of the main character's dead body with an account of the character's origin and basic concept. But there is a crucial, albeit subtle difference. "A Rag, a Bone, a Hank of Hair" focuses on recapping the whole of Captain Britain's history up to that point, telling the story of several distinct runs and attempting to reconcile them into a coherent history. "The Anatomy Lesson," on the other hand, is focused almost entirely on dissecting the events of Wein and Wrightson's 1972 *Swamp Thing* #1.

This leads towards the issue's other major antecedent in Moore's work—his lengthy tenure writing twist ending stories for *2000 AD* (a form, it should be noted, that has its roots in the EC horror comics that *House of Secrets* emulated). Like many of Moore's *Future Shocks* and *Time Twisters*, "The Anatomy Lesson" favors an elliptical structure. It starts and ends with a character, Jason Woodrue, standing in his Washington apartment, with the first and last pages being structural mirrors of each other—a backdrop in which Woodrue's face is cut up into multiple small square panels and a trapezoidal set of panels that overlap these panels depicting Woodrue in long shot, staring out his apartment windows, which are cut into a set of small, square frames so that the square panels underneath serve not only as frames of a comic but as a literal depiction of Woodrue's face from outside of his window. To the right of each page is a vertical stack of panels that are arranged like the window panels featuring Woodrue's face, but that depict another event. The first and last lines are identical: "It's raining in Washington tonight."

As with Moore's elliptical *Future Shocks*, however, the point is not so much the fact that the beginning and end of the story match, but rather that upon reaching the end of the story and revisiting its first image the reader is in a profoundly different place due to some surprise revelation. As is typical of the structure, the first page ends by setting up a mystery, the solution to which will hinge on the surprise. In this case, Woodrue describes "the old man" (who turns out to be Sunderland, the villainous corporate leader who spent most of Pasko's run trying to kidnap Swamp Thing) and imagines him "pounding on the glass right about now." Woodrue muses on whether there will be blood. "I like to imagine so," he admits. "Yes, I rather think there will be blood. Lots of blood. Blood in extraordinary quantities." This monologue juxtaposes the vertical strip of panels on the page's lower

Figure 113: The first and last pages of "The Anatomy Lesson" structurally mirror each other, a classic Alan Moore trick. (From Saga of the Swamp Thing #21, *written by Alan Moore, art by Steve Bissette, Rick Veitch, and John Totleben, 1983)*

level, which also show a view of a man through a window, specifically one pressing desperately against the glass as, over the course of three panels, the glass is steadily covered with extraordinary quantities of blood.

This sequence raises a number of questions such as "Who is this man?" and "Why is he being brutally murdered?" the answers to which will presumably fill the remaining twenty-two pages. Having set up the mystery, then, the comic proceeds to a flashback that makes up the bulk of those pages. Despite the fact that the issue was not promoted as a jumping on point for new readers, and would in reality only inherit the dwindling audience that existed for the comic, Moore is careful to structure this sequence to work for people who have never read a page of *Swamp Thing* before. It is not until the third page that Swamp Thing himself is introduced, and then as the bullet-ridden corpse seen at the end of "Loose Ends." Like the image of the man dying against the glass, Swamp Thing is presented as a mystery—a problem to solve. In this case, the problem does not appear to be "Who is this person?" but rather a more metafictional problem—how is this comic going to deal with the fact that its main character is dead?

And yet Moore answers this, in many ways, the wrong way round, spending the next ten pages carefully analyzing the question of who Swamp Thing is, going over the origin story repeatedly. This is structured as a series of rhetorical questions and answers. Initially the mystery is why Alec Holland became the Swamp Thing when nobody else who had been exposed to the famed bio-restorative formula was turned into a plant. Woodrue examines Swamp Thing's body closely, discovering that he has human-like organs inside of him, but that these organs are just vegetable matter and can't possibly function. Finally, after a brief bit of exposition about planarian worms, which were at the time in vogue in popular science news due to a study (ultimately revealed to be fatally flawed) in which the worms were trained to run a maze, then ground up and fed to other worms who seemed to then learn to run the maze faster, Moore gets around to dropping his major twist: in fact Alec Holland was killed by the explosion, and his corpse was flung into the swamp where the bio-restorative formula caused the plants that fed on Holland's decomposing body to absorb his consciousness. As Moore explains it, "We thought that the Swamp Thing was Alec Holland, somehow transformed into a plant. It wasn't. It was a plant that thought it was Alec Holland!"

From this revelation at the halfway point of the issue, Moore begins working backwards towards his opening, explaining why Woodrue is standing in his apartment thinking about the death of the old man who hired him to figure all of this out. Woodrue explains how the old man immediately and cruelly fired him, declaring that he had no further use for him and that "there are others who can be paid to see the work through to its conclusion," and that Woodrue proceeded to sabotage the building's security systems, locking all of the doors and turning off the freezer unit in which Swamp Thing was stored.

This leads to the issue's second, and more bleakly funny twist, the solution to the story's page three mystery: how is the comic going to handle the fact that its main character is dead? The answer, it finally turns out, is that by reexamining and altering the nature of the character's origin, Moore also quietly and without fanfare changed the nature of his death. As Woodrue reflects, the old man "should have let me finish. He should have listened. Then I'd have been able to explain the most important thing of all to him. I'd have been able to explain that you can't kill a vegetable by shooting it in the head." And indeed, the old man hasn't; Swamp Thing rises, reads the report that reveals that he is genuinely a monster with no hope of ever regaining a humanity he never had, and, in fury, kills the old man. And so the comic returns to its initial image, the main character restored and the order of things completely upended, an immaculate and intriguing slate for Moore to construct new stories upon.

The first of these new stories is a three-part story that further explores the character of Jason Woodrue. Woodrue is not merely a plant scientist, as "The Anatomy Lesson" makes clear, but rather the human identity of the Floronic Man, a minor plant-based villain within the DC Universe. Picking up several months after "The Anatomy Lesson," this arc features Woodrue studying Swamp Thing as he reacts to the revelations of "The Anatomy Lesson." At the start, Swamp Thing is not in a good way—as Woodrue explains it to Abby and Matt, "He's given up on being human. It got to be too much for him and he had to let it go. He's withdrawn. He's a vegetable. He hasn't moved in a fortnight. He's put down taproots and stopped pretending to breathe." Meanwhile, in sequences that go within Swamp Thing's mind, he has a series of visions in which he steadily abandons the vestiges of his humanity—abandoning his love for Linda Holland, coming upon a bunch of worms feasting upon the corpse of Alec Holland and leaving only his humanity for Swamp Thing to eat, and finally opting to discard the last of his humanity, symbolically represented as a skull and a few vertebrae imploring Swamp Thing to "Get up! C'mon! Get moving! This is the human race! You have to keep running or you get disqualified!"

Meanwhile, the Floronic Man executes a scheme to commune with the world of plants into which Swamp Thing is sinking, an experience that drives him mad and leads him to embark upon an elaborate scheme of the sort more generally associated with super-villains. He begins in a town of 559 people called Lacroix, where he seals the population within their houses and allows the vegetation to grow wild. "In almost all of the houses," Moore's narration explains, "there were one or more potted plants. These began to accelerate their photosynthetic processes, pumping out pure oxygen at an alarming rate. As they became hyperoxygenated, the people within the houses grew excited and nervous without knowing why. At 2:15, someone lit a cigarette," the result of which was the incineration of the entire town.

Figure 114: Shattered by realizing he was never actually human, Swamp Thing sinks back into the swamp. (From Saga of the Swamp Thing #22, *written by Alan Moore, art by Steve Bissette and John Totleben, 1983)*

Figure 115: At peace with his vegetable nature at the end of the arc, Swamp Thing greets the rising sun. (From Saga of the Swamp Thing #24, written by Alan Moore, art by Steve Bissette and John Totleben, 1984)

Woodrue explains that this is the beginning of a plan to eradicate the entirety of the animal population of the planet so as to create "another green world, as there was at the beginning, before the beasts crawled up out of the oceans. Those long, green centuries where no bird sang, where no dog barked, where there was no noise! Where there was no screaming meat!!"

"I thought of Martin Heidegger and his idea that true humanity comes with not bowing to the external world. I decided again that I should never bow to my own morality."
–Alan Moore, *Marvelman*, 1984

The effect of Woodrue's scheme to create so much oxygen that animals die out, however, is traumatic to the Green, where Swamp Thing now resides, and, between his fury at Woodrue's tainting of the place he retreated to and the terrified screams of Abby Cable as she is attacked by plants, Swamp Thing is driven to return and confront Woodrue. The core of this confrontation is an argument between Woodrue and Swamp Thing, in which Woodrue rants more about how he is saving the planet from the animals that are destroying it, while Swamp Thing argues that the death and destruction wrought by Woodrue is itself "the way of man." The argument concludes when Swamp Thing confronts Woodrue with the question of who "will change the oxygen back into the gasses that we need to survive when all the men and animals are dead," at which point Woodrue's sense of communion with the world of plants falters, and he cracks and runs away. Abby summarizes this as, "He realized that the plants couldn't survive without man, and so the plants backed down." Swamp Thing concurs, but asks, "Will your people do as much?" But however much Swamp Thing may consider himself to be separate from Abby's people, he is animate now, and accepts that his place is not to simply sink into the green, but to live in the swamps, experiencing the vibrant ecosystem, and the arc ends with a splash page of

Swamp Thing standing arms spread wide to greet the rising sun.

It is not, to be sure, a subtle ending. The didactic nature of Swamp Thing's rhetorical defeat of the Floronic Man and his barbed question to Abby are in fact crashingly obvious, although in a way that productively flags the fact that, going forward, *Saga of the Swamp Thing* will be an unabashedly ecological comic. But what is subtler is the degree to which this stems out of Moore's larger and more surprising decision to spend quite a lot of effort sincerely exploring the question of what it would be like, from a psychological perspective, to be a walking plant. The entire ecology debate between Woodrue and Swamp Thing is framed as the practical application of the more spiritual experiences both characters have within the Green. The second issue of the arc, entitled "Another Green World" (an homage to a Brian Eno album, as is relatively typical of Moore), demonstrates this well—it ends with Swamp Thing finally arriving to confront Woodrue, but this is ultimately framed as a response to, and an extension of, Swamp Thing's initial meditations on the fact that "there is a red and angry world. Red things happen there. The world eats your wife, eats your friends, eats all the things that makes you human. And you become a monster. And the world just keeps on eating. I couldn't take that… being eaten. I couldn't take the red world. So I walked out, and I left my body behind, and I'm somewhere else now. Somewhere quiet. Somewhere green and timeless. I drift the cellular landscape stretching beneath me… eerie. Silent. Beautiful." And when Woodrue is finally defeated it is not merely a realization that Swamp Thing is right, but a proper fall from grace in which Woodrue loses his psychic connection with the plants of the world. Any ecological truth, in other words, is merely an extension and consequence of the psychic life of vegetables.

It is worth pausing to look at the other vegetable with a rich inner life in these three issues, namely Woodrue. As with his run on *Captain Britain*, Moore takes a visible delight in playing with the larger world of the character. But where in

Captain Britain he drew almost entirely from the past history of that specific character, within *Swamp Thing* he played freely with the entire sweep of the DC line. Given this, it's interesting that he began with the Floronic Man, a minor villain who had made a grand total of seventeen appearances in the twenty-two years since his creation, the bulk of them as a supporting player in a super-villain team. He first appeared simply as Jason Woodrue, serving as the villain for the 1962 first issue of *The Atom*, where he is described as coming "from a dimensional world close to our own which is inhabited by wood nymphs, dryads, nereids, air sprits and flower-spirits," and where he attempts to use plants to take over the Earth. In his fourth appearance, fourteen years later, he transforms himself through an elixir to become a living plant and fights the Green Lantern for two issues before settling down for a several year stint in the Secret Society of Super-Villains, where he mostly played second fiddle to a malevolent talking gorilla. (Although to be fair, almost every DC Comics villain has at some point played second fiddle to a malevolent talking gorilla.)

He was, in other words, a character that essentially nobody cared about. Admittedly Moore did not have access to a deep and impressive bench of plant-based villains who could fill the specific plot role he needed. But even among those options, the Floronic Man was nowhere near DC's most famous plant villain—Moore could easily have used Pamela Isley, aka Poison Ivy, a plant scientist/femme fatale from Batman's rogue's gallery. Instead Moore consciously opted for a ridiculously obscure villain, who he builds into a thoroughly massive threat. This choice to draw from the history of DC comics in an obscure and marginal way immediately positions *Swamp Thing* at a slightly orthogonal angle to the rest of DC Comics, clearly flagging it as a comic that is not going to interact with the larger line in a straightforward or entirely predictable manner.

Moore pays this off in the conclusion to the Floronic Man arc in *Saga of the Swamp Thing* #24, titled "Roots." In this issue Moore introduces some exceedingly high profile guest stars: the Justice League of America. At this moment in DC's history, the Justice League consisted of Superman, Wonder Woman, Green Lantern, The Flash, Green Arrow, Hawkman, Aquaman, Zatanna, and Firestorm—some of the company's biggest properties, in other words. Certainly all of them—even Zatanna and Firestorm—were on a basic level more familiar and recognizable characters than Swamp Thing himself to your average early 1980s DC reader. But Moore, having spent four issues making *Swamp Thing* stand at an odd remove from the rest of the line, employs them in an unexpected manner. The issue opens with images of the Watchtower—the orbital base of the Justice League—and narration saying, "There is a house above the world, where the over-people gather. There is a man with wings like a bird... There is a man who can see across the planet and wring diamonds from its anthracite. There is a man who moves so fast that his life is an endless gallery of statues... In the house above the world, the over-people gather." The narration slots firmly into Moore's well-established iambic style that he uses to give sections a mythic heft. ("there is a house above the world..." "there is a man who moves so fast...")

But it's significant that this narration is being applied to the familiar DC characters, thus putting them at a strange and alien remove. The use of the phrase "over-people" is a reworking of the more familiar "superhero," or, more literally, "Superman," returning to the Nietzschean roots of the name in the idea of the übermensch, which most literally translates to "overman." This is a theme Moore had already explored in *Marvelman* by positioning the character as the product of Project Zarathustra, and is a recurring theme in Moore's superhero work. As he put it in a 1984 interview, "That's the origin of the superman concept, and it's a fascist ideal"—a theme he would reiterate in his famed 2014 "last interview" when he proclaimed that "the origin of capes and masks as ubiquitous superhero accessories can be deduced from a close viewing of D.W. Griffiths' *Birth of a Nation*," a film largely about valorizing the Ku Klux Klan.

Moore emphasized this remove in his instructions to Bisette and Totleben on how to draw the heroes, saying to "draw them with their faces shadowed—make them a bit more mysterious." Bisette and Totleben further emphasize the sense that the superheroes simply don't quite belong in this world by portraying Woodrue's face on the monitors as he explains his mad scheme in a relatively photorealistic style, thus creating a visual disparity between him and the Justice League. All of this is used to build up the idea that the Justice League is completely powerless in the face of Woodrue's plan—as Green Arrow says at the end of the sequence, "What you're saying is, 'We get to lose this one. This time we finally strike out.' Man, I don't believe this! We were watching out for New York, for Metropolis, for Atlantis... but who was watching out for Lacroix Louisiana?" The effect is to slyly increase the stakes of the issue's main plot—the climactic showdown between Swamp Thing and Woodrue—by stressing that it's a threat where not even the Justice League can help. But it also serves to make the Justice League have the same relationship to Swamp Thing that Swamp Thing has to the Justice League—that of weird and slightly strange forces that hover at the edge of the world. And when, at the end of the issue, Woodrue comes crashing out of the Swamp Thing's world and back into the world of the Justice League (where he belongs), he's shown to have been driven mad by the experience: he sprays human skin onto his distorted and human face covered in bark and insists that he broke his arm "doing something normal, driving a car, fishing, one of those things us men do" while the liquid skin drips down off the thorns that have grown out of his chin.

With five issues under their belt, the Moore/Bissette/ Totleben team was clearly making waves at DC. Impressed with the book, DC began running house ads for it in its other comics, starting in March of 1984. These ads coincided with the start of Moore's second arc, which drew heavily from the

*Figure 116: Jason Woodrue makes an unconvincing case for his humanity.
(From* Saga of the Swamp Thing *#24, written by Alan Moore, art by
Steve Bissette and John Totleben, 1984)*

ideas proposed by Bissette and Totleben, to the point where the trade paperback credits them as co-plotters. The major idea that Moore worked from was one of Bissette's, who drew on the experience of his then-wife in working at a school for autistic children to propose setting a story at a similar institution. Secondarily, Bissette and Totleben had an idea for a fear monster inspired in part by Francisco Goya's famous print "The Sleep of Reason Produces Monsters," a title Moore appropriated for the first issue of his second arc.

This print is the forty-third of eighty in a series Goya titled *Lo Caprichos*. Created in 1797, the series consists of satirical attacks on what Goya viewed as the "innumerable foibles and follies" of late 18th century Spain. Many of these were practical critiques—Goya depicted child abuse, female vanity, and the excesses of the clergy, all with exaggerated grotesqueries that bled in and out of the monstrous depictions of witchcraft that litter the prints. "The Sleep of Reason Produces Monsters" is the most famous print in the series, depicting Goya himself asleep at his desk and haunted by unsettling beasts that drift forward from the shadows behind him. The message is straightforward enough, and put forward in the title—an alliance with Enlightenment reason against the ignorant darkness that opposed it. Taken as part of the larger social critique of *Lo Caprichos*, it presents the grotesque excesses that he depicts throughout the series as coming from a willful ignorance—as the product of rejecting reason. Crucially, it is not that reason drives away monsters, but rather that reason's absence creates them, a point reiterated by the longer epigraph to the piece, generally translated as "fantasy abandoned by reason produces impossible monsters: united with her, she is the mother of the arts and the origin of their marvels."

In this regard, Goya adopts an almost completely opposite position from his contemporary, William Blake, for whom reason is embodied in the form of Urizen, "a shadow of horror" who is "self-closd, all-repelling" born out of the void at the edges of Eternity. As Urizen contemplates his

Figure 117: Goya's "The Sleep of Reason Produces Monsters." (1799)

Figure 118: Urizen writing his "books formd of metals," a description that applies equally well to Blake's copper engravings. (The Book of Urizen Copy G, Object 1, written 1794, printed 1818)

selfhood he acquires form, until he emerges from the darkness, speaking of his desire to create "a solid without fluctuation." And so Urizen creates a world, saying:

Here alone I in books formd of metals
Have written the secrets of wisdom
The secrets of dark contemplation
By fightings and conflicts dire,
With terrible monsters Sin-bred

It is, in other words, precisely the awakening of reason as represented by Urizen (who, like many of Blake's mythological figures, gets his name from a pun, in this case the phrase "your reason") that produces monsters.

And yet in the end Blake's position is not as far from Goya's as it might appear. It is not straightforwardly the case that Urizen is evil so much as it is that Urizen unbound is destructive. At the climax of his unfinished epic *Vala, or the Four Zoas*, order and peace is restored to Eternity when Urizen abandons his mad quest to fix and define the nature of all things and is instead reunited with his Emanation, Ahania, who represents pleasure, which Blake views as the true "food of Intellect."

Ahania cast off her death clothes
She folded them up in care in silence & her brightening
    limbs
Bathd in the clear spring of the rock then from her
    darksom cave
Issud in majesty divine Urizen rose up from his couch
On wings of tenfold joy clapping his hands his feet his
    radiant wings
In the immense as when the Sun dances upon the
    mountains
A shout of jubilee in lovely notes responding from
    daughter to daughter
From son to Son as if the Stars beaming innumerable
Thro night should sing soft warbling filling Earth &

heaven
And bright Ahania took her seat by Urizen in songs & joy

For both Goya and Blake, in other words, some sense of balance is required—it is just that Goya fears the passions of man running unchecked, while Blake fears the prison of law and religion woven by reason.

"It's where Darkseid fell through existence to his doom. Leaving hell deserted. And there, in his absence, the first flower grew. So begins the myth of a new creation. Apokolips reborn as New Genesis."
–Grant Morrison, *Final Crisis*, 2009

And in another sense, Blake is closer still to Goya, on an almost literal level. It is, after all, once Urizen has been bound by Los, the fallen, human form of Urizen's opposite number, Urthona, that Los's emanation, Enitharmon, is split from him and gives birth to the monstrous serpent Orc. Orc, within Blake's mythology, is the spirit of revolution, and makes his most substantial appearance in *America a Prophecy*, the first of Blake's three "continental prophecies," in which Blake reworks the recent political history of the world into another iteration of his mythology. As its title suggests, *America a Prophecy* reworks the recent history of America, specifically the American revolution. It is manifestly not a straightforward retelling of history, not least because of the presence of various gods and monsters. And yet nevertheless the major figures of the American revolution are present within the poem. It opens, for instance:

The Guardian Prince of Albion burns in his nightly tent,
Sullen fires across the Atlantic glow to America's shore:
Piercing the souls of warlike men, who rise in silent night,
Washington, Franklin, Paine & Warren, Gates, Hancock & Green;
Meet on the coast glowing with blood from Albions fiery Prince.

Appearing to this gathering of American political figures is Orc, who is accused by Albion's angel of being a "Blasphemous Demon, Antichrist, hater of Dignities; / Lover of wild rebellion, and transgresser of Gods Law." Orc, for his part, proclaims:

> The fiery joy, that Urizen perverted to ten commands,
> What night he led the starry hosts thro' the wide
>   wilderness;
> That stony law I stamp to dust: and scatter religion abroad
> To the four winds as a torn book, & none shall gather the
>   leaves;
> But they shall rot on desart sands, & consume in
>   bottomless deeps,
> To make the desarts blossom, & the deeps shrink to their
>   fountains,
> And to renew the fiery joy, and burst the stony roof.

In place of Urizen's law, then, Orc offers the belief that "every thing that lives is holy, life delights in life; / Because the soul of sweet delight can never be defil'd." Albion calls upon the colonies to rise up against Orc, but "Silent the Colonies remain and refuse the loud alarm," and instead they declare independence, with Boston's Angel asking

> What God is he, writes laws of peace, & clothes him in a
>   tempest
> What pitying Angel lusts for tears, and fans himself with
>   sighs
> What crawling villain preaches abstinence & wraps
>   himself
> In fat of lambs? no more I follow, no more obedience pay.

And so the American Revolution breaks out, overthrowing the chains of Urizen. At first glance, given Blake's larger ideological predispositions, this ends triumphantly, with Orc's fire threatening to engulf Europe as well. The European countries try

> to shut the five gates of their law-built heaven
> Filled with blasting fancies and with mildews of despair
> With fierce disease and lust, unable to stem the fires of
>   Orc;
> But the five gates were consum'd, & their bolts and hinges
>   melted
> And the fierce flames burnt round the heavens, & round
>   the abodes of men

presaging the second of Blake's continental prophecies, *Europe a Prophecy*. And yet beneath the surface all is clearly not well in the world. As the poem draws to its conclusion, the images turn dark and sinister, with scenes of despair and suffering. And for all the revolution's lofty ideals, the description given is hardly encouraging.

> Fury! rage! madness! in a wind swept through America
> And the red flames of Orc that folded roaring fierce
>   around
> The angry shores, and the fierce rushing of th' inhabitants
>   together;
> The citizens of New-York close their books & lock their
>   chests;
> The mariners of Boston drop their anchors and unlade;
> The scribe of Pensylvania casts his pen upon the earth;
> The builder of Virginia throws his hammer down in fear.
> Then had America been lost

It becomes all too clear that the revolution is not straightforwardly a good thing.

In practice, this reflects Blake's steady rejection of the idea of a charismatic, leader-driven revolution, viewing that as, in the end, a reiteration of the underlying problem of Urizen and his egotistical desire to control. Ultimately, for Blake, a revolution based on authority is doomed to failure.

And so the monstrosity of Orc becomes a strangely ambivalent thing, simultaneously doomed to failure and necessary for the world.

A similar ambivalence pervades Moore's story. At the climax, when the simian fear monster and another monster battle within the school, Swamp Thing tells Abby to take the child whose fear the Monkey King is feeding upon and flee to the swamp. Abby protests, asking, "What about you? There are those two monsters, and…," but Swamp Thing interrupts her, proclaiming icily, "Three Monsters." The third monster is, of course, Swamp Thing himself, a fact that casts the arc's initial declaration that the sleep of reason produces monsters in a new and different light.

The other monster, after the Monkey King and Swamp Thing, was another suggestion/request on the part of Bissette and Totleben, who were eager to draw a character named Etrigan, created by Jack Kirby during his brief period working for DC (as was the Monkey King, actually). This period followed his falling out with Marvel in 1970 over the fact that Stan Lee continued to get more and more public attention and credit. In late 1969, Kirby had attempted to negotiate an ongoing contract with Marvel, frustrated that for all his contributions to the company he was still being paid as a freelancer, that he didn't get sufficient creative control over his work (most particularly the Silver Surfer, which he had created entirely on his own, only to have Stan Lee effectively take over the character), and over a series of broken promises by the ever-changing Marvel management, most notably a promise to match whatever settlement was reached with Joe Simon over copyright to Captain America in exchange for Kirby testifying in Marvel's favor in Simon's lawsuit. When the contract offer arrived, Kirby found it derisory, and proceeded to sign a contract with DC Comics to begin producing work with them.

Upon arrival at DC, Kirby was given leave to create an expansive set of concepts and books generally referred to as the Fourth World saga. With covers proudly boasting "Kirby is here!" the series spoke volumes about the clout and acclaim Kirby had within the industry. But under the hood, the comics also revealed how strange a place DC was at the time. For all their evinced pride at having hired Kirby, they also were having every single drawing of Superman he did for his work on *Superman's Pal Jimmy Olsen* (which he took on to fulfill DC's request that he work on at least one existing title) redrawn by artists like Al Plastino, a late forties Superman artist who wasn't even doing other work for DC, much to Kirby's chagrin. And so when the Fourth World books did not generate the sales DC had hoped from their new star artist, they quickly (and again to his chagrin) moved him to other titles.

The first among these was a request that Kirby create a horror title. This was not a natural fit for Kirby or an assignment he was enthused about, but Kirby obliged, creating a book called *The Demon* that debuted in June of 1972, two months before Wein and Wrightson's *Swamp Thing* #1. Etrigan was originally a demonic servant of Merlin tasked at the fall of Camelot to protect a portion of an ancient magical tome. After the fall, Etrigan turned to human form and lived for centuries under the name of Jason Blood, although with clouded memories that kept him from realizing his immortality. Eventually, however, Blood is lured to the crypt of a mysterious castle where he discovers an inscription reading "Change! Change, o' form of man! / Release the might from fleshy mire! / Boil the blood in heart of fire! / Gone! Gone!—The form of Man! / Rise, the demon Etrigan!" This transforms Blood at last back into the demonic Etrigan, just in time to fight off Morgan le Fay, who has been pursuing him since the fall of Camelot to learn its secrets. From there Jason Blood and Etrigan proceed to have a fraught relationship in which Blood simultaneously fears and relies upon Etrigan's power as they investigate and stop various supernatural goings on. The series ran for sixteen issues (the Monkey King debuted in #4) before it too was cancelled, and Kirby continued to float around DC for a bit

Figure 119: For all that DC boasted of having Kirby's talents, they insisted on having his Superman redrawn, as his take was considered too radical.

Figure 120: Jason Blood transforms into Etrigan for the first time. (From The Demon #1, *by Jack Kirby, 1972)*

doing odd jobs and creating more characters before he finally got frustrated and returned to Marvel at the end of his contract.

Moore, Bissette, and Totleben were hardly the first people to draw from Jack Kirby's store of creations in the years after Kirby's departure from DC, but it is nevertheless hard not to see the decision to use one of Kirby's characters, and, perhaps more to the point, to proclaim at the end of the arc, "This story is dedicated with awe and affection to Jack Kirby," as an act of staking out an ideological position. Kirby was always one of the most inventive and original creators in comics, and his work had an odd and visionary quality, especially in the Fourth World saga, which is perhaps the greatest instance of someone creating a new mythology wholesale since William Blake. Essentially everyone in comics recognizes Kirby as one of the greats, but there's a marvelous ambition on Moore's part in so quickly identifying his *Swamp Thing* run as a sort of spiritual cousin to Kirby's work. (Kirby, for his part, praised Moore's iconoclasm when they shared a panel with Frank Miller at the 1985 San Diego Comic-Con.) But the parallels go deeper than Moore could possibly have known in 1984. The frustrations that characterized Kirby's career, from his feeling that he wasn't adequately compensated given the amount he'd done for Marvel to his lack of creative control at DC, are merely some of the most infamous moments in a long history of labor exploitation in the American comics industry. These issues were ones that Moore and his collaborators were passionate about, and the arc of Kirby's career at DC, from early days being feted as a visionary genius to eventually leaving in disgust and frustration over DC's restrictive editorial policies, bears visible parallels to the arc of Moore's career, right down to their five-year duration.

It is perhaps unsurprising, then, that the most vibrant component of Moore's second arc is Moore's treatment of Etrigan. Certainly it's one of the elements Moore took the most care with. He describes in one interview how, in writing the character, "I settled myself down in front of a mirror and I closed the blinds so the neighbors didn't see or become suspicious and phone the police or anything," and then begin a sort of acting exercise to figure out how the character would talk: by hunching over and imagining himself talking through large fangs, with a speech impediment. He combined this with an innovation introduced a few months earlier by a Len Wein-penned issue of *DC Comics Presents* whereby Etrigan's speech was all delivered in rhyming couplets (as opposed to just his iconic "Change! Change o form of man" speech and one or two other rhyming couplets Kirby threw in), so that Etrigan's first appearance in the second issue of the storyline opens with an extended monologue in sonnet form:

> The toys about the nursery are set
> for idiot chaos to arrange at whim.
> He drools and ruins lives, his chin is wet
> and old or young, it matters not to him.
> The gracious lady and her root-choked beast
> have come to save the innocents from harm,
> to spare them from the monkey's dreadful feast.
> What noble souls they have! What charm!
> And see! The children's uproar brings to life
> their guardians: that most dedicated breed!
> Yet she betrays her husband, he his wife,
> though both of them are kind to babes in need.
> Should innocence be mollycoddled thus?
> I fail to see the reason for the fuss

and so it continues for a few more stanzas. It is perhaps no surprise that Moore would excel at writing Etrigan, given that his speech patterns allowed Moore to slip into the iambic rhythm he usually relies on to make a passage bigger and more portentous.

"God will bury you. Nature will bury you. Time will bury your bones unseen. Total and absolute. Infinite amplitude. Til all the black is ripe in green."
–Seeming, "The Burial," 2014

The second arc introduced other sizable elements of Moore's run as well, however. On a story level, it continues a plot that Moore inherited from Pasko regarding Matt Cable and his descent into alcoholism. Moore has Cable get into a drunken car crash that kills him, only for a mysterious spirit appearing in the form of a fly to offer to save him; the fly then crawls into his mouth, seemingly possessing him. On a practical level, meanwhile, it introduced a new editor for Moore in the form of Karen Berger, who would edit the remainder of his *Swamp Thing* run before going on to oversee the recruitment of other British writers and artists to create comics in a similar vein. Of the editors that Moore has worked with, there are perhaps none that he praises as unreservedly as he does Berger, who remained essentially the only figure at DC that Moore would actually speak to all the way until her departure from the company in 2013. It is tempting, especially given Moore's tendency to complain about editors who he feels overstep their bounds, to suggest that Moore's fondness for Berger was simply because she was inclined to get out of his way and let him tell the stories he wanted to tell, and it certainly is true that Berger gave Moore considerable creative freedom and generally backed and supported his instincts. But the interplay between them was always much more subtle than that—a fact that would be demonstrated clearly by Moore's next story arc.

But having completed seven straight monthly issues of transformative and groundbreaking horror comics, Bissette and Totleben were by this point in need of a break before starting on a new arc. The production schedule of American comics takes into account that few artists can actually maintain a monthly pace of twenty-three pages, especially not as more and more detailed and intricate art styles became

Figure 121: Matt Cable, dying from a drunken car crash, is possessed by a demonic force in the form of a housefly. (From Saga of the Swamp Thing #27, written by Alan Moore, art by Steve Bissette and John Totleben, 1984)

Figure 122: Shawn McManus's approach to drawing Swamp Thing was noticeably more cartoonish than Bissette and Totleben's. (From Saga of the Swamp Thing #28, 1984)

increasingly popular with readers. Accordingly, the norm is to draft fill-in artists. Often these stories are what are known as inventory stories—ones solicited with the express purpose of being kept until the production schedule slips behind—other times they're simply stories written as a break from the overall serialized narrative. In either case, they are typically self-contained, single-issue stories that do not rely on other plot elements—stories featuring a guest star or retellings of the main character's origin are both common approaches. And so when the schedule grew tight after the Etrigan arc, Shawn MacManus was brought in for "The Burial," a story that in effect recapped Swamp Thing's new origin, with Swamp Thing finding himself haunted by the ghost of the real Alec Holland, and thus crawls the swamp for his bones in order to give him a burial. Neil Gaiman suggests that the point of the story is as "a celebration of and memorial to the original Len Wein and Bernie Wrightson" *Swamp Thing*, and this is certainly one of the things the story is doing, but it serves a second and pragmatic purpose as well. With the series' new direction gaining considerable buzz, reintroducing the book's new premise and re-explaining the relationship between Moore's stories and the traditional Swamp Thing readers might be used to was just a savvy move. Having, over the course of seven issues, made the title a subject of incredible acclamation, it was just plain time for an issue that worked as a jumping on point.

MacManus gave "The Burial" a cleaner, crisper style that throws Bissette and Totleben's tense and scratchy style into relief, such that the story feels as though it has taken a step backwards towards Wrightson's art, especially in the original *House of Secrets* short story. Under MacManus's pencil, Swamp Thing becomes a slightly cartoonish character, his mossy face given an added range of expression so that he can gape, horrified, at the ghosts around him. The story is a slender thing, to be sure, but a needed breather after seven issues of white-knuckled cutting edge horror. Moore, for his part, noted MacManus's more cartoonish style, and developed an idea for future use.

By this time, the success of Moore's *Swamp Thing* work had caused some major shifts to the overall shape of his career. Moore started in 1979 eager to make £42.50 a week—the figure he'd been receiving when on welfare. *Swamp Thing*, however, paid $50 a page, which worked out to around £850 an issue, or, divided over a month, nearly £200 a week, more than quadruple his initial benchmark for success, and solidly above the average income in the UK at the time. And it was not as though *Swamp Thing* was occupying his every waking hour. In fact, Moore could work out scripts fairly quickly. The script for *Swamp Thing* #29, for instance, was written in two days—a particularly tight turnaround, but still an illustration of how much other work Moore could fit in if he wanted to.

But financial success once again allowed him to pick and choose his assignments, much as the beginning of *Skizz* had allowed him to finally drop the time-consuming and comparatively ill-paying *The Stars My Degradation* a few months earlier. As mentioned, Moore stopped doing short stories for IPC as soon as his *Swamp Thing* work commenced. A year or so after starting *Swamp Thing*, Moore also dropped *Captain Britain*, frustrated both with Marvel UK's less than prompt payments and the sacking of Bernie Jaye. Two months later, in August of 1984, he dropped *Marvelman* after an explosive blow-up with editor Dez Skinn, although he would continue to write *V for Vendetta* until *Warrior* finally went under in February of 1985. For the time being he continued his *2000 AD* work, starting a new project, *The Ballad of Halo Jones*, in July of 1984, and contributing a few short stories featuring the ABC Warriors and the Ro-busters for the 1985 annual.

The same month that *Halo Jones* started, Moore published what would turn out to be one of the most historically significant issues of his *Swamp Thing* run. Following MacManus's fill-in, Moore planned to have Bissette and

Totleben draw "The Nukeface Papers," an arc about nuclear pollution. Karen Berger, however, felt that this was not the right move for the book's momentum, and had Moore shelve the story, which led Moore to quickly develop a story featuring the return of Swamp Thing's one significant recurring villain, Anton Arcane. On one level, this move threatened to render the book formulaic. With the exception of "The Burial," all of Moore's *Swamp Thing* issues since "The Anatomy Lesson" had been three-part story lines following a relatively consistent pattern whereby the first issue features some malignant presence infecting the world, the second brings Swamp Thing to the point of confronting this presence, and the third finally resolves the plot. Repeating this basic story structure with a villain who had made a big return just ten issues earlier at the end of Martin Pasko's run... feels at first glance a bit stale, as if Moore's grand revolution of American comics really just consisted of finding a slightly new formula to milk to death.

It is not that the Arcane arc is a bad story. On the contrary, it's quite effective. The first issue, *Saga of the Swamp Thing* #29, titled "Love and Death," in which Abby steadily goes mad under Arcane's psychic assault, has a grim and unsettlingly visceral sense of horror that outstrips any of Moore's earlier work on the title. On a superficial level this visceral horror stems from Bissette and Totleben's depiction of Abby curled up on the floor in shades of red and sickly yellow, with insects crawling all about her as Moore's narration describes, "She couldn't get rid of the smell. In the shower she used up all of the soap, the shampoo, the bubble-bath, the perfume... the smell was still there." But the issue's horror exists beneath the surface. Over the course of the story Abby's descent into madness is explained through a series of flashbacks in which she comes to realize that something is deeply wrong with her husband. Eventually she concludes, correctly, that he's undead and possessed by something, revealed in a grotesque double page spread at the issue's end to be Anton Arcane. This double page spread, in

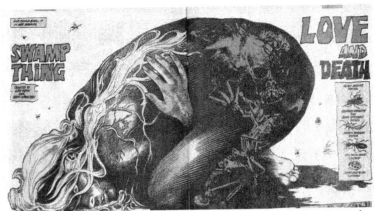

Figure 123: *Abby's rape is metaphorically represented by the invasion and infestation of her body with insects.* (From Saga of the Swamp Thing #29, 1984)

Figure 124: *This two-page spread, revealing that Abby had been the victim of zombie incest rape from Anton Arcane, proved to be of remarkable historical importance.* (From Saga of the Swamp Thing #29, written by Alan Moore, art by Steve Bissette and John Totleben, 1984)

which her demonically possessed husband grabs her by the hair as she's surrounded by a group of reanimated corpses, revealed now to be rotting zombies, and answers her question of "What do you want me to say?" with the grotesque incest pun of "Just say uncle," proved, for several reasons, to be a historical turning point.

For one thing, it was one of Moore's first engagements with a theme that would recur across his career—and with a frequency that would ultimately provide one of the most common lines of criticism of his work: rape. Indeed, the incestuous rape of a character via the spiritual possession of her husband's dead body is a strong contender for the single most horrific and disturbing rape in Moore's oeuvre—a body of work in which it does, indeed, have an awful lot of competition. This would be true even if Bissette, Totleben, and colorist Tatjana Wood hadn't outdone themselves in the gruesome and insect-ridden artwork, simply on the basis of the conceptual horror. With the artwork, it is a scene that is unprecedented in mainstream American comics—one that makes S. Clay Wilson's cartoonish tableaus of demonic orgies look like lighthearted fun in comparison.

This was, of course, the point. In a lengthy response made in 2014 to criticisms about the prevalence of rape in his comics, Moore notes that in 2013, "There were 60,000 rapes in the UK. I'm assuming that this is reported rapes, and that actual incidents of rape are possibly two or three times as high. There were a further 400,000 cases of sexual assault, and a frankly horrific 1.2 million cases of domestic abuse. Leaving aside the sexual assault and domestic abuse figures and just focusing on the rapes—which is of course rather my 'thing'—I would have to say that I do not recall the sixty thousand homicides that occurred in the U.K. last year, possibly because—well, they didn't, did they?" He goes on to note that, given this, it is telling that in fiction the rates are reversed such that violent death is considerably more common than rape. "Why," Moore asks, "should sexual violence be ring-fenced when forms of violence every bit as devastating are treated as entertainment? If I may venture an answer to my own question, might it be because the term 'sexual violence' contains the word 'sexual', a word relating to matters traditionally not discussed in polite society?" Moore suggests that the failure to engage with the prevalence of rape constitutes "the denial of a sexual holocaust, happening annually" before declaring that he "could not, in all conscience, produce work under those limitations without at least attempting to change or remove them. Presumably, my current critics would have done differently, and indeed, as I remember, most people in the field found it more convenient simply not to address issues of sex or sexuality—or those of race, politics, gender and any other matters of social substance, for that matter."

The point, in other words, is that Moore opts to depict rape specifically because of its horror, and furthermore because he views that horror as the flipside of his interest in depicting "consensual and relatively joyous sexual relationships" as part of his conscious decision to "along with political and social issues… make sexual issues a part of my work." The demonic rape of Abby is included specifically because of how utterly horrific it is. And yet given this, the criticism of Moore's handling of rape are in many ways solid. While Moore is clearly committed to the depiction of rape as something awful, the truth is that he rather egregiously ducks the consequences of depicting it. Abby dies midway through the issue following the revelation of her rape, and when she is resurrected in the 1985 *Swamp Thing Annual* it is with no memory of what happened. For all that "Love and Death" focuses on her trauma, the subsequent issues can fairly be criticized for being a fairly banal saga of men taking vengeance on other men for terrible things that have been done to women. In this regard the rape is troublingly severed from the corresponding issue of survivorship. It becomes an object of spectacle as opposed to a real experience to be engaged with, so that its horror is not the lived experience of rape but rather the conceptual horror of the basic phenomenon of rape. Once the immediate and traumatic agony of her rape is over, Abby becomes little more than a prop for another plot.

"These precious things; let them bleed now. Let them wash away.
These precious things; let them break their hold on me."
–Tori Amos, "Precious Things," 1992

In many ways this distinction underlies the entire debate over Moore's use of rape and, more broadly, its consequences for the subsequent history of American comics. Moore, after all, had already criticized the depiction of sexual violence in comics back in his "Invisible Girls and Phantom Ladies" essay in *The Daredevils*, where he blasted the tendency for comics to "start dishing up evil, sordid little adult fantasies," particularly highlighting the use of bondage. In that essay, Moore recalls "a particularly charming Michael Fleischer story that appeared in DC's *Brave and Bold* [sic] during which the usually quite capable Black Canary spent almost the entire issue tied to a chair wearing only her underwear, while the villain of the piece delivered such memorable and sensitive dialogue as 'You squirm so prettily, my dear.'" The issue ends with Black Canary saying, "Liberated ladies aren't supposed to say things like this, Batman, but you know what? You're my hero!" as she kisses him. In the face of the use of sexual violence as a form of overt entertainment in which the reader is meant to take the same sort of pleasure as the sadist who is tying up nearly naked women, Moore's decision to use rape to produce one of the single most horrific moments in his entire *Swamp Thing* run can, for all its genuine flaws, still reasonably be seen as a form of progress.

The bigger problem, and one that hangs over every individual instance of Moore writing about rape without quite connecting directly with any of them, is that Moore's commercial success would eventually lead to a wave of imitators who embraced his more explicit style while discarding trifling things like the underlying commitment to feminism that led Moore to want to depict rape as a serious and genuine object of horror. The result is a dreadful litany of comics that are more in line with Michael Fleischer's Black Canary story than Moore's horror tale, only without Moore's decision to stop short of actually depicting the rape on-panel. Rape, in other words, simultaneously became permitted in comics and, more disturbingly, trivialized. And for all his good intentions, Moore's failure to engage meaningfully with the consequences of Abby's rape means that it fits squarely within this tendency. Beyond that, the nature of the horror Moore employs can reasonably be accused of moving the attention away from the horror of the sexual violence: the swarms of insects, the zombies, and the fact that the double page spread is the point in the narrative where it finally becomes clear that the story features a major character return are all rather more loudly trumpeted than the rape, and are the issues that the remainder of the storyline opts to focus in. The result is that the rape serves as a means of emphasizing another terror, as opposed to Moore's stated goal of actually being depicted as a horrific thing in its own right. Put another way, there's only so serious your depiction of zombie incest rape can be.

But for all of this, the truth is that "Love and Death" is still a marked improvement for a comics industry in which stories like Fleischer's were and are the norm. "Love and Death" is a twenty-three page meditation on traumatic experience. However much it may push rape to the margins of the story, it is still a story that is overwhelmingly concerned with depicting Abby's experience as being unfathomably awful. While the nature of paraphilia is such that it is surely inaccurate to declare that nobody has ever been sexually aroused by the "say uncle" double page spread, it's clear that Moore, Bissette, and Totleben are not only making no effort to depict Abby's ordeal as sexy, they are actively trying to make it appalling and upsetting. Sure, there are flaws, but many of the criticisms that can be leveled against this specific depiction of rape are ones Moore will address, to varying degrees of success, over the remainder of his career, and, indeed, over the remainder of his *Swamp Thing* run. Regardless of them, "Love and Death" is at least a clear and sincere attempt at serious engagement with sexual violence in keeping with Moore's defense that "these are important issues, to which I have been visibly turning my attentions for the past three or four decades" and that "I have given these matters a certain amount of thought during that time." Indeed, given that "Love and Death" marks the first time that Moore depicts an actual rape instead of an attempted one, it must be recognized that Moore's decades of thought on the subject are, at this point, in their early stages and that some development and maturing of his approach is to be expected.

It is also worth noting that explicitness and seriousness are in no way correlated. Indeed, in his lengthy defense of his use of rape as a theme Moore approvingly cites a 1954 story published by EC Comics that dealt with rape "without referring to the actual crime except by implication." This story, "A Kind of Justice," saw print in *Shock SuspenStories* #16, and is one of the most shockingly and disturbingly intense stories that EC Comics ever produced. It opens with a girl named Shirley, lying on the floor of a dilapidated shack crying as a shadowy figure stands over her saying, "You tell anybody... and I'll kill you!" The caption explains around what happened: "She'd been waiting, alone... and the next moment she'd not been alone. He'd appeared out of the darkness and she'd seen the look on his face. He'd forced her to the old shack by the quarry. She'd pleaded and screamed. And now it was over. But it would never be over for her... because she'd never forget..." Shirley gets up, traumatized, and staggers home, where her mother realizes what's happened, but Shirley, terrified by her rapist's threat, refuses to say who did it.

For all that it cannot name what happened to Shirley, the story hammers home the awful brutality of it. Shirley avoids taking the bus home, hiding behind a tree because "she was too ashamed for people to see her," and when she refuses to say who did it her father shouts, "Who are you trying to protect? I'll find out if I have to beat it out of you!" And so her father drags her to the police, where the story's one seemingly decent character, Sheriff Judson, interviews her. Again she doesn't answer, and so Judson and his deputy go through town looking for suspects, finally arresting a man from out of town sitting in an all-night diner. With little to no pretext, they arrest the man, which leads to Shirley's father bringing an angry mob to the police station. After a good cop/bad cop routine to elicit a confession from the man, Judson proceeds to tell the mob that he's confessed, then offers to bring Shirley, whose father has dragged her to the police station to make an identification, home so she doesn't have to watch what happens. The mob beats the man to death in his cell while he screams about how Judson promised to protect him. Finally, the scene cuts to Judson driving Shirley home, where he tells her, "You were smart not to talk, Shirley! Remember! You tell anybody... and I'll kill you!"

This is brutally, cruelly effective, highlighting the awful and corrupt ways in which power works. It is, to be sure, an incendiary story, but it is precisely that incendiary nature that has over time secured the reputation of EC Comics as one of the most daring and important comics publishers of its era. Indeed, Moore's extended defense of his depiction of rape is in many ways simply a detailed expansion of the argument William Gaines made to the United States Senate Subcommittee on Juvenile Delinquency the same month that "A Kind of Justice" came out. In this hearing Senator Estes Kefauver displayed the cover of that month's *Crime SuspenStories*, saying, "This seems to be a man with a bloody ax holding a woman's head up which has been severed from her body. Do you think that's in good taste?" Gaines's response was as memorable as it was emphatic: "Yes sir, I do—for the cover of a horror comic." In other words, depictions of disturbing and upsetting material are the point

Figure 125: Rape as depicted in a 1954 EC story. (From Shock SuspenStories *#16, written by Carl Wessler, art by Reed Crandall)*

Figure 126: William Gaines was famously forced to defend this cover in front of the US Senate.

of horror comics. Rape included, not just for Moore, but for Gaines.

Unfortunately for Gaines, his defense fell on unsympathetic ears. This is perhaps unsurprising, given the way in which EC's output, at its best, angrily skewered those in power. For all that the nominal focus of the Senate hearing was on the violence in comics, the larger issue was a moral panic whipped up by psychologist Frederic Wertham, whose recent book *Seduction of the Innocent* condemned the American comics industry, accusing its depictions of crime and violence of leading children into juvenile delinquency on the grounds that many of the children he encountered as a psychiatrist read comics. Wertham's book is infamous for many of its claims, particularly his argument for the existence of a homoerotic subtext to the relationship between Batman and Robin, which he described as "a wish dream of two homosexuals living together." And yet for all that Wertham's censorious instincts are rightly mocked, the truth is that many (though certainly not all) of his actual readings were well-grounded. The popular comics of the early 1950s were often violent, lurid, and anti-authoritarian—and truth be told, there is some pretty massive homoerotic subtext to Batman and Robin. The biggest problem with Wertham was not that he was wrong about what was in the comics—it's that he didn't like lurid anti-authoritarian stories.

Certainly this is borne out by the eventual resolution of Wertham and Kefauver's crusade. As is usually the case with these things in the United States, since the First Amendment clearly protects publishers' rights to publish the material in question, the industries in question instead agree to self-censor to avoid bad publicity. In this case the major publishers formed a trade organization that appointed Judge Charles Murphy to create a code of conduct for the comics industry. This became the Comics Code Authority, which became de facto law due to the near-universal agreement of distributors to refuse to carry any comics not bearing the seal noting that a comic was approved by the Authority. Murphy's criteria for the Code was, in practice, an attempt to crack down on exactly the sort of stuff that EC was doing. Crime and horror comics—which is to say the bulk of EC's output—were consciously targeted. Zombies, vampires, ghouls, and werewolves were all explicitly forbidden, and large swaths of the Code seemed as if they were written to forbid "A Kind of Justice" specifically. Among the rules that "A Kind of Justice" would have broken were: "Crimes shall never be presented in such a way as to create sympathy for the criminal, to promote distrust of the forces of law and justice," "Policemen, judges, government officials, and respected institutions shall never be presented in such a way as to create disrespect for established authority," "In every instance good shall triumph over evil and the criminal punished for his misdeeds," "Illicit sex relations are neither to be hinted at nor portrayed," "Seduction and rape shall never be shown or suggested," and "Sex perversion or any inference to same is strictly forbidden." It is clear here that the point is not merely to prevent the depiction of sex and violence, but rather to demand that comics only be used as tools to promote established order and the status quo. The Code's true purpose is made explicit in the declaration that established authority must always be presented positively.

In practice, the letter of the law was incidental. Under Murphy, the Code operated with a breathtaking and idiosyncratic license that, at least until the company was forced to abandon publishing comics in 1955, was mostly used to target EC specifically. Famously, Murphy objected to a story published in EC's *Incredible Science Fiction* #33, reprinted from a 1953 issue of *Weird Fantasy*. The comic is a parable about racism, with an astronaut inspecting a planet populated by robots to see if it's ready to join the Galactic Republic, only to conclude that it is not because of the systematic discrimination of blue robots on the part of the orange robots. Having reached his conclusion, the astronaut departs the planet, with the final panel revealing that the astronaut is black. Despite not violating any of the Code's stated rules, Murphy demanded the astronaut be recolored as white, a demand Gaines flatly refused, although this was a pyrrhic victory at best given that *Incredible Science Fiction* #33 was the last comic EC published. (They only managed to continue publishing *Mad* by refashioning it into a magazine, which put it beyond the Code's regulatory reach.)

Over time the Code loosened slightly, with some of its more absurd restrictions being removed, but incestuous zombie rape of the sort Moore wrote for *Saga of the Swamp Thing* #29 was still, in their view, a bit much, and they proceeded to veto the issue. It is this incident, more perhaps than any other, that highlights the quality of Moore and Berger's working relationship. First, for all that Moore's complaints about editorial interference might suggest that he prefers editors to simply stay out of his way entirely, it is worth highlighting that the only reason "Love and Death" exists as *Saga of the Swamp Thing* #29 is that Berger nixed his intended next story on the grounds that Moore should continue to focus on the growing relationship between Swamp Thing and Abby before exploring other avenues. But when Moore's story was targeted by the Code, Berger was quick to back it, and convinced the rest of DC's editorial hierarchy to simply publish the issue without the Code stamp and, starting with issue #31, to simply stop submitting Moore's book for Code approval in the first place. It is this ability to push for improvements to a book but to also fiercely defend the creators' vision that earned Berger such respect from Moore (and, ultimately, from the bulk of the War's combatants, where she enjoys the rare status of being liked and respected on essentially all sides). From Moore's perspective, Berger had won for him a triumphant victory— as he put it a few years later, when asked his feelings on beating the code, he replied, "Given the insufferable size of my ego, what do you think I think of it? It's something that gives me immense pleasure and an overwhelming feeling of smugness every time it crosses my mind."

"With each terrible death and resurrection, Crafty knew that by his torment, the world was redeemed. It seemed there was nothing that could truly kill him, and while he lived there still remained the hope that one day he might return and on that day overthrow the tyrant God and build a better world."
–Grant Morrison, *Animal Man*, 1988

After its initial splash of controversy the Arcane trilogy resolved more or less predictably, albeit with the substantial wrinkle of Arcane killing Abby. Ultimately Matt Cable wrests control of his body back and casts Arcane back down to hell before using the last of his lingering superpowers to bring Abby back from the dead. Unfortunately, Matt is only able to revive her body, leaving Swamp Thing to journey into the afterlife to rescue her soul from hell, where Arcane condemned it. This journey is depicted in *Swamp Thing Annual* #2, a forty-page saga called "Down Among the Dead Men." Moore has described the story as an attempt to provide "a preliminary map—a rough map—of the DC supernatural territories," which is as good a description as any for a spiritual journey into the DC Universe versions of heaven and hell. Structurally speaking, the story is intensely episodic—Swamp Thing allows his consciousness to sink into the Earth, and then further into the realms of death. There he proceeds to meet a series of minor supernatural characters from DC history alongside a series of short encounters with various entities in the realms he explores. The two most notable of these are a scene where he meets Alec Holland in heaven, finally getting to exchange words with the man he thought he was, and a scene in which he meets Arcane, who is being tortured by vast numbers of insect eggs hatching inside his body. As Swamp Thing walks on, Arcane begs him, "Huh-how many years have I buh-been here?" and Swamp Thing turns, a beautifully cruel smile on his face, and answers simply, "Since yesterday."

These short scenes pack a reasonable emotional punch, but in many ways it is the larger canvas that is interesting in

"Down Among the Dead Men," and particularly the set of characters Moore selects to serve as Swamp Thing's guides, which included the return of Etrigan alongside three other characters from DC's long history. First among them is Deadman, a character created in the late 1960s by Arnold Drake and Carmine Infantino for *Strange Adventures*, a long-running title that, over the years, wandered around through many premises and presentations but was, in the late sixties, a supernatural fantasy book. Deadman was the circus name of Boston Brand, a trapeze artist murdered during a performance, but who was allowed to remain as a ghost who could possess the bodies of people by a goddess named Rama Kushnu (a bastardization Rama and Krishna, both incarnations of Vishnu) so he could hunt his killer. In many ways Deadman is most notable for providing the first ongoing work for Neal Adams, who would go on to become the iconic comics artist of the 1970s for his dramatic compositions, which often featured pages of angled, non-rectangular panels drawn from low-to-the-ground perspectives that, combined with a style honed by years working on photorealistic drama strips syndicated to newspapers, gave his characters a staggering, larger than life presence. Deadman himself is a ridiculous character, not least due to his appearance as a gaunt, white corpse in a circus outfit, who suffered from the same problem Moore identified in Swamp Thing whereby the seeming premise of the series (in this case Deadman's quest to find his killer) could never be resolved or else the series would end (since Deadman's unlife explicitly lasts until he finds his murderer). But as with the original run of Wein/Wrightson Swamp Thing tales, there is much to like in the original run of stories.

The second character Moore dusts off is altogether more strange: John Broome and Carmine Infantino's The Phantom Stranger, who first appeared in a six-issue series bearing his name in 1952, where he featured in a variety of short stories all of which had basically the same plot: initially some apparently supernatural event occurs, bringing misfortune to

Figure 127: *Neal Adams's inventive page layouts and dramatic angles revolutionized American comics art.* (From Strange Adventures #207, *written by Carmine Infantino and Jack Miller, 1967*)

Figure 128: *In Moore's proposed origin for him, the Phantom Stranger was an angel whose wings were torn off and who was sent into exile to walk the Earth.* (From Secret Origins #10, *art by Joe Orlando, 1986*)

people; at a moment of crisis, the Phantom Stranger appears out of nowhere and resolves the situation, generally revealing it to have a mundane explanation. After a sixteen-year gap, he appeared again in an issue of *Showcase*, then got a second series in which he was reworked as an actually supernatural character. Through all of this, the Stranger pointedly never received anything like an origin story or explanation of where he came from, a conceit that gave him a certain appeal.

Moore, when writing the character, tended to imply that he had some Biblical origin, and indeed in 1987 wrote one of four possible origin stories for the character in *Secret Origins* #10, alongside Dan Mishkin, Paul Levitz, and Mike Barr. Moore's story is structured as two parallel stories, told on alternating pages, covering essentially the same ground on different scales. The first is the story of a member of New York's red-beret wearing Subway Angels, a volunteer organization founded in 1979 to patrol the increasingly dangerous New York Subway, while the second is set around the fall of Lucifer. In both, the protagonist is torn between two rival factions, fails to commit to either, and is brutally rejected by both as a result. The stories converge in the final two pages as the Phantom Stranger appears to the protagonist of the Subway Angels plot after he has been beaten and helps him up, giving a solemn speech about how "lonely inside our separate skins, we cannot know each other's pain and must bear our own in solitude. For my part, I have found that walking soothes it; and that, given luck, we find one to walk beside us… at least for a little way."

Finally, Moore introduces the Spectre, a Golden Age hero who served as God's vengeance, best known for a run of ten issues in the mid-70s written by Joe Orlando and Michael Fleisher, with art by Jim Aparo, which vented Orlando's frustrations and anxieties after being mugged with the Spectre meting out gruesome punishments to criminals that skirted the edge of what was permissible under the Comic Code of the time. It is not that any of these characters are particularly obscure, although none had been in particularly active use prior to "Down Among the Dead Men," with the Phantom Stranger, who had previously had a backing feature in *Saga of the Swamp Thing* during Pasko's run, being the closest thing to a regularly appearing character. What the characters really had in common, however, was that they (along with Swamp Thing himself) would have featured in the comics of Moore'schildhood and adolescence. All of the characters had prominent runs in the late 60s/early 70s that stood out distinctively in the era, and Moore was at the perfect age for them. They are certainly not the only characters Moore loved, but they nevertheless have ties to a common moment that Moore was both celebrating and updating for the present day. Which was in many ways the point of the exercise. "Down Among the Dead Men" is in no way a complete collection of DC's mystical and supernatural characters, but it is a thorough enough one, and Moore, by lashing them together into a single framework, makes a tacit demonstration that his by now clearly successful approach to writing *Swamp Thing* was not some fluke, but rather a viable approach to a particular sort of comic in general. And it is telling that "Down Among the Dead Men" roughly coincided with the point where Moore began to get other work at DC.

With "Down Among the Dead Men" both being an oversized story and one published as an Annual, meaning that it came out the same month as *Swamp Thing* #32, another fill-in issue was needed to keep the book on schedule. Having given Shawn McManus a story that was rather frustratingly ill-suited to him in "The Burial," Moore was eager to give him something actually tailored to his cartoonish style, so he penned a bespoke story called "Pog" that serves as one of the oddest installments of Moore's run. As Moore explains it, the idea came to him while he was brainstorming "characters that live in swamps—and I just put Pogo."

Pogo was a newspaper strip written and drawn by Walt Kelly that featured the characters of Pogo the Possum and Albert the Alligator, initially created in 1941 for Dell Comics' *Animal Comics*, but made more famous as an editorial page comic in the *New York Star* and, starting in 1949, as a nationally syndicated comic. The strip is in the grand tradition of American "funny animal" comics and cartoons that accompanied and, gradually, replaced minstrelsy's role in American comedy. Pogo is an everyman sort of possum living in the Okefenokee Swamp on the Georgia/Florida border along with a menagerie of absurd friends and companions, of which Albert Alligator is the most prominent. The comic's strengths are severalfold. For one, Kelly is a gifted cartoonist whose figures are reliably both expressive and ridiculous. For another, Kelly's command of language was exquisite in a way few, if any of his contemporaries (or indeed imitators) could match. His characters speak in an invented vernacular long on misspellings and malapropisms, proclaiming things like, "Us must git our e-quipments quipped up afore the expedition pedooshes," and an annual tradition of fractured Christmas carols, the most famous of which began, "Deck us all with Boston Charlie / Walla Walla, Wash., an' Kalamazoo! / Nora's freezing on the trolly / Swaller dollar cauliflower alley-garoo!"

Kelly turned these strengths to effective satire, skewering the establishment of American politics in most every direction, most famously in his character "Simple J. Malarkey," a caricature of anti-Communist crusader Senator Joseph McCarthy. When, in a typically Kellyesque series of events, *The Providence Bulletin* declared that it would drop the strip if Malarkey appeared again, Kelly responded by simply having the character appear with a paper bag over his head. This was only the most famous of many times Kelly found himself in trouble with the papers distributing his strip, and eventually he settled on the tactic of creating a second set of strips whenever he was doing something controversial. These strips would feature many of the same political points, but in a toned down and subtler manner often featuring cute rabbits as the characters. Kelly, for his part, was open about the practice, making it clear that if readers saw *Pogo* strips featuring cute bunnies then their newspapers were engaging in censorship.

But for all that *Pogo* was overtly and satirically political, it was also appreciably broad in its targets. Kelly liked to claim that he was opposed to "the extreme Right, the extreme Left, and the extreme Middle," and Kelly's satire, even when it took aim at specific figures, tended to suggest that everyone was in the same absurd and slowly sinking ship, and that the problem with the world was the people in it. This is best exemplified by the most famous quote to come out of the comic, the punchline to a poster Kelly, a committed environmentalist, created for one of the earliest celebrations of Earth Day. The strip features Pogo and another character walking across the swamp, then pulls back to show the mass of litter and junk that they've been walking across as Pogo glumly comments, "We have met the enemy, and he is us."

Moore's *Pogo* homage, fittingly, returns to the ecological themes that characterized his earliest issues of *Swamp Thing*, and that would come to characterize his best work on the title. The story features a ship of aliens drawn by McManus in a cartoonish and Kellyesque style, and given a wordplay-heavy way of speaking that similarly evokes Kelly's work. "Don't be unmembered to tell the Tadling see if old strigiforme is fetchable nowabouts," Pog, the leader of the aliens says at one point, before breaking off to marvel at the swamp in which they have landed: "A new Lady! A new Lady as envirginomental as the old one!" Eventually the aliens encounter Swamp Thing (who, in this issue, speaks only in an incomprehensible string of symbols), and explain to him their origin, telling him how on their planet (which they call the Lady), "There was one solitribal breed of misanthropomorphs who refused to convivicate with elsefolk. They constructed their own uncivilization, and excluded anykind else from joining it. They were the loneliest animals of all. They took our Lady away from us." He goes on to explain the horrible things these animals did, running medical experiments and, worse, killing and eating the other

Figure 129: Arguably the most famous Pogo strip was Walt Kelly's poster for the 1971 Earth Day.

Figure 130: "Pog" ends on a bleak and funereal note that deftly mends the Walt Kelly pastiche with Swamp Thing's *remit as a horror comic. (From* Swamp Thing #32, *written by Alan Moore, art by Shawn McManus, 1984)*

creatures until Pog and his shipmates set forth in their ship *Find-the-Lady* to find a new Lady on which to live, which Pog believes that they have now done.

In response, Swamp Thing sadly takes Pog to Baton Rouge to show him the nature of the planet on which they have landed—a silent sequence of humans cooking and eating meat, which Pog stares at in dumbstruck horror before weeping and crying out, "They can't own this Lady too! We were going to be happy here!" Swamp Thing and Pog rush back to the swamp, but are too late to save one of Pog's crew, a cute alligator-looking alien named Bartle, from being killed by attacking gators in the swamp. After a funeral for Bartle, Pog and his crew return to their ship and fly off, still looking for a planet unspoiled by man, which gives the story a bleak finish that is both surprising and effective.

Actually, in many ways the whole story can fairly be described as surprising, coming as it does an issue after Abby's death. It is, to be fair, clearly an inventory story of the sort that comics run periodically. What is surprising is not so much the existence of the story as the juxtaposition—the fact that *Swamp Thing* #31 ends with a splash of Swamp Thing cradling Abby's dead body, and *Swamp Thing* #32 opens with cartoon animals on a spaceship. Even with "Down Among the Dead Men" between them to tie up the actual plot threads, this is quite a leap to take over a month. But, of course, that variety and flexibility was central to what worked in the Wein/Wrightson issues of *Swamp Thing* that established the character in the 1970s. In many ways the point of "Pog," aside from telling an effective and self-contained story, is to claim that mantle of versatility.

"It slithers up towards the Svadishtana Chakra, just three finger-breadths below the navel, corresponding to the lunar sphere of dream, imagination, sexual fantasy… opening inside us, a six-petal lotus, an ecstatic flowering of possibilities, fantastic, sensual, limitless… and the snake moves. And the snake turns."
—Alan Moore, *Promethea*, 2000

Which, in the larger context of *Swamp Thing* at this point, is valuable. Moore's first year of *Swamp Thing* was largely made up, after all, of three storylines, each three issues long, that were, while terribly innovative in the larger context of what DC was doing at the time, relatively similar to each other. A reader could be forgiven, coming off of "Down Among the Dead Men," for assuming that they knew what the book was capable of and what sorts of things it might do. "Pog," in this regard, is a startling wakeup call notifying the reader that the book could do things that were not just surprising but were in fact completely out of left field. In practice "Pog" marks an extreme—Moore would never again do anything quite so completely out of keeping with anything before or after it again on *Swamp Thing*. But it was an extreme that mapped a profound and varied territory, which Moore, in practice, planned to explore in short order.

Bissette and Totleben, however, were still running behind, and so Moore's planned next issue had to be postponed on short notice, resulting in a plan to run a reprint in issue #33. Moore, on the fly, suggested instead that if Berger had an artist who could do twelve pages in two weeks, he could come up with something, and, with twenty-four hours' notice, crafted a twelve-page story that could serve as a frame for the original Wein/Wrightson "Swamp Thing" short story from *House of Secrets* #72. Moore's frame story, titled "Abandoned Houses," features a dreaming Abby's visit with Cain and Abel at the titular Houses of Secrets and Mystery, integrating those two hosts into the larger DC Continuity. There, Abel relates to her the events of the reprinted story in order to teach her that, as he puts it, "Alec Holland was not the first thing to walk the swamps," although since this revelation happens in a dream, Abby proceeds to forget it at the end of the story.

"Abandoned Houses" was followed by another issue with a strong claim to be the best single issue of Moore's *Swamp Thing* run, entitled "Rite of Spring." Having liberated the book from the censorship of the Comics Code, Moore was, unsurprisingly, eager to explore this freedom. And more broadly, having heaped considerable trauma upon Abby, including her horrific rape in "Love and Death," Moore was perhaps eager to take her story beyond the mere fact of her trauma and to a place of reparation and healing. This would be part and parcel of a larger plot Moore had in mind to develop Abby, a character he noted that he'd always been fond of. "Not that she'd ever really stood out that much as a character," Moore clarified, "but I liked the hair. It's distinctive; the white hair with the black stripe. Yeah, that looks good. So there's no reason why she couldn't be made into a much more interesting character." And so Moore had decided, early on, that he would develop Abby as a love interest for Swamp Thing. Having, with the Arcane trilogy, gotten rid of Matt Cable as a character by putting him into a seemingly irreversible coma, he was free to explore this idea. Given this confluence of goals and possibilities, Moore settled on the obvious solution of devoting the bulk of an issue of *Swamp Thing* to an exploration of psychedelic vegetable sex.

Even without the Comics Code, of course, Moore could not plausibly have gotten away with a traditionally graphic sex scene under the DC banner. Beyond that, to do so would in many ways go against what he had been developing with the book. Swamp Thing, by this point, was defined heavily by his connection with the vegetation and by the sorts of spiritual quests into the Green that he took in the aftermath of "The Anatomy Lesson" and again in "Down Among the Dead Men." To frame his intimacy with Abby primarily in the purely physical act of copulation would go against this aesthetic. To frame their intimacy as another sort of spiritual quest, on the other hand, was savvy in the extreme, allowing him to do an extended sex scene that bypassed genitalia entirely.

And so, after some charmingly awkward exchanges in which Abby reveals her feelings for Swamp Thing, Swamp Thing exudes a tuber from his chest and gives it to Abby to eat. Almost immediately, Abby's worldview begins to dissolve into a vibrantly colorful kaleidoscope of imagery, so that the swamp appears to be "all of fire... millions of birthday candles." As Swamp Thing explains, "You ate the fruit, Abby. You absorbed a little of my consciousness... my perceptions." As he explains this, the panels slowly curve sideways, rotating so that by the end of the page the book must be held sideways to read, which leads to a seven-page sequence that depicts their shared experience in a series of landscape pages. Within this format, Bissette and Totleben are free to cut loose and revel in the stylistic experiments they wanted to, crafting decadently intricate double page spreads to house what is in effect an extended prose poem by Moore.

The content of this prose poem eroticizes the pulse of nature within the swamp, describing Abby's experiences in the externalized terms of biology and ecology. "Below the water the sudden cold frottage of fish skin, slick and silver against my instep... It twists, flickers, disappears. The bubbles rise... The threadlights, a blazing cat's cradle, inside me, inside him," Moore writes, as Bissette and Totleben place his words in a winding path of black John Costanza letters across a wash of Tatjana Wood blue just over where Swamp Thing and Abby's hands touch to frame the nose of Swamp Thing's face unfolded across the two-page spread. "In him, I ride the amber sap, oozing through miniature labyrinths. Clusters of insect eggs burn like nebulae, suspended in their unique and vine-wrought cosmos... Through him, I sprawl with the swamp, sopping, steaming dragonflies stitching neon threads through the damp air surrounding him... Beyond him I wrestle the planet, sunk in loam to my elbows as it arches beneath me, tumbling endlessly through endless ink." The words descend across the pulsing rhizome rays extending out from a sun of Swamp Thing's eyes, gazing out as Abby, naked and green, mounts the very world itself, her legs wrapped around it, pulling it into herself, floating in the endless void of blackness in her own hair, above a golden curl that wanders down across the page to turn to a chittering

Figure 131: The page orientation rotates as Swamp Thing's psychedelic tuber takes root in Abby. (From Swamp Thing *#34, written by Alan Moore, art by Steve Bissette and John Totleben, 1984)*

Figure 132: The famous psychedelic vegetable sex sequence in "Rite of Spring" is laid out as double page spreads in which the pages are in landscape orientation, giving Bissette, Totleben, Costanza, and Wood a sprawling canvas in which to set Moore's prose poem. (From Swamp Thing *#34, 1984)*

worm as "the bark encrusts my flanks. The moss climbs my spine to embrace my shoulders... we... are... one creature... and all... that there is... is in us." Until at last it all ends in a rainbowed spread of narrow panels arced along the curve of a spider's legs, an orgasmic burst of unity extending out of Abby and Swamp Thing's heads as their mouths close in around the jewel-encrusted heart of the fruit that fuels their union, while "underground, buried claws wound the soil... savage furrows fill with moisture... a fish twists... the bubbles rise... the world pulses... and shudders... with life... and death... with tide... and magma... with me. With him." And then, at last, the panels bend again and the colors normalize. Abby fixes the strap of her tank top, looks at Swamp Thing, and asks, "Does this... uh... does this mean we're going out?"

They kiss, embracing in a tender splash page, and the next issue begins with a splash of Swamp Thing sitting beside his sleeping lover, staring out at the pink and purple dusk while "to the east, paperboys have wearied halfway through their rounds, dumping their remaining papers somewhere discreet and telling the newsagent he must have miscounted. The dead headlines dance upon a lukewarm wind, monochrome tumbleweed bowling through the failing light." These papers blow across the background of the page, and Swamp Thing watches them "flap like huge moths, crippled by their own weight, hopping clumsily amongst the black trees. Their pages are full of obsolete tragedies and discarded faces; all the carefully logged hysteria of a world he no longer belongs to." Now his life is entwined only with Abby, who "mumbles three dream-submerged syllables, but does not wake, and he is content beneath a darkening and volcanic sky. The swamp engulfs them. It is their own damp cosmos, and the troubles of the world beyond seem no more than the whispered conversations of distant madmen..." And from this prologue page, Moore launches into the story he'd planned for *Saga of the Swamp Thing* #29, back when he was still ostensibly writing for the Comics Code, "The Nukeface Papers."

"Hey, you guessed my name. Why would we be so coy with the miracles, Cassandra? Maybe because we didn't want to scare the shit out of you."
–Kieron Gillen, *The Wicked + The Divine*, 2014

"The Nukeface Papers" provides an interesting split between its two installments. The first issue, when it was published, was basically a six-month old script, the story having originally been intended for publication in July of 1984. In many ways the first part shows this—it follows the basic structure Moore used for the first issues of his preceding three arcs, with the storyline's threat intruding upon and infecting Swamp Thing's world. In this case the threat is the eponymous Nukeface, a drunken derelict who has become deranged by and addicted to the nuclear waste buried in his hometown of Blossomville, Pennsylvania (a thinly veiled version of Centralia, Pennsylvania, a town destroyed by an underground fire in a coal mine that is expected to continue burning for the next quarter-millennium), and who has come to the bayou because his stash in Pennsylvania has been cemented over and new waste is being deposited in the swamp instead. Swamp Thing dreams of Blossomville as Nukeface approaches, seeing a place where "something bright and awful kissed the world, and left its smeared blue lipstick-print. The soil is curdled, and all that grows, grows wrong. In a skin of black cinder, puddles reflect fire, red and wet and glistening like sores." Disturbed, he goes to investigate, only to be touched by Nukeface, who leaves a blue and bubbling wound on Swamp Thing's body as he collapses. By the time the issue saw print, though, Moore had stretched his wings creatively, and so the second part, published in February of 1985, had an altogether different tone.

Even the first issue, however, showed a passion for formal experimentation. Throughout the story Bissette adds scraps of newspaper that flutter in the breeze or float in the waters of the swamp, rotting. These newspaper fragments are not mere illustrations, however—instead, Bissette inserts photographs of actual newspaper clippings he saved up, so that the issue is a collage of real headlines about environmental pollution combined with Bissette and Totleben's art for the story. "As Jones said during his Erie visit, a toxic waste dump site, located anywhere in the area, could be a major source of new jobs," one clipping reads. "A French cargo ship that sank off the coast of Belgium Saturday night was carrying containers filled with a form of uranium used to make fuel for nuclear reactors," reads another. Others are more fragmentary—one talks about "shoddy work and forged documents" in relation to the unfinished nuclear power plant in Marble Hill, Ohio, while another describes an unspecified nuclear disaster that involved seven hundred radioactive pellets left in a truck "which became dangerously 'hot,' emitting 50 rads of radiation every hour." There's an out of context quote by a "Mr. Sotelo" who says, "It's OK, we're still alive. Maybe the doctors exaggerated the danger." Other headlines talk of familiar disasters like Three Mile Island and Bhopal.

All of these, it is worth stressing, were real events. The Bhopal disaster, for instance—referenced in several headlines in the second part of "The Nukeface Papers"—happened just two months before that issue was published, on the night of December 2nd/3rd, when a pesticide plant owned by Union Carbide's Indian subsidiary released a cloud of deadly chemical gas along with other chemicals. This was not the first industrial accident at the plant, which had a history of incidents going back to 1979, but by December of 1984 the plant was in such poor repair that the bulk of its safety systems were completely offline. The accident was caused when water entered an overfilled tank of methyl isocyanate, which caused a rapid chemical reaction accelerated by iron that had leached in from rusting pipes. The tank rapidly heated, resulting in a rise in pressure, and emergency venting released nearly 75% of the gas within the tank. The official and immediate death toll killed nearly four thousand people,

Figure 133: Steve Bissette worked physical newspaper clippings into his pencils for "The Nukeface Papers." (From Swamp Thing #35, written by Alan Moore, art by Steve Bissette and John Totleben, 1985)

Figure 134: Nukeface triumphant, in a grotesque parody of Swamp Thing's pose at the end of Moore's first arc. (From Swamp Thing #36, written by Alan Moore, art by Steve Bissette and John Totleben, 1985)

along with causing a 300% increase in the stillbirth rate and a 200% increase in neonatal mortality. Causes of death included choking, pulmonary edema, and reflexogenic circulatory collapse, and autopsies further showed victims suffering from cerebral edemas, necrotizing enteritis, and other similarly awful effects. Overall estimates of the death toll, taking into account those who died subsequently of conditions caused by the disaster, go as high as sixteen thousand. Union Carbide eventually paid $470 million in damages, or roughly 5% of their 1984 revenue.

But the formal experimentation of the newspaper clippings crosses over to the writing itself in the second part, which is told in a style bearing an obvious debt to Akira Kurosawa's *Rashomon*, with seven separate characters each getting a section devoted to their perspective on events, culminating in a Nukeface section in which he comes to realize that he won't be able to get more of his nuclear waste from Louisiana. "There's gotta be some more of it out there someplace," he figures, and he "don't care if I gotta look in every state, every town… every street, dammit! It's there, boy. I know it's there… perseverance and determination, that's all it takes… Heads up, America, here I come!" he declares, leading to a final splash page grotesquely parodying the climactic panel of Moore's first arc with Nukeface, arms spread wide, greeting a sky now full of Steve Bissette's newspaper clippings.

But in many ways the bigger plot point comes in the two sections written from the perspectives of Swamp Thing and Abby. In them, Swamp Thing lies in agony after being contaminated by Nukeface's touch. "Throughout the long paralyzed night my mind is caught in a gauze of delirium," Swamp Thing narrates. "With the first light of dawn, I notice that my arm has gone. The day passes slowly. During the afternoon, a hole appears in my stomach. Soon my lower half will be detached. As it starts to decay, my head fills with ice-blue nothingness." He tries to call out to Abby with his mind, and as night falls again she reaches him, and they talk briefly.

"I tell her what I plan to do," he explains, "and then my lower jaw falls off, and after a while, I die." Later, at the end of the issue, the same scene is told from Abby's perspective, revealing that Swamp Thing's plan is to try to build himself a new body, but with no certainty of success, as he festers away to nothingness, dying for the second time in sixteen issues.

By this time, Moore had solidly established himself as a hot writer in American comics. February, 1985, in fact, proved a very big month for him: he published sixty-one pages with DC comics, netting him £637 a week from that alone—fifteen times the £42.50 he sought to make five years earlier. On top of that, he began writing backup features for Howard Chaykin's *American Flagg* and saw the second part of *The Ballad of Halo Jones* commence publication in *2000 AD*, along with the final installment of *Warrior*, which featured the still-continuing *V for Vendetta* (as well as Grant Morrison's debut of a Dez Skinn-designed feature called *The Liberators*). In terms of work published in ongoing, serialized comics (as opposed to things like *Lost Girls*, where several hundred pages of material saw print all at once), this marks the most productive month of Moore's entire career.

There is, however, a strong case to be made that it is the next month, March of 1985, that was the more *important* month in Moore's career, that being the month that he introduced the character of John Constantine to *Swamp Thing*. This would prove to be an act with significant ramifications, both for DC and for Moore's own life. For all the eventual importance of the character, however, his conceptual origins are almost comically idiosyncratic. At the root of it is the fact that Steve Bissette and John Totleben were big fans of The Police, and Bissette in particular "liked Sting, because he had a great face and I was a big fan of the movie *Quadrophenia*, where he plays Ace Face." Bissette and Totleben had in fact already included Sting in the background of a scene in *Saga of the Swamp Thing* #25, and, as Bissette tells it, "We wrote Alan, and said, 'We're going to put Sting in the comic, and Alan, you better make it a character, because he's not going to go away. We're going to make him more and more visible, whether you like it or not.'" Moore was apparently suitably amused by this impetuous demand, and created a character for Bissette and Totleben, albeit not modeled off of Sting in *Quadrophenia*, but rather off of his appearance in *Brimstone and Treacle*.

The difference between these is considerable. *Quadrophenia* is a 1979 film adaptation of a rock opera by The Who that, somewhat curiously, removed most of the actual musical bits. It featured Sting as Ace Face, a charismatic Mod thug who, in an iconic scene, completely fails to give a damn about a judge criticizing the Mods for being violent thugs and casually pays off his hefty fine out of his wallet, to the amusement of all the other slightly less cool Mods. *Brimstone and Treacle*, on the other hand, is a 1982 adaptation of an unaired Dennis Potter television play. The script dates back to 1976, having stopped off as a stage play in 1977, and features a middle-aged couple caring for their near-adult daughter after she was severely disabled in an accident. Their lives are turned upside down by Martin Taylor, played by Sting in the film, a con man who worms his way into their house by taking advantage of their fractured marriage and then rapes their daughter before being chased off into the night, after which the daughter miraculously recovers, only to reveal that she remembers her father cheating on her mother.

Unlike Ace Face, who went through the world with an archly cool bluster, Martin Taylor is a scheming trickster figure. Sting's view of the character was that he was the literal Satan, a possibility the film flirts with, although its ending also suggests that he may be an ex-priest of some sort (thus making the film a cousin of "A Kind of Justice," and, impressively, a far grimmer one). The script is, like much of Dennis Potter's work, a piece of dark absurdism in the classical, theatrical sense. Potter is fond of including dream sequences and exaggeratedly staged sequences, often with musical accompaniment. In *Brimstone and Treacle*, most of these sequences focus around Martin Taylor, including a

Figure 135: Sting as Martin Taylor in Brimstone and Treacle. *(1982)*

Figure 136: John Constantine on his first appearance, ironically not drawn by Bissette and Totleben. (From Swamp Thing *#37, written by Alan Moore, art by Rick Veitch, 1985)*

disturbing scene in which he prays with the wife, who glows beatifically even as Taylor's prayer is accompanied by stagey flashes of lightning and her daughter screams in increasing terror. This gives Taylor a strange power within the film—he breaks the fourth wall in small, subtle ways, seeming to be aware of the sort of story he's in even as the people around him remain oblivious.

As introduced, John Constantine is a similar trickster figure with a slyly self-aware relationship with the genre in which he appears, arriving in the comic boasting about how he understands who Swamp Thing is better than even he does. Initially, very little is clear about him beyond that he is British, knows a reasonable amount about the supernatural, and is talking to people about some imminent apocalypse. Unlike Martin Taylor, he's not straightforwardly malevolent—indeed, by the end of his storyline in *Swamp Thing* he's been emphatically revealed to be, on balance, a good guy, albeit a ruthless one who will do whatever it takes to stop the dark forces he confronts. Throughout his story, there are various comments about some horrific event in Newcastle that left deep scars on Constantine and several other people, and by the end of this arc Constantine has cost several people their lives and cruelly betrayed several more, although, to be fair, the world is saved in the process.

Whatever pop culture artifacts he emerged out of, however, the creation of John Constantine would prove to be an act with tremendous ramifications. For all that Moore's brief period working for DC would have an incredible impact on the American comics industry and the world, there are actually precious few enduring characters that Moore created for DC. He sold them *V for Vendetta* and created *Watchmen* for them, but these works (at least when he wrote them) existed outside the shared universe that makes up the bulk of DC's publications, and were, at least from Moore's perspective, creator-owned projects. When working on what Moore understood to be company-owned properties at DC, and indeed in general, Moore preferred to play with the depth of existing concepts, treating company-owned properties as an occasion for textual play. As he put it in the introduction to the first collected edition of his *Swamp Thing* comics, "The continuity-expert's nightmare of a thousand different super-powered characters coexisting in the same continuum can, with the application of a sensitive and sympathetic eye, become a rich and fertile mythic background with fascinating archetypal characters hanging around, waiting to be picked like grapes on the vine." And when in DC's vineyards, Moore was generally happy to restrict himself to creating blends out of what had already been planted. With the exception of John Constantine.

But what a vine to plant. John Constantine comics were published essentially non-stop since Moore's departure from *Swamp Thing*, when Jamie Delano's *Hellblazer* started up alongside the Rick Veitch era of *Swamp Thing*. Essentially every significant figure in the War has written the character at one point or another. Grant Morrison, Neil Gaiman, and Warren Ellis all wrote issues of *Hellblazer*, as have most of the more marginal powers: Garth Ennis and Peter Milligan both have sizable runs, for instance. The only major figure not to have actually written Constantine is Kieron Gillen, who reacted to DC's 2012 cancellation of *Hellblazer* by noting that, "Part of me also thinks 'you're not a real British Comics Writer unless you've written *Hellblazer*.' So that's me doomed," although as Gillen has also noted of his first arc of *Phonogram*, "*Rue Britannia* may as well be *Hellblazer*," which is accurate enough, and applies equally well to his run on *Journey into Mystery*. Beyond merely having a long-running comic with an impressive array of writers, however, Constantine has also proven a profitable character for DC's larger corporate owners, who spun out a quasi-successful movie version and, in 2014, a short-lived television series based on the character.

> *"How to be a magician: Simple. Declare yourself a magician, behave like a magician, practice magic every day."*
> –Grant Morrison, "Pop Magic!", 2003

It is also notable that for all that Moore is known to spit invective at his former employers for, as he memorably put it in one interview, "going through my trashcan like raccoons in the dead of the night" in lieu of actually coming up with new ideas, Moore has never demonstrated any particular animosity over the continual use of John Constantine. As Moore himself notes, "I understood that when I had finished with [Constantine] that it would just be absorbed into the general DC stockpile," and even provided a blurb for Brian Azzarello's 2000 run on the title (a favor Azzarello repaid twelve years later by writing two *Before Watchmen* books). "I've never objected to that," he stresses, in an interview where he elsewhere rails against DC's propensity for doing "crappy Green Lantern stories" that were "based upon an eight page story of mine from twenty years ago," further highlighting that Constantine, at least, is a character he's at relative peace with DC's continual use of.

What makes this particularly interesting, however, is that Constantine is also clearly a character of considerable personal significance to Alan Moore. Although the character certainly was created in part to satisfy Bissette and Totleben's desire to draw Sting, Moore further explains that he has "an idea that most of the mystics in comics are generally older people, very austere, very proper, very middle class in a lot of ways. They are not at all functional on the street. It struck me that it might be interesting for once to do an almost blue-collar warlock. Someone who was streetwise, working class, and from a different background than the standard run of comic book mystics. Constantine started to grow out of that." These are words of considerable significance coming from someone who, throughout his entire career, has vocally identified with his working class background and who, in his later career, became a self-proclaimed magician. Moore's later description of Constantine as a "wide boy occultist" furthers this sense, as does Moore's direction in the script to Constantine's debut in *Swamp Thing* #37, where he specifies that the character should carry a "faint air of menace" perhaps not entirely unlike that generated by being immensely tall and having mildly terrifying quantities of hair.

It is, in other words, not unreasonable to suggest that Constantine was always devised in part to effect a permanent alteration upon the landscape of DC Comics. Having by this point spent considerable time playing with the DC Universe's more mystical and cosmological aspects, Moore inscribed a fundamentally new sort of character and perspective into the comics—one who was enough of a charming rogue to last and thus to provide an enduring approach to comics. If a quarter century of writers followed that approach and continued telling stories about a character whose basic iconography and philosophy are inexorably linked to Moore's worldview, well, this is hardly something that can be called a problem or a downside.

Certainly Constantine proved to be a powerful creation within Moore's own life, in that Moore actually met him on two separate occasions. The precise timing of these two encounters is difficult to pin down. Moore first described the initial encounter in a 1993 interview: "One day, I was in Westminster in London—this was after we had introduced the character—and I was sitting in a sandwich bar. All of a sudden, up the stairs came John Constantine. He was wearing the trench coat, a short cut—he looked—no, he didn't even look exactly like Sting. He looked exactly like John Constantine. He looked at me, stared me straight in the eyes, smiled, nodded almost conspiratorially, and then just walked off around the corner to the other part of the snack bar. I sat there and thought, should I go around that corner and see if he is really there, or should I just eat my sandwich and leave? I opted for the latter; I thought it was the safest. I'm not making any claims to anything. I'm just saying that it happened." In a subsequent 2009 interview, he dated this to the "early 80s, when I'd just introduced the character," which introduces some confusion given that the character was first introduced in the back half of the 1980s, but would nevertheless seem to clearly date the encounter well before

Moore's conscious and active engagement with magic, and, given that Moore, in talking about the encounter, also talks about Constantine's physical appearance "in the comics at the time" (in explicit contrast to how he may or may not look in the present comics, which Moore suggests he hasn't read), it would seem to date it firmly in the 1985-86 period in which Constantine made his first string of appearances. Moore's second account of this encounter is even more emphatic, stressing how he did not simply feel that "this is somebody who looks quite coincidentally quite like John Constantine," but how "it was much more exact than that, I was thinking, 'That's John Constantine, who is a fictional character that I created.' At that point he looked at me, smiled, winked, and walked off to take a seat around the corner." Moore subsequently emphasized this, saying that there was "an intimacy and a knowing quality to the wink. It was exactly the kind of wink that any kind of fictional character might give to their creator."

Moore's accounts of the second encounter are on the whole briefer. His first description of that came in 1999, where, after describing the initial sandwich shop encounter, he said, "Years later, in another place, he steps out from the dark and speaks to me. He whispers, 'I'll tell you the ultimate secret of magic. Any cunt could do it.'" He followed up on this description in the 2009 interview, clarifying that the "other place" he alluded to a decade earlier was in fact a magical ritual he conducted with other people. "I'd just stepped out of the room and popped downstairs to make some tea," he explained, "and I was just passing through the kitchen when all of a sudden in the darkness on the left side of my head… it's very difficult to describe this, but it was clearly that somebody had struck a match in the darkness, and this lit up the face of John Constantine in the sudden halo of the match flare. And he, in a typically amusing way, told me the ultimate secret of magic, very memorably, in one very short five-word sentence, and then blew the match out and vanished." He clarified that while his first encounter with

Constantine was "a real daylight event," this second encounter was "a purely internal event that happened only within my mind, but they both seemed to be John Constantine to me." Moore does not provide further information for this second encounter, but it must have occurred sometime between the commencement of Moore's active magical work in November of 1993 and his first recounting of it in April of 1999, roughly a decade after the first.

These two events dramatically heighten the already powerful sense that Constantine serves, if not as a straight authorial insertion akin to, say, Grant Morrison's King Mob or Kieron Gillen's David Kohl, than as a figure who is intimately linked to Moore himself. But it is also worth noting that Constantine's life outside of Moore is a genuine one—Moore is his creator, but other writers, most notably Jamie Delano and Garth Ennis, are on the whole more responsible for the character as he is currently known. And even within Moore's life, there is a sense of independence to Constantine. He first appeared to Moore of his own accord, and even his second, more magically significant appearance was not one in which he was deliberately and consciously summoned. But even as he suggests that Constantine independently manifested in a real and literal sense within a Westminster lunch spot, Moore also emphatically refers to himself as John Constantine's creator. While John Constantine has taken on a life of his own in many senses, then, it is important to note that this life is one lived by someone with numerous ideological and aesthetic similarities to Alan Moore, and one that continues to haunt the corporation that Moore would eventually come to furiously shun, wrecking whatever subtle havocs he pleases.

Given this, it is significant that Constantine's first appearance in *Swamp Thing* #37 (ironically drawn by Rick Veitch, given it was the desire of Bissette and Totleben to draw Sting that led to the character's creation) corresponds with the second of three times that Swamp Thing comes back from the dead within Moore's run. Just as the first return in "The Anatomy Lesson" served to fundamentally reconceptualize Swamp Thing, so too does "Growth Patterns" alter the character. Part of the alteration is of Swamp Thing's own making—his plan to come back involves growing himself a new body, and thus much of the issue, set over the course of just over two weeks, consists of Swamp Thing slowly reforming under the care of Abby, who finds his tiny bud-like form in the swamp and brings him home to water him. These portions of the issue consist of charming and sweetly loving interactions between Swamp Thing and Abby, such as a scene in which Swamp Thing finds himself frustrated at deficiencies in Abby's lawn care, complaining to himself that "she should water the soil and not me. If the droplets magnify the sunlight, I shall burn," and that the insecticide she uses to get rid of the aphids (which he finds annoying in their own right) hurts. "Perhaps," he muses, "I should concentrate on developing vocal apparatus so that I can tell her where she is going wrong," which, the next day, he does, leading Abby, with a small smile, to quip, "Well, pardon me. How about 'Thanks for all the water?'"

Swamp Thing's rebirth is narrated in parallel with sequences introducing John Constantine as he visits a number of friends and allies in pursuit of information about some unknown apocalypse, described by each of them in differing terms, which will prove to be a major feature of Moore's run going forward. Finally, on the thirteenth day of the story, Constantine journeys to Louisiana and confronts Abby, blackmailing her into letting him talk to Swamp Thing. There he highlights the greater potential of Swamp Thing's regrowth, pointing out to him that he can "let your body die in one place" and "regrow it in another on the other side of the country," thus allowing Swamp Thing to instantaneously travel across the world. In doing so, Constantine suggests a much larger and more substantial conception of Swamp Thing that goes far beyond just being a mass of vegetable matter that mistook itself for Alec Holland, calling him the "last plant elemental in the entire bloody world," a claim that also sheds light on the "Abandoned Houses" story that interpolated Wein and Wrightson's original Swamp Thing story, and Abel's claim that "Alec Holland was not the first thing to walk the swamps."

This newly established power of transportation accomplishes one of the revisions to the character concept Moore had identified when taking on the series in the first place. "Another point that struck me," Moore says, was "that we had to come up with a better way for the Swamp Thing to travel around, rather than constantly moving around the country upon freight trains or in the boot of a car or in some truck. It was tedious." Giving him the ability to effectively teleport is, in other words, part of the steady transition away from the Wein/Wrightson approach towards the character. Even without an extended explanation or definition, the phrase "plant elemental" is evocative in terms of its potential. But that potential is significantly different than the original brief of "swamp monster." The implications of this are as intriguing to Swamp Thing as they are to the reader—he's quickly hooked by Constantine's apparent knowledge, and agrees to Constantine's deal that if Swamp Thing meets him in a town called Rosewood, just outside of Chicago, he'll tell Swamp Thing more about what he is.

"I am not talking about meatballs. I am talking about STEAK!"
–Diamanda Galas, "Wild Women with Steak Knives," 1982

This serves as the beginning of the so-called "American Gothic" arc (the name was never actually used in the comics), a storyline in which Constantine leads Swamp Thing on a tour of the United States to confront various classic horror tropes like vampires and werewolves. The timing is apropos—Moore had taken his first trip to the United States in August of 1984, midway through the Arcane arc of *Swamp Thing*, and the same month that *Marvelman* ceased publication in *Warrior*. There he had hobnobbed with DC executives and gotten variously praised and treated as a bit of a golden boy. He hit it off with some of the DC staff—particularly his editor, Karen Berger, and Julius Schwartz, a longtime DC editor who impressed Moore by having the signature of H.P. Lovecraft in a scrapbook, as he'd served as his literary agent late in Lovecraft's life. Others proved chillier—Paul Levitz, a fanzine writer who had steadily ascended into upper management at DC, referred to Moore as his "greatest mistake," a line that, whatever was meant by it in 1984, has bottomless depths of iciness in hindsight.

And so it was hardly a surprise that Moore would opt to explore the American-ness of his newfound success. And, given that his success was as a horror writer, a tribute to American horror must have seemed wholly appropriate. The choice of Rosewood, Illinois was not an arbitrary setting either. Indeed, the first story of the arc was a rather barbed thing, especially in the context of Levitz's strange words. Martin Pasko, early in his *Swamp Thing* run, wrote a story set in a town called Rosewood that featured Swamp Thing fighting vampires, with a father and son sacrificing themselves to flood the town and drown the vampires. Returning to Rosewood, Moore retcons this conclusion, having Constantine explain that there were vampires who hid out in freezers in the supermarket, and who were thus untouched by the running water and could simply wait for the water to become still before emerging. "They're living down there, in Rosewood, totally unmolested," Constantine explains. "Having a stable community has opened up lots of opportunities for them. They can settle down, after years of hiding. They can breed."

And so, suitably chastened over his failure to adequately clean up the vampires the last time he encountered them, Swamp Thing trudges into the water to fight underwater vampires. This goes poorly, however with Swamp Thing being efficiently dismembered by the vampires' newly hatched giant fish monster. But where this would have been a significant problem in any past issue of Swamp Thing, it instead comes after two issues that have stressed the increasing ease with which Swamp Thing can build a new body, and his reaction to being killed by a giant fish is relatively casual. "It is my own fault," he thinks. "I am too human in the way I think... in the way I fight. I must learn to exploit the possibilities of what I am." And so after some reflection, he proceeds to reach out over the entirety of Rosewood, incarnating not in a regular sort of swamp monster body, but as an entire landscape, resulting in a fantastic half-page panel from Bissette and Totleben in which Swamp Thing's visage is stretched out across an entire hillside as he moves the earth, rerouting the river into the lake and making the water run once again, destroying the vampires once and for all.

This is, of course, tremendously cheeky. Moore in effect reframes an event from before he took over the book just to show how utterly trivial and silly a threat it is within the context of his new approach. The overall point of the exercise is clearly, as with several previous stories, to break with the past publication of *Swamp Thing*, but in this instance the comparison is aggressively direct. Moore is no longer just ripping up the past, he's pointedly highlighting the difference and positively boasting about what his version of *Swamp Thing* can do that previous runs couldn't. Moore is in effect criticizing the Pasko run for the measly nature of its threats, and pointing out that his own vision of Swamp Thing is so wildly powerful that some pesky vampires simply don't register.

This sort of negative example carries real weight. The basic plot of the American Gothic arc, "Swamp Thing tours America and encounters stock horror tropes," is, after all, the default mode of *Swamp Thing*, underlying both the original Wein/Wrightson run on *Swamp Thing* and Pasko's run. And while Moore may have contrived to remove the clumsy mechanism of having Swamp Thing jumping freight trains to travel (as he did when arriving in Rosewood the first time), it's still not instinctively clear why the American Gothic arc is a good idea as opposed to the point where it is clear that Moore is out of ideas and has nothing better to do than the most generic *Swamp Thing* stories imaginable. By initially leaning into that critique through revisiting a past *Swamp Thing* story to explicitly show how things are different now, Moore immediately justifies the larger exercise.

The effectiveness of this statement rests in part, however, on the fact that Moore makes sure to outdo Pasko's story in other ways as well. Pasko's story is ultimately focused on the people of Rosewood fighting back against the vampires, treating the vampires as wholly knowable and predictable—so much so that there's not even any descriptions of their horror that can be quoted in order to demonstrate their inadequacies. Their function within the issue is to be generic monsters, to facilitate Pasko's plot about a man so obsessed with fighting them that he sacrifices his entire family to do it. But Moore, despite the fact that he is writing a story that trades in part on the fact that a bunch of vampires aren't actually a significant threat to Swamp Thing anymore, goes to considerable length to make the vampires scary. The vampire fish monster gets a lengthy description of how it is "massive and bloated, gorged upon its siblings… it pulses and takes stock of its surroundings. It licks pulp from dreadful, splattered talons, and considers what to do next," for instance. Moore similarly engineers a sequence that plays on many of the same themes of Pasko's story: Moore inverts one of Pasko's scenes, where a kid is attacked by his vampirized mother, into a scene where a vampiric child kills his mother and mocks his ineffectual father, which plays out with far more perversity and cruelty. Perhaps most impressively, Moore includes a scene that attempts to generate empathy for the vampires. "Why must we be destroyed?" the vampires ask as they are disintegrated by the running water. "We asked for so very little. Only a home that we could call our own, some livestock to provide our food, and a safe place to raise our children." The effect is that Moore not only demonstrates that he's moved past stories like Pasko's, he also casually

Figure 137: Swamp Thing regrows a body that is an entire mountainside. (From Swamp Thing *#39, written by Alan Moore, art by Steve Bissette and John Totleben, 1985)*

Figure 138: Phoebe walks through the misogynistic supermarket contemplating the Red Lodge. (From Swamp Thing *#40, written by Alan Moore, art by Steve Bissette and John Totleben, 1985)*

demonstrates that he can do such stories better than Pasko can as well.

One consequence of Moore playing out this gambit over the course of the two-part vampire story, however, is that he forecloses a large number of other story possibilities. After stories like "Rite of Spring" and the initial Floronic Man arc that demonstrated new possibilities, the vampire story was notable as a story that actively tried to close the door on a sizable category of adventures. This is a dangerous game—no matter how emphatically and convincingly Moore demonstrates the flaws of the story structure, the fact remains that *Swamp Thing* has fewer possibilities at the end of issue #39 than it did at the start. Swamp Thing has become so thoroughly powerful that physical confrontation has become essentially irrelevant to the book. The category of things that can be meaningfully treated as threats to Swamp Thing seems, in other words, significantly reduced. And so in many ways the decision to make the next stop in the "American Gothic" tour a werewolf story is surprising, given that werewolves are acutely physical threats.

But *Swamp Thing* #40, "The Curse," in fact goes a long way towards demonstrating the sort of threat that Moore imagines Swamp Thing facing. On one level, the plot of "The Curse" is simple enough: Swamp Thing arrives in Kennescook, Maine just in time to confront Phoebe, a woman who has turned into a werewolf and gone on a rampage. But the nature of the threat in "The Curse" is not really Phoebe herself, but rather the social structure in which she exists and that fuels a rage that can only be expressed by turning into an eight-foot tall snarling death beast. The story opens with Phoebe shopping, buying menstrual pads, and the atmosphere is one of claustrophobia. Moore focuses on the package of the pads, on which "a laughing woman runs through endless fields beneath a cornflower sky," while the branding proclaims that these particular menstrual pads are "for freedom," a description that clashes jarringly with the paralleled description of the (fictional) Pennamaquot tribe of

Native Americans, which, in Moore's description, constructed a Red Lodge "upon stilts, that its dark and sullen female power should not taint the Earth." The purpose of the Lodge is to isolate the tribe's women during menstruation—within it the women "were forbidden to stand, or lie down, or see the moon. They could touch nothing, even themselves.. they ate from sticks, like lepers, and the gourds that they sipped water from were afterwards smashed and buried without trace."

Phoebe imagines the Pennamaquot women's rage at their situation, "their anger, in darkness turning, unreleased, unspoken, its mouth a red wound, its eyes hungry... hungry for the moon" as she walks the aisles—as "the checkout lady places the package in a paper bag, as if to protect her other groceries," as she walks past a massive sign advertising the "Autumn Morn disposable douche, with the gentle scent of white flowers... for the real woman in you," and as she passes another advertising the wares of a porn shop, with its images of "numb-eyed women [who] stare through zippered leather masks." Later, as she and her husband entertain guests, her husband jokes about the Lodge, saying, "It was where the Indians sent their squaws when they started getting cranky around that time 'o the month," and one of her guests pipes up to insist that his wife not eat any more cookies because "She's still trying to get her figure back after the kid... and that was two years ago," and throughout this, Phoebe's rage festers until finally, when her husband confronts her over dinner being late, she transforms into a werewolf and begins rampaging through the town.

The implication of all of this is made explicit in the story's climax, where Swamp Thing confronts Phoebe and tries to help her. "I am woman," she proclaims. "I seek release from this stifling place that has been built for me." On its most basic level this refers to the Red Lodge whose psychogeographic ghost haunts Kennescook, but more broadly it clearly refers to the systemic oppression that is depicted throughout the issue—one that goes beyond the material cruelty of the Red Lodge and into the bizarre dualism with which the female body is treated, on the one hand eroticized and objectified, and on the other thoroughly rejected, with its natural functions declared shameful and disgusting things—a curse from which women are encouraged to seek freedom, a freedom that only serves to leave them ready to be objectified and, should they fall short as objects, to be mocked as poor Joannie is for the awful crime of her body changing after giving birth. And faced with all of this, and with the fact that her rage is useless in destroying it, Phoebe opts to fling herself upon a display of steak knives, the image of which provided the issue's opening panel, with the cruelly ironic slogan, "Here's good news for housewives!"

Swamp Thing's role in all of this is ultimately to bear witness to it. Just as Phoebe, for all her animal fury, cannot simply eliminate the systemic oppression of women, nor can Swamp Thing, for all his power. When Phoebe demands release, Swamp Thing is forced to admit that he cannot help her, and it is in the face of this that she chooses to kill herself rather than continue suffering under her rage and indignity. This serves to demonstrate the sort of threat that Swamp Thing, with his newfound powers, is best matched up with: one in which the underlying problem is not simply a villain in need of punching, but a systemic issue that cannot actually be confronted directly... like the reality of female oppression.

"I is not want for come no more alive by fire, as like to this. It is not right. It is more hurt as I may hold."
—Alan Moore, *Voice of the Fire*, 1996

"The Curse," however, was not an uncontroversial story. Indeed, it generated so much response that the letter pages of both *Swamp Thing* #45 and #46 were devoted entirely to it. For the most part, however, these letters were in favor of the story. The only outright critical letter in *Swamp Thing* #45 comes from a gentleman in (ironically) Northampton, Massachusetts, and complains that Moore repeats the phrase "hungry for the moon" too often, objects to the story's generality in speaking for all women, and moans about the display of steak knives being unrealistic ("No market worth its liabilities would ever, ever, never-ever display its cutlery so dangerously"). Of these three complaints it is, in an idiosyncrasy typical of the sorts of comics readers who wrote in to DC letters pages in the 1980s, the steak knives that seem to be the biggest problem. Another letter, however, takes issue with the ending of the story, while still generally praising it.

This sentiment is shared by one of the two letters presented in *Swamp Thing* #46. This letter, by Mindy Newell, takes up most of a page, and Moore offers an equally long response. Newell's objection is straightforward—that Moore's decision to have Phoebe kill herself is a weak cop-out of an ending. Newell writes, "I also understand that you were trying to point out to our male audience that women don't deserve to be treated in such a horrific manner... that you were striking a blow, not just for equal rights, but for equal *understanding*. But," she continues, "how can there be equal understanding between partners when one of them lies dead under the howling moon?" She goes on to point out that Phoebe's husband has almost certainly learned nothing from the incident. "My best guess," she offers, "is that he will mourn for a time, but sooner or later the guilt he feels over Phoebe's suicide will turn to callous anger... 'Oh, well, she was always a bit loony anyway.'" Continuing her critique, she asks rhetorically, "Why does Phoebe kill herself? You can beat around the bush all you want, but in the end she killed herself because she was born a woman. Great message, Alan," she adds, dripping with sarcasm. (All of which said, Newell ends her letter by noting that she'll be voting for the story in all the major awards, which provides needed context to her sharp criticism—criticism that Moore admits is "a valid reaction to the story" and taking the blame for any misinterpretations that the story leaves itself open to.)

When answering a letter expressing similar criticism in *Swamp Thing* #45, Karen Berger declared, "Phoebe killed herself because it was the only freedom she felt she had; one lone, suppressed, repressed, uninformed, isolated woman living in Nowhere, U.S.A., where women are generally more visibly persecuted than their educated, independent counterparts in the city. Phoebe's choice of suicide may have been her only relief, sad and unfortunate as it was. It wasn't in any way meant to imply or represent a statement or action for women as a whole." Moore, in his typically lengthy reply, makes a similar observation, saying that the fact that Phoebe is "a furious and slavering werewolf should have been enough to tip off the reader that what we were dealing with here was simply one aspect of a woman and her nature rather than trying to imply that this howling and ultimately self-destructive monstrosity was in some way the exclusive true face of womankind." In Moore's view, the reason behind the suicide ending was that *Swamp Thing*'s audience is primarily made up of men, and "that a downbeat and pessimistic portrayal was more likely to stick in the mind and have repercussions."

Put another way, then, Moore's contention is that for a horror comic, an unsettling and not entirely satisfying ending is not merely appropriate, but largely preferable. And, as Moore puts it, "I wanted to suggest that the mistreatment of women either physically or psychologically was something that went back a long way, something that had almost become completely institutionalized as part of our social outlook. That, as I see it, is the curse, along with the adjacent Catch-22 that even when women can express their anger, they're only allowed to do it in male terms, by which token they've already lost." In this regard, Moore views Phoebe's suicide as a deeply flawed solution that "preserved a certain integrity" in the character, inasmuch as her death is at least on her own terms. And this is certainly supported by the issue itself, where her death is described as "a poor kind of moonlight," a description that at once grounds Phoebe's actions in the larger werewolf mythology and emphasizes its inadequacy as a solution. (In truth, nobody raises the most cutting objection to the resolution of "The Curse," which is to ask why it is that the plight of the modern woman is squared away in a single issue while a story about underwater vampires that mostly serves to demonstrate why underwater vampires just aren't that interesting is stretched out over two issues. Much of what Newell and others object to in "The Curse" could have been squared away if the issue did not have the lingering sense that the primary reason Phoebe flung herself at a display of cutlery was that she'd reached the end of page twenty.)

What is not immediately obvious from Newell's letter, however, is why it and Moore's response are given the lion's share of a letter column, and a letter column that is the second column devoted to the issue in question at that. The answer, although it's not clearly acknowledged on the letter page, is that Mindy Newell is not a random reader, but another writer at DC Comics and a protégé of Karen Berger's who is perhaps best known for being the first ongoing female writer of *Wonder Woman*. Given Newell's admission at the end of her letter that she considers the story tremendously praiseworthy, it is important not to overemphasize the degree to which the letter represents a feud within the DC stable, but it's also worth noting that for the second story in a row, Moore found himself at odds with other parts of DC. (A small footnote to all of this—Newell submitted a question to a 2015 interview Moore did on Goodreads just to say "Hi," to which Moore responded warmly.)

To some extent, of course, critiquing America was the entire point of the American Gothic arc. And it is not that Moore was falling out with DC, at least not yet. Indeed, he was still actively producing work for the company, including, the same month that "The Curse" came out, an issue of *DC Comics Presents* that had Superman and Swamp Thing meeting, with Swamp Thing saving Superman from a fatal Kryptonian fungal infection. But for all of this, the sense of an inevitable and perhaps unavoidable tension between Moore and his American publishers was rising.

This was not, however, because Moore was doing anything different than what he'd been doing. Regardless of its success, it's clear that with "The Curse" Moore returned to the approach he'd used in "The Nukeface Papers": a heavily politicized horror in which whatever issues of the day Moore was passionate about were adapted into comic book monsters. Indeed, after its initial vampire two-parter, all of the stories within the arc are framed around political issues that have been paired with other classic horror monsters. "The Curse" was his engagement with feminism, and was followed immediately by another two-part story, this time matching up zombies with the history of racism and slavery in America. The result was not entirely successful—Moore flatly described it as "a failure" that "didn't really work" because it "ended up not quite saying what I'd wanted to say," which is on the whole a fair assessment. Moore's claim that he sat down "to try to analyze what I'd done wrong and work out ways that I could avoid making that mistake again," however, seems in many ways to implicate the technical aspects of Moore's writing instead of putting the criticism where it belongs on this arc: on the fact that Moore, being an English writer whose only actual direct experience with the United States consisted of a week-long trip to New York City and Vermont, neither of which, notably, are the Louisiana Bayou, was perhaps not in a good position to cast bland platitudes about how the solution to the long and awful legacy of American slavery is to "break this terrible cycle" of violence so that everyone can (presumably) just get along. Similarly, the final story in the "American Gothic" arc, "Ghost Dance," a ghost story set in a lightly reskinned version of the famed Winchester Mystery House, is clearly a well-intentioned story that is marred by a crashingly unsubtle, albeit sympathetic, "guns are bad" message.

As with "D.R. & Quinch Go to Hollywood," the crux of the problem here is that Moore is writing stories that are trying to be about America, but are instead only engaging with superficial cultural representations of America. It's not that Moore is wrong in condemning racism and gun violence, nor that these are inappropriate topics for horror stories. Rather, it's simply that Moore barely manages to engage with them on anything other than the most obvious and superficial level. Moore's best work on *Swamp Thing* is animated by his ability to find new perspectives to take on things, most obviously in his complete and radical reinvention of the basic character of Swamp Thing himself. But with much of the "American Gothic" arc Moore is unable to get his teeth into the material to any substantial extent. And at times he strays into the actively offensive—however defensible the feminist aspects of "The Curse" are, for instance, there's little that can be said in defense of the depiction of the Red Lodge as a fundamental wound in the psychogeography of Kennescook. The Red Lodge (and similar institutions) existed in several Native American cultures, but their purpose was not to imprison the unclean women, but rather to create a sacred space defined by women for what was viewed as a moment of supreme power for them. The suggestion that the lodges were focused primarily on shame was, in practice, projected onto them by European colonists whose culture actually did have centuries of history of treating menstruating women as "unclean," and who thus assumed that the indigenous populations they observed held the same attitudes. Ironically, in other words, in identifying some fundamental American horror rooted in the pre-colonial history of the continent, all Moore actually does is repeat the cultural slanders that his colonialist ancestors made when they were systematically slaughtering the indigenous American population.

Even these relatively weak issues, however, contain moments of inventive cleverness. The first page of *Swamp Thing* #42, for instance, features a gleefully grim joke in the form of five wide panels, stacked from top to bottom of the page, showing a cut-out view of the interior of a coffin that contains a mostly decomposed skeleton. Caption boxes

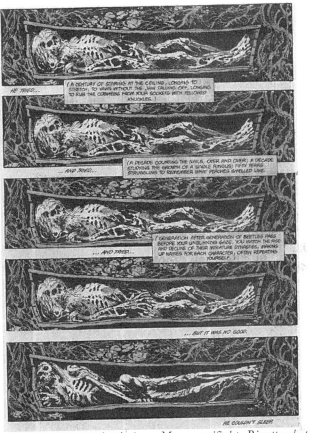

Figure 139: In his script for the issue, Moore specified to Bissette what the Beetles were doing in each panel, starting by indicating that they should be "doing whatever it is that beetles do under the ground — go to church, lend each other power tools, deliver newspapers, stuff like that" and then that they should be "scampering up the orbit of one eye socket perhaps before embarking upon a trip across the ochre planetoid of the skull," and that in the third panel "another beetle [is] standing to one side considering whether to become a Jehovah's Witness or not," while in the fourth "the beetles are all worrying about the recession." In the fifth panel description, however, he notes, "I don't care what the beetles are doing. They haven't lived up to their original promise as supporting characters and I've grown weary of them." (From Swamp Thing #42, *written by Alan Moore, art by Steve Bissette, John Totleben, and Ron Randall, 1985)*

describe "a century of staring at the ceiling, longing to stretch, to yawn without the jaw falling off" and the occupant's "decade counting the nails, over and over" and "fifty years struggling to remember what peaches smelled like," as well as "generation after generation of beetles," watching "the rise and decline of their miniature dynasties, making up names for each character." Meanwhile, underneath each panel is a second caption. These captions form a clean diagonal line from the top left to the lower right of the page. "He tried... and tried... and tried... but it was no good," they say, before reaching their mordant conclusion: "He couldn't sleep."

Between the two-part zombie story and "Ghost Dance" are a pair of one-offs. The second of these, "Bogeyman," is a minor tale of a serial killer who encounters Swamp Thing, which is enlivened by the opening pages where Swamp Thing awkwardly attempts to visit Abby in her home, mulching up unexpectedly from her tub. The first, however, "Windfall," published in *Swamp Thing* #43, is one of the most interesting stories of Moore's run. In many ways, "Windfall" is a sequel to "Rite of Spring." Like that story, it engages explicitly with psychedelia, telling the story of two people who come into possession of one of the tubers that grow on Swamp Thing's back. What is perhaps most notable about "Windfall," however, is that the story's protagonist is a drug dealer. Swamp Thing himself only appears in the first four panels of the strip, which show one of the tubers dropping off his back. At thatpoint it's picked up by an aging hippie named Chester (complete with Grateful Dead shirt) who may or may not be physically modeled off of Bryan Talbot's Chester P. Hackenbush. Although at the time of the story Chester is, as he puts it, "doin' ten days brown rice, tryin t'clean my system out, y'know," he's clearly a man with an extensive interest in ethnobotanicals and psychedelics, such that two separate people come to him looking for drugs.

"Tripping on 500 mushrooms might loosen your astral sphincter a little, but it will not generally confer upon you any of the benefits of the magic I'm discussing here."
—Grant Morrison, "Pop Magic!", 2003

The first is a man called Dave, whose wife Sandy is dying of cancer—she has only a day or two left to live, and in excruciating pain at that. Although Chester is not sure what (if anything) the tuber does yet, besides suspecting that it might be somehow related to datura, he offers Dave a piece. Immediately after Dave leaves Chester gets his second visitor: a boorish guy named Milo who declares bluntly that "I feel like getting screwed up tonight" before simply taking the biggest piece of the tuber without paying for it.

At this point in the comic a ten-page section begins, which alternates between a page telling Dave's story and a page telling Milo's. This is, in essence, a contrast between a good trip and a bad one. The one half, featuring Dave's wife Sandy, mirrors "Rite of Spring" in many regards, both on the level of dialogue (Sandy proclaims, "It's all life. You. Me. Felix. Everything. It's all the same thing," while Abby says, "Everything's alive and... and it's all made from the same stuff,") and in terms of art, albeit with a different focus. "Rite of Spring" acknowledged the intrinsic link between death and life, with a section where Abby experiences life from the perspective of a rat fighting another rat, describing how "my enemy's blood erupts to fill my mouth with molten copper," and concluding that "there is no contradiction... only the pulse. The pulse within the world." But "Windfall," as befitting its subject matter, expands on it, as Sandy realizes that "icicles, snowflakes, they're all unique. They've each got their own beautiful shape, and when they melt it's gone forever. That's where I am now... icicles are frightened of the sun. There's no need. There's no need for all this fear," and views her own death as part of a global process where eventually the individual snowflakes and icicles "run together and lose their individuality, becoming a puddle, a lake, an ocean, merging with all the other droplets." Sandy's experience gestures back towards "Rite of Spring," linking sex and death tacitly as she describes how "we spend our lives, pressing our bodies against each other, trying to break the surface tension of our skins, to unite in a single gleaming bead... it's almost as if we know."

Milo, meanwhile, does not have quite so good a time of it. In his hallucination, he relives the origin story of Swamp Thing: he feels himself burning as he's thrown out of a bar, and lands in a puddle in which, as he gets up, he sees his own reflection twisted into Swamp Thing's visage. At this point he begins hallucinating a variety of monsters from the past history of Swamp Thing (reaching back all the way to a clockwork monster from the Wein/Wrightson *Swamp Thing* #6) as he rants, "This is what the world's really like, isn't it? I can see it now. We're all monsters," and goes on about how "everything just dies and rots, gets fulla bugs, mindless bugs, eatin' each other... it's horror. It's all horror," before he's ultimately hit by a truck he imagines to be driven by Anton Arcane. His experience echoes the "American Gothic" arc in which "Windfall" is embedded, as he envisions "a city, a continent, a whole planet full of torture, madness, death," and such contrast re-establishes the twin themes and principles underlying Moore's overall tale.

The story ends with both Dave and an unnamed friend of Milo's coming back to Chester to relate what happened— Dave in order to tell him that he "gave my wife's last moments some meaning" and that he "ought to feel good about that," while Milo's friend complains, "You gave Milo that stuff, you as good as killed him," before asking if Chester has any more. Chester decides that "this fruit... it's like some kinda cosmic litmus paper, right? You eat it, an' it tells you whether you're a bad person or a good person," before being left alone with the last slice, and the decision of whether to try it. "I think I'm a good person," he muses as Country Joe and the Fish's "Bass Strings" plays. "I mean, that's what I try to be... I don't abuse the planet, or other people, and I'm

Figure 140: Sandy's psychedelic death evokes "Rite of Spring." (From Swamp Thing #43, written by Alan Moore, art by Stan Woch and Ron Randall, 1985)

Figure 141: Milo has a bad trip and encounters old Swamp Thing monsters.
(From Swamp Thing #43, written by Alan Moore, art by Stan Woch and
Ron Randall, 1985)

never violent or anything... but, like, I still eat meat, and I sometimes think some pretty bad things... I said some stuff to Suzanne before she left, and I wish I hadn't said it. I was so bitter. But hell," he concludes, "there's worse people than me." But ultimately, after considering the last piece, Chester puts it back on the plate and opts not to face whatever cosmic revelation it might offer him.

Chester's status as an occasional drug dealer with an interest in psychedelics, to say nothing of his shaggy hippy demeanor, evokes Moore's own background significantly. In many ways, "Windfall" seems to exist to make the point that Moore made in a 2009 interview, where he criticized recreational drug use, noting that psychedelic drugs like psilocybin "were sacred at one point, which meant that you weren't supposed to eat them unless you were properly initiated in a tradition, you'd done your Eleusinian Mysteries or whatever." More bluntly, as he put it, "In our current society, the only context we have to take drugs in is a leisure context, which a lot of time is disastrous." Certainly there's a tacit moral judgment in "Windfall" between the legitimate use of psychedelics and the thrill-seeking junkies that Chester (and, clearly, Moore) have no regard for.

But it's important to note that Sandy's trip—the one that is presented as the good trip—is very much about rejecting an easy dualism between life and death. Given this, treating the two trips as a straightforward moral parable about the proper use of drugs is misleading. What Milo hallucinates may be horrific and ultimately fatal, but it's also in line with the frequent themes of the comic. Indeed, Milo's trip is not that different from the experience of the serial killer in the next story—both characters encounter (symbolically or otherwise) Swamp Thing, triggering an ultimately fatal existential crisis as they confront his monstrosity and thus their own. The idea of a fundamentally sick world is at the heart of the tour Constantine forces Swamp Thing to go on, so he can see "the blackness within this continent." Monstrosity is as fundamental to Moore's story as the idea of nature's balance, and while Milo's methodology in drug use may be criticized, it would be wrong to suggest that his trip is somehow untrue or wrong.

Likewise, it is not as though Moore dismisses the value of a bad trip. In the same 2009 interview, he talks about a time when he and Melinda Gebbie tripped together, where "just for a few seconds, I was a boy of about seventeen, and I was dying in a trench just outside Ypres. It was the small hours of the morning—that grey bit just before dawn when the birds are singing. I was lying on my left side up against the side of the trench because my right foot was infected with maggots. It didn't hurt, but it itched. Unbelievably. And there were other kids, teenagers, slumped up against the other side of the trench and some of them were asleep, I knew, and some of them weren't. And I'd never had sex with a woman in my life. The woman I had the closest relationship with emotionally was my sister—I don't really have a sister—who I was missing profoundly and wishing I could see her one more time." The experience disturbed Moore so much that, as he describes it, "I couldn't get myself under control for about three-quarters of an hour. I couldn't stop crying, because I'd just suddenly realized that the First World War had happened." This is, by any reasonable definition, a bad trip, and yet, reflecting on the experience, Moore rejected the idea that what he'd experienced was a past life. "The feeling that I have," he explains, "is more 'was everybody *everybody*?'," leading him to ask, "Is there some huge commonality? Are we all the same person? Is this all God talking to himself?"—a line of questioning that parallels "Windfall," where Sandy concludes that the world is "all the same thing, like an ocean, but all divided up and contained in separate bottles."

In other words, while there clearly is a cautionary element to "Windfall," there's also, as one would expect from Moore, a clear embrace of psychedelia in the fullest sense, good trips and bad. Indeed, given the focus on balance within the good trip segments, this seems self-evident. In this regard, even though "Windfall" is a break from the larger "American

Gothic" storyline that it's placed within, it's still pointing towards the same overall conclusion—a five-issue arc about the apocalypse. This is, it is worth stressing, something that was set up from the very start of the storyline. In Constantine's first appearance, he comes to visit Swamp Thing after getting a variety of reports suggesting that some sort of cataclysmic event is going to take place in a year's time. The details are sketchy, but it apparently involves a South American cult of some sort that's going to use "all the old frighteners" to "increase the belief levels" of the world and unleash some greater nemesis. Constantine briefly lists said frighteners, and the list corresponds pretty much exactly to the stories that then unfold: "werewolves, vampires, haunted houses," and "dreams." And sure enough, in May of 1986, exactly twelve issues on past Constantine's first appearance, comes a story in which a South American cult unleashes an awful supernatural terror upon the universe. This five-issue apocalypse arc forms the second half of the "American Gothic" storyline, although there's a clear transition between them— the first portion diagnoses the psychic sins of America through classic horror monsters, whereas the apocalypse arc submits those sins for eschatological judgment.

The first part of this story, however, connects to a far larger part of DC Comics history, namely Marv Wolfman and George Pérez's epic *Crisis on Infinite Earths*. This story, published as a twelve-issue limited series, was a watershed moment in the history of comics. It came about due to the confluence of two seemingly unrelated things: the fact that DC Comics took place in a multiverse consisting of infinitely many parallel universes, and the fact that over the course of the 1970s and 1980s American comic book retailing had steadily transitioned from being dominated by newsstands and other magazine vendors to being dominated by shops focusing exclusively on comic books.

"In the beginning there was only one. A single black infinitude, so cold and dark for so very long that even the burning light was imperceptible. But the light grew, and the infinitude shuddered, and the darkness finally screamed, as much in pain as in relief."
–Marv Wolfman, *Crisis on Infinite Earths*, 1985

This tendency began in 1972 when a bookshop owner and comics convention organizer named Phil Seuling created East Coast Seagate Distribution after negotiating deals with most of the major comics publishers to allow him to buy comics at a deep discount in exchange for the comics purchased being nonreturnable. Because this dramatically decreased the risk for publishers (who were, as ever, facing declining sales), this proved acceptable to the companies. Seagate then arranged to ship those comics to specialty shops. Over the course of the ensuing decade, this eclipsed newsstands as the primary means of distributing comics, in no small part because Seagate could routinely get comics to shops a week faster than the newsstands got them, a fact that comics fans quickly picked up on, bringing more traffic towards the specialty shops and away from newsstands. In 1973, the direct market consisted of approximately 25% of comics sales. A decade later, it was newsstands that made up only 25% of the market, and the industry was awash in regional distributors all in competition with one another.

One consequence of this was a fundamental shift in the nature of comics readers. Whereas in their early days American comic books were read by a wide general audience, the direct market sold entirely to people who were dedicated enough comics fans to go to a shop stocking specifically comics, as opposed to people who happened to pick them up from a magazine rack at the supermarket. This accelerated a general trend that existed since the rise of semi-organized fandom in the late 60s, creating a smaller but more highly engaged readership. Comics companies quickly capitalized on this, creating titles designed for dedicated fans.

A basic truism of comics fans, however, is that they are prone to a certain measure of obsessiveness, particularly on the matter of maintaining consistency across multiple comics. This was one of the great strengths of Stan Lee's approach to comics, which was always careful to show that all of the Marvel books took place in a shared universe and to make sure events in one book were, if appropriate, reflected in others. But DC, owing to its decades longer history, had a much more ad hoc approach to continuity. Although some of its superhero titles, most notably *Batman*, *Superman*, and *Wonder Woman* had been published continually since World War II, most had been retired in the aftermath of the war when superheroes declined in popularity, and were not revived until after the formation of the Comics Code, when superhero comics were seen as a suitable genre to continue telling the sorts of adventure stories that had previously appeared in the now-banned crime comics. DC, in reviving its superheroes under the editorial eye of Julius Schwartz, used many of its old World War II-era character names, but gave them all revised origins and concepts. So, for instance, where the World War II-era character the Flash was a college student named Jay Garrick who fell asleep in his laboratory and inhaled chemical vapors that gave him superhuman speed, the 1950s iteration of the character was a police scientist named Barry Allen who, working late one night, had a case full of chemicals explode all over him in a lightning strike.

In 1961 DC published *The Flash* #123, which featured a story entitled "Flash of Two Worlds!" In this story, Barry Allen accidentally travels between universes, appearing in a parallel Earth in which Jay Garrick, the comic book character that inspired his costume and name, is actually a real person, with whom he teams up to stop several World War II-era Flash villains. This comic introduced the idea of the DC Multiverse, which was eventually formalized to place the World War II-era superheroes on a world designated Earth-2, while the contemporary ones existed on Earth-1. This quickly led to the proliferation of many more universes, until, as Marv Wolfman described in an essay at the start of the first issue of *Crisis on Infinite Earths*, "DC Mythology, which had grown helter-skelter over the past 50 years, had become rather convoluted." These problems compounded themselves, as the default solution to any continuity problem was to declare that whatever story didn't fit took place on yet another alternate earth, compounding the problem and, worse, becoming increasingly impenetrable to new readers.

Crisis on Infinite Earths was designed to clean up the morass of DC history and allow the line to move forward with a single, unified world that would incorporate all of the various parts of the multiverse into a coherent whole. The product of four years of research on Marv Wolfman's part and the willingness of George Pérez to draw frighteningly detailed panels with dozens of minor characters in them was such that practically every character in the history of DC could be incorporated into the story. (Swamp Thing, for his part, appears in the last panel of page ten of issue #4, alongside Sergeant Rock and two of the Easy Company, delivering his only line, "Yes... the Earth... has changed... become dark... corrupt.")

It is ironic, then, that the plot of *Crisis on Infinite Earths* is one of the most ludicrously impenetrable and convoluted things ever put to page. It concerns the conflict between two godlike beings, the Monitor and the Anti-Monitor. The former of these had been appearing in cameo roles throughout DC's line in the years leading up to *Crisis on Infinite Earths*, including a brief appearance in *Swamp Thing* #31, the final part of Moore's Arcane story, while the latter was a new villain introduced for *Crisis* itself. Both had their origins in the creation of the Multiverse, with the Anti-Monitor existing on a planet called Qward within an antimatter universe originating in some 1960s Green Lantern comics, and wanting to destroy the entire Multiverse. The Monitor recruits a bunch of heroes to defend the Multiverse by merging all of the universes into one, but his plans are derailed when his assistant, Harbinger, is possessed by one of the Anti-Monitor's shadow creatures and kills the Monitor. It turns out, however, that the Monitor had planned for this eventuality and projects the last five Earths of the Multiverse into a Limbo universe. With the assistance of Alexander Luthor from Earth-3 (where heroes are villains, such that the Justice League of America is replaced by the Crime Syndicate of America, but where, correspondingly, villains are heroes, resulting in Lex Luthor sending his infant son to Earth-1 as the universe ends at the start of *Crisis*, in a sly parallel of Superman's origin story) the now-recovered Harbinger leads an attack on the Anti-Monitor that delays his plans, at the cost of Supergirl's life. Meanwhile, the Flash dies stopping another scheme of the Anti-Monitor's, which results in him being flung across time where, as his body disintegrates, he tries to offer warnings to heroes, explaining a series of mysterious appearances he'd been making prior to his death. Undaunted, the Anti-Monitor travels to the dawn of time as a massive alliance of supervillains tries to conquer the Multiverse. This latest scheme is defeated by the Spectre, who battles with the Anti-Monitor using the combined powers of all of DC's magical characters to fight against him, which drains the power of all of the superheroes. The result is the creation of a singular universe in which elements of the remaining five worlds are juxtaposed, including both the Earth-1 and Earth-2 versions of Superman. At this point the Anti-Monitor attacks yet again, dragging the singular Earth into the antimatter universe and proclaiming, memorably, "You whimpering fool, it already is too late! From the moment you set foot on Qward—you sealed your own fates! This is the day the Universe dies!" He's finally defeated once and for all (until his next appearance in 1999) by the trio of Alexander Luthor, the Earth-2 Superman, and the Earth-Prime version of Superman (Earth Prime originally being intended as the real world of the DC Comics readership, introduced in *The Flash* #179 in 1968, but eventually given a Superboy in *DC Comics Presents* #87 in 1985), who, along with the Earth-2 version of Lois Lane, secretly saved by Alexander Luthor when the various Earths merge, retreat into a paradise dimension outside of the universe, allowing the newly formed singular Earth to continue on with no memory that there had ever been a multiverse save on the part of the Psycho-Pirate, a 1960s enemy of Doctor Fate and Hourman who was a Silver Age remake of a Justice Society of America villain from 1944 who controlled emotions through the magical Medusa Masks, and who had been an ally of the Anti-Monitor throughout *Crisis on Infinite Earths*.

In the years following the comic's publication, the various comics DC published rebooted to reflect this new continuity. These reboots led to one of Moore's two engagements with *Crisis on Infinite Earths*, a two-part Superman story entitled "Whatever Happened to the Man of Tomorrow?" that served as the final Superman story before the post-*Crisis* reboot. The origins of this story lie in Moore's second trip to the United States in 1985, where he was a guest at San Diego Comicon. There he heard from Julius Schwartz that he intended to transition to the reboot of Superman by doing an issue of each of Superman's two titles at the time, *Action Comics* and *Superman*, that would pretend to be the final issue of the comic. As Schwartz tells it, upon hearing this Moore "literally rose out of his chair, put his hands around my neck, and said, 'If you let anybody but me write that story, I'll kill you.'" Moore, for his part, wrote in 2004 upon the occasion of Schwartz's passing, "How, now, am I supposed to contradict a classic Julius Schwartz yarn? So, all right: it's true. I picked him up and shook him like a British nanny, and I hope wherever he is now, he's satisfied by this shame-faced confession." (Other classic Julius Schwartz yarns include his sexually assaulting Colleen Doran.)

On art duties for "Whatever Happened to the Man of Tomorrow?" was, at Moore's request, Curt Swan, whose immaculately clean lines defined Superman's square-jawed and uncomplicated heroism of the preceding three decades. "Whatever Happened to the Man of Tomorrow?" would end up being Swan's last piece of regular work for the company, however, as *Crisis* and the subsequent reboot of the Superman franchise was used as an excuse to push Swan out in favor of a thirty years-younger and then-trendier artist, in this case John Byrne, who would himself be steadily ushered to the junk heap of once-hot artists several decades later. Moore also opted to frame the story using a gimmick dating back to the 1950s under the editorial tenure of Mort Weisinger (one of the least pleasant editors to work with in comics history, famously described by Roy Thomas as "a malevolent toad"): advertising elaborate and ridiculous premises for comics on the covers, often coming up with them prior to actually writing the story inside, which left writers to subsequently come up with stories that explained why, for example, Superman was setting fire to the dressing gown Jimmy Olsen had gotten him for Father's Day while saying, "I'm sorry I ever adopted you as my son." Eventually this got difficult enough that Weisinger concocted the idea of declaring stories to be "imaginary stories" that existed outside of continuity, and thus could be used to do things like tell the story of Superman's death, which of course could never happen inside the comics themselves.

And so "Whatever Happened to the Man of Tomorrow?" opens with one of the more famous passages ever written by Moore, which proclaims, in an ornate and old-fashioned script selected by letterer Todd Klein, that "This is an IMAGINARY STORY (which may never happen, but then again may) about a perfect man who came from the sky and did only good. It tells of his twilight, when the great battles were over and the great miracles long since performed," and proceeds to tease much of the plot of the subsequent two issues before concluding that the story "begins in a quiet midwestern town, one summer afternoon in the quiet midwestern future. Away in the big city, people still sometimes glance up hopefully from the sidewalks, glimpsing a distant speck in the sky... but no: it's only a bird, only a plane. Superman died ten years ago. This is an IMAGINARY Story... Aren't they all?"

It is worth highlighting the degree to which this is, within the context of 1986 DC Comics, actually controversial. Certainly John Byrne, who was inheriting the Superman books after this, did not like it, and complained years later about how he cannot hear the phrase "imaginary story" "without a snide and ennui soaked voice whispering in my ear 'but aren't they all?'" Indeed, he suggests that Moore's preface to the story "goes most deeply to the root" of "the many things that can be seen to have gone wrong with American superhero comics." His reason for this remarkable claim is that, "When we ask 'Aren't they all?' we are looking behind the curtain. We are seeing that the Emperor has no clothes." While Byrne's concern about the prospect of readers looking behind the curtain at that particular moment is wholly understandable, given that what they'd see was Byrne taking the job of an acclaimed thirty-year veteran of the industry who had just been unceremoniously fired, it stands in marked and, more to the point, ideologically grounded contrast with Alan Moore, who noted that when he first got into comics at the age of seven he "was probably preoccupied with the characters themselves. I wanted to know what Batman was doing this month. Around about the time when I reached the age of say twelve, perhaps a lot earlier, I became more interested in what the artists and writers were doing that month," a viewpoint that marks, for Moore at least, an active and conscious interest in the exact artifice of comics that Byrne wants to sweep under the rug (at least when talking about comics aimed at people who are not fairly young children, which, it is fair to say, few comics in the age of the direct market actually were).

"Whatever Happened to the Man of Tomorrow?" is, as one might expect given Moore's approach, very much invested in the narrative game that it is playing. It has two almost entirely contradictory jobs to do, and it does this by being actively concerned with the gap between them. On the one hand, it is self-consciously an epic tale of Superman's last and final battle, where "his enemies conspired against him and of that final war in the snowblind wastes beneath the Northern Lights," in which "all the things he had were taken from him save for one." On the other, it's a disposable "imaginary story" that everybody reading knows is not actually final, but just marking time before the big John Byrne reboot comes in next month. And so Moore makes the story about the very impossibility of its own existence, starting the story with a journalist interviewing Lois Lane (now Elliot) about Superman's now decade-old death. By foregrounding that fact at the start, Moore seems to fly in the face of the story's lack of genuine finality. But because of the peculiar circumstances of the comic, serving as the last comic before a reboot that isn't going to pick up where Moore's story leaves off, but is rather going to declare that Moore's story and every previous Superman story are no longer part of the Superman canon, Moore instead seems to be taking a sort of grim advantage of the situation. Since nothing he does is going to "count," so to speak, Moore can do any terrible things he wants. And so the comic is in many ways an unrelentingly grim parade in which all of Superman's great villains come back, deadlier than ever before, and wreck untold havoc.

But, of course, given the existence of decades of imaginary stories, this isn't actually a new sort of power. It's not even the first time Superman died, with Jerry Siegel and Curt Swan having killed him in a 1961 imaginary story. As much as Moore may play at the idea that his story is different because the Byrne reboot is imminent, this is ultimately a trick on Moore's part. The key fact is the nature of the story's grim parade. As with much of Moore's work in American superhero comics, "Whatever Happened to the Man of Tomorrow?" is based on playing with existing concepts. This was, after all, the point of requesting Curt Swan for art chores: to make the story look like the decades of Superman stories in which its characters were developed. Moore doesn't just tell a grim and apocalyptic story, in other words: he tells a grim and apocalyptic story that is unmistakably a Superman story. Indeed, the story is almost gratuitously a Superman story, positively relishing in getting every single major Superman villain and supporting character into the plot somewhere. Even Superman notices this; the story's climax comes when he realizes that there's one villain who hasn't appeared yet, and that this villain must therefore be responsible for everything that's happened.

All of this exists to set up the real question Moore is examining with the story, which is what it means to try to craft an epic and apocalyptic narrative out of Superman in particular. And it is here that Moore pulls his best trick, ultimately opting to reject the premise. The story's main plot ends with Superman being forced to kill Mr. Mxyzptlk, the five-dimensional imp he realizes is behind all of this. (Mxyzptlk's motive is one of the most charmingly pointless imaginable—after two thousand years of being a mischievous imp, he's grown bored and decided to spend two millennia being evil instead.) Wracked with guilt, Superman proclaims, "Nobody has the right to kill. Not Mxyzptlk, not you, not Superman... especially not Superman!" And so he opts to walk into the chamber of his Fortress of Solitude where he keeps the Gold Kryptonite, which will permanently strip him of his powers, and then, apparently, he walks out into the frozen wastes to die.

At this point the story returns to its frame narrative of the interview with Lois, who politely shows the journalist the door, leaving Lois, her husband Jordan, and their infant child Jonathan alone. They talk, with Jordan telling stories of work today. "Old Dan Hodge brought in some snapshots of his grandchildren," he says, "and we're working on this old '48 Buick at the moment, trying to get her working. She's beautiful." Pressed by Lois on a criticism of Superman that he'd voiced earlier in the story, Jordan claims, "He was overrated, and too wrapped up in himself. He thought the world couldn't get along without him." But as he claims this,

Figure 142: Alan Moore tasked Curt Swan with drawing a creature that his captions described as indescribable. Swan was apparently unphased. (From Action Comics #583, 1986)

Figure 153: The last Superman story defers its ending. (Written by Alan Moore, art by Curt Swan and Kurt Schaffenberger, from Action Comics #583, 1986)

the image focuses on Jonathan playing with the bucket of charcoal for the fire: he picks up a chunk, holds it, and finally drops a diamond back into the bucket. Lois, meanwhile, suggests that they might sit in "bed with a bottle of wine. And after that, I figure we just live happily ever after. Sound good to you?" And so the comic closes with Jordan standing at their door, closing it towards the reader, and winking at them, answering simply, "Lois, my love... what do you think?" In other words, far from being an apocalyptic story with a downbeat ending, the story is in fact about how Superman earned a retirement to where he got to do the things he really loves, which is to say, to be an ordinary man, working in an auto shop. The story does not mark the end of Superman at all—clearly their son is going to grow up to be a superhero in his own right. The story both serves as the finale for an entire era of Superman comics and as a demonstration that this finale is completely and utterly unnecessary.

First and foremost, then, this story is a love letter on Moore's part to Superman comics and, more broadly, to DC. But the context of the love letter is both revealing and important. However good Moore's story is, it only exists because DC was at the time actively seeking to jettison all of the past stories Moore is drawing on in favor of a single, unified, and self-consistent account of Superman and, ideally, everything else within DC. Moore is, in other words, ostentatiously winning the battle when the larger war has already been lost to the likes of John Byrne. Moore's full-throated celebration of Superman only gets to exist in an elegiac context, as the flexibility and playfulness with which Moore could craft his story was precisely what the *Crisis*-mandated reboot was designed to excise from the character, and indeed, to excise from the company as a whole. Not two years later, Moore himself would break ties with DC.

Moore's other engagement with *Crisis on Infinite Earths*, as mentioned, came in the pages of *Swamp Thing*. This was another consequence of the direct market's transformation of the American comics industry that is worth remarking upon:

the crossover. Since *Crisis on Infinite Earths* was designed to impact every comic being published by DC, it was assumed that everyone buying any DC comics would buy it. And to this end, virtually every comic DC published ran at least one issue that, at least superficially, tied into the larger story. (It is worth emphasizing the word "superficially" here—*Crisis on Infinite Earths* also led to fandom coining the term "red skies crossover" to describe several of the crossovers, which consisted of perfectly ordinary issues of their respective comics where, in one panel, someone would remark on how the sky was red and ominous, perhaps as if some crisis were coming, before getting on with whatever they were doing.) For *Swamp Thing*, this was issue #46, entitled "Revelations." The timeline of this crossover is, however, vexed, and more to the point, vexed in a way that highlights the logistical problems underlying *Crisis on Infinite Earths*. "Revelations" features a sequence in which Swamp Thing visits the Monitor's satellite. This is the same context in which Swamp Thing appeared in *Crisis on Infinite Earths* #5, released in May of 1985, the same month as the second part of Moore's underwater vampire story. But "Revelations" did not come out until December of 1985, two full weeks after *Crisis on Infinite Earths* wrapped up.

In many ways, however, *Crisis on Infinite Earths* is just a backdrop for "Revelations." Moore has Swamp Thing travel around the world to see what it's like in the face of the apocalypse, leading to a two-page spread in which he sees "horrors and marvels" that "could not be counted," allowing Moore to offer descriptions like, "A jackboxer from the Manhattan saltbogs of 5070 had managed to bring down a young ichthyosaurus with his whorpoon, but the alligators were closing in fast," "a woman with a pulpy orange growth upon her shoulder stumble unwittingly into a field of water hyacinths. As they parted and she sank into the water beneath, the growth opened its mouth and began to bellow," and, "there was laughter and weeping and somebody was screaming for somebody else to hold their hand, please,

please, just hold their hand…" None of these images have any corollary within *Crisis on Infinite Earths*—they don't refer to specific scenes in the way that Swamp Thing's appearance on the Monitor's satellite do. Rather, they're flavor: attempts to depict what it's like to witness the end of the world.

"We all woke up, the day after the world ended, and we still had to feed ourselves and keep a roof over our heads. Life goes on, y'know?"
–Alan Moore, *Promethea*, 2005

But the tie-in to *Crisis on Infinite Earths* consumes only the first of five issues about the end of the world, and it would be a mistake to treat the Moore's apocalypse as coextensive with *Crisis*. Rather, Moore's story piggybacks upon that cataclysm, casting his apocalypse as an echo of the larger one. As Constantine explains within the narrative, "This sort of physical destruction is bound to cause temporary disturbances on the psychic plane. Our problem is that there are people who anticipated the disturbance and plan to take advantage of it." For Swamp Thing's part, he experiences it as "the whimpering that people made deep in their souls. He heard the bedlam of a mass mind faced with extinction." Within Moore's later cosmology this would seem to suggest an apocalypse within Ideaspace, although it's important to note that the conflict is presented as taking place in the DC Universe's Ideaspace, which is at best a tiny subset of Ideaspace proper.

Much of Moore's work on *Swamp Thing* has engaged with this precise point. Moore explicitly sought to use *Swamp Thing* to engage with "the reality of American horror." In his view, "What frightens people these days is not the idea of a werewolf jumping out at them, it's the idea of a nuclear war." In truth, Moore's engagement with the apocalypse went beyond mere nuclear war (which he never touched on directly in *Swamp Thing*, although it was a substantial theme elsewhere in Moore's DC work), and to the larger idea of the human capacity to destroy their own habitation in a number of ways, an image that ties in with the larger ecological themes of *Swamp Thing*.

So Moore's apocalypse is framed, ultimately, as a conceptual apocalypse—as a nightmarish consequence of the very idea of the apocalypse and of the way in which the horrors Moore engaged with throughout his run on *Swamp Thing* loom over the culture. But this conceptual apocalypse is still grounded in specific ideas. The Brujería, the South American cult that Moore has unleashing this apocalypse, is described as having "existed for centuries in the forests of Patagonia, at the southernmost tip of South America." They are, in other words, positioned at the root of the Americas as a whole. The "darkness at the heart of this continent" that Moore spent the entire "American Gothic" arc presenting, in other words, finds its most fundamental expression here—a dark and twisted cult lying at the deepest base of the entire land. (That this fits into the same tradition of demonizing and exoticizing indigenous American populations that Moore perpetuated in "The Curse" is, of course, a deeply frustrating failure on Moore's part.) It is in this regard worth noting that the Brujería's scheme is in many ways an echo of Moore's own plotting. "Using their influence," Constantine explains, "they've forced the dark stuff to the surface, all over the world. I only showed you the trouble spots I thought you could learn from." These trouble spots, of course, constituted the "American Gothic" arc, a point hammered home by Bissette and Totleben's art, which recaps these threats. "Each incident," Constantine continues, "has increased the general belief in the paranormal by degrees, until the whole psychic atmosphere is like a balloon ripe for bursting." In other words, the Brujería have created a bunch of typical horror stories in order to create an atmosphere of tension. This tacitly allies the Brujería with Moore, who, as a writer, has been enacting this exact plan: a series of traditional horror stories serving as a prelude to an eventual apocalypse.

The unleashing of this horror in "A Murder of Crows," in *Swamp Thing* #48, comes when one of Constantine's allies,

Judith, betrays him to the Brujería and agrees to serve as their messenger. This involves a ritual in which Judith vomits out her intestines and allows her body to shrivel until only her severed but still talking head remains. The Brujería then place a black pearl in her mouth, at which point her head steadily transforms into a bird, a process that is laboriously and disturbingly described, at which point the bird is released to summon the nameless dark power by delivering the pearl held in its mouth to a distant destination. Although this transformation is presented as a physical corruption ripe with body horror, the fact that it is brought about via Judith ingesting an unnamed root places it in the larger thematic tradition of psychedelic plants within Moore's *Swamp Thing*. It is, in other words, inexorably linked with the bad trip—the negative, monstrous aspect of the spiritual plane.

But the summoning of this dark power doesn't come until the third issue of the arc. The second, coming between it and the *Crisis* tie-in, presents an equally important aspect of this setup. In it, before journeying to the Brujería's cave, Constantine takes Swamp Thing to the Parliament of Trees, also located in South America, in this case at the source of the River Tefé in the Amazon. Here Moore pays off an idea introduced in "Abandoned Houses," revealing the resting place of all the past plant elementals of the world and allowing Swamp Thing to seek communion with them. In yet another sequence of psychedelia, Swamp Thing allows his mind to meld with that of the parliament, where he asks the "eternal trees" about the coming apocalypse and "how to use my power to its best advantage." The Parliament recoils, saying, "Power? Power is not the thing. To be calm within oneself, that is the way of the wood." When Swamp Thing expresses doubt, saying that he has "seen much that is evil... it preys upon my mind. I wonder if nature can be just to allow such things," the Parliament further rebukes him, telling him that "Flesh doubts. Wood knows. If you wish to understand evil, you must understand the bark, the roots, the worms of the earth. That is the wisdom of an Erl-King.

Aphid eats leaf. Ladybug eats aphid. Soil absorbs dead ladybug. Plant feeds upon soil. Is aphid evil? Is ladybug evil? Is soil evil? Where is the evil in all the wood?" And with that, Swamp Thing is cast out of the Parliament, much to his horror.

Taken together, these issues mirror the basic structure of "Windfall," with "The Parliament of Trees" serving as Sandy's half of the story and "A Murder of Crows" serving as Milo's. These two aspects of the spiritual experience are, at least superficially, being pitted against each other, and yet in the Parliament's answer there is already the setup for this debate's inevitable resolution. This resolution occupies the final two issues of the arc, culminating in the oversized *Swamp Thing #50.*

These issues, perhaps surprisingly, return the focus to the larger DC Universe. With the Brujería's messenger released, Constantine is forced to drop to plan B—preparing to battle the entity they've summoned once it arrives. This involves Constantine and Swamp Thing parting ways again to handle parallel tasks. Constantine, for his part, meets with various mystical figures within the DC Universe: Marv Wolfman and Gene Colan's Baron Winters; John B. Wentworth and Howard Purcell's Golden Age creation Sargon the Sorcerer; a character created for *Action Comics* #1 by Fred Guardineer called Zatara, along with his Gardner Fox/Murphey Anderson-created daughter (and Justice League member) Zatanna; the pre-Superman Siegel and Shuster creation Doctor Occult (who shows up uninvited); and finally Arnold Drake and Bruno Premiani's Steve Dayton, "the world's fifth richest man," who created a helmet to increase his mental powers and who goes by the name of Mento. This latter character's inclusion was foreshadowed back in *Crisis on Infinite Earths* #4, where Constantine meets with him in a more or less contextless eight-panel scene (wedged between a scene with Batgirl and Supergirl and one in which Pariah, a character created for *Crisis*, witnesses more earths dying— which is most of what he does in the story), an appearance

Figure 144: Judith turns into a bird, a scene of splendid psychedelic body horror. (From Swamp Thing *#48, written by Alan Moore, art by John Totleben, 1986)*

Figure 145: Zatara bursts into flames, his top hat sickly and hilariously unaffected. (From Swamp Thing *#50, written by Alan Moore, art by Steve Bissette and John Totleben, 1986)*

that was followed up on by an equally cryptic sequence in *Swamp Thing* #44 ("Bogeymen"). Swamp Thing, on the other hand, reconnects with the various characters he met back in "Down Among the Dead Men" in order to confront the being on the spiritual plane.

The oversized *Swamp Thing* #50, which was also Steve Bissette's final issue as the book's primary penciller, finally offers this confrontation, with a series of supernatural beings attempting to defeat the summoned entity and failing before Swamp Thing finally saves the day. While this is going on, Constantine and his allies watch via Mento's psychic powers, narrating the events and, as Constantine explains it, channeling their magical energies to help Swamp Thing and his allies, which results in the incineration of both Sargon and Zatara due to psychic backlash from the blackness. The confrontation itself consists of four characters fighting their way to the gigantic shadow at that is the nameless entity, where they are grabbed and forcibly drawn into it to confront it.

These four confrontations are depicted as sequences in which the characters float in an immense blackness, which addresses them in turn, asking each a question. They in turn answer and, as the shadow finds their answers unacceptable, are cast out. First is Etrigan, to whom the shadow explains, "Before light, I was; endless, without name or need of name. Then light came. Witnessing its otherness, I suffered my first knowledge of self, and all contentment fled. Tell me, little thing. Tell me what I am." Etrigan, for his part, explains that the darkness is "Evil, absence of god's light, his shadow-partner, locked in endless fight." But the shadow is unimpressed, claiming all Etrigan has taught it is fatalism and inevitability, and that these are not what it needs. Next is Doctor Fate, a Golden Age magical character, who, when asked "Little Thing, what is evil?" replies, "Evil is a quagmire of ignorance that would drag us back as we climb towards the immortal light. A vile, wretched thing, to be scraped from the sandals like dromedary soil." Again, the shadow is unimpressed, saying that Doctor Fate has only taught it contempt and casts him out. At last comes the Spectre, who, asked the same question as Doctor Fate, proclaims that "Evil exists only to be avenged, so that others may see what ruin comes of opposing that great voice, and cleave more wholly to its will, fearing its retribution," to which the shadow says that the Spectre has taught it only vengeance and casts him out. At this point it appears that all hope is lost, and even the Phantom Stranger seems to give up. But Constantine, for his part, demands to know what Swamp Thing is doing and shouts, "This is what I prepared him for!" Swamp Thing, for his part, walks willingly into the blackness.

Here, then, Moore sets the stage for his larger philosophical confrontation. Having identified a fundamental rot within this new continent in which his tales are to be unleashed, he has now brought an apocalyptic force to devour it. More than that, he has lent this final judgment a moral rightness. To Doctor Fate's contempt, it quite reasonably asks, "Am I so low, then, and is he you serve so high that there can be no possibility of respect between us?" And to the Spectre's suggestion that evil exists only to be punished, it asks, "What of the tortured eons I endured, unable to broach this maddening brilliance and quiet the pain it woke in me? Do they not demand retribution?" In this final question, the darkness brings up a fundamental and previously unspoken aspect of Moore's story. The darkness is, by this point, being portrayed as the nothing in which God created light, an event that has tortured it with knowledge of self ever since. This has parallels in the basic idea of an American darkness and of the Brujería. The depiction of them as existing in the furthest reach of the continent raises the question of what exists in the rest of the continent. The answer, of course, is the product of European colonialism, which led to the overthrow and oppression of the indigenous population to which the Brujería belong. This colonialism is mirrored in the darkness's pain at being invaded by light, and the angry vengeance that it comes to demand serves as a metaphor for the oppressed and subaltern indigenous populations. The darkness is not evil, in this analogy, but rather a righteous demand for justice on the part of the deeply aggrieved, with the European light being the true villain of the piece.

And yet having engineered this conflict carefully over the course of more than a year of comics, at the final moment Moore opts to avert it. Swamp Thing, when faced with the darkness's question about the nature of evil, at first reflects on the evil he witnessed during the "American Gothic" arc: "Its cruelty... the randomness with which it ravages... innocent... and guilty alike." But then he comes to the council given by the Parliament of Trees, admitting that he did not understand their answer. "And yet," he says, "they spoke of aphids eating leaves, bugs eating aphids, themselves finally devoured by the soil, feeding the foliage. They asked where evil dwelled within this cycle and told me to look to the soil. The black soil is rich in foul decay... yet glorious life springs from it. But however dazzling the flourishes of life, in the end, all decays to the same black humus... Perhaps evil," he finally concludes, "is the humus formed by virtue's decay... and perhaps... perhaps it is from that dark, sinister loam that virtue grows strongest?" This answer, at last, is satisfactory to the darkness, which allows Swamp Thing to leave freely while it reflects upon what he has said, and then finally confronts the light, depicted as a double page spread of two massive hands reaching towards each other. The scene is narrated by Dayton, who is driven hopelessly mad by the experience and left unable to describe it. Instead Moore offers only the cryptic words of the Phantom Stranger, who says, "The light and shade are still everywhere around us... only the conflict between them has altered," and later muses, "In the heart of darkness, a flower blossoms, etching the shadows with its promise of hope... in the fields of light, an adder coils, and the radiant tranquillity is lent savor by its sinister presence. Right and wrong, black and white, good and evil... all my existence I have looked from one to the other, fully embracing neither one... never before have I understood how much they depend upon each other."

Within this ending there is a kernel of interesting observation that Moore, in his usual obliquely unchanging manner, would return to in his later career when, for example, he had Promethea wonder, "If Qlippoths are husks left when good departs, does that mean evil isn't a real thing, in itself? It's just an absence of good, like dark's an absence of light?" or when, in *Snakes and Ladders*, he writes that "the profane and sacred are both one, and that the salt of the earth and its scum are struck from the same coin, and in our lowest depths, the worst abyss of us, there is a light." There are, to be sure, profound implications to this sort of thing—it's an insight not unlike that of William Blake when he wrote in *The Marriage of Heaven and Hell*, "Without Contraries is no progression. Attraction and Repulsion, Reason and Energy, Love and Hate, are necessary to Human existence. From these contraries spring what the religious call Good & Evil. Good is the passive that obeys Reason, Evil is the active springing from energy. Good is Heaven. Evil is Hell."

And yet for all of this, there is something frustratingly hollow about the resolution. There is no describable change effected by Moore's resolution. Good and evil are said to have the same relationship as ever, although the Phantom Stranger concedes that perhaps "a different light has been cast upon" it. But within the confines of DC's superhero line, in which the comic is tacitly grounded, this seems set to mean little. A "no-score draw," as Constantine describes the outcome, inherently favors the side that had power at the outset—that is, the light that has banished the darkness to a point depicted as "a chaotic inferno with neither land nor sky" beyond the edges of reality itself. DC Comics and its multitude of superhero franchises will continue to embrace "good," and by extension to embrace the status quo. The light will always retain its tacit allegiance with entrenched power structures, and the darkness will never have its vengeance for the light's invasion of it.

The fundamentally conservative nature of this ending is stressed by the issue's final page, which returns to Cain and Abel. Abel reflects upon the situation: "Nearly all our stories revolve around good struggling against evil... darkness against light... what will become of the stories? Without that ancient conflict to fall back on, what will they be about?" Cain's answer, of course, is to shove his brother off a cliff to his death with a wisecrack about how he's "sure we'll think of something," a moment that reiterates the complete lack of change offered by this resolution. This is not, as Moore would later write in *Promethea*, a conceptual apocalypse with the real possibility of transforming the world. Rather, it's a damp squib—a whimpering end of the world wholly devoid of bang.

It is not fair, however, to frame this as a failing on Moore's part. For all that he was rapidly becoming the golden boy of DC Comics, Moore was never going to be allowed to fundamentally and irrevocably alter the nature of the DC Universe, and he was certainly not naive enough to think otherwise. He had, after all, by this point, already had his plans for a story called *Who Killed the Peacemaker?* This story would provide a sweeping and transformative take on some obscure superheroes that DC acquired when it bought out the failing Charlton Comics in 1983, but was vetoed by DC on the grounds that it would render the characters unusable, which resulted in the proposal being reworked as *Watchmen* with original characters that could be cordoned off from DC continuity, with the first issue coming out the month after *Swamp Thing* #50. The idea that he was going to get away with destroying heaven and letting the primordial darkness reign once more was unlikely to have seriously crossed his mind.

"I feel that I have become an essential part of some incomprehensible biological process. The house is an organism hungry for madness. It is the maze that dreams."
—Grant Morrison, *Arkham Asylum*, 1989

Indeed, his next story arc, a three-issue tale that brings Swamp Thing into conflict with Batman, is largely about reiterating this precise point. It is easy and tempting to draw a dividing line between *Swamp Thing* #50 and the story that commences with *Swamp Thing* #51. DC does exactly that in the six-volume collected editions of Moore's *Swamp Thing* that are how most readers encounter the text these days, ending the fourth volume, *A Murder of Crows*, with issue #50, and commencing the fifth, *Earth to Earth*, with #51. And there is a marked shift in tone between the apocalyptic battle on the shores of hell itself that takes place in issue #50 and the much smaller scale story of Swamp Thing attempting to rescue an imprisoned Abby that follows it. But the two stories are considerably more enmeshed than they appeared. In many ways, it makes more sense to look at the entire run from "Growth Patterns" back in *Swamp Thing* #37 to "The Garden of Earthly Delights" in *Swamp Thing* #53 as a single seventeen-issue arc that runs from the return of Swamp Thing following the second time Moore killed him to the character's third death under Moore.

In this reading, the turning point in the arc is the transition from the "American Gothic" storyline to the apocalyptic one, with the three-issue Batman story serving as a thematic reprise of the apocalypse. Certainly the Batman story overtly responds to the apocalypse plot, with Swamp Thing laying siege to Gotham City after discovering that Abby has been arrested there. Swamp Thing's anger is framed as a rage in which he loses sight of the very council from the Parliament of Trees that he just employed to save the entirety of creation. As he howls in fury after discovering what's happened to Abby, the captions repeat the Parliament's advice: "Power is not the thing. To be calm within oneself, that is the way of the wood. Power tempts anger, and anger is like wildfire. Avoid it." The narration continues, "Out in the swamp, the monster raged and trampled, and roared his lover's name, and promised war," when just a few pages earlier he mused to John Constantine, "The war is over. I am home at last. What could possibly anger me now?" And so Swamp Thing's attack on Gotham is framed as an echo of the war just fought and, perhaps more importantly, as a sort of alternate ending—a conscious counterpoint to the sense of universal harmony envisioned by the ending of *Swamp Thing* #50.

Beyond that, the Batman arc has its seeds in the apocalypse arc, specifically from a subplot in issues #47 and #48. *Swamp Thing* #47 ("The Parliament of Trees") is bookended by scenes in which a sleazy photographer sells photos he took of Abby and Swamp Thing kissing (which he obtained after beginning to secretly photograph Abby undressing) to a local newspaper. The next issue, in which the Brujería transform Judith into a bird, ends with a series of panels in which Judith, now a crow, flies outwards from the page, eventually filling the entire panel with black as Constantine narrates the fact that "The bird's flown and the message is on its way, and the bad luck will take us all. Each and every one of us, all on a one-way losing streak." But instead of ending on a note of cosmic apocalypse, the next two panels proceed to zoom out, first to swirls of black on a white background, which are revealed in the final panel to be Abby's hair. This then leads to the issue's actual cliffhanger, which is not the Brujería's release of the crow but rather Abby's arrest as a sex offender due to the newspaper photos. "You been out in the swamps shackin' up with something that ain't even human," the cops explain as they take her away. "And now we got the whole story in black and white. Although from where I'm standin'," the cop goes on, "it's mostly black," a comment that coincides with the end of another sequence of panels zooming in on the newspaper headline closer and closer, until the black print on the white page overwhelms the panel, resulting in a solid black panel akin to that produced by Judith's flight two pages earlier.

This parallelism frames Abby's arrest both as the consequence of the Brujería's successful ritual and as an expression of the same darkness. Or, more accurately, it frames the nature of Abby's arrest—sexual puritanism—as an expression of the same darkness. The precise nature of the metaphor is perhaps slightly elusive, however. On the surface the crime for which Abby is arrested parallels miscegenation laws. The moment where Abby's lawyer suggests that she claim that she was "forced into a repulsive relationship by this monster" certainly does invoke the age-old stereotypes whereby relationships between black men and white women in the American south were portrayed as necessarily being rape, which often resulted in vigilante murders—a history (clumsily) explored in the two-part zombie story of the "American Gothic" arc. But given the larger context of Moore's career and the fact that interracial relationships, although still severely stigmatized, were not really pressing news issues in 1986, it seems equally likely, if not more so, that the incident is meant to invoke the legal persecution of homosexuality, that being an issue Moore was a passionate activist about throughout the 1980s. This latter reading is supported by the specific nature of the charge—Abby is "being charged under those laws of this state usually reserved for people who have carnal relationships with farm animals"—and by a scene in *Swamp Thing* #51 that depicts selections from the mail (and in one case a brick thrown through the window) that Abby is subjected to while she waits for trial, harassment that causes her to flee to Gotham, where she's arrested, provoking Swamp Thing's siege. One notes that the writer has been praying for Abby, but says that "you have <u>lay down</u> with a <u>beast</u>, and you are an <u>abomination</u> in his <u>sight</u>," phrasing that invokes Leviticus 18:22, which (in many translations) famously uses the word "abomination" to describe same sex relations. Another reads: "Deer slut, What is the matter you cannot get a reel man so you have infercourse with anything it is to bad your husband is in a comma he wood wup yur ass you are an ugly pig," phrasing that invokes the harassment of lesbians, particularly in its threat of male "corrective" violence.

Regardless of what specific metaphor is chosen for this, however, the larger point is that Abby is imprisoned as part of a crackdown against sexual freedom. This is as fundamental an evil as exists within the ethics of Moore's *Swamp Thing*, amounting as it does to a complete rejection of all the truths revealed in "Rite of Spring." And Moore goes to lengths to establish that in this regard, at least, Swamp Thing is wholly justified—he makes sure that Batman ultimately sides with Swamp Thing, claiming angrily that the refusal to release Abby constitutes an insistence "on the letter of the law over love and justice." Batman challenges Gotham's mayor, who protests that "we can't make exceptions to the law," to "start rounding up all the other non-human beings who may be having relationships outside their species," suggesting that he should "arrest Hawkman and Metamorpho... and there's also Starfire, from the Titans. Her race evolved from cats, I believe... the Martian Manhunter, obviously. Captain Atom... and then of course there's what's-his-name... the one who lives in Metropolis." In making this appeal, Batman tacitly positions the entire DC Universe, down to Superman himself, as being on the side of sexual freedom, which firmly entrenches Swamp Thing's fury not as a righteous anger, but as a righteous anger intrinsically supported by the larger comics line.

But what is in many ways more interesting than the nature of what drives Swamp Thing to forget the Parliament of Trees' words and to go to war is the nature of the warfare he wages. After erupting into the Gotham City Courthouse out of a rose that Abby was handed by a supporter on the way in, he gives them an hour to release her, proclaiming, "I have tolerated your species for long enough. Your cruelty and your greed and your insufferable arrogance... you blight the soil and poison the rivers. You raze the vegetation till you cannot even feed your own kind, and then you boast of man's triumph over nature. Fools, if nature were to shrug or raise an eyebrow then you should all be gone. I want my wife. You have one hour." And when, after an hour, Abby is not returned to him, he unleashes the full extent of his power upon the city, instantly causing it to become overrun with vegetation. "The sidewalks begin to bleed emerald. Moss dribbles up the sheer sides of glass towers and the ghettos are burning with orchids. Stalled cars, ugly with buckled wings and broken antennae, become monuments of fabulous and surreal beauty in seconds. Spewing from choked drains and gratings, Eden comes to the city."

The phrasing on this last sentence—that this new jungle of Gotham is "Eden"—reveals an important ideological point. Although the story remains emphatic that Swamp Thing's siege of Gotham is an instance of him wrongly succumbing to the temptation of power, it is altogether more subtle on the nature of Gotham City under Swamp Thing's brief reign. The imagery of the third issue of the story is bold and, in its own way, as apocalyptic as anything from the preceding storyline. "In Coventry the residents' protection group creep through an overgrown department store bristling with guns and tension. In the cosmetics department an escaped tiger treads carefully through the spilled lipsticks," one description of the city goes, while another describes "the topsoil of the park where lean cats stalk fruit-fattened birds and drunkards fall in love amongst the nectarines." But on balance this overgrown Gotham is portrayed as a sort of paradise—within a day there are pilgrims coming to the city, and 15% of the population has apparently decided that they prefer this new Gotham. Swamp Thing's psychedelic tubers are shown to be sprouting throughout the city, giving the many residents an opportunity for spiritual enlightenment. "The city," Swamp Thing ponders, "is changed into a thing of subtle marvels. Across the street, children pick pure white lilies from the awning of a sex cinema, and play at weddings, parading silently between the silent trees. Wine dribbles from a phone booth crammed with grapes, and the mouths of subways breathe a rare, delicate perfume." Swamp Thing quickly acquires supporters, who are also given voice. A teacher talks about how her class studied the way rain forests produce oxygen, and "how they'll all be gone within forty years. One kid asked, 'What will we breathe then?' I couldn't answer him. That's why I'm behind the Swamp Man." Others say that "he nices up the area and he's got the administration sweating blood." Those opposing Swamp Thing, meanwhile, are portrayed as dunces and fools—the mayor, notably, makes reference to Ronald Reagan's famously daft claim that "Trees cause more pollution than automobiles do," a moment that makes it abundantly clear where Moore's sympathies lie in the matter.

Inevitably, of course, the status quo is maintained. Moore wasn't going to be allowed to level one of the DC Universe's major cities and replace it with a post-scarcity utopia any more than he was going to be allowed to destroy heaven. Ultimately Batman succeeds in persuading the mayor to free Abby, and Swamp Thing relents. The world returns to normal. Nevertheless, the nature of Swamp Thing's siege is unnerving. It is notable that Batman makes an attempt to forcibly stop Swamp Thing by attacking him with defoliant early in issue #53, but is trivially repelled, with Swamp Thing creating an army of bodies and physically beating Batman. Batman goes to the mayor and demands he release Abby because there are "no other options. That thing out there is very nearly a god. It can crush us." The degree of power that this outcome gives to Swamp Thing is remarkable. The entire concept of Batman is that he figures out ways to defeat all manner of threats. For him to throw up his hands and declare Swamp Thing a quasi-god is unsettling. Given the way in which this story is a tacit extension of the previous apocalypse, it is tempting to read this as an illustration of the new relationship between good and evil. And in a sense it is—Commissioner Gordon describes the overgrown Gotham as a "savage Eden," and it is clearly a world with no shortage of serpents; he also describes it as a "green hell."

"[Anarchy has] become a kind of shorthand standing for the breakdown of society and order into screaming chaos; into a Hieronymus Bosch

Figure 146: Gotham as a "savage Eden." (From Swamp Thing #53, written by Alan Moore, art by John Totleben, 1986)

Figure 147: The Garden of Earthly Delights, by Hieronymus Bosch.

landscape populated by looters, berserkers, giants with leaking boats for
feet and eggshells for a body."
–Alan Moore, "Fear of a Black Flag," 2010

This ambivalence is reflected in the title of this last issue, "The Garden of Earthly Delights," after a triptych painted in the late 15th/early 16th century by Hieronymus Bosch. The painting consists of three distinct panels, following the general convention of the form in that era and moving from a depiction of the Garden of Eden in the leftmost panel and the Last Judgment in the right. The first panel depicts God presenting Eve to Adam, which flows smoothly into the largest panel, the center one, continuing the skyline across the gap so as to give a sense of this image emerging directly from the first one. This center panel depicts the titular garden as a scene of vast, libidinous excess. Nude figures embrace within a transparent globe that is itself the fruit of a plant, birds the size of people frolic in the stream, vast phallic and yonic towers emerge out of the lake, there are men with heads of fruit, and men riding fantastic beasts, all spilling out across the panel in an overwhelming, breathtaking spectacle of man and nature in seeming harmony. Finally there is the rightmost panel, which breaks from the flow of the skyline, depicting a night scene in hell in which people are inventively and grotesquely tortured. The overall message, at least initially, appears to be an anti-materialist one that considers the earthly delights of the central garden but that ultimately concludes that these delights, which stem out of the original temptation of the flesh in the Garden of Eden, lead only to demonic ruin.

And yet the entire physical object that is *The Garden of Earthly Delights* cuts visibly against this interpretation. The actual physical triptych is a massive thing, more than seven feet tall and nearly thirteen feet wide, painted on a trio of solid oak panels that are hinged so that the left and right panel can close over the center panel, revealing a fourth image on the outer doors. The triptych itself is the size of one hundred and ninety-five comic book covers, such that one could spread every page of every issue of *Swamp Thing* from "Loose Ends" through the end of the Etrigan arc over it and still have room for half of "The Burial." And, of course, the entire visual pleasure of the piece is based on its sense of sprawling excess—on the incredible sense of detail and intricacy presented. Whatever Bosch's intended meaning, a topic with centuries of criticism asserting motivations ranging from political allegories about the gardens at the Palace of Coudenberg, to detailed symbolic readings based on Bosch's supposed membership in heretical occult sects, to prosaic readings that treat it as a wholly straightforward and direct piece of medieval religious art, the material object that is *The Garden of Earthly Delights* stubbornly insists on a pleasure of seductive and overwhelming wonder.

This view of the piece is further reinforced by its exterior painting, a depiction of the Earth during its creation, specifically on the third day, after the creation of vegetation. The world exists as a vast and empty place, painted in a monochromatic grey-green that blends rock and plant together such that it is impossible to tell where one starts and the other leaves off. Encased within its crystalline globe, the world is silent. But in the upper left of the image sits God, overseeing the world's creation, and moreover, being absolutely dwarfed by it, barely the size of a single tree or rock within it. It is the vacant earth and the beginnings of teeming life that grow within it that dominate the scene, even before it is opened up to reveal the first images of man inside. This sense of a vast and teeming planet continues into the first panel, where Adam and Eve are surrounded by wondrous beasts, where birds wind their way through an ornately carved rock formation, and where out of the waters of Eden rises an extravagant fountain with a clear resemblance to the phallic towers of the second panel. And even in Eden, sex and death are present—throughout the panel the beasts feed upon each other's flesh, and Eve's posture as she is presented to Adam, thrusting her chest and

Figure 148: Details from The Garden of Earthly Delights. *a) Eve's seductive pose from the left panel. b) People cavorting lasciviously in the middle panel. c) One of the many bizarre sights in the rightmost panel.*

hips forward as she kneels before him, speaks volumes.

Given the sense of vastness of the earth and the life within it, the second panel of humanity and nature cavorting in harmony seems almost wholly inevitable. Indeed, it seems like the natural moral conclusion to what appears in the previous two images. The lushness of the material world is presented as being so vast it exceeds the scope of its creator. If this is so, what possible purpose could humanity have beyond surrendering their bodies to the world? In this reading, the final panel is not a consequence of the center panel, but an alternative—a fact highlighted by the breaking of the skyline that stretches over the first two panels. It is telling, after all, that the people being tormented in hell appear to be engaged in material pursuits: they are gamblers and musicians, and the nightmarish visions within hell come not from the natural world, but from human creation: knives, chamber pots, and musical instruments. It is only in hell that there is any depiction of civilization—a smoldering city that stretches out into the background, in marked contrast to the twisting towers of the Garden, which seem, like the transparent globes of fruit and the animal carapaces in which people burrow, to be as much products of nature as of man.

From this perspective, then, *The Garden of Earthly Delights* becomes a work not so much about rejecting materialism as it is about rejecting the trappings of human society in favor of the vast world of nature. It is, in other words, a piece that very closely parallels the plot of Moore's own Gotham triptych, in which it is ultimately the assumed social order of Gotham that is rejected by Swamp Thing in favor of a world where humanity gives itself over to the limitless pleasures that nature offers. The "green hell" that Commissioner Gordon sees within this world is not just due to the its potential for savagery, but because, as in Bosch, it is the existence of the Garden of Earthly Delights that allows for all of the laws and systems of man to be rejected and cast down into hell. (Were one feeling ambitious, one might even describe this as "a different light" being cast upon the relationship between good and evil.) As Moore summarized in a later interview, "Even though mankind can cover nature and smother the wilderness with a layer of concrete and cement, even though mankind can erect huge, powerful, and impressive-looking buildings, underneath our feet, underneath the buried pipes and the buried cables, nature is still there. The wilderness is still there. And though man might boast of having conquered nature, that's not the case, for if nature were to shrug or to merely raise its eyebrow, then we should all be gone." The human systems of the world that populate and, perhaps more importantly, shape Bosch's hell are, in the end, mere parasites suckling upon the unfathomable vastness of nature.

But in all of this, there is still an edge of cruelty—a sense that there is something wrong with Swamp Thing's ascension. Perhaps it is merely the incoherent protests of civilized humans unwilling to face the truth that Swamp Thing reveals to be self-evident, but it is also worth noting that Swamp Thing's siege of Gotham mirrors the Floronic Man's scheme in Moore's first *Swamp Thing* arc. Where Woodrue took control of the plants of the world in order to destroy humanity, Swamp Thing does so to dictate the terms of a new equilibrium with humanity, thus tacitly answering his challenge to Woodrue at the end of *Saga of the Swamp Thing* #24. And like "Roots," this is witnessed by a traditional superhero who is nevertheless powerless to stop it—in this case Batman, ironically the one major DC hero not present "Roots." Nevertheless, there is a moral critique to be had here, and it is one that Moore threads throughout the story: the fact that Swamp Thing succumbed to the anger that is power's temptation and in doing so betrayed the way of the wood. It is, in the end, the same crime committed by Woodrue—that of using power to accomplish your own ends.

And so having transgressed, Swamp Thing is thusly punished; all of this plays out over the backdrop of Dwight Wicker, last seen in Moore's first issue, and originating all the way back in the Pasko run, who shows up in Gotham pursuing Swamp Thing for the murder of General Sunderland in "The Anatomy Lesson." Wicker hires Lex Luthor to find a way to kill Swamp Thing, which he accomplishes by creating a device that will disrupt Swamp Thing's ability to tune into the world's vegetation, removing his ability to exit his body in the event of an attack. Utilizing a combination of this device and an abundance of napalm, Wicker assassinates Swamp Thing as he reunites with Abby outside the courthouse, having finally withdrawn from inhabiting the city itself and into a single, destroyable body.

By this point, of course, this has gotten to be something of a habit for Moore. But that is in many ways the point— Moore's run frequently mirrors its own past events. The Floronic Man's attack on Lacroix is reiterated as Swamp Thing's siege of Gotham; the parallel trips of "Windfall" (itself a mirror of "Rite of Spring") repeat as "The Parliament of Trees" and "A Murder of Crows." And, of course, this is now the third time that Moore has killed Swamp Thing. By this point the death of the lead character is recognizable not so much as a significant problem to the narrative as it is a transitional point. Swamp Thing's first death in "Loose Ends" and "The Anatomy Lesson" served as the transition away from Pasko's attempt to mimic the Wein/Wrightson stories of old and towards Moore's psychedelia-tinged ecological horror. His second over the course of "The Nukeface Papers" and "Growth Patterns" marks the transition towards a much more expansive sense of what Swamp Thing's powers are, making him no longer just a bipedal vegetable, but a functional deity. And so any savvy reader would, upon seeing Swamp Thing's third death, assume that this marked yet another transitional point in Moore's story.

Accordingly, Moore leans into this sense, taking two issues before having Swamp Thing reappear in the comic, with *Swamp Thing* #54, "The Flowers of Romance," not featuring the character at all. Instead, staying in the vein of Dwight Wicker's unexpected return, Moore reintroduces Liz

Tremayne, a supporting character for much of Pasko's run unseen since "Loose Ends" three years earlier. Liz has seemingly had a rough time of it, being psychologically abused by Dennis (a development Moore set up in "Loose Ends"), who has convinced her that Sunderland is still hunting them and that everything poses a massive and terrible danger—so much so that at the start of the issue she spends forty minutes "sick with indecision" trying to decide if it is safe to plug in a television set while wearing rubber gloves and oven mitts to protect herself from electrocution, and only doing so because she is desperate for human contact after Dennis goes out for three days. Moore lingers on these scenes, allowing them to play out with a considerable and visceral horror that is unsettling in ways little else in Moore's run, and certainly little else in horror comics is. In many ways the scenes, even though they do not actually contain any direct sexual violence, fall into the larger pattern of Moore's depiction of rape, but there's an edge and anger to them that goes beyond even that, finally paying off the myriad of abusive relationships Moore had been depicting in *Swamp Thing* since the beginning, including Abby and Matt's. Moore had been building to this story for years, having talked as early as 1984 about it in response to a question about drawing on real-world, contemporary aspects of society to craft horror stories. "I'd tell you a contemporary horror story," Moore replies, "but I'm going to use it as the Liz and Dennis storyline, and I don't want to give too much away. However, it's something that really happened to a cousin of mine. It's about the destruction of one human being's whole personality by another. That's an example of human evil that, to me, is more frightening than any number of demons from hell." Moore reiterates this at the start of the issue's script, describing it as "a completely bloody mind-grinding horror story to hear," and detailing the horrors actually inflicted upon his relative (in fact a cousin's sister-in-law, as opposed to a cousin), many of which he lifted directly for the issue.

Liz's tentative steps towards independence in Dennis's absence lead her to discover that Dennis had lied to her about Abby and Swamp Thing's death, which causes her to seek out Abby, who has returned to Houma following Swamp Thing's death. She is pursued, however, by Dennis, who ultimately chases Liz and Abby out into the swamp with a machine gun. Liz ultimately works her way around a flower-covered bog, which Dennis foolishly runs into, sinking underwater and water-logging his gun. As he advances upon them, boasting about how he "waded through puddles wider than this in 'Nam'" and telling Abby that she "spoiled a beautiful romance, bitch, and I'm gonna club your brains right out." But as he gloats, a crocodile advances out of the swamp; he's ultimately ripped apart by the animals. What is really significant, however, is the panel in which the crocodile makes its appearance, slowly emerging amidst the flowers, which spread across his snout so as to frame his red eyes and nose into a mirror of Swamp Thing's iconic visage, thus tacitly admitting that Swamp Thing remains alive.

"I love the way science SOUNDS. I love the ideas for their art. There's a crazy beauty about a theory of dimensional structure that assembles itself into a snowflake, or the idea that reality is a two-dimensional plane of information and the 3-D universe is a hologrammatic side effect. And that's how I write science fiction. I use the sound of the ideas and then make it all up. And then it all comes true anyway."
–Warren Ellis, 2004

This is confirmed in the next issue, which focuses primarily on Abby's attendance of a memorial service for Swamp Thing, and in which she comes to terms with her loss. At the end of the service a man comes up to her and introduces himself as Boston Brand. He explains that he's "checked out all the places he might have ended up," and says that as far as he can tell, Swamp Thing isn't in any afterlife. The issue ends with four pages of page-tall narrow panels that zoom out from Abby leaving a rose upon Swamp

Figure 149: Swamp Thing's face appears in implication. (From Swamp Thing #54, *written by Alan Moore, art by Rick Veitch and Alfredo Alcala, 1986)*

Figure 150: The steady pan out from Gotham towards the planet on which Swamp Thing's consciousness has landed. (From Swamp Thing #55, *written by Alan Moore, art by Rick Veitch and Alfredo Alcala, 1986)*

Thing's memorial, out to the city streets, out to the planet, and finally across the cosmos. Captions narrate Abby's final acceptance of her lover's death, in which she misunderstands the words Deadman said to her. "Maybe a wino's delusion is the best thing I have to cling to right now," she thinks. "Perhaps when we die, there's another world somewhere. Perhaps there's a heaven so big it has room for someone like you. I hope so. I hope you're there now. Goodbye, my love. Goodbye." At which point the steady pan out finally arrives, galaxies away, at a crater on an alien planet. With a "*sklitch! pwack scluc kwilp thap pletch*," a figure emerges, stark blue and made of alien vegetation, but nevertheless, clearly the Swamp Thing.

This marks the beginning of Moore's final arc on *Saga of the Swamp Thing*—a nine-issue story about Swamp Thing's return to Earth. By this point, as Moore puts it, "I'd done nearly all my original ideas on the book, all the ones that Steve and John had contributed to, all the ones I'd subsequently come up with—I'd pretty much done everything that I'd wanted with the character." The final arc, then, was designed as "this big space storyline" where "I'd get all of my science-fiction Swamp Thing ideas out of my system." Moore did not even write all nine issues, with both Steve Bissette and Rick Veitch (who Moore had by this point tapped as his successor on the book) chipping in fill-in stories. Bissette's, in *Swamp Thing* #59, exists mainly to heap further indignities upon Abby at the hands of Anton Arcane, while Veitch's (slotted between Moore's final space-based story and the issue where Swamp Thing finally returns to Earth) gives Swamp Thing an adventure with Jack Kirby's New Gods.

Moore's ideas for sci-fi based *Swamp Thing* stories broadly fit into two categories: experimental stories that extended the psychedelic approach that characterized much of Moore's *Swamp Thing* work, and stories that let Moore play with a few more DC properties he'd been a fan of in his youth. The first issue of the arc, in *Swamp Thing* #56, fits into the former category. Entitled "My Blue Heaven," the story features Swamp Thing on a planet teeming with plants and insect life, but with no intelligent life whatsoever. In total isolation, Swamp Thing explores the world, contemplating the vast blue landscape and the different shades: "The color of African skin... of shadow on snow... of a jay's throat... the color of saxophones at dusk... of orbiting police lights smeared across tenement windows... of a flame's intestines... of the faint tracery of veins beneath the ghost flesh of her forearm's underside... of loneliness... of melancholy." He experiments with different types of bodies, growing a body with air sacs that can float across the landscape, and growing a second body with which he can play chess (although every game ends in stalemate). Eventually he grows a doppelgänger of Abby, and an entire duplicate of Houma over which he can serve as demiurge. But within his soulless vegetable city he finds a version of John Constantine (appearing "at the corner table" of the Houma diner "alone in the concealing shadows," a description that echoes Moore's first encounter with Constantine in a sandwich shop) who points out to him that he is merely talking to himself. Unable now to avoid seeing the artifice of his creation, Swamp Thing destroys his world in a fit of rage and finally flees, without knowing if there is anywhere he can possibly land, and concluding that death is preferable to this isolated hell.

In many ways this echoes Moore's third issue of *Swamp Thing*, "Swamped," in which Swamp Thing nearly loses himself in the green as he reels from the revelation that he is not in fact Alec Holland. As in "Swamped," Swamp Thing encounters a wealth of phantasms and mirrors of his past life, and nearly loses his identity in the face of them. But whereas in "Swamped" he is ultimately happy to surrender himself to the green, finding it a place where he can at last be at peace and be happy, in "My Blue Heaven" his memory of and love for Abby renders the equivalent solitude unbearable, a testament to the breadth of change the character has undergone in the thirty-five issues since "Swamped."

Having completed his meditations, Swamp Thing proceeds to jump through a series of other alien worlds, which Moore uses to explore the possible intersections between Swamp Thing and the science fiction in DC's line of comics. First is a two-issue story featuring Adam Strange, a present-day human created by Julius Schwartz and most associated with the 1950s/60s sci-fi anthology series *Mystery in Space* (from which Moore derives the title of the arc's first issue), who occasionally traveled from Earth to the alien planet of Rann via the Rannian's "Zeta Beam" and had space adventures in the Buck Rogers/John Carter tradition. Moore matches up Strange with another set of DC aliens, the Thanagarians, who discovered a substance called Nth metal that defies gravity, and used it to dress up in hawk costumes, which provided the Silver Age origin story for Hawkman. The story is a fairly standard bit of space opera with few ideas save for Moore's obvious love for the characters involved (Strange's run in *Mystery in Space* ran from 1959-65, or from the ages of six to twelve for Moore, while Thanagar first appeared in 1961, and got his own series in 1964).

After the Bissette-penned fill-in issue, Moore continues with an issue titled after a David Bowie song, "Loving the Alien," which serves as an opportunity for John Totleben to engage in a more experimental art style than he'd previously been able to, and lets Moore stretch into one of the most avant garde plots he'd written. The issue is constructed entirely in splash pages, with no dialogue to speak of, but is rather narrated by a mysterious alien entity, part flesh, part machine, floating in space and seeking a mate. Only Totleben's art, drawn as a series of psychedelic collages that often feature only the vaguest implication of Swamp Thing's figure, makes it clear who the "ghost" is that haunts the narrator's insides. Moore's narration, meanwhile, is an extended exercise in writing from a profoundly alien perspective. "How shall I say it," the narrator writes, "how to describe the effect this last bare fact worked in me? He was of my flesh. I was melted by the implications. Yes... yes, that is it! 'Melted.' Not for my body, that was not melted, save for the unchanging magma, boiling ceaselessly around my nuclear core. Not my body, but rather my mind; my psychostructure; my self. My self is what melted. All the precisely indexed data, sucked greedily from the computer systems of a thousand doomed alien vessels; all my art and science and neurosynthesis; the logarithms and sines; the very formula of what I am… melted." It's a strange and slightly disorienting account of what is, in effect, the alien creature falling in love with Swamp Thing when he attempts to incarnate out of the plant matter that is the alien. The story is in most regards an interesting experiment as opposed to an entirely successful one, but nevertheless demonstrates Moore continuing to aggressively push himself even as he was bringing his time on *Swamp Thing* to a close.

The final portion of the outer space arc comes in *Swamp Thing* #61, a story called "All Flesh is Grass." On one level this story is another excuse for Moore to play with a personal favorite concept within DC. But on another, it is an attempt to invert the premise of *Swamp Thing* and find a new way to do horror stories with it. This is not insignificant. Depending on the particulars of one's definition, it is possible to argue that the last time Moore actually wrote a horror story in *Swamp Thing* was "A Murder of Crows," all the way back in *Swamp Thing* #48. Certainly it has not been the dominant mode for the title to work in for some time. But in "All Flesh is Grass," Moore finds a genuinely new way to attack the genre. The premise is that Swamp Thing finally makes it to the planet J586, suggested by Adam Strange at the end of that story, where it might be possible to fix Swamp Thing's ability to communicate with plants so that he can talk to the Earth again. Unfortunately, as he materializes on J586, he realizes too late that all of the plant life on the planet is in fact sentient, and that he has built his body and consciousness out of thousands of living people, all of whose identities collide with his own, driving him hopelessly mad. Veitch depicts the scene in a nightmarish double page spread in which Swamp

Figure 151: John Totleben's experimental artwork for Swamp Thing *#60. (Written by Alan Moore, 1987)*

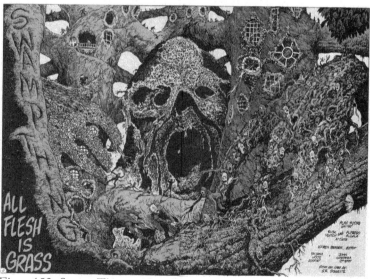

Figure 152: Swamp Thing accidentally incarnates as a grotesque assemblage of other people's bodies. (From Swamp Thing *#61, written by Alan Moore, art by Rick Veitch and Alfredo Alcala, 1987)*

Thing's hands are formed out of screaming and horrified alien faces, while Moore narrates the psychological distress of the people trapped within Swamp Thing's body. "The horror swiped blindly, gestured inarticulately, nothing but amok. In each hand a polite and well-mannered family clenched into a fist of bitterness and recrimination. The horror ran, palms damp with angry tears, fingers quarrelling."

Rescuing J586 from Swamp Thing's rampage is Medphyl, the sector's representative to the Green Lantern Corps. The Green Lantern Corps extends out of the Silver Age revamp of Green Lantern, away from the iconography of orientalist adventure and towards an expansive concept in which Green Lantern is just one of a vast organization of what are in effect intergalactic police, each patrolling a sector of space emerging conically out of the planet Oa, at the center of the universe, where the Green Lantern Corps is headquartered. Moore had long been fond of the concept, and his Order of the Black Sun back in his aborted 4-D War storyline for *Doctor Who Monthly* was, by his own admission, him nicking the concept on the assumption that he would never actually get a chance to write a Green Lantern story of his own.

This was, obviously, an incorrect assumption. Indeed, "All Flesh is Grass" is not even the only opportunity Moore had to write Green Lantern stories. During his time at DC, he wrote a trio of short stories featuring the characters. These stories in many ways resemble DC Universe versions of his *Future Shocks* for *2000 AD*—all are short stories featuring twist endings.

The first, "Mogo Doesn't Socialize," pairs Moore with Dave Gibbons for a story about a Green Lantern named Mogo and why he doesn't attend meetings of the Green Lantern Corps. It features Bolphunga the Unrelenting, who is said to possess "the strength of a Denebian Dozerbull, the endurance of a Lalotian Lava-Limpet, and the intelligence of a bed of kelp." Bolphunga decides that he will destroy the feared and powerful Green Lantern known as Mogo, and lands upon the planet on which Mogo is known to inhabit.

Over the course of three pages Bolphunga searches for Mogo, but finds nothing save for a series of vast and carefully cut clearings. Eventually, mapping the planet, he realizes the awful truth: that the clearings form the insignia of the Green Lanterns, and that Mogo is not a being upon the planet but is in fact a sentient planet, which in turn explains why Mogo never shows up at meetings: "His gravity field, you see. It would pull Oa apart."

A similar sense of wit pervades Moore's third Green Lantern story, "In Blackest Night." In this one, a Green Lantern named Katma Tui must explain to the Guardians how she was unable to find a Green Lantern to serve "in the black and lightless void known as the Obsidian Deeps." The problem, Katma explains, is that the being she found, Rot Lop Fan, was unable to understand the idea of a Green Lantern, since, residing in the Obsidian Deeps, he has no ability to comprehend the concepts of color or light. And so Katma Tui is forced to translate the concept, replacing the idea of a lantern with a bell, and the color green with the tone F-Sharp, which Rot Lop Fan finds particularly "soothing and restful." And so instead of the Green Lanterns' traditional oath, Rot Lop Fan proclaims that "In loudest din or hush profound / my ears catch evil's slightest sound / let those who toll out evil's knell / beware my power: The F-Sharp Bell!" And so, she explains to the Guardians, "I did appoint a worthy protector to the Obsidian Deeps... however I'm not sure if he qualifies as a member of the Green Lantern Corps, for in truth he's never even heard of us!"

"In the darkest part of the swamp, he pauses. A monstrous black bird flaps overhead, momentarily eclipsing the sun. LaBostrie feels his skin crawl and moves on. Below, in the green tank of swamp water, something stirs. And rises."
–Grant Morrison and Mark Millar, *Swamp Thing*, 1994

But it is in most regards the second of his three Green Lantern stories that is most interesting. One of two collaborations he did with Kevin O'Neill while at DC, the story, entitled "Tygers," tells of the death of Abin Sur, the predecessor to Hal Jordan as the Green Lantern for Earth's sector of space. The story is notable for several reasons. For one, it is the story that Moore was referring to in later interviews where he accused DC of "going through my trashcan like raccoons in the dead of night." The story responsible for provoking that comment was a 2009 Green Lantern-based crossover written by Geoff Johns, which actually owes relatively little to "Tygers" save for featuring some characters from the alien planet on which it is set, although it is true that an extended prophecy given within "Tygers" has been extensively mined by both Johns and other writers for story concepts.

For another, as its title suggests, the story owes a considerable debt to William Blake. The bulk of this debt is subtle—no actual Blakean concepts or images appear within the story, and although Kevin O'Neill draws a number of memorably grotesque and bizarre horrors in the story, his style in "Tygers" is far from a straightforward imitation of Blake, nor even an homage. O'Neill's art is nevertheless striking, and in many ways he comes closer to the spirit of Blake by doing his own strange and visionary style instead of an imitation. The shambling creature Quill of the Five Inversions, whose prophecies ultimately lure Abin Sur to his demise, is an astonishingly gruesome and monstrous figure who, though he has no obvious counterpart in Blake's art or mythology, bristles with an unsettling power that few other artists could provide.

In a happily generative coincidence, the name of planet upon which Abin Sur is so fatally tempted, Ysmault, is, upon its first mention, split across two lines by letterer John Costanza, causing it to become hyphenated as "Ysm-Ault," a spacing which reveals the hidden word "Ault," which is the surname of Donald Ault, a prominent American scholar specializing both in William Blake and in the comics of Carl Banks, creator of Scrooge McDuck. Ault's most famous work at the time was his 1974 text *Visionary Physics*, which argues that rather than just being a convenient bogeyman that Blake famously rails against when he rejects "single vision & Newtons sleep," it is instead more accurate to consider Blake's work as an elaborate response to Newton, whose system Blake views as "providing a usurpation of and substitution for the very vision he himself is trying to communicate."

Ault traces the evolution of Blake's engagement with Newton, from its earliest form in *The Book of Urizen*, in which the demonic figure of reason, Urizen, is described via what Ault describes as "several obviously Newtonian concepts: the 'void,' 'all-repelling,' 'this abominable void,' 'this soul-shudd'dring vacuum,' 'measurement,' 'dark revolving,' 'globes of attraction,'" as well as "several more obscure allusions, such as 'the rolling of wheels / As of swelling seas,' referring to Newton's reduction of the motions of the tides to the motions of revolving planets," to a later model in which Newton and Urizen are equated with Satan, who "has tricked fallen man" into subscribing to their system, which Blake recognizes as having a sinister but potent appeal to the Imagination. Blake's response rejects the very idea of systems, instead dividing experience into "symbolic 'States' which preserve the integrity of the individual identity yet which 'abolish' systems" in favor of a world of endless change and infinite differences that exists in simultaneous Eternity.

This evolution of Blake's response is also visible in his treatment of the possibility of a decisive overthrowing of Urizen, from Los's failed attempt to bind him in *The Book of Urizen* to Blake's ultimate rejection of Orc and the charismatic revolution he augurs in *America a Prophecy*. Both, ultimately, merely offer new systems that purport to replace the Newtonian one, but that ultimately only reiterate the flawed fixity of Newtons sleep. Instead, Blake embraces an altogether more variable and strange system. A similar move takes place in Moore's final two issues of *Swamp Thing*, in which he returns to the questions of eschatology and revolution that he explored in the issues between Swamp Thing's second and third deaths.

These final two issues return to the dualistic structure that has recurred in Moore's *Swamp Thing* since "Windfall." The first, titled, in Moore's typical elliptical fashion, "Loose Ends (Reprise)," alternates between a tour of several of the secondary characters from throughout Moore's run, checking in on Matt Cable and Wallace Monroe, as well as looking at Abby, Chester, and Liz, and on Swamp Thing's vengeful return as he hunts down and takes grotesque vengeance on those responsible for his most recent death. The issue ends with Swamp Thing finally returning to Abby, leading into Moore's final issue, "Return of the Good Gumbo."

Where "Loose Ends (Reprise)" focuses on Swamp Thing as an essentially wrathful figure, with the character almost entirely absent from the issue, appearing only in his chakra-based spirit form in a two-page spread early on in the issue prior to his final page reunion with Abby, "Return of the Good Gumbo" offers an entirely more merciful figure. The issue is framed by a description of Gene LaBostrie, a man in a Louisiana village who punts across the swamp, musing on how "it is as if the spirit has departed from this land. The children cry and give no explanation. Prematurely aged by Spanish moss the trees stand sulking, waiting for a word of reconciliation no one can pronounce. Each day's sun seems less willing to begin its labored, struggling ascent towards the shadeless pinnacles of noon, less eager to drive back the ebb-tide night across the swamps and turn their mirror-ribboned streams to chrome." This monologue's call for some lost spirit is tacitly answered by the next page, a literal splash page of a bird landing in the water in front of Abby and Swamp Thing reclining beneath a tree and besides the story's title.

Throughout the issue, Swamp Thing ponders the question left broadly unanswered by the Gotham City triptych. "Am I not a god?" he asks. "I could touch all the world with gorgeous wilderness as I touched Gotham. Could transform this planet to a sphere of colors, perfumes, and full bellies. Anything." Abby, meanwhile, talks of her time working with Chester in an ecological activist group, but bemoans the slow progress. "There was talk about dumping waste here, but we kicked up, so they abandoned the idea. Uh, well, that is, they dumped it someplace else," she admits. "Sometimes, I think for us to really help the environment, we'd need a different world." The observation causes an awkward silence, broken when Swamp Thing grows a tuber for her to eat and they make love for the first time since his return.

This lovemaking is depicted in a return to the iconography of "Rite of Spring," which flows into a sequence in which Swamp Thing sits awake next to her and continues to reflect on the question of whether to save the world by overthrowing it. He thinks over the death of Alec Holland that gave him birth, and thinks about the Parliament of Trees, "a dynasty spanning the eons, reaching back to times before mankind, whose only record now is etched on sheets of coal, far underground. A dynasty of gods." Pages recount the epochs of life on Earth, as Swamp Thing wonders why his predecessors did not simply keep the Precambrian Eden clean of animals, or why in the Silurian age they "never made this world a cool Piscean paradise, nor when the fish with legs boiled up from the Devonian mud did they impose reptilian utopia." And each eon is shown to have its plant elemental, a vegetable creature befitting the fauna of the age, from fish to dinosaur (finally giving Bissette a chance to draw one), until at last there is a panel of Swamp Thing standing and watching the sun rise.

"Is this," he asks, "what it means to be a God? To know, and never do? To watch the world wind by, and in its windings find content? If I should feed the world, heal all the wounds man's smoldering industries have made, what would he do? Would he renounce the wealth his sawmills bring, step gently on the flowers instead, and pluck each apple with respect for this abundant world in all its providence? No. He would pump more poisons, build more mines, safe in the knowledge that I stood on hand to mend the biosphere, endlessly covering the scars he could now endlessly inflict." And so he yields, averting wrath and revolution. Instead he goes deep into the swamp and builds from trees and flowers a home for him and Abby to retire to. Declaring her his princess, he summons a lily pad to serve as a raft, and they sail out to their new home together, arms entwined. They say their farewells to Liz and Chester, who are ecstatic for their friends. Swamp Thing embraces Liz, seeing her for the first time in many issues, and gently reassures her as she continues to heal from the traumas inflicted upon her. And with that they walk out into the swamp, together, as Chester and Liz hold hands and face the future.

From there the scene cuts to the sleazebag photographer whose images of Abby and Swamp Thing led to so much trouble, as he tries to get Gene LaBostrie to tell him where the Swamp Thing can be found. LaBostrie feigns to not speak English, "spreads his hands in mimed apology, then shoves his craft out" to guide him home. "Do they think money's everything?" LaBostrie contemplates. "The only yardstick that life's quality is measured by? Yes, yes they do, and that is why they are so very poor." And as he thinks this, he catches sight of Swamp Thing, a shadow in the grass, waving at him, and LaBostrie, drawn to look like Alan Moore himself, waves a final farewell to the character upon which he made his reputation in America, and upon five years of comics that would prove to change the world forever.

And that is it. No fiery retribution, for all of Moore's obvious rage. Whatever darkness sits within the heart of this new world, Moore opts to let it remain there, perhaps in the hope that it will, as Swamp Thing suggested, breed some greater virtue. There is no fury of Orc—no red flames melting the heavens nor plagues creeping upon burning winds. Whatever apocalypse Moore might have envisioned and considered, in *Swamp Thing* at least, in the end he declines to bring it down upon America, even symbolically. Instead there is what Moore describes as "a kind of 'happy ever after'

Figure 153: The reunion of Swamp Thing and Abby is portrayed in a sort of bayou-pastoral style. (From Swamp Thing #64, written by Alan Moore, 1987)

Figure 154: Alan Moore waves goodbye to the longest single run of comics of his career. (From Swamp Thing #64, 1987)

ending" where "Swamp Thing and Abigail just go and grow themselves a fairy-tale household in the swamp and, as far as I'm concerned, they live happily ever after." And so on the final page of Moore's run Gene LaBostrie, and in turn Moore, returns home, "walks down his village street and lets the laughing children tease him, grabbing at his trailing coat. In every garden cabbages and onions grow so big and succulent a man might cry. The cooking smells and fiddle strains are tangled in the summer air, both equally as sweet. Good god is in his heaven. Good gumbo's in the pot. LaBostrie moves his black-fringed lips in something very like a prayer: 'Laissez les bontemps rouler.' Please. For us. For all of us... Laissez les bontemps rouler." And with that, Moore brought his longest engagement with American comics to a polite and benedictive end: a prayer for peace.

There is no sense in which this prayer was answered.

Chapter Nine: V for Vendetta (The Warrior Years)

"Please. For us. For all of us... Laissez les bontemps rouler."
—Alan Moore, *Swamp Thing*, 1987

Moore's final issue of *Swamp Thing* came out in June of 1987, one month before the famously delayed *Watchmen* #12. One month later, Grant Morrison, who had spent the preceding two years steadily building a comics career by almost perfectly duplicating the steps of an early-career Alan Moore, took on his first ongoing assignment for *2000 AD*, a conscious response to Moore's work and an overt effort to rewrite the territory that Moore had just established; less than a year after that he would make his own leap to America with a blatant attempt on DC's part to copy the success they had with Moore on *Swamp Thing*. Moore, on the other hand, would do two further projects with DC before acrimoniously parting ways with them: a Batman story with Brian Bolland, and the concluding third of *V for Vendetta*, a project rescued from the wreckage that was *Warrior*. This comic, a bracing adventure story about the violent overthrow of the government by an anarchist terrorist, is exactly the unsparing howl of rage against the systems of the world that *Swamp Thing* ultimately declines to be.

From its first installment, back in 1982, amidst Moore's earliest works, *V for Vendetta* crackles with mad gusto. The first page brazenly sets a scene with all the fascist gusto of *2000 AD*'s Judge Dredd, only with none of the broad comedic satire that characterized that strip. Instead it is an all too familiar near-future world, recognizably just a few of history's happenstances removed from the world of its readers. It is a few months shy of sixteen years in the future, with an unsettlingly phrased radio broadcast identified as the "Voice of Fate." The language, quietly evoking Moore and Lloyd's previous collaboration on a story for *Doctor Who* that featured the evil plastic alien Autons, is plastic and stilted: it is "the fifth of the eleventh, nineteen-ninety-seven," a declaration that is followed by a bizarrely precise weather forecast promising that "the weather will be fine until 12:07 A.M. when a shower will commence lasting until 1:30 A.M." Note the care with which Moore sets up the unsettling nature of this—the first number is weirdly over-specific, whereas the second is a nice, round number like one would expect from a weather forecast. This broadcast is contrasted with David Lloyd's starkly monochromatic art, which begins with a soaring skyline before cutting to a mass of people heading home in wide shot. A third panel focuses on a detail from the image, a CCTV camera pointed at the street, atop a sign that proclaims, "FOR YOUR PROTECTION."

From this introduction, the art and voiceover both take a turn for the dark. We are told that "the Brixton and Streatham areas are quarantine zones as of today," as militaristic men patrol a jet-black street in an equally jet-black car, their authoritarian uniforms pillars of light within the film noir abyss. "Productivity reports from Herefordshire indicate a possible end to meat rationing starting from mid-February 1998," and note the contrast to the date earlier on the page, while a scared-looking girl applies make-up. The productivity reports are, it is instantly obvious, bullshit. There is no chance of meat rationing ending in February of 1998, and the crap apartment of the unnamed female hammers home the point that this is a world that in just sixteen years has gone to complete shit. Immediately a Moore devotee gets the sense of

Figure 155: Moore's choice of CCTV cameras all over London as a signifier of fascism proved disturbingly prescient. (Written by Alan Moore, art by David Lloyd, from "The Villain" in Warrior #1, 1982)

Figure 156: The semiotically dense first glimpse of the Shadow Gallery. (Written by Alan Moore, art by David Lloyd, from "The Villain" in Warrior #1, 1982)

Roxy from Moore's later *Skizz*—the squalid and resignedly accepted life of poverty's misery, far worse in this world than the slice-of-life Birmingham of 1983.

The page's last panel is a wide shot of a man approaching a mirror, seen from behind, and too far from the mirror for his face to be visible. He is bisected by shadow, half-white, half-black, and his own figure bisecting the psychedelic Rorschach Blot of a carpet. The mirror is a bulb-lit vanity clearly from an actor's dressing room. Atop it are a wig and mask. The walls of the room are plastered with posters for classic films, but with a clear cinephile's selection. The horror super-cast of Basil Rathbone teaming up to kill the Boris Karloff's monstrous but sympathetic Frankenstein (his last turn in the part), who tragically obeys only the villainous and psychotic blacksmith Ygor (played by Béla Lugosi), sits next to a poster for the decade-later James Cagney vehicle *White Heat*, in which Cagney scintillates as a mad gangster. Next to them is a poster for the 1932 *Murders in the Rue Morgue*, also starring Lugosi as a marvelously mad scientist. A bookshelf on the opposite side of the room contains four books with visible titles: Thomas Moore's *Utopia*, Harriet Beecher Stowe's *Uncle Tom's Cabin*, Karl Marx's *Capital*, and Adolf Hitler's *Mein Kampf*. The captions continue, talking about a police raid upon "what is believed to be a major terrorist ring," adding another layer to this rich collage of ostentatious villainy both glamorous and monstrous, white and black as the page itself.

The scene continues upon the second page, with the unnamed female and the male both getting dressed, the man pulling on gloves and a grinning alabaster mask, then standing revealed before the mirror, all theatrical flourish, wide cloak and dramatic hat. To his right, a close-up of the poster for *White Heat*, the caption of the radio broadcast's sign-off obscures some of the poster, so that it reads simply "Jimmy ... in his New Hit from Warner Bros." Below it, a second placard, all 1930s' cabaret lettering, proclaims: "Chapter One / THE VILLAIN." The left-hand adjacent panel features the young girl, her face an alabaster mask of worry as she checks her makeup one last time, implicit plural to the chapter's title. As Moore is working within the British tradition of short chapters from which he found liberation in DC's twenty-two page periodicals, he opts to split the page between this and a second scene, a transition Lloyd emphasizes by leaving the top two rows of panels dominated by whites, and the bottom two anchored by blacks. A man smokes a pipe and stands against the corner of a brick building. Moore indulges in one of *V for Vendetta*'s handful of non-diegetic narrative captions, laying out a moral thesis statement on which to pin this entire procession of lurid and uncensored mischief. "Parliament's cold shadow," Moore writes in familiar iambs, "falls on Westminster Bridge and she shivers. There was power here once, power that decided the destiny of millions. Her transactions, her decisions, are insignificant. They affect no one... except her." The third person feminine pronoun refers to the woman seen applying makeup. "Mister," she asks, Zelda Estrella lettering the dialogue box smaller than the text of the captions. "...Uh...would...would you like to...uh..." she stammers, awkward and pathetic, "sleep with me or anything?... I mean... uh... for money?" she finishes, meekly, confirming the narration's assessment of her insignificance.

The third page opens with a reverse shot of the man she's tried to pick up, who smiles thinly and proclaims her efforts "the clumsiest bit of propositioning I've ever heard." He suggests that she's not been doing this long, and she confirms with a wince, "I must be really terrible," and, "It's my first night." She's got a job, she explains, but it doesn't pay enough, and she really needs the money—a familiar litany of working class misery, in other words. "I'm sixteen," she insists, heartbreakingly, "I know what I'm doing." The man points out that she does not, in fact; he reaches into his trench coat, pulls out a badge, and explains, "If you did you wouldn't have picked a vice detail on stakeout."

With this, his colleagues step from the shadows, five men

employed to take in one harmless would-be prostitute, while the "Fingerman" (as the woman calls him) explains that prostitution is "a Class-H offence. That means we get to decide what happens to you. That's our *prerogative*." The woman begs them not to kill her, her letters becoming small and meek again, framing the propaganda poster of whatever sick regime this is, its slogan stamped "STRENGTH THROUGH PURITY PURITY THROUGH FAITH." She pleads that she'll "do anything you want," but the pigs explain to her how this will actually work: "You've got it all wrong, miss. You'll do anything we want and then we'll kill you. That's our prerogative," he repeats, by way of explanation, and Lloyd draws a narrow-paneled close-up of her wide-eyed, tear-stained face on the verge of rape, in the style of Frank Miller's beautifully sliced rectangles of noir beauty in *Daredevil*.

We then go out to a wider panel in which the cloaked figure, unseen since the title card, stands, again cast half in brilliant white and half in printer's shadow, and begins to speak his rhyme: "The multiplying villainies of nature do swarm upon him," he proclaims, beginning to quote an account of Macbeth's valor in combat from the first act of Shakespeare's play, while one of the Fingermen begins the question, "Who the hell...," a note on which the page ends, marking the halfway point of the installment.

The fourth page opens with a scene of confusion—the masked man advances forward, continuing his monologue from Macbeth, while the Fingermen attempt to block his path and speculate as to his identity, suggesting that he's "some kinda retard got out of a hospital," and warn him that he's "in trouble, chum. Big trouble... This woman is a criminal. We're police officers. She's wanted for interrogation, so keep your...," but before the man can finish his sentence, the nature of the scene shifts out from under him. The second row of panels begins with a panel of a man holding a detached hand, staring at it as he completes the thought from the preceding panel: "hands off?" The masked man is gone from the panel, his cloak billowing behind him, showing that he's already moved on from this scene. The next panel shows where—the detached hand is still visible in the top left of the panel, but the image is dominated by the masked man, shown from behind, cloak still furling out behind him as he charges towards the girl. The cloak fills most of the frame, and it is impossible to tell exactly what he's doing, but the expression of agony on one of the Fingermen's faces and the way in which the other one seems to have been thrown backwards suggests violence. "Disdaining fortune with his brandished steel, which smoked with bloody execution, like Valour's minion carved out his passage till he faced the slave," the masked man continues as he reaches the girl, who stares at him, meekly saying "oh" in the smallest of letters. The masked man faces to the right, implicitly completing the motion implied by his rushing out of shot at the first panel in the sequence. Having reached her, he turns to the Fingermen, firing off tear gas and disappearing amidst their confusion.

It is this confusion that opens the fifth page, as the man holding the detached hand asks, "I got his hand. What shall I do with his…" Once again, he does not get to finish the thought, this time due to the hand's unexpected and fatal detonation. "Oh Jesus," one of the two surviving Fingermen says in horror, trying to figure out how his steadfast and reliable gig as a beat cop for a fascist authority has unexpectedly turned into a massacre at the hands of a ridiculously dressed man quoting Shakespeare. "We've got to find him," the other says firmly, "or the Head will have our guts." But the mysterious figure has already exited the scene—in the six panels of the Fingermen reacting to his attack, he is visible in only one, where they are shown in a long shot from above and behind, while in the foreground the man's boots and cape are visible, depicted in pure and unadulterated black.

It is not until the page's third row of panels that the masked man makes a full return, sitting on a roof top with the girl he's just saved from a grisly death, the Houses of Parliament and Big Ben visible across the Thames in the

Figure 157: Lloyd cuts from a close-up on Evey's terrified face to the reveal of V, lighting stressing his moral ambiguity. (Written by Alan Moore, art by David Lloyd, from "The Villain" in Warrior #1, 1982)

Figure 158: The artist signs his work. (Written by Alan Moore, art by David Lloyd, from "The Villain" in Warrior #1, 1982)

background. "You... you rescued me!" she exclaims, "like in a story! I don't believe it. Wh-who are you?" The man's reply is given in a panel consisting of a close-up of his masked face, his eyes further shrouded by the shadow of his hat brim. "Me?" he asks. "I'm the king of the twentieth century. I'm the bogeyman. The villain. The black sheep of the family," drawing a tacit link with the accoutrements initially seen in what might either be described as his lair or his dressing room and their common thread of embracing ostentatious villainy and discarded radicalism, whether generally socially acceptable as with *Utopia*, totally socially unacceptable as with *Mein Kampf*, or in a trickier space in between as with *Capital*. Understandably puzzled by his overtly cryptic answer, the girl asks what he's doing hanging around Westminster at night, to which the man explains, "Tonight is special. Tonight is a celebration. A grand opening. Were you never taught the rhyme?" he asks.

This leaves only Moore's sixth and most audacious page. It opens with an extreme close-up on the man, so that only one slit eye of his mask and its painted black curl of an eyebrow is visible. He intones the aforementioned rhyme: "Remember, remember, the fifth of November, the Gunpowder Treason and plot. I know of no reason why the Gunpowder Treason"—and at once, for any of the readership for whom the mere shape and visual of his outfit and mask was not sufficient to identify the character he is playing, he stands revealed as a man dressed in a Guy Fawkes costume.

> *"We would look out of the window every morning to make sure the bitch hadn't put Daleks on the streets yet."*
> –Warren Ellis, on Margaret Thatcher, 2011

As he provides the final three iambs of his rhyme, "should ever be forgot," the tacit promise of this costume is suddenly and triumphantly realized. The panel displays the man from behind, so that the audience looks over his shoulder towards the Houses of Parliament, which are in the midst of exploding. The remains of what was once the clock tower burst outwards, black fragments shattering against the white background of the explosion, the circles of the clock faces still implied in the negative space of the devastation. This is followed by another extremely narrow panel, showing the girl's shocked reaction with a close-up of one bulging eye—notably the left one, where the man's eye two panels earlier was the right, implicitly constructing a completed face framing the destruction of London's single most iconic landmark. "The Houses of Parliament," the girl exclaims. "Did you do that?"

"I did that," the man replies simply. And as he does, the narrative captions return: "The rumble of the explosion has not yet died away as from far below comes the rattle of smaller reports. And suddenly the sky is alight with…" it trails off, and the trail of thought is continued by the girl, looking up joyfully at the sky and shouting, "Fireworks! Real fireworks! Oh god, they're so beautiful!" And they are—eleven cumshot explosions over the noir night, arranged in an eponymous V. The narration continues over a panel further subdivided into four narrow columns depicting Londoners staring at the spectacle. "And all over London," it says, "windows are thrown open and faces lit with awe and wonder gaze at the omen scrawled in fire on the night." A final panel shows the man and woman in silhouette. "There," the man declares. "The overture is finished. Come. We must prepare for the first act." "Me?? B-but… Oh. Okay," the woman replies." "It is precisely 12:07 A.M. It begins to rain," the narration concludes. "To be continued," reads the title card.

In just six pages, then, Moore presents a dystopian future that is intensely grounded in the political reality of the time, introduces his two main characters, casts his lot with theatrical villains, and then blows up the Houses of Parliament. It is one of the most shocking and effective openings in comics, made even more impressive by the fact that the script was completed in July of 1981, at which point

Moore's published output consisted of *Roscoe Moscow* and the start of *The Stars My Degradation* for *Sounds*, two years' worth of *Maxwell the Magic Cat*, a dozen short stories for *2000 AD*, and some work in *Doctor Who Weekly*, none of which really suggested a writer capable of such an invigorating story.

Ultimately, two things contribute to the sense of radicalism. The first is how well-grounded in the present of 1982 Britain *V for Vendetta*'s dystopia is. The basic suggestion that Britain could be less than fifteen years from a fascist takeover is fundamentally unsettling. In the third installment, during a scene where Evey tells V her life story, Moore finally establishes that date as 1992, just a decade in the future. It is true that the prophesied details were quickly discredited—the *V for Vendetta* timeline assumes a Labour victory in the next General Election, with the fascist government rising to power because the (presumably) Foot government made good on an election promise to remove nuclear missiles from British soil, resulting in them being the only country to survive a 1988 nuclear war. And yet for all that some of the details were off, *V for Vendetta* was surprisingly prescient, most famously in its depressingly accurate prediction that by 1997 the streets of Britain would be lined with surveillance cameras to capture the population's every move. Similarly significant is the decision to ground Evey's past in the material reality of 1982. Evey grew up on Shooter's Hill, in the South of London, the home, of course, of Moore's friend and colleague Steve Moore, to whom Evey's father bears a marked resemblance in the photo Evey shows V. V alludes to "the recession of the eighties" as history, but it was of course a current event to the readership. The result of all of this is that the world of *V for Vendetta* is, while not the reader's own, inextricably connected to it—a world the reader is obliged, within the narrative, to treat as a serious cultural possibility.

The second factor, then, is the unwavering way in which the narrative takes seriously the idea that in the face of such a world, violent terrorism might be a reasonable action. Over time, this became one of the primary themes of *V for*

Vendetta, with the final chapter, published by DC Comics, focusing heavily on the moral legitimacy of violence as a tactic. But in the early installments it is difficult to have anything but sympathy for V and his titular vendetta. Certainly the first installment, for all that its title explicitly proclaims V to be the villain of the piece, is firmly on his side. The movie posters of the films, in which the most memorable characters are villainous raving lunatics, that adorn his Shadow Gallery make this clear, as, more bluntly, does the fact that the alternative to V, as presented in that installment, is a bunch of would-be rapists with badges. The thrilling denouement, blowing up Big Ben, is provocative, but it is clearly something the reader is meant to find thrilling. And it is thrilling, simply because Moore identifies an argument that is both tremendously compelling and yet widely treated as "improper" to speak aloud, namely that blowing shit up is, on the whole, a perfectly reasonable response to Thatcherism.

In this regard, as Moore is quick to admit, he is slotting into a grand British "tradition of making heroes out of criminals or people who in other centuries might have been regarded as terrorists." Elsewhere he notes that this tradition "goes back to Robin Hood, Charlie Peace, and Dick Turpin. All of these British criminals that actually are treated as heroes." The sentiment, it's clear, was shared by David Lloyd, who suggested to model the protagonist on Guy Fawkes because that would "look *really* bizarre *and* it would give Guy Fawkes the image he's deserved all these years. We shouldn't burn the chap every Nov. 5th but *celebrate* his attempt to blow up Parliament!" Moore, for his part, claims that upon receiving this suggestion, "Two things occurred to me. Firstly, Dave was obviously a lot less sane than I'd hitherto believed him to be, and secondly, this was the best idea I'd ever heard in my entire life."

But Moore is also quick to point out, when asked whether V is a hero, "We called the very first episode 'The Villain' because I thought there was an ambiguity there that I wanted to preserve," and, when pushed in a 2012 interview, makes clear V's violent tactics are "something I don't sympathize with," and that "of course" people should not actually go and blow up the Houses of Parliament, although he also notes that this is largely a plot point introduced in Book Three, and that the matter is left morally ambiguous prior to that point. That is not, however, to say that it isn't addressed. Indeed, the ninth chapter of Book One is entitled "Violence," and features as one of its central scenes Evey confronting V about the fact that he used her offer to help him to make her an accomplice to murder. V's response is typically oblique—he points out that it was Evey who offered to help V, and cryptically quotes Thomas Pynchon's *V*, but otherwise declines to engage with Evey's moral dilemma. Evey, for her part, comes back to V later in the issue, and apologizes, admitting that she "was trying to get out of taking the blame," but also emphatically declares that she won't be involved in killing again, a vow V witnesses in utter silence.

But these two scenes are interspersed among several others that also reflect on the titular theme of the chapter. It opens with Eric Finch, the detective hunting V, going over autopsy results, along with a cold and clinical discussion of the physical manifestation of violence: "The wound's been cleaned up a little, Eric," Doctor Delia Surridge explains, "but you can see that it has a fairly ragged edge. So you're right, it isn't a knife wound. It looks like something's been punched through the skin with incredible force." Later, there is a scene between Derek Almond, the head of the Finger, and his wife Rose, which culminates in a scene of domestic violence as Derek hits Rose and screams at her, "I don't have to take any of this crap from you! Not any of it!" And rounding out the issue is V finally coming for Dr. Surridge, who has been expecting him ever since Eric Finch gave her a rare rose that V had left at the scene of an earlier murder, and who has spent the issue remembering an image of a man, completely black in silhouette, framed by a massive fire behind him. When she realizes that V has come for her, she sits up in bed, and says, "It's you isn't it? You've come… you've come to kill me." V confirms this, and Dr. Surridge breaks down, saying "Oh thank God. Thank God."

And so Evey's non-debate with V over the use of violence is positioned in the context of a wealth of violent acts. There is no easy and straightforward moral conclusion to be drawn from all of these scenes. The incident between the Almonds is clearly horrific, but the clinical and detached description of the dead Fingerman's wounds at the outset and the subtleties implicit in Delia's joyful embrace of her imminent demise are altogether more ambiguous. They are certainly not things the reader is meant to look upon as straightforwardly pleasurable, but they are also not easily read as condemnations of the very idea of violence. Yes, Moore eventually arrives at the position that violence is categorically unacceptable, but crucially, this takes place years after the strip started, and after Moore and Lloyd have moved the comic from being published in the UK to being published in the US. It is not fair to call it an unexpected plot development, but it is fair to say that the strip could have developed in other directions.

But this is true of *V for Vendetta* in a more general case as well. The strip was conceived and the script for the first installment written in 1981, while the final installment didn't see print until 1989. Any project would drift and evolve over that sort of time period, even before one considers the degree to which Moore's career evolved over those eight years. Certainly the strip gradually grows more stylistically confident over time. Moore and Lloyd determined at the outset that they would keep narration to a minimum and entirely eliminate sound effects and thought bubbles. Moore, in the early chapters, still uses narration for key events, but he gradually manages to eliminate them entirely, using them for the last time in the fourth installment, where he narrates the effect that changing the person who delivers the periodic "Voice of Fate" broadcasts has on the British population. After that, Moore finds ways to communicate information by giving the role of narration to specific characters. From the beginning of his career Moore displayed an instinctive understanding of the way in which words and images could be used to provide two parallel streams of information, but this skill takes a visible leap forward in the seventh installment of *V for Vendetta*, "Virtue Victorious," published in November of 1982, where he runs narration from the corrupt Bishop of Westminster as he prays before engaging in sexual relations with someone he believes to be a fifteen-year-old girl, but who is in fact an undercover Evey sent by V. "Dear God... thou who has granted us reprieve from thy final judgement, thou who has provided us with that most terrible warning, help us to be worthy of thy mercy," the bishop intones, while the art shows events from an entirely different scene as V kills the bishop's guards and makes his way to his window.

The effect is a common one in Moore's repertoire, using the contrast between text and image to communicate things that neither can communicate on their own. But by November of 1982, the closest thing he had done to this sort of contrast was "The English/Phlondrutian Phrasebook" with Brendan McCarthy for *2000 AD*, in which humorous sayings from a hypothetical tourist guidebook for an alien planet are juxtaposed with scenes from a nightmarish visit to said planet. But "Virtue Victorious" does not use its contrast for comedy, or, at least, not for any straightforward comedy, and the point is not the contrast between the bishop's words and the images, but the way in which the two intersect and resemble each other. The bishop is praying for divine forgiveness for the child molestation he's about to commit, but when he speaks of "the evil one who is surely come amongst us in this, the hour of our greatest trial," the images of V fighting his way through the guards give clear double meaning to these words.

"Institutions and authorities designed for the far simpler reality of just a hundred years ago have burst their banks; have found their timework

Figure 159: Moore juxtaposes the Bishop's prayers with V's attack. (Written by Alan Moore, art by David Lloyd, from "Virtue Victorious" in Warrior *#7, 1982)*

principles inadequate to a flash influx of revelation, an unruly torrent carrying us all struggling towards the edge of a Niagra future in amidst our driftwood debris of outmoded ideologies."
–Alan Moore, birthday greeting to Chelsea Manning, 2014

The sequence is not unprecedented—it is in many ways simply a refinement of the technique Moore was using back in the first installment, where he had V quoting Macbeth while slicing his way through the Fingermen threatening Evey. But the refinement is in this case significant, with the text and images in "Virtue Victorious" coming from two distinct scenes that are allowed, in effect, to play simultaneously. As the comic went on, Moore grew even more confident, eventually doing away with most of the dialogue and words entirely and giving Lloyd stretches of pages at a time in which the storytelling is entirely visual, or, to use an example from Book Two, a chapter in which the only dialogue comes from television broadcasts playing out in the background. These are in some ways small potatoes compared to the expansive formal and stylistic experiments that Moore would later become known for, but nevertheless, the advancement within the course of the serial is significant, and it's not surprising that Moore refers to the comic as "one of the first real major breakthroughs I made in terms of my own personal style."

But for all that *V for Vendetta* evolved formally, it's clear that the overall outline snapped into place fairly early, and Moore's setting up of the larger theme of violence and its legitimacy in Book One is clearly aimed at allowing further exploration of that theme at a later date. In this regard it is perhaps significant to note that the chapter entitled "Violence" was not actually Moore's first attempt to do a chapter with that title. The first attempt came four chapters earlier, when he wrote a script for the fifth chapter, to be published in *Warrior #5* in September of 1982. As David Lloyd tells the story, this script was the lone time on *V for Vendetta* that he "saw something [Moore had] written for it that failed to slot into place like the perfectly machined component I always expected him to manufacture," and that it seemed rushed and generic. Moore, for his part, immediately asked Lloyd what he'd thought of the script when they talked, then cut him off at "Well, erm" to say that he agreed and would write a different one.

The bulk of the abandoned script consists of two paralleled sequences—one of Evey and V sparring in the Shadow Gallery, and the other of a training operation focused on capturing or killing V, overseen by Derek Almond. The former consists of V taking dirty shots at Evey—striking her when her back is turned as she massages her leg from an earlier blow. Eventually Evey, enduring a lecture from V about how she's improving, but "must learn not to be so predictable. The essence of success is surprise," finally snaps—Moore describes her as "boiling with suppressed fury" and notes to Lloyd, "I don't know if you've ever been a beginner at a martial arts class and had the shit stomped out of you by people far better than yourself, but if you have then you'll know how Evey feels. She is trembling with impotent rage"—and knees V in the crotch. He staggers back, leaning on the mantelpiece in pain, and limps off telling Evey, "That was very good... never fight people on their own terms. You're learning."

The parallel sequence, on the other hand, hinges on a well-rehearsed and well-drilled takedown exercise in which the central twist is the revelation that the character the audience is initially allowed to believe might be V (Moore specifies that the first cut from the Shadow Gallery to the training exercise should be "sudden and very confusing") is in fact a cop. The sequence ends with a cut from Almond drilling his forces to the Leader, named for the first time as Adam Susan, consulting with the computer, Fate, on the likelihood of Almond's plan succeeding (Fate assesses the odds of success at 78.055%), and Susan ultimately decides to enact Fate's plan. The script ends with another narrative caption reading, "His name is Adam Susan. He is called the

Leader. But Fate has spoken, and he does as he is told. Immediately."

As with the later chapter entitled "Violence," the purpose of the script is clearly to juxtapose these two instances of violence. But unlike the actual published "Violence," there is no moral dimension to the violence on display. Both acts of violence are simulations. They are not being pitted against each other in any moral sense, but rather in a purely tactical and instrumental sense. The only question is which approach is more effective—Almond's well-drilled operation, or V's embrace of unpredictability. In this regard the implicit answer is perhaps too simple, with V's methodology clearly serving as a response to the rigid approach of Almond and his Fingermen. Indeed, this simplicity pervades the unused Chapter Five, and it's not hard to see why Lloyd objected to a script that, in his view, leaned too heavily on a cliché martial arts scene and "didn't really take us very far."

But the nature of the abandoned script's take on violence is indicative of the terms in which Moore was conceiving of the series at this stage. The issue of violence is clearly entirely instrumental. The chapter is only concerned with the question of what approach to violence is more effective, an issue it treats as fundamentally tied to the underlying conflict between V and the fascist regime, and isn't even broaching the question of violence as a moral issue at this point. More to the point, by the time it does approach violence as a moral issue, it is purely as a question of two different approaches to being a revolutionary terrorist. Even as it becomes a moral question, in other words, it still remains a fundamentally instrumental discussion about tactics—a secondary issue to the book's main themes.

These themes are rendered most explicit in the chapter Moore wrote to replace the abandoned "Violence" version of Chapter Five, entitled "Versions." The chapter is presented as two monologues, each presented as a discrete whole; there is no cutting between them. The first is by Adam Susan, and is in effect an extended version of the final beat of the abandoned script. It consists of Susan reflecting, in interior monologue, on the nature of his life as he approaches his headquarters, walking into the office past the Hitler salutes and ascending the elevator to his private chamber, where he communes with the computer Fate. He proclaims bluntly, "I believe in survival, in the destiny of the Nordic race. I believe in fascism." He goes on to explain this, using the traditional fascist image of a set of bound twigs and the metaphor of "strength in unity" that it represents. "I will not hear talk of freedom," Susan declares. "I will not hear talk of individual liberty. They are luxuries. I do not believe in luxuries. The war put paid to luxury. The war put paid to freedom."

Susan is, however, quick to point out that he does not allow himself the luxuries he denies others. "I sit here within my cage and I am but a servant," he insists. He goes on to clarify that he loves and serves Fate. "I stand at the gates of her intellect and I am blinded by the light within. How stupid I must seem to her. How childlike and uncomprehending. Her soul is clean, untainted by the snares and ambiguities of emotion. She does not hate. She does not yearn. She is untouched by joy or sorrow. I worship her, though I am not worthy. I cherish the purity of her disdain. She does not respect me. She does not fear me. She does not love me." The section ends with a gradual closeup of Susan's face as he proclaims, "Fate... Fate... I love you," and then a wide shot of him, alone and isolated with his computer lover/ruler.

The second section is a monologue from V directed to the statue of Justice atop the Old Bailey—a statue that Susan stares at as he drives past at the start of his own monologue. V's monologue takes the form of an imagined dialogue with Justice, with V filling in her dialogue. V explains to Justice that he once considered himself in love with her ("Please don't think it was merely physical. I know you're not that sort of girl," he reassures her), but that he has since moved on to someone else. "What? V!" he imagines Justice saying. "You have betrayed me for some harlot, some vain and pouting hussy with painted lips and a knowing smile." But V retorts

Figure 160: Adam Susan, ensconced within his lover, magnificently isolated. (Written by Alan Moore, art by David Lloyd, from "Versions" in Warrior *#5, 1982)*

Figure 161: V stares up at his lover. (Written by Alan Moore, art by David Lloyd, from "Versions" in Warrior *#5, 1982)*

that it was in fact Justice's own infidelity—her fling with "a man in uniform... with his armbands and jackboots!"

"You are no longer my Justice. You are his Justice now," V proclaims, and says that he too has another mistress. "Her name is Anarchy, and she has taught me more as a mistress than you ever did! She has taught me that justice is meaningless without freedom." Justice, on the other hand, he dismisses as a "Jezebel" and sneers, "I used to wonder why you could never look me in the eye. Now I know." And so V departs, leaving his former lover "a final gift"—a heart-shaped box—at her feet before walking away, at which point, as is wont to happen with V, the box spectacularly explodes, destroying the statue of Justice. "The flames of freedom. How lovely. How just," V muses as he looks back at his handiwork.

For all that this is markedly different from the abandoned script, there are similarities. For one thing, "Versions" ends with a one-page epilogue of Eric Finch trying to question the seemingly hopelessly insane Louis Prothero about V that is, with only a few minor changes to the dialogue, the first page of the abandoned "Violence" script. More substantively, however, both "Versions" and the unused "Violence" are based on the use of two parallel scenes, one of V and the other of the fascist regime. But where "Violence" cut back and forth between the two scenes several times, "Versions" keeps the two strands separate, having them meet in the chapter's third page, in which the first four panels are devoted to the tail end of Adam Susan's version, the last four to V's, and the middle panel to an establishing shot of the Old Bailey. It is, in other words, an altogether more rigid structure, and marks the first of many times in Moore's career that he turns to a formalism to help him with a misbehaving script.

"Nomax the Revel! Nomax the Breaker of Rules!"
–Grant Morrison, *Annihilator*, 2014

The more rigid structure, along with the title and declaration of each monologue as "first version" and "second version" puts considerably greater emphasis on the idea of V and Susan as representing contrasting visions of the world. But this gets at the more significant difference between "Versions" and "Violence," which is that where "Violence" contrasted V and the fascists on the basis of their tactics, "Versions" contrasts them on a more fundamental philosophical level. And for all that the comic is clearly on V's side, it goes out of its way to present Susan's position, if not quite sympathetically, at least credibly. Moore has talked on several occasions about the effort he put into writing the fascist characters, and specifically about how this evolved over the course of working on the series: "I'd look at a character who I'd previously seen as a one-dimensional Nazi baddy and suddenly realize that he or she would have thoughts and opinions the same as everyone else," for example, and about how, for all that fascists were in practice his real-life political enemies, "In fact fascists are people who work in factories, probably are nice to their kids, it's just that they're fascists. They're just ordinary."

In this regard, perhaps the most significant thing about "Versions" is the way in which it depicts, in effect, three possible choices. The first is Adam Susan's embrace of Fate, which is on one level a literal object in the form of a computer, but on another is clearly meant to include the abstract concept, the notion that outcomes are pre-determined by some outside and higher power being fundamentally in line with the ideology of fascism. The second is Justice, who both V and (in V's telling at least) Susan aspire towards, but which is also, ultimately, suggested to be a tool of fascism. And the third is V's new mistress, Anarchy, who is, as he puts it, "honest. She makes no promises and breaks none." The debate, in other words, is not even about the practical manifestations of anarchism or fascism as political ideologies, but about the abstract values themselves, with V's position being, in effect, that Anarchy, unlike Fate and Justice, cannot be corrupted. It is, in other words, specifically because Anarchy exists on an almost purely ideological level, with no materialist "promises," that it is valued. This is a significant change from the original "Violence" script, which focused almost entirely on the pragmatics of the conflict between V and the fascists, and goes a long way towards answering David Lloyd's longstanding curiosity as to "why Alan hadn't met the exacting standards I knew he always expected from himself" on the unused chapter—because it represented, on Moore's part, a fundamental misunderstanding of what his own comic was about, and it was not until he worked through that misunderstanding with "Versions" that he finally realized that *V for Vendetta* was not primarily a book about appropriate tactics of resistance, but rather a book about why resistance is valuable in the first place.

For all that Moore's style evolves over the early installments of *V for Vendetta*, however, it remains the case that Book One is in many ways a simple and straightforward thing. This is perhaps inevitable. Moore only came to fully understand the comic over the course of writing Book One, after all. Nevertheless, the fact remains that Book One is in effect a fairly simple revenge plot focusing on the eponymous vendetta. It jumps around a couple of perspectives in a clever way, but in the end it's just the tale of an anonymous vigilante killing a bunch of fascists, with a reveal of his origin story at the end. There are moments of real cleverness—the tenderness between V and his final victim, for instance, is surprising and genuinely unsettling, especially after the cruel yet thrilling poetic justice dished out to, for example, the Bishop of Westminster, who's killed with a poisoned communion wafer that V challenges him to transubstantiate. And V's origin, as a concentration camp survivor apparently driven mad by an experimental hormone-based treatment that killed the other forty-seven test subjects, is suitably chilling, playing off of the World War II origins of the superhero genre to which *V for Vendetta* is tacitly connected, but drawing from the darkest and most horrific parts of that iconography. But ultimately, for all that V talks about an underlying philosophy to his actions, Book One of the story is focused entirely on a personal vendetta, the nature of which is revealed in the telling, which makes it a somewhat self-absorbed narrative.

Book Two, however, which commenced with a prelude in *Warrior #12*, published in August of 1983, is an entirely different story. Where the first book was on the whole a straightforward action story, the second book is an altogether more complex thing. This is clear from its opening section, entitled "This Vicious Cabaret," and presented as a series of images of various characters as they left off at the end of the previous installment, juxtaposed with narration on V's part in the form of a cabaret song, with sheet music for the vocal line composed by Bauhaus's bassist, David J. It's an aggressively experimental opening, but in some ways its most radical aspect is clear only in implication. The structure of "This Vicious Cabaret" consists of windows on all of the major characters: Eric Finch, the "policeman with an honest soul that has seen whose head is on the pole" and who "grunts and fills his briar bowl with a feeling of unease"; Adam Susan, the "master in the dark nearby" who "inspects the hands with brutal eye that have never brushed a lover's thigh but have squeezed a nation's throat"; Evey, who "doubts her host's moralities" but who "decides that she is more at ease in the land of doing-as-you-please than outside in the cold"; and, perhaps most significantly, Rose Almond, battered widow of the now late Derek Almond (killed by V in the climax of Book One), who the lyrics prophesize "will be dressed in garter and bow-tie and be taught to kick [her] legs up high in this vicious cabaret," an addition that presages her becoming a significant character in a way that she was not in Book One.

But in many ways the most notable thing about "This Vicious Cabaret" is the character who isn't quite depicted, V himself. It's not that V is absent from the chapter, but rather that he looms over it: as a pair of hands playing the piano; in tight close-ups on his mask; or in a series of panels in which he appears within a crowd scene and, eventually, adjusts one of the figures, revealing them all to be plastic dummies. This is an apt enough metaphor—although he's the title character and ostensible protagonist, V spends this prelude markedly outside the world upon which he comments. In some ways this has always been true—V's mysterious nature requires, after all, that the narrative never get too far into his head, and even Book One regularly opted to focus on other characters, which really is a sensible move when one considers that the title character has a completely static face and a habit of talking in quotes.

But Book Two ultimately sidelines him even further. The first installment consists entirely of a conversation between V and Evey that culminates in V blindfolding Evey and leading her outside. It's an elaborate sequence in which Lloyd's panels draw ever closer on Evey, so that it's impossible to tell what's happening to her or where she's being led, while a recorded voice begins reciting bits of dialogue from Book One, specifically the scenes in which Evey offers to help V, and her later vow not to kill anymore. Eventually Evey removes the blindfold in frustration, discovering herself to be standing outside on a street, with V seemingly standing in the middle of the road a few feet away. But V, after reciting a bit of dialogue from Enid Blyton's *The Magic Faraway Tree* and answering Evey's earlier question as to whether he was her father (he denies it), turns out to not be V at all, but to just be a mask, hat, and cloak draped around a wooden stand with a tape recorder underneath, with the chapter ending on a wide shot of the street, Evey barely distinct in the midground asking, in tiny Jenny O'Connor letters, "V?"

The second chapter, driven by an internal monologue on the part of Rose Almond at her late husband's funeral, only features V in nine panels, in which he visits an old movie theater and takes a film poster for a film called *The Salt Flats*, which appears in every regard to be a perfectly ordinary film poster like many of the others that V has in the Shadow

Figure 162: Evey abandoned, her isolation emphasized by the long shot. (Written by Alan Moore, art by David Lloyd, from "The Vanishing" in Warrior *#13, 1983)*

Figure 163: V's monologue is illustrated primarily through real-world photographs, directing it as much towards the real-world reader as its fictional audience. (Written by Alan Moore, art by David Lloyd, from "A Vocational Viewpoint" in Warrior *#16, 1983)*

Gallery, except for a handful of details like the fact that it was apparently nominated for Best Picture in 1986 (three years after the comic's publication), and that the film's logo is curiously in the exact same font as another series appearing in *Warrior*, Steve Parkhouse and John Ridgway's *The Spiral Path*.

The third and fourth installments are largely focused on V. The first, "Video," is the aforementioned segment consisting almost entirely of dialogue from television broadcasts, in which V breaks into the broadcasting station and takes control of the television broadcast, while the second, "A Vocational Viewpoint," consists entirely of the monologue V subsequently delivers to the people of England, telling them, "I'm not entirely satisfied with your performance lately... I'm afraid your work's been slipping, and... well, I'm afraid we've been thinking about letting you go." He reminisces about "the day you commenced your employment, swinging down from the trees, fresh-faced and nervous, a bone clasped in your bristling fist." But, V complains, humanity has a "basic unwillingness to get on within the company. You don't seem to want to face up to your real responsibility, or to be your own boss." He allows that "the management is very bad" and that "we've had a string of embezzlers, frauds, liars and lunatics making a string of catastrophic decisions," but even this he blames on the broad population who "appointed these people" and "who gave them the power to make decisions for you. While I'll admit that anyone can make a mistake once, to go on making the same lethal errors century after century seems to me nothing short of deliberate." And, V insists, humanity had a choice. "You could have stopped them. All you had to say was 'no.' You have no spine. You have no pride. You are no longer an asset to the company." But, he says, he will nevertheless give people "two years to show me some improvement in your work" before armed guards finally burst into the room he's broadcasting from and open fire on him, sending him toppling through a window to his apparent demise.

This bracing chapter serves two main purposes. The first is a more thorough statement of the book's philosophical themes, which goes considerably further than "Versions," the previous chapter to spell them out at any length. This, along with the shift in focus to include Rose Almond as one of the series' primary characters, speaks to the way in which Moore was trying to broaden the sense of what *V for Vendetta* could do in the second book. The second is to give the main character an impressive send-off before he's largely removed from the strip. The possibility that V has actually died is not entertained for long—the reader discovers in the next installment that the dead man is in fact Roger Dascombe, the fascist regime's minister of propaganda, and Rose Almond's new lover following V's murder of her husband. But save for a two-panel wordless appearance at the end of Chapter Six in which his face isn't even shown, and a four-page completely wordless fill-in chapter drawn by Tony Weare instead of David Lloyd, V made no appearances between his apparent death in *Warrior* #16, published in December 1983, and the February 1985 issue, *Warrior* #26, where he appears unexpectedly in a final page splash. This was also the final issue of *Warrior* entirely, and V would not appear again until the final two installments of Book Two were published by DC in November 1988's *V for Vendetta* #7, nearly five years after he essentially disappeared from his own strip.

The eight chapters between V's broadcast and his re-emergence are for the most part focused on Evey, although Chapter Five opens with a four-page section focusing on Eric Finch's enforced vacation after he angrily decked Almond's replacement at the Finger. The remaining two pages introduce a new character—a small time criminal named Gordon who, in the chapter's final panels, turns out to be housing Evey, unseen since V abandoned her in a street four chapters earlier. The next few chapters focus on her life with Gordon up until he's killed when a deal goes wrong and she attempts to avenge him before apparently being arrested.

*"We gasped upon Devonian beaches, huddled under Neolithic stars.
Spat blood through powdered teeth, staining each other as we kissed.
Always we loved. How could we otherwise, when you are so like me, my
sweet, but in a different guise?"*
–Alan Moore, "The Mirror of Love," 1988

The most interesting of these is probably Chapter Six, "Variety," which takes place within The Kitty-Kat Keller, a gentleman's club in which an unnamed dancer goose-steps to a fascist cabaret song while Evey observes the various patrons: Rose Almond being tossed out because her card is overdrawn, an associate of Gordon's named Robert being told by Almond's replacement at the Finger that he'll no longer be honoring their deal to keep his elderly mother out of a home ("Homes? They're gas chambers!" Robert exclaims, to which Creedy responds, "Not gas. If you want the truth, Robert, there's just three good South Ken boys with iron bars"), and another associate from Scotland named Ally Harper, who will turn out to be Gordon's murderer next chapter. This selection of petty and everyday degradations offers a perspective not really seen yet within *V for Vendetta*, one that pays off its original conception as a 1930s mystery strip in the noir tradition, and culminates in Robert having a breakdown, shouting to the bar, "We shouldn't have to live like this!" and "I wish the bastard bomb had 'it bastard London. That's what I wish. I wish we were all dead!" at which point the Fingermen in the bar surround him and beat him. Evey and Gordon head out to the street, sickened by what they've seen, with Evey asking Gordon, "He's right, wasn't he? We shouldn't have to live like this," to which Gordon replies, "No, kid, we shouldn't. What are you going to do about it?" as the perspective pulls back to reveal V on a rooftop above, a tacit answer to Gordon's question.

But in many ways the heart of Book Two, and indeed of *V for Vendetta* as a whole, is the four chapter stretch following Evey's apparent arrest for attempting to murder Gordon's killer. The first is a hallucinatory dream sequence entitled

"Vicissitude" in which the various men in Evey's life—her father, Gordon, and V all blur together along with the bishop who was going to molest Evey when she went undercover for V, which becomes an unsettling dreamscape of exploitation and degradation that ends with her being grabbed by V (in a panel Lloyd tellingly draws to perfectly mirror her arrest in the previous chapter) and waking up in a prison cell. The next chapter, "Vermin," depicts Evey in a squalid cell, obsessing over a rat, and finally being taken out and interrogated over her associations with V and her attempted murder of Harper, although they instead accuse her of planning to murder Creedy, on the grounds that he is "a frequent customer of the Kitty Kat Keller." They then blindfold her and shave her head and dump her back in her cell with the rat. "Only now I don't mind the rat," she narrates, "because I'm no better." In the chapter's closing panels, she discovers a letter, scrawled on toilet paper, written by a woman named Valerie.

The next chapter, "Valerie," is one of the most extraordinary works of Alan Moore's career. The timeframe in which it takes place is left deliberately vague, a fact emphasized by Evey's narration on the first page: "I know every inch of this cell. I know every pitted indentation in the rough plaster like I know my own body. I don't know where I am. I know it gets dark and then light; that I wake then sleep; that time passes measured in hair growing back beneath my arms where they won't let me shave. I don't know what day it is." Her only comfort and sanity is the letter she found at the end of the previous chapter. "I read her letter," Evey continues, "I hide it, I sleep, I wake, they question me, I cry, it gets dark, it gets light, I read her letter again… over and over…" while the art depicts her seated in front of a bowl of water, with a guard who shoves her head into it to torture her, hammering home the cruel and cyclic nature of her abuse.

The text of the letter had in fact begun at the end of the previous installment, in a panel drawn from Evey's perspective when she discovered it. Its desperate tone mirrors

Evey's own misery. "I have a pencil," Valerie writes, "a little one they did not find. I am a woman. I hid it inside me. Perhaps I won't be able to write again, so this is a long letter about my life. It is the only autobiography I will ever write and oh god I'm writing it on toilet paper," a harrowing set of details that reinforces the sense of routine depravity implicit in this regime of pointless and repetitive torture, such that the single interrogation depicted within it stands in for countless others before and after.

The second page opens with a close-up of the page shown at the end of the previous chapter before continuing the text of Valerie's letter, with the art switching to some fill-in work from Tony Weare (who previously drew a few pages of Chapter Five, as well as the interstitial "Vincent") depicting the autobiography Valerie narrates. She was born, the letter says, in 1957, twenty-four years before Evey, in Nottingham. "I met my first girlfriend at school," she says. "Her name was Sara. She was fourteen and I was fifteen but we were both in Miss Watson's class. Her wrists. Her wrists were beautiful," Valerie says, as Weare draws a close-up panel of two feminine hands resting comfortably and intimately against each other.

She tells of coming out at the age of nineteen when she "took a girl called Christine home to meet my parents." Weare, whose scratchier and looser style results in somewhat more expressive faces than the eye-bulging grotesques of David Lloyd, depicts the shocked reactions of her parents, and Valerie confirms that "my mother said I broke her heart. But," she continues, as Weare draws a landscape shot of Valerie standing at a rail, looking over a pond, with roses growing in the foreground, "it was my integrity that was important. Is that so selfish? It sells for so little. But it's all we have left in this place. It is the very last inch of us…" and then the final panel returns to David Lloyd's art, picking up in the exact instant that the first page left off, with Evey's head plunged into the water, as the narration concludes, "Within that inch we are free."

With this, the scene returns to Evey's torture. Her head is

held underwater for one more panel before her interrogator curtly says, "Alright," and she is yanked back up, water streaming from her face, contorted in pain. "Let's review the facts," her interrogator says, and he outlines a wholly erroneous account of how "Codename V" gave her orders to murder Peter Creedy. Her interrogator is entirely faceless, depicted by Lloyd as a straight black silhouette over a starkly white panel, so white that it swallows the outline of his text bubbles. He never asks what happened, but merely presents a narrative and gives her the opportunity to assent to the lies within.

Evey does not, insisting, "No! No, please, that isn't true." Her interrogator, in a show of mock pity, simply says, "Oh dear. Rossiter." It is not a question, and the guard behind Evey responds with a simple "Sir." Evey begins to scream and beg, but to no avail—the guard grabs her by the back of the head and shoves her face back into the water, drowning her again. The narration from Valerie's letter starts up again: "London: I was happy in London."

And so the action cuts back to Valerie's story, with another page of her autobiography presented as text: "In 1981 I played Dandini in Cinderella. My first rep work. The world was strange and rusting and busy with invisible crowds behind the hot lights and all that breathless glamour." She talks of her early forays into London's gay scene, and her frustrations with and sense of alienation from it. "So many of them just wanted to be gay. It was their life. Their ambition. All they talked about. And I wanted more than that," she says. In 1986, she says, she got a role in a film called *The Salt Flats*, where she met a woman named Ruth and began an affair. "We lived together," she says, "and on Valentine's Day she sent me roses, and oh god we had so much. Those were the best years of my life."

This section, for attentive readers, offers a number of clues as to what is happening. V stole a film poster of *The Salt Flats* back in Chapter Two of Book Two, and the image of roses has throughout the book been closely linked with V, who left flowers beside his early victims, and who spent his time in Larkhill gardening and growing roses. The significance of this is further emphasized by the next panel: shown from behind, Valerie and Ruth cuddle on a sofa and watch the news, with three roses in the foreground. "In 1988 there was the war," Valerie narrates, "and after that there were no more roses. Not for anybody." The penultimate panel of the page shows a massive parade of men in Norsefire uniforms, marching left to right across the panel, such that the final panel, another shot of the guard drowning Evey, serves as the symbolic head of their pack.

The fifth page returns to the scenes of Evey's torture, as she's pulled out of the bowl, blindfolded, and shoved back into her cell. But the text continues Valerie's story: "In 1992, after the take-over, they started rounding up the gays. They took Ruth while she was out looking for food. Why are they so frightened of us?" she asks. As Evey is tortured and shoved around, Valerie talks about how Ruth was tortured into giving up Valerie's name and claiming she'd been seduced. "I didn't blame her," Valerie insists. "But she did. She killed herself in her cell. She couldn't live with betraying me. With giving up that last inch." Valerie tells of her own capture—of how "they shaved off my hair. They held my head down a toilet bowl and told jokes about lesbians. They brought me here and gave me drugs. I can't feel my tongue anymore. I can't speak. The other gay woman here, Rita, died two weeks ago."

This last point once again serves as a clue for attentive readers, being the second mention of Rita within *V for Vendetta*. The previous one came up at the end of Book One, as Finch is reading Adam Susan excerpts from Dr. Surridge's diary of her time at Larkhill, which include the off-handed comment that "Rita Boyd, the Lesbian, died at tea-time. During the autopsy we found four tiny vestigial fingers forming within the calf of her leg." Given that V burnt Larkhill to the ground in his escape, it is impossible that Valerie's toilet paper autobiography could have survived, or

Figure 164: The marching Norsefire guards, with the one torturing Evey symbolically at the front of the pack. (Written by Alan Moore, art by David Lloyd, from "Valerie" in Warrior #25, 1984)

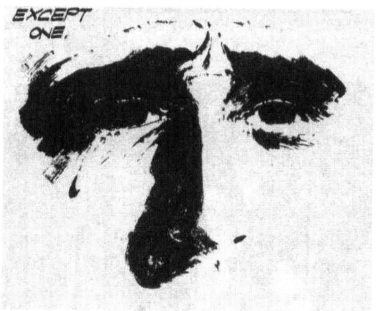

Figure 165: Evey's last inch. (Written by Alan Moore, art by David Lloyd, from "Valerie" in Warrior #25, 1984)

that Evey could actually be imprisoned there. But this clue is subtle and overwhelmed by the images of Evey's degradation and the stark, awful blacks of the cell she is shoved back into. "It is strange that my life should end in such a terrible place," Valerie's story continues, "but for three years I had roses and I apologised to nobody. I shall die here. Every inch of me shall perish." The page ends with a medium shot of Evey, contorted in pain within her darkened cell as Valerie states, "Except one."

After these five pages alternating between illustrating Valerie's life and illustrating the horrors of Evey's captivity, the chapter concludes with a final page that alternates between them. "An inch," Valerie writes, over a reprise of the panel of Valerie and Sara's hands touching in Miss Watson's class. "It's small and it's fragile and it's the only thing in the world that's worth having. We must never lose it, or sell it, or give it away. We must never let them take it from us." This, over a small panel of Evey's weary and exhausted face reading the letter yet again.

This is followed by a reprise of Valerie standing by a pond watching the birds, a rosebush behind her: "I don't know who you are, or whether you're a man or woman. I may never see you. I will never hug you or cry with you or get drunk with you. But I love you. I hope that you escape this place." The art switches back to Evey, now in medium shot, sitting on her wooden cot, the toilet paper scroll hanging from her hands, an isolated and haggard figure in her chiaroscuro cell. "I hope that the world turns and that things get better, and that one day people have roses again." Valerie makes her final appearance in the next panel, a close-up of her, still standing at the rail, watching the ducks. "I wish I could kiss you." The letter is signed "Valerie," the text positioned in the top-right corner of the panel. In the bottom-right, a final note—a single "x" to represent the kiss she can never give to the reader she will never know she has.

The art cuts back to Evey for the final row of panels, her face in shadow, a single tear visible, the narration returning to her instead of simply her quoting Valerie. "I know every inch of this cell," she thinks, as she holds the scrap of toilet paper up, her face shrunken and lined with wrinkles that should be impossible for a woman who is only sixteen years old, and kisses it softly on the x. "This cell knows every inch of me." And a final panel, her eyes and nose, weathered, single tear still suspended on her face, the edges of it simply fading out to the stark and infinite whiteness of the page.

"Except one."

"With language now under surveillance he resorts to code. Stealth prophecy. Boils down oppression and resistance into glowering essences, to barbarous names."
–Alan Moore, *Angel Passage*, 2001

"Valerie" is followed by "The Verdict," the last chapter of *V for Vendetta* to be published in *Warrior*. The chapter opens with Evey being offered the opportunity to confess to her "crimes"—that she was kidnapped by V, "systematically brainwashed by means of drugs and torture" and "frequently subjected to sexual abuse," that she aided him in "the unlawful killings of Roger Dascombe, Mr. Derek Almond, Dr. Della Surridge, and the Reverend Antony Lilliman, Bishop of Westminster," and that "the above statement is genuine, and that it was not signed by means of intimidation." This last statement is rather clearly untrue, however, as when she declines to sign it she's told that she'll be taken "out behind the chemical sheds" and shot.

And so Evey returns to her cell and reads Valerie's letter again, waiting for Rossiter to come and take her to her execution. She's given one last chance to sign the statement. "You could be out in three years. Perhaps they'd find you a job with the Finger," she's told, but she declines once again, saying, "Thank you, but I'd rather die behind the chemical sheds." And so her guard proclaims that "there's nothing left to threaten with" and tells her that she's free. Shocked, she turns around and sees that her cell door is open and unguarded. She stumbles out through the compound, realizing that all the soldiers and guards are just dummies and tape recorders. Finally, she pushes through a door and comes into the main room of the Shadow Gallery, where V stands waiting for her and says simply, "Welcome home."

Part Two of *V for Vendetta* ultimately had two further chapters, both of which saw first publication in DC Comics' *V for Vendetta* #7 in 1988, although the first of them, "Values," was written and drawn for the never-published *Warrior* #27. It continues the exclusive focus on Evey, resolving the rather striking cliffhanger on which the series was hung for nearly four years. It starts with a close-up of Evey, shocked by the revelation, as she breaks down sobbing, "Yuh-you hit me, and, and you cut off my hair... it was *you*. It was just *you* all this time... you... tortured... me... oh, you tortured me... oh god, why?"

To this V replies, "Because I love you. Because I want to set you free." As Evey erupts in horror at this claim and sputters, "You say you want to set me free and you put me in a prison." He explains, "You were already in a prison. You've been in a prison all your life... happiness is the most insidious prison of all." He continues telling her how she's free now, while she grows increasingly frantic and panicked. "Woman, this is the most important moment of your life. Don't run from it." She doubles over, says she can't breathe. "You were in a cell, Evey," V says. "They offered you a choice between the death of your principles and the death of your body. You said you'd rather die. You faced the fear of your own death, and you were calm and still. Try to feel now what you felt then." She lies in his arms saying, "Oh, Oh, I can feel it... oh what is it... oh, I'm going to die, I'm going to burst... I... uh... oh God... I felt... huhh... I... felt... like... an angel." Finally he takes her out onto the roof, where she stands nude in the rain. "V..." she says, "everything's so... different. I... I feel so..." and V reassures her, "I know. Five years ago, I too came through a night like this, naked under a roaring sky. This night is yours. Seize it. Encircle it within your arms. Bury it in your heart up to the hilt. Become transfixed. Become transfigured. Forever."

This, as the final chapter of Part Two renders explicit, serves as Evey's initiation—the point at which she comes to fully embrace V's anarchist ideology. (In it, V also explains what attentive readers would have figured out in the "Valerie" chapter, namely that Valerie was the woman one door down from V in Larkhill.) But more to the point, it is the first time Moore has written a magical initiation into one of his comics, although he was still years off from actually having the aesthetic and philosophical framework to consciously craft it as such. Nevertheless, the overall structure is visibly that of the descent into the abyss, confrontation with ego-death/Choronzon, and subsequent rebirth. It is also worth noting that this is clearly the most important sequence in *V for Vendetta*, at least in terms of emphasis. Five straight chapters are devoted to Evey's experience in prison, starting with the dream sequence of "Vicissitudes" and ending with her rain-soaked transfiguration. One could even argue six chapters by counting "Vengeance," which, as an all-Evey chapter, is not an unreasonable claim either. In comparison, the entire arc from Evey offering to help V to the end of Part One is only six chapters, and contains sequences featuring at least eight different characters. Nowhere else in *V for Vendetta* is there anything nearly as long and singularly focused as V's extended manipulation and psychological warfare against Evey. Its thirty-six pages form nearly fifteen percent of the total narrative.

And yet, strikingly, there is no moral debate anywhere within *V for Vendetta* about V's kidnapping and torturing Evey. This is striking, given that the moral debate over killing is ultimately what Moore would opt to focus the story's climax on, and yet none of V's murders are as unsettling as his treatment of Evey. The fact that the reader is shown Evey's treatment sincerely, as though all is as it appears, is tremendously affecting, especially when one recalls that the comic was being serialized monthly, such that the amount of time the reader spends genuinely believing Evey is in a fascist prison undergoing the sort of authoritarian interrogations for which the adjective "Kafka-esque" was coined is not merely twenty pages but the better part of four months. And this is clearly a concept that genuinely disturbs Moore, because he was already planning Liz Tremayne's storyline in *Swamp Thing*, which he described in terms that could equally well apply to what V does to Evey: "The destruction of one human being's whole personality by another." When talking about it in terms of *Swamp Thing*, he called it "an example of human evil that, to me, is more frightening than any number of demons from hell." So the basic horror of what happens to Evey is such that the revelation that it's all for Evey's own good and her subsequent thanking of V "for what you've done for me" is not really enough to counterbalance it.

But equally, that's the point. It's unfair to suggest that Moore gives V a moral pass on this. But it is nevertheless the case that while the narrative eventually sides against V on the issue of killing, it never really does on the issue of torturing someone at length to convert them to your ideological position. It may be unsettling, but it comes closer to being praised than condemned. It is easy to make too much of this—Moore, in several interviews, says something to the effect of, "Although the artwork was very black-and-white, with no shades of gray, I thought that one of the most interesting things about the strip was that morally there was nothing but gray." Surely the torture of Evey is the ultimate example of this. But equally, there is something revealing in the fact that this is not one of the issues Moore chooses to move out of the realm of ambiguity upon the story's resolution. Ultimately, one suspects that Moore is not entirely willing to commit to the idea that the searing radiance of spiritual enlightenment need be consensual. Certainly this position is compatible with *V for Vendetta* as a whole. The story may not go to the theatrical extremes that V does within it, but its overall purpose is clearly to unsettle the reader's assumed beliefs about the world and to get them to seriously consider anarchist revolution as a solution to their ills. And it is worth highlighting the word "theatrical," as ultimately, from the moment he exiles her to the end of Book Two, that's what V's psychological assault on Evey is: an act of elaborate theater. At the end of the day, Moore is clearly in favor of using art to terrorize people into spiritual enlightenment.

William Blake, of course, was much the same. Floundering in the early stages of his career, and roiling with his visionary, revolutionary politics, Blake felt the noose tightening in more ways than one. The aftermath of the French Revolution led to a crackdown on dissidents in England—a 1792 Royal Proclamation specifically condemned "seditious writings." At the time Blake was open about his politics, composing but never publishing the first part of what was intended to be a seven-book poem about the Revolution. But in time Blake's outward vigor dimmed. It was not that he lacked courage—quite the contrary, he boldly printed *America a Prophecy* under his own name. And yet the same year, he (quite wrongly) predicted that he would not survive five more years, and speculated, "If I live one it will be a Wonder." But Blake was always particularly terrified of being persecuted for his beliefs, both political and religious, and this found succor with his revulsion as Revolution gave way to Terror. Modifying the printing techniques he'd developed for *The Marriage of Heaven and Hell* and *Songs of Innocence*, Blake began composing his Continental Prophecies, which were at once more radical and more cryptic than *The French Revolution*.

This esotericism had an unsettling yet compelling effect. Freed of merely crafting commentary on existing events, Blake's mythic reworkings of history and revolution provided something more like an idealized form of revolution—one that reached beyond the immediate circumstances of his time and instead got at the very heart of social and political change. Blake was no longer writing anything so trite as allegory. The word he chose was terrifying in its boldness: prophecy. Blake is not describing history, but the shape and way in which the world will—might—can change. This is not art about persuasion, or political commentary, but about revelation—about revealing the shape of the end of the world.

And yet the turn from explicit political commentary to something more shrouded and occult is carried over in the works themselves. Neither his mythic reworking of the American Revolution nor its sequel, *Europe a Prophecy*, tell stories of revolutions that fix the world, or even necessarily improve it. Instead they simply serve as another turn through Blake's increasingly complex mythology—indeed, the same year that *Europe a Prophecy* saw print, Blake also put out *The Book of Urizen*, the start of a completely different cycle of books. Just as the American Revolution falls short because, ultimately, Orc is an inadequate figure, the French Revolution as depicted in *Europe a Prophecy* turns gradually rotten as the book unfolds.

The central character of *Europe a Prophecy* is Enitharmon, here making her first substantive appearance within Blake's system, having been mentioned in passing in *America a Prophecy*. Over the larger course of Blake's mythology, Enitharmon is one of its most central female figures, serving as the counterpart to Los/Urthona, the creative urge and the closest thing Blake's mythos has to a protagonist. This is a complex role to play, not least because Blake's vision of femininity is a complex and not always entirely pleasant thing. In this regard, it is also significant that *Europe a Prophecy* opens with a prelude that itself continues the prelude of *America a Prophecy* in narrating the story of Orc, this time talking about "the nameless shadowy female" who "rose from out the breast of Orc" and who addresses Enitharmon. Blake would later develop the character of the shadowy female into a fallen form of Vala, the fearsome emanation of gentle Luvah (whose own fallen form is Orc), and she would come to play a key role in his mythology, particularly in *The Four Zoas*.

"With dolorous hissings & poisons round Enitharmons loins folding,

coild within Enitharmons womb the serpent grew casting its scales."
–William Blake, *The Book of Urizen*, 1794

Vala opens *Europe a Prophecy* by railing, "O mother Enitharmon wilt thou bring forth other sons? To cause my name to vanish, that my place may not be found." She speaks of how she, "sitting in fathomless abyss of my immortal shrine," looks up at heaven and the stars and seizes "their burning power" so she can "bring forth howling terrors, all devouring fiery kings. Devouring & devour'd roaming on dark and desolate mountains In forests of eternal death, shrieking in hollow trees."

But Enitharmon, she claims, foils her in this. "I bring forth from my teeming bosom myriads of flames," she says, "and thou dost stamp them with a signet, then they roam abroad and leave me void as death." But the prelude ends with a strange sense of hope, with the shadowy female asking "who shall bind the infinite with an eternal band? To compass it with swaddling bands? and who shall cherish it With milk and honey? I see it smile & I roll inward & my voice is past."

This prelude poses an interesting ambiguity, especially when taken in light of the remainder of *Europe a Prophecy* and, for that matter, of Blake's mythology. Vala/the shadowy female is not generally a positive figure, but rather an embodiment of nature (itself a complex concept within Blake's system), and a warlike death goddess. She speaks of herself as, "My roots are brandish'd in the heavens, my fruits in earth beneath Surge, foam, and labour into Life, first born & first consum'd! Consumed and consuming!" Ultimately, she will prove responsible for Albion's fall. And yet it is difficult not to see her as a sympathetic figure in this exchange with Enitharmon—her revolutionary, destructive spirit is the obvious tonic to Urizen's ghastly order. And it is worth stressing that it is Blake's most famous image of Urizen, as the Ancient of Days, that serves as the frontispiece to *Europe a Prophecy*, a fact that further strengthen's Vala's moral legitimacy.

Similarly, over the course of *Europe a Prophecy*, Enitharmon is far from a sympathetic figure. She awakens in "the deep of winter," as Urizen flees to "the distant north" and "strong Urthona takes his rest." In response, the Urizen's children awaken Orc, vowing that "we will crown thy head with garlands of the ruddy vine." (This passage also illustrates one of the extreme challenges of parsing and interpreting Blake's work. The awakening of Orc comes within a passage that begins "The shrill winds wake! Till all the sons of Urizen look out and envy Los:", the colon clearly indicating that what follows is a monologue delivered by the sons of Urizen, who speak of how "we may drink the sparkling wine of Los." And yet this passage ends with a five-line stanza,

> Arize O Orc from thy deep den
> First born of Enitharmon rise!
> And we will crown thy head with garlands of the ruddy vine;
> For now thou art bound;
> And I may see thee in the hour of bliss, my eldest born.

This last line, in the first person singular, cannot be spoken by the sons of Urizen, and must be either Los or Enitharmon, and yet at no point in the monologue is there any other indication of a change in speaker. This sort of thing is alarmingly common in Blake.

And yet despite this, the obvious assumption that Blake is somehow sloppy in his work simply does not hold—the meticulous attention to artistic detail and the painstaking, extensive revisions made to his work belie any account of his work that suggests that it is anything less than precise. Rather, it depicts a worldview that rejects the idea of single vision—a sort of textual version of cubism in which a multiplicity of states of being are simultaneously described and depicted.)

"The horrent Demon rose, surrounded with red stars of fire, whirling about in furious circles round the immortal fiend. Then Enitharmon down descended into his red light," communing with Orc's fearsome spirit. In the wake of *America a Prophecy*, with its ultimate rejection of Orc, this is an unsettling prospect to say the least. This communion with Orc brings about "the night of Enitharmon's joy," during which Enitharmon decides that women will have dominion over the world. She bids her sons, Rintrah and Palambron:

> Go! tell the human race that Womans love is Sin:
> That an Eternal life awaits the worms of sixty winters
> In an allegorical abode where existence hath never come
> Forbid all Joy, & from her childhood shall the little female
> Spread nets in every secret path.

This commences a period of eighteen hundred years—a figure that reaches, essentially, from the birth of Christ to Blake's present day—in which Enitharmon sleeps, and the world is captured within "a female dream." This period is, to say the least, not a happy one. The council house in which Albion's Angels assemble is destroyed, and the world plunges into materialism, with man being shackled by the five senses and the Angel having "turn'd the fluxile eyes Into two stationary orbs, concentrating all things. The ever-varying spiral ascents to the heavens of heavens were bended downwards; and the nostrils golden gates shut." The infinite becomes a serpent, and pity becomes "a devouring flame" such that mankind flees and takes shelter "in forests of night" (a significant phrase, to say the least). The result is chilling: "God a tyrant crown'd."

This is the tyranny of Urizen implicitly foreshadowed by the frontispiece, leading to a world torn between Urizen's tyrannical law and Orc's violent upheaval. Blake describes a frantic struggle among Albion, Orc, and Urizen to seize and blow upon the trumpet that will bring about the last Judgment, but all fail. Instead, "A mighty Spirit lea'd from the land of Albion, Nam'd Newton; he siez'd the Trump, & blow'd the enormous blast!" Newton, as ever, is an antagonistic figure within Blake's work, representing, in his

Figure 166: A year after writing Europe a Prophecy *Blake used the phrase* "The Night of Enitharmon's Joy" *as a title for a bespoke painting. (1795)*

Figure 167: The Ancient of Days, the frontispiece of Europe a Prophecy. *(Copy K, Object 1, created 1794, printed 1821)*

vision, an irrevocable turn towards Urizenic materialism, with "Newtons sleep" being the counterpart to dreaded "single vision." His successful trumpeting of the horn of judgment reflects the awful state of the world after Enitharmon's eighteen hundred year slumber. She calls upon her sons and daughters, who represent a complex and often debated set of viewpoints on sexual politics of the late eighteenth century, the details of which Blake, in a 2014 séance, openly admits "were probably overly determined by the degree to which I wanted to sleep with women who weren't my wife at the time." (Numerous critics, it should be noted, directly associate Enitharmon with Blake's wife, Catherine, who for her part is an enormously complex figure in her own right deserving of considerable examination.)

It is here worth pausing and clarifying the chronology of events in this cycle of Blake's prophecies. *Europe a Prophecy* is, recall, the sequel to *America a Prophecy*. And yet over the course of *Europe a Prophecy* Blake retells a history of the entire Christian age of Europe, with this history emerging out of Enitharmon's communion with Orc, the spirit of revolution unleashed and set upon Europe at the end of *America a Prophecy*. That poem was a symbolic reworking of the history of the American Revolution, and even that occurred, historically, near the end of the eighteen-hundred-year sleep of Enitharmon. And yet at its conclusion *Europe* returns to being a chronological and quasi-historical sequel to *America*, resolving with Orc launching another attack upon Urizen's order of things: "But terrible Orc, when he beheld the morning in the east / Shot from the heights of Enitharmon / And in the vineyards of red France appear'd the light of his fury." With this, the French Revolution breaks out, Los returns and "reard in snaky thunders clad: And with a cry that shook all nature to the utmost pole, Call'd all his sons to the strife of blood." This is a bold call for revolution, certainly, and a seemingly vocal embrace of the upheavals to England's south. In this regard, at least, Blake and Moore are on the same page—the similarities between Orc and V's twin campaigns of terror and insurrection are ultimately unavoidable.

And yet a revolution born of Orc has already been undermined by Blake, just as it would ultimately be rejected by Moore in *Swamp Thing*. Indeed, for all the revolutionary fire with which Blake's continental prophecies so obviously burn, it is striking that Blake never actually endorses anything so crass as an actual political movement. There are some he holds in particular contempt, perhaps most obviously the entire apparatus of organized religion, which he associates with the hated Urizen and Newton. And yet the long reign of institutional Christianity and its failures are, within *Europe*, just as associated with Enitharmon. This further speaks to a certain perversity within Blake's work—his decision to represent Christianity in terms of a feminine figure is visibly subversive, in a way that goes beyond any simple allegorical readings whereby, for instance, Enitharmon represents the feminine figures of Eve and Mary, the classical virgin/whore complex embodied in the Kabbalistic image of Binah, which Moore describes as where "form becomes possible." To link the entire history of Christianity with a goddess figure is, in a real sense, to reject it and propose something akin to his earlier nuptials between heaven and hell. And yet this subversive religion is also rejected, as is revolution, and everything else.

And so in the Continental Prophecies we have an odd sort of revolution—what Moore, in *Angel Passage*, described as "voice suppressed, lips stitched, the vision has nowhere to turn save inwards." But he could equally well have said that it was a revolution that had been pushed "to the very last inch of us," where "it's small and it's fragile and it's the only thing in the world that's worth having. We must never lose it, or sell it, or give it away. We must never let them take it from us." Which is all another way of saying that Blake, like Moore, was an anarchist.

The precise meaning of this claim is, it must be admitted, a challenge to pin down. Moore himself traces the history of anarchism from ancient Greece through to the present day, and in a 2010 essay for *Dodgem Logic* entitled "Fear of a Black Flag," offers a partial catalogue of the "bewildering profusion of anarchist subdivisions, categories and splinter movements with radically different views" including "Communist Anarchists, Free market Anarchists, Egoist Anarchists, Anarchists Green or Syndicalist, Post-Left or Feminist, Anarchists Insurrectionary or Pacifist. Then there's Anarchy Without Adjectives which sounds entirely sensible despite the fact that the words 'Without Adjectives', used here as a descriptive phrase, are actually performing all the functions of an adjective." When this diversity of viewpoint is extended historically, to try to encompass not just Moore's own evolving views, preserved in amber in the earliest chapters of *V for Vendetta* and expounded, quite separately, nearly thirty years after the strip's beginning in an underground magazine bearing the name of his own failed mid-seventies fanzine, but also the views of William Blake some two centuries earlier, it's clear that any attempt at a rigorous philosophical position is going to be doomed before it gets off the ground.

Certainly Moore, in "Fear of a Black Flag," declines to cast his lot with any explicitly named anarchist tradition. Instead he returns to first principles, noting that "as often proves to be the case with words, the Greeks most definitely had one for it, in this case anarchos, meaning 'without rulers'," which is an accurate enough account of the word's etymology. Moore, as befits his autodidactic status regarding this philosophical tradition, ultimately ends the essay on the same note, describing the ancient Athenian process of sortition, "which is basically a type of government by lottery. In all decisions that concerned the state a jury would be randomly appointed from all parts of the community by drawing of straws or lots. This jury would then listen carefully to an informed debate presenting both sides of the argument, just as a jury does during a court case. After this a vote is taken on the matter and the jury is dissolved." Moore muses on the advantages of this, noting that "no special interest groups or corporations can buy influence in the government if no one knows who government will be until the next time that the straws are drawn. No jury would be likely to vote in a set of special privileges for the jury, such as being able to claim back expenses on the paddocks for their unicorns, when they themselves would no longer be jurors when these perks were ushered in." But for all that Moore praises this particular system, it is ultimately presented only as one of many similar proposals to emerge out of the millennia of anarchist thought that he summarizes.

"Sounds like a wishful past, all jungled over, a heroic run and the what-for of everything fuck simple."
—Alan Moore, *Crossed +100*, 2015

This includes not just the ancient Greeks and Taoist Sages, but the word "anarchy" as a 1642 coinage within the English language, used to dismiss Oliver Cromwell's New Model Army, along with Pierre-Joseph Proudhon's nineteenth century idea of mutualism and Max Striner's individualist anarchism from the same century. He turns also to Mikhail Bakunin's Collectivist Anarchism, with was an important predecessor to Marxism, along with Peter Kropotkin's rejection of private property, and, more contemporarily, Hakim Bey (who in addition to being an anarchist and pedophilia advocate was an open sorcerer, defining the concept as "the systematic cultivation of enhanced consciousness or non-ordinary awareness and its deployment in the world of deeds and objects to bring about desired results").

But for the purposes of understanding Blake, perhaps the most important thinker Moore touches upon is William Godwin, whose *Political Justice*, in Moore's account, advocated "that the individual act according to his or her individual judgement while allowing every single other individual the same liberty." *Political Justice*, more properly titled *Enquiry Concerning Political Justice and its Influence on Morals and Happiness*, was published in 1793, the same year as *America a Prophecy*, and Godwin and Blake traveled in similar circles—Blake did a series of illustrations for Godwin's future wife Mary Wollstonecraft's *Original Stories from Real Life* in 1791, for instance. (Godwin and Wollstonecraft's daughter, also named Mary, would go on to have a significant career of her own, largely under her married name, acquired from "Ozymandias" poet Percy Bysshe Shelley.) Blake followed Godwin no more than he did any other man, but the intellectual similarities are clear enough.

For Moore's part, at least in terms of *V for Vendetta*, the most obvious contemporary in anarchist thought is Colin Ward, whose *Anarchy in Action* was first published in 1973, when Moore was working with the Northampton Arts Group, putting out zines while writing spoken word pieces like "Old Gangsters Never Die," submitting a doomed proposal for "a freakish terrorist in white-face make-up who traded under the name of the Doll and waged war upon a totalitarian state sometime in the late 1980s" to future *Starblazer* publisher DC Thomson, dreaming up his sci-fi epic *Sun Dodgers* and the character of Five, "a mental patient of undefined but unusual abilities who had been kept in a particular room, room five," and meeting Phyllis Dixon, who he quickly married the next year. Ward offers a summary of anarchist thought on a wealth of issues, including specific topics like housing and education, packaged as an avuncular sales pitch. (His preface begins, "How would you feel if you discovered that the society in which you would really like to live was already here, apart from a few little, local difficulties like exploitation, war, dictatorship, and starvation?") Certainly Ward's thought coincides with Moore's in plenty of places: his blunt summary of the contemporary education system as being akin to that of ancient Sparta—"training for infantry warfare and for instructing the citizens in the techniques for subduing the slave class"—is easy enough to parallel with Moore's condemnation of his own education as a curriculum of "punctuality, obedience, and the acceptance of

Figure 168: The cover for the third issue of The Northampton Arts Group Magazine, *featuring an early iteration of Alan Moore's concept for "the Doll." (c. 1973)*

monotony," just as his declaration that anarchist theories of education are based on "respect for the learner" parallels Moore's observation that anarchism would require people "be educated to a point where they were able to direct their own lives without interfering in the lives of other people."

But ultimately, Moore, like Blake, is not one to lay out anything so banal as a singular policy proposal, or to endorse a specific ideology. Indeed, to do so would ultimately be contrary to what he was trying to accomplish. In numerous interviews, Moore has described the philosophical foundation of *V for Vendetta* as coming out of his belief that "the two poles of politics were not Left Wing or Right Wing. In fact they're just two ways of ordering an industrial society and we're fast moving beyond the industrial societies of the 19th and 20th centuries. It seemed to me the two more absolute extremes were anarchy and fascism." And fascism's central premise, as Moore puts it in *V for Vendetta*, is "Strength in Unity." And so presenting a singular, clear template of beliefs for others to follow would end up on the exact opposite end of the spectrum from where he wants to be. As he put it in a later interview, while talking about anarchy and fascism, "I don't necessarily want anybody to believe the same things I believe." And Blake's refusal to offer any straightforwardly positive alternative can be taken in largely the same vein.

Instead, anarchism can in many ways be described more as an aesthetic. Certainly that's the sense that Moore gives at the start of "Fear of a Black Flag," where he describes the associations of the word *anarchy*: "men in capes and broad-brimmed hats clutching black bowling balls with fizzing fuses and the helpful legend BOMB scrawled on the side in white emulsion," "a Hieronymus Bosch landscape populated by looters, berserkers, giants with leaking boats for feet and eggshells for a body," and "an ultra-violent and demented version of Spy vs. Spy, adapted from a screenplay by Rasputin and the Unabomber." These are not ideological principles, but images, not unlike the quotations and movie posters that make up so much of V's initial characterization.

This highlights another key similarity between *Europe a Prophecy* and *V for Vendetta*, which is that both were eventually augmented with writers' statements answering, as Moore puts it (in his essay entitled "Beyond the Painted Smile" that saw print in *Warrior* #17, the March 1984 issue of the magazine, between Chapters Five and Six of *V for Vendetta*, but written in October 1983, the month Chapter Two was published), the question asked "at every convention or comic mart or work-in or signing" by some "nervous and naive young novice," namely, "Where do you get your ideas from?"

In Blake's equivalent statement (a four-stanza poetic plate added as Object 3 to *Europe a Prophecy* Copy H, one of two copies made in 1795, a year after first publication, and retained in Copy K, the most lushly colored of them, printed in 1821), he tells how "a Fairy mocking as he sat on a streak'd Tulip" attracted his attention by singing a song about how

> Five windows light the cavern'd Man; thro' one he
>   breathes the air;
> Thro' one, hears music of the spheres; thro' one, the
>   eternal vine
> Flourishes, that he may recieve the grapes; thro' one can
>   look.
> And see small portions of the eternal world that ever
>   groweth;
> Thro' one, himself pass out what time he please, but he
>   will not;
> For stolen joys are sweet, & bread eaten in secret pleasant.

Blake snuck up on the Fairy and caught him in his hat, thus binding the fairy to his service in the manner of such things. Blake then proceeded to ask the Fairy a rather idiosyncratic question: "What is the material world, and is it dead?" The Fairy laughed, and said:

> I will write a book on leaves of flowers,
> If you will feed me on love-thoughts, & give me now and
>   then

A cup of sparkling poetic fancies; so when I am tipsie,
I'll sing to you this soft lute; and shew you all alive
The world, when every particle of dust breathes forth its
    joy.

    Blake obliged, gathering flowers as he walked with the Fairy, and as they did the Fairy showed him each one and "laugh'd aloud to see them whimper because they were pluck'd," hanging around Blake "like a cloud of incense." Blake went inside, took out a pen, and the "Fairy sat upon the table, and dictated EUROPE." (When asked in 2014 whether this account was actually true, Blake sardonically replied, "As true as this answer is.")

    Moore's explanation, on the other hand, is a detailed account of the collaborative process between himself and artist David Lloyd as they refined ideas for the 1930s mystery story commissioned by Dez Skinn for the forthcoming *Warrior.* And yet for all that this appears, on the surface, the simpler and more straightforward explanation, it is in a sense the far thornier one. *Europe a Prophecy* came wholly formed, dictated by a fairy, its entirety explicable by that one act, uncanny as it may be. But *V for Vendetta* had an enormously complex history that was the result of months of refining ideas and throwing new ones into the hopper. Moore mentions dozens of influences over the course of "Behind the Painted Smile," each of which in turn has a branching root system of causes and influences, all of which exist alongside other sources to which *V for Vendetta* self-evidently owes considerable debt and their own webs of influences and precedents.

    Nevertheless, the question of how this object came to be is unavoidable. It is, after all, one of the twin plastic smiles that form the bulk of Moore's direct political impact upon the world. It is the work that would go on to be directly and consciously appropriated to provide a symbol employed by anarchist and countercultural protest groups on a global scale. It has a strong case, of all of the spells cast in the course of the War, of being the one that would go on to have the single greatest impact. And of all the spells cast, it is the one whose influences are, perhaps, the purest. Its characters are original creations of Moore and Lloyd. For all the influences that exist, it is unlike, say, Moore's run on *Swamp Thing*, where he worked primarily with existing characters. It also dates to such an early point in Moore's career that it can legitimately be said to bear little to no influence from the rest of the War. The only major combatant to have done any work predating *V for Vendetta* is Morrison, whose stuff Moore almost certainly had not seen when he began work. Moore's work was not yet informed by his growing sense of mistrust towards the comics industry—he was still nothing more than another jobbing freelancer trying to get out of a banal and dead-end job. *V for Vendetta*, in other words, is simply the product of two British men in their late twenties/early thirties who wanted to make a living doing comics. To understand anything that subsequently happened in the War, then, it is necessary to understand that process.

In Moore's telling, as mentioned, it was very much David Lloyd's idea to model V's visual look upon Guy Fawkes, after spending some time trying more conventional designs. Before Lloyd hit on the idea, the design had been modeled after police uniforms (at the time it was thought V might have infiltrated the police force). As Moore describes it, "it had a big 'V' on the front formed from the belts and straps attached to the uniform, and while it looked nice, I think both Dave and I were uneasy about falling into such a straightforward super-hero cliché." Certainly the Guy Fawkes image was more visually striking, but its import goes beyond that. Upon reading it, "all of the various fragments in my head suddenly fell into place, united behind the single image of a Guy Fawkes mask." Clearly Lloyd had hit upon something substantial.

And yet Guy Fawkes himself is hardly a promising figure for what Moore was trying to accomplish with *V for Vendetta*. Yes, he did notably try to blow up the Houses of Parliament, but his reasons for doing so and his larger plan are hardly ones Moore would sympathize with. Fawkes, simply put, was a militant Catholic who wanted to assassinate King James I and make England a Catholic nation again, undoing Henry VIII's foundation of the Church of England. Fawkes converted to Catholicism in his teenage years following the death of his father and his mother's remarriage to a Catholic. In 1591, at the age of twenty-one, he relocated to the continent and fought for Spain in the Eighty Years War against the breakaway Dutch Republic. He was among the soldiers at the Siege of Calais in 1596, and by 1603 he was viewed as officer material. At this point he adopted the Italian equivalent of his name, rebranding himself Guido Fawkes, and traveled to Spain to seek King Philip III's support for a Catholic rebellion in England following the 1603 ascension of King James and union of the Scottish and English Crowns.

At this time the fines levied against practicing Catholics were a significant source of income for England, and James was emphatic in his denunciations of Catholics, especially after his discovery that the pope had secretly sent a rosary to his wife. The resulting crackdown included the expulsion of all Catholic priests from the country and a step up in the enforcement of the fines, which led to considerable discontent among Catholics. Among those unhappy was Robert Catesby, who began recruiting co-conspirators for a plot against the king. Among the first of these was his cousin, Thomas Wintour, who traveled to Spain in early 1604, where he met Fawkes, recruited him, and returned to England with him that April.

The core of Catesby's plan was to blow up the Houses of Parliament during its opening, killing the bulk of Parliament and James I at the same time. This was to coincide with the incitement of a revolt in the Midlands, and with the kidnapping of the Princess Elizabeth, who lived in Warwick and was thus conveniently positioned for the Midlands-based conspirators to pop over and kidnap. Elizabeth was eventually to be installed on the throne to serve as a Catholic monarch. Fawkes, as the participant with the most military experience, was placed in charge of managing the explosives, which were steadily smuggled into a cellar beneath the Houses of Parliament. An outbreak of plague delayed the opening of Parliament from February 1605 to October, and then, subsequently, to the 5th of November, 1605. This, however, proved sufficient delay that an anonymous letter ended up tipping off James I to the conspiracy, and he tasked Lord Chamberlain Thomas Howard with conducting an exhaustive search of the Houses of Parliament. These uncovered Fawkes beside a pile of firewood, which he managed to explain away. A second search headed by Thomas Knyvet in the early hours of November 5th, however, uncovered Fawkes in cloak and hat, and he was arrested, foiling the plot.

"Earth 43: A world of darkness and fear where super-vampires rule the night as the BLOOD LEAGUE."
–Grant Morrison, *Multiversity Guidebook*, 2015

It is not that this is entirely unsympathetic. Fawkes himself was a Catholic supremacist, but he fit into the same centuries-long tradition of religious dissidence in England that would eventually produce William Blake. And as David Lloyd noted, the basic cheek of trying to blow up Parliament is rather appealing.

But it is not so much Fawkes the man that is most relevant to the development of *V for Vendetta* as it is the holiday that sprung up in the wake of the plot. After it was uncovered, the public was encouraged to celebrate the plot's failure by lighting bonfires. The next January, Parliament passed the Observance of 5th November Act, which established a standing holiday commemorating the King's survival. This holiday persisted, not least because in 1688 William of Orange's arrival in England to overthrow James II happened to land on November the 5th, the day after his birthday, giving the holiday another resonance. Over time the custom of bonfires came to incorporate first burning the pope in effigy, and then, somewhat more moderately, burning Guy Fawkes in effigy—a tradition that led to the creation of the Guy Fawkes mask.

The holiday also, in the 19th century, gradually became more associated with the working class, a transition that led away from the celebration of victories of the monarchy and towards a more anti-authoritarian approach. Over the course of the century, Fawkes found himself incorporated into popular fiction, starting with William Harrison Ainsworth's 1841 novel *Guy Fawkes*, which rehabilitated Fawkes into a more sympathetic character who, by 1905, was appearing as a hero in illustrated books like *The Boyhood Days of Guy Fawkes; Or, the Conspirators of Old London.* This was very much the spirit in which Moore was introduced to the holiday—he talks of how "when parents explained to their offspring about Guy Fawkes and his attempt to blow up Parliament, there always seemed to be an undertone of admiration in their voices, or at least there did in Northampton."

Moore and Lloyd's intercession proved well-timed. Moore mentions that the autumn of 1981, when they were developing *V for Vendetta*, was the last year that the mask was widely available before it was "phased out in favour of green plastic Frankenstein monsters geared to the incoming celebration of an American Halloween." The specific dating of this transition is surely exaggerated by Moore, but it is true that the particulars of the Guy Fawkes holiday was in decline at the time, with it gradually becoming more known as Bonfire Night. (Moore notes that this was unsurprising following "a summer of anti-Thatcher riots across the UK.") Moore and Lloyd, then, found themselves in the fortuitous position of having based their comic on an image that was popular enough to be immediately recognizable, but that was also losing its stature such that they could imbue it with meaning relatively unfettered by its material past.

So what matters about Guy Fawkes is ultimately the way in which a symbol of radical and transgressive rejection of

Figure 169: An 1870s effigy of Guy Fawkes built by a London fruit vendor.

Figure 170: Police blocking the street during an anti-Thatcher riot in Brixton. (Photograph by Kim Aldis, licensed under a Creative Commons Attribution-Share Alike 3.0 Unported license.)

institutional power gradually became a more ambivalent symbol while also shedding most of the particulars of what that initial rejection actually consisted of, such that he became, in effect, a sort of socially sanctioned symbol of general insurrection. Combined with the image of the Guy Fawkes mask itself, which allowed Moore to render his central character a faceless and expressionless cipher, the idea allowed him a main character who embodied not any specific ideology, but rather a sort of generic objection to all ideologies—an approach summed up by Moore's decision to title the first chapter of *V for Vendetta* "The Villain" and to give V his line proclaiming, "I'm the King of the Twentieth Century. I'm the bogeyman. The villain. The Black sheep of the family"—in other words, the rejection of authority implicit in anarchism.

But what is striking about V and the Guy Fawkes mask is its connection to an authorized rejection of authority. The 19th century transformation of the Fifth of November into a working class holiday fits into a longstanding tradition of carefully controlled rebellion common to the British children's comics like *The Beano* and *The Dandy*. Guy Fawkes Night was, in many ways, a structural mirror of any given installment of *Dennis the Menace*—both feature a gleeful subversion of the social order with lots of explosions and mayhem, but more importantly, both also promptly end: *Dennis the Menace*, generally, with the reassertion of authority implicit in Dennis being spanked; Guy Fawkes Night by the rollover of the calendar onto another grim Victorian workday. Guy Fawkes represents a sanctioned rebellion—a specific place that institutional power allows dissent to exist, largely to keep it from existing anywhere else.

As Moore recognized, the fact that rebellion is an assumed part of the social order is itself a source of power. And Guy Fawkes serves as an effective image of this simply because of the sheer degree of rebellion he represents. If an attempt to blow up Parliament and assassinate the king can be recuperated into society as an authorized rebellion, the space available to rebellion is, perhaps, larger than it initially appears. And indeed, this helps explain why Lloyd's Guy Fawkes suggestion caused the entire concept to click together for Moore. In "Behind the Painted Smile," Moore recalls a list he made of things he wanted to include or reflect in *V for Vendetta*. The list he offers in "Behind the Painted Smile" reads: "Orwell. Huxley. Thomas Disch. *Judge Dredd*. Harlan Ellison's *'Repent, Harlequin!' Said the Ticktockman*. *Catman* and *Prowler in the City at the Edge of the World* by the same author. Vincent Price's *Dr. Phibes* and *Theatre of Blood*. David Bowie. The Shadow. Night-Raven. Batman. *Fahrenheit 451*. The writings of the *New Worlds* school of science fiction. Max Ernst's painting 'Europe After the Rains'. Thomas Pynchon. The atmosphere of British Second World War films. *The Prisoner*. Robin Hood. Dick Turpin…"

This is, obviously, a somewhat ludicrously diverse list, and that is in many regards the point. Everything upon the list is indeed reflected within *V for Vendetta* to some extent, and most (though not all) feature some consideration of a singular figure rebelling against an authoritarian regime, to varying degrees of effect, and, perhaps more notably, with various degrees of skepticism about that rebellion. But as Moore explains, "There was some element in all of these that I could use, but try as I might I couldn't come up with a coherent whole from such disjointed parts." But after Lloyd's Guy Fawkes idea was mooted, the connection Moore was looking for finally emerged—the British "tradition of making heroes out of criminals." In a 2005 interview, Moore went further, highlighting how many of the characters along these lines are "sociopaths" who are "thoroughly unpleasant," noting that "we love a gallant rogue and we also love a murdering, psychotic, horrific travesty of a human being. I thought that maybe I could exploit this."

This fascination with the intersection between the marginalized and mainstream elements of culture and with the notion of authorized rebellion also sheds light on one of Moore and Lloyd's collaborators in *V for Vendetta*, David J, who wrote the music for "This Vicious Cabaret" and who went on to record an official *V for Vendetta* EP featuring his own rendition of "This Vicious Cabaret" along with a setting of the cabaret song from "Variety" and some instrumental pieces. David J would go on to be a member of Moore's magical society (The Moon and Serpent Grand Egyptian Theatre of Marvels), contributing to Moore's five spoken word workings in the 90s and early 00s, and so it is worth pausing to unpack his contributions to Moore's earlier career, and, for that matter, Moore's early contribution to David J's career, which began in earnest, like Moore's, in 1979 with the formation of the band Bauhaus.

In many ways, Bauhaus was just a subtle alteration on several previous bands that had formed in Northampton, generally featuring some combination of David J, his younger brother Kevin Haskins, and Daniel Ash. In late 1978, Haskins and Ash formed one with bassist Chris Barber and a friend of Ash's, Peter Murphy, as the vocalist. (Murphy, despite the fact that he had no musical experience to speak of, in Ash's opinion, looked right for a lead vocalist.) After a few weeks, however, Ash decided Barber was not really working out, and instead invited David J to be their bassist. J suggested the band's name based on his love of the German art school of the same name, originally proposing Bauhaus 1919 (the year of the school's foundation) before shortening it to simply Bauhaus, and they played their first official gig as a New Year's Eve show (having previously crashed a Pretenders show when they brought their own amps to the union hall where the band was going to play and played their own set).

Two days later, while biking home from a warehouse job, David J had an idea for a lyric, and stopped to jot it down on the back of a series of address labels. He took it to rehearsal that night, and Ash matched it with a chord structure based around a sliding barre chord that left the E and B strings open. Haskins added a bossa-nova drumbeat (J notes that "he had been taking lessons from an old jazz guy, and this was one of the two beats he knew"), and J opted for a simple walking bassline, over which Murphy sang the lyric: "White on white, translucent black cape's back on the rack... Bela Lugosi's dead." As J describes it, "we all just fell in with each other. It was as if we had been playing this strange song for years." They debuted it the next day at a gig in Kingsthorpe, and went into the studio to record it and some other tracks a couple of weeks later.

Given that the song was in effect the product of a jam session, the sweep and scale of the studio version is perhaps not entirely surprising. It is, however, undoubtedly impressive: the song clocks in at nine-and-a-half minutes long. The melody is driven entirely by David J's baseline for the first ninety seconds, starting with him plucking the first note of his three-note bass line, then beginning the walkdown, letting each of the three notes hang. Only after those first ninety seconds is there any variation, and that just consists of him filling in the extra beats of each measure with repetitions of the note as Ash adds a trilling guitar effect with a hammer-on. The chords don't make an appearance until 2:20; the vocal line waits until nearly the three-minute mark. There's another ninety seconds of vocal-free ambience at five minutes, and the last two minutes are also almost totally wordless, and indeed mostly just feature Haskins's drumming with occasional bass interjections from David J. These long expanses in which the song is left to its simple and sparse instrumentation, augmented only by some echo effects whipped up by Ash after studio engineer Derek Tompkins taught him how to use a delay unit, give the song an ethereal tone that suits its vampiric subject matter. Equally crucial, however, is Murphy's voice—a luscious baritone that hits the exact mix of austerity and camp necessary to sell a song about the star of the 1931 Universal *Dracula* film that includes lines like, "The virginal brides file past his tomb, strewn with time's dead flowers, bereft in deathly bloom," and repeated chants of "undead undead undead." As Alan Moore put it, "Jay's bass and Haskins' drums provided the music with its elegant and powerful metal skeleton, while Murphy's hard, haunting voice and Ash's molten glass guitar provided its white, jewel-studded flesh."

"None more goth."
–Kieron Gillen

The result was a minor hit that stuck around in the independent charts for two years and, perhaps more significantly, marked the birth of goth music. Sticking with the period aesthetic from which they got their name and first single, Bauhaus quickly forged a distinctive visual style that drew from German Expressionism coupled with periodic trips to antique stores to pick over "piles of moth-eaten Victorian velvet (in both the ladies and gentleman's departments)" as J puts it. This aesthetic was particularly eye-catching in their live shows, thanks to Graham Bentley's lighting design, which used stark industrial lighting and strobes to flood the stage with light that emphasized their monochromatic wardrobe. All of this served to highlight, in Moore's words, "the riveting stage presence of Peter Murphy as he writhes against his live backdrop of searing white light and contorted shadows"—a stage presence that would go on to become one of the defining images of goth culture when director Tony Scott used the song and Murphy's performance for the opening credits of his classic 1983 vampire film *The Hunger*, with Murphy gyrating against and tearing at a wire mesh, a libidinous monster playing homage to the cinematic tradition Scott's film succeeds.

Moore, indeed, was one of the band's early boosters, giving them one of their first pieces of national press in February of 1980 when he gave them a half-page writeup in *Sounds*, some eight months before their first full album, when they were still riding high on the back of two singles and a Peel session. Entitled "Phantoms of the Teenage Opera," the piece concludes by proclaiming the band to have "a sound as clean as a razor, and a vision that doesn't need dressing up in angry rhetoric or android accessories to make a point. Their

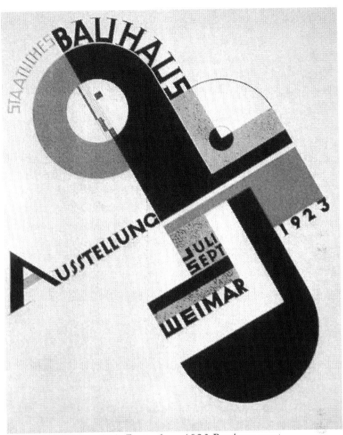

Figure 171: Poster for a 1923 Bauhaus event.

Figure 172: Peter Murphy in The Hunger. *David J's bass is visible on the left.*

music may have the shadow of the tall steel over it, but that's a heartbeat you hear throbbing in the background, not a ring modulator. On yer bikes, the rest of you. Here comes the night shift." Moore would also write the liner notes for the band's second album, *Mask*, under the pseudonym Brilburn Logue:

> "This is for when the slats of the night slam shut on you, for when the radio is broken and crackles like uranium orchids, for when the Föhn-wind rattles the telegraph wires like a handful of bones, and this is for when dream ambulances skitter through the streets at midnight. In the amusement arcade a sailor whose muscles writhe with pornography, doubled up, his vomiting emeralds. Elsewhere a black man with brass teeth and a swallow skin tie is laughing and laughing and offering poisoned candy floss to the children. This is for when your cuff gets caught in the cogs of an urban evening, for when your vision is frayed and you don't have any more lust. This is for the wasp-woman. This is for the torturers' wives with their thumbs blue as billiard chalk. This is for all the mathematicians who got mixed up in the dream gang. This is for when you get caught in a sleep riot, this is for when your jism turns to platinum, for when the television is full of murder, for when the sky is out of order, for when your room is crawling with cheap poetry. This is for when your veins are singing with indigo, for when the radiator is full of fever, for when your sex is full of voodoo, for when your clothes are imaginary, for when your kitchen is dead. This is for when your flesh creeps and never comes back."

Moore's support for the band is hardly surprising—they were, after all, Northampton locals. Indeed, one can read Moore's liner notes for *Mask* as a sort of primitive ancestor of his Nighthampton dreamscape from *The Show*, and the strange and dreadful nature of the place was one of the first things Bauhaus tried to capture in their music. The title track of their first studio album, "In the Flat Field," with its howled chorus of "I get bored, I do get bored in the flat field" is about, as J puts it, "the quotidian mundaneness of life in Northampton, and the desire to escape that flat existence." And yet for all of this, Murphy's lyrics gives a sense of strange wonder to the place:

A gut pull drag on me
Into the chasm gaping we
Mirrors multi-reflecting this
Between spunk-stained sheet
And odorous whim
Camera eye-flick shudder within
Assist me to walk away in sin
Where is the string that Theseus laid
Find me out of this labyrinth place.

But the mutual connection to Northampton had a practical effect too, which is that Moore knew the band personally. David J had frequented an occasional event that Moore helped run (along with a guy who alternately went by the names of Pickle and Mr. Liquorice) called the Deadly Fun Hippodrome, that J described as "a mad anarchic surrealist cabaret," and even played with Moore in an ad hoc band called the Sinister Ducks one afternoon when the scheduled entertainment failed to materialize. J had been slightly too young for the Arts Lab proper, but stuck around in the avant-garde scene of Northampton that Moore emerged out of, producing, for instance, a fanzine called *TV Murders* with Mr. Liquorice and Alan Moore. (Liquorice describes it as "kind of an anti-fanzine in that it featured no reviews or gig listings of any kind. Only surrealistic cut-ups and montages.")

That a man who proposed naming his band after a German art school would have an investment in the avant-garde is perhaps unsurprising. And this is further reflected in the band's music, which always balanced its self-consciously punk rawness with an art-school level of self-awareness. Both *Mask* and their third album *The Sky's Gone Out* contain songs assembled in an "exquisite corpse" style—indeed, the latter song is actually called "Exquisite Corpse." For the first one of these, simply called "1. Jay 2. Murphy 3. Haskins 4. Ash," each member of the band contributed a short track composed to an agreed-upon drumbeat, with the resulting song stitching them together. "Exquisite Corpse" went with an even less restricted approach, dropping the drum track and letting the members run wild. They also produced an experimental film called *Consequences* with the same approach, and although J describes this as "extremely self-indulgent and overlong," the fact that it exists reveals the commitment to this sort of self-consciously avant-garde style.

This inspiration comes to a creative head in the second track of the band's final album of the 1980s, *Burning from the Inside*, an homage to the French playwright Antonin Artaud, whose post-surrealist manifesto of the Theater of Cruelty remains one of the most radical visions of that medium ever espoused. In December of 1982, the band engaged in an "attempt to raise his spirit through a ritualistic performance" in Chicago: with the band stripped to the waist and covered with UV-sensitive paint, they performed a concert that consisted of only of the song "Antonin Artaud," wherein they deliberately stalled on the repetition of the line "red fix" for more than twenty minutes in an attempt "to induce a trance-like state in the audience and ourselves," with the audience having been instructed to bring some sort of percussion instrument to participate in the performance themselves. The goal, as J explains it, was "to break through the usual restrictions of a rock gig, where the audience is distinctly separate from the band," so as "to attain a state of shared transcendence" and "shatter conventional perception through a violent, jarring, primitive rite, one that would go beyond 'performance' and become something shamanic, disturbing, and ultimately liberating. (We were, it has to be said, four very intense young men.)"

It will not escape attention that this description is self-evidently an act of magic and an aesthetic predecessor to J's later magical workings with the Moon and Serpent Grand Egyptian Theatre of Marvels. This was not a coincidence.

One of the singles off of *The Sky's Gone Out*, "Spirit," was, in J's explanation, about a quasi-supernatural entity that attended the band, which he describes as "a kind of supportive daemon that could only be evoked if we were all in tune with each other." The lyrics of the song make it clear that this is conceived of literally, giving the spirit voice as it explains:

> Tonight I could be with you
> Or waiting in the wings
> Lift your heart with soaring song
> Cut down the puppet strings

while also threatening that

> The stage becomes a ship in flames
> I tie you to the mast
> Throw your body overboard
> The spotlight doesn't last.

The song ends with Murphy repeatedly intoning "Call the curtain / Raise the roof / Spirit's on tonight" before turning into a repeated chant that "we love our audience," in what is difficult to take as anything other than a straightforward act of summoning.

A similar sort of spiritual invocation eventually emerged out of the song "Who Killed Mister Moonlight," a "surrealistic ballad on *Burning From the Inside* inspired in part by the murder of John Lennon," the title character of which was eventually taken by the band "as being representative of the dreamy, poetic aspect of Bauhaus." J would end up taking the lead vocal on the song, and would go on to use its title for his memoir. This was, in practice, because Peter Murphy was ill during most of the production of *Burning From the Inside*, which led the album to be mainly assembled by his bandmates, with him providing lead vocals later. This deepened the sense of division between Murphy and the rest of the band that had been growing for some time, and hastened the band's dissolution during the tour following the album. The other three eventually reunited as Love and Rockets, but not before J recorded and released the *V for Vendetta* EP in 1984.

But not all of the influences on *V for Vendetta* were so radically countercultural. Indeed, one of the biggest, from which the series would eventually draw the title of its third part, was almost ostentatiously mainstream: the work of Enid Blyton. Blyton was an exceedingly prolific British children's writer in the early 20th century best known for her *Famous Five* and *Secret Seven* series, but for the purposes of *V for Vendetta* it is one of her lesser series, the *Magic Faraway Tree* series, that is most relevant. That series debuted in 1939 with *The Enchanted Wood*, which told the story of Jo, Bessie, and Fanny, who live near a large forest, which turns out to be the eponymous Enchanted Wood. (H.P. Lovecraft, describing the Enchanted Wood in *The Dream Quest of Unknown Kadath*, says: "In the tunnels of that twisted wood, whose low prodigious oaks twine groping boughs and shine dim with the phosphorescence of strange fungi, dwell the furtive and secretive Zoogs; who know many obscure secrets of the dream world and a few of the waking world, since the wood at two places touches the lands of men, though it would be disastrous to say where. Certain unexplained rumours, events, and vanishments occur among men where the Zoogs have access, and it is well that they cannot travel far outside the world of dreams. But over the nearer parts of the dream world they pass freely, flitting small and brown and unseen and bearing back piquant tales to beguile the hours around their hearths in the forest they love. Most of them live in burrows, but some inhabit the trunks of the great trees; and although they live mostly on fungi it is muttered that they have also a slight taste for meat, either physical or spiritual, for certainly many dreamers have entered that wood who have not come out.") Within it, they find the Faraway Tree, whose "top reaches the far-away places... sometimes its top branches may be in Witchland, sometimes in lovely countries, sometimes in peculiar places that no one has ever heard of." From this point the series becomes about the various adventures they have climbing the tree and going to the various lands along with their magical friends Moon-Face and Silky.

"His dirty white gloves were wrapped around her throat, gloves that had whip-steel in them where the fingers ought to be. Her eyes, her beautiful green eyes were starting to bug out, inflated with pain and horror. Death was turning her face into a field of pale and sickly violets."
–Alan Moore, "Night Raven: The Cure," 1982

These adventures are written in Blyton's characteristically straightforward prose style, which Colin Welch famously described as that of "the first successful writer of children's books to actually write *below* her audience," that the BBC wouldn't let programs invite Blyton on the grounds that she was a "tenacious second-rater" who produced "mediocre material," and that her voluminous output was the work of genius only because "anyone else would have died of boredom long ago." This is certainly a harsh assessment, but it is in truth difficult to argue. Consider, for instance, her account of the group's adventures in the Land of Take-What-You-Want, in which "if you want anything, you can usually get it there for nothing." At one point, the adventure goes as follows:

'Do you want a nice fat lion, Jo?' asked Silky, as a large lion wandered by and licked Silky's hand.
'No, thank you,' said Jo, at once.
'Well, what about a giraffe?' said Silky. 'I believe they make fine pets.'
'You believe wrong then,' said Bessie, as a tall giraffe galloped past like a rocking-horse. 'Nobody in their senses would want to keep a giraffe for a pet.'
'Oh, look!' cried Fanny, as she came to a shop in which stood a great many large and beautiful clocks. 'Do let's take a clock back home!'

This is, to be clear, par for the course for Blyton. In the 1943 sequel *The Magic Faraway Tree*, Blyton creates a land not entirely dissimilar to the Land of Take-What-You-Want: the Land of Do-As-You-Please. In it, Jo drives a train, Fanny gets everyone elephants to ride, and Dick (a new character in this book) goes swimming. Then Moon-Face gets an idea for something to do:

> 'Let's dig an ENORMOUS castle!' cried Moon-Face. 'Then we can all sit on the top of it when the sea comes up.'
>
> 'We can't,' said Silky, suddenly looking sad.
>
> 'Why not? Why not?' cried Jo in surprise. 'Isn't this the Land of Do-As-You-Please?'
>
> 'Yes,' said Silky. 'But it's time we went back to the Faraway Tree. This land will soon be on the move—and nice as it is, we don't want to live here for ever.'
>
> 'Gracious, no,' said Jo. 'Our mother and father couldn't possibly do without us...'

This portion of the book makes an appearance in the first part of *V for Vendetta*, with V reading it to Evey as a bedtime story before leaving to kill Delia Surridge. Its significance is straightforward enough—the Land of Do-As-You-Please is clearly a vision of an anarchist society, and is indeed what V comes to call the society he brings about over the course of the story.

But the use of such a ruthlessly establishment piece of "literature" is significant in its own right, further cementing Moore's implicit case that the anarchic tradition he's espousing is an integral part of British culture. By taking the ridiculously contrived and sudden departure from the Land of Do-As-You-Please and juxtaposing it with V murdering someone, Moore highlights the possibility that is fundamentally unspeakable within Blyton's bland and anodyne tale: that one doesn't have to leave the Land of Do-As-You-Please, and that anyone in their right mind would want to live there forever. And so the sort of revolutionary freedom that Moore espouses is revealed not as some external force trying to destabilize British society, but as something that's slumbering deep within Albion's psyche.

But perhaps more significant is the way in which this viewpoint can be said to have been lurking within British comics in 1982. It is worth noting that although Moore includes it in his 1983 catalogue of inspirations, many of these later interviews downplay what might fairly be called the most obvious inspiration for *V for Vendetta*, especially given Moore's existing career at the time he created it: *Judge Dredd*. Moore, after all, had become a frequent contributor to *2000 AD* by the time *Warrior #1* came out, and was specifically drawn to the satirical aspects of the comic, which Dredd was in many ways the epitome of. And *V for Vendetta* can easily be read as a straightforward inversion of *Judge Dredd*. Where Dredd is an eternally-masked figure embodying absolute and unwavering authority who's presented as the hero of his stories while constantly being undermined and revealed as the fascist monster that he is, V is an eternally-masked figure embodying complete and utter rejection of authority, initially presented as the villain of the piece while tacitly endorsing his position. In many ways, the entire strip is a logical iteration of the British comics industry as it existed when Moore was writing it—a revision of the industry's most popular character that makes its point directly, instead of through irony-laden satire.

This is particularly unsurprising given the publication it was appearing in. *Warrior* was, by design, the brasher cousin to the rest of the market. Its first issue opened with an editorial titled "Freedom's Road," in which editor Dez Skinn boldly proclaimed that "while the large comics publishers seem to be in a period of creative regression, we hope our attempt, our one little magazine in a sea of others, will spark off enough interest to get things moving again." In a later interview, Skinn explained that, after leaving Marvel, he wanted "to stop doing quantity and start doing quality," and so "took the team I had built up at *House of Hammer*, *Doctor Who*, and *Hulk* (the comics I'd produced previously) and said to them, 'Okay, let's do it again but for ourselves this time.'"

This latter quote indicates the complex sort of waffling Skinn was engaged in. On the one hand, the "for ourselves this time" attitude suggests the sort of soaring iconoclasm whose promise is implicit in the title "Freedom's Road." It positions *Warrior* as a sort of cousin of *Near Myths*—a magazine that would fuse the intelligence of the underground with the accessibility of the mainstream. It also had a practical aspect: *Warrior* was, unique in the mainstream British comics industry, a creator-owned publication, which meant that, for instance, Steve Moore and John Bolton owned *The Legend of Prester John* and *Father Shandor, Demon Stalker* and would be in a position to profit directly from any success the properties had. In fact, this was part of *Warrior*'s business plan—Skinn stood to profit from any foreign publication or larger success as well, and every strip was designed with an eye on that market, so explicitly that Moore, when developing a proposed *Warrior* strip called *Nightjar* with Brian Talbot, noted that Talbot should plan the art so that it would be easily colorized for foreign markets: "I know this sounds like a remote shot, but Dez is very definitely gearing himself up towards finding space in that kind of market."

But in some ways the really revealing thing is Skinn's explicit decision to model the contents of *Warrior* on his previous success with Marvel UK's *Hulk Comic*, with several of the strips in *Warrior* being direct mirrors of those in *Hulk Comic*, often with the same creators, such as Steve Moore and Steve Dillon's *Laser Eraser and Pressbutton*, a clear reworking of the pair's Nick Fury strip in *Hulk Comic*, or Steve Parkhouse's *The Spiral Path*, which was modeled directly on the *Black Knight* strip he'd done for *Hulk Comic*. As Skinn freely admits, "We were not really trying to create something new." This points at an important aspect of Skinn's editing of *Warrior*, which was that he was, in a number of ways, extremely conservative and cautious. He once argued with Moore over whether to tone down the language in one comic, rhetorically asking Moore, "Why offend even one reader?" to which Moore strenuously objected, pointing out that "the alternative is to gear your entire product to the most squeamish and prudish member of the audience." Moore, while outlining *Nightjar* to Talbot, noted that "we *do* have to appeal to people with some pretty base sensibilities. Dez, for one." This made Skinn an awkward editor for an iconoclastic publication like *Warrior.*

It also serves to expose, underneath the vast web of influences upon the strip, the actual pragmatic reason why *V for Vendetta* came into being, which is that along with his clones of the Nick Fury and Black Knight strips, Dez Skinn wanted a version of another one of his *Hulk Comic* strips, a 1930s noir strip by Steve Parkhouse and David Lloyd called *Night Raven.* The strip was a triumph of the sort of conceptual minimalism that characterizes British comics. Its debut was a three-page story in which the eponymous masked vigilante crashes a meeting of crime bosses and successfully picks them off one by one, grabbing the last one by the head and branding him with his sigil, leaving him catatonic. The strip is bookended by the two trademark phrases of the strip—its opening line of "Night-time in the city..." and the note that Night Raven leaves with his last victim that reads simply, "where brooding darkness spreads its evil wings the Night Raven stings!"

These two lines constitute, in practice, the entire concept of *Night Raven* as a strip. The character is not given any sort of origin or explanation. The city is never named. There is no sense of context—subsequent strips simply find new corners of the city in which Night Raven can bust new sorts of crime. All of that is visibly extraneous. The purpose of *Night Raven* is simply to allow for a three-page slice of action in a pulp noir aesthetic. In this regard, the creators could hardly have been better chosen. Steve Parkhouse is one of the unheralded greats of the British comics industry—one of those whose style is so particularly focused on the structures of British comics that he never broke out elsewhere. Which is to say, he's a particular master of the ultra-short form. His stories often hang together best, strangely, when read as continual narratives, but on an individual chapter level they're unparalleled, and *Night Raven* exemplifies this in its discarding of everything that isn't immediately relevant to creating a compelling action scene. And the noir setting brings out Lloyd's strengths, allowing him to use large patches of shadowy blackness and giving him lots of action sequences, while also blunting his biggest weakness by not requiring a large variety of facial expressions and by making the slight grotesqueness of his characteristic bulging eyes an appropriate part of the tone.

Night Raven ran for fourteen installments in *Hulk Comic* under Parkhouse and Lloyd, and then for a further six with John Bolton replacing Lloyd on art (due, apparently, to Stan Lee's distaste for Lloyd's work) for a Yellow Peril-infused adventure pitting Night Raven against "Yi Yang, leader of the Dragon Tong... radiant as a rose, but with a heart as cold as steel," at which point it became a casualty of *Hulk Comic's* steady transition to being a US reprint comic like the rest of the Marvel UK stable. It was, however, popular enough to merit continuation as a series of text features, first in *Savage Action*, and then, when that title was merged into it, in *Marvel Super-Heroes*, where it appeared alongside the Dave Thorpe *Captain Britain* strips. These features, by Paul Neary and Alan McKenzie (writing under the Marvel UK house pseudonym of Maxwell Stockbridge), were fairly generic stories in the pulp fiction milieu, following straightforwardly from the *Hulk Comic* strips. ("It was New Year's Eve," begins one of Paul Neary's stories, entitled "Killing by Numbers." "The party-going jet-setters whiled away the hours approaching midnight, as the snow fell softly into the concrete canyons of the city. The drifting flakes blotted the squalor and disrepair of the tenements and alleyways from view, but it could never eradicate the deeper, spiritual decay that festered in the souls of the city's underworld.")

Once *Warrior* emerged with their tremendously successful *Night Raven* clone, however, Marvel UK was quick to respond, putting Alan Moore in as writer of the text pieces. Moore, as is his wont, commenced revamping the character. In typical fashion, Moore brought back supporting characters from the strip's history, including crime reporter Scoop Daley from Lloyd's last arc and the return of Yi Yang, who he established as Night Raven's iconic villain. In similarly typical fashion, he continued by killing Night Raven off, albeit with a twist, with Yi Yang infecting Night Raven with a toxin that, as Moore describes it in his first story, "corrodes the flesh and eats away at the brain until your whole world is just filled with pain and horror and madness. And then it kills you. Fifty years later." Moore also hit upon the idea of giving the stories a clear narrator other than Night Raven, thus putting the central character at a slight remove to make him "charismatic and unknowable." This is played to its best effect in Moore's second story, "White Hopes, Red Nightmares," which tells of a psychotic man named Howard Bates in 1957 who adopts Night Raven's identity and starts murdering people he believes to be communists while Night Raven himself is semi-amnesiac and reeling from Yi Yang's poison, but it's a common element in all but one of Moore's five tales (and the only one it doesn't apply to is a one-parter concerned almost entirely with major plot developments).

"It was a voice of thunder that answered the question—a drawling twang in a forbidden tongue we'd only ever heard in banned movie reels."
–Grant Morrison, *Multiversity: Mastermen*, 2015

Over the course of Moore's stories, Night Raven suffers from the disease until he finally obtains a cure, at which point he realizes that Yi Yang had only done all of this to give herself an enemy. ("How does an immortal kill herself?" Night Raven ponders in the story where he's finally cured. "She sets about creating a weapon, perhaps unconsciously, responding to that barely audible voice inside her that pleads

Philip Sandifer

Figure 173: Night Raven causes the antagonists to kill their own man by putting a Night Raven mask on one of them. (Written by Steve Parkhouse, art by David Lloyd, from Hulk Comic #1, 1979)

Figure 174: V causes the antagonists to kill their own man by putting a Guy Fawkes mask on one of them. (Written by Alan Moore, art by David Lloyd, from "The Vacation" in Warrior #18, 1984)

for extinction. She creates a weapon that might just be able to kill her.") This also let Moore gradually move the setting up to the present day, which has obvious appeal to anyone seeking to use the character in future stories since it enables teaming him up with other characters in the Marvel stable. Having accomplished this, however, and with Moore backing away from Marvel UK work due to his dissatisfaction with Bernie Jaye's dismissal, Moore, again characteristically, handed the text pieces over to Jamie Delano, giving him his first professional credit.

V for Vendetta, however, fell a long way from *Night Raven*, although certainly similarities were maintained, most obviously the faceless and implacable nature of the lead characters, although V eventually did get the origin story that Night Raven lacked. The most obvious of these is the change in setting from the 1930s to the present day—a change prompted by Lloyd's request to not have to keep doing a bunch of historical reference. Moore proceeded to mull over the nature of the 1930s noir setting, and concluded that the appeal "was rooted in the exotic and glamorous locations that the stories were set in... seedy waterfront bars, plush penthouses dripping with girls, stuff like that. All the magic of a vanished age." And, further, that "it might be possible to get the same effect by placing the story in the near future as opposed to the near past," thus giving the story its futuristic setting, which Moore then combined with an abandoned idea he'd submitted to *Starblazer* publisher DC Thomson, about a white-faced terrorist called the Doll fighting a near-future totalitarian dictatorship, which set Moore and Lloyd upon the path that would eventually lead to Moore's aforementioned list of would-be influences and Lloyd's Guy Fawkes idea.

This accounts for almost all of the conceptual genesis of *V for Vendetta*, save for one detail, namely how it is that Moore came to be the writer on it. The most obvious person to pair with Lloyd on a *Night Raven* clone, after all, would have been Steve Parkhouse, although Parkhouse was already employed writing and drawing *The Spiral Path* for *Warrior*. The explanation for this is relatively simple, however: David Lloyd wanted Moore. They had already worked together on some of Moore's *Doctor Who Weekly* strips, and Lloyd clearly believed in Moore's talent, having opted to interview him for the Society of Script Illustrators newsletter, despite his extreme greenness at the time. Skinn had no problem with Lloyd's suggested writer, presumably in part because Skinn was already entertaining a pitch from Moore for the strip that Skinn intended to be the centerpiece of his new magazine, a revival of Mick Anglo's 1950s character of Marvelman.

Where Moore got the *V for Vendetta* job due to Lloyd's intercession, *Marvelman* he landed more or less entirely on the strength of his idea for it—an idea that, to be fair, he'd been working on and refining for sixteen years at that point. As Moore tells it, he was on holiday at the Seashore Caravan Camp in Yarmouth at the age of twelve, relishing the fact that the coastal regions of the UK had slightly different comics distribution than what was available in Northampton, and that there were thus a wealth of new comics to read. And on his 1966 holiday, this included both a *Young Marvelman* annual and *The Mad Reader*. The latter of these contained Kurtzman and Wood's iconic "Superduperman" [See Chapter 6—Ed]. The former contained a selection of Mick Anglo's *Marvelman* stories, published between 1954 and 1963.

The origin of Marvelman is legendarily complex. The story begins in the United States in 1940 with the publication of Fawcett Comics' *Whiz Comics* #2 (which, unusually, was actually the first issue of the magazine, although it also had two issue threes, so in a sense it all worked out in the end), featuring the debut of Captain Marvel. Captain Marvel was a fairly straightforward attempt to capitalize on the success of DC's Superman, to the point of having a cover in which the character hurls a car, much like Superman does on the cover of *Action Comics* #1. The story within, however, had a markedly different tone. It opens with a young boy trying to sell a newspaper to a mysterious figure in a trench coat and fedora, who asks him, "Why aren't you home in bed, son?"

The boy explains that he's homeless and sleeps in the subway, at which point the man exclaims, "Follow me!" The boy for some reason does, at which point "a strange subway car, with headlights gleaming like a dragon's eyes, roars into the station and stops. No one is driving it!" The man reassures the boy, telling him that "everything has been arranged," and so the boy gets on the train, which takes them to "a platform resembling the mouth of a weird, subterranean cavern." At this point, the mysterious man vanishes from the narrative entirely, and the boy walks past statues representing the seven deadly enemies of man (in fact the seven sins) and meets "an old, old man, sitting on a marble throne." He introduces himself as Shazam (and a bolt of lightning strikes as he does), and explains that this is an acronym for Solomon Hercules Atlas Zeus Achilles Mercury. Shazam has apparently been using (respectively) the wisdom, strength, stamina, power, courage, and speed of these gods "to battle the forces of evil which every day threaten to extinguish man from the face of the Earth," but he's grown too old to continue, and so has decided that the boy, Billy Batson, will now have to fight evil in his place by speaking his name and transforming into Captain Marvel. At this point Shazam is crushed by a massive block of granite, and Batson returns to the world above ground, where he foils the evil plan of Doctor Sivana, who wants to destroy all radio stations.

The character was a breakout success, at one point becoming the most popular superhero in the United States, outselling even Superman. This led DC to sue Fawcett on the grounds that Captain Marvel was simply a ripoff of Superman, a case that wound its way through the courts for twelve years until 1953, at which point Fawcett, bled dry by legal fees and the post-War decline of superhero comics, opted to settle the case and cease publishing Captain Marvel, at which point DC licensed and eventually bought the character. (This lawsuit, it should be reiterated, was what Kurtzman and Wood's "Superduperman" was parodying.) The shutdown of Captain Marvel in 1953, however, gave the

British comics publisher L. Miller & Son, who had bought the rights to publish black and white reprints of *Captain Marvel* in the UK, a significant problem, in that their most popular comic had abruptly ceased to exist.

To deal with this, L. Miller & Son paid one of their writer-artists, Mick Anglo, to create a replacement character. Anglo stuck pretty closely to the original material. Instead of Billy Batson there was Micky Moran. Instead of a wizard there was an atomic scientist. And instead of saying "Shazam" the character's magic word was "Kimota," which was of course "atomic" backwards. Other than that, however, the character was a near-exact lift of Captain Marvel, and when he made his debut in the newly retitled *Marvelman* #25, he didn't even get an origin story beyond a caption box that explained, "A recluse Astro-Scientist discovers the key word to the Universe, one that can only be given to a Boy who is completely honest, studious, and of such integrity that he would only use it for the powers of good. He finds such a Boy in **MICKY MORAN**, a Newspaper Copy Boy, and treats him in a special machine which enables him to use the secret. Just before the Scientist dies he tells **Micky** the Key Word which is **KIMOTA. MICKY MORAN** remains as he ways, but when he says the Key Word **KIMOTA** he becomes **MARVELMAN**, a Man of such strength and powers that he is Invincible and Indestructible."

It would be a gratuitous exaggeration to suggest that *Marvelman* was particularly good. Far from it—the strip never really developed beyond its origins as a *Captain Marvel* knockoff. Nevertheless, it was the one British-created superhero of any significance, and retained a certain nostalgic cachet as a result. And so when Moore happened upon a collection of Young Marvelman stories (Marvelman, like Captain Marvel, had a pair of child sidekicks/spinoffs) alongside "Superduperman," he had an idea. He was aware that *Marvelman* had long since gone out of print, and found himself imagining what the character might be up to these days. This intersected with the idea of a superhero parody, and he found himself musing on the idea of a version of Marvelman who had forgotten his magic word.

This, in turn, intersected with Skinn's developing plans for *Warrior*. He viewed his quiet revival of Captain Britain in *Hulk Comic* as one of its biggest successes, and furthermore wanted to make sure he had a superhero comic in the mix. As he put it, "I wanted one of the six strips to reflect Marvel, to gain a slice of their audience, with something uniquely British." Given that, Marvelman was really the only character available. Skinn first offered the strip to Steve Parkhouse, and then, when he wasn't interested, to Steve Moore, who also wasn't interested, but who noted that he had a friend who would be hugely interested—Moore having just mentioned it in his Society of Strip Illustrators interview with Lloyd as a dream project. Skinn, however, was understandably cautious about giving what he intended to be one of the marquee strips in his magazine to an untested writer, and so Moore wrote up a pitch outlining his ideas for the character.

Moore's pitch begins with several paragraphs outlining his general philosophical take on the character and on how he could best "bring what was basically a silly-arsed strip into line with the Nineteen-Eighties." This required grappling with the nostalgia involved in reviving the character. As Moore observed, "Nostalgia, if handled wrong, can prove to be nothing better than sloppy and mawkish crap. In my opinion, the central appeal of nostalgia is that all this stuff in the past has gone. It's finished. We'll never see it again... and this is where the incredible poignance of nostalgia really comes from." Moore's solution was to juxtapose the nostalgia for Marvelman with the "cruel and cynical Eighties," arguing that "the resultant tension will hopefully provide a real charge and poignance." Further, Moore was eager to make the strip work as good science fiction, which, in his view, meant that the strip's fantastic premise "should stem from one divergence from reality," which, he explained, would be "the crashing of an alien spacecraft in 1948."

At this point, Moore begins a lengthy explanation of his

revamped mythology for the strip. At the heart of it was the character of Emil Gargunza, Anglo's transparent substitute for Doctor Sivana. In Moore's conception, Gargunza was a Brazilian scientist who made his name in eugenics research before contracting for the Third Reich and subsequently defecting to the UK at the end of the war. This led to him being put in charge of investigating the 1948 spaceship crash, in which he discovered alien bodies that appeared to be two bodies fused together. Gargunza figures out that these aliens have the ability to switch between two bodies, and thus to transform into beings of tremendous power, and commences figuring out how to do this with human bodies so as to create superheroes. He does so with three orphans associated with the Royal Air Force (his employer), keeping them under strict observation and testing their abilities by feeding them false memories of being silly cartoonish superheroes. In 1961, he terminates the experiment, detonating a nuclear weapon in their immediate proximity to kill them.

Instead, however, his oldest subject, Micky Moran, survives in his human form, but he's forgotten how to transform into a superhero. He grows up, gets married, gets a job, and at this point Moore proposes to pick up his story in an episode entitled "A Dream of Flying." Moore outlines a plot that begins with Moran having a joyful dream of flying that turns ugly as he's engulfed in some sort of fireball. Moran awakens and heads to work as a freelance journalist, covering the opening of a nuclear power station, but haunted by the dream. Terrorists attack the power plant, attempting to steal plutonium so they can build their own hydrogen bomb. Moran, held hostage, sees the word "ATOMIC" reflected in a door, and reads it backwards, out loud, suddenly transforming himself into Marvelman. The terrorist next to him simply drops dead, burnt to death in the force of Marvelman's transformation. Seven feet tall and blue, he trivially cleans up the terrorists and flies away, joyful at being a superhero again.

Moore then goes on to outline some future plots, starting with one in which Kid Marvelman turns out also to have survived, but in his superhero form, which he remained in, growing rich and powerful with his secret abilities and becoming, in Moore's words, "a nasty amoral son-of-a-bitch." He also suggests an arc in which Gargunza's employers take an interest in the newly returned Marvelman after he visits the grave of Dicky Dawson, Young Marvelman, followed by one in which Marvelman confronts Gargunza himself. "This should take us well into the stage where we're selling the film rights and printing up the T-Shirts and similar," Moore quips, although this would more or less have been true save for a series of creative conflicts and poor investments. "I'll worry about what comes next when I get that far." Moore then suggests Dave Gibbons or Steve Dillon as artists—both had in fact already been sounded out but were uninterested—and notes that he could rework the idea with a Marvelman pastiche, perhaps called Miracle Man, if the rights proved unavailable. This pitch sufficiently impressed Skinn that he asked Moore to write a first installment on spec that, if Skinn liked it, would land him the job.

(The last point raised in Moore's pitch raises a significant issue in turn: the character of Marvelman was created by another company, and Skinn had to make sure he did not infringe upon their copyrights. This fact would end up causing a series of problems for over thirty years until Marvel Comics finally solved them all by rounding up everybody who might have had rights to the character and paying them off over the course of 2009-13. The result of this decision— entirely necessary given the eventual mess into which the legal situation had by that point degenerated—means that the actual legal situation has become a sort of superposition of competing claims, none of which had or ever will have their day in court, having been rendered irrelevant in the face of Marvel's expenditures, and all of which are now essentially irrelevant, no matter how much ink was spilled over them back in the day.

Regardless, it appears that what happened was as follows. At the start, there were only two plausible entities who might have held the copyright to Marvelman: L. Miller & Sons and Mick Anglo. The former had gone out of business in 1974, without taking any action with the rights. This left Mick Anglo. Skinn, for his part, concluded that Anglo had no rights to the character, and that it was thus in the public domain. This is not entirely straightforward, as Anglo had, in 1977, reprinted a page of *Young Marvelman* art in an anthology called *Nostalgia: Spotlight on the Fifties* and added a copyright notice. Certainly Anglo is, in the wake of Marvel's resolution of the matter, the "official" person who held the rights prior to Marvel, with Marvel's deal to acquire the character having been made with Anglo, followed by them settling with all of the creators involved in the property over the course of the 1980s and 90s to republish their specific stories. But this is, notably, merely the way in which Marvel presented a process that really amounted to paying everybody who might plausibly sue over the rights enough money to promise that they wouldn't. But regardless of what the eventual 2009 resolution of the rights saga was, in 1981 Skinn concluded that Anglo's work had been a work-for-hire. All the same, he contacted Anglo to ask for his permission, which Anglo appears to have given without any expectation of payment, although Skinn did pay Anglo for reprinting some of Anglo's stories in the 1984 *Marvelman Special.*

This also, however, raises the question of Moore's own intellectual property rights. The entire concept of *Warrior* was that, unlike their work for companies like IPC or Marvel UK, Moore and the other contributors would retain creative ownership. This also applied to Marvelman, although, as a previously created character, it was somewhat more complex than with *V for Vendetta*. The understanding that everyone had at the time was that the rights were split between Moore, Leach, and Quality Publications, which is to say, Skinn. Over the next decade, these supposed rights would be traded around among the writers and artists as they came and went, a process that would eventually become a key component of a legal dispute between Neil Gaiman and Todd McFarlane, before, like everything else, being superseded by Marvel's "pay everyone" plan. Nevertheless, the question of exactly how Skinn obtained these rights was not entirely settled. Moore's recollection is that Skinn told him he'd purchased the rights from the Official Receiver, who owned them following L. Miller & Son's 1963 bankruptcy. This is, it should be noted, precisely the sort of detail Moore is not always great about recalling. If that was Skinn's explanation to Moore, it was clearly a fabrication, not least because L. Miller & Son did not go bankrupt in 1963 or, indeed, at all. And Moore has not been subtle in suggesting malfeasance on Skinn's part, bluntly saying that "my opinion—for what that is worth—is that there was knowing deceit involved in the Marvelman decision." But for all of this, it is worth stressing a key fact about Skinn's conduct, namely that he, through all of this, never would have thought about what he was doing in terms of creating a watertight legal case for the purposes of resolving a thirty-year-long intellectual property dispute. From his perspective, once Mick Anglo gave his blessing to the project—and it's clear that he did—the rights were settled, and as long as, at any given point, everyone who might sue was satisfied and not going to do so, that was more than sufficient for the purposes of publishing *Warrior*, although it would turn out that he had not adequately considered one other company with a potential legal claim in a character called Marvelman.)

Moore's script was a fairly direct adaptation of what he suggested in his pitch, to the extent of containing sections of the pitch as caption boxes, and was sufficient to get him the job. The artist chosen for the project was Garry Leach,

Figure 175: Marvelman's joyous return. (Written by Alan Moore, art by Gary Leach, from "A Dream of Flying" in Warrior *#1, 1982)*

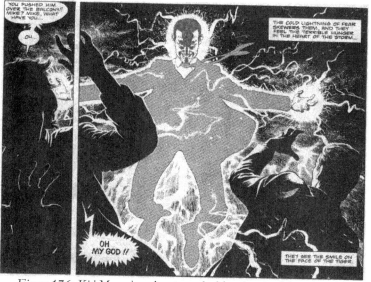

Figure 176: Kid Marvelman's return, darkly mirroring Marvelman's. (Written by Alan Moore, art by Garry Leach, from "When Johnny Comes Marching Home" in Warrior *#3, 1982)*

recommended by David Lloyd, and who had previously worked with Moore on "They Sweep the Spaceways," one of his *Future Shocks* for IPC. Leach drew the first three installments of the strip, which covered Moore's initial script. One issue focused on Marvelman coming back to explain what was going on to his/Moran's wife, which gave Moore an opportunity to recap Marvelman's canonical origin story and how a superhero came to be a middle aged journalist (Liz Moran laughs at the absurdity of the story, upsetting Marvelman, who protests, "This may, damn it... this does sound silly in 1982, but in the fifties it made perfect sense"). Another introduced Kid Miracleman/Johnny Bates, which ends with the revelation that Kid Marvelman has gone bad in a series of caption boxes as he unveils himself: "The cold lightning of fear skewers them, and they feel the terrible hunger in the heart of the storm... they see the smile on the face of the tiger."

The next installment of *Marvelman* marked the point where things started to go wrong for *Warrior* and, indeed, for the strip. Skinn's original plan was to do a Summer Special of *Warrior*, which would include a *Marvelman* strip called "The Yesterday Gambit" in which Moore would flash-forward the plot line. It was to consist of three sections: a frame story drawn by Steve Dillon featuring Marvelman's exploration of an alien-built underwater structure called Silence, with a mysterious figure called Warpsmith; and a pair of sections in which Marvelman fights past versions of himself, one from during the adventure where Gargunza attempted to kill him, and one set between the first and second issues of *Warrior*, the former drawn by Paul Neary, the latter by Alan Davis. After drawing power from his encounters with his past selves, Marvelman and Warpsmith are attacked by Kid Marvelman, leading into a cliffhanger. This plan, however, was scuttled.

Unfortunately, *Warrior* was running into financial troubles from the start. Sales on the first issue had only been 40,000 or so, which was far lower than Skinn had hoped for. On top of that Leach was proving to be a slow artist, and deadlines on

Marvelman were imperiled from the start. The result of all of these problems was that the Summer Special and the fourth issue of *Warrior* were hastily merged together into one, which resulted in confused numbering and further harmed sales. This began the long and slow descent into failure for *Warrior* as payments grew increasingly late and increasingly small, resulting in various creators abandoning *Warrior* for more lucrative and reliable work.

The first to do so was Leach, who was finding the amount of time that *Marvelman* was taking and the pay *Warrior* was offering an unsatisfying combination. He stayed onboard as part of the magazine's design team but after one more installment in *Warrior* #5 he handed off art duties to Alan Davis, inking Davis's first two strips to smooth the transition. These three installments concluded the Kid Marvelman story, with the character ending up far more disturbing than the merely "amoral son-of-a-bitch," instead becoming an actively homicidal sociopath who casually kills his secretary and assistant, which Leach gruesomely depicts through a startlingly disturbing caption box of Moore's that reads, "Her name is Stephanie. She likes Adam and the Ants. Her boyfriend's name is Brian. She collects wedgewood. Her insides have turned to water. She is only human." Kid Marvelman also proves far more powerful than Marvelman, having had years to master his powers, and over the course of Leach's last strip and Davis's first, pummels Marvelman nearly to death. The fight prompts a series of phone calls (depicted in small inset panels) responding to "a signal that has been anticipated for nearly eighteen years," and result in a character named Sir Dennis Archer exclaiming, "Oh God. They're back. The monsters are back." But in the course of his brutal beating of Marvelman, Kid Marvelman makes a crucial mistake, gloating, "I beat him!! He thought he was bloody great and I beat him to a whimpering pulp!! And now I'm going to finish him off! Me! His adoring junior protege! Me. Kid Marvelman."

As this happens, Moore narrates: "Kid Marvelman.

Johnny Bates. He was human once. But he's forgotten all that. He has forgotten the curious hurts and joys of humanity. He has forgotten the warmth of bodies locked in love, forgotten the painful beauty of children. He has forgotten the primal terror that hides in the heart of the lightning, of the thunder. He should not have forgotten the thunder." For "Marvelman" was to Johnny Bates what "Kimota" was to Micky Moran—the word that transformed him back and forth between his identities. It causes him to suddenly change back into a small and terrified child, seemingly no longer dangerous (although this assumption on Marvelman's part has already been undermined for the reader by the flash forward in "Yesterday's Gambit").

Leach's last involvement with *Marvelman* came in *Warrior* #7, published in November of 1982, eight months after the magazine's debut. It appeared alongside installments of *The Spiral Path*, *Shandor*, *Demon Stalker*, *Laser Eraser and Pressbutton*, a Paul Neary strip called *Madman* that had debuted in *Warrior* #2, and the "Virtue Victorious" installment of *V for Vendetta*, in which Evey helps V bring down the pedophilic Bishop of Westminster. Entitled "Secret Identity," the strip served as a transitional beat between the Kid Marvelman story that had just resolved and the story of Evelyn Cream and Project Zarathustra, set up in the denouement. It would also, idiosyncratically, be one of the major causes of Moore's eventual departure from the strip just under two years later.

"We're not gods from space who can survive planetary impacts and physics bubbling down into chaos and clashing timelines. We're just human."
–Warren Ellis, *Supreme: Blue Rose*, 2015

The eight-page strip jumps among settings, starting with Sir Dennis Archer shortly after briefing the sapphire-toothed Evelyn Cream on his mission. Archer reflects on the events of October 12th, 1963, when they blew up the Marvelman Family. The second page has Mike and Liz out on Dartmoor, getting ready to test Marvelman's powers. Liz brings a stack of American superhero comics, and reads off possible powers he could have. The third goes to Johnny Bates, now in the hospital, catatonic. The scene shifts to inside Bates's mind, where Kid Marvelman berates him as a "snot-nosed little pratt" and a "snotty little virgin." Then it cuts back to Marvelman and Liz investigating his powers, trying to figure out exactly how they work and how, for instance, the impact of a massive boulder falling on him doesn't drive his feet into the ground at all. Page five has Evelyn Cream (with caption boxes that explain how he has figured out that Marvelman must have been one of the reporters at Larksmere, that the transformation probably resulted in some sort of energy transfer, and that the terrorist with burns was probably closest when it happens) arriving at the hospital. This is followed by one more page of the Morans: Marvelman has turned back into Mike, and the two of them drive off; as they do, Liz tells Mike, "I've missed my last periods and I'm going to have a baby and it isn't yours it's Marvelman's."

The final two pages form a single scene depicting Cream's encounter with the terrorist, who lies in his hospital bed, heavily bandaged. As Cream enters, he wakes up and murmurs, "Huh? Whaddayou want, chocolate?" Cream communicates with him by writing on a notepad, promising not to kill him if he answers his questions. He proceeds to ask enough questions to identify Marvelman's secret identity, then explains to Steve that he was lying about the promise not to kill him. He smothers him in his hospital bed and calmly walks out.

Upon getting the script for this issue, Skinn raised some concerns, specifically about the words "virgin," "periods," and "chocolate," and asked Moore to change them. Moore, with his characteristic regard for anything he perceived as censorship, pushed back against the note, arguing that "they were natural, they were part of the characterisation," and that "*Warrior* was aimed at a fairly intelligent readership, we hadn't had any complaints," (which, in Skinn's account, was not true—they had in fact just lost distribution in WH Smiths because of a mother's complaint over the *Zirk* strip in *Warrior* #3) and that getting prudish was therefore senseless. Skinn pushed back, leading to the "Why offend even one reader?" question, and finally offered a compromise whereby Moore would change one of the three. Moore took umbrage with this: if it didn't matter which one he changed, then none of them could actually be that bad. To which, in his account, Skinn asked him to change one purely so Skinn could avoid losing face, at which point Moore flatly refused.

This was at the time a mere hiccup in the relationship between Skinn and Moore, but it seems to have been a turning point in Moore's opinion of Skinn all the same. Not, to be clear, in his relationship with *Warrior*—indeed, he kicked off 1983 by essentially picking up a third strip in *Warrior #9*. In addition to "Violence" and *Marvelman*, he contributed a strip entitled "Cold War, Cold Warrior" about more aliens of the same race as Warpsmith from "Yesterday's Gambit," and featuring art by Gary Leach. It reveals Warpsmith to be a member of the teleporting race of aliens called the Warpsmiths of Hod, and tells a story of espionage and deception in the vein of his aborted *4-D War Cycle* for *Doctor Who Monthly*.

(Indeed, it's a reasonable hypothesis that a substantial portion of the larger plot surrounding the Warpsmiths, and, by extension, the elaborate shared continuity for the *Warrior* strips that was dreamt up but never put into place by Alan and Steve Moore, was based in part on the abandoned *4-D War Cycle*. In the timeline they wrote out [which also establishes Gargunza as the creator of Fate, and decides that *V for Vendetta* takes place in an alternate timeline that diverges when Mike Moran does not rediscover his magic word at Larksmere] one of the earliest events listed is "The Chronarchy (a race like Earth-2 Time Lords) attack the Warpsmiths of Hod. Warpsmiths wipe out all but a few of the Chronarchy with Death-Cats, the ultimate weapon provided by the Rhodru Makers." The Rhodru Makers are also referred to in "Cold War, Cold Warrior," and, along with the Qys [the alien race whose crash landing provides Gargunza the ability to create Marvelman], form a significant portion of the future history. The tone is clearly different, not least because of the rather ludicrously named "Death-Cats," but the overall shape is visibly similar to the Time Lord/Black Sun/Sontaran conflict spelled out in the *4-D War* strips, and, given the comparison of the Chronarchy with the Time Lords and the timing of Moore's departure from *Doctor Who Monthly*, it seems more likely than not that the future timeline was based in part on reworkings of those ideas. Ironically, the one place where this shared continuity is at all referenced in the stories, a joke about Ginda Bojeffries that appeared in the final installment of *The Stars My Degradation* can, if one is sufficiently determined to count cameo appearances and crossovers, be used to argue that *Doctor Who* itself is part of a shared continuity with Axel Pressbutton and, if one takes the unused timeline at face value, *V for Vendetta/Marvelman*.)

Warrior #9 also featured, in its last panel, the debut of the character of Big Ben ("The Man with No Time for Crime"), created by Dez Skinn, but given to Moore to launch within *Marvelman*. It is fair to say that Moore did not exactly do the character any favors. Skinn had intended the character to be another tent pole of the magazine, and put him on the cover of *Warrior #10*, in which he made his full debut. But Moore introduced him as a failed attempt to recreate Marvelman, portraying him as mentally unstable and considerably less powerful, with the main character ultimately dispatching him with a single blow. Big Ben would eventually start appearing as a regular feature in *Warrior*, but only once the writing was largely on the wall for the magazine.

Even issues #9 and #10 revealed problems, however. They were, between them, the only two installments to come out in the first half of 1983, with February, March, and June seeing no issues, and issue #10 covering both April and May. The magazine made it back to a monthly schedule in July, publishing six consecutive monthly issues before missing the first two months of 1984, but it was clear that there were still toubles. Moore, nevertheless, wound down what he labeled as Book One of *Marvelman* in *Warrior* #11, and, after a month-long gap filled with a Young Marvelman story, commenced Book Two in *Warrior* #13—a story that would still be in progress when Moore left the strip a year later in August of 1984. This story, as stated in Moore's original pitch, brought Marvelman back into conflict with Dr. Gargunza, and for the most part, like almost everything following Leach's departure from the strip, focused heavily on the task of relaying the complex backstory that Moore had worked out and giving Marvelman his new origin.

By the time Moore left, however, the wheels had well and truly started to come off. In May of 1984, to fill a month's gap between *Warrior* #18 and #19, Skinn put out a title called *Marvelman Special* that consisted primarily of reprints of old Mick Anglo stories featuring the character. This, however, turned out to push the patience of Dez Skinn's previous employers too far. Marvel UK had thus far remained silent about one of their competitors publishing a character named Marvelman, but in their view publishing a comic that actually had their company name in the title was simply a bridge too far, and they commenced sending lawyer's letters to Skinn, which he reprinted, along with his replies, in the final two issues of *Warrior*.

These events led to a further souring of Moore's relationship with Marvel, which had already become strained following Bernie Jaye's dismissal. While his relationship with Skinn had by this point deteriorated completely, whatever outrage Moore had towards Skinn was overshadowed by his sense that it was fundamentally unfair for Marvel to object to publication of a character whose use of the word "Marvel" in his name went back further than the company's did. This frustration was amplified by the difficulties going on in trying to sell *Marvelman* and the other *Warrior* strips to US distributors, which were being complicated by fears over what Marvel would do. Moore, using the only leverage he had available, wrote Archie Goodwin, a senior editor at Marvel, informing him that unless Marvel backed down from their threats (and specifically allowed US reprints to go out under the title *Marvelman*) he would refuse to work for them again and would forbid reprints of his *Captain Britain* work. Goodwin, in Moore's account, sent word of this to then-editor-in-chief Jim Shooter (described by Moore as "another one of these comic book industry führers," in contrast to Goodwin, "a wonderful writer and a wonderful editor"), whose response was to throw the memo away.

This had at least one, if not two major consequences. The first was that Moore's suggested alternate title of *Miracleman* (drawn, among other places, from his *Captain Britain* work) was used for the eventual US reprints and continuation. The second and more uncertain one was Moore's falling out with Alan Davis, who felt that Moore's decision to make a stand over the name "Marvelman" by refusing to allow reprints of their *Captain Britain* work was unfair. Davis was at the time still working his warehouse job alongside his comics work, and was well aware that breaking out into the American market as Brian Bolland, Dave Gibbons, and Alan Moore already had would be lucrative. As Davis put it, "It was an opportunity to get my work seen by an American market." Further complicating matters, Davis hadn't even heard about this from Moore, but found out five months later from Jamie Delano.

This chronology, however, presents some problems. Moore left *Captain Britain* in June of 1984, one month after the publication of *Marvelman Special*, and three months prior to Marvel's letter to Skinn. The precise date of Moore's letter to Goodwin is difficult to pin down; it appears to have been somewhere in early 1985. But by early 1985 Davis had already broken in at DC, his first issue of *Batman and the Outsiders* coming out on March 21. Furthermore, Davis recalls Moore suggesting Delano as a writer in response to Davis's being hired by DC for an *Aquaman* miniseries (the miniseries never happened, and Davis was given *Batman and the Outsiders* instead). This means that Davis must have been aware that he'd already been noticed by American publishers months in advance of Moore's letter to Goodwin, although it must be noted that Davis's recollections of this period are at least somewhat confused, since he reports that his first meeting with Delano came when Moore brought him over to watch the last episode of *Boys from the Black Stuff*, which Davies had taped for him on early VHS equipment, despite that episode airing two years earlier than all of the other events discussed. Nevertheless, it's clear that Moore and Davis's falling out was more complex than simple anger over denied reprints.

By this point, however, Davis had already left *Marvelman* in frustration at Skinn's slow payments, which had led to Davis withholding a finished installment from Skinn. This could have, in theory, been overcome—Skinn had replaced the artist on *Marvelman* once already, and by this point every other strip besides *V for Vendetta* had either undergone creative changes, ended, or both. Except that, at virtually the same time, Moore and Skinn's relationship finally disintegrated beyond the point of salvation. Moore had soured on Skinn ever since the censorship squabble around issue #7, and had come to view him as someone who, as he later put it, "wanted to be Stan Lee. He wanted to be the person who got all the credit, whose name was on the whole package." But the breaking point came in a meeting at the Quality Publications offices, in which Moore brought up the censorship of issue #7. As Moore tells it, Skinn denied the incident ever happened. "At this point," Moore explains, "I was halfway across the office, and Steve Moore and Garry Leach were saying, 'Leave him, Alan, he's not worth it,' and at that point I ceased my work for *Warrior*. It was just that I couldn't have someone lying about me and my honesty."

But this was also not strictly speaking true. Moore refused to do further work on *Marvelman*, but he continued to write *V for Vendetta* for five installments after his last *Marvelman* strip ("...And Every Dog It's Day," in which Marvelman finally confronts Gargunza, only to learn that Gargunza can force him to transform back to human form, and which ends in a cliffhanger splash of Gargunza unleashing Marveldog to attack Mike Moran). It is fair to ask, then, why Moore applied different standards to the two strips, continuing one within *Warrior* for as long as the magazine existed while terminating the other.

This is especially true because the period in question was one where Moore was bringing a number of projects to a close. He ended his *Captain Britain* work in June, finished his last *D.R. & Quinch* in May, and then pulled *Marvelman* in August. Taken in the context of his ceasing work on *Future Shocks* for *2000 AD* in the wake of the *Swamp Thing* job, a different picture of why he was dropping projects starts to emerge—especially given that this is around when DC would have started offering him additional opportunities. Certainly that's Alan Davis's contention when he states bluntly, "Alan clearly quit both *Captain Britain* and *Marvelman* at virtually the same time but claims external, unconnected reasons for both. Isn't it simpler to accept that with *Swamp Thing* and new offers from DC—which were far better paid—the volume of work increased to a point where choices had to be made. I know I, amongst many other creators, was hoping for a call from DC."

But this "pure self-interest" theory of Moore's actions still doesn't explain why he persisted with *V for Vendetta* in *Warrior*, which would have been just as low-paying. Some of it, surely, is that Lloyd was keen for it to continue ("I was very happy to keep doing it because Dez was still paying me money") and that, more importantly, he was passionate about the work: "Nothing was more important to us… it was ours. And we could do what we liked with it." And there was, to be sure, a practical consideration—the project had a planned ending that, once reached, would allow it to find new life as a stand-alone volume. Whatever *Warrior*'s flaws, it was at least adequate to the task of funding the work's completion, and if Lloyd was happy with its payment, well, he was the one who most needed the money. *V for Vendetta* was still his main job, as opposed to a passion project to be done on days he didn't have any *Swamp Thing* work to do.

> *"There is a moment of crystalline silence. The storm holds its breath. And so it begins…"*
> —Alan Moore, *Marvelman*, 1982

Nevertheless, this highlights a truth, albeit an obvious one, about Moore's tendency to have professional relationships come to unhappy conclusions, which is that his positions aren't based on pure and absolute principles that override all other concerns. It is indeed often, though certainly not always the case, that Moore's principled stands are also for positions that benefit him. The observation by Alan Davis and others that his stands are often much more about his benefit than his collaborators' is a fair one. Again, there are certainly many cases where Moore has taken a stand for his collaborators, but there are undoubtedly times when he's put his own interests first. Equally, however, it is clear that Moore is genuinely invested in his principles. He walked away from *Doctor Who Monthly* at a point in his career when he could hardly afford to give up work, and the magnitude of some of his stances, most notably his refusal of money from film versions of his work, makes it difficult not to credit the stated principles behind them. But this is how principles work, in reality, and there is no contradiction in the fact that financial success makes the risks inherent in principled stands more manageable.

It is also worth noting that there is a meaningful distinction between the question of why Moore stopped working for a given publisher and why he never returned. There is no real doubt that the reason Moore stopped writing *Captain Britain* was a combination of not needing a low and erratically-paying gig anymore and not enjoying it as much following Bernie Jaye's departure. There is also no doubt that the reason Moore never returned to work for Marvel was their handling of the Marvelman trademark issue. A similar logic applies to Dez Skinn and *Warrior*. What led him to wind down his work for the magazine, and what in years since has come to characterize his attacks on Skinn, are distinct.

Whatever the subtle nuances of Moore's decision-making, the matter was largely moot. Just five issues after the last *Marvelman* strip saw print, *Warrior* folded with issue #26. By this point, its star had fallen quite far. The six features in *Warrior* #26 are, aside from *V for Vendetta*, unheralded strips by minor figures such as Grant Morrison, whose resume at the time was even thinner than Moore's had been when he landed *V for Vendetta* and *Marvelman* (and Moore was conspicuous as the only name in *Warrior* #1 who wasn't already an established industry name). Despite only having published a couple stories in a defunct Scottish magazine, a local newspaper strip, and a series of space combat-heavy *Starblazer* issues, with most of these credits being several years old by 1985, Morrison had been on Skinn's radar for a bit. He had, unsolicited, sent Skinn a script for a Kid Marvelman story entitled "October Incident: 1966."

For many years, this script was one of the great lost artifacts of the War, but in 2014 Marvel, seeking to bring attention to their flagging reprint series of Moore's *Marvelman/Miracleman* material, published the *All-New Miracleman Annual* #1, which consisted of two stories—a new Peter Milligan/Mike Allred collaboration and a Joe Quesada-illustrated adaptation of Morrison's by then thirty-year old script. In many regards this adaptation is less interesting than the reprinting of Morrison's original script in the back matter for the Annual. Quesada's adaptation is artistically capable—Quesada talked in interviews about how he tried to adopt "a somewhat European comics approach," specifically citing Moebius and Sergio Toppi as influences. "I traditionally enjoy using a lot of black and shadow in my work," he explained, "but I intentionally forced myself to work in an open style." Part of this, along with the basic need for a $4.99 high-profile annual to have a decent number of story pages, meant that

Morrison's script, which was written with the idea of being a standard-length strip in *Warrior*, is expanded to eleven pages, four of them full-page splashes.

This has the effect of slowing the pace of the story considerably, which is a significant problem for Morrison's script, which was on the slow side to begin with. Morrison calls for twenty-nine panels, which would make for a roughly five-page story. (In comparison, the final six *Marvelman* strips Moore penned for *Warrior* are 41, 38, 38, 33, 33, and 26 panels respectively, each over six pages, and it is notable that the last of these featured two splash pages, which is by *Warrior* standards ridiculously decadent.) On top of that, the plot is aggressively straightforward—a priest, in 1966, walks along a beach where he'd seen some awful event three years past, recalling "memories of fire in the sky and of glory that blazed white as the sun on the night the old dragon was cast out of heaven," memories the reader quickly realizes are of Kid Marvelman falling from Dr. Gargunza's nuclear trap. As he kneels on the beach and prays, he is visited by Kid Marvelman, who, after a brief conversation, incinerates him. At six pages, this would have been a slender bit of filler, although it's no more disposable than, for example, the five-page Alan Moore/John Ridgway "Young Marvelman" story that saw print a year earlier in *Warrior* #12.

And for all the script's frailties—frailties that are hardly unexpected for someone working on what would have been his tenth multi-page professional credit, roughly the equivalent of Moore's contribution to the 1980 *2000 AD Sci-Fi Special*, "A Holiday in Hell"—it is, at least, a capable execution of Moore's aesthetic for *Marvelman*, which was always one of the strips he wrote in his distinctive caption-heavy style. Morrison captures the effect well, framing his story with two extended and suitably portentous narrations. "It was the dream," the story opens, over an image of the priest walking along the shore. "The dream had come back after three years. He knew it was a warning when he woke to the grey light and the wind. The days of the revelation were come upon the world and something unclean was abroad. Something venomous was walking the quiet roads and the lonely pathways, something cold and far from human. He prays to the almighty that it will pass him by," a beginning not entirely dissimilar to that of the start of Book Two of *Marvelman*, "Catgames," which opens, "Downwind, a scent, a strong scent… a **wrong** scent. Thick, powerful urine and bitter, rotting metal… rotting metal? Something bad. Something big. Something coming." And while it is true that Moore's *Marvelman* strips tended to move at a somewhat more energetic pace, even Morrison's languid pacing can credibly be explained as Moore's influence if one imagines Morrison's script as an attempt to bring some of the more dread-laden horror pacing of Moore's *Swamp Thing* work back home to *Warrior*.

While Moore's influence on Morrison's script is obvious (and entirely understandable, given that Morrison was pitching a strip meant to fit seamlessly into Moore's overall narrative), it is not as though Morrison did not have ideas of his own. Perhaps the most compelling comes in his account of 1966 Kid Marvelman's appearance in the description of the fourth panel, which describes him as having a Beatles-style haircut and "wearing a black vinyl short raincoat, black poloneck jumper, black drainpipe trousers and black chelsea boots. His face is strong and cruel with high cheekbones and slanting eyebrows. He is smiling in a slight, wicked way. His body is slim. He looks like a mod angel of death." Morrison later, in the interview which led Quesada to realize that the 1984 script survived and could be revived, japed that "I made the teenage mod Johnny Bates look exactly like me, forever damning myself as Moore's Devil." This is perhaps overstating the case, inasmuch as an actual visual image of teenage mod Johnny Bates was not actually realized until thirty years later, but there is unmistakably a basic truth to it, and when Quesada came to illustrate the script he used a 1984 photograph of Morrison as a goth-mod brooding by the Ayrshire shore as reference for Bates, finally allowing

Figure 177: The 1984 photograph of Grant Morrison Joe Quesada used as reference for Kid Miracleman.

Figure 178: Kid Miracleman, drawn as Grant Morrison, proclaims the apocalypse. (Written by Grant Morrison, art by Joe Quesada, from "The October Incident: 1966" in All-New Miracleman Annual #1, 2014, from a 1984 script.)

Morrison his longed-for damnation.

There is something more than slightly dramatically appropriate about this act, which comes late enough in the war that it is impossible to understand it in any context other than a magickal attack, with Morrison forcibly inserting himself into Moore's seminal work to wreak havoc. Under this reading, however, the mad hubris of Kid Miracleman is a striking and indeed troubling thing. "The apocalypse has arrived," Kid Morrisonman gloats at the terrified priest. "I can do any bloody thing I want and you can't stop me, you pathetic old witch doctor!" And yet for all the unsettling bravado of the move, there is also something strangely self-defeating about it. Morrison's attack upon the conceptual territory of *Marvelman* comes long after Moore had fled the scene—indeed, the nature of the deals Marvel cut to pre-empt any legal action over the copyright status of the character meant that they were unable to actually publicly acknowledge who had written the 1980s comics they were publishing with lush new digital coloring, with all of the issues of their *Miracleman* series crediting the stories to simply to "the Original Writer," which left Morrison to embrace the role of the taunting devil only to find the figure he meant to taunt conspicuously absent, leaving him with all of the confinement of damnation and none of the liberation, a mad god ruling a kingdom of just under 22,000 sales, less than that month's installment of Kieron Gillen and Jamie McKelvie's *The Wicked + The Divine*, and with frankly less potential for digital and trade paperback sales to boot.

But this outcome was perhaps inevitable given the historical space Morrison was attempting to revise. Three separate accounts of exactly what happened with "October Incident: 1966" exist. These are in several regards impossible to reconcile, but the broad strokes are nevertheless the same—Skinn liked Morrison's script enough to suggest to Moore that they might run it, Moore indicated displeasure with this plan, and the idea was dropped, leaving the script unpublished until 2014. The earliest account of this came in

2001 when George Khoury interviewed Dez Skinn for *Kimota! The Miracleman Companion*, and Skinn mentioned Morrison's submission. As Skinn tells it, "Grant came in at the tail end of *Warrior* and wanted to try his hand at 'Marvelman' as Alan Moore had stopped writing it," and describes Morrison's submission as "a Kid Marvelman story, about a discussion between Kid Marvelman and a Catholic priest." In Skinn's account, he thought the script was "bloody clever" and forwarded it to Moore, who declared simply "nobody else writes Marvelman," which led Skinn to tell Morrison, "I'm sorry. He's jealously hanging on to this one." Regarding Morrison's reaction to this, Skinn said that he "did have an answer, but again, I shouldn't really speak for him."

But Skinn's interviews must always be taken with a grain of salt, and this one is clearly no exception. His description of Morrison's story is of one where "Kid Marvelman argued a very good case against organized religion. Nobody was flying, no beams from anybody's eyes." This is, as the 2014 release of the script demonstrates, flatly untrue. The extent of Kid Marvelman's case against organized religion is, "Jesus only walked on the water. But me... I walk on the air," a line accompanied by Morrison's panel description, "Track in towards the young man, whose feet are seen to be leaving the ground ever so slightly," which is to say, flying, or, as Morrison has it two panels later, "hanging in the air as though in parody of the crucifixion. Lightning is crackling around his outstretched hands," a description that Quesada, ironically, ends up fulfilling with a panel of Kid Marvelman with lightning crackling out of his eyes. Given that nearly every detail Skinn remembers about the content of Morrison's "brilliant" script is completely wrong, it is difficult to completely credit his overall account of events.

"They were friends once, these creatures of near unimaginable power. Now, horns locked, they fight to the death in the pounding rain. There is passion here, but not human passion. There is fierce and desperate emotion, but not an emotion that we would recognize. They are titans,

*and we will never understand the alien inferno that blazes in the furnace
of their souls. We will never grasp their hopes, their despair. Never
comprehend the blistering rage that informs each devastating blow. We
will never know the destiny that howls in their hearts, never know their
pain, their love, their almost sexual hatred. We are only human, and
perhaps we will be the less for that."*
—Alan Moore, *Marvelman*, 1982

A second account emerged in 2010 in the documentary
Grant Morrison: Talking with Gods, where Morrison himself
relates the story with occasional interjections from a separate
interview with Skinn. Morrison and Skinn tell of Morrison
stopping by the *Warrior* offices with, as Morrison puts it, a
"Kid Marvelman spec script" that Skinn immediately
purchased, in what Morrison described as "a really good jump
for me." Morrison is blunt about what happened: "Alan
Moore had it spiked. He said it was never to be published,"
an event Morrison credits for the "slight antagonism" that
exists between the two creators. Morrison goes on to claim
that Skinn, following his falling out with Moore, "asked me to
continue *Marvelman*," an opportunity he was tremendously
excited by, but when Morrison wrote Moore asking for his
blessing, he received back "this really weird letter" that began,
"I don't want this to sound like the softly hissed tones of a
Mafia hitman, but back off," and then threatened Morrison's
future career if he carried on.

This account of events was flatly denied by Moore three
years later in an interview with Lance Parkin for his
biography of Moore. In it he says that Morrison's version of
events "has no bearing upon reality at all" and defies anyone
to produce such a letter. Moore recalls Morrison's script:
"Dez had rather sprung it on me out of the blue, and it didn't
fit in with the rather elaborate storyline that I was creating,"
and explains that he was "almost 100 per cent certain that I
never wrote any kind of letter to Grant Morrison, let alone a
threatening one." Skinn separately clarifies to Parkin that for
his part, "I never saw or asked to see the letter Grant got,"

but that he "enthusiastically sent Grant's wonderful little cameo story up to Alan Moore, ill-aware of his growing possessive paranoia." It is worth noting, however, that Moore and Skinn are, in these interviews, conflating what Morrison depicts as two separate events—Moore's spiking of Morrison's spec script, and the separate instance of Morrison being offered the opportunity to take over the main *Marvelman* strip.

One significant discrepancy arising among these accounts is the question of exactly when Morrison's spec script arrived. Skinn recalls the script coming after Moore had left *Marvelman*, which would place it in August of 1984 or later. But Moore's departure from the strip had been a quiet thing that was not publicly announced, and when Skinn did make a public statement (in an editorial that was spread out over the final two issues) acknowledging that *Warrior* was no longer publishing *Marvelman*, he gave the impression that the problem was Marvel's legal action over the *Marvelman Special* and not the fact that he'd fallen out with the writer, a situation that would not really have suggested to Morrison that there was a vacancy to be filled. Given that the detail of Morrison submitting "October Incident: 1966" in response to Moore's departure comes entirely from Skinn, as opposed to from Morrison himself, it seems on the whole more likely that Morrison simply pitched a fill-in story akin to the five-page "Young Marvelman" story in *Warrior* #12 or the "Vertigo" and "Vincent" installments of *V for Vendetta*, this being, if nothing else, a far more reasonable thing for a writer looking to break in to pitch, as Morrison would surely have realized based on his previous industry experience.

Notably, Skinn, Morrison, and Moore are all in agreement over how Morrison was notified that "October Incident: 1966" would not be used, with the news being relayed by Skinn. But the reasons for this are trickier. Moore's explanation—that the strip did not fit with his storyline—is largely unpersuasive: nothing in "October Incident: 1966" is difficult to reconcile with the rest of Moore's story, and

Morrison took care to set it in a period where nothing was really going on in Moore's timeline, with Young Marvelman being dead and Marvelman proper in his amnesiac phase. Skinn's explanation that Moore was jealous and paranoid fits with his general depictions of Moore, but this also means that it fits too heavily into the general pattern of Skinn denying that he'd done anything the least bit unreasonable in his dealings with Moore, which, given that Moore was one of a half-dozen major names in British comics to have been driven away from *Warrior* due to some aspect of Skinn's handling of the business side, is not entirely credible either.

But if Moore felt a bit paranoid about Skinn's suggestion of taking on a new writer for the strip, it's hardly difficult to understand why. This period coincided with the negotiations for the deal that would eventually bring Marvelman to US publisher Eclipse Comics under the title *Miracleman*. Given that Skinn had by this point lost almost all of the impressive talent that had launched *Warrior*, with only Alan Moore, Steve Moore, and David Lloyd remaining from the original masthead, and given that Moore and Skinn had an increasingly fractious relationship, Moore would hardly have been unreasonable in fearing that Skinn was looking, in effect, to experiment with the possibility of replacing him with a writer he might have an easier time controlling. A firm line in the sand to avoid any sort of precedent for people other than him writing Marvelman would have been a prudent defense against this possibility, and one that he could readily enforce given that, under the then-current understanding of the copyright situation, he owned a share of the character.

But this in turn raises a major question about Morrison's account of events, specifically his claim that he was offered the opportunity to take over as the regular writer of *Marvelman* after Moore's departure. Simply put, this seems virtually impossible. For one thing, it is notable that neither Skinn nor Moore offer any support for the claim, but instead treat the question of Morrison and Marvelman as a topic that consists purely of the script to "October Incident: 1966." For another, it does not fit the established timeline of events for *Marvelman/Miracleman* at all—the idea that Skinn was simultaneously negotiating a US continuation of the comic with Eclipse (a deal signed in September of 1984, the month after the last Moore/Davis *Marvelman* strip was published) and attempting to negotiate a continuation in *Warrior* with a completely unknown and untested writer is ridiculous on the face of it. Skinn stood to get far more money out of a US sale, that having always been a major part of the *Warrior* business plan, and he surely would not have endangered that deal by offering Morrison a job, especially given that it wasn't his to offer in the first place. The *Marvelman* copyright was at the time universally understood to be split among Skinn, Moore, Davis, and Leach, which meant that three people beyond Skinn would have had to sign off on giving the strip to a new writer, at least one of whom, Alan Moore, was clearly not going to agree to that.

And yet Morrison's recollection of events is shockingly thorough, complete with the "softly hissed tones of a Mafia hitman" line, which, it must be said, is a characteristically Moorean turn of phrase. Could Moore have separately reached out to Morrison over "October Incident: 1966" in order to warn him off of pitching for other people's characters? This would have been a strange course of action for Moore, but he had only recently met Morrison at the October 1983 Glasgow Comics Mart and given him career advice, and it is at least theoretically possible that he continued to do so. If such a letter did exist, however, it is worth asking how fairly Morrison is capturing its tone and content. The "Mafia hitman" line sounds like Moore, but it sounds like Moore making a sardonic joke akin to his description of Scotland as a place where "incest, murder, and cannibalism" are "still very much a part of everyday family life." In other words, even if one does give Morrison the supreme benefit of the doubt and allow that, despite clearly inventing a job offer from Dez Skinn that could never have existed, he really did receive the letter described, it seems more likely that Moore was offering sincere advice on the wisdom of attempting to interject one's self into someone's ongoing and creator-owned project than that he felt compelled to separately intimidate an unknown writer he'd already had Dez Skinn tell off. And, ultimately, while the Mafia hitman line sounds a bit like Alan Moore, so does "the only answer is the sound of dream thunder echoing down the days as the memories come stealing... memories of fire in the sky and of glory that blazed white as the sun on the night the old dragon was cast out of heaven."

But whatever the details of what happened to Morrison's "The October Incident: 1966" script in 1984, Dez Skinn was still in dire need of new writers, so he tapped Morrison to take over the writing of a strip called *The Liberators* for *Warrior* #26. *The Liberators* had debuted in *Warrior* #22, with a Skinn-penned story called "Death Run" that featured a team of rebels led by a scantily clad female leader. The story juxtaposed action shots of the rebels' progress with captions from an unseen figure directing them on what to do—a figure revealed at the end of the story to be the heroine's brother, who has been captured and is being converted into a "wardroid." The story ends with the woman blowing up the base, herself, and her already lost brother.

Morrison's story, "Night Moves," serves as a prequel to "Death Run," and is, it must be said, a reasonably impressive debut from Morrison. Certainly it's the second best thing in *Warrior* #26 by a considerable margin. Morrison immediately set about improving the property, taking care of business Skinn had overlooked like bothering to give the characters names. Playing on the post-apocalyptic punk aesthetic developed by artist John Ridgway for the characters, Morrison gave them a slightly idiosyncratic dialogue style, not so strange as to be distracting, but enough to give the strip a sense of texture—things like, "I've been around and over, talking with stones. This is some bad place here, Shanni." And Morrison repeats his effective imitation of Moore's caption boxes, giving his story a suitably ominous opening narration: "The darkness is coming. An animal bursts into being, realizes its lungs are not made to breathe oxygen, and dies silently. The sky is a sullen, bruised red as the sun goes down. The darkness is coming." The result is a credible action strip helped considerably by the fact that it still has the reliably excellent John Ridgway on art duties.

A second Morrison-penned installment of *The Liberators*, entitled "Angels and Demons," was also prepared, but due to *Warrior* going under it did not see print until 1996. This strip continues to build on the universe of *The Liberators*, jumping among three separate groups of characters in its six pages. The bulk of the stories feature the main group of rebels being attacked by a Wardroid, while separate sections follow the character of Frisk, who has a strange flashback to what appears to be the 20th century while scavenging through the ruins of Westminster; another scene shows the conversion of someone into a Wardroid. The latter section, where one of the villains muses, "How must it seem to surrender the tracks and pathways of your mind to our searching fingers? To feel thought sparks retreat along neural branches down into the lightless brain root?" anticipates numerous images in Morrison's later work, from the interrogation of King Mob by Sir Miles in *The Invisibles* to the mind control fetish erotica of "The Story of Zero" to Darkseid's victory in *Final Crisis*. The former, on the other hand, gestures towards further complexities in the vast and never realized shared timeline of the *Warrior* strips, not least in the presence of a line of dialogue within the flashback where one character says, "We're the children of the project. We're the coming race... the Supermen," a line that seems to invoke the Nietzschean rhetoric of Dr. Gargunza in Moore's *Marvelman*, who names his superhero project Project Zarathustra, and, prior to stumbling upon an old *Captain Marvel* comic and taking inspiration from it, referred to the Marvelman family as his "over-men." (The Nietzschean roots of Moore's *Marvelman* were also, it should be noted, name-checked in "October

Incident: 1966.")

To be sure, the strip still has problems. The world of *The Liberators* feels too big, like there's a surplus of smaller good ideas masking the lack of an actual hook or concept for the series. But this is hardly Morrison's fault. "Death Run" gave him a meager foundation to build on—it was basically a *Future Shock* that Morrison was told to somehow build an entire continuing story around. Morrison's work on *The Liberators* does more than could be reasonably expected with the property, and it's clear he's giving real and intelligent thought to the genuinely difficult topic of how to transform the story into something functional. It is also worth stressing the basic ignominy of the job description: Skinn was at this point simply creating concepts, writing mediocre and vague first installments, and then handing them off to other writers to develop. But if any of the concepts broke out as *V for Vendetta*, *Marvelman*, and *Laser Eraser and Pressbutton* were on the brink of doing, it would be Skinn who would be their legal creator and who would reap the bulk of the benefits, even as writers like Morrison did the actual work of taking Skinn's half-formed ideas and making them into things anyone cared about. Skinn, who to this day profits from the sale of the *V for Vendetta* Guy Fawkes masks despite his sole contribution to the story being that he asked David Lloyd to do a 1930s mystery strip and approved Alan Moore as a writer for said strip, was by this point clearly taking his self-appointed role as the British Stan Lee to a crudely logical conclusion. The only difference was that Lee was always capable of turning a profit off the exploitation of his creative partners, whereas *Warrior* went under after its twenty-sixth issue, meaning that Morrison, despite his obvious talent, would have to wait until the next year for further opportunities in comics to present themselves.

Chapter Ten: The Bojeffries Saga

"He's only dreaming in his tank. Anyway, now that you've chosen to stay and take part in our little experiment, you may be wondering how much of what you're about to experience is real."
–Grant Morrison, *Multiversity: Ultra Comics*, 2015

This is in many ways something of a curious footnote to Moore's *Warrior*-era career. It constitutes a total of twenty-four pages of comics, and is arguably most notable for being the answer to the mildly challenging trivia question, "Alongside *V for Vendetta* and *Marvelman*, what's the third series Alan Moore created for *Warrior*?" Much of this is down to the fact that *The Bojeffries Saga* is markedly out of keeping with the general tone of *Warrior*. This is often ascribed to the fact that it is overtly a comedy, as opposed to an action-heavy adventure strip, but this does not really capture the full scope of its strangeness. From the start, comedy was a part of *Warrior*—the first issue, in fact, featured a two-page comedic bit by Steve Moore and Dave Gibbons called "A True Story?" and firmly in the mould of *Tharg's Future Shocks* from *2000 AD*, while later installments included overtly comedic stories like Hunt Emerson's "Stir Crazy." Beyond that, *Laser Eraser and Pressbutton* always had a consciously humorous streak to it, especially on the occasions when it was replaced with a *Zirk* strip. Nor can *The Bojeffries Saga*'s status as a comedy explain its marginal status within Moore's overall career. Yes, Moore's serious work is generally the material that attracts the most critical attention, but it's hardly as if *D.R. & Quinch*, to take the most obvious example, is a relatively ignored and minor part of Moore's career. Indeed, if anything Moore's ultra-violent alien miscreants get somewhat more attention than they deserve, despite clearly being a comedy.

But what *D.R. & Quinch* and most of the other comedies in *Warrior* have in common that sets them apart from *The Bojeffries Saga* is that they are all comedic versions of the action-adventure strips that are *Warrior* and *2000 AD*'s bread and butter. For example, "A True Story?" is the tale of a cartoonist who, as he ponders the idea of a time loop, is sucked into a dimensional portal in his teacup by Grongad, Tyrant of the Ninth Dimension, and tasked with saving Grongad from a slave revolt, a task he fails at utterly. The now freed slaves are perfectly happy to send him back, except that they send him back to the precise moment Grongad took him from, which, as he observes, means that he'll be stuck in a time loop, a fact confirmed by the last panel, a repeat of the one right before the cartoonist was abducted. It's funny, but crucially, it's a funny strip about a slave revolt in the Ninth Dimension.

The Bojeffries Saga is markedly different. Yes, its cast includes a werewolf, a vampire, a Lovecraftian horror, and a woman who claims to be able to "arm-wrestle against the gravity-pull of a black hole" because she's "infinitely powerful," a statement that, given the rest of the family, is not entirely outside the realm of plausibility. But this cast of supernatural characters is dropped into an aggressively mundane setting where the joke is often based upon the sheer irrelevancy of their supernatural power. Ginda Bojeffries, for instance—the infinitely powerful woman—is never shown using any of her power. Instead she brings it up in contexts such as complaining about how men are sexually intimidated by her "because their fragile male egos don't like the thought of me being infinitely superior to them in every detail" and yelling furiously at them for any perceived slight, such as her reaction upon being called "young lady" by one character, to which she angrily points out, "I have thoughts and feelings too, you know," accuses him of finding "the idea of a female who can cause nuclear explosions by squinting up one eye threatening to your manhood," boasts that she "can create a uni-cellular life-form using only the ingredients found in malt vinegar," and slams the door in his face.

Certainly, figuring out how best to present *The Bojeffries Saga* to his readers was an obvious challenge for Dez Skinn. By the time of its debut in *Warrior* #12, it was clear that Moore was the breakout star of the magazine, and so the debut of a new strip by him was an obvious thing to put on the cover of the issue. But the two taglines given to it on the cover are inscrutable choices, to say the least. The first, "A soap opera of the paranormal," is at least a reasonably accurate description of it, and one Moore uses internally for the second installment of the story in *Warrior* #13, but it rather crucially withholds just how much emphasis should be put on the "soap opera" part. (It is worth noting that in the British context, this phrase would have evoked more than just the usual associations with ongoing and slightly tawdry drama. As a genre, British soap operas are largely associated with the working class, with the country's two most popular soaps at the time of *Warrior* #12 being *Coronation Street*, a show that had been running since 1960 about the people living on a terraced street outside Manchester, and *Emmerdale Farm*, a show set in the Yorkshire Dales that debuted in 1972.) The other description, which proclaims that *The Bojeffries Saga* "makes Monty Python look like a comedy," is simply baffling. For one thing, the claim, when actually looked at, would appear to suggest a contrast between Monty Python and *The Bojeffries Saga* whereby the former is funny and the latter isn't. For another, however, as comparisons to other comedies go, Monty Python is markedly far different from what *The Bojeffries Saga* is doing.

It is not that there are no similarities between Monty Python and *The Bojeffries Saga*. There absolutely are, not least, as Lance Parkin observes, the fact that Trevor Inchmale, the viewpoint character used to introduce the family in the first *Bojeffries Saga* story, is the sort of character that Monty Python member Michael Palin made his career playing. And more broadly, both fit into a coherent tradition of British comedy—a tradition that Brian Eno, interviewed by Alan Moore, proclaimed to be the country's "great export"—and have attendant similarities from that. Nevertheless, the differences are both fundamental and revealing. The five British members of Monty Python all had Oxbridge educations, with Michael Palin and Terry Jones both attending Oxford, while Graham Chapman, John Cleese, and Eric Idle all came up through the Cambridge Footlights theater club. (The sixth member, Terry Gilliam, was an American expatriate, but attended a private liberal arts school and worked in advertising before leaving the country.) And while Monty Python's comedy is often described as "anarchic," its default mode is still basically to find comedy in the travails of a sane and reasonable man in the face of ridiculous absurdity. This is, after all, the basic structure of most of the troupe's most famous moments, both on their television show *Monty Python's Flying Circus* in sketches like "Dead Parrot" or "The Spanish Inquisition," and in their films, such as the Black Knight sequence of *Monty Python and the Holy Grail*. The sense of the anarchic tended to come less from the content of individual sketches and more from the way in which they were assembled to make episodes of *Monty Python's Flying Circus*, with the troupe employing the Spike Milligan-honed technique of cutting sketches off seemingly midway and linking them with Terry Gilliam's surrealist collage-based animations.

But none of this is particularly close to *The Bojeffries Saga*, which doesn't engage in avant garde structural techniques and is not especially concerned with the travails of sane and reasonable people. Even the first installment, a story in two

Figure 179: Ginda Bojeffries takes offense. (From "The Rentman Cometh" in Warrior #12, *written by Alan Moore, art by Steve Parkhouse, 1983)*

Figure 180: Trevor Inchmale introduces both The Bojeffries Saga *and several possible novel titles. (From "The Rentman Cometh," in* Warrior #12, *written by Alan Moore, art by Steve Parkhouse, 1983)*

parts entitled, respectively, "The Rentman Cometh" and "One of Our Rentmen is Missing," and which has the vaguely Palinesque character of Trevor Inchmale, ultimately lands far from the standard "sane man railing against a mad world" setup. Its plot—a rentman attempts to investigate a house in seeming arrears only to discover a rabbit hole of impossible weirdness that culminates in him being transformed into a bowl of petunias by a senile Lovecraftian horror—is certainly in the same vein, but this obscures as much as it reveals. Trevor Inchmale, the rentman in question, is ultimately portrayed as being just as ridiculous as the Bojeffries family. The story's opening gag is a series of wide panels in which he is depicted biking down a street as he thinks to himself, "'Call me Inchmale.' 'Rentman!' 'Rent is My Business.' 'The Rentman Cometh.' 'The Old Rentaroonie.' 'Rent Asunder!'" A caption box helpfully explains: "There are many interesting ways in which to spend your mortal existence. Trevor Inchmale favours inventing titles for his forthcoming autobiography." This sets the tone for a story in which the joke is not so much the absurd set of circumstances that Inchmale faces as it is Inchmale's fundamental deficiency in being able recognize the absurdity in front of him; when he sees, for instance, Raoul the werewolf return home as a wolf, Inchmale simply assumes the Bojeffries are guilty of "keeping of pets without council permission." The story is largely a farce, with increasingly absurd consequences emerging from humorous misunderstandings on the part of a character who can be relied upon, regardless of the situation, to be a complete idiot.

A potentially more accurate antecedent to *The Bojeffries Saga* within the history of British comedy is *The Young Ones*, a BBC Two sitcom that debuted in 1982, the year before *The Bojeffries Saga* launched. While Moore himself has never cited it as an inspiration, comedian Lenny Henry, when writing the introduction for the 1992 Tundra Publishing collection of *The Bojeffries Saga*, described the strip as "bringing an anarchy and weirdness to comics similar to the kick up the ass that *The*

Young Ones brought to television." And while there are still obvious differences—most blatantly that *The Young Ones* features no overtly supernatural elements (although it's certainly not a strictly speaking "realistic" series either, with characters routinely doing things like surviving decapitations)—this is, on the whole, probably a more reasonable comparison than Monty Python, if only because *The Young Ones* is, like *The Bojeffries Saga*, at heart a show about a bunch of weirdos living together, albeit in this case a couple of University students and not a family of supernatural creatures.

But in some ways more relevant than the subject matter is simply the attitude of *The Young Ones*. The show emerged out of the alternative comedy scene that formed around The Comedy Store, a London comedy club more or less contemporaneous with the War (and subsequently at The Comic Strip, a club formed when several prominent alternative comedians split from The Comedy Store), and which, more broadly, shared the post-punk aesthetic of most British counterculture of the period. The style was explicitly political, formed in conscious opposition to the dominant mode of British stand-up comedy at the time, and took particular umbrage towards the tendency of overtly racist and sexist humor. But more than that, alternative comedy was based on a fundamental transition in the basic style and structure of comedy. Instead of focusing on comedy's roots in the old music hall tradition, alternative comedians were generally writer-performers who worked outside of the old-fashioned "joke" structure and focused exclusively on originally composed material instead of classic and well-worn gags.

But for all that Monty Python, as a troupe of writer-performers, marked an important antecedent to alternative comedy, the new movement was least in part defined by contrast to its Oxbridge-steeped style. Indeed, Alexei Sayle, the MC at The Comedy Store when the alternative comedy scene was forming, and one of its most prominent members, cites a 1984 episode of *The Young Ones* that featured appearances from several comedians who came up through the Cambridge Footlights group a generation after Cleese and Chapman did as the "turning point" in the alternative comedy scene, at which it started moving towards the political center and away from the radical political ideas that he'd envisioned for it.

> *"See, this is my point. It's like all the small towns up here all think they're magic villages."*
> —Warren Ellis, *Blackcross*, 2015

Sayle's shock is not entirely fair. (It should be stressed that Sayle is clearly poking fun at his own political intransigence as much as he's offering a serious history of the alternative comedy scene, describing how, upon turning up at the studio to discover the guest stars, he "railed at the writers," saying, "The whole point of what we were doing was surely to challenge the smug hegemony of the Oxford, Cambridge, public-schoolboy comedy network, as well as destroying the old-school working men's club racists," to which, in his telling, the writers replied, "That was just you, we never subscribed to your demented class-war ravings.") It is, after all, not as though the alternative comics were by and large from less privileged backgrounds than their similarly transgressive predecessors in Monty Python. Rik Mayall (who wrote for the series and played the entitled anarchist asshole Rick) was born to a pair of drama teachers, while Ade Edmonson (who played the sociopathic punk Vyvyan Basterd) had an international upbringing in places like Bahrain, Cyprus, and Uganda before he ended up attending a private school, and both went to the University of Manchester, as rigorous an academic institution as exists in the UK.

All the same, the cultural differences between the University of Manchester and Cambridge are genuine, and speak to a larger difference in approach between *The Young*

Ones and Monty Python. *The Young Ones* is not, by and large, a show that concerns itself at all with the notion that there might be such a thing as a sane world. Its conflicts are generally between equally absurd figures, such as the eternal hatred between Rick and Vyv. Indeed, this gets at the heart of the comedy in *The Young Ones*, which is often about the ruthless mockery of the excesses and pretensions of the very left-wing politics that animate it. Instead of being a show that pokes fun at the absurdity of the larger world, it is a show that pokes fun at the absurdity of its own audience, skewering the punks and hippies that the show appeals to. And in this regard, at least, Lenny Henry's comparison with *The Bojeffries Saga* is on target. What is crucial about *The Bojeffries Saga* is not, ultimately, its supernatural weirdness, but the conceit of this bizarre family living in terraced council housing. It is a setting that is heavily grounded in Moore's own upbringing. As Moore put it, he was "trying to convey the sense of these working-class traditions that you were aware of but didn't understand the reason for it. The normal rituals and traditions that came with an ordinary family life… it's all autobiographical, in that all families look a bit weird and monstrous when you're growing up in them."

This last notion—the idea of monstrous families—further highlights the fact that, for all that *Warrior* pushed the comparisons to British comedy, there are rather more obvious antecedents to *The Bojeffries Saga*. Many have pointed out the similarities to *The Addams Family*, which began as a series of cartoons in *The New Yorker* by Charles Addams before more famously receiving a television adaptation in the 1960s that ran for three years and sixty-five episodes on ABC, and to *The Munsters*, a fairly blatant knock-off on CBS from the same period. These similarities are, it's true, fairly straightforward. All three are comedies focused on a supernaturally endowed family whose humor comes from juxtaposing the supernatural with the mundanities of everyday life. But they are far from the only three texts to mine that basic territory, and Moore, in interviews, has pointed to other sources, saying that "when thinking of influences, I'd have to include Henry Kuttner's Hogben family stories," and further admitting that "of course there were things like *The Addams Family*, *The Munsters* and all of those TV monster family shows, but the Henry Kuttner stories were probably at that point the predominant influence."

Kuttner was an American writer who Moore elsewhere describes as "one of fantasy and science fiction's most accomplished and intelligent voices, as well as one of its least celebrated." This fact is not particularly hard to account for—his career only ran for twenty years before his death in 1958, and in addition to his own name he used seventeen separate pen names, a decision that makes Steve Moore's in hindsight unfortunate decision to publish some of his best-known work under what Moore describes as his "mystifying" Pedro Henry pseudonym look like a genius stroke of self-promotion. Despite the brevity of his career, Kuttner amassed a number of credits, both on his own and with his wife, C.L. Moore (who he met after sending her a fan letter under the mistaken assumption that she was a man), including a bevy of Golden Age *Green Lantern* stories.

And Alan Moore is hardly the only writer to have a soft spot for Kuttner: Richard Matheson dedicated *I Am Legend* to him; Ray Bradbury credits him with a vital assist in one of his first stories, dedicating his first short story collection to him; Roger Zelazny cites his influence on his *Amber* series. More immediately relevant to the War, William S. Burroughs directly quotes Kuttner in *The Ticket That Exploded*, and Neil Gaiman, in 2013, took to Kickstarter to help fund a reprint of the Hogben stories that Moore cites as the major influence on *The Bojeffries Saga*. These consist of five stories—one in 1941 in which the Hogben family makes a small appearance, and then another four published over two years from 1947-49, one under his own name, and the other three under the Lewis Padgett pseudonym he used for much of his work with his wife.

Their premise is simple enough: they tell of the misadventures of the eponymous Hogbens, a group of genetically mutated hillbillies of somewhat mysterious origins, although it's clear that they are centuries old based on Saunk Hogben's narration whereby he mentions, "Maw always had a soft spot fer the man that helped us get outa London. Named Little Sam after him. I fergit what his name was. Gwynn or Stuart or Pepys—I get mixed up when I think back beyond the War between the States." This sort of droll joke, trading on a narrator who understands the story he's in less well than the reader, is the basic currency of the Hogben stories, which are full of vaguely implied jokes like the description that opens the second Hogben story, "Pile of Trouble": "We called Lemuel 'Gimpy' on account of he had three legs." ("Pile of Trouble" was, in fact, Gaiman's first exposure to the Hogben stories, in Kuttner's collection *Ahead of Time*. Gaiman recalls, "I don't think I knew it was meant to be funny—all I know is that I loved it completely and utterly, that it became part of my personal mythology, and that the book vanished shortly after.") It's a style of humor that's fairly similar to that of *The Bojeffries Saga*, with obvious similarities to, for instance, Ginda's casual declaration that "I can turn a cream egg into a diamond and then eat it anyway. I can arm-wrestle against the gravity-pull of a black hole. I'm infinitely powerful."

But perhaps the most obvious connection between the Hogben stories and *The Bojeffries Saga* is simply in the basic plots of their respective first installments. The first proper Hogben story, "Exit the Professor," concerns an encounter between the family and "Perfesser Thomas Galbraith" (as he's referred to throughout the story), a biogeneticist from New York who, upon discovering the Hogbens, who is taken aback by the implications of their existence and who proclaims that "you've got to be studied, for the glory of science and the advancement of mankind." This suggestion goes down poorly with the Hogbens, particularly with their grandfather, who proclaims that "none of you may go to this New York. The moment we leave this haven, the moment we are investigated, we are lost." This sets off a chain of comic misadventure as Saunk attempts to get rid of the professor without violating the family's promise to Sheriff Abernathy that they wouldn't kill anyone "for a while, at least," which finally culminates in the Hogbens shrinking Galbraith and stuffing him in a bottle. The similarities to the plot of the first *Bojeffries Saga* story are obvious: both serve to introduce their eccentric families through the eyes of a meddling outsider who is eventually and unusually disposed of via a dramatic transformation. And, given that Moore is open about Kuttner's influence on *The Bojeffries Saga*, this is surely not an accident.

But it is equally important to note that, for all the importance that the Hogben stories had on the early development of *The Bojeffries Saga*, the series quickly developed its own voice and approaches. Originally, Moore was "planning on giving a tip of the hat to Henry Kuttner's original story. I think we ran a preview that included a character called Hogben Henry, as we were still thinking of it as an episodic, continuing story. I think he was some sort of American cousin who would have turned up for an apocalyptic showdown in the final end of the arc." But plans quickly changed. "As the story went on," Moore explains, "I realized it was influenced a lot less by things like Kuttner or *The Munsters* or *The Addams Family*, but by a lot of the British absurdist playwrights of the 50s and 60s."

While Kuttner's influence on *The Bojeffries Saga* may have waned after the comic's initial creation, it is an influence that came full circle when Steve Parkhouse was tapped to provide illustrations for the Neil Gaiman-fronted reprinting of the Hogben stories in 2013. In one sense this was an odd fit. Yes, Parkhouse illustrated the Hogben-derived *Bojeffries Saga*, and has done numerous other pieces of humor work over the course of a long career, but given the idiosyncratically American tone of the Hogben stories, the selection of such an idiosyncratically and specifically British writer to illustrate the project is, on the surface, slightly strange. But then, that sort of thing basically defines Parkhouse's career, which is one that has constantly flitted about the edges of the War thus far.

It was Parkhouse who penned the *Black Knight* strip in *Hulk Comic* that bridged the gap between the original *Captain Britain* comic created by Chris Claremont and Herb Trimpe and the Dave Thorpe/Alan Davis revival that Alan Moore eventually took over. Parkhouse, for his part, was proud of the *Black Knight* work, saying he "wanted to claim back the characters from the Americans," and recalling a "holiday on the Isles of Scilly, famed for their prehistoric burial grounds" where he sat "on a headland gazing out to sea, with nothing but the open Atlantic between me and the Eastern seaboard of America; and the whole story landed in my lap. It seemed like fate. I'm in love with Britain and the British myths. It's my link to the traditions of storytelling. The landscape holds the secrets of so much Celtic lore."

It was also Parkhouse who co-created *Night Raven*, a strip he is less fond of, calling it "silly and ill-considered," while admitting, "I don't care much for genre entertainment—but I'll do it if I'm asked," and acknowledging that "David Lloyd seemed to get some kind of buzz out of it," which perhaps illuminates part of the electricity of *V for Vendetta*, the strip Lloyd and Moore co-created to fulfill Dez Skinn's brief of a *Night Raven* clone for *Warrior*.

And it was Parkhouse who assumed writing of the *Doctor Who Monthly* lead strip after the Moores' acrimonious departure following their falling out with Alan McKenzie over Steve Moore's writing of Absalom Daak features—a job that Alan Moore has suggested he was tacitly being set up to inherit from Steve Moore. Parkhouse became in many ways the iconic writer of the *Doctor Who Monthly* (and later *Doctor Who Magazine*) comic in the 1980s, penning, among others, a memorable story featuring Peter Davison's version of Doctor Who called "The Tides of Time," in which he delighted in challenging Dave Gibbons with "the idea of starting a story with a village cricket match" before expanding out to "a

Figure 181: Mythic Britain in The Black Knight. *(From* Hulk Comic *#1, written by Steve Parkhouse, art by John Stokes, 1979)*

Figure 182: The ancient hill where Ruad hides Galbrain, one of many lush and mythic landscapes in The Spiral Path. *(From* Warrior *#1, by Steve Parkhouse, 1982)*

potential epic, ranging through so much scenery, from one end of the galaxy to another," and tone for Colin Baker's Doctor Who called "Voyager," which gave John Ridgway an opportunity to draw a richly ornate dreamscape that became, in the eyes of many fans of the series (a group Parkhouse describes as "a generation whose predilections frankly mystified me" based on their fetishization of "power hungry aliens versus an emotionally challenged and sexually inhibited hero") the greatest comic version of *Doctor Who* ever made.

> *"Alien architecture. Made by giants for a never-ending war. Perpetual war."*
> –Grant Morrison, *Nameless*, 2015

Parkhouse, like his fellow Steve Moore, is one of the great strange men of British comics. Both serve to give the subtle and unsettling sense of the British comics industry prior to 1979 as a sort of graveyard of strange magicians, a vast collection of visionary weirdos content to be near-completely overlooked. Although Parkhouse does not share the Moores' or Morrison's active and public identification as a magician, he is as self-evidently one as exists. This is perhaps most clear in *The Spiral Path*, his often overlooked fantasy strip for *Warrior*. Like his *Black Knight* and *Doctor Who* work, there is an oddly shamanistic quality to *The Spiral Path*—it is a comic that is based heavily on intense visuals, at times at the expense of entirely clear plotting.

On one level, *The Spiral Path* is a fairly straightforward bit of sword-and-sorcery fantasy in the tradition of Conan the Barbarian, or, to pick something perhaps somewhat closer to its conceptual terrain, Elric of Melniboné. It opens with a bombastic narration about how "the land of Tairngir had been invaded by hostile forces... after many years of battle, King Galbrain was deposed, his armies destroyed by magic and madness. Sick and dispirited, the King and a handful of warriors took flight and now approached the furthermost borders..." and the first installment largely focuses on

Galbrain's travels as he meets a druid, Ruad, who shelters Galbrain in "an old hill dwelling" full "of mine-workings and tunnels." Galbrain obligingly retreats, at which point it is revealed that the armies that have been pursuing Galbrain have followed, and there are thousands marching upon the hill.

But the story this seems to set up—of a King fighting to reclaim Tairngir against seemingly insurmountable odds— never quite materializes. Galbrain is essentially absent from the remainder of the tale. The next two chapters focus primarily on the twin sacrifices of the druid Ruad, who first sends his crow, Caed, to fly forth, tying a message to his leg and telling him, "Bear this spell with you, in the hope it may reach the ears of the one who dreams us all... the one who may some day awaken," and the warrior Nuada, who dies facing a fearsome giant. The story then drifts to cover the transformation of Caed from a crow to a human being with the help of a mysterious druid and his daughter. The druid, however, is killed in the attempt when he's possessed by one of the lords pursuing Galbrain, the undead Artûk. And so the unnamed druid's daughter, Bethbara, sets off with Caed to parts unknown, taking up another few installments, until they're separated and have parallel mystical experiences. The strip ends, after twelve installments, with Caed slaying Artûk and, as prophesized, taking his place as a "king of terror and death" at the head of his undead army, while Bethbara becomes a queen of seemingly equal and opposite power. At the bottom of the last page a caption proclaims, "Here ends the first twist in *The Spiral Path*—a sequel, *The Silver Circle*, may appear at a later date," which, as it happens, it did not.

Holding together this somewhat disjointed tale is Parkhouse's moodily rich art, which makes rich use of dark blacks and thickly hatched shadow. Parkhouse favors a fairly wide angle on the action, confining closeups on his character's faces mostly to small panels, with the majority positioning characters in the midground so as to allow him to fill his pages with lush portraits of his mythic landscape. This is punctuated by occasional bursts of symbol-laden surrealism, especially during the portion of the story in which Caed and Bethbara have their parallel vision quests, with Parkhouse working firmly in the same sort of ornate fantasy style that John Stokes used when illustrating his *Black Knight* strip in *Hulk Comic*, or that John Ridgway (who inked the final installment of *The Spiral Path*, presumably to help Parkhouse with the twin deadline of that and "The Rentman Cometh" for *Warrior* #12) would later provide for "Voyager" in *Doctor Who Magazine*.

It is perhaps unsurprising that *The Spiral Path* is so untidy given how difficult it was for Parkhouse, who described it as "a painful, lonely, and psychologically damaging experience." He describes its method of composition bluntly: "No fucking script. I just drew the frames as they occurred to me. I hoped that some spirit would show through the agony—that I would be rescued by my guardians. It was a long, dark night of the soul that lasted over a year." This is not, to be clear, simply hyperbole. *The Spiral Path* is a magical work in the same sense that *The Birth Caul*, *The Invisibles*, or *Somnium* are. Parkhouse explains that "Artûk, Lord of the Slain had appeared to me in a dream and nearly claimed my life. I tried to exorcise him by capturing him on paper—but I didn't really get a handle on it. Part of me still shudders at the memory of *The Spiral Path*. I never worked that way again."

And while Parkhouse may have been scared away from such overt magical workings by *The Spiral Path*, he winds his way through the future of the War. He eventually works with Grant Morrison on *The Invisibles*, drawing one of its most memorable issues, "Best Man Fall," a comic Parkhouse describes as "a tour-de-force" that "reinforced all my feelings that comics can compete with novels, TV and cinema as long as there is a writer of real quality at the helm," as well as doing art for *Big Dave* during Morrison's co-editorship of *2000 AD* for the aptly named Summer Offensive, relishing the opportunity to return to the "controversial and contentious and largely satirical" tone of the classic Mills and

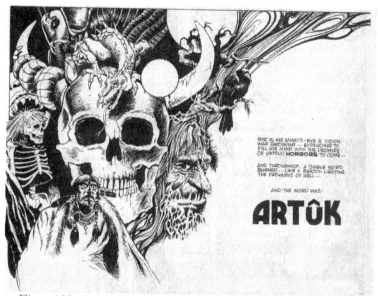

Figure 183: *Artûk, Lord of the Slain, who appeared to Parkhouse in a dream and nearly killed him. (From* The Spiral Path *in* Warrior *#3, by Steve Parkhouse, 1982)*

Figure 184: *Trevor Inchmale's asymmetrical glasses make him immediately recognizable as a character. (From "The Rentman Cometh," in* Warrior *#12, written by Alan Moore, art by Steve Parkhouse, 1983)*

Wagner strips for the magazine. And he makes a brief cameo on Neil Gaiman's *The Sandman*, inking Michael Zulli's pencils for the "Men of Good Fortune" fill-in within *The Doll's House* arc, an experience he describes as "working like crazy to contain Michael Zulli's manic pencilling. He pencils like a spider on speed."

In terms of *The Bojeffries Saga*, Moore is unequivocal in his description of Parkhouse's contributions: "Steve Parkhouse is the main vision behind the strip." Specifically, he reflects fondly on working with an artist "who grew up on the same *Beano* and *Dandy* illustrators that I did. You know, the Paddy Brennans and the Ken Reids and the Leo Baxendales, and who kind of worked that into their style." And Parkhouse's style for *The Bojeffries Saga* owes a clear debt to those illustrators, and more broadly the tradition of cartooning they belong to. The Bojeffries all have distinctive silhouettes and unique body shapes, from Ginda's blocky frame and bowl haircut to Jobremus's eternally slouched posture, along with little touches like Trevor Inchmale's asymmetrically rimmed glasses.

But Parkhouse's art is doing something much subtler than just cartooning. Generally, the point of the distinctive silhouettes in cartooning is to facilitate the artist's use of a simpler, cleaner line. If a character is recognizable simply by the outline of their head, one doesn't have to make the other details of the character particularly ornate—an expressive set of eyes and a mouth will generally do. But Parkhouse, although his character designs owe a huge debt to cartooning, still employs the detailed line of his other work. In particular, Parkhouse continues to draw the richly detailed backgrounds that characterized his work on *The Spiral Path*, except that instead of drawing lush portraits of mythic Britain, Parkhouse is drawing sweeping landscapes of British urban sprawl. Indeed, Moore and Parkhouse open "The Rentman Cometh" in such a way as to focus on this, with three wide panels of Trevor Inchmale biking down the street followed by a double-sized establishing shot of the skyline, the terraced houses of the Bojeffries' neighborhood giving way to tower blocks and industrial landscape in the background, all meticulously hatched and shaded.

Similarly, the second *Bojeffries* story, "Raoul's Night Out," has a wide panel of a terrace skyline as its second panel, and another large architectural panel at the end of its first page, this time depicting the eccentric jumble of structures that make up the factory at which Raoul works. The story's second part, meanwhile, both opens and closes with a skyline panel, with caption boxes providing a wry narration of events. ("In the smeared and glimmering tooth-mub of the night, the moon hangs suspended like a partially dissolved Disprin..." the strip opens.) In fact, every installment of *The Bojeffries Saga* has at least one panel in which Parkhouse draws a wide shot of some architecture, generally, though not exclusively, terraces. The effect is to make a specific landscape of Britain as important and defining an element of *The Bojeffries Saga* as the actual characters.

It is therefore worth pausing to consider the nature of terraced housing, since it is so clearly a major signifier within *The Bojeffries Saga*. From a strictly architectural standpoint, terraced housing refers to rows of houses featuring identical floorplans and shared side walls, either "through terraces," which had a back door, or "back-to-backs," which also share their back walls with the next row of houses over. However, for the purposes of *The Bojeffries Saga*, the social history of terraced housing is more significant and revealing than the architectural history. The terraced style is associated with a particular period in the long history of British class relations, starting in the Victorian era when they were the preferred style for industrial revolution-era workers' housing, particularly in the textile industry. Their existence was in many ways an extension of the basic logic of the industrial revolution itself—an attempt to replace the slums with efficiently stamped out housing. The underlying ethos was Victorian in the extreme, harkening back to that old belief that that what poor people really needed was to work hard—

Figure 185: A very British skyline. (From "Batfishing in Suburbia" in
Dagoda #8, 1986)

Figure 186: The incomprehensible factory in which Raoul works. (From
Warrior #19, written by Alan Moore, art by Steve Parkhouse, 1984)

the terraces were poorly constructed, dark, and small houses that served little purpose other than containing people who were not, at that precise moment, working.

The style took off in the wake of World War I, when the army discovered, to its alarm, that the fighting-age population of British cities was generally in appalling health, a state of affairs blamed on urban poverty. This resulted in the Housing Act of 1919, which gave money to local authorities to construct new housing, leading to the rise of the council estate, which, at the time, was generally constructed in terraces. But in the wake of World War II and the extensive bomb damage to British cities a new vision of housing policy took hold, first with the New Towns Act in 1946, which, in Northampton at least, resulted in the abrupt bulldozing of the council estates in favor of new developments meant to attract a better sort of worker from London, and then, over the 1950s and 60s, in the steady turn towards the brutalist tower block.

So for Moore and Parkhouse to actively invoke the terraces in 1983 was not merely a specific cultural reference, it was a specific cultural reference to a working class landscape that was already largely gone. Moore notes that one of his favorite things about *The Bojeffries Saga* is the way in which it serves as "a kind of history of British culture, the incidental British culture that is kind of embedded in that narrative. How long has it been since there was a rent man? Or giro checks? There's all these things that don't exist anymore." Indeed, by the time of the last *Bojeffries Saga* story, this will largely become the explicit point of the series. But it's an idea that's in the strip from the start. The entire premise of "The Rentman Cometh"/"One of Our Rentmen is Missing" is that the Bojeffries have been living in their eccentric house for ninety years without paying rent or anyone noticing. They're an artifact of the past idiosyncratically embedded in the present.

The theme is similarly present in the second *Bojeffries Saga* story, "Raoul's Night Out," which, as the title suggests, primarily focuses on Raoul, the werewolf, with only Jobremus and Ginda representing the rest of the Bojeffries clan, and who only appear on two of the twelve pages. The rest of the characters involved in the farce are Raoul's coworkers at Slesidge & Harbuck Ltd Staunchion Grinding and Light Filliping. (Moore notes that the name was selected to evoke the experience of walking past factories where "you don't know what they do in there, and you suspect the people who work there don't know either," an image that similarly evokes a sense of a rapidly disappearing past.)

The story also marks a subtle evolution to the underlying format of *The Bojeffries Saga*. The plot is still basically that of a farce, but instead of focusing on one character in a traditional "idiot" role, he layers together a set of absurd misunderstandings incorporating several characters, all of whom are, in their own ways, complete dunces. But what's in many ways more important than the change in comedic structure is the nature of the characters involved. The first story was, at the end of the day, essentially a Hogben story transplanted to working class Britain, with the focus firmly on the eccentric family and Trevor Inchmale as an intrusion from the mundane world. But "Raoul's Night Out" is a story about working class Britain into which a single werewolf has been inserted. This allows Moore to engage in a fairly direct satire of the working class. For instance, among Raoul's coworkers is Colin Council Estate, who introduces his girlfriend Sheena to Raoul by saying, "Society's rejected 'er because she's got '****' off' tattooed on her forehead" (a fairly straightforward homage to Vyv of *The Young Ones*).

"All Coppers are Rascals."
–Ol' Bill, *Dodgem Logic*, 2010

The move to looking at the larger culture in which the Bojeffries exist allows Moore a considerably sharper sort of satire. The main thrust of "Raoul's Night Out" is a night out with Raoul and his coworkers that goes wrong for a number of reasons, not least of which is that Colin consulted his diary to tell Raoul that it was a new moon without bothering to mention that, as Sheena puts it, his "***** diary is four ***** years old" and that he hasn't "bought one since the *** Pistols disbanded." This, rather awkwardly, results in Raoul turning into a wolf in the middle of dinner, which causes the further deterioration of a situation already made fraught when Raoul passed on a pamphlet given to him by his coworker Stanley to another one of his coworkers, George, completely oblivious to the fact that Stanley's neo-Nazi propaganda ("Did Himmler Discover Radium?" one article asks) might go down poorly with George, who is black. By the story's end George and Stanley are in the midst of a furious row, Little Nigel (who Moore, in an interview, describes as "a teddy boy dwarf") is discoursing at length about his habit of going to the Yachting Club and molesting women while pretending to be drunk, and Raoul is a wolf, at which point the cops burst through the window of the restaurant, take one look at the situation, and proclaim that "it's fairly obvious what the source of the trouble is here" before violently beating George and dragging him off. ("Y'know, I'm not racial predjudice, but they ent the same as us, are they," muses Little Nigel to Stanley afterwards.)

But for all that "Raoul's Night Out" goes for incisive comment on British racial politics, its main focus is simply on the odd ritual of the night out with one's coworkers. The story ends with Raoul returning home and telling Jobremus the story of the night, to which Jobremus sadly shakes his head and says, "Honestly, our Raoul… you are a gret wally… I dunno why you bother to *go* every year if it's always the bloody *same*," at which point caption boxes take over: "The evening was still, save for the faint whirring noises that the streetlamps made if you pressed your ear to them and the distant, poignant coughing of a consumptive housemartin. Goodnight, everybody. Goodnight." The joke, in other words, isn't just that British cops are racist or that punks are not the most reliable people ever born, but rather that this sort of farce is perfectly ordinary—as Moore put it, "I didn't have to reach back so far in my memory to bring out Raoul's Night Out. That was thinking back to my late teens and early twenties where I was in the world of work and experienced work nights out for myself, which were always kind of nightmarish, if oddly entertaining in other ways."

"Raoul's Night Out" was the final *Bojeffries Saga* strip to appear in *Warrior*. It was not, however, the final *Bojeffries Saga* strip in general. The degree to which one finds this surprising is perhaps a matter of perspective. From one angle, it would have been odd for it not to continue, given that Moore's other two *Warrior* strips found new homes after the magazine's implosion. But the migration of *Marvelman* to Eclipse and *V for Vendetta* to DC was, in each case, due to the acclaim and popularity those strips had attracted, and this acclaim was based on a specific and ultimately narrow view of Alan Moore's style as a writer whereby his "serious" works with inventively gruesome violence and high body counts are considered his most important. *The Bojeffries Saga* was, self-evidently, not going to follow precisely in the footsteps of Moore's other *Warrior* strips. More to the point, at the time of *Warrior*'s collapse *The Bojeffries Saga* consisted of just twenty-six pages of material. There aren't really any other examples in Moore's career of something that short getting followed up on years later, and certainly none that are comedic in nature.

And yet not only was *The Bojeffries Saga* followed up on, it has the distinction of being the work in Alan Moore's career with the single longest span between its first and last installments, with thirty-one years separating "The Rentman Cometh" and the final *Bojeffries* story, "After They Were Famous." But for all of this, there is no point in Moore's career where *The Bojeffries Saga* can ever be called a major concern—at its most active period, Moore and Parkhouse produced thirty-four pages over three years, and those were the same three years during which Moore started *From Hell*, *Big Numbers*, and *Lost Girls* and wrote both *Brought to Light* and *A Small Killing*. And so *The Bojeffries Saga* is in the curious position of simultaneously being able to demonstrate the entire expanse of Alan Moore's career and never really giving a particularly good sense of it. In this regard, it is possibly the most revealing and significant document of the pre-War period.

Moore and Parkhouse's first return to the terraces came in 1986, when they penned a four-page prologue to "The Rentman Cometh" for Fantagraphics' *Dagoda* entitled "Batfishing in Suburbia," described as "a preface to the American edition." Its main purpose is to engineer a subtle but significant shift to how *The Bojeffries Saga* introduces itself. Appending it to the start of the story means that instead of being introduced to the world through Trevor Inchmale's fatal encounter with the uncanny, the story is introduced in terms of the Bojeffries, specifically a sequence in which Jobremus and Reth engage in the traditional family pastime of batfishing, which is to say, of fastening a harness onto a drunken moth and using it as bait to catch bats, a ritual Jobremus, recalling when Podlasp took him batfishing, describes as "a turning point in a boy's life." In the middle of this is a brief sequence—just over a page in length— introducing Trevor Inchmale as he's scolded to go to bed by his mother (with whom he apparently lives), who proclaims, "I know what you're doing in there! You'll ruin your eyesight, that's what you'll do." What he is doing, of course, is reading nineteenth century rent records and discovering the arrears of the Bojeffries, a rent arrears of such a staggering amount that, once he goes to bed, causes him to remark, "Something's happening in my pyjamas." Meanwhile, back on the roof of the Bojeffries house, Reth catches his first bat, upon which Jobremus exclaims, "This is grand! This is what England's all about! Family traditions passed on from generation to generation, like the monarchy." They manage to reel the bat in, at which point Jobremus bashes its head against the chimney and throws it away, as "after that, they're not much good." Reth, puzzled, asks what the point is. There's an awkward pause, Jobremus instructs him to drink his Bovril, and a caption box intones, "The night wore on, and a fine drizzle of ironies in the small hours led to a bout of serious events just before morning. All the next day there were scattered circumstances. That's how it was in England."

The effect of this is to ground the world of the Bojeffries as the central reality of the strip, as opposed to starting with a mundane (albeit clearly eccentric) figure. True, there is nothing supernatural revealed about the Bojeffries in this strip; the practice of batfishing is clearly ridiculous, and the idea of making sure that a moth harness is "not too tight around the crotch" is clearly outside the realm of human possibility, but it nevertheless falls markedly short of lycanthropy. All the same, it removes any sense that this might be a story about Trevor Inchmale, who, structurally, is clearly the (equally absurd) antagonist of the piece (although the connection between the two narratives is merely implied). But perhaps the more significant change is one of tone— rather than have the first thing the reader learns about the Bojeffries be that they're a century behind on rent and have a psychotically violent woman named Ginda in their family, the reader sees a silly but nevertheless idyllic vision of the family. Perhaps more to the point, however, it demonstrates an idyllic vision of the British landscape that the Bojeffries inhabit. "Batfishing in Suburbia" is particularly long on landscapes, with fifteen panels over the course of its four pages giving Parkhouse plenty of opportunities to draw skylines and architecture, almost all of it in a soft moonglow, providing a particularly vivid effect in the colorized Tundra collection. In the collected editions, the story is followed by a splash page of the Bojeffries house from the perspective of its back garden, thus on a cliff face overlooking the sea, with gulls circling and the moon shining bright behind the chimney, the face of Trevor Inchmale carved out of the rocks, making the sense of the Bojeffries' world as a sort of loving nostalgia unmistakable.

The next wave of *Bojeffries Saga* work spanned 1989 to 1991, and came out in Garry Leach and Dave Elliott's *A1*, an anthology out of which sprung a couple of odd little footnotes to the War, including a second Moore/Leach *Warpsmiths* strip entitled "Ghostdance," a Glenn Fabry-illustrated Axel Pressbutton strip from Steve Moore, and, in the third issue, another of the handful of times Alan Moore and Grant Morrison were published in the same magazine as Morrison and Dom Regan's "The House of Hearts Desire" saw print alongside the *Bojeffries* strip "A Quiet Christmas with the Family." The five *Bojeffries Saga* installments to see print in *A1* divide into, essentially, two categories. The first are three strips in the same general vein as "Raoul's Night Out"—character pieces that take a single member of the Bojeffries clan and look at them to the near-exclusion of all other family members. The first of these, "Festus: Dawn of the Dead," tells the story of the vampiric Festus over the course of three days as he tries to go about his basic business without any untimely incinerations, a task he fails spectacularly at, suffering fates such as being branded by the cross upon a sweet bun, or terrified by a paperboy offering him the *Mirror* or the *Sun*. The second, "Sex with Ginda Bojeffries," largely does what it says on the tin, making humor out of Ginda's fundamental misunderstandings regarding sex, such as her attempt to fake orgasm by shouting, "Listen... I'm making short, sharp cries, like an animal in pain! Ouch. Ouch, my paw! Ouch," and ending with a caption describing how "somewhere, a biological clock chimed the hour. As a familiar and unpleasant weight rolled on top of her, England lay back, closed her eyes, and thought about sex..."

The third, "Our Factory Fortnight," is something of a special case. On the one hand, it is another character-focused piece, this time looking at the world through Reth's eyes, and focusing specifically on the annual Bojeffries family vacation to the Sparklesands caravan camp. ("Apparently, since last year there's been a full enquiry to find out exactly *why* the sands were sparkling, and now everybody's advised to hire lead wind-breaks and all the deckchairs have had to be

Figure 187: Ginda Bojeffries applies her unorthodox seduction techniques. (From "Sex With Ginda Bojeffries" in A1 *#2, written by Alan Moore, art by Steve Parkhouse, 1990)*

Figure 188: Paperboys serenade the terraces. (From A1 *#4, 1990)*

encased in concrete until the year six thousand," Reth notes.) In addition to the ink wash, "Our Factory Fortnight" is a structural experiment, written not as a straight comic, but as series of eighteen pictures and captions, in the style of countless low-rent British comics annuals and summer specials (the latter of which were generally published specifically so that they could be sold in vacation towns like the one depicted in "Our Factory Fortnight," which, indeed, features Reth dreaming about such comics).

> "The Hoop was a massive dead end in which to dump America's unemployed. Called a 'Poverty Reduction Programme', it didn't reduce poverty… it just meant that people no longer had to look at the poor."
> —Alan Moore, The Ballad of Halo Jones, 1985

The other two A1-published Bojeffries Saga strips were "A Quiet Christmas with the Family" and "Song of the Terraces," both of which moved away from the single character spotlight. The former is a relatively straightforward strip in which Moore and Parkhouse run through the obvious gags surrounding the idea of a Bojeffries family Christmas: Raoul eats a reindeer, Grandpa is upset to be given a gift token for a pet store instead of a sacrifice of white goats, and Festus is incinerated when Reth excitedly proclaims, "God bless us every one." The latter, on the other hand, is one of the most interesting and formally inventive Bojeffries Saga stories to date. Described as "a light opera with libretto by Mr. A. Moore and full orchestration by Mr. S. Parkhouse," the strip is formatted as a musical, beginning with the chant of a paperboy as he walks down the terraced street, identifying the paper of choice of each house he walks past: "Sun, Sun, Sun, Sun, Sun, Guardian, Sun." He is quickly joined by further paperboys, taking up his chorus and adding in descriptions of the papers' contents:

Page three, transfer fee, 'Is your man a sex bomb?'

Which M.P.'s been compromised outside a Gent's in Wrexham?
Outrage, sports page, 'Di: her secret vices!',
Someone out of *Neighbours* whose domestic life's in crisis...

In time the original paperboy takes up a new verse, imploring the reader to

> when letter boxes snap
> pity the little chap
> who does not write the crap
> but is its victim.
> For while the world's asleep
> he works to earn his keep
> lest, with poll-tax so steep
> his folks evict him.

At this point, things really get going as the first actual member of the Bojeffries family appears, with Raoul stepping out and singing his own tune about going to work, with other men quickly joining in and singing about how "we've little dicks and big dogs / and we're not too fond of nig-nogs / but we whistle as we make our way to work" as Raoul declares:

> At veekends I vill shop for shelving down at M.F.I.
> or vatch a fourth diwision team at play
> I'd like to vin der futball pools und then retire und die
> so I vhistle as I go to vherk each day!

As their section finishes, out comes Ginda, who sings:

> There are six hundred women in this council cattle pen
> with nought in common save for their biology,
> who thus in conversation tend to stick to kids and men
> and other horrid facts of gynecology.

Her verse quickly turns to a parody of Alfred, Lord Tennyson's "Charge of the Light Brigade, as "on into the Valium and the shadow of Dreft rode the six hundred," at which point Ginda's song takes on a structure of describing these women:

> Six hundred scratched recordings of Ken Dodd and
> "Happiness"
> six hundred breakdowns, and, when life is done
> six hundred lame obituaries in the local press
> that read: 'The angels called and off went Mum.'

Meanwhile, the women of the estate begin their own verse in parallel with Ginda's:

> The three-piece-suite we bought last week will probably see us
> out
> Life's Mills and Boon must reach its final pages
> We think Death sounds quite nice: we've no idea what Life's
> about
> and we haven't had a good lie-in for ages.

Next up are the car alarms, proclaiming their basic futility, at which point Ginda, the paperboys, Raoul, and the men and women of the estate all return, singing in parallel until in unison they all proclaim, "THIS IS OUR TERRACE SYMPHONEEEEEE!!," at which point Jobremus leans out the window and tells them off for making such noise.

The strip is notable in several regards. First is simply its structural inventiveness—it is by some margin the most technically accomplished *Bojeffries Saga* strip. It also, more than any other *Bojeffries Saga* story, gives Steve Parkhouse the extended opportunity to draw architecture, given that it is set in the street, such that a row of terraced houses is the backdrop for nearly every panel—indeed, the strip features a credit offering "special thanks to Raymond and Fiona of Architects Plus." But in some ways more important is the general change in tone that "Song of the Terraces" demonstrates—a turn away from a sort of nostalgic lampooning of working class Britain and towards something much angrier and more directly cynical. Moore says there as "always been a cutting edge to the Bojeffries," specifically noting the commentary on racism in "Raoul's Night Out," but adds that "generally in the early stories, the humour is probably more affectionate, I think. Even while I am rueing the horrific institution of the works night out, I can still find something kind of dopey and endearing about it, whereas in the later ones," he explains, he has generally "become less tolerant about some of the things that I think are ridiculous or even repulsive about culture."

This becomes even more pronounced in the final and longest *Bojeffries Saga* strip, "After They Were Famous." This strip, first published in the Top Shelf/Knockabout collection of *The Bojeffries Saga*, had a long genesis—the project dates to around 2008, and the story is set in 2009, when the script was finished, but Parkhouse took considerable time illustrating the twenty-four pages, and it did not actually come out until 2014, more than twenty years after "Our Factory Fortnight." The delay between script and art was, in some ways, fortuitous, as it meant that *The Bojeffries Saga* retained its slight remove from time. Talking about the way in which the early installments looked at a rapidly vanishing culture, Moore noted, in an interview to promote the 2014 collection, that "even in the most up to date story, *Big Brother* is still on Channel 4 and David Cameron is still in opposition. It's these ephemeral things about our culture and the way it's changed over the years that end up being the most poignant things about the Bojeffries." But poignant is, in some ways, an odd term for "After They Were Famous," a strip that is absolutely withering in its assessment of the culture of its time.

The central premise is straightforward: the strip simply makes the gap between it and the last strip explicit and explores what might have happened to the Bojeffries in the intervening years. This opens with a Channel 4 documentary purporting to give an update on the family, starting with a set of six television-shaped panels as the documentary starts, and then cutting to a splash page of the derelict Bojeffries family home, one of the strip's few really big pieces of architecture, and a clear comment on the fundamental decline of the cultural institutions *The Bojeffries Saga* originally existed to satirize. Indeed, this sense of decay is tangible throughout the strip, with Parkhouse's art style having evolved over the thirty years of the Bojeffries, moving away from both the ornate detail and cartoonish clarity of the early strips and towards a much scratchier, rougher style. "After They Were Famous" also forgoes the straight black and white style of most of the previous *Bojeffries Saga* strips, instead going with a grey ink wash that is often coarsely applied, giving the strip a splotchy, slightly disheveled look that, while slightly off-putting at first glance, is an effective match for the sense of cultural decay implicit to the strip.

From this opening, the strip goes through a fairly linear account of the current fates of the family, with varying degrees of entertainment value. Reth has become a wealthy author on the back of a memoir about his family, which led to his ostracization and the family's relative disintegration. Jobremus has simply made a generational shift in British poverty, living in a tower block with a woman named Shardnee and her five children—he sits, clad in a tracksuit, on a dilapidated sofa giving his interview while Shardnee eats first the bulk of a pizza and then the box it came in. One of her children tells him, "You're a paedo. Gimme your mobile or I'll tell mum you're a paedo and then she'll well stab you up, you paedo," a demand Jobremus unhesitatingly gives in to. Festus, under the name Britney Sutcliffe, is the vocalist for the goth band Pram of Shit, Boiby is now providing power to most of England and Wales, and Ginda is a Labour MP with a propensity for snapping necks in the name of parliamentary debate.

Finally, having introduced all of this, the strip cuts to Raoul, happily oblivious to the entire world around him, when he runs into Colin and Sheena from "Raoul's Night

Figure 189: The dilapidated ruins of the Bojeffries family home. (From "After They Were Famous," in The Bojeffries Saga, *written by Alan Moore, art by Steve Parkhouse, 2014)*

Figure 190: Raoul walks through the rapidly changing landscape of contemporary Britain. (From "After They Were Famous," in The Bojeffries Saga, *written by Alan Moore, art by Steve Parkhouse, 2014)*

Out." Sheena, it transpires, has been a contestant on *Big Brother* since her last appearance ("They adored me having '**** off' on my forehead. I mean, thank heavens it wasn't 'fuck'.") and they encourage Raoul to give it a try, given that Slesidge & Harbuck went out of business fifteen years ago because "nobody could remember what staunchion grinding was." Raoul returns to the Bojeffries house, which is demolished while he sleeps, and, after wandering through London (a sequence that provided Moore's favorite moment of the strip, a panel "of him walking down a flooded street, up to his waist in water, with all the Police rescue boats helping people in the background. Then in the next panel he's in a different part of town, where he's dripping wet but there's no water. He doesn't appear to have noticed the town is flooded, because he wouldn't, as he's Uncle Raoul.

On the other hand, there was something in that panel that seemed to me to speak to the fact that the landscape around us is altering now with blinding speed and we take that blinding speed of change as the norm and we try to deal with that and get along as normal, even if the situation around us is becoming increasingly abnormal. I know that's a lot to read into a single panel and it was certainly not what I intended when I wrote it, but the way it came out there was something poignant in that, that we are walking through a flood without a care in the world."), makes it to the *Big Brother* auditions, where he gets brought on to *Celebrity Big Brother* due to the mistaken impression that he's Meryl Streep (who apparently played him in the disastrous film adaptation of Reth's book). Indeed, it turns out that this year's edition of *Celebrity Big Brother* simply consists of the entire Bojeffries clan, in a perfect reconstruction of their old house, which turns out to be the doing of Podlasp, now a television executive. After a few pages of mining this for humor (Festus, for instance, quickly murders Reth for his book), the strip ends, with a familiar caption box narrating that "as our plummeting standards meet the rising ocean coming the other way, we kiss England on the cheek and say goodnight... and then, come the morning, we leave silently before England awakens. Because she's a minger."

While the differences between "After They Were Famous" and "The Rentman Cometh" are non-trivial, in most regards it is the similarities that are more apparent. The strips demonstrate a lifelong fascination with the working class culture of the United Kingdom—an aspect both of Moore's background and career that is on the one hand essential to any thorough understanding of him, and on the other at least relatively difficult to discern from any of the major works from this phase of the War. Class issues are certainly relevant with some frequency—they're quietly at the heart of both *Skizz* and *D.R. & Quinch*, and lurk in the background of *Swamp Thing* and *V for Vendetta*, for instance. But they are not issues that leap from the page and announce themselves as major concerns upon even the most casual reading the way they do in *The Bojeffries Saga*.

This, in turn, reveals a larger flaw in the basic idea of attempting to understand Moore and the War through the lens of the "major works." A narrative of Moore's cultural conquest that begins with *Roscoe Moscow* and continues up through his breaking out into the American market and the commissioning of *Watchmen* is easy enough to construct, and is even a true story, such as it is. But its truth comes from the fact that it is constructed from a point well into the War, after the consequences of the early skirmishes have largely played out—it is a truth, in other words, based on selecting the historical events that ended up having the most future impact, not on describing the events of the early 80s as they seemed to be happening at the time. In the fog of war, before it was clear to anybody that there even was a War, there was no such narrative of steady ascent. There was only a young man in Northampton trying to feed his family through means other than jobs he found soul-destroying. And so alongside the road from *Sounds* to *Swamp Thing* is another altogether more idiosyncratic path—one that contains many more things like *The Bojeffries Saga*, and often just as fascinating.

Consider, for instance, Moore's three-page contribution to Marvel UK's *Not the World Cup: The Official Souvenir Brochure*. The piece envisions a television interview between Ted Drinkproblem and "the controversial star player of the Republic of Santa Mafiosa, Ricardo del Wolverine," who shares a variety of helpful football tips such as how best to foul opposing players. ("Many beginnairs assume that eet iz best to foul the pairson 'oo 'az the futbaal. Not so. Eet iz far bettair to creepul the smallest and weakest playair, whether 'ee 'az the baal or not," del Wolverine explains, before advising that it's best to hit the player with a four-by-two and, if necessary, finish him off with an industrial rock drill while the ref isn't looking.) The piece ends in a blaze of bewildering homoeroticism as del Wolverine demonstrates in detail how to go about kissing your teammates, working his way up the host's arm while singing Barry Manilow's "Feelings."

The history of Alan Moore criticism could stretch for centuries into the future without anyone even calling this piece a hidden gem, little yet a major work. (Although the suggestion that scoring goals is best accomplished by calmly showing the goalkeeper a photograph of his family being menaced by a mobster with a Tommy Gun is a pretty good gag.) And yet within these three pages an entire secret history quietly unfolds—one that encompasses the very existence of *Not the World Cup: The Official Souvenir Brochure*, a bit of ephemera characteristic of the British comics industry's often charmingly low-rent sensibilities—sensibilities without which *Marvelman*, for instance, would never have existed.

And this is before one looks into the cultural importance of football, a sport whose history in many ways is literally and directly the history of class relations in Britain. The notion of a ballgame involving one's feet originates in numerous cultures, but the specifically British game dates back to at least the 9th century, where a version is referenced in the *Historia Brittonum*, which also provides the earliest reference to King Arthur. Originally played as a Shrovetide festivity in which neighboring towns and villages would attempt to drag an inflated pig's bladder across the open space between the towns, with the objective being to get the ball into the neighboring town. The game had few rules—teams could be of unlimited size, and the allowed means of moving the ball were apparently anything that did not result in murder or manslaughter—but was nevertheless a recognizable antecedent to the modern game. The game survived numerous attempts to ban it over the centuries, generally on variations of the principle that it was inappropriate for poor people to have that much fun. Eventually and inevitably, however, the game was co-opted and codified by rich people, with public schools gradually establishing a set of rules until, in 1848, at an eight-hour meeting of representatives from various schools, what are now known as the Cambridge Rules were written down. These formed much of the basis for the rules created fifteen years later by the nascent Football Association.

Over time, the Football Association's control over the sport grew. In 1872, they organized the first edition of the FA Cup, which the Wanderers won in an upset victory over the Royal Engineers after Engineers player Edmund Creswell broke his collarbone, effectively reducing the team to ten men as the concept of substitutions had not yet been introduced. The popularity of this event led to virtually all of the clubs in England wanting to join, and by extension agreeing to the FA-dictated ruleset. But while the FA had regulatory control over the game, the game continued to enjoy popularity among the working class, due largely to the fact that the basic requirements for playing it were little more than an open space and a ball, objects which even the most deprived areas of Britain could scrounge up. In 1822, a northern club, Blackburn Rovers, reached the final of the FA Cup for the first time, and in 1885 the Football Association finally caved to the inevitable and allowed for professional players, a move that benefitted clubs in working class areas, where amateur players had difficulties balancing the game with their workdays, a challenge not shared by the posh public schoolboy amateurs of the southern clubs.

As the game spread across the world over the course of the 20th century, this dualism whereby a wealthy elite regulates (and ultimately profits from) the game while the working class provides the bulk of the players was mirrored wherever the game sprouted, which eventually became enough countries that, in 1904, FIFA, an international version of the Football Association, was founded in Paris, and, in 1930, organized the first World Cup. The 1982 edition of this tournament was played in Spain, with England maintaining their general record of limping pathetically out of the competition, this time going out in the second round after a pair of 0-0 draws with West Germany and Spain. But the fact of England's mediocrity at yet another sport they'd invented did not detract from the event's popularity, with no end of souvenir merchandise being produced, including Marvel UK's humorous *Not the World Cup*.

More to the point, football, in England, consists of a hierarchy of numerous leagues, starting from what was in 1982 the Football League First Division, but is now the FA-independent Premier League, and continuing down through what are now twenty-four tiers, with four hundred and eighty separate leagues and divisions containing around seven thousand teams running from the Premier League, with internationally recognized icons like Manchester United and Chelsea, all the way down to the Mid-Sussex Football League Division Eleven, where the Scayne's Hill Reserves fight it out with Crawley United for the possibility of promotion to the twenty-third tier of the pyramid, the Mid-Sussex Football League Division Ten. The sheer size of this structure, with a football team for every seven square miles, or one for every 7500 people, means that football is woven into the basic cultural fabric of the country. As with *The Beano* and *The Dandy*, English football is just something you have, like rickets.

And so, of course, this was always reflected in the country's comics, with football comics being a staple of the British comics magazine for virtually the entire history of the industry. The iconic example of the genre is *Roy of the Rovers*, an IPC strip originating in *Tiger* in 1954, before spinning off to headline its own comic in 1976. It chronicled the adventures of Roy Race, a lifelong football fan who made his debut for his beloved Melchester Rovers, rather improbably, in a European Cup final after an injury to the team's regular striker, and scored the winning goal. This provided a template for decades of subsequent stories, which generally featured similarly improbable and heroic victories won with nothing more than good old-fashioned British sportsmanship and grit. Indeed, the importance of football to the national culture is crucial to understanding why, of the numerous violent and over-the-top strips in *Action*, it was *Look Out for Lefty* (originally drawn by Moore's *Not the World Cup* artist, Barrie Mitchell) that, for most of the magazine's glory days, attracted the most controversy—because unlike the sympathetic Nazi of *Hellman of Hammer Force* or the continual explosions of red mist that *Hook Jaw* offered, *Look Out for Lefty* offered a sympathetic portrayal of working class violence grounded firmly in the material realities of the working class, and, more to the point, in the real specter of football hooliganism, which had left Leeds United facing a ban on European competition after their fans rioted during and after their defeat by Bayern Munich in the 1975 European Cup final less than a year before *Action* made its debut.

So even though his contribution to *Not the World Cup* is not particularly good, and even though it is clearly not a strip Moore was particularly enthused about, it was nevertheless a work that is situated deep in the specifically British comics industry that Moore both grew up reading the products of and sought employment in. This industry, it is important to recall, was the sole industry he aspired to work in when he started out, and while it's clear he'd spent time thinking about the idea of working in American comics, Len Wein's fateful

Figure 191: *Football was not necessarily the most natural subject for Moore. (From "Not the World Cup," illustrated by Barrie Mitchell, 1982)*

Figure 192: *Captain Airship One electrocutes Winston Jr. for masturbating. (From "Captain Airstrip One" in* Mad Dog #10, *written by Alan Moore, art by Chris Brasted and SMS Quill, 1985)*

phone call in May 1983 was still sufficiently out of left field that his initial reaction was to assume the caller "was David Lloyd doing a funny voice." The career that Moore imagined was much closer to the one implied by a writer who dashes off glossaries of trucker lingo for the *BJ and the Bear Annual* and humor strips about football in amidst the *Future Shocks* and puppet fiction for skin mags, and perhaps by things like his pair of fumetti for *Scream*—a career in which the opportunity to write *Skizz* for *2000 AD* would be a highlight and not a footnote, and one that is perhaps perfectly embodied by a 1980 photo of Moore inking a *Roscoe Moscow* strip hunched over an old ottoman because the heat had gone off in his upstairs office.

That, after all, was the sort of career enjoyed by his mentor, Steve Moore—a career Moore later described in *Unearthing* thusly: "The days grind forward measured in worn-out typewriter ribbons. In 1974, he lands a gig at Thorpe & Porter's *House of Hammer*, scripts *The Legend of the Seven Golden Vampires*, captions oozing his still-burgeoning obsession with Cathay. 1975, he's writing endless children's annuals, documenting the Sex Secrets of Bangkok for a soft-core relaunch of *Tit Bits*, ducking furtively behind the mystifying pseudonym of Pedro Henry. When the work is thin, down to the Croxley onion-skin, he'll work a day or two for Bram Stokes at the relocated *Dark They Were and Golden Eyed* along the faintly miserable defile of St. Anne's Court." And while one might be tempted to argue that a writer of Alan Moore's skill and caliber was never going to be confined to such meager grounds, one might also recall Moore's description of Blake in Felpham: "Their cottage, once the early beatific ozone rush is gone from the sea air, is damp and poorly humid. Mildewed pointillism bleeds into the stipple of his miniatures. Angry at his subservience to a lesser writer, to a lesser man, he comes to loath the thing that he depends upon. Hayley, his patron, is a self-inflated mediocrity and yet so generous. The work, the fine commissions, portrait cameos of poets. He can see them, funeral processions of giant phantoms on the Sussex shore. Milton and Dante, Chaucer, William Cowper lost and broken, shying at the bar of his own lunacy. A lesson there. His drawing paper cockles with the damp. He put a brave face on it all, one of the only faces he has left."

"There's not much left of Maria. The wind from tomorrow is scouring her away. The talons of the old world are reaching up out of the dirt for her ankles. She can barely remember what hope and peace felt like. She dreams of those infinite childhood Augusts when she didn't know anything and nothing was coming and wakes up with cold in her bones."
—Warren Ellis, *Injection*, 2015

This vision is not some mere alternate history of a world where there never was a War, where Moore's Scottish devil had no great master whose career he could imitate, where a Hampshire journalist never gets a vital lesson in writing comic scripts, and where a young man from Essex and a games journalist from Bath don't have a comics industry waiting to receive the next British genius with open arms. Rather, it is a career that happened alongside the familiar narrative of Moore's chain of successes from 1979 to 1986—a career that consists of nothing more or less than the sum total of works that don't fit into the tale of Moore's relentless march to success, and even some, like much of his *2000 AD* work, that do.

And it's important to stress that Moore really did spend a lot of time in the odd and marginal corners of British publishing. Indeed, Moore was a semi-frequent contributor to fanzines, a scene he also boosted through his fanzine reviews and write-ups of conventions for Marvel UK, primarily in *The Daredevils*. In fact, one of his fanzine contributions, a five-page comic for the magazine *Mad Dog* entitled "Captain Airstrip One," rather neatly bridges the gap between Moore's talking about fanzines and participating them. The comic expands upon the eponymous Captain Airstrip One, who is Moore and Davis's creation for Marvel UK, the alternate-universe Captain Britain of a world based on George Orwell's *1984*. The strip is a humor strip largely structured like what Moore called his "list" stories for *2000 AD*—a fairly linear exploration of the humor implicit in the idea of an Orwellian superhero—for instance, having him crash through a window to help deal with little Winston Jr.'s propensity for smut-think by electrocuting him to death. But for all its disposability— the strip is firmly an amateur production—it adds a useful point to the larger tapestry of Moore's *Captain Britain* work, affirming his inherent suspicion of the basic idea of a Captain Britain by demonstrating directly that the archetype need not be considered in the least bit heroic.

Elsewhere, Moore contributed the script for the final installment of *Moonstone*, an ongoing superhero sci-fi story in the fanzine *Fantasy Advertiser*, in which he also wrote a lengthy four-part essay entitled "Writing for Comics," an essay worth looking at in some detail simply because of the level of direct insight it provides into Moore's general approach to comics at what can fairly be called the zenith of his early career. The piece was serialized over four issues of *Fantasy Advertiser* from August 1985 to February 1986, and makes mention of a variety of Moore's early stuff, from his *Future Shocks* to his DC Comics work, including a fleeting mention of the then still-forthcoming *Watchmen*. Like any guide to writing, it is idiosyncratic in the extreme—for all that Moore insists, "Above all, I don't want to produce anything that smacks even remotely of 'How to Write Comics the Alan Moore Way'" (an allusion to the popular *How to Draw Comics the Marvel Way*, which, as Moore goes on to point out, is better described as "How to Become a Lackluster John Buscema Clone"), the approach described is clearly particular to Moore and Moore alone.

At the heart of this idiosyncrasy is Moore's focus on creating comics with "relevance to the rapidly altering world in which the industry and the readers that support it actually exist," engaging in curiously eschatological musings about how "whether for better or worse, society as we understand it will be going through some almost incomprehensible changes during the next 40 years. Assuming these changes are survivable (and there seems little point in assuming anything else), and assuming that we have a future, then we are eventually going to have to cope with it." None of this is untrue—the possibility that Moore's sense of what the next few decades of history would bring has, in hindsight, proven fairly accurate—and yet it is difficult to imagine many other comics writers who approach the question first and foremost from the angle of humanity's basic survival. Beyond that, the essay is heavily discursive—Moore spends several paragraphs, for instance, discussing the Peter Greenaway film *The Draughtsman's Contract*, which is particularly striking given that he introduces the film by noting that he's never seen it. (Despite this rather glaring gap, the point he uses the film to illustrate, which is that novels and comics allow the reader to set the pace at which they consume the work, thus allowing for greater "literary complexity" than films, where one is "trapped in the rigid framework dictated by the film's running time," is a cogent one.)

This sort of extreme "from the ground up" approach permeates the entire essay, which largely espouses the very intellectual, almost structuralist approach to comics that one would expect from reading many of Moore's interviews. It is not merely the musings on the particular structural benefits and drawbacks of specific media, but things like an extended dissection of the difference between what a story is about and the plot of the story. (He illustrates this with the example of his *Swamp Thing* story "The Curse," which is "about the difficulties endured by women in masculine societies, using the common taboo of menstruation as the central motif," but whose plot concerns "a young married woman moving into a new home built upon the site of an old Indian lodge and finding herself possessed by the dominating spirit that still resided there, turning her into a form of werewolf.") In some ways, the work resembles one of the most famous "how to write" guides ever produced, Edgar Allan Poe's "The

Philosophy of Composition," in which Poe describes in improbable detail the decision making process that led to the writing of "The Raven"—especially in the lengthy section towards the end of the essay in which he meticulously works through the composition of a *Superman* story he did with Dave Gibbons called "For the Man Who Has Everything."

It is not that any of his insights into why that script works are wrong—indeed, Moore executes a cogent analysis of why a story that has indeed been widely praised as one of the greatest Superman stories ever told (and was in fact anthologized in a collection titled exactly that) worked. But as with Poe's insistence that "I saw that I could make the first query propounded by the lover—the first query to which the Raven should reply 'Nevermore'—that I could make this first query a commonplace one—the second less so—the third still less, and so on—until at length the lover, startled from his original *nonchalance* by the melancholy character of the word itself—by its frequent repetition—and by a consideration of the ominous reputation of the fowl that uttered it—is at length excited to superstition, and wildly propounds queries of a far different character—queries whose solution he has passionately at heart—propounds them half in superstition and half in that species of despair which delights in self-torture—propounds them not altogether because he believes in the prophetic or demoniac character of the bird (which, reason assures him, is merely repeating a lesson learned by rote), but because he experiences a frenzied pleasure in so modelling his questions as to receive from the *expected* 'Nevermore' the most delicious because the most intolerable of sorrow," Moore claims, "Since I'm aware that pages 2 and 3 are on left-hand and right-hand pages respectively, it would seem advantageous to save any big visual surprise until page 4, so that the reader doesn't see it until he turns over. Thus page 3 ends with a teaser. Having entered the Fortress, the three heroes are staring at us in surprise and dawning horror, looking at something off-panel that we cannot see. This hopefully suggests something sufficiently intriguing to get the reader to turn over to page 4. Since there's an ad break immediately after page 4 and since I quite like having a full-page splash panel, just to give the title of the story and its suggested premise some weight and moment to signify that the story has started in proper, page 4 is the splash. Thus, on the fourth page, we see what Batman and Robin and Wonder Woman are seeing: Superman, standing there frozen with a hideous black-red growth spilling from his breast," there is a faint sense that he is not so much describing his process as patting himself on the back after the fact for having come up with something so clever.

But this slightly overwrought tendency is largely undercut by a sort of self-deprecating practicality, such as his observation, after working out the first half of the comic and how he wanted it to end, that "this meant that pages 26 to 36 were left for the final climactic battle between Superman and Mongul, which seemed about the right sort of length," or his account of Mongul's motivation where he says that he "wants Superman out of the way so that he can take over the universe or whatever these tyrant types usually aspire to." Similarly, the fact that this intricate description of his thinking on one particular script comes after many pages of detailed analysis of the comics industry in general, in which he thoughtfully and carefully dismantles common pieces of advice like the claim that a character should be able to be summarized in fifteen words makes it more believable when he suggests that he applied similar thought to the particular details of a script, not least because he is evidently able to jot off such thorough remarks upon both for a fanzine like *Fantasy Advertiser* at more or less the height of his career. If nothing else, one can compare the process Moore describes to surviving artifacts like his initial pitch for *Marvelman* or to his infamously thoroughly thought out scripts and see the similarities.

It is also worth pointing out that Moore, revisiting the essay in 2003, explicitly advised readers to "work without a safety net" and "ignore everything I said in this essay's opening chapters about thinking through your plot and structure and characterization before embarking upon the story," noting that "when you are a writer of some experience and prowess, it should be well within your capabilities to simply launch yourself at the deep end with a good opening idea and then trust your own mysterious processes to let plot and structure and nuances of character emerge from the narrative as you go along," and revealed that this was how he was presently working on comics, explicitly citing *Promethea* #12, an issue he describes as having "a structure so intricate and unlikely that I'm still not entirely sure how we accomplished it" as being written that way. Nevertheless, the fact remains that when, in 1984, Moore boasted that "I know quite a bit about writing comics" and that "there are maybe a dozen people in the Western world who know as much or more than I do about writing comics," he had, on the evidence, a solid case. This is, ultimately, one of the basic truisms of Moore's writing: he is an enormously cerebral writer, or, as Grant Morrison less charitably puts it, one whose writing "built its own splendorous crystal labyrinth," but was as a consequence "stifling."

Elsewhere in the UK fandom scene is Moore's contribution to Gary Spencer Millidge's 1985 benefit anthology *Food for Thought*, which also included Grant Morrison's Gideon Stargrave two-pager "Famine." (This is, in fact, one of two pieces Moore wrote for charity books addressing the African famine, having also penned three pages for Marvel Comics's *X-Men: Heroes for Hope*, a writers and artists jam that also comprises one of the two occasions on which Moore has worked with Marvel Comics proper, as opposed to their UK division or an alternate label such as Epic Comics. Moore's pages, illustrated by *Heavy Metal* veteran Richard Corben, feature the X-Men character Magneto suffering a psychic attack.) Entitled "Cold Snap," with art by Bryan Talbot, it is a bitterly cynical piece that echoes many of the ecological themes of *Swamp Thing*, only from a more humorous angle. It opens with narration, "It was early evening in the late cretaceous. Chalk-heavy seas covered most of north-western Europe. But nobody minded. WGBK were showing reruns of 'I Married a Hypsilophodon' and, somewhere, trilobites were lending each other money. There was the faintest of nips in the air..." Over four pages, it continues in a similar vein, showing the domestic life of Steve and Eilleen, a pair of dinosaurs waiting out what they admit is a particularly harsh winter. The power keeps going out, it seems, although this is framed mainly in the familiar terms of 1980s politics, with Steve grousing about how they "never should have elected a lesothosaurus. I mean... what do we know about him? Nothing!" and grousing to his neighbor, Roger, about "all this energy crisis shit in the paper." Eilleen suggests that she "was talking to Alice's girl—the one who's in college—and she says that we're using up our resources too fast," but Steve and Roger are quick to dismiss this on the grounds that Alice's girl is a lesbian. Sure, it's a bad winter, but as Roger notes to Steve as they trudge back through the snow in from a failed attempt to dig up Steve's push mower (which is frozen solid to the ground), "it's not the end of the fucking world."

It's a good strip, and Moore is characteristically willing to say as much, although he is gracious enough to offer the credit to Talbot, who he says "did a masterful job," reflecting on how Talbot did the illustration "on one of his last pieces of duotone," a type of drawing board that could be used to efficiently add hatching to a piece. But Moore's enthusiasm is perhaps unsurprising, given that it's one of only a few opportunities he's had in his career to collaborate with Talbot. (Talbot also illustrated one of his *Future Shocks*, "The Wages of Sin," and a *Ro-Busters* story for the *2000 AD* 1983 annual, as well as one of his Superman text-pieces. Talbot also contributed character designs for *Ragnarok*, a largely awful independent animated film for which Moore provided some storyline work.) This was clearly something of a pity for Moore, who, in a letter to Talbot in the process of another

Figure 193: Cretaceous climate change skeptics. (From "Cold Snap" in Food for Thought, *written by Alan Moore, art by Bryan Talbot, 1985)*

Figure 194: The opening to Nightjar, *unpublished for twenty years. (From* Yuggoth Cultures #1, *written by Alan Moore, art by Bryan Talbot, c. 1983, published 2003)*

project, an abandoned supernatural horror strip for *Warrior* to be entitled *Nightjar*, reflected on how enthused he was to be working with Talbot because "this will be the first time I've worked with an artist whose background is as solidly rooted in the underground as my own is."

Nightjar ultimately became a casualty of Moore's falling out with Dez Skinn, who, for his part, insists that he "was never very keen on *Nightjar* (hated the name) and Bryan was another slow—or busy—artist, so it would never have happened in *Warrior*." Talbot ultimately only completed two and a half pages of the strip, with another page partially completed, but roughly twenty years after Talbot had started the page, William Christensen at Avatar got in touch and asked if he still had the unfinished pages. Talbot did, and Christensen proceeded to commission Talbot to finish the strip, reprinting it along with the script and Moore's letter to Talbot about the development of it in the first issue of theanthology *Yuggoth Cultures*, collecting various Moore obscurities with newly commissioned adaptations of some of his poems and song lyrics.

The resulting strip is a straightforward thing—mainly a slab of exposition that starts with ten-year-old girl watching her father die, a death that Moore, in typically florid captions, describes as "a dirty death, stumbling and falling amidst the yellow grass and rusted pram wheels, eyes rolling, white foam flecked on blackening lips" as a man whom the audience is told is the Emperor of all the Birds is "murdered by sorcerers." The strip then jumps forward eighteen years as the girl, Mirrigan Demdyke, receives a lecture from her dying grandmother (memorably depicted by Talbot as an old woman with her eyes sewn shut), who explains that her father was not killed fairly under the rules of magic, as he was not killed by a single opponent, but by a cabal of seven sorcerers conspiring against him. Outraged by this travesty, Mirrigan swears that she will kill the seven, who are introduced at patient length by her grandfather, starting with "Hart Wentworth, whose soul is like a monstrous slug, crusted with sapphires, thrashing contentedly in the tarpit of his own vileness" and ending with Sir Eric Blason, the new Emperor of all the Birds, who Moore leaves relatively undescribed in the comic, but notes in the script is "a member of parliament" with "power on a level that drug-addled ninnies like you and I can scarcely conceive."

It is not a setup long on subtlety, and the unreconstructed revenge narrative does seem to support Moore's response to Talbot's suggestion a few years later that they revive the strip, namely, as Talbot puts it, that Moore had "moved on and was capable of better work," although to be fair, *V for Vendetta* ultimately evolved from straightforward revenge narrative to something more interesting, and the possibility certainly exists that Moore would have similarly enlivened *Nightjar*. Certainly much of the conceptual territory was subsequently revisited, most obviously with, as Talbot points out, "his concept of an urban sorcerer eventually manifesting itself in the form of John Constantine." But to both men's regret, this was as close to a major project together as they ever came.

"The world must be warned about those ducks. It's all true."
–Translucia Baboon, quoted by Neil Gaiman, 2004

The underground scene through which Moore and Talbot came up provided another major component of Moore's shadow career—work which can be described as stemming out of the Arts Lab scene he participated in between his expulsion from school and the commencement of *Roscoe Moscow*, a scene that, while it formally wound down in the mid-70s, introduced Moore to a number of creative partners with whom he produced work alongside his early comics career, mostly in the form of a series of bands with varying degrees of extremely minor success. The first and least successful of these was his 1978 effort The Emperors of Ice Cream, with saxophonist Alex Green and, in a near-miss, David J, who answered Moore and Green's ad in the *Northampton Chronicle and Echo*, only to ultimately decline due to being invited to join Bauhaus. The Emperors, at least in their first iteration, fizzled, with Green describing them as a "dream band that never got beyond rehearsals," although Moore would revive the name nearly fifteen years later for a second try.

More successful were The Mystery Guests, a band that Moore was not actually a member of, but which consisted of several familiar figures from Moore's orbit, most notably Green and Pickle/Mr. Liquorice. Moore's description of the band in a 1981 *Sounds* article is vivid, to say the least, describing the reaction to their music as "violent and schismatic, divided mainly between those who merely loathed them and those who wished them actual physical harm. A few, it must be said, had the wit to appreciate that the abrasive and cruel music, coupled with the sniggering delirium of the lyrics displayed the early thrashings of a monstrous and disturbed genius." A fanzine review of a concert where they shared a bill with Bauhaus gives a similar sense—the reviewer remarks, "Someone told me that they're excellent musicians in their own right while another source revealed that they'd got a bet on to try and clear the floor (which they almost succeeded in doing)."

Moore penned lyrics to one and a half songs for The Mystery Guests. His full song, "Wurlitzer Junction," which resurfaced from essentially complete obscurity on the *Nation of Saints: 50 Years of Northampton Music* CD included with the first issue of *Dodgem Logic*, is an ostentatiously disjointed number that pairs a straightforward punk guitar line with a consciously dissonant keyboard line in the style of a Wurlitzer organ. Moore's lyrics are oblique, mixing slices of working class life ("I keep the wallets and I stack the tacks behind the factory / I do not do it for remuneration / In fact the lack of tax is actively unsatisfactory") with moments of slight foreboding ("Why don't you take me to the imaginary zoo? / You'll be on the News at Ten / Where ambulance men give empty views"), mixed into an almost but not completely meterless verse. (Moore notes that he's particularly proud of rhyming "bachelor" and "manufacturer.") The other, "The Merry Shark You Are," consists of a first verse written by Moore ("You never hear the bomb that hits you; anesthetic / Here's a steady man with thoughts like shrapnel / You piss in the dark just like / the Merry Shark you are") and a second by Mr. Liquorice ("And if she's dead she died in flames / In cheap hotel rooms where the petrol scent remains / What becomes of slim young women / Born at best on best-forgotten days?"). The two songs were independently released in 1980 where, in Moore's words, they "immediately soared to the furthermost pinnacles of obscurity."

A third band, The Sinister Ducks, first formed when Moore, Alex Green, David J, and a fourth member, Glyn Bush ("who happened to be passing through town that particular lunch hour," as Moore explains) stepped in to fill an afternoon slot for Mr. Liquorice and Moore's Deadly Fun Hippodrome in the summer of 1979. As Moore describes the experience, "Mr. Liquorice asked me if I could possibly form a super-group and be on stage in ten minutes time. Being pretty drunk, this seemed to me a viable proposition." A second performance took place two years later at another Mr. Liquorice event, this time actually going as far as preparing material the day before the performance instead of in a ten minute rush. The show was most memorable for a song called "Plastic Man Goes Nuts," which featured, for a vocal line, the severed head of a talking doll toy that was held up to a microphone rigged to provide post-processing effects while, as David J puts it, "Alan would stare at it with malicious intent. Experimental!"

After another two years, the band released a single consisting of two tracks, an A-side entitled "March of the Sinister Ducks," and a B-side consisting of a recording of "Old Gangsters Never Die," by this point a decade-old piece that had already been repurposed once when it was incorporated into the aborted *Another Suburban Romance*. This is one of two recordings of Moore performing the piece that exists, the other dating from when Moore was a guest on spoken word artist Scroobius Pip's *Distraction Pieces* podcast in 2015 and performed it on Pip's request. Unlike the Sinister Ducks recording, which featured a musical backbeat and saxophone line, with Moore affecting an ostentatious American accent, the *Distraction Pieces* version is performed without accompaniment, with Moore opting for his natural accent, reworking the narrator from the force of sinister arrogance of the 1983 recording into a quieter figure who seems to almost yearn for the deaths he describes. This change reflects not only the passage of more than forty years since Moore first wrote the piece, but also Moore's evolving opinion of it, with Moore reflecting that it is "a series of beautiful images relating to old gangster films, old gangster mythology" but that "they don't actually say very much," and that "the words exist as a carrier of a kind of mood." Accordingly, his performance abandons the attempt to define a character. Instead, Moore gives individual images room to breathe and stand on their own—indeed, following Moore's impromptu performance, Pip singles out Moore's use of pauses and gaps for praise.

"March of the Sinister Ducks," meanwhile, is an original piece for the single, and is simply one of the most delightfully bizarre things ever produced by the War. It consists of just under three minutes of urgent warnings about the evils of ducks sung over a guitar and piano backing, with Alan Moore contributing both the gregariously baritone vocal line and most of the quacking noises that litter the track. The song steadily develops from its initial ridiculousness, noting that "everyone thinks they're such sweet little things (ducks, ducks, quack quack, quack quack)" and that "you think they're cuddly but I think they're sinister (ducks, ducks, quack quack, quack quack)" before eventually warning about how the ducks are "sneering and whispering and stealing your cars, reading pornography, smoking cigars (ducks, ducks, quack quack, quack quack)" and that "they smirk at your hairstyle and sleep with your wives (ducks, ducks, quack quack, quack quack) dressed in plaid jackets and horrible shoes, getting divorces and turning to booze" before finally proclaiming them "web-footed fascists with mad little eyes (ducks, ducks, quack quack, quack quack)."

But for all that it emerged out of Moore's art lab connections, the eventual Sinister Ducks single owed no small debt to the comics world as well. The front cover was an inventively bizarre piece by Kevin O'Neill, while the back cover featured the work of Savage Pencil, who shared the comics page of *Sounds* with Moore. Beyond this, the single also contained an eight-page comic adaptation of *Old Gangsters Never Die*, with art by Lloyd Davis. It's a bizarre set of collaborators and, for that matter, a bizarre single, utterly unconcerned with any sort of commercial success. Instead, it exists fairly obviously for no reason other than to entertain the people creating it, a monument to nothing save for Alan Moore's sense of what might be fun, which, notably, was spot-on.

This also goes a long way towards describing Moore's contributions to magazines like *Honk*, an American anthology published by Fantagraphics. Moore's contributions include his first work with Eddie Campbell, a three-page text piece entitled "Globetrotting for Agoraphobics" for which Campbell provides half a dozen single-panel cartoons as illustration. The piece is a humorous attempt to address, "What we can do for agoraphobiacs in our midst? How can we ease their suffering? How can we help them see themselves as useful members of society, rather than as nuisances who get in the way when the Gas-man wants to read the meter in the cupboard under the stairs?" He goes on to suggest that what agoraphobics really need is a trip around the world, which, given the obvious difficulties involved, is, in his account, probably best accomplished by sticking a paper bag over their head and trying to persuade them that they're on a globetrotting trip without actually taking them outside of their apartment—by employing tricks like, in order to get them to think they're on a plane, sitting "them in an armchair that is situated so as to be facing the wall from less than a

Figure 195: Kevin O'Neill's cover to the "March of the Sinister Ducks" single.

Figure 196: Eddie Campbell illustrates the proper handling of agoraphobia. (From "Globetrotting for Agoraphobics" in Honk #4, *1987)*

foot away, requiring that the knees be tucked up under the chin in an uncomfortable position, where they will remain for the next eight hours." From there it's just a small matter of following Moore's suggestions for specific countries, such as his account of how to recreate Sweden in your kitchen: "Seating your by-now-world-weary explorer in the chest freezer, fill the sink with blancmange and then try vigorously to unblock it using a conventional plumber's suction cup while asking them what they think of the live sex show."

Moore's other contribution to *Honk* is a reprint of a piece earlier published by Knockabout Comics, originally with illustrations by Savage Pencil, although the *Honk* version was illustrated by Peter Bagge. Entitled "Brasso with Rosie," the piece is one of the few—and by some margin the earliest—openly autobiographical pieces that Moore has written. It is, to be sure, an exaggerated and at least partially fictionalized piece—Moore's claim that an elderly relative of his was once "totally immobilized when a thoughtless spouse decided to hang mirrors upon either side of the tiny, damp-scented room in which he customarily sat, presenting the luckless dotard with an infinite succession of doppelgangers arrayed to either side of him," which lead him to believe that he had "been granted some form of X-ray vision, enabling him to see through the peeling walls and into the identical living rooms of his neighbors," and that "he remained like this for twenty years," is, for example, surely overstating the case by at least half a decade.

"Outside the horses walk on cobbles, ringing in the city's burdened, swollen heart. Cars follow and then more cars; cyclone flow of noise and fume and colored steel. The factories are born, thrive briefly, turn to husks as the hand-lettered signs above the shops give way to corporate logo."
—Alan Moore, *The Birth Caul*, 1995

But underneath the comedic exaggeration is a sardonic and vivid account of the texture of Moore's childhood, featuring no shortage of details that Moore would go on to revisit in later works, such as his claim that "while it was true that before I was ten years old I had been hung from a tree by my wrists, whipped with barbed wire and buried alive by my schoolchums, there were also moving and poignant memories that I shall carry with me forever," an account he would eventually revisit in his magical working *The Birth Caul.* Indeed, "Brasso with Rosie" discusses birth cauls in the context of his grandmother's "elaborate and obsessive system of Juju and Counter-Juju," claiming here that she in fact had an "extensive collection" of them that was discovered after her death, as opposed to, in his later account, simply having his mother's caul.

A similarly autobiographical piece appeared in Myra Hancock's self-published magazine *Myra,* with illustration by, of all people, Myra Hancock. Entitled "A True Story," it's a deliberately shapeless narrative that starts with a couple pages about a childhood acquaintance of Moore's named Christopher Martin. Moore begins by telling the story of getting into a fight with Martin and punching him, then digresses through some school-age antics, always focusing on odd details, such as the fact that Martin "idolised Manchester United and collected programmes with their picture in the middle. In one, Paddy Brennan's right testicle was clearly visible." Halfway through the second of the strip's five pages, Martin contracts Hodgkinson's Disease. By the end of the third page, he's dead. The third page focuses on Moore and his friends' reaction to the death, which is as drably mundane as everything else in the strip. The piece concludes with Moore running into one of his old friends in the post office and going for coffee, where they reminisce. "He told me that Gavin now has a wife, two kids, and multiple sclerosis," Moore narrates. "I told him that Jon's divorced now, and has a job in the police force. We both had a good laugh, without being quite sure why." And with that, the strip ends, all the drama of confronting death at a young age ultimately expressed only in the trivialities of day-to-day life, which is,

Figure 197: Alan Moore's family as depicted by Peter Bagge. (From "Brasso With Rosie," in Honk #2, 1987)

Figure 198: Moore sardonically depicts the banality of a childhood friend dying of cancer. (From "A True Story" in Myra #8, *written by Alan Moore, art by Myra Hancock, 1986)*

after all, the context in which such things truly exist in the first place.

It is worth pointing out that these independent, small-press works are essentially the only place in which Moore engages in any degree of autobiography. Indeed, in a 2003 interview with Moore, Eddie Campbell enumerated the sum total of autobiographical works of Moore's that had appeared by that point, counting only four works: the last chapter of *Voice of the Fire*, *The Birth Caul*, a piece called "Letter from Northampton" that Campbell describes as "a lightweight page in a mag called *Heartbreak Hotel*," and "Brasso with Rosie," which Campbell notes Moore declined to let him reprint with the interview. Moore, for his part adds "A True Story" to the tally, while pointing out that the last chapter of *Voice of the Fire*, despite being autobiographical, avoids the first person singular entirely. (These days you'd have to add *Jerusalem* to the list as well, of course.) He also acknowledges "a certain reluctance to appear on the page myself," while conceding that "it's really just my particular great vanity to try and conceal my great vanity." But the fact that Moore does not often write directly about his own life does not mean that this life is any less immediately relevant to understanding his work, and, more to the point, his actions over the course of the War, a topic of growing concern as the actual outbreak of hostilities looms.

Many of the basic facts are well known. Moore was born on November 18th, 1953, in Northampton. His parents were working class—his father worked as a manual laborer at a brewery, where he earned £780 a year—about £20,000 today; his mother worked at a printer's. He lived in a council house in the Spring Burroughs region of the town, a network of streets built over the old moats and forts of Northampton Castle, demolished in 1662, with both his parents, his brother, and his grandmother, although shortly before he was born there had been a seven more extended relations living with them. The house was by no means luxurious—it had neither an indoor toilet nor hot water, although it did have electric lighting, which put it ahead of many of the houses in the area. His life was certainly not one of intense deprivation—his family was always able to make basic ends meet and still provide him with a bit of pocket money—but this was in no way a universal experience for the area. Moore is usually sardonic about this, as in his quip that "there were a great many families who were probably, looking back, incest families, where even the dog had the same hairlip," but occasionally lets slip a detail regarding the degree of deprivation that existed around him, such as the existence of families that couldn't adequately feed themselves and "whose children had that sort of dull gray skin that I came to associate with undernourishment."

While Moore has not written at any great length about his upbringing—although, obviously, it comes up in several interviews—there exists a surprisingly good alternative. Moore's first-form French teacher was Jeremy Seabrook, who, the year after teaching Moore, penned *The Unprivileged*, which was the first book in a still-ongoing career writing about poverty. This career would have a global scope, chronicling poverty in India and elsewhere, but *The Unprivileged*, subtitled "A hundred years of family life and tradition in a working class street," was semi-autobiographical, with Seabrook telling the history of his own family and upbringing, which took place only a few streets and fourteen years removed from that of his eventual pupil. (Indeed, Moore notes in the short film *Don't Let Me Die in Black and White* that his family at large comes from the same street as Seabrook.) Interviewed by Lance Parkin, the first scholar to uncover the connection, Seabrook did not remember Moore specifically, but nevertheless remarked on the character of the Burroughs, an area defined by the then-declining shoemaking industry, saying that "the shoe people were generally narrow, suspicious, mean, self-reliant, pig-headed, but generally honourable and as good as their word."

And so while *The Unprivileged* is not, as such, a book about Alan Moore, it is nevertheless profoundly revealing. It is not fair to call it the book Moore would have written about his childhood, but given the biographical similarities of Moore and Seabrook, it's still one that offers numerous parallels to Moore's life. Seabrook, for instance, describes the superstitious nature of the area's inhabitants—the way that "one or two older members of the family still assert that they are able to work harm against those they dislike simply by the power of their will," and talks about how his family's superstitions "seem sometimes to have the power to transport me, their slightest more matter-of-fact observations serving as magical incantations, to impossible and fabulous times, when even the wild flowers and birds in Polebrook Woods had a profound and urgent significance for those who lived close to them," a description that not only seems to prefigure Moore's eventual psychogeographic approach to magic, but that matches his account of his grandmother's "kitchen corner voodoo" whereby "knives crossed on the dinner table, as an instance, heralded the forthcoming destruction of the house and its immediate neighborhood by a rogue comet. To avert this peril, the catastrophically crossed cutlery had to be struck forcibly by yet a third knife," a prime example of Seabrook's observation that "nearly all of their superstitions connected with the natural world were warnings of imminent death, sickness or loss." Elsewhere, Seabrook talks about the complex rules of divination that existed around the sparks and embers of the fire, noting that this "ancient elemental source of so many superstitions was frequently consulted as an infallible means of divination," and in doing so almost seems to call *Voice of the Fire* (in which Moore namechecks Seabrook) into being.

Similarly, Seabrook provides a litany of idiosyncratic dialect of the region, generally "unaltered Anglo-Saxon," describing his family talking "of the *slommakin* neighbors *glining* at you from behind the curtains, the *mardy*-arsed children and the *blarting* women having a tune (crying) over nothing, Vera *glawning* around (A S *ginian*, to yawn) as if she wasn't sharp, the smoke *puthering* out from the grate when the wind blew down the chimneys, the old man *golloping* his food, Gran *scratting* about like a blue-arsed fly, the kids *yawping* and *grizzling* in the *jitties*, the sister who *takes tut* over nothing, people *flacking* in and out of the house all day long, the roads all *claggy* with mud, the *shutting-in* of the day," an aspect of life that Moore recalled influencing *The Bojeffries Saga*, saying, "There were the peculiarities of speech, the little things that your parents or someone that you knew would say. I remember that the expression 'Duzzy' that was used in the first episode, that was something peculiar to my first wife's father, who would use it instead of saying 'bloody', or something like that. It was one of those evasive semi-swear words, which I thought sounded peculiar so I stuck it in the *Bojeffries*."

But there is a significant difference in approach here. For Moore, these oddities of speech are an object of wistful nostalgia—an artifact of what Moore, a decade after creating *The Bojeffries Saga*, described as a "terraced landscape which is becoming increasingly at risk and endangered, and which probably won't be here too much longer." But for Seabrook, this dialect is a considerably more sinister detail. "It was possible," he reflects, "to imagine a vigorous and independent dialect, but none of it was of recent evolution." He documents the way in which the Green Street culture was simply an ossified relic of a pre-urban culture, shuffled off to the terraces in a feat of Victorian social engineering: "The language altered little with the immediate change from country to town. It took several generations for the Anglo-Saxon words relating to their craft to fall into oblivion. Some of our family had been thatchers, or *thackers* as they called themselves, and they continued to use words like *yelm* for straw, *dike* for ditch." Not only was the vocabulary itself archaic, so was the entire tone of speech, with pronunciations that hailed from "the traditional Anglican speech of Mercia, which predated by many hundreds of years anything resembling standard English." This was not, in other words, a lively dialect, but a decayed relic. As Seabrook puts it, "They could not allow that people adopted another linguistic usage for any other reason than snobbery. It was assumed that theirs was the only natural speech." Only in the terraces' final generation did this begin to change, so that "the old find themselves suddenly speaking an unintelligible tongue. All at once the stylized ritual phrases, the mummified images, the fixed inflexions and cadences are full of a plaintive lamenting music. The old are aware of an inability to make themselves understood, even to their own children, and they realize that they will be the last ones to use the dialect."

"It flows out of me, and I don't understand it and I don't know where it's from, but it's there and undeniable and mine and I get to share it. I get to share it with everyone. This? This is as good as it gets. I feel small and holy, and the part of me that hasn't disappeared in the storm I've unleashed is whispering… This is worth it."
–Kieron Gillen, *The Wicked + The Divine*, 2015

This sort of sympathetic revulsion towards the culture of Green Street is characteristic of Seabrook's book. He returns constantly to the closed-mindedness of the area's inhabitants, describing their hatred of abstract art as "the anger of anyone brought abruptly face to face with ideas which he has no use for, but which he finds form the very basis of someone else's philosophy. They did not admit it willingly that anything exceeded their ability to understand, and in consequence violence had to be done to everything they encountered in order to accommodate it." This resulted in attitudes characterized on the one hand by intense suspicion towards "other people [who] were sure to abuse your hospitality, take advantage of your kindness and exploit your generous nature," and on the other by an intense desire "not to be beholden to anybody." He describes one group of relations simply as "mean. Of them it was said that 'they'd bottle a fart and use it again if they could'. Tom's mother was extremely reluctant to throw away anything she had used personally, and even left the water she had washed in cooling greyly for

Figure 199: *Alan Moore stands in front of Green Street for the Channel 4 documentary* Don't Let Me Die in Black and White *(1993).*

Figure 200: *Alan Moore (right) enjoying his happy childhood.*

hours in the enamel bowl in the sink. Once they found some mice-droppings in a sack of flour, and they spent the whole night extracting the tiny black grains from the bag before offering the tainted powder for sale the following morning." The sense of anti-intellectualism and insularity is profound, a theme Seabrook circles back to again and again, concluding, "The life of the streets had a devitalizing effect, and did not allow of any departure from a rigidly fixed pattern of behaviour and relationships." But for all of this, he speaks movingly of the plight of his family and neighbors, explaining in the book's final passage how, when the terraces were finally bulldozed in favor of some new vision of social engineering, the now displaced residents were "shown the error and irrelevance of their faith by those who have access to greater truths, and who tear the veils from the eyes of others, veils that prove to be not veils at all, but living membranes, the removal of which leaves nothing but empty and bleeding sockets."

Moore, for his part, is not quite so condemnatory towards his upbringing, or at least, not consistently so. In a 1990 interview with Gary Groth for *The Comics Journal*, he described himself as having had "a very happy childhood," for instance. But he is elsewhere just as scathing as Seabrook: in the *Mindscape of Alan Moore* documentary he describes it as "a monochrome world with limited opportunities," talking about how British comics like *The Beano* and *The Dandy* failed to appeal to him because "they presented a world that was almost indistinguishable from the world that I lived in," and how the "bright, garish 4-coloured" world of American superhero comics appealed in contrast because it offered a sense of escape. Obviously, over the course of his life, this escape was one he managed, thoroughly escaping his class background, and while he has lived his entire life in Northampton, that is by this point firmly a choice, as opposed to, as Bauhaus would have it, an inescapable flat field of boredom. And, more the point, this escape is clearly the entire point of his comics writing career—a concept that is inseparable from his desire to get out of dead-end and soulless jobs in favor of making his living creating art.

It is also, of course, not the norm. Boys from the Burroughs do not, as a rule, become powerful sorcerers numbered among the great literary figures of their era, or, indeed, find any other form of escape from working class poverty. Some of this, of course, is luck, an irreducible component of any narrative of social mobility. Nevertheless, two factors in Moore's life and attitudes seem particularly significant. The first of these is that Moore always had a broader vision than the parochial one described by Seabrook. Moore's father was a voracious reader, and both of his parents prioritized literacy for Moore. Beyond that, as Moore explains, "I was left more or less to map out my own universe. I was looked after and cared for and all the other things that a child should have, but in terms of my inner life, or my intellectual life, I was largely left to my own devices. Which suited me just fine. I knew where the library was; I knew where I could find information if I wanted it. I was developing my own tastes which largely centered around comic books and juvenile science fiction novels. I was allowed to go my own way and make my own decisions." This mix of intellectual encouragement and freedom to explore stands in marked contrast to the sorts of worldviews Seabrook describes.

It is, however, in no way sufficient to explain Moore's trajectory. Certainly it is sufficient to explain how Moore came to do well on his Eleven Plus exam, earning him a place at the Northampton School for Boys, the local grammar school. (The vagaries of the British education system are a rare instance of a digression too big for this project, but the term "grammar school," at the time, was defined by the Education Act 1944, which also set up the Eleven Plus exam, and described the most prestigious of three categories of schools, focusing on a traditional academic curriculum, with students sorted based on their performance on the exam.) This was the generally accepted path for social advancement—a fact that exists in the same tradition as the Victorian terraced houses and their subsequent demolition in favor of brutalist high-rises. It was also not a path that Moore took to. For all the broadening of his worldview that his literary childhood had given him, he had remained blissfully unaware of the striated subtleties of the British class system. As he tells it, "Entering grammar school was the very first time that I'd actually realized that middle class people existed. Prior to that I'd thought that there were just my family and people like them, and the Queen."

This new category of person had generally gone to considerably better schools than the working class primary school Moore had attended, and Moore quickly went from being the star pupil to being among the lower reaches of the class rankings, beginning a path of steady alienation that culminated in his expulsion at the age of seventeen. Moore is open about the degree to which he is responsible for his washing out of the class ladder, admitting that, in the face of his steadily declining class rank, "I decided, pretty typically for me, that if I couldn't win then I wasn't going to play. I was always one of those sulky children, who sort of couldn't stand to lose at Monopoly, Cluedo, anything." But this wry self-deprecation exists alongside a more ideological position—Moore also described his education in *The Birth Caul*, saying, "The real curriculum is punctuality, obedience, and the acceptance of monotony, those skills we shall require later in life. Oblique aversion therapy to cure us of our thirst for information and condition us so that thereafter we forge an association between indolence and pleasure," a critique that, once again, is not entirely unlike that of Seabrook, who put the grammar school's "unacknowledged curriculum" as one of "advanced snobbery and social climbing."

For a while, at least, Moore and his social circumstances maintained something of a détente. He was not a star pupil by any measure, but he rarely got in trouble, save for being busted smoking occasionally, and the banning of the poetry magazine he worked on, *Embryo*, after it published a poem containing the word "motherfuckers." But come the dawn of the 1970s, the situation deteriorated rapidly. First came the New Towns scheme, which resulted in the bulldozing of his terraced street and his family being relocated. This was a traumatic process, to say the least—Seabrook opens the final chapter of *The Unprivileged* with a description of the abandoned terraces: "The street is condemned now, and the wind blows through the derelict houses... everything has been left as it stood. A dead bird lies in its cage in the window, a dusty tray of butterflies impaled on pins hangs obliquely on a parlour wall, milk bottles in congealed cream rings stand on the scrubbed deal tables... in each interior the abandoned belongings remain like those of refugees overtaken by a sudden disaster; a stained striped flock mattress, fragments of rosy china vases and teapots and Coronation mugs of five reigns, blue-eyed Victorian Jesuses in gilt frames suffering the little children to come unto them, a Monarch of the Glen, school prizes awarded to the names of old men and women for Diligent Study and Application—*Isabel's Secret* or *A Sister's Love*, stories abounding in hospices and orphans and untimely deaths and little girls in frilly pinafores taking the place of Mamas who'd been called home, serious and stoical at eight years old." (Another Moore/Seabrook parallel, this time to Ginda Bojeffries description of "six hundred lame obituaries in the local press that read: 'The angels called and off went mum'" in "Song of the Terraces.")

Just six months after the family was moved, Moore's grandmother, the first magician he ever knew, died. Moore is unequivocal about the cause: "Being moved from the place where you got your roots was enough to kill most of these people. Yeah, I mean, the place where I'd grown up was more or less completely destroyed. It wasn't that they put anything better there; it was just that they were able to make more money out of it without all these bothersome people." Two weeks later, Moore's expulsion. "Within a fortnight it can all fall down, the luminous Wurlitzer palace of our youth: no luck, no school, no happy home. The job down at the skinning yards where men with hands bright blue from caustic dye trade nigger jokes. The tide comes crashing in and sweeps us all away," he writes in *The Birth Caul.*

It didn't, of course. Despite being unwilling to thread the needle of state-sanctioned social mobility and thrown upon the world's blunt engine, with no visible prospects save for soul-destroying menial jobs that seemed designed for no purpose other than breaking any independent spirit or energy for a life of the mind he might still entertain, Moore nevertheless plotted his escape. Mere intelligence was insufficient to the task. This would require some other discipline—some other point of character.

Unsurprisingly, a key clue can be found in Seabrook, who, in discussing the songs and hymns that were sung at family Christmases, notes, "The only people from their own class who appeared in these compositions were wastrels and drunkards who came to a bad end or pious and sober artisans who had signed the pledge of temperance and who behaved themselves lowly and reverentially towards their betters." This is a reference to the age-old distinction between god's poor and the devil's poor—the one made by Puritan philanthropist Thomas Gouge when he explained that "I am not against the relieving of all beggars, some of them I know are blind, others lame, aged, and past their work; these impotent poor, in regard of their present condition, are objects of charity; but not the impudent poor, who have strength enough to work and will not, those canting vagrants who are the burden of the earth, and the same of the kingdom, for these I have no charity: Neither had the apostle St. Paul, who towards God's poor was full of compassion; but for the Devil's poor, he gave this command, 'That if any would not work, neither should he eat," and by Victorian minister Hugh Stowell Brown, who, in his *Lectures to Working Men* distinguishes between "God's poor [who] are those who are poor through no fault of their own" and "another and a very different class, viz.—the Devil's poor," who "are to

God's poor as ten to one, or more probably a great deal more than that," and who have "a cunning, a mean, a hardened, or a ruffianly look, about which there can be no mistake; their faces are enough to hang them."

This was, of course, the exact same sort of distinction made by Moore's headmaster after his expulsion, who, as described before, wrote a letter of un-recommendation to any and all schools Moore might have wanted to attend, declaring that he was "corrupting influence" and "sociopathic." So this was the label Moore was now branded with. But within this label Moore found and carved out his own sort of freedom— the same sort of freedom he explored in the development of *V for Vendetta* when he probed the cultural "tradition of making heroes out of criminals." And it is this that is, perhaps, the key fact to understand about Alan Moore—the realization without which no aspect of his career or his actions during the War make the slightest bit of sense: he's a con man.

This is, after all, a well-trodden image within the British working class landscape. The specific term would be "spiv" or perhaps "wideboy," as in "the wideboy occultist I'd created some years previously for a U.S. comic book." And there are, perhaps, few images more finely suited to a working class man who quite literally makes things up for a living. Certainly it is an identity that Moore seems to inhabit well— one he alludes to when he disclaims that "in my work as an author, I traffic in fiction. I do not traffic in lies, although I'll admit that the distinction is a nice one." It is implicit in his early career admission, no doubt with a satisfied grin, that "just between you and me, I'm grossly overpaid," and in his blurb for Lance Parkin's biography, in which he proclaims that it "belongs on the bookshelf of any halfway decent criminal profiler." It is a self-image that is immediately evident in the twinkle in his eyes when, in a 2012 interview, after he explains that he'd only sold the film rights to *From Hell* and *League of Extraordinary Gentlemen* because he assumed the films would never get made, the BBC interviewer accuses him of "trying to get money for old rug," and he agrees with unbridled enthusiasm. It is the implicit link in his first Northampton novel, *Voice of the Fire*, where he transitions from his story of murderous huckster Alfred Rouse to the book's final chapter, in which he himself is the tacit narrator with a line repeated across the two chapters: "They're buying it." And perhaps most obviously, it is the logic behind one of the first acts of his career, his use of the Curt Vile and Jill de Ray pseudonyms for a spot of welfare fraud that is, in hindsight, blatantly a two-fingered statement of intent to Thatcher's Britain.

It is only when this is understood, for instance, that Moore's propensity for falling out with former friends and colleagues begins to make sense. To Moore, "artist" and "con man" are in effect synonyms (as, of course, is "magician"); it is not merely that he views himself as one, but that the idea that there might be any other way to view one's self as an artist simply does not register. This explains things like his statement, "I still don't get a lawyer to look at [my contracts], because that seems to me mistrustful. Yes, I know that sounds stupid, given that it's obviously an industry I mistrust, but I really do prefer to be working with people on the assumption everyone's being honest with each other. I'd rather not work with people than be in a continual state of mistrust." It is a view that has its roots in the sort of endless suspicion described by Seabrook—not entirely dissimilar to the way that his family "never trusted articulate people, and always held 'the gift of gab' in great contempt." To Moore, anyone who wants to set up elaborate rules for a transaction is presumably doing so in order to swindle him, whereas anyone willing to work on a simply negotiated handshake deal can be trusted as a fellow grifter. And likewise, when Moore's understanding of a deal is violated and he feels that he has been done wrong by a colleague, he reacts with all the righteous and ruthless fury of a criminal whose sense of "honor among thieves" has been betrayed, until, over the course of his career, his set of friends and colleagues slowly concentrated into a set of people he considered reliably like-minded in their basic roguishness.

And so at last a true understanding of Moore's career before the actual commencement of hostilities within the War comes into focus, at least from his own perspective. It is not a narrative of assent or conquest at all, but a snowballing long con that begins with some petty welfare fraud and gradually escalates, the stakes and payoff growing and growing until, preposterously, a wideboy from the Spring Burroughs found himself the golden boy of one of the two biggest comics companies in America, writing a magnum opus that would change the world forever. And, in turn, last the inevitability of what was to follow at last becomes clear. It would end like any well-executed con: with burnt bridges and a thief on the run.

Chapter Eleven: The Ballad of Halo Jones

"Our skullbabies will always tight the day for peoplekind."
—Alan Moore, *Crossed +100*, 2015

There is, however, one final beat to the buildup of this mad caper—the work that would end up as Moore's farewell to the mainstream British comics industry in which he made his name. This is *The Ballad of Halo Jones*, an ongoing strip for *2000 AD* published in three separate runs. The first, published as Book One, ran for three months beginning in July of 1984, one month after Moore ceased work on *Captain Britain* and *Marvelman*, and alongside the publication of *Swamp Thing* #29, the infamous zombie incest rape issue. The second launched in February of 1985, the same month when Moore began work on *American Flagg* and when *Warrior* ended, and again ran for three months. And the third, Book Three, began in January of 1986, one month after Moore's tie-in issue to *Crisis on Infinite Earths* and one month before *Miracleman* commenced in the US, and ran until April, two months before *Watchmen* debuted.

The strip's existence marks an obvious and in many regards overdue shift in Moore's status within IPC's roster of *2000 AD* writers. Of the UK comics companies with which Moore worked, IPC was the last to give him an ongoing, waiting until after he was already writing *Captain Britain* and winning massive acclaim for his work in *Warrior*, and even then offering him nothing more interesting than "can you write us an *E.T.* ripoff," an unpromising request that Moore shaped into the better-than-you'd-expect *Skizz* along with artist Jim Baikie, one of the many eternal journeymen of British comics. Subsequently, one of his *Time Twisters*, "D.R. & Quinch Have Fun on Earth," done with frequent collaborator Alan Davis, got expanded to a series of recurring stories. But once Moore started making waves in the US market, IPC (mindful of how it had lost both Brian Bolland and Dave Gibbons to DC) finally deigned to offer him a relatively free hand to create a concept of his own design.

Teaming with Moore for the new strip was Ian Gibson, who had worked with Moore on his early *Future Shock* "Grawks Bearing Gifts." Gibson's style was distinctive, mixing a cartoonish and exaggerated sense of figure and facial structure with scratchy and moderately dense line work that gave it a vivid edge. The result was particularly well-suited to humor strips, and indeed, prior to *The Ballad of Halo Jones* Gibson was most associated with the ongoing *Sam Slade, Robo-Hunter*, chronicling the adventures of a humorously taciturn bounty hunter on the trail of various robots. But Gibson's style had been a longstanding part of *2000 AD*, and his career was far more diverse than just humor. Indeed, he illustrated two of the eight parts of *The Robot Wars*, the first major *Judge Dredd* story arc, including the final installment, where he got to show off another key aspect of his work, his skill at baroque futuristic tech in the grand Kirby Machine tradition. (Indeed, Gibson even includes a straight-up Kirby homage in the finale as the strip's villain, the messianic carpenter robot Call-Me-Kenneth rants triumphantly, bathed in Kirby Krackle.)

Moore and Gibson were both mindful of the fact that although *2000 AD* had an unusually large female readership, the magazine was overwhelmingly dominated by male characters. For instance, Prog 374, immediately prior to the debut of *The Ballad of Halo Jones*, featured exactly three female characters across the entire issue—Chief Judge McGruder in

Judge Dredd, who appears for two panels; a woman who has her necklace stolen, also in *Judge Dredd*; and a background figure in a scene at a train station in a *Time Twister*. They get forty-nine words of dialogue among them. It is not that Prog 374 is a bad comic, nor indeed that *2000 AD* was in the mid-80s; as Moore put it, "In my admiration for *Judge Dredd, Strontium Dog, Robo-Hunter* and all the rest I stand second to no man, feeling that the world in general and *2000 AD* in particular would be a poorer place without them. Rather, I think I was motivated by a desire to fill in some of the holes left between those strips."

But the problem Moore identifies runs deeper than just *2000 AD*, published out of the Youth Group within IPC, which launched comics with strictly delineated demographic targets. *2000 AD* was a boys comic, along with *Action* and *Battle Picture Weekly*. Girls, on the other hand, were meant to read things like *Misty*, *Tammy*, and *Jinty*. The titles are, mercifully, misleading as to the quality of the publications. Indeed, compared to many gendered divisions among children's entertainment the gender division within IPC was solidly not awful; girls comics were not devoted exclusively to romance strips and advice on doing your nails or anything like that. *Misty*, for instance, was primarily made up of supernatural/horror strips such as *Journey into Fear*, about a pair of siblings being manipulated by an evil car yearning to return to its days of being owned by a gangster; *Tammy* largely offered over-the-top stories in the grand Victorian tradition of awful things happening to children, with titles such as the frankly astonishingly named *Slaves of War Orphan Farm*; while *Jinty* was largely stories with a sci-fi bent, including the Pat Mills number *Girl in a Bubble*, in which a girl is kept in a plastic bubble, ostensibly because she has no germ resistance, but in fact as part of a sinister experiment. (*Jinty* also included *The Blind Ballerina*, a strip Moore fondly recalls for a cliffhanger in which the eponymous ballerina pirouettes, unaware that she's on the M1 motorway with a lorry barreling towards her.) Nevertheless, there was a clear division.

More to the point, however, by this time the girl's line had largely been decimated—*Jinty* got merged into *Tammy* in 1981, with *Misty* following suit in 1984, before *Tammy* was finally merged into *Girl* a few months later on the insistence of Youth Group director John Sanders, who cancelled it despite its high sales as an act of revenge against the editor, a prominent activist within the National Union of Journalists who had just been involved in a strike. But it was not as though the rapid dwindling of female-targeted titles was being made up by a broadening of the boys titles. Instead girls were effectively being shut out of the medium entirely. And so Moore and Gibson's desire to introduce a strip that featured female characters in the lead roles was a pointed and necessary course correction.

Moore and Gibson were further invested in making sure they wrote about the right sort of female character. As Moore said, "I didn't want to write about a pretty scatterbrain who fainted a lot and had trouble keeping her clothes on. I similarly had no inclination to unleash yet another Tough Bitch With A Disintegrator And An Extra 'Y' Chromosome upon the world. What I wanted was simply an ordinary woman such as you might find standing in front of you while queuing for the check-out at Tesco's." In this regard, at least, Moore had obvious prior form, having done much the same thing with Roxy in *Skizz*, but this time, instead of focusing on a woman in contemporary Britain, Moore focused on a woman in the sort of exaggeratedly grotesque sci-fi world that might be described as "typical *2000 AD* fare."

The other major creative decision going in—and one that would prove in some regards a problematic one—was that the strip should be done without caption boxes to provide narration. Exactly whose idea this was is not entirely clear. Gibson, certainly, takes credit, saying in one interview that "*Skizz* had had so many caption boxes! I said I don't want any explanations in *Halo Jones*, any kind of thought balloons or caption boxes telling everybody what's going on." But a second interview, in which Gibson also takes credit for suggesting the idea of him working with Alan Moore, doing a comic focusing on a female lead, and coming up with the first story, Gibson gives a somewhat less credible account: "I told Alan that I thought we could get away with making the story 'self explanatory' in the way that we figure some things out (in our lives) only after the event. I never see any panels floating in the sky to warn me that 'I'm in for a big surprise' or any handy 'little did he know' notes attached to the lampposts. And Alan agreed that it would be a nice change in comics." This is somewhat harder to swallow, not least because of the suggestion that Moore was likely to write such crass captions in the first place. And indeed, while *Skizz* did use caption boxes to provide free indirect speech narration for both Skizz and Roxy (mainly for Skizz, and in the early portion of the comic when he's wandering alone and hasn't learned English, so as to highlight the alienness of his perspective on the mundane world, such as when he watches a wrestling match on TV and reflects that "the ape creature's primitive vu-box displays more of the madness, fills his head with more of the harsh, raucous cries"), Moore was by this point most of the way through *V for Vendetta*, where he used the same caption-free style Gibson was requesting, making Gibson's suggestion that he was in some sense making Moore work against his instincts tenuous at best.

All the same, it's notable that Moore does not claim any credit for this decision in the course of discussing the strip's origins in the introduction to the first *Halo Jones* collection, instead describing it as a mutual decision between him and Gibson, who he openly credits with "providing as many of the main concepts and the small touches as I myself," and so the strong sense that Gibson is embellishing the tale (a sin that Moore is, to say the least, well-acquainted with) ought not be taken as evidence that Gibson did not push for this. Indeed, the process for *The Ballad of Halo Jones* was on the whole particularly collaborative, with Gibson visiting Moore in Northampton for a several-day-long cannabis-fueled brainstorming session of the sort that makes any attempt to delineate who came up with what fruitless.

"I want to see eight thousand words. Printable words. I still remember that essay you wrote when the Beast got elected. I do not want to see the word 'fuck' typed eight thousand times again."
–Warren Ellis, *Transmetropolitan*, 1998

Moore, in any case, took to the approach with gusto. The obvious touchstone was Howard Chaykin's *American Flagg*, a comic published by First Comics, an alternative press outside of Chicago that was among the first generation of independent publishers to distribute comics via the direct market. Launching their line in 1983, founders Mike Gold and Ken F. Levin sought mainstream talent that might be interested in working on creator-owned projects. They quickly settled on Howard Chaykin, by this point a veteran of over a decade in the American industry, but always something of an outsider due to his disinterest in the popular genres of superhero and horror comics.

Instead Chaykin was largely a science fiction artist who, in his own words, was interested in drawing "guys with guns, guys with swords, and women with big tits." His work appeared in both indie venues like *Heavy Metal* and a graphic novel adaptation of *The Stars My Destination*, but also in mainstream titles like Marvel Comics's *Star Wars* adaptation and their *Micronauts* series. Given the opportunity to pitch for First Comics, he proposed a satirical dystopia about a world in which the American government has decamped to Mars and left the country (and ultimately the world) under the control of the massive Plex corporation. The resulting comic is ostentatious in the extreme, with Chaykin reveling in the creative freedom available to him from a publisher with no interest in the Comics Code Authority. *American Flagg* is long on sex, with the main character being Reuben Flagg, a former television star from a show called "*Mark Thrust, Sexus Ranger*," described as "the provocative adventures of a fearless vice cop walking the mean streets of an unarmed, untamed and sexually transmitted disease riddled sector of a great urban metroplex," who has been assigned to patrol the streets of Chicago.

The most immediate problem upon his arrival is the periodic warfare between two gogangs ("anarchist terrorist motorcycle clubs"), the Ethical Mutants and the Genetic Warlords, whom every Saturday night after the airing of the popular program Bob Violence commence a wave of destructive violence at the local mall. Flagg uncovers the fact that the violence is due to subliminal messages within Bob Violence, and manages to put an end to it, but this only begins the process of Flagg's gradual discovery of the sheer corruption and insane plans of Plex. The tone has obvious similarities to *Judge Dredd* in *2000 AD*, although this is less a matter of mutual influence and more simply one of common sources, with both fitting smoothly into a long tradition of brash sci-fi satires. (Indeed, a more obvious antecedent is probably Chaykin's friendship with Frank Miller, who was working on his own sci-fi dystopia *Ronin* for DC Comics around the same time.) But what is most interesting about the strip is Chaykin's technical virtuosity. Chaykin's world is full of nuance and detail—as Moore puts it in *Writing For Comics*, Chaykin "worked out the brand names and the TV shows and the attitudes to fashion and the political problems, and then he just went straight into the story and let the readers pick it up as they went along. In the first issue of *Flagg* we see snatches of TV shows and advertising billboards that give us a much more real impression of the way that these people think and live than any amount of explanatory caption boxes would have."

The comic's glory days are generally agreed to be its first twelve issues, after which Chaykin gradually lost interest in the title and eventually handed it off to other writers, including Alan Moore, who wrote a series of backup stories beginning in issue #21. Moore's arc opens with a pastiche of his own classic "The Anatomy Lesson" in miniature—an eight-page story called "The Hot Slot" that's bookended by a man barricaded in his office as some ghastly monster claws and pounds at the door outside. In the middle section of the story, the man explains his predicament over the course of a phone conversation: apparently, the problem is that Max, the man barricaded in his office, has been airing reruns of Mark Thrust, and has found himself with a bit of a problem regarding the advertising. Specifically, it's working too well, particularly in the second advertising slot, which comes immediately after the point in the program in which Mark Thrust is engaged in sexual congress. The slot initially went to "Fields O' Foam" bubble bath, and, due to a particularly effective cut between the episode and the ad, this led to a massive surge in Fields O' Foam sales. Eventually the approach is figured out by other advertisers, and the slot becomes hugely expensive. The problem, as Max explains, is that "our company seems to have been responsible for depraving the entire population of this city," with the entire city becoming, as Max puts it, a bunch of "fornicating maniacs." In particular, "there's a seven foot tall tumescent Samoan trying to beat my office door down."

Whether or not he did this as a deliberate riff on "The Anatomy Lesson," "The Hot Slot" is in many ways typical of Moore's writing, in that it's a piece driven by its structure, in this case an iteration of Moore's favored elliptical approach whereby the story starts and ends in the same place. But Moore's ability to plan his *American Flagg* arc that carefully quickly dissipated as his intended four-part story got stretched out to seven, requiring, in Moore's words, "some very strange things out of desperation to fill the extra pages of story," and a resultant loss in structural sharpness. "I think it has a moral behind it somewhere," Moore suggests, "if you can wade through all the naked flesh and decapitations," which is about fair.

Although *The Ballad of Halo Jones* predates Moore's work on *American Flagg*, it was well into Chaykin's landmark first year on the title, and the influence is clear, both in style and

Figure 201: *The first page of* American Flagg *is a dense blend of fictional brand names and news reports that throws readers in at the deep end. (By Howard Chaykin, 1983)*

Figure 202: *Ian Gibson's expansive sprawl of sci-fi tech, opening* The Ballad of Halo Jones. *(From* 2000 AD *#376, written by Alan Moore, 1984)*

substance. Moore did not merely avoid explaining the story via caption boxes, he largely avoided explaining it at all, forcing the reader to piece together the nature of the world as the story goes. The opening two-page spread, done as the two color pages of Prog 376, featured a vast tableau of futuristic technology, all rendered in Gibson's characteristically Kirbyesque style, with a voiceover from an unseen media personality named Swifty Frisko, who reports how the "Algae Baron Lux Roth Chop" is considering but leaning against preventing the E.S.S. Clara Pandy, "last of the famous Krupp-Corona 'S'-Series" from disassembly, and how the arrival of said ship is likely to cause "ozjams around east-am for the next hour," as well as how the Proximan "Mr. Bandaged Ice That Stampedes Inexpensively Through a Scribbled Morning" will henceforth be known as "Procurator Bandaged Ice That Stampedes Inexpensively Through A Scribbled Morning Waving Necessary Ankles." The page ends with a close-up of the eponymous Halo Jones.

But for all that is revealed in this first page, there is surprisingly little sense of what it means. None of the future technology is contextualized or explained. And this is true not only in the sense that the reader does not know precisely what an Ozjam or a Krupp-Corona 'S'-Series ship is—these, after all, are the sorts of sci-fi terminology that a *2000 AD* reader can reasonably be expected to make sense of without any context. The question of what, exactly, the reader is looking at and what sort of world this is are largely avoided. The reader is given detail but not context. The first installment continues in a similar vein, introducing things like the Different Drummers (who apparently all nod in unison, rather unsettlingly) and the Proximans (armless lizards who are apparently an immigrant population, with all the prejudices that implies), but never really explaining what world holds all these strange things. Tellingly, the name of the place, the Hoop, appears only once in the entire first installment, and then only in the context of the phrase "hoop-scoop," which is apparently a thing that "Rumble-Jacks" do.

"I wanna live with Halo Jones. I wanna home that's miles from home. I wanna drugs from the Twilight Zone. I wanna never never never never never never never say no."
–Shriekback, "Malaria," 1985

The result of this is that the first thing the audience learns about Halo Jones's world is not what it's like, but rather the fact that she wants to get out of there, and that everybody else in the world does too, but, as her friend Rodice puts it, "Even if you do get out it's no good, 'cause no matter how far you get, they'll fetch you back here and bust you to pieces." Past that, as with *American Flagg*, the world is introduced more through the media playing in the background than through characters explaining it to each other. (Not that Moore avoids blatant exposition entirely—not long after the disorienting opening spread, for instance, Moore has several characters straightforwardly explain the Different Drummers to each other, despite the fact that all of them are seemingly familiar with the group and have no reason to provide this exposition.)

This continues throughout. Nowhere in Book One is there anything that quite serves as an explanation of the Hoop and how it works. This is not, to be clear, a flaw: *The Ballad of Halo Jones* is not a story about the Hoop and how it came to be. (In point of fact, it's a scheme to move the unemployed—or "increased leisure citizens," to use the preferred euphemism—out of sight and out of mind. This isn't really established until Book Two, however.) It's about what life on the Hoop is like, which is to say, about a soul-crushing dead end designed to serve as little more than a human landfill. In this regard it's just an iteration of a trope that has already appeared numerous times in the course of the War, generally as an analogue for Thatcher's Britain in some form. And Moore, by avoiding an approach to the Hoop with any perspective other than the ground-level view offered by Halo and her friends, keeps the focus firmly on the experience of living in such a place.

And so Moore writes a story that is, for five of its ten installments, about a shopping expedition gone wrong. (As Gibson puts it, "I told Alan that the best way to get to know a place is to go shopping in it.") The point of this is to highlight the material reality of living in the Hoop—the fact that even a simple shopping trip because you're running low on food is a lengthy affair that requires careful planning to avoid the scheduled riots (another obvious debt to *American Flagg*). And this, in turn, serves to set up the final three parts, in which Halo and her friend Rodice return home to find that one of their two housemates has been brutally murdered and the other has opted to join the Different Drummers, which finally motivates Halo to stop just talking about getting out and to snag a job on the Clara Pandy (rescued by Lux Roth Chop after all) and get out.

Unfortunately, the strip ended up getting off to something of a rough start. For all that *American Flagg* belongs to the same satiric tradition as *2000 AD*, its worldbuilding techniques, even in the considerably simplified forms that Moore uses them, are rather more technically sophisticated than the magazine usually goes for. The result was a lot of confused readers. On top of that, the aggressively low stakes of the story proved a turn-off, and although Moore and Gibson had outlined a nine-book epic in which Halo would bounce from adventure to adventure, nothing in the first book really gestured at that or gave much of a sense of where this story of a girl who wanted to get out of where she was might be going. The result was that, despite the prominence of its creators and a prominent place in the magazine, *The Ballad of Halo Jones* did poorly in IPC's weekly surveys of readers to see what strips they were enjoying.

Despite this, IPC decided to commission a second book, partly because Moore and Gibson's reputation was sufficient to make a second chance worthwhile, and partially because, while the readers might not have been on board, there was still considerable excitement within IPC for the concept, and, as Moore puts it, the editors "were anxious to find out how it all turned out," a wish that would ultimately be frustrated anyway. But although they commissioned a second book, IPC had some specific editorial notes for Moore and Gibbons. The first of these was that the book should be more violent, the lack of action being viewed as part of the first book's poor reception. The second was an instruction "that the strip should be more intelligible." Moore was, to say the least, unimpressed with both requests, and though he did not, as he had by then done with both Marvel UK and Quality Communications, sever ties with the company over it, it is clear that the development of Book Two of *The Ballad of Halo Jones* was not an entirely pleasant experience.

Moore can hardly be faulted for some measure of frustration. In the US he was making far more money and working under the long editorial leash of Karen Berger, who was willing to back him against the Comics Code Authority and to let him do an issue of psychedelic vegetable sex. Whereas IPC was giving him grief over the fact that *The Ballad of Halo Jones* was slightly less hand-holding in its exposition than its readers expected, and he was being given directives that he surely viewed as little more than demands that he dumb the strip down just because it had not been an immediate smash hit. For all that *The Ballad of Halo Jones* represented IPC's belated recognition that Moore was A-list talent, they were still visibly unaware of the caliber of writer they had and were eager to micromanage. It was plainly disrespectful of the sheer degree of talent that Moore had demonstrated by this point in his career, all the more so coming after the belated and mildly insulting offer of *Skizz* long after Moore's abilities were clearly established.

Nevertheless, he persevered with the project. It was, of his UK jobs, the best-paying, and he did have a longstanding affection for the magazine, so this is perhaps unsurprising. But more even than he cared for *2000 AD*, one suspects that

Moore cared for Halo Jones. It is worth recalling that his initial motivation in starting a comics career was the impending birth of his eldest daughter, Leah, who was by 1985 seven years old, and her sister Amber, four. And it's clear that his sense of parental responsibility was a fundamental part of his decision. As Moore put it, "If I didn't make the jump now, once the baby was born I'd never have the nerve to do it. Once I've got a pair of hungry eyes staring up at me saying, 'Feed me,' then, you know, I'd probably stay where there was security. And also, if I did that then, this is what I'd be teaching my children. I'd be teaching my children that there was a ceiling to what they could do or what they could be." Leah was now around the age he'd been when he started reading comics, and Moore's awareness of the way in which the comics he loved were hopelessly skewed towards male readers was surely something he'd thought of in terms of his own daughters and the options they had (and, more importantly, didn't have) to read comics that might inspire them as the ones of his youth had him. (Tellingly, when filmed in 1987 for the "Monsters, Maniacs, and Moore" TV documentary he did a sequence where he read "A Cautionary Fable," his twisted Hilaire Belloc riff, to the girls.) The editorial structure at IPC that so frustrated him was also, with its rigid delineation between "boys comics" and "girls comics" and its subsequent abandonment of the female audience, the entire point of *The Ballad of Halo Jones* as a project. And so despite the insult, Moore continued.

Moore handled the editorial injunctions cleverly. For the violence, he incorporated a hostage situation into the second installment, and an extended action sequence after Halo's robotic dog Toby turns out to be a murderous stalker. Neither are intrusive, and were sufficient to mollify Moore's editors. The issue of complexity, meanwhile, was mostly going to solve itself. In Book One, Halo was in a world she was familiar with, and so Moore, in telling the story from her perspective, declined to offer much exposition. But in Book Two, and indeed, for the remainder of *The Ballad of Halo Jones*,

Halo would be in new and unfamiliar settings that she would have to understand, and that the reader would thus discover alongside her.

To further clarify things, however, Moore wrote a prologue to Book Two in which Halo Jones's adventures are discussed in a lecture at the Institute for Para-Historical Studies 1400 years after her death. This conceit allowed Moore to recap the events of the first book in a straightforwardly exposited manner, describing the abject poverty of the Hoop via an explanation of the government policies that created it, as opposed to just depicting it. More to the point, however, it allows Moore to abandon any pretense of subtlety in terms of the strip's main theme. An entire page of the prologue is turned over to allowing the lecturer to explain how the entire point of Halo's story: "She wasn't anyone special. She wasn't that brave, or that clever, or that strong. She was just somebody who felt cramped by the confines of her life. She was just somebody who had to get out," and how her most famous quotation was her claim, "Anybody could have done it."

But the innovation for Book Two that would have the most impact was the addition of the character Glyph, Halo's cabinmate. Introduced mainly in the third installment of Book Two, "I'll Never Forget Whatsizname," Glyph explains that as a side effect of repeated treatments to remake their body as they continued to vacillate over whether they wanted to be a boy or a girl, Glyph reached a state where their entire personality had been erased and people simply stopped noticing them entirely, to a supernatural extent. "Finally, my landlady forgot I was living in my apartment," Glyph narrates, "and leased it to another family. I protested, but they didn't notice. Eventually, I moved out. I walked through the crowded streets and nobody even looked at me... they just stared straight through me. It was as if I'd somehow slipped beneath the threshold of human awareness." Although the story relies unpleasantly on the stereotype that transgender people are prone to regretting their transitions (the first of many questionable depictions of transgender people over the course of the War, although one that has to be taken in the context of being written in 1985), it's tremendously effective, with Glyph's narration trailing off as they tell Halo and Toy, her other cabinmate, that they're "just grateful to you for taking a moment to listen... I don't ask for much—maybe you could just say 'hello' every once in a while, or ask me how I'm feeling. You could say things like 'Nice day, Glyph,' or 'Hi there, Glyph!' Or, uh, I could tell you some jokes... or, uh..." only to realize that Halo and Toy have long since wandered off from the conversation to watch holosoaps, forgetting all about Glyph, who slowly slinks away as Toy boasts that she's "just naturally interested in people."

"One of the Culacoons detaches himself from the main herd and rushes screaming at the nearest mollusk. He stabs the exposed violet membrane over and over with his spear. Everyone cheers. Soon, his fellows join in, each assaulting the snail-thing of their choice. The atmosphere is overwhelmingly masculine."
–Alan Moore, "A Man's World," 1985

Glyph's tragedy (an act of self-sacrifice to save Halo and Toy from Toby's attack, with neither of the two noticing or remembering Glyph afterwards) serves in many regards as a mirror for Halo's own arc over the course of Book Two, which tracks her voyage on the cruise ship The Clara Pandy. Halo plans to meet Rodice on the planet Charlemagne after a year's journey, a meeting that hangs over the entire arc from the first installment, which is narrated in the form of a letter from Halo to Rodice as she passes Pluto on her way out of the solar system. But upon reaching the appointed meeting place at the story's end she discovers that Rodice changed her mind after Halo's departure and is still back on the Hoop. Angry and betrayed, Halo responds to Rodice's promise that "I'll tell you everything when you get back to the Hoop" by proclaiming that she won't be coming back to the Hoop and

Figure 203: The crushing isolation of Glyph. (From The Ballad of Halo Jones Book Two *in* 2000 AD #408, *written by Alan Moore, art by Ian Gibson, 1985)*

Figure 204: Halo drinking at a bar, far from home, after learning that Rodice chose to stay behind on the Hoop. (From The Ballad of Halo Jones Book Two *in* 2000 AD #415, *written by Alan Moore, art by Ian Gibson, 1985)*

hangs up, which leaves her, in her own way, as isolated and cut off as the forgotten Glyph.

Certainly the character was a success. In stark contrast to Book One's chilly reception, it quickly became obvious that the profound and crushing sense of isolation and loneliness that Glyph represented had struck a chord in readers. "The response to this story," Moore says, "of a terminal nonentity was surprising in its intensity and I think that, maybe, that was the episode where we finally got the readers on our side." Certainly IPC was finally on side, commissioning a third run of *Halo Jones* and this time asking for a twenty-part saga instead of the ten-part runs of the first two books. Moore, however, was too busy with his DC work to commit to that, and so it was set at fifteen parts.

The third book of *The Ballad of Halo Jones* saw Moore and Gibson tackling a particularly iconic trope within *2000 AD*, namely the war comic. As Moore wrote, "Future war has always been the most popular topic among the *2000 AD* readership, and it seemed to me that the time was ripe for a story that looked at the concept of war in the future from a slightly different angle to the more traditional one." This angle, at least in *2000 AD*, was best embodied by Gerry Finley-Day's *Rogue Trooper*. Finley-Day was in many ways the epitome of the IPC establishment. He joined the company in the early 70s and, like Pat Mills, got his start on girls comics, editing *Tammy* (where he'd created "Slaves of War Orphan Farm") before following Mills to work on *Battle Picture Weekly* and *Action*, and finally becoming one of the mainstays on *2000 AD*, first as the writer on *Invasion!* Before going on to pen a variety of titles for the magazine. But it is *Rogue Trooper*, the story of a genetically enhanced soldier who had the digitally preserved consciousnesses of his fallen comrades embedded into his equipment, that proved his most enduring creation for the magazine.

Finley-Day, however, could be difficult to work with. His scripts were infamously sloppy (an early typo in *Invasion!* in which Finley-Day attempted to have Bill Savage escorting men across a plain led to the coining of the word "scrotnig," subsequently a favorite term of Tharg the Mighty), and the general attitude was, as Alan Grant put it, that he "was really good at coming up with ideas," but "didn't know how to realise" them. Grant, who'd had to near-completely rewrite his scripts for *Harry 20 on the High Rock*, more bluntly describes taking the scripts to editor Steve MacManus and saying, "We can't print these scripts the way they are—the sentences don't make sense, the word balloons are way too long," and having to cut around sixty percent of the scripts to make them work. Dave Gibbons, Finley-Day's initial collaborator on *Rogue Trooper*, gave a similarly scathing assessment, explaining how he broke from his usual practice of lettering stories he did art on because "I got so pissed off with the scripts on *Rogue Trooper* that I didn't even want to read them. Steve would précis the script, give me a plot and I would draw it from that. Then someone else would letter it, because I couldn't bear to read the words, quite honestly." And so, over the course of the 1980s, Finley-Day steadily found himself eased out of the magazine, with his last contribution being a *Rogue Trooper* arc that ended in Prog 449, two weeks prior to the debut of *The Ballad of Halo Jones* Book Three.

Certainly this strip gives a sense of why Moore might have wanted to approach the idea of a futuristic war from a different angle. The story is a labored and contrived number in which a peace conference between the long fighting Southers and Norts is disrupted by a surprise alien attack, resulting in the Southers and Norts allying to fight this new (and almost wholly unexplained) threat, with the final panel featuring Rogue Trooper cheerily lobbing a grenade and exclaiming, "This is gonna be like old times! Nu Earth at war, and me in the middle of it!" It is not, to say the least, a subtle and nuanced take on the horrors of war. And this was in keeping with *Rogue Trooper*; Gibbons had rapidly became disillusioned with what he called a "dreadfully written" comic after helping create it, remarking, "It never quite went the way I wanted or hoped. I imagined somebody on a long-term quest to find out where they came from and who they were, against this kind of wild west background. But it turned out more like, 'Eat Leaden Death, Nort Scum!' That's never been my favorite kind of war story."

Moore, on the other hand, was interested in returning to an older tradition of war comics: "Among the majority of future war strips that I had come across, none came even close to matching the depiction of inhumanity and misery conjured up by Pat Mills and Joe Colquhoun's masterful *Charley's War*." This was a 1979-debuting strip in *Battle Picture Weekly* featuring the exploits of Charley Bourne, a working class lad in the usual mould for *Battle Picture Weekly*—scrappy and possessing a strong sort of practical common sense that is (of course) far more valuable than any sort of book learning. But while the setup of the strip is bog standard for a British war comic (Charley enlists at the age of sixteen, lying about his age, but forgetting to change his birthday on his paperwork), the tone is markedly different. *Charley's War* made no bones about the horrors of World War I, with Colquhoun and Mills both meticulously researching the period so that the actual war content reflected the awful intensity of the actual First World War.

The strip also contained Mills's trademark satirical streak, which became particularly savage in the sections set in England. This included an extended story arc set in London while Bourne is on leave, featuring Blind Bob, a Crimean War veteran. Bob is a classically grotesque character of the sort common in British comics, and he provides no shortage of comedic moments over the course of the story, but it's a fundamentally tragic story about an old man, disabled in the service of his country and largely left to rot, which ends with Bob throwing himself in front of a truck in (tragically mistaken) despair at the prospect of being sent to a workhouse after being integral to saving London from zeppelin raids. It's at once darkly funny and an absolutely scathing indictment of the treatment of veterans.

Figure 205: Gerry Finley-Day's last panel of Rogue Trooper, *which illustrates much of what frustrated Dave Gibbons about the strip, and much of what Alan Moore wanted to avoid in doing a war story with Halo Jones. (From* 2000 AD *#449, art by José Ortiz, 1985)*

Figure 206: The famous and brilliantly bleak end of the Mills/Colquhoun run of Charley's War. *(From* Battle Action Force, *1984)*

A similar tone exists in Pat Mills's last contribution to the strip, which flashes forward to "thirteen years later... January, 1933. Charley was one of the many ex-servicemen who had been unable to find a job and spent years on the dole." The strip then shows Charley harangued by Mister Bickers from the Labour Exchange, who angrily reminds him that "if any child does a newspaper round or does errands, the money must be deducted from his father's dole" and demands to inspect the Bournes' larder. It ends with Charley musing to himself, "We fought the war to end all wars... so our kids wouldn't have to go through the same thing... that's what makes it all worthwhile," as he walks past an old soldier selling matches and a newspaper salesman who proclaims that Adolf Hitler has just been elected Chancellor of Germany.

Moore was interested in bringing this sort of approach to futuristic warfare, feeling that "since warfare seems to become increasingly horrifying with each passing generation" it was strange that comics were "only capable of bringing home the full gut-wrenching impact when describing the conflicts of the past." He had prior form in this regard, of course: he'd already written a pair of *Rogue Trooper* stories for the 1983 and 1984 *2000 AD Annuals*, both of which looked at the psychological consequences of war, a marked departure from the usual tone of a *Rogue Trooper* story. But there's a considerable difference between introducing and killing off a psychologically scarred character over the course of a six-page strip and a fifteen-part look at a future war of his own devising, and Moore unsurprisingly went considerably further with *The Ballad of Halo Jones*.

The central horror of future war that Moore imagines, occupying the eighth through thirteenth installments of Book Three, involves the planet Moab, "the single biggest non-gaseous planet so far encountered by humanity." Slightly larger than Jupiter, the planet has massive gravity, requiring all combat to take place in massive gravity suits, rendered by Ian Gibson as massive, vaguely mushroom shaped things that look more than faintly ridiculous. But underneath the rather outlandish visuals (which, along with a healthy degree of gallows humor from Halo, keep the strip grounded in its satirical lens) is a solidly gruesome concept. Moab's gravity is such that exposure to it instantly reduces soldiers to bloody smears if there is any failure in their gravity suits, including, of course, being struck by a bullet. Even grislier, the gravity in the actual combat zones is sufficient to cause massive time dilation, so that in combat events happening even a couple dozen meters away seem frozen in time, slowly accelerating as one approaches them so that, as Halo describes it (in a caption box, Moore having by this point thoroughly abandoned the structural constraints of Book One), "The bullets inch forwards. The spray of arterial crimson descends gradually—a slow, hideous dew," until finally one is in the thick of the terrifyingly deadly action.

The result is a chillingly effective metaphor for the fog of war, as a seeming snapshot of combat (as it appears at any given moment to those outside the high gravity zones) dissolves into chaos and viscera. Adding to the impact is the disorienting passage of time when one is in combat, so that Halo's first excursion into the Crush (as it's called), a five-minute skirmish from her perspective in which she runs to an artillery position and back, in fact takes two months outside. This means that whenever Halo emerges there's a new leadership structure, and any casualties among her unit have long since been mourned and become old news. It becomes impossible for soldiers to actually follow the larger events of the war, as everything becomes a blur; entire years of war and politics pass outside the Crush over the course of a week or so for Halo, until suddenly one day all the fighting just stops, and Halo and her fellow soldiers emerge to find a lone cleaning woman who explains that the war has been over for weeks, ever since Earth's economy collapsed.

This psychological disorientation mirrors Halo's own state as she reels from the death of Toy, her old friend from the Clara Pandy, who died in combat on Halo's previous deployment as Halo tried to drag her injured body back to

Figure 207: The awful brutality of war on Moab. (From The Ballad of Halo Jones Book Three *in* 2000 AD *#462, written by Alan Moore, art by Ian Gibson, 1986)*

Figure 208: A post-traumatic Halo contemplates cold-blooded murder. (From The Ballad of Halo Jones Book Three *in* 2000 AD *#458, written by Alan Moore, art by Ian Gibson, 1986)*

base for medical attention, not realizing by the end that she was dragging a corpse with her. Halo goes on leave shortly after, but finds herself in an utterly self-destructive state, unable to find any employment other than the military, and finally reenlists after finding herself idly fantasizing about murdering an old woman in cold blood for sport. It's a shocking portrayal of post-traumatic stress, grounded in the same brutal social realism that saw Mills depicting Charley Bourne on the dole in 1933, and, for that matter, in a Britain where Thatcher had only recently gone to war with Argentina for some obscure islands as crushing unemployment sparked riots at home.

"First, there is Brahma, the self-aware immensity, from whose thought-substance are created all known and unknown things."
–Grant Morrison, *18 Days*, 2015

This parallel is, of course, in no way incidental. *The Ballad of Halo Jones* was, from the beginning, rooted in social commentary on Thatcher's Britain. This was in many ways the point, the satirical tradition of *2000 AD* being one of the things that endeared it to Moore in spite of the numerous frustrations. The Hoop was just another variation on the terraces of Moore's childhood: a place built for poor people to die in with as little fuss as possible for the rest of the world. The callous disregard for the safety or well-being of its residents and the cruel farce that there might be any jobs for them anyway was, as with the best strips in *2000 AD*, and indeed the best science fiction, nothing more or less than Moore looking outside his own window and describing what he saw from an oblique angle, an approach perfectly suited to Gibson's brilliantly grotesque blend of realism and cartooning. And the focus on the economic realities continues to be at the heart of the strip in Book Three, which uses its prologue chapter to depict Halo's decade-long downward spiral after leaving the Clara Pandy, a vicious cycle of unemployment and claustrophobia that slowly leads her to a life of petty crime and alcoholism. It's in this context that Halo's enlistment in the military is shown, making it clear that this is an act of desperation—the only way out of the galaxy that Halo can find. In this regard, notably, Moore surpasses his model *Charley's War*, which never really looked at the economic conditions that make the military an attractive career option, not to mention tying all that into its overall portrait of the horrors (both material and psychological) of war, and it is hardly surprising he considers Book Three the high point of *The Ballad of Halo Jones*.

Book Three is also, however, the endpoint of *The Ballad of Halo Jones*. This was not the original plan; Moore and Gibson had at least some degree of an outline spanning nine books in total, although few details have emerged. Gibson has, in the thirty some-odd years since Book Three, done a couple illustrations of Halo that have been speculated to reveal unused plot details, but these are not entirely reliable barometers: one suspects that his portrait of Halo as a scantily clad slave of some sort was not in keeping with Moore's plans, and a nude illustration of her he did that was briefly to be sold as a print at the Bristol Comics Expo before hastily being withdrawn on the insistence of Rebellion (*2000 AD*'s latest owners) amidst some furious backpedaling on Gibson's part about whether it was ever meant to be Halo (the convention certainly unambiguously sold it as such, and Gibson admits to naming the piece "nude Halo") was, as Moore rather charitably put it, "quite the opposite of what the character was meant to be."

Moore, for his part, has suggested that Book Four would have involved Halo as "a female space pirate," and that he intended to continue aging Halo through the books until, in the final book, she would be an old woman on "some planet that is right at the absolute edge of the universe where, beyond that, beyond some sort of spectacular lightshow, there is no space, no time." Moore explains that "Halo Jones, after spending some time with the rest of the immortals, would have tottered across the landing field, got into her spacecraft, and flown into the psychedelic lightshow, to finally get out." The particulars, in any case, were never realized, and although upon completing Book Three Moore declined to rule out ever returning to the character, he has since hardened this position to an absolute refusal to work with *2000 AD*'s owners, saying, in his most recent comments on the matter, that "I've cut me ties with all those things" and numbering Halo among the "comics work I am very very distanced from."

Despite this, it is not fair to say that Moore left IPC in a huff. Indeed, he returned thirty-four progs after the end of Book Three to do a one-page gag strip featuring Halo Jones for the magazine's five hundredth issue, the last work he would end up doing for the company. A look at the dates offers a far more basic reason why he might not have hurried back to do *The Ballad of Halo Jones* Book Four: he didn't have to. Two months after Book Three wrapped, *Watchmen* started, and it quickly became clear that Moore was going to be making quite a lot of money off of it. (In fact, the book would end up making Moore outright rich.) At every major step along the path of his ascension, Moore had taken the opportunity to downsize work where he found the pay to frustration ratio unsatisfying, and the start of *Watchmen* was no different—Moore ended *Maxwell the Magic Cat* around the same time, for instance. Simply put, Moore would surely have been asking himself about the merits of working for IPC rates even if he weren't frustrated with the editorial experience on *The Ballad of Halo Jones*.

All the same, there was an ethical dimension to this. *Watchmen* wasn't just better paying than *2000 AD* work; it was, in his understanding at least, a creator-owned work on which he was given heavy editorial freedom. IPC, on the other hand, was an infamously conservative company with a poor track record in how it treated its creative personnel. Notably, their contracts gave no royalties for reprints, which meant that the collected editions of Moore's comics—the format where *Watchmen* looked set to be an enduring source of income—gave him no royalties unless he wrote introductions for the volumes, which would get him a piddling 1%. This, combined with his frustrations with his editors, made it easy to understand why Book Four of *Halo Jones* was not a priority for Moore, not least because he was intending to move the story away from the editor-friendly war setting, a move that was surely going to provoke another flurry of editorial pressure to add more action sequences.

This position rapidly hardened to an ethical redline for Moore. At first Moore wouldn't do more work on *The Ballad of Halo Jones* until he was given ownership of the property; then, just to make sure his bluff wouldn't be called, he added the caveat that Judge Dredd be returned to Wagner, Mills, and Ezquerra, which was obviously never going to happen. This too is hardly surprising. Moore was well aware that his name sold books on its own merits, and IPC was profiting gamely on that fact without giving him any meaningful share of the money. This was flatly exploitative, and exploitative in a way that would have been acutely galling to Moore's working class leftist sensibilities, especially as he looked out at a Britain where Thatcher had just a year earlier broken the back of the National Union of Mineworkers during a high profile strike. And this was hardly irrelevant to events at IPC. John Sanders, the head of the Youth Group at IPC when *2000 AD* was started and later the managing director of IPC's comics line, was virulently anti-union, complaining bitterly about the "union's smash and grab behavior" and praising Thatcher's efforts to break the back of the labor movement. This sort of attitude would surely have been sickening to Moore, and once he had the financial security to not have to submit meekly to such exploitation he simply stopped doing so.

More surprising, perhaps, is why IPC (and, subsequently, Fleetway, who bought IPC's comics division in 1987) didn't make any significant effort to keep Moore on board. The reason is on the whole simple, however: that's just not the sort of company IPC was. The idea of paying their creators more was completely alien to them. According to Sanders, "We needed all rights because the Youth Group only made realistic profits by re-using material at no cost... my attitude was if you don't want to work for us, there are plenty of other markets for you." This last claim sits at an odd juxtaposition with his statement, in the same interview, that "we had 50 per cent of the market, and [DC Thompson] had the other 50 per cent," but then, when has the person explaining to an artist why they don't deserve to be paid ever told the truth? Except, of course, that by 1987 there finally were other markets, and the UK to US pipeline that DC was rapidly building was taking its toll on the magazine as major creator after major creator found their time occupied with American comics that paid more up front and offered royalties for reprints. Moore was, in the end, merely the first of many talents that IPC and the rest of the British industry lost to the international market.

"The night before returning to America, I wandered into the desert and ate a ball of hashish I'd been given in Tibet. The ensuing vision transformed me. Wading through powdered history, I heard dead kings walking underground; heard fanfares sound through human skulls. Alexander had merely resurrected an age of Pharaohs. Their wisdom, truly immortal, now inspired me." –Alan Moore, *Watchmen*, 1987

More broadly, IPC's attitude was that it was *2000 AD* and its associated characters that sold comics, not individual creators. This was perhaps obvious given that even providing credits for creators had been a fight (with, predictably, John Sanders being opposed), and when credits were provided creators were described as though they were interchangeable robots. The stars of *2000 AD* were its fictitious editor Tharg the Mighty, Judge Dredd, Nemesis the Warlock, Rogue Trooper, Sam Slade, and the others—not the people who had created them. And so, perhaps unsurprisingly for a company whose modus operandi was to publish thinly veiled knockoffs of popular media, IPC's attitude was largely that if Moore was going to be uppity, they'd just hire new people to write like Moore. And as luck would have it, they even had somebody on hand: Prog 463, in addition to featuring the twelfth installment of *The Ballad of Halo Jones* Book Three, featured the IPC debut of Grant Morrison on a *Tharg's Future Shock* entitled "Hotel Harry Felix."

There is no way to reasonably deny the fact that Morrison's short pieces for *2000 AD* owe a heavy debt to Alan Moore. "Hotel Harry Felix" features an alien life form that takes the form of thoughts and ideas, a concept Moore had already explored in "Eureka." His second, "The Alteration," is a two-pager featuring a man on the run who is caught by monsters and turns into one, only to have it turn out that he was actually a monster who had contracted "humanitis" and was being cured, a joke not entirely dissimilar to Moore's two-page "Return of the Thing." His fourth, "Some People Never Listen," bears more than a passing resemblance to Moore's "The Bounty Hunters." His seventh, "Wheels of Fury," featuring an AI car that turns into a jealous lover, is almost a straight reworking of the Moore/Gibbons "The Dating Game," in which a city's central computer becomes a jealous lover. "Fair Exchange" uses the same joke that concludes "D.R. and Quinch Have Fun on Earth" of a comedic misunderstanding in which an alien is presented with something that is secretly rude graffiti in its native language, while the two-part "Fruitcake and Veg" is a more or less straightforward repeat of the basic joke of *D.R. & Quinch*, including a section where the narrator reflects, "People say to me, 'Mr. Sweet, what is it that makes you commit senseless and irresponsible acts of wanton destruction? What made you become the deranged homicidal maniac we've come to know and love?' Well it's a fair question. So I always give them a fair answer. I say it's my upbringing, I tell them society's to blame... and then I blow 'em up!" And the similarities continue right up to Morrison's final *Future Shock*, "Big Trouble for Blast Barclay," a Flash Gordon riff that echoes Moore's "The Regrettable Ruse of

Rocket Redglare," and which even has the same artist, Mike White. All told, out of fifteen short pieces Morrison wrote for *2000 AD*, around half have pronounced similarities with Moore's work.

Certainly in light of facts like these it is easy to see why Alan Moore might have eventually concluded that Morrison was serially ripping him off. It is equally easy to construct a variety of defenses. Yes, Morrison uses ideas that resemble Moore's. But, for instance, in "Fruitcake and Veg," the Quinchian soliloquy comes in a story that also includes a group of armed revolutionaries who try to liberate vegetables from slavery and a monarchic potato. The story as a whole, in other words, is not a *D.R. & Quinch* knockoff in any meaningful sense, but rather one that uses one aspect of Moore's *D.R. & Quinch* as a component of something different. (Of course, the evil vegetables bear no small resemblance to the plot of *The Stars My Degradation*...) And indeed, it's worth recalling the degree to which the second *D.R. & Quinch* tale incorporated large swaths of the plot of *The Utterly Monstrous, Mind-Roasting Summer of O.C. and Stiggs*. The truth is that neither Moore nor Morrison have ever been shy about wearing their influences on their sleeves.

It's also the case that Morrison often does very different things with the ideas than Moore does. This is perhaps clearest with "Big Trouble for Blast Barclay," his Flash Gordon pastiche. As stated, there are obvious similarities to "The Regrettable Ruse of Rocket Redglare"—indeed, it's arguable that it's the most straightforward and unreconstructed Moore lift of Morrison's career. But there are also appreciable differences that give the stories genuinely different perspectives. Moore's story is one of faded glory and nostalgia turned sour. The story is essentially a tragedy, its final twist serving as ironic justice to punish Redglare for succumbing to temptation. "Big Trouble for Blast Barclay," on the other hand, has Barclay suffer an entirely undeserved fate at the hands of a purely malevolent foe. Redglare's fate is a severe but intelligible consequence of his actions, whereas

Barclay and his allies are brought down when a DHSS Snooper catches Barclay engaging in welfare fraud because he claims supplementary benefit, which requires he be available to work every day, whereas in reality he's jetting off to the Crab Nebula. Barclay points out that "they don't pay you to be a hero of the spaceways," but to no avail, with a crowd of supporters rapidly turning on him and accusing him and his allies of "livin' off the backs of the taxpayers" and of being "scroungers."

It's worth stressing the degree to which this is a fundamentally different approach. Moore adheres to the logic of Flash Gordon stories and pushes it to new places based on stretching its rules to a breaking point. Morrison, however, combines Flash Gordon with an extrinsic logic. The idea that the hero will eventually grow old and fat is not something *Flash Gordon* itself engages in, but it is still a sensible extension of the basic idea of the character. The idea that the Thatcher-era Department of Health and Social Security might show up and nick the hero for benefits fraud, on the other hand, is not something that is supposed to come up in a Flash Gordon story. Indeed, that's the entire point—that it's a completely absurd scenario for a Flash Gordon-style hero to end up in. And this absurdity is at the heart of the story's unsubtle commentary upon Thatcher's Britain, highlighting the cruelty of the crowd (who serve as the ones the end revelation—that the DHSS snooper is in fact an alien imposter who has been preparing the way for an invasion of evil alien hamsters—is meant to punish).

But perhaps the most important thing to point out is that while roughly half of Morrison's *Future Shocks* have pronounced similarities to Moore's, half don't. Yes, Moore is self-evidently one of Morrison's major influences, but it is equally self-evident that he is not the only influence. It's not that all of these Moore-free stories are blindingly original ideas. "Danger: Genius at Work," for instance, is a crashingly unsubtle dystopia about a world where "everyone looks the same, gets the same wages, lives in the same sort of house,"

Figure 209: Where Moore used Flash Gordon to satirize itself, Morrison uses it as a vehicle to satirize Thatcher's Britain. (From "Big Trouble for Blast Barclay," in 2000 AD #516, written by Grant Morrison, art by Mike White, 1987)

Figure 210: John Hicklenton's visionary weirdness elevated "The Invisible Etchings of Salvador Dali" to greatness. (In 2000 AD #515, written by Grant Morrison, 1987)

all in the name of total equality. (Indeed, in the story's one solid gag, everyone is also given the same name: Terry.) Among the things forcibly equalized is intelligence, and the story follows the brilliant Theophilus Pritt as he is forcibly dumbed down to ordinary intelligence for coming up with too many clever inventions. It's at once cliché and painfully self-indulgent, coming across as nothing so much as another writer whining about his under-appreciated brilliance.

More successful, while still clearly derivative, is "Return to Sender," an iteration of an oft-appearing subgenre of strips in which a beleaguered comics writer encounters fantastic obstacles in successfully completing and submitting his work. Morrison's take on the material is endearingly gonzo, stuffed with an elaborate litany of ideas. They are, to be sure, not all his—two plot points (a race of very small aliens who are casually wiped out by contact with a comparatively giant human object and a human phrase that's coincidentally a massively offensive insult in an alien tongue) are taken from the same sequence in Douglas Adams's *The Hitchhiker's Guide to the Galaxy*, for instance, yet the story is still genuinely entertaining.

But there are also stories where Morrison excels with genuinely clever and well-executed ideas. "Curse Your Lucky Star," for instance, is a solid story about a doomed effort to get rid of a man named Jeremy Chance who has freakishly good luck, but always at the expense of other people, resulting in an endless chain of catastrophes around him. It's decided that the only thing to do is to put Chance into suspended animation and blast him off into space, but this only causes his luck powers to shift him billions of years into the past where he gets caught up in the formation of Halley's Comet, which promptly smashes into the planet, killing everybody on Earth (except, of course, Jeremy Chance). It's a classic *Future Shock* that mines some good gags out of its premise before wrapping it up in a finish that's at once clever and inevitable.

And then there is "The Invisible Etchings of Salvador Dali." Of Morrison's fifteen *Future Shocks*, it is both the strangest and the most visibly Morrisonesque. The story runs for three pages, with the first two focusing on the adventures of the unnamed narrator as he traverses a world of surrealist horrors to recover the eponymous etchings. Morrison is adept at coming up with compellingly weird images like a rain of narwhals or Albert Einstein with "a wheelbarrow full of clouds," and artist John Hicklenton turns out to be just as creative, stuffing panels with a motley of bizarre and disturbing images, all realized in a brutal and viscerally grotesque style. The final page makes the unsurprising revelation that the narrator is in fact a mental patient, only to then reveal that the world has been reshaped by a "reality bomb" that has turned the world into exactly the same sort of surrealist landscape that the patient dreams of, and that the people at the hospital are preparing to wake him up in the hopes that he can cope with the world gone mad. Between the sly double twist and Hicklenton's vividly visionary weirdness the strip numbers among the best in the entire history of *Future Shocks*, and makes it clear that Morrison has a vibrant creative vision all his own.

All the same, it's undeniably the case that Morrison was applying this vision to the task of following in Moore's footsteps. Morrison makes no secret of the fact that his return to comics was inspired by Moore's work on *Marvelman* and the aesthetic possibilities it offered. And while the British comics industry was not so large that there were a great variety of paths into it, it's telling that Morrison largely recreated the specific path of Moore's ascent while writing comics visibly in the same basic mould as Moore's. But more than it reveals anything about Morrison's creative faculties, this simply reveals the fact that Morrison was a shrewd businessman. He saw that Moore was having more career success than any other writer in the history of the British comics industry and so engineered a career that would give him the same success. As Morrison puts it, "To get work with

Marvel UK and *2000 AD* I suppressed my esoteric and surrealist tendencies and tried to imitate popular styles—in order to secure paying jobs in the comics mainstream. There is a reason those pieces were written in a vaguely Alan Moore-ish style and it's because I was trying to sell to companies who thought Moore was the sine qua non of the bees knees and those stories were my take on what I figured they were looking for."

But Morrison had more good fortune than just having an obvious figure to model his career on: his arrival on IPC's radar coincided almost perfectly with Moore's departure from the company. Which meant, in effect, that the job of being Alan Moore was, as far as *2000 AD* was concerned, open. Accordingly, Morrison's *Future Shocks* apprenticeship was markedly shorter than Moore's. Where Moore spent two-and-a-half years and forty short stories to earn the privilege of writing a cheap rip-off of a popular sci-fi property, Morrison needed only fifteen shorts over a period of just under a year and a half before he was given an ongoing series. Indeed, in a fitting irony, Morrison was asked to do a superhero strip for *2000 AD*, a direct reaction to the success that Moore was having in the US with *Watchmen*.

Which leaves little to do save to move on to that monolithic entity. It is in many ways difficult to conceptualize a magickal war in the traditional vocabulary of battles and victories, but there can surely be no effort to do so that does not conclude that *Watchmen* is its largest single conflagration. Certainly it marks the point where the drums of war give way to full-on combat. But the shape of that conflict is impossible to define, a fractal geometry where every act of precise measurement reveals nothing save for more measurements to take. This is, of course, the inevitable nature of a war that rages through what Moore will come to define as Ideaspace. A conventional, material war exists to be fought over defined territory—a physical geography that can be measured and bounded. But in Ideaspace, where any piece of terrain has an infinite number of adjacent points, the idea of a fixed and determined battlefield is wholly useless.

This is, of course, the heart of what a magickal war is. When fighting for control over an endlessly shifting terrain, the construction of certainties, however fleeting, are the only weapons that make sense. This is, perhaps, what Moore ultimately meant when, in *V for Vendetta*, he spoke of ferociously defending that final inch of selfhood against a hostile world. Certainly it is what William Blake meant when he proclaimed that he "must create a system or be enslaved by another mans." And it is no surprise, then, that both Moore and Blake ultimately resorted to the same tactics in their respective Albionic Wars, abandoning all hope of defining the territory in which they fought in favor of radical and complete control over their definitions of themselves, ultimately transfiguring themselves into the very psychic landscape for which they battled.

And for Moore, *Watchmen* is the radiant blast of nuclear fire in which he is transformed from mere flesh into eternity. From the vantage point of history this seems inevitable, the precision engineering and meticulous craft of *Watchmen* pointing resolutely towards that outcome as though there was never any other possibility. It does not seem as though the particular world that *Watchmen* holds in microcosm, detonated within the particular psychic domain of Ideaspace in which it sits, at the particular historical moment at which it landed, could ever have had any consequences other than the precise and exact ones that unfolded. It is as though Moore existed for this exact ascension, designed to be the exact piece of territory that he is.

And yet in setting this point as the one from which the narrative finally reaches *Watchmen*, a strange truth emerges. Consider the end of Book Three of *The Ballad of Halo Jones*. After emerging from the Crush to find that the war has abruptly ended, Halo, still reeling from all that she's seen and done, enters what she knows to be an ill-advised affair with General Luiz Cannibal, her overall commander during the war, who in turn finds himself on trial for war crimes. In the course of the trial, however, Halo discovers not only that Cannibal is guilty of the war crimes, but that a seemingly innocent action she took back on the Clara Pandy had made her an unwitting accomplice to his crimes—something that is all the more upsetting to her because it took place before she ever chose to involve herself in the war. It is a powerful moment that speaks to the way in which war implicates far more than just its ostensible combatants, a pressing concern in the wake of the Falklands and the sinking of the ARA General Belgrano. And so, after sabotaging Cannibal's gravity suit just before he goes back out into the Crush one last time, thus dooming him, she steals his shuttle, and goes where she always goes and wants to go: out.

It is a strange irony that for all the inevitability of *Watchmen* and all its meticulous symbolism, Alan Moore himself clearly had no idea what he was doing. War was in most regards the last thing that Alan Moore wanted to be involved in. He was, after all, nothing more than a con man with a scheme to make himself and his friend Dave a quick buck by making some stuff up about superheroes. And yet he crafted the most devastatingly effective bomb imaginable and dropped it at an almost unimaginably perfect target. The result is that he is at once caught up in the blast, made irrevocably complicit in a decades-long chain of grueling conflicts, and liberated by it. He gets out, achieving both financial and creative independence for the rest of his life, and is trapped forever in the War's gravity, crushed to nothing save an ugly smear of blood. And so as the War erupts with awful inevitability, the searing light of *Watchmen* bursts forth, and in the blinding deadly flash a single image becomes terribly and horribly clear:

End of Book One

About the Author

Philip Sandifer lives in New York and writes about many things, some of which take place on this plane of reality. In particular, he is the author of *TARDIS Eruditorum*, a sprawling history of *Doctor Who*, and *Neoreaction a Basilisk*, a savage journey into the heart of the eschaton.

He blogs at eruditorumpress.com.

Made in the USA
Charleston, SC
18 December 2016